Making Love
Last Forever

Making Love
Last Forever

GARY SMALLEY

W PUBLISHING GROUP

www.wpublishinggroup.com

A Division of Thomas Nelson, Inc.
www.ThomasNelson.com

Unless otherwise indicated, Scripture quotations used in this book are from the Holy Bible, New International Version (NIV). Copyright © 1973, 1978, 1984 International Bible Society. Used by permission of Zondervan Bible Publishers.

Anecdotes and case studies presented in this volume are composites of actual cases. Names and other details have been changed to protect identities.

Library of Congress Cataloging-in-Publication Data
  Smalley, Gary.
  Making love last forever / Gary Smalley.
  p.   cm.
  Includes bibliographical references and index.
  ISBN 0-8499-1194-X
  1. Marriage.   2. Intimacy (Psychology)   3. Love.
  4. Man-woman relationships.   I. Title.
  HQ734.S6863   1996
    306.7—dc20
                                                                 96-21566
                                                                      CIP

Printed in the United States of America

Dedication

I dedicate this book to several outstanding families, all of whom made this book possible. Without them believing in me and investing so much of their resources in my work, this lifelong project would never have been realized.

Steve and Shannon Scott

Jim and Patty Shaughnessy

Bob and Marjorie Marsh

John and Nima Marsh

Dave and Leslie Marsh

Ed and Laurie Shipley

Jeff and Karen Heft

Ben and Marion Weaver

Frank and Katie Kovacs

The staff at American Telecast

Contents

Acknowledgments

I wish to thank a number of dear people who have made this book possible. First my wife and three children who had to put up with all my trial-and-error methods of building a healthy marriage and family. They were willing to take several different paths with me until we found the ones that worked best for us. We're all still great friends and enjoying our adult lives a lot more because of our journey together.

Most importantly, I wish to thank Larry Weeden for his outstanding ability to capture my thoughts and desires within each chapter. His wordsmanship is greatly appreciated and his loving and gentle attitude made the whole project a very pleasant experience.

Thank you, thank you, thank you doesn't begin to express my deep appreciation to Joey Paul and F. Evelyn Bence for their outstanding editorial help in the final stages.

Mike Hyatt, my literary agent, of Wolgemuth and Hyatt, has not only been a very caring friend over the years, but he has worked diligently with me to prepare this newest manuscript. Our involvement goes all the way back to his University days when my wife Norma introduced him to Gail, his wife to be. Also, his commitment to help in all the promotional developments has been superb.

None of this project could have been started without the inspiration and encouragement of the men and women of American Telecast. They are the ones who produced all three of our TV infomercials, "Hidden Keys to Loving Relationships" with Dick Clark, then, Connie Selecca and John Tesh, and our last one with Kathy Lee and Frank Gifford. Without them the four million plus videos would not be floating around the world. Particularly, I'd like to thank Steve and Shannon Scott, Jim and Patty Shaughnessy, the Marsh family, and all the other employees of their outstanding company.

Another very important group of people on this project were four psychologists who not only teach on the graduate level, but who are warm, personable, and loving men: Dr. Rod Cooper, Dr. Dan Trathen, Dr. Gary Oliver, and Dr. Ken Canfield. I thank them for the many insights they gave me over the last few years. These men all helped me develop my video series for national TV, eighteen sessions in all. They met with me for days at a time and imparted their wisdom and research. Then after I had taken their instruction and developed each session, they would again listen to my sessions and evaluate the accuracy and validity of each session. In short they have not only greatly enriched my life over the past few years, but they have been truly great friends in stretching me to learn so many terrific new things about marriage and life. Dr. Canfield presently has the single largest database of fathering research of any marriage and family center in the world. The other three men all have regular counseling responsibilities, teach in a graduate school of psychology, and help with an organization that hopes to inspire and challenge almost one-half million men to become more loving to their families and to learn how to relate better in their spiritual lives.

Then there's Dr. John Trent who is not only a good friend, but the one who first introduced me to the best personality inventory I have ever studied. He has an unusual grasp of this concept and I'll always be indebted to him for his inspiration, love, and instruction.

I also want to thank Bill Butterworth for his help in the initial stages of our project. He had a great ability to help me retell my own stories with humor. Randy Marshall also gave me excellent assistance with stories and jokes.

Then I wish to thank the many couples who allowed me to review each chapter with them week after week as we were developing it. Terry and Janna Brown, Rick and Trish Tallon, Todd Ellett, Chris and Sonja Meyer, John and Karen Hart, Chris Zervas, Jack and Sherry Herschend, John and Lisa Clifford, Amy Davis, Smith and Gail Brookhart. Then, following this unique group's help, I had another large focus group of men and women critique each chapter after the book had been finished. Terri Felton and Terri Norris headed this delightful group. They were great. They met for an entire day and rated each chapter and gave suggestions on how to improve each one.

Thanks to my publisher, Word, (all of them, who also read and helped in the final stages of editing and marketing).

All in all, this has been the most involved project I have ever under-taken. It has taken almost two years of writing and over twenty years of gathering the information. But, I'm very aware that this project could not have happened without hundreds of precious individuals helping in the process. Thank you for your valuable help!!

Getting the Most from This Book

If you keep your eyes open to three specific things while reading this book, I believe you will get far more from the suggestions offered here.

First, stretch your mind to at least entertain the idea that you are fully responsible for your own quality of life, no matter what your circumstances have been, are, or may become.

Second, be open to the idea that falling in love with life is the best way to equip yourself to stay in love with your spouse—forever. To help you do this, I've divided this book into two parts offering separate sets of principles. The first half of the book is based on this critical truth: You will never know the deep satisfaction of a life-long love with your spouse if you are not first in love with life. In this half of the book I'll give you five ways to enrich your own life. Then, in part 2, I'll present eight practical helps for understanding and, yes, loving your mate. These principles hold and can bring about positive change in a relationship whether or not your spouse is willing to make personal changes in his or her lifestyle or attitude. Having said that, of course, the ideal is for the two of you to work together at improving your relationship.

Third, read through the entire book while marking sections that strike you as: *Yes, this describes me or a dynamic in my marriage. I need to hear this out.* Then go back to the marked pages that apply to you; reread them and work through those issues. Look for deeper insight as you go for a love that lasts forever.

As you work through the book I'll give you pointers for tapping resources at hand—family, friends, and coworkers—to help you follow through on many of the ideas shared within these pages. And the books referenced in the endnotes are additional invaluable resources. You don't have to live with the gnawing feeling that the happiness you discover will never last. Love and contentment can!

You'll see that everything I teach or write about has a basic theme. I'm always trying to expose the age-old struggle between the life-giving principle of honor and the destructive emotion of anger that too often creeps in when we don't get what we expected. I see honor and anger as being opposites, at two ends of a pole. Each of us can make daily choices about which emotions we will experience. When we choose anger over honor, we unknowingly (or knowingly) welcome the stress-producing, life-draining, divorce-creating thoughts that lead us down a path of personal and relational destruction. But choose honor, and you choose life.

Over the past five years, I've had a learning-curve explosion. It's as if I'm back in graduate school. I don't know what hit me; maybe it's the vitamins, or could it be that wonderful Ozark Mountain air, but my hunger to learn has rocketed. This newfound knowledge has greatly expanded my understanding of many principles I've written about in the past. You'll see the exciting new aspects I've discovered lately and have shared in seminars across the country and on videotape. Thousands of couples can tell you these principles have worked wonders. And with every passing year, as I learn more about myself, my family, and the human race, I understand the truths at a deeper level. This book reflects that growth, that comes as we choose to face new challenges placed before us.

I urge you to join me on this journey to forever-love.

Making Love
Last Forever

Part I

The Love-for-Life Factor: How to Fall in Love with Life

The first step toward achieving the deep satisfaction of a lifelong love with your spouse is learning to love life itself—every part of it, good and bad, harsh and rewarding. But just how do you nurture this attitude, this exuberant *joie de vivre?*

Here in part 1 of *Making Love Last Forever* I present five key choices that are placed before you. Your decisions in these areas can mean the difference between (1) Your full celebration of life's journey and love, or (2) A disastrous collision that can sink your love into the depths of despair.

To help get you off to a quick start, in chapter 1 I'll share love's best-kept secret. Then I'll describe five "icebergs" that have the potential to sink your marriage—and the choices you can make to navigate around those icebergs and ensure a safe and rewarding marriage journey for you and your mate.

In chapter 2 I'll show you how to detect your own level of anger, one of the most dangerous icebergs. The average person has little or no idea how damaging forgotten or ignored anger can be—alienating loved ones, sabotaging relationships. Worse yet, most people don't even know how much destructive anger they're carrying around—and from past experiences, everyone has some degree of buried anger. Like a ball and chain, it weighs one down. But we can choose to break free of that destructive anger; I'll show you how. Then in chapter 3 I'll describe seven ways to release anger's control over you and your relationships.

In chapter 4 I'll show you a second choice. You can choose a disastrous route—ignoring the value of any trials that come your way, or you can choose to see that every painful encounter contains a "pearl of love" you can add to your life to build a priceless collection. When we face hardship, we don't have to get bitter. We can choose to use the hardship to make love grow bigger and better.

In chapter 5 we discuss the perils of "putting all your eggs in one basket." I'll show you how you can choose to diversify your life interests and increase your chances for remaining satisfied with life and for staying in love.

Chapter 6 shows two great truths that have transformed my and my wife's attitudes and increased the safety we feel with each other because we've learned to avoid our past patterns of sabotaging our love. I'll share how we've chosen to not allow people and circumstances to "take away" our love for life because we've seen how this can lead to a relational disaster.

Finally, in chapter 7 I'll discuss the choice of establishing your own personal spiritual journey. Being disconnected from a living and loving God is like untying and pushing away a life jacket, thinking we're better off without it. God's love is the fuel we need to move into warmer water, away from damaging icebergs.

After discussing these five choices to help you avoid the icebergs and choose to fall in love with life, in part 2 I'll give you the best ways I've found to celebrate your love and enrich your relationship with your mate. Most of these principles will also improve your relationships with children and friends.

When you assume full responsibility for your present and future, you come to a place where you—like thousands of others—can make a deep commitment to your spouse and your kids: "I don't want to be bound to the past anymore. I want a 'new generation,' a fresh start."

When you do, you'll be taking the first step on the journey to forever-love.

1

Love's Best-Kept Secret

If I were to ask the question: "What is human life's chief concern?" one of the answers we should receive would be: "It is happiness." How to gain, how to keep, how to recover happiness, is in fact for most . . . . at all times the secret motive of all they do, and of all they are willing to endure.
                                                                        —William James

Will our love last forever? It's the hope of every starry-eyed bride and groom who clasp hands and say, "I do."

If your marriage is anything like mine, a few years after the wedding, you or your spouse—or both of you—were wondering why you had ever chosen this person to live with. "Till death do us part"? Impossible! "To love and to cherish"? You've got to be kidding!

I take much of the blame for the first disastrous years of my marriage. I was a wounded young man who had learned wounding tactics from my wounded, angry father. I knew how to lash out, clam up, lecture, and get my own way. In response to my tirades, my wife, Norma, learned how to cope.

But for Norma and me . . . something happened on the way to "forever." We discovered the principles I present in this book. We set a new course that has renewed our love and deepened our relationship. Today after thirty-one years of marrage, we are in love—with life and with each other.

Is it really possible to marry and then see that starry-eyed love actually get better? Yes.

Restoring a Wrecked Relationship

Whenever I see love win out in a marriage that looked hopeless, my confidence is increased, and I've found ways to help almost anyone stay in love despite impossible odds. Take this seemingly "shipwrecked" relationship:

Who would have thought that John and Sharon would reconcile and eventually enjoy a good marriage? It was eleven o'clock one night when the phone rang. Norma and I were already in bed. At the other end of the line was John, a popular, local business executive. He was locked in a major argument with his wife, Sharon, and the dispute was so fierce that he was glaring and saying things like, "I'm sick of trying. I want to get on an airplane and fly to another state. I just don't have any energy left to stay with this woman." Before he took such a drastic step, however, he was making this one last attempt to reach out for help. "Is there anything you can do for us?" he asked. "Can we come over tonight and talk with you?" Norma and I had a quick discussion, and we invited them to come over.

John and Sharon made their way to our home, and the argument continued in front of us. The issue they were facing was serious: John was addicted and out of control sexually, and to add insult to injury, he had given Sharon a sexually transmitted disease. She was nauseated by his behavior and disgusted with him.

Despite the gravity of the situation, a couple of things happened that night that are comical in hindsight—especially if you like seeing Murphy's law lived out. For instance, at one point in their arguing, Sharon kicked our coffee table, driving it toward me and causing it to cut my leg. At another point, Sharon was nearly breaking my fingers in an effort to get out of my grasp so she could run outside and attack John. (Norma had taken him into the front yard in the hope of cooling things down a bit.)

By 12:30 or 1:00 A.M. I had been beaten up, yelled at, and deprived of sleep, so I felt I had earned the right to say something to this couple. (They hadn't allowed us to give them any advice yet.) I began, "Well, as I've listened to both of you, I think there's something you can start working on even tonight."

But John looked at his watch and said, "I am so tired. I am so discouraged. I don't have any more energy. I've got to leave."

And with that they both left. I fell asleep that night thinking, *This will never work out.*

I share this extreme case because unfortunately more than 50 percent of the marriages in this country end in divorce—and it doesn't have to be that way. In time John and Sharon acted on most of the principles I've shared in these pages—and their relationship turned around. When things had cooled down, we met several more times, and we helped them connect with a counselor who specializes in their particular conflict. Finally John accepted the need to address the issues head-on with their counselor and with the help of a small support group. He came to understand that he had used illicit sex as medication for the pain of being hatefully rejected by his dad and of knowing his marriage relationship was weak. For her part, Sharon came to understand how her anger had blocked her ability to establish any type of meaningful relationship with John. She didn't understand how conflict can be the doorway to deeper intimacy.

Now, several years later, this couple whose relationship was so critically fractured is together and, believe it or not, they are in love. What's more, John and Sharon are helping other couples discover the joy they found as they made the midcourse adjustments that renewed their love.

I trust your marriage is far from being on the rocks. Maybe you're reading this book simply because you want to do everything you can to make a new marriage last a lifetime—or because you want to revive a love that seems a little off course. You can avert the loss of your love by heeding certain warnings and choosing to make small changes to get yourself back on course. Later I'll show you five important choices that can make the difference between disaster and a satisfying voyage.

Not long ago I was bowled over as I was reminded of how every aspect of my life is influenced by the choices I make. This particular wake-up call had to do with my physical condition, but the lesson I learned opened my eyes to these five choices.

The Lesson of the *Titanic*

When it comes to my blood-pumping heart, I know I'm a high-risk patient. My dad died of a heart attack in his fifties. One brother died of heart failure at fifty-one. My oldest brother had a massive heart attack at fifty-one and has since had another. Now that I'm fifty-five, my own medical exams have prompted the doctor to shake his head with concern.

For years, although I knew our family history, I chose to believe that I didn't need to pay much attention to the doctor's preventive (I called it drastic) advice, though at Norma's insistence I did occasionally get myself to the Cooper Clinic in Dallas, which specializes in heart-related matters. Recently I was in Texas for another exam. After all the tests had been completed, I sat in the doctor's office, listening and laughing, trying to make light of some of the results. Then I noticed that the doctor had a painting of a ship hanging on the wall. In a joking way, I pointed to it and said, "That's the *Titanic*, isn't it?"

The doctor didn't miss a beat. Playing along with my jovial mood, he nodded and said, "It's interesting that you'd bring that up. Do you know why I have it there?"

"No," I responded.

"Do you know much about the *Titanic*, Mr. Smalley?"

"No, I don't," I admitted, walking into his trap. I know it's at the bottom of the ocean; that's about it."

"Well," he explained, "the experienced captain of the *Titanic* was warned six separate times to slow down, change course, and take the southern route because icebergs had been sighted. But he ignored all six specific warnings because he was the captain, and he thought, *This ship is unsinkable* . . ."

"I had no idea the ship received that many warnings," I said, still not seeing where he was leading me.

". . . then *rip*—the ship hit the iceberg. It went down quickly and disastrously," he said. Then he leaned across his desk and looked me straight in the eye. "And how many times have you been warned about your heart?" he demanded.

"Lots of times," I replied weakly as his point struck home.

"And when will you take it seriously and change course?" he asked.

As a result of that conversation, I've made some basic lifestyle changes that have great potential for improving my health and prolonging my life. Almost anyone can make small adjustments if he or she believes it will make a lasting positive difference.

If you change course when warned, you can avoid disaster—and then celebrate the voyage. It's the strongest principle anyone can learn from the *Titanic*. And it's also the best-kept secret of making love last forever. If we tune our ears and eyes to the warnings, we can change much more than our life expectancy. Here in part 1 of this book, I give you my sighting of five icebergs that can sink your love forever. Only you can make the choice to heed those warnings and change the course of your voyage. In part 2, I'll share eight thick "steel" linings that will make it nearly impossible for your love boat to sink.

I've designed this book to help you *stay* in love with your mate but also to *fall in love with life*. What does loving life have to do with loving your spouse? Much of what you read in the first half of this book is based on this truth: *For your love to last forever, you must be in love with life*. Think in terms of the oxygen-mask instructions given by airline flight attendants. They say that passengers flying with children or others who need assistance should fasten their own masks first before trying to help someone else. If you don't make the choice to reach for oxygen for yourself, there's no point in your trying to help anyone else. You won't have the strength or ability to do it. That's how it is with love: Learn to love your own life first, and then you have the resources to give and receive love.

Your life or your marriage doesn't have to hit the rocks—the icebergs or immovable objects that can sink your love. Your discontent can be a warning you can heed. *Change course. Avoid disaster. And celebrate your life and love together—a long and gratifying voyage*.

Note what I didn't say. Love's best-kept secret is not *change (or exchange) your spouse* or *change your job* or *change your address*. It's *change your own course*. Even small changes in your behavior can lead to major changes in your life—no matter what your past, no matter how much pain you've plowed through. In the same way, even small personal changes can have enormous positive effects on your marriage, according to research on the crucial factors that keep a couple happily married.[1] (Personally, this gives me great hope, because, though I'm calling for change, no one's talking about sainthood!)

You Can Choose to Get on Course

Do you want to know the deep satisfaction that comes from being in love? It's simple. It's your choice.

My choice? you're thinking. *But you don't know what I've been through. You don't know what I have to live with. You don't know my mate!*

I agree this may be a hard truth to swallow, because it also means you no longer have any excuse to be miserable! I hated the idea at first. For more than half my life, I would find all kinds of reasons why I wasn't fulfilled and in love. I could place blame with the best of them. Then, little by little after age thirty-five, I started seeing what so many had already said about our enjoyment of life and our love being in our own hands.[2]

Someone who continually blames problems on others or on his or her circumstances becomes what author Stephen Covey calls "the reactive person." Reactive persons allow others to rob them of their quality of life. Covey sees another group of people as *proactive*. They're ones who believe "as human beings we are responsible for our own lives. Our behavior is a function of our decisions—our choices—not our conditions. We can subordinate feelings to values. We have the initiative and the responsibility to make things happen."[3]

One of my favorite writers in this area is Dr. Harriet Goldhor Lerner. A chapter in her book *The Dance of Anger* could convince anyone that one's marital happiness is mostly in one's own hands.[4] She also says that putting our energy into changing another person to enhance our own enjoyment of him or her is a solution that "never never works."[5] If we focus our attention on adjusting someone else's life so we can find happiness, we fail to exercise the only power we have for enriching our own lives: the power to choose for ourselves. In short, here is the formula: (1) We can't change other people. (2) We can choose to make changes in ourselves. (3) As changes occur in ourselves, people around us usually adjust their responses and choices according to our new behavior.

If this seems too hard for you to take right now, please withhold judgment until you've finished the next few pages. Then see if it doesn't make more sense.

To flesh out this truth, let's look at someone who chose to take responsibility for his own emotional well-being. When Richard first came to see me, he was not a happy man. Picking up the phone to call a counselor was a first step in acknowledging that his dissatisfaction with life was a warning that something was wrong. He was frustrated, disappointed, and fearful things were never going to change. And yet a wee bit of hope for something better prompted some changes in his life.

Richard was in his fifties, a husband and dad, a classy dresser, and the president of his own large company. After more than thirty years of marriage to Gail, he'd grown tired of her nagging and hatefulness. But he had also grown tired of expecting Gail to change and meet his relational needs, as she had in the early days of their marriage. And even though he hated the thought, he was contemplating divorce. But before he took that drastic step, he sought out and acted on my advice.

After the usual counselor-client preliminaries, I asked what had brought him to me. He answered, "I'm aware of my part in messing up with my wife and kids. I've spent so much time building this company. Now I recognize that even though it's late, I want to have a better relationship with them. I'm very successful financially, but I'm not very happy, and neither are my family members. I don't know how to go about changing things, especially after being the way I've been for so many years."

Then he added something highly significant. "I didn't have much of a relationship with my own dad," he said. "In fact, he was always too busy for me, just the way I've been with my family."

Right there was a key factor in Richard's past failure as a husband and father. His own dad had never built a close relationship with him, and that pattern probably had gone back for several generations. So Richard's model as a parent was weak, and Richard didn't get the opportunity to see a man loving his wife. His grandfather's example as parent and husband got passed from generation to generation. As a result, Richard didn't know any other approach.

If Richard had been hooked on the blame game (where you "win" by finding someone else to blame for everything wrong in your life), he could have stopped his growth at this point. With a little bit of new insight, he could have said, "Okay, it's mostly my father's fault!" Or he could have said, as so many workaholic people do, "But I was providing for my family! I did it all for them so they could have a better standard of living. If they can't understand my good motives, it's their problem. Hang this 'relationship' bit."

If Richard had chosen to blame his father for his own problems, he might have had some justification. Research has shown that people raised under strong, controlling, and rejecting parents may, in turn, reject and control their own families.[6] But Richard was no longer looking for a scapegoat. He took responsibility for his response to the way he had been parented. At this point Richard learned two powerful truths:

1. What I am today is because of the choices I've made in the past.

2. I am 100 percent responsible for all the choices I've made.

Richard began to distance himself from the age-old rationalization: *The devil made me do it.* Richard no longer was going to empower his father to ruin his relationships. He took responsibility for himself. He said things like, "No more, Dad; I'm not going to follow your example any longer. I'm going to discover what I need to do for myself and for my wife and children and finally find satisfaction in these vital areas of my life." All he needed was some guidance to start avoiding the icebergs and sail toward warmer seas.

Richard was also willing to start the process of adjusting his own life before his oh-so-irritating wife changed. As a counselor, I love situations like that where I can jump right in the middle of a gigantic mess and try to help turn it around. So I said, "Let's start with your kids. I'll go with you, and we'll go to see one child at a time. We'll just talk to your children. Let's face the truth about what has happened between you and them. Let's find out what we can do."

(Incidentally, most wives love it when they see husbands rebuilding their relationships with their children. It can offer hope to the wife that the husband is serious about changing his relationships, especially the one with her.) When Richard told Gail his plans, she was doubtful but indeed encouraged.

The first call went to their twenty-seven-year-old son, a graduate student. Robert agreed to meet with us, so we flew to the city where he lived and met him in a hotel room.

We sat and made a lot of small talk, and then as moderator I said, "Robert, your dad has asked me to help both of you restart your friendship. Could I ask you to begin by rating where your relationship with your dad is today? Rate it from zero to ten—zero meaning 'rotten relationship' and ten meaning 'great relationship.' Your father really wants to know how you see your relationship with him."

Robert stammered uncomfortably as if he felt unsafe. He fidgeted for a while before he said, "Well, about a two or three."

As low as that number was, I knew his totally honest rating would have been a zero or one.

Richard responded, "Son, I'm not surprised with that at all. I know I never spent the time I needed to spend with you, and I really feel bad about that." And then this dad said, "Son, I've come to tell you sincerely that I want to be your friend. I've missed a lot of years, and I feel terrible about that. I've never known how to be a good father and friend. As you know, with my dad, I just never learned how. But I want you to understand that I'm here today because I want to find out from you what it will take to be your good friend."

Big tears welled up in Robert's eyes, and an awkward silence instantly filled the room. No one wanted to talk. We all just sat there hoping someone would break the ice. Then, without coaching, Richard stood up and walked over to his son. Robert also stood. As they faced each other, Richard said softly, "Son, for years I've wanted to say that I love you, but every time I tried, something always seemed to block me. But today, in front of a friend, I want to say to you . . . I love you with all my heart. I've always been proud of you, and I hate myself for not saying it. Why have I been so mute? I do want to be your good friend, and I just hope it isn't too late."

Robert threw his arms around his dad, and they just held each other, melting in each other's arms. (Of course, I was bawling.) After a few minutes, they sat down, and Robert stared at his dad for a while. Then he said, "All my life I've longed for you to say what you've said today, but, to be honest, I never thought it would happen. And here you are, sitting in this room, saying the things I've wished for. Dad, thanks for coming."

Before we left, Richard asked for and received his son's forgiveness. Then Richard asked, "How can we start to get to know each other and build a real friendship?"

"Why don't we play golf today and talk about it?" Robert suggested. "Let's begin with that." And that's what they did.

In the months that followed, Richard and Robert spent more time together. And although I didn't go with him again, Richard also went on to meet with each of his other children. I later heard from them about how excited they were that "my dad still thinks enough of me to want to become my friend." Dads, it's amazing how powerful our words are. Never take them lightly!

Richard changed course to avoid the first destructive iceberg. In the next chapter you'll see what Richard, along with John and Sharon, began to avoid and how their love and marriages moved into warmer water. Richard and his children and wife are still working at their relationships. They've made progress—because of one person's initiative to go for something better.

The Future Is Yours!

Richard did two key things—the same two things I had to do in pursuing satisfaction in life and love in spite of a painful past—the same things we all need to do. He took responsibility for his own future choices, and he accepted the reality of the past while choosing to live beyond it.

Taking Responsibility for One's Own Future Choices

To change the course of his marriage and his relationships with his children, Richard first owned his own problems and took full responsibility for his future with a clear plan of action. In other words, he had to accept the fact that we're responsible for our present and future. Our future is a reflection of our past and present choices. How we handle unhealthy things from the past, the current state of our marriage, our children, our friendships, our job, and so on is up to us. Wherever we find ourselves, the buck stops with us! Whatever it takes, we need to be willing to grab the reins of the future and say, "Somehow, some way, I'll find what I need to have a good life for myself and my family!"

In one sense I see humans as being like cars. When young, we had "warranties"—reasonable expectations—that our parents and others could fix most of our problems for us. But as adults, our warranties are up. We've gone the years and covered the miles. We have to say, "If this thing called 'my life' breaks down, I'm the one who has to get it fixed."

That's what Richard did. He assumed the responsibility to make things right. He didn't blame his father for being a poor role model. Nor did he blame his career for keeping him away from home so much. That approach would have been the surest route to continuing failure. He did need to understand the lasting effect of his heritage, as I had to do when faced with my own heritage, discussed below. But then he needed to ask, "What do I do to overcome my past?"

Accepting the Reality of the Past and Choosing to Live Beyond It

The second course correction Richard made was to accept the truth of his past. He looked realistically at what his father had done to him, and he decided to take the good and discard any of the bad as he saw it. He didn't want his past to control his present and future.

I know what it feels like to grow up with an angry father. I know that my dad's behavior affected me, along with my brothers and sisters. At times, I used to wish things would have been different. But they weren't. So now I have to take what was given to me and do the best I can with the available resources. This has truly been a releasing and joyful experience as I've come to realize I'm free to take the counsel of others—friends, family, books—and decide to do what I believe is best for me and my family. I don't have to waste time wishing things had been different. I'm free to **choose how I will respond** to everything that happens or doesn't happen to me.

While we can't succeed by blaming the past for our current unhappiness, we do need to understand and interpret our inherited tendencies so we can consciously grow beyond them. If we don't, I've found that we usually remain "frozen" at a lower maturity level.

A personal illustration: On one of our first family trips to Hawaii, Norma, the kids, and I were all excited about hitting the sand and being together. As we prepared to go down to the beach for the first time, however, I was delayed for some reason. Everyone else wanted to get going. But I explained, "I'm just not ready."

"Okay," they said, "we'll go on ahead. Come find us when you're ready. We'll be right down here." They pointed up the beach.

"Sounds fine," I told them. About half an hour later, I left the hotel room and went looking for my family. I walked up and down the beach as far as I could go in both directions, but I couldn't find them. As time went on, I started feeling irritated and hurt. *Wait a minute*, I thought. *We're here in Hawaii as a family to be together, and they've deserted me! I've been rejected!*

Basically, I was pouting and showing my immaturity. I never did find them, so I went back to the hotel and waited impatiently. Eventually they came in, and I was sulking. "What's wrong with you?" they asked.

"You left me," I said glumly.

"We told you where we were going," they responded.

"Yeah, well, I went there, and you weren't there," I accused them.

"We meant that other beach just a little farther down," they said.

"Well, that wasn't very clear!" I insisted, unwilling to be appeased. After that, I wasn't speaking to anybody. Thank God for our son Greg, who has always had the capacity to confront his father.

"Dad," he said cautiously and respectfully, "I thought you wanted a 'new generation' with our family—to be a better father than your own dad was in a lot of ways."

"I do," I insisted, glaring at him.

"Well, Dad," he said, "is this really the kind of example you want to pass on to me?"

"No," I had to admit grudgingly. "And I realize I've asked you guys to help me when I'm not responding well."

Now, here's the really interesting thing. My wife said, "You know, this is exactly how your father acted when he was upset. He would be angry, sulk, be silent, and close everyone out." And she had said to me in the past, "The worst thing you do to me is when you become silent, because then I feel we're not connected." That was my way of punishing the family when I wasn't happy with them, and that was also some of my dad coming out in me.

Greg was in high school when this conflict occurred, and as it escalated, he intervened. "Okay," he said, "let's get this solved. Let me hear your side, Mom . . . Now let me hear your side, Dad . . . Dad, don't you understand what you did here? . . . Okay, Mom, do you understand? Good. That fixes it." He actually helped us solve that minor skirmish. No wonder he's now working on his doctorate in counseling!

By handling the situation so directly and drawing the comparison to my father, my family made me see the level of immaturity at which I was stuck. It's important to take such a look at our level of maturity from time to time. And when we find ourselves thinking only of ourselves, a lot of that can be traced right back to our past. One expert says the worst thing a husband can do if he wants his love in marriage to last is to close out the family with the "silent treatment."[7] That was me. But I don't have to let this type of behavior continue. I understand my past, but I'll be hanged before I will allow it to determine my future!

The Challenge

What about you? Have you come to the place where you're agreeing and willing to take full responsibility for the quality of your own life? Can you—like John and Sharon and Richard and Gary Smalley—turn away from the blame game, no matter how difficult your past has been, and embrace the great, freeing truth that *you will be as content as you choose to be*? I trust you will, and I know that if you do, the rest of this book is going to be like a trip to a buried treasure chest for you. You'll find insights all along the way that will help you to make your life the best it can be.

If you're a victim of abuse, you're probably going to need help to deal with your situation and to rediscover love for life and love for your spouse. And if others react negatively to the changes you try to make, the going won't be easy. But even then you still choose your own response to each situation, and you, too, can decide to be persistent and hopeful. If you do, I can almost guarantee your future will be better than your past.

The next two chapters discuss the critical choice of draining unresolved anger from your life. This anger causes more pain, drowns more marriages, sinks more children than any other power I know. It's the mother of all "icebergs." You'll not only see the damage it does, but you'll see how you can keep it far removed from you and your loved ones.

Forever-Love Principles

1. Forever-love does not work to change or exchange a spouse. Instead, it realizes, "If something's wrong, it's up to me to change my response and my mind-set."

2. Forever-love believes that even small behavior changes can lead to major improvements in relationships.

3. Forever-love is possible, no matter what your circumstances.

4. Forever-love calls for courage to move beyond the status quo.

5. Forever-love says the future = hope.

6. Forever-love says, "I'll take responsibility for my own choices—past, present, and future."

7. Forever-love accepts the reality of the past but lives beyond the blame game.

8. Forever-love *can't* change the weather. It *can* choose how to respond to the weather.

9. Forever-love is willing to move beyond inherited, intergenerational negative patterns.

2

The Number One Enemy
of Love: Unresolved Anger

*Individuals or whole peoples can gnaw on old grievances, remembering them
again and again, renewing them obsessively until the shape of memory and desire
is permanently warped along the lines of anger.*

—William Stafford[1]

There's a major destroyer of love on the loose; I've found it to be the leading cause of divorce and the single greatest thief of one's love for life. It may
already be at work in your life and marriage.

This destroyer is *forgotten, unresolved anger*—not just the kind that gnaws
at one's stomach night after night but also the type that quietly disappears.
At least I used to think it disappeared. But when we bury anger inside us
. . . *it's always buried alive!* Then, when we aren't even aware of its presence,
it does its damage, destroying like rust on a car, like moths in a dark closet.

But it doesn't have to remain buried; it doesn't have to wreak its havoc
in our lives and relationships. There is hope—when we choose to rout it out.

Anger—Buried Alive

Let me tell you how anger worked its damage in the life of a friend,
Larry, who for nine years was angry at me. He tried to say the anger would
go away, but it didn't.

At one time we were great friends. Then I sensed there was a wall between us. We were still casual friends, and I attributed any distance between us to the fact that we no longer lived in the same city; we now lived halfway across the country from each other. And anyway, I figured that if there were anything between us, he would talk about it.

Well, not long ago, I was staying in a hotel in the town where Larry lives. While I was there, I got a call from him. "We've got to talk," he said.

"All right," I answered, "about what?"

"I've been upset with you for about nine years now," he answered, amazing me. As he went on, I was even more appalled. "I've been really angry with you all that time, and I can't shake it," he said, his voice quivering. "I've tried to tell myself I would get over it in time, but it won't go away. I think about it a lot. Now it's affecting what I do in my job and my other relationships too. I don't want to live like this anymore. I have to get this thing resolved. Can we meet?"

Words like that from a friend make you sick to your stomach. As Larry spoke I asked myself over and over, *What did I do? What does this involve?* Of course I agreed to meet with him.

We got together in a restaurant, and there the story came out, though it took about five hours. Larry cried, I cried, and at one point it got so emotional that his nose started bleeding. One messy scene! But he finally got out this deep anger he had been carrying for all those years.

The problem had grown out of a decision we had made nine years before: Together we were going to confront a guy with whom we both had major disagreements. This was a very serious situation, and we were both equally upset. We went to see the man, and when we got there, the guy said to me, "I'll discuss the problems you and I have with each other, but I'd rather not have both of you ganging up on me."

So I talked it over with Larry, who agreed to leave the conversation—and the scene. I remember, as we parted, telling Larry I was sorry and that we would talk later. But as things turned out, Larry thought I had sided with the other guy and deserted him as my friend. I had actually doubled Larry's anger. I left him with his anger toward the other person unresolved and unintentionally I also added hurt to his anger.

So Larry walked away thinking, *How could Gary have done this to me? We were going to talk to the man together, and he just discarded me like I'm not of any value.* Yet I had never understood what I had done or how my friend felt about it until that day in the restaurant.

When I heard his feelings and how the incident had affected him for nine years, I grieved deeply. I had not intended to give more loyalty to our adversary than to my good friend.

Fortunately, our relationship was healed that day. We cried together, hugged each other, and sought each other's forgiveness. The anger was finally drained out of my friend but not before he had suffered depression and other signs of unhappiness for nine years. And since that time, we've gone on to develop a deeper friendship than ever before.

Some might say that Larry was overreacting and in time would have gotten over it. That's what he had thought would happen, but it didn't. There are thousands of people who wish they could shake off the effects of old offenses, but the truth is, many just can't. And because they aren't able to get over it, the damage continues inside them, sometimes for years.

Before you dismiss this chapter as being not for you because you're not an angry person, let me point out that most of us bury our anger so quickly that we don't know what we're doing. Then it does its sneaky damage. It often leads to our lashing out at others. Or it gets turned inward, where it can become depression. Some may pretend it's simply not there, but it is.

This chapter is designed to take a close look at anger, what causes it, and the massive havoc it wreaks. The next two chapters will help you drain away as much destructive anger as you need to.

Anger Springs from Three Separate Emotions

Anger is an emotion. Like all of our emotions, there's nothing wrong with it in and of itself. It's our human response to something that occurs, or at least to our perception of that occurrence. In fact, some anger is good; we *should* get angry when we see an injustice or when someone is trying to violate our personal property lines. In such cases, our anger is what motivates us to take appropriate action. But after anger motivates us to do something good, we can't afford to let it linger inside us. We have to get it out. Anger is a good emotion when it gets us moving, but if we let it take root, we set ourselves up for a great deal of potential harm.

Dr. Howard Markman of Denver University, a leading expert in the prevention of divorce, gives a strong warning about hidden anger. He reminds us that all those little discussions that just don't seem to get resolved and continually provoke an inappropriate outburst—issues that don't necessarily call for heated feelings, such as whether the toilet paper rolls from the top or the bottom or whether the toilet seat is up or down—are usually driven by anger that's just below the surface. No matter how many times a couple tries to resolve those issues or enter into deeper intimacy, the anger can keep them apart and in turmoil.[2] Living with angry people is like living in a minefield. If you say or do the wrong thing, *kaboom!* They explode all over everyone. And you're left thinking, *Oh, I had no idea that one thing I did would cause such a reaction.*

Actually, anger is a secondary emotion, not a primary feeling. It arises out of *fear, frustration, hurt,* or some combination of these three. For example, if someone says something harsh to us we first feel hurt and *then* anger. When we strip the word *anger* down to its deepest level, we see a thread that runs through this entire book—*unfulfilled expectations.* Frustration is not receiving what we had expected from other people or from circumstances.

Hurt is when we don't hear the words or receive the actions we expected from other people or from circumstances. And fear is either dreading that what we expect will not come as we wish it to or expecting that something bad is going to happen. In his book *Banishing Fear from Your Life*, Charles Bass clearly explains, "The process by which fear provokes anger is relatively simple: we use anger to cope with fear." He goes on to tell a wonderful story of counseling a couple "who interacted with a fear/anger reaction." From the husband and wife he heard two completely different stories. Here's the husband's version:

> Every time I come home, Mary is waiting for me with a chip on her shoulder. I hate to go home. As I drive home, I get more and more tense. When I get home and see her waiting for me with her hands on her hips, it just makes me mad, and I tie into her before she can get the jump on me.

The wife's story:

> Joe is always mad at me over something. . . . He always comes home in a bad temper. I really have to stand up to him to defend myself.[3]

For both people a smoldering anger was fueled by fear—of the other's anger.

There's a wonderful line in the classic Christmas carol written by Phillips Brooks. "O Little Town of Bethlehem" refers to "the hopes and fears of all the years." If those hopes aren't realized and those fears *are* realized—anger can settle in. Anger at ourselves. At specific others. At the more generic world. At God. We feel the need to blame our unhappiness on someone or something.

Anger is our choice. We choose to respond in anger when something happens to us that's outside of our control. It's a normal response, even a good response, when it's controlled. But we are the ones who choose to hold on to anger or to let it go. We can choose to see its powerful potential for destruction and take the steps to reduce it within us. Otherwise it's an iceberg sinking our love.

A Dangerous Substance

Anger should not be welcomed as a heart-guest. When we allow anger to linger and settle in, it brings harm not only to ourselves but also to those around us. Just think of all the times you've felt frustrated, hurt, or fearful. Is it your practice to ignore these emotions or to face them and then walk past them?

Think of anger as a sticky, bad-smelling, dangerous substance that can be compressed and stuffed into something like a spray can. Different people have different-sized cans—and different degrees of compression—depending on how much anger they're carrying and for how long.

What happens? Angry people tend to go around spraying their anger on other people. The spray is felt by others as meanness, insensitivity, negativity, and general offensiveness, and the "sprayers" may not even realize how they're behaving or how it affects other people. They just keep spraying in every direction everywhere they go like skunks that constantly feel threatened. And anger spray stings like an acid that burns.

How do we respond when we get sprayed by someone else's anger? Too often, without even thinking about it, we make the unhealthy choice of letting ourselves marinate in the angry person's spray. (Then we also begin to emit the foul odor.) After a while, it starts seeping inside us and filling our anger can. When this happens in families, anger is passed down from generation to generation, wreaking intergenerational havoc.

Sometimes a debilitating anger starts in childhood, perhaps with some sort of abuse. I have to confess that in the past, I had a big anger can that too often exploded on my wife and kids. The anger started to compress when I was a child because, as I already mentioned, my dad sprayed me often from his anger can. Since I was the youngest child, my brothers and sisters actually got sprayed a lot more than I, but I got my share.

My daughter made me aware of what I was doing when she confronted me one day about the way I treated my son Michael, who was in high school at the time. "Dad," she said, "you're so critical of Michael, of little things he says and does. You're really going to hurt him."

That took me by surprise. Frankly, I hoped she was exaggerating the seriousness of the situation. So I went to Michael, told him what his sister had said, and asked, "Is that true?"

"Yeah," he answered.

"Really?" I said, still not wanting to believe it.

"Dad," he said with great feeling, "I've had enough criticism for a lifetime!"

Then I had no choice but to accept the truth of it. And that realization helped me continue to drain my own anger and deal with it so I could stop the generational pull inherited from my dad. Again, our anger may be buried, but it's buried alive, destroying our own happiness and our relationships—unless it's routed out.

Have you ever wondered why there's so much abuse and violence in our country today? A lot of this anger that leads to violence started with parents who didn't know the effects that anger was going to have on their children. I expect that most of these parents were also unaware that their anger level had anything to do with nurturing their children. But consider the implications of this story: A prison volunteer got the idea that the prisoners might like to send Mother's Day cards to their moms. So she wrote to a greeting card company and asked it to donate some cards.

The company responded graciously and generously and, sure enough, those hard-bitten men gobbled them up. The demand was overwhelming! The volunteer ran out of cards before she ran out of sons who wanted to send expressions of love to their mothers.

Well, Father's Day comes just one month after Mother's Day, so the woman figured that was such a success she would do the same thing for Father's Day. She contacted the card company, and once again it honored her request.

The woman let the prisoners know that free Father's Day cards were available, then she waited for the men to rush in and get them. And do you know how many of those felons, many with a history of violence, asked for a card this time? Not one. Not a single prisoner wanted to express love to his dad. And that's when the woman learned that such men usually carry a deep resentment and even hatred toward their fathers—many of whom were absent from their sons.

The Consequences of Unresolved Anger

Even if your anger never turns violent or illegal, it can prove destructive—as it did for my friend Larry, as it has for me, and as you'll see from the consequences of unresolved anger I describe in the next few pages.

Distance from Other People

One of the most common results or symptoms of deep anger is relational distance, an unwillingness and inability to let others get close. It seems to block our ability to give and receive love. You're sincerely trying to develop a satisfying and loving marriage, but the anger spray in either you or your mate can greatly inhibit your efforts. Consider this truly unfortunate story of a couple that had been married about seventeen years:

The husband knew things were not going well; he wanted to do something about it, and he asked me for help. Because he lived in a different state, we had to communicate by phone and letter. He would describe a difficult domestic situation, and I would suggest something he could do to improve the relationship. A few days later, he would call and say, "I tried that, Gary, but it just doesn't seem to work. She didn't respond well at all."

We went back and forth like that several times, and after a while, I started to get a little irritated with him. *What's the matter with you? I thought. Can't you get this?* But that's not what I actually said. I'd suggest he try a little different approach.

A week later I would receive a letter stating, "Gary, I really want to love my wife, but I can't seem to do it."

This long-distance counseling continued off and on for about three years. Sometimes I wouldn't hear from him for months. And then one day he called to say, "I really appreciate all your help, but I'm leaving my wife."

I can't stand that kind of call! I dislike divorce, and I dislike losing a couple I've been trying to help. *Failure!* I thought. Again, that's not exactly what I said to him. I asked, "Why are you giving up?"

"Well," he answered, "when I woke up this morning, she was standing by the bed with a knife in her hand."

Whoa, I thought, *that could motivate a person to leave, couldn't it?*

But why didn't this husband's effort work? Why did their relationship get to the point of knife-wielding and eventually divorce? The one time I talked with the wife, I discovered an extreme bitterness toward her mother because of a series of childhood incidents. For years, without even realizing the implications, she had carried this deep-seated anger toward her mom, and it poisoned her relationship with her husband. She had been so hurt by her mother that she had decided unknowingly that she was never going to let anyone get close enough to hurt her again. No matter what advice I gave her husband and no matter how hard he tried to love her, his efforts were doomed. She simply wouldn't let him get near her heart. It's as if angry people can't allow others to get too close! The unhealed hurt holds them at arm's length, sabotaging relationships.

The irony is that *after* the divorce, the woman went to a counselor who specialized in uncovering anger, and he helped her overcome the deep bitterness she felt toward her mother. She learned how to forgive her mom. Through their children, this divorced couple eventually became good friends, but in the meantime she had remarried, so the damage to that first marriage was permanent.

Why hadn't the woman sought counseling earlier? She simply didn't know how much her anger was influencing her attitude and behavior; nor did she realize how much distance anger—very old anger—can create in a relationship.

The process can work like this: We are hurt. That hurt creates anger that's not dealt with; it fills our anger can. Now we grow cautious, unable to trust; our fear might cause us to reject others before others reject us. The pain may linger only in our unconscious minds, but we automatically try to keep others at a safe distance. Whenever people get too close, our anger can starts spraying, usually sabotaging relationships through negative words or actions.

Many people I've counseled or who have attended my seminars have run up against this. A man—like the one whose seventeen-year-long marriage ended in divorce—will get fired up in one of my sessions and decide, *I'm going to go home and love my wife and children better.* But when he gets home and tries to be a better husband, his wife resists and pushes him away emotionally. Why? Often it's because she was hurt in the past, and as a result her anger can is relatively full and she simply doesn't feel comfortable with the idea of her husband getting closer to her.

This distancing mechanism can neutralize the positive perks that someone else tries to give. My good friend Dr. Gary Oliver was counseling with a couple whose divorce was going to be final in a week. He told them he wasn't a miracle worker; looking for a last-minute solution to their problems, they said they were willing to try anything.

So Gary got alone with the husband and said, "I'd like you to give it a shot—admittedly a long shot. For the next seven days, I want you to praise your wife very specifically three times a day. Write down what you say. Then we'll meet again and see what happened."

Seven days later the three met again. Gary asked, "Have things changed much in the last week?"

"Nothing much is different," the wife said.

Gary asked the husband, "What did you do differently?"

"Well, I praised my wife twenty-one times this week," he reported.

"What?" she protested. "How can you say that?"

"I did," he insisted. "I wrote them all down."

"Why don't you read the list to us?" Gary suggested.

The husband pulled out his sheet of paper and read off all twenty-one praises.

Now here's the interesting thing. As the man read, his wife just shook her head in amazement. She had never heard even one of them in the entire week. It was as if he had gone to make a deposit in her bank account and found a sign saying "bank closed." When she realized he had, in fact, praised her all those times, she reached over and touched him tenderly for the first time in months.

Why was she blind to his attempts to show her love? Because people like her who have too much anger deep inside tend to neutralize the positive things that happen to them. They simply can't see or hear them.

In any relationship, this tendency to miss the positive and accentuate the negative is a very destructive force—one fed by chronic anger. Marital experts Drs. Howard Markman, Scott Stanley, and Susan Blumberg highlight the fact that negative beliefs and interpretations can powerfully filter out the positive and leave one seeing only the negative. It's such a destructive force, they call it one of the key danger signs for a marriage.[4]

Are you aware of how your angry moods may be affecting how you see others? Having this automatic distancing mechanism is like living inside a relational box made of thick plate glass. Anyone who tries to become more intimate with a "hidden-anger" person seems to smash into this glass barrier. And then when the offended one tries to move closer to others in relationship, the glass plate seems to magnify the "outsider's" image; this can scare the angry person into moving back to a "safer" distance.

Unfortunately, when you're in relationship with someone who retains old anger that predates your relationship, you can feel as if you've just eaten a restaurant meal and then been handed a bill for ten thousand dollars. You explain to the waiter that there's no way your bill could be so high, maybe even joking about how you couldn't possibly eat that much.

But then the waiter says, "Your bill is ten thousand dollars because we want you to pay for everyone who has eaten here today. Is that okay with you?"

"No, that's not okay!" you insist.

Yet that's exactly what people (perhaps you or your spouse) do when they hold too much anger inside. They make others—often it's their spouses or family members—pay the "bill" for those in the past who have offended them.

When you're around these hidden-anger people, you can just sense that these are folks you can't get close to. In such cases, sadly, everyone the hidden-anger person knows pays. That's why it's so important to get the anger out as soon as possible.

This may be the main reason why people from divorced homes have such a hard time staying married. Their own anger level pushes the mate away and sabotages the marriage. Dr. Scott Stanley told me these children of divorce typically were never able to access their anger, bring it to the surface, and solve it. They kept it bottled up inside.[5]

And if these children said to themselves, *I'll never be like my dad or mom when I get married,* they almost assuredly predicted the failure of their future relationships. Why? Because their harsh determination is frequently fueled by unresolved anger. The cycle can go on generation after generation as angry kids become angry adults who have kids of their own.

We each have to face our past and check the level of our own anger. We can stop this generational pull of ruined relationships by taking responsibility for reducing the level of anger within ourselves. (To assess your own level of hidden anger, see the anger inventory at the end of this chapter.)

Distance from God

A second consequence of unresolved anger can be spiritual blindness or feeling particularly distanced or alienated from God. A recent Gallup poll revealed that over 90 percent of Americans say they believe in God. That's great as a base, a starting point. But in my counseling, I've observed some reverse correlation between anger and faith: It seems the greater a person's unresolved anger, the more difficulty that person has in developing a meaningful spiritual life. The spiritual side of life offers us love and asks us to be loving and sensitive toward others, but anger appears to darken the heart, making it impossible to see the "call" or receive the love offered us from God. Anger can function like an automatic rheostat, turning down the spiritual light that could be shining within and from us.[6]

I experienced this myself when I was deeply angry at one man—at one time a coworker—for more than six years. I had little desire for or interest in spiritual things; I didn't want to be with other people who were worshiping God; I had sparse spiritual insight; I was also discouraged and at times depressed. I didn't recognize the cause at the time, but when I finally started getting my own anger out, I saw how much it had affected me in this area. With the release of the anger, my spiritual interest and satisfaction with life returned.

Distance from Oneself

Another consequence of unresolved anger is a lowered sense of self-worth. In this case the anger and low self-worth are so intertwined and so circular that it's hard to separate causes and effects. Let's say that a child's—or an adult's—personal sense of being or of his or her personal boundaries was drastically, maybe repeatedly, violated. Hurt, frustration with feeling helpless, and fear lead to anger. And that anger can set in and take this form: *I can't be worth much if others—and "life"—treat me like this.* The anger prompted by someone else's actions or attitudes can quickly become blame or guilt—directed at oneself. Such anger turned inward can become depression.

Take another example, this one of children of divorce. The initial question, *How could Mom and Dad tear apart our home?* might be answered, *Maybe I'm to blame. Maybe they don't love me and don't want to be around me.* In her book *Children of Divorce*, Debbie Barr notes, "If a preschooler has fleetingly wished any disaster upon a departing parent, the child's guilt may multiply."[7] As a result the child's self-worth plunges; his or her anger compresses. Again, ultimately these children tend to follow the same path as their parents did. After they marry, they sabotage the relationship and try to keep their spouses from hurting them again.

Dr. Earl D. Wilson makes this observation: "Anger can be a cover-up for guilt." I would add that this can be legitimate or illegitimate (false) guilt. Wilson goes on to tell a brief anecdote of a client named Bob who had quite a temper and who always kept his girlfriend at a distance. Wilson ends the discussion by saying, "After some time in counseling, Bob was able to see that the reason he couldn't accept Janice's compliments about him was that he saw himself as anything but nice. He had to deal with this guilt and his feelings of failure (anger at himself) before he was ready for a close relationship."[8]

The greater the pain we carry inside, the greater the temptation to engage in addictive behaviors to get relief—temporary relief. The addictive behavior can include an unhealthy addiction to another person. According to Dr. Scott Peck, unchecked anger is a critical element in the most common psychiatric disorder: People with a passive-dependent personality disorder come to believe that they cannot live a quality life without being cared for by another person. Passive-dependents set themselves up for emotional bankruptcy, because no one can ever fill them. No amount of positive praise or affirmation is ever enough. They are endlessly angry because people are continually disappointing them.

They're locked into a pattern of living where they must have others, but when they get them, they smother them and usually kill the relationship. They find someone else, and the same thing happens. As they continue to fail, their anger—fueled by hurt (feeling abandoned) and frustration (feeling a failure) and fear (of being alone)—can alienate them from themselves and others, eating away at them just as if they actually turned on themselves and gnawed at their ankles until they reached the bone.[9] Is anger destructive, or what?

The cycle of anger and the sense of low self-value feeding off each other also can produce physical problems. Many people today go to the doctor and complain of backaches, neckaches, or headaches. But when the doctor looks into it, he or she can't find any physical cause of the pain. And some doctors are concluding that this epidemic of aches and pains may be the outworking of buried anger.

This anger alienates us from our own bodies. Consider the results of tests with students in medical school and law school in the 1960s. By using basic personality tests, hostility was measured. Twenty-five years later the students were tracked down. By the age of fifty, only 4 percent of the low-ranked "easygoing" lawyers and 2 percent of the doctors had died. Lawyers who had ranked high on hostility had a 20 percent mortality rate; doctors, 14 percent.[10]

Anger in the form of chronic hostility has also been clearly and strongly linked to heart disease. Those who are more hostile are more susceptible to heart attacks—the leading cause of death in our country.[11] Hostile anger can boost heart rates, raise blood pressure, and lead to increased clogging of the arteries. What's worse, the risk of heart attack seems to be greatly increased during the two hours following a bout with anger.[12]

Keep in mind, these are just some of the physical risks of anger. When you think about all the problems anger and hostility cause in relationships, you really get the full picture of how destructive this emotion can be if it's not handled correctly.

Distance from Maturity

This last distance caused by unresolved anger is connected to all those previously mentioned. Unresolved anger freezes our emotional maturity level near where it was when the hurtful offense occurred. I discussed this briefly in chapter 1. Let's suppose your parents divorced when you were twelve. You were devastated, and your anger can began to fill. In all likelihood, you also got stuck near that emotional level. You may have an adult body, but you've probably got the heart of a wounded twelve-year-old.

Maybe you're not the angry person but you live with one. In that case, you may find yourself asking from time to time, *Why is he so childish?* or *Why does she say those off-the-wall, immature things that hurt us?*

For example, a father says to his six-year-old, "Hey, son, get that quarter out of your mouth. It's been on the floor and has germs all over it!"

But the wife immediately responds, "Oh, Jimmy, that's okay. Don't worry about it. Even germs can't live on what your father earns."

Where might a juvenile, cutting remark like that come from? Most likely from a big can of unresolved anger that started to develop when the woman was young herself. Inside, she's still a hurting, angry child.

Anger Has the Power to Keep Us Miserable

Read that subhead again and allow the truth to sink in: Anger has the power to keep you miserable.

Think back to my friend Larry, whom I offended and who stayed angry with me for nine long years. All that time, he was continually replaying his videotape of my offense. He was seeing my face and hearing my words of betrayal over and over, and the pain was fresh almost every time. That event and my behavior were exerting a tremendous, debilitating influence on his life long after I had forgotten the entire incident. He was actually empowering me to keep him miserable. He allowed my offense—which happened on one particular day—to go right on offending him day after day for nine years. (*Gary really did that to me!*) He unwittingly allowed me to control him.

Fortunately, he finally took the healthy steps of contacting me, getting his anger out in a good way, and restoring the relationship.

Unresolved anger and blame can imprison us and bind us and make us miserable at heart and miserable to live with. Conversely, there is truth to the song that says, "Freedom is a state of mind." You can break free of unresolved anger. You may need further insight and support to break free, but that freedom is available. And it is a key to staying in love with life and for life.

Reason for Concern . . . and Hope

The good news about all this deep, destructive anger is that there's hope for the future. It can be resolved. Whether it's you or a loved one—perhaps your mate—who struggles with this, there are healthy, freeing steps that can be taken. The anger we've kept for so long can be drained away; damaged relationships can be mended. In the next chapter, I'm going to show you just how this can be done.

For now, I hope you can see how unresolved anger is a very serious problem that demands attention. When I stop to consider all the damage caused by buried anger—the countless divorces and other broken relationships, the millions of violent crimes, the uncountable mean-spirited words and actions and the resulting hurt feelings that breed more anger, the physical pains and the billions of tax dollars spent to treat them—I'm amazed and appalled. I trust you are too.

But it's my hope that by this time you share my conviction that we've got to see our anger for what it is and choose to deal with it in a healthy way. We simply can't let anger stay inside us, unresolved, and build up over two, three, or more years. The price is too high. So please take the anger inventory that follows to see just what your current level of anger is. Then move on to the next chapter and see how to get this hidden destroyer of relationships under control.

The Anger Inventory

All of us have some unresolved anger remaining in us at all times, but the key is to reduce it to as low a level as we can. While this is not a scientifically constructed test, you may find it can give you some idea of where you stand in regards to your anger or your potentially anger-producing background. This is not a pass-or-fail evaluation but rather an aid to help you reduce the size of your own anger can. You may wish to discuss your results with your mate, a friend, or a trained counselor.

To take the inventory, simply rate each statement below, on a scale from 0 (very low) to 10 (very high), for how much it applies to you. Then look to the following chapters for help in dealing with your level of anger.

_____ 1. I have frequently recurring minor health problems.

_____ 2. I tend to have difficulty remaining close to people. Others have even said I am "cold."

_____ 3. I continually fail to see the pitfalls in business deals.

_____ 4. I have little interest in religious matters.

_____ 5. I have many doubts about the existence of God.

_____ 6. I tend to see religious people as "a bunch of hypocrites."

_____ 7. I tend to be judgmental or overly critical of people.

_____ 8. I have a general inability to see my own shortcomings.

_____ 9. My image is very important to me. What I wear and drive are big concerns.

_____ 10. I often struggle with feelings of low self-value.

_____ 11. I often fail to see that my words or actions hurt the feelings of others.

_____ 12. My parents divorced before I turned eighteen.

_____ 13. I think one or both of my parents drank too much alcohol.

_____ 14. My parents seemed addicted to drugs or other substances.

_____ 15. My parents abused me.

_____ 16. My parents seemed too distant or neglectful to me.

_____ 17. I felt that my parents were too controlling of me.

_____ 18. I often struggle with feelings of discouragement or depression.

_____ 19. I seem to be at odds with several people for long periods of time.

_____ 20. I tend to be overly controlling of my mate, children, or friends.

_____ 21. I have general feelings of anxiety; I can't put my finger on what it is that I'm uneasy about.

_____ 22. I have sometimes thought about suicide.

_____ 23. I have had a hard time forgiving others when they hurt or frustrate me.

_____ 24. I have a hard time confronting others when they hurt me, and I know that I'm not that good at getting my anger out.

_____ 25. I find myself overly busy most of the time.

_____ 26. I find it easier to blame others than to take responsibility for my mistakes.

_____ 27. I often overreact to what others say or do to me.

_____ 28. I feel I'm motivated far too often by fear of failure.

_____ 29. I often wish people who have hurt me could be punished somehow.

_____ 30. I frequently think that I've been cheated out of important areas of life.

_____ 31. I get into fights with others that sometimes result in physical aggression, such as throwing things, slapping, or hitting.

_____ 32. I don't really trust anyone other than myself.

Now add up the thirty-two numbers—your rating.

My total score: _____

If your total score is more than 100, the next two chapters are especially important for you. If your score is more than 200, you may want to see a counselor who is trained in helping people uncover and deal with anger.

Finally, as an additional help in assessing your level of anger, list below the people toward whom you hold anger, and rate your anger toward each on a scale from 0 (very low) to 10 (very high):

_____

_____

_____

Forever-Love Principles

Our list of forever-love principles continues from the previous chapter:

10. Forever-love does not welcome anger as a heart-guest.

11. Forever-love knows the destructive, alienating power of anger.

12. Forever-love says no to anger's misery and yes to inner freedom.

3

Seven Ways to Unload Unresolved Anger

Most of us, unfortunately, . . . say things like: "He made me so mad." "You really get to me." "Her remark embarrassed me terribly." "This weather really depresses me." . . . We are content to blame others, circumstances, and bad luck. . . . [But] we can rise above the dust of daily battle that chokes and blinds so many of us; and this is precisely what is asked of us in the process of growth as a person.

—John Powell[1]

As we saw in the preceding chapter, unresolved anger is that videotape of past offenses that keeps playing over and over in our minds, doing incredible damage to us and to everyone around us. We simply must deal with it—eject the tape, if you will. It may not be easy, but it's possible. There is a way to do it. If Linda could make it work, I believe anyone can.

Linda, a college student, came to me for help. She was discouraged, depressed, and visibly losing stamina. "I can't go on like this," she said. "I'm so miserable!"

"What's troubling you so much?" I asked.

"This is really embarrassing," she replied. "I've never told anyone because I just know that somehow it's going to come back and hurt me even more in the future."

"I'm here to help," I assured her. "I want to listen and do whatever I can."

She paused a moment, deciding whether she could trust me. Then, through tears, she told her secret: Her father had sexually abused her over a period of years. "I can't get over it," she said. "It has wiped me out and destroyed so much of my life that I don't know what to do about it. Is there anything you can do to help?"

As we talked, her negative emotion came pouring out from an understandably deep cistern of anger toward her dad. By coming to me and facing the deep pain within, she was finally able to take responsibility for her response to her father. What had happened to her was not her fault. But she was now responsible for how she would handle the memories and negative emotions resulting from the abuse that was beyond her control. She was choosing to confront the past.

The deep anger in her ran a continual "replay of tapes" of past offenses. It was in her power to eject the tapes, quit the damaging reruns, and go on to a new level of emotional maturity where she could fall in love with life and with someone special.

Remember what we discussed in chapter 2: Anger is a secondary emotion that arises out of fear, frustration, hurt, or some combination of these three. If someone disrespects us, for example, we first feel hurt and then we choose anger over other options, such as denial, forgiveness, or using the circumstance to lead us to personal growth.

That means that those three underlying emotions—fear, frustration, and hurt—can be seen as warning lights as bright as the "check engine" sign on a car's dashboard. Or they can serve as warning signals as clear as those received—and ignored—by the captain of the *Titanic*. When we see a warning light, we have a choice. After a hurtful, fearful, or frustrating experience, we can move in one of two directions: toward getting better or toward getting bitter.

Some of us, like Linda, have ignored the warnings for so long that a deep-rooted anger has started to destroy any happiness we ever had. But for Linda—and anyone reading this book—it isn't too late. By going to a counselor for help, Linda was acting responsibly, wisely, and humbly—unlike the cocksure captain of the ill-fated *Titanic*.

Well, all of us have warning signals in our lives. Ignore them at your own peril! Keep steering and pushing on your course without stopping, and you'll burn out your engine, hit a relational iceberg, or both.

I explained these things to Linda and asked, "What do you want from life? Do you want to be better? Or do you want to hold on to the negative and grow increasingly bitter?"

"I want to get the negative stuff out of my life. I want a better life. I want someday to have some joy in my life."

"Okay then," I said. "Let me take you through the steps that helped me deal with my own anger."

Switch word pictures with me once again and think of anger in terms of that dangerous substance that's compressed into a spray can. Some of these steps, or tools, will drain a little anger at a time while others may let out half of it all at once. Some bring immediate results while others give help over a longer period. Even though some may cause you to think, *I don't know if I can do that*, let me assure you that none of them is impossible. I've seen all of them work for me and thousands of others. Try them. After several weeks you'll find yourself saying, *You know, I don't have that same sick and empty feeling I had before*. Why? Because your pressurized anger is going, going, nearly gone.

You may contemplate the most obvious way to get the pressure out of the can: letting it explode in one violent rip. But let me caution that you are the "can" that may well be hurt in the blast! I hope instead you'll consider the healthier steps I suggest here.

Linda was willing and even eager to learn practical ways to live a life free from bitter anger. I gave her the seven steps that follow.

1. Define the Offense

Think about it. Aren't most of your actions motivated by the desire for gain or the fear of loss (or a combination of the two)?

Those hopes and fears—expectations and losses—can trigger anger. We get angry because someone (maybe even our own mortal, inadequate self) is taking something away from us that we don't want to lose, or else we're being denied something we want to gain. We blame something or someone for a loss—maybe even the loss of an unfulfilled dream or the loss of our peace of mind. The first step is to analyze and define exactly what happened, what you've actually lost or were denied.

As we analyzed Linda's anger in this light, I asked her, "What did you lose that led to your anger? If you can write it down—name it and try to look at it objectively—that alone can begin to drain out some anger."

I use the word *objectively*, but I acknowledge that here we're naming the offense in somewhat *subjective* terms. Naming a perceived loss can bring clarity and lead to healing. What did Linda perceive her loss to be?

Linda recognized a number of losses, but the two biggest ones really stood out. For one thing, she felt that her father had taken her childhood away from her—had stolen it from her, in fact. But the worst pain came from the feeling that he had taken her future, especially her future husband.

"What do you mean by that?" I asked.

"Well, I can't date anybody," she said, looking at the floor. She paused for a minute, unable to continue.

"Take your time," I offered gently.

She nodded silently, and tears filled her eyes. Finally she took a deep breath and said, "I feel so unworthy; I feel that if I meet the right guy, someone I really like, as soon as he finds out what happened to me, he'll think I'm trash."

Again she paused. I could see her body start to shake. At last she sobbed, "Nobody is going to want me or stay with me, because I'm not worthy of anyone!"

Those agonizing feelings of despair and shame growing out of her deep sense of loss produced many of the symptoms of anger: making her keep her distance in relationships, feeling alienated from God and from herself. She first needed to name her pain, to try to look at it from outside herself, much as I once had to do . . .

In the last chapter, I referred to a man toward whom I was very angry for six years. When I looked at that situation and tried to name my loss, I realized I felt he had stolen some of my dignity. Maybe deeper than that, because we were coworkers and our conflict made me feel I couldn't stay in the same organization, I also felt he had taken my future. I had enjoyed that job—had thought I was finally where I wanted to be in life—and then, because the place "wasn't big enough for both of us," I felt deeply resentful.

Another personal story leads into my second point. When my brother Ronnie, four years older than I, died at the age of fifty-one, I was angry with him for months. He had been an angry person himself; he was generally distrustful of people and somewhat explosive at times. He didn't like doctors, so he refused to get checkups the way he should have.

I would tell him, "Ronnie, heart trouble runs in our family. We've inherited this. You've got to get your cholesterol and your heart checked."

But he would respond, "I don't like doctors. They rip you off." And he would refuse to go.

Finally he had a heart attack and had to go to the doctor. But even then, he wouldn't follow the doctor's instructions for how to take better care of himself. He figured, *I'm strong. I'll be all right.*

We were just getting to be closer friends when he died, and I got angry. Getting past that anger took time, and it meant I had to face the reality of my loss: I had lost a brother and a friend. Just admitting what I had lost and allowing myself to feel it (see step 2, described below) helped a lot to get rid of my frustration and anger.

What about your own anger? Think of the things others have done that are still playing on that videotape in your mind. What did they take away from you or deny you?

2. Allow Yourself to Grieve

The second step in unloading anger is to allow yourself to grieve your loss. You've identified and written down what happened in the offense. Now accept that your pain—your sense of loss—is real; this person—your mate, boss, friend, parent, or maybe even yourself—did take something from you or deny you something. Don't minimize it! He or she didn't treat you with respect. Say the words: "You hurt me!"

You are angry, so look at it realistically. It's not only okay to grieve your loss, whatever it is, for a period of time, but grieving is also essential for your healing.

Elisabeth Kubler-Ross found that people go through stages of grief whenever they learn of their impending death: denial, anger, bargaining, depression, and acceptance. M. Scott Peck adds that we go through these same stages of grief every time we're about to grow in psychological or spiritual maturity.[2] If the conscious, grieving process feels painful, think of it in terms of final results: You're about to have an important "growth spurt" in your life. At the final stage of acceptance you will be able to say, "Yes, I can live with the loss; I can see beyond the loss."

Many people refuse to grieve their losses. They stay stuck in denial, the first grief stage. They try to be happy and say, "I'm strong. I'll get over it in a hurry." It's much healthier to allow yourself to hurt for a while. As they say, De-nial is not a river in Egypt! It's more like quicksand. Some serious offenses or losses need to be grieved—the pain acknowledged and released little by little, like slowly letting the air out of a balloon. Depending on the magnitude of loss, it can take months. That's a vital part of releasing your anger, something a woman named Wendy was unaware of.

Wendy was a stay-at-home mom until her youngest child went to school. Then she took a little nest egg she had set aside and used it to realize a dream: She opened a small coffee shop. She knew the risks going in, but she wanted to give it a try.

After fully investing her time and energy for four hard months, Wendy was forced to close the shop. The money ran out. She was so disappointed. Through her sadness, she experienced serious mood swings. Her kids noticed how quickly she snapped at them for the least little thing.

But the brunt of her anger was saved for her husband, Ron. Through no fault of his, Wendy became increasingly hostile and cold to him. She tried her best to avoid being with him—for a reason she couldn't put her finger on. It became an extremely trying time in their marriage.

Wendy's eyes opened only after she recognized her denial. She needed to allow herself the freedom to grieve the loss of her business venture. And then her family relationships, which had grown distant, slowly returned to their former closeness. We're mistaken when we believe the only grieving to be done is after the death of a loved one. We must grieve the loss of relationships, projects, personal goals, work-related issues—just about any loss. It's essential for emotional health.

Now let's return to Linda's story. Week after week in our counseling sessions, I simply allowed her to express her deep anguish. There were times when she would ask me, "Will the pain ever end?" Her "grief therapy" certainly could not be described as "brief" therapy! She needed several months to start the healing because her loss was so great.

The most dramatic change in her grief came the day I asked her to relive her childhood feelings as she remembered them. We focused on one particular time when she lay on her bed feeling deep shame and hatred for her dad. During a three-hour session with a great many tears and much anguish I listened to her pain—a young girl whose body had been violated and whose heart had been crushed by the man whose duty it was to protect, cherish, and nurture her. I had to fight back my own desire to go after him with a baseball bat. To put it mildly, I was getting angry myself!

Linda even found that grieving—continuing to acknowledge the pain and loss—was needed after things started to get better for her. Her experience was something like that of a woman who called me one day and said, "Mr. Smalley, I have a very serious problem, and I need to talk to someone. I'm in danger!"

Frankly, I didn't know if I wanted to get involved if there was physical danger, but I finally agreed to meet with her.

"I appreciate your meeting with me," she said when we got together.

"My husband, who is well known in this community, is doing something illegal. I can't live this way anymore. I'm extremely angry about what he's doing and the way he treats me. I've got to expose this so I can get help myself. But I don't know what he's going to do to me—or to you—if he finds out I've told you."

I sat there thinking, *Thanks a lot, lady. This is great! Is he part of the underworld or something?*

She went on to describe what her husband was doing. I knew who he was, and although it was a scary prospect, I decided that the best approach was for his wife and me to confront him. "Maybe he'll respond well and do the right thing," I told her hopefully.

The two of us did confront him, and although he resisted initially, I'm happy to say that he surprised me by eventually responding well and straightening things out. But the reason I tell this story is that the wife— and this is perfectly normal—still had her anger even after her husband had turned around. I could help her realize what she had lost and go through a grieving process, but she had to express the pain. Only then did her anger start to drain away. This was also true for Linda, whose pain would reappear now and then even after she started to heal.

In dealing with your own anger, it's best to face it. And don't cut short your need to grieve.

3. Try to Understand Your Offender

The third step in resolving anger—trying to understand your offender— may seem impossible and the benefits of it incomprehensible. It may take awhile, but as soon as you can do it, I assure you, it can speed your release. Some of the healing power of this step is just in trying it. As you attempt to understand the person and why he or she might have committed the offense, you set a process in motion: You may well see how your offender could have acted out of his or her own hurt.

This step has meant a lot to me personally. When I took it, it was like draining half of my anger can at once. Let me explain. Remember the man I was angry with for six years? I was so tied up inside that I would wake up early in the morning thinking things like, *I'm going to get revenge* and *I hope something bad happens to him today.* I was grinding away, playing the old tape in my head. Then one day, a person I was counseling came in with an article clipped from a magazine. The client said, "This article really describes me and tries to help people like me understand how they can get better. Would you read it? Maybe it will give you a better understanding of me, and you can use some of the ideas to help me."

"Sure," I said. I took the article home that night, though frankly I wasn't thrilled with the idea. But as I started to read it, I was amazed. I thought it described my own offender to a T! It was the first time I had any understanding of him and why he might have acted as he did. *So that's why he was such a jerk to me,* I thought. *That's why he did all those things. It makes all the sense in the world. No wonder!*

As I gained some understanding of the potential pain in his life, I actually felt twinges of compassion for him. I hadn't planned it or expected it at all. But realizing his hurtful actions toward me could be caused by his own hurtful experiences helped me see everything in a whole new light. He was an anger-filled, sabotaging man.

Stephen Covey calls what happened to me a "paradigm shift"—an entirely new perspective on a particular subject. He gives a personal example to illustrate a complete change in attitude. He was on a train when a man boarded with his children. The kids were irritating all the other passengers, including Covey. But when Covey found out that the man's wife had just died and the family was coming from the hospital, Covey's attitude changed instantly and utterly.[3]

That's somewhat like my experience. As soon as I understood for the first time just how wounded my offender might be, my attitude changed; a great pressure behind my anger was released.

Let's say your father offended you. Then at some point you find out about his own history—how his father and mother and maybe his grandfather treated him. That new information gives new insight into why he acted the way he did toward you. And as you make that discovery, you will practically feel some of the resentful emotions draining from you.

My son Greg saw this happen in a dramatic way. As a counselor, he specializes in child therapy. One time he was helping a nine-year-old girl who was feeling rejected by her father. Greg recognized that the problem went beyond the little girl; it was a family system problem. So he asked the dad, "Will you come in and meet with us?"

"Fine," the man said, not knowing what Greg had in mind.

The father joined them for a session, and during the conversation, Greg asked the girl, "What would you really like from your dad?"

Her teary eyes gazed downward, and she said softly, "I would love for my daddy, just once, to tell me that he loves me."

The man immediately replied, "Honey, you know I love you."

Big tears rolled down her cheeks as she looked up at him and said, "Yeah, Daddy, but I would just like to hear it."

Her dad's heart broke. Through his own misty eyes, he told her, "Honey, for some reason I can't say that. I never heard it when I was growing up. I never heard my mom or dad tell me they loved me, so I don't even know how to say it. I'm sorry, Honey, but I just can't say it."

The little girl was sobbing now as she said, "Daddy, I really wish you would!"

At that point Greg suggested, "Why don't we practice right here? Why don't you say it to her right now?"

The man felt awkward and uncomfortable, like being asked to propose marriage in front of an audience. But seeing how important it was to his daughter, he said, "All right, I'll try."

Then with great tenderness, he reached over and took his child's hand. "Honey," he said with difficulty, barely able to look at her, "I just want to say that I love you." With that, he started sobbing. The girl was still crying too. And then Greg started in, so that all three of them were crying tears of love and joy and understanding for both of the hurting children in that room.

When the daughter realized that her father had never heard words of love from his own parents, she could understand, and it amazed both men when she said, "So that's why you couldn't say you love me! That makes sense. Daddy, you lived in a home like the one I live in." That insight instantly drained some anger from her life. And fortunately in this case, the offender—her dad—was willing and able to move beyond his own hurt and say the things he needed to say to heal his child.

What that father learned—that you can choose to move beyond the limitations of your childhood—is something I had to learn as well. As an adult, I was in a meeting once when we were supposed to write out the first time we heard our fathers praise us. As I sat there, I thought, *Okay. Let's see. Uh-huh.* I couldn't think of a single time I had heard words of praise from my dad! Then I thought, *This must be something that has affected me for sure.* And I realized that I had always had a hard time praising other people.

Had that stopped me from ever praising others? No. It had been difficult, but I had learned to do it. And the more we practice the positive, in spite of the way we were raised, the easier it gets. But as in the case of that girl's father, we might need a counselor or a support group to provide a safe environment for our first attempts.

This step was another major turning point for Linda. When I found out that her father had come from an alcoholic family, I felt sure that an understanding of what that meant to her father could help her own recovery.

Linda's grandfather was an alcoholic. And addictive people usually don't know how to and usually can't develop close-knit, meaningful relationships. They generally ruin most of their relationships and send their children into the world with major empty holes in their hearts. It's as if children of alcoholics are missing part of their relational ability. The resulting pain these children feel can cause them to seek out a medication in the form of addictions of their own.

Linda's father was sexually addicted, from a pornography habit to the incest he inflicted on her. She was, in some ways, like a drug to him—as alcohol had been to his father. I tried to help her see his pain and understand why he acted the way he did. That insight wasn't all she needed for her own healing, but it did allow her to release a big chunk of her anger. She saw that he was as wounded by his dad as she was by hers, but in a different way. He wasn't just setting out purposefully to "steal her childhood." His actions reflected his own deep pain and emptiness.

For myself, I gained yet more understanding of the power of trying to understand an offender when I went to speak at a major university. I was supposed to address several groups of faculty, administration, and students, and we gathered in an austere, formal room for the first meeting. They were a serious-looking group, and as I got up and started to speak, I could see that things weren't going well. I was trying to be funny, and they weren't laughing. As far as I was concerned, the session couldn't end soon enough.

About halfway through, things got even worse. A woman stood up with a real hostile look on her face, and she said, "This upsets me. I can't hear any more of this!" And she stormed out of the room.

I was instantly hurt. *Is that offensive, or what?* I thought. Her behavior ruined the rest of the session for me. I had no desire to continue. I only wanted to disappear through a trapdoor, run to my rental car, and get out of there. I figured maybe everyone else in the room felt the same as that woman, and she had been the only one brave enough to stand up and say what they all were thinking. That's what her outburst did to me. But I managed to stumble through the rest of my presentation.

Afterward, I was really feeling low, drained of energy. There was a big gap between what I had expected and what I had actually experienced. My frustration and hurt warned me that anger was close at hand. But I decided to face this head-on. *I'm going to find out why she would be so rude and offensive to me. There has to be some reason.* I knew there must have been some hostility in her life because she had clearly sprayed me with her "anger can."

I asked someone about the woman and learned she was director of a university department and a leading spokesperson for the women's movement. As I made my way to her office, I thought, *Whoa! Should I really do this?* But I kept walking, right up to the receptionist. I respectfully asked, "May I see your boss for a couple of minutes? I'd just like to talk with her."

The receptionist checked for me, then came back and said, "No, she's not able to see you now. She's real busy."

"Could you ask her one more time?" I pleaded. "Tell her I won't take more than five minutes. I just want to ask her an important question."

The receptionist checked again, and this time she told me, "Okay, she can give you five minutes. That's it."

I walked into the office, and the woman glared at me as if to say, *What are you doing here? Didn't you get enough abuse already? Do you want more?*

"I want to thank you for what you did," I started.

Yeah, right, her look said.

"You got my attention, as you can well imagine," I explained, "and I would love to know what you heard in my talk that you reacted to so strongly. You see, I speak all over the world, and maybe what bothered you bothers other people, too, and they're just not telling me. So I'd really like to know what disturbed you."

"Oh," she said. "Well, you . . ." She talked about this and that and so on. But then, within three or four minutes, she started to cry and tell me how angry she was with one of her colleagues. "I hate this person," she told me, continuing with a litany of his offenses.

As I sat there listening, I thought, *Wow! This is one angry person.* All her emotion seemed to be wrapping around my neck and choking me, it was so strong. But I just let her vent, listening carefully and saying things like "Bless your heart" and "Oh, you have to put up with that?"

Next came an even bigger surprise. After a few more minutes she asked me, "How many more times are you speaking on campus?"

"Two more," I said, wondering what she had in mind.

"I'd like to go with you and introduce you," she said.

"Really?" I replied, shocked.

"Yeah," she said with a smile.

Just a short while before, she couldn't stand me. Now she was my buddy, and all because I had listened, shown some compassion, and helped her to see some things she could do to resolve her anger! What's more, *understanding what had made her so angry released the anger starting to churn in me because of her outburst.* My time on campus had started with the making of a new enemy, but it ended with the making of a new friend.

Remember, when someone has offended you, it's often (not always) spray from his or her own anger can. When that's the case, you're dealing with a person who has probably unknowingly placed himself or herself at a distance from others, God, self, and maturity. And you can choose not to allow that person to exercise control over your life.

Try this step: Make the effort to understand the individual's background and motivation. Let your new understanding of that person's pain and life-difficulty drain some of your anger.

4. Release Your Offender

This step in dealing with anger involves giving up your desire for revenge, releasing your offender from your wish to get even. This step sometimes comes "naturally" once you have understood some of the causes of the offensive behavior toward you.

Releasing your offender can drain several ounces of resentment at once, and it usually involves learning how to forgive. The original definition of *forgiveness* actually means that you untie or release someone. As long as you remain bitter and unforgiving, you're tied to that person with emotional knots. So being untied involves a conscious and deliberate release of the offender through an act of forgiveness.

It's a good idea to say the words out loud, preferably with someone else present, because then the impact is more powerful. In my forgiveness of the coworker who had so offended me, I said the words aloud but alone. I took several hours, and I relived those situations in which I had felt such deep hurt. In my mind's eye I was with him again in those painful incidents, but I was also observing "from a corner of the room." In this private scenario, as we came to a place where he had given offense, I would stop him and say, "I forgive you. I'm untying you from the emotional ropes that have held me to you. I release you. I'm not responsible to you anymore, and you're not responsible to me. It's over for us. I'm going to turn my life in a different direction. I'm not going to run that video in my mind anymore; I'm pushing the eject button. I won't wish harm on you any longer. You're a wounded person; I may not know the source of all your own anger or wounds, but I hope someday you find your own healing. In the meantime, your woundedness is no longer my fault. You blamed me, but I receive your offensive behavior toward me as your sick way of showing your woundedness."

I experienced many emotions during those hours, but I felt that I got a lot of anger out. And about a week later, I realized I was enjoying a new sense of release and freedom because of what I had done. My own anger can had shrunk, and I wasn't feeling so miserable anymore; nor was I spraying others so much. That reminded me that we either release those who have hurt us or else our anger can consume us, and that's too high a price to pay for hanging on to bitterness. Wanting revenge—something bad to happen to the other person—will only heap more anger on ourselves, and we'll potentially get more anger-spray in return.

An important though difficult part of releasing someone is giving up the expectation that the person will eventually see the error of his or her ways and take the initiative to make things right with you. This was a big hang-up for Linda. Her father had emotionally and physically abused her, and she kept expecting that someday he would turn around, recognize his error, and do something wonderful for her.

"Someday my dad is going to tell me he loves me," she insisted. "He's going to hug me and admit he was wrong. I know it's going to work out—like in a fairy tale."

I knew that wasn't likely to happen. From what she had told me about him, I was sure her father had his own enlarged anger can. You can't expect nice things from people with big cans of anger compressed by their own deep wounds, so you've got to release them from that expectation. It's as if they live in darkness and can't see what they've done. For quite some time, Linda couldn't understand that her expectations were unrealistic. Finally I got through to her when I said, "Linda, please walk over to that lamp, put your arms around it, and give it a big hug."

She gave me a funny look, but she got out of her chair and followed my instructions.

I asked her to sit down again, and then I asked, "How long will it take for that lamp to come over to you and return your hug?"

"A long time," she answered with a grin. "It never will."

"And why won't it?" I asked.

"It's unable to," she said.

"That's right, Linda," I told her. "And your father isn't able to do what you want, either, because of his own conflicts. You've got to give up waiting for that wish to come true and turn your own life around. He's a little wounded kid in adult skin. He has a huge hole in his heart. That hole makes him unable to see your wounds."

I also told her a story of the battleship out cruising on a very foggy night. A lookout reported that he saw the light of another ship directly ahead. The captain ordered, "Radio that ship and tell it to turn twenty degrees to port."

The call went out, but a message came back, "No, YOU turn twenty degrees to port."

The captain was a little irritated by that, so he commanded, "Listen here. I'm the captain of a battleship, and if you don't veer off right now, I'll see that you're through in the navy."

This time the message came back, "Sir, you may be a captain of a battleship, but I'm a seaman first class in charge of this lighthouse, and I'd suggest you veer off in a hurry, or you're all history! Sir."

Most people who have hurt us are like that lighthouse. They're not going to change course and become more loving. They're stuck in place like a rock! Either we turn away from them by releasing them from our anger, or we head for disaster.

The next step has so much potential for draining anger that I've devoted a whole chapter to it. But I'll give you an overview here.

5. Look for Pearls in the Offense

This tool in overcoming anger is to search for "hidden pearls" in the offense committed against you. The idea here is that some good can come out of any bad situation—if you'll just look for it. Find the good, and you can be grateful for it. And . . . gratitude and anger can't coexist. This is yet another step that can drain a lot of anger all at once. It's an alternate choice you can make in how you respond to hurt, fear, or frustration.

As I looked back on my journey to releasing anger toward my coworker, I realized that a lot of good had come from a "bad" situation. For example, because I was hurt by what happened, I developed a greater sensitivity and compassion as a counselor. The way things worked out, my leaving that job (what I'd perceived as the "loss of my future") opened gigantic new doors for me to write, speak, and counsel.

Would I want to go through that same kind of pain again? No way! But it's in the past, and I can now be grateful for the good that came from it.

There's a lot more to be said about pearl-hunting in the next chapter. Keep reading.

6. Put Your Feelings in Writing

Another helpful step in working through anger is to put your feelings in writing in the form of a letter to the person who offended you. I'm not saying you have to mail the letter. But when you spell out your hurts, frustrations, and fears, researchers say it's almost as if your anger is released through the ink of the pen. You may not feel the effect immediately, but you can in time.

What do you write? Clarify what you lost or were denied—what it is that caused you pain and has led to your anger. Talk about your resultant feelings. Express your desire to set aside—and live beyond—your anger and know the freedom that comes with forgiveness. And one of the best things is to state how you would like your offender to respond.

Normally, I don't encourage people to send such letters to—or confront—their offenders; the offender usually reacts badly and increases the offense. It can make the problem worse for everyone involved.

As an old proverb says: Do not reprove a fool, or he will hate you and spread all sorts of lies about you.[4] Foolish people (often angry, emotionally blind people) can't see most of their own faults and shortcomings. Being confronted with their hurtful actions and words can threaten them with so much pain that they may respond by lashing out—hating you for forcing them to look at what they cannot face; they may subsequently do whatever they can to discredit you.

But Linda, the young woman who was abused by her father, wrote such a letter, and she went ahead and mailed it to him. She knew it was risky; he could have hurt her doubly by denying he had ever abused her. Or the letter could have been read by someone else; that always complicates things. But we both thought the risk was worth taking in this case in the hope that she could be further healed.

I'm happy to say that her dad responded better than either of us had hoped. When he got her letter, he called her immediately. His first words were something like, "Honey, I've waited all these years to talk about this, but I never could. I couldn't admit what I had done because it was too painful. I have suffered for years. When you told me in your letter that you had forgiven me and released me, I was so grateful!"

A short time later, they had a tearful reunion full of hugs and healing. I had told Linda at one point that I didn't think her father would ever be capable of responding in such a way, and I'm happy to say that this time I was wrong.

As Linda continued to heal, she met a fine young man and eventually married. (I was honored to be a part of her wedding.) She's now a very caring and loving wife and mother. A negative intergenerational cycle has been broken.

Again, as I said before, I generally advise against mailing a letter written to an offender. But just writing the letter can help unload some of your resentment whether or not you mail it.

7. "Reach Out" to Your Offender

This last step in resolving anger may well be the hardest. It doesn't come naturally, and it requires a huge act of the will, not to mention a high degree of maturity and love. But when you're able to do it, it can release a lot of anger.

What does this involve? Finding some way to help in the healing of the person who offended you. Again, I suspect this sounds impossible, but I've seen its benefits to those who can get to this point.

Recently, I talked with a young woman about helping someone who had offended her. She had been deeply hurt in a dating situation while in college, and she admitted, "There's no way I can ever take part in trying to heal the man who wounded me."

"I understand that," I said. "I know you may never be able to do this. I'm not saying you should do it. But I'm saying that if you can come to the place where you can have some compassion for the man because of the pain he's also been through, it can provide a great healing for you. Guaranteed: He is a wounded man, sick and in need of healing. I've tried to do this myself for people who have offended me; it has been very emotional, but I could feel my anger releasing. But I know it won't be easy for anyone."

It's never easy to reach out in a loving way to those who have hurt us. A man named Earl realized this when he took steps to reconcile with his father. Already in his late thirties, Earl realized that some of his own coldness to his wife was due to his upbringing by an alcoholic father. He realized he needed to work through his anger toward his dad, whom he felt had "cheated" him out of a portion of his youth.

Earl talked the situation over with his wife and decided, *My dad's an out-of-control alcoholic, but maybe I can do something as the son. I don't want to keep passing on the same unhealthy behavior to my wife and kids, so I'm going to start the ball rolling.* This involved a conscious change in his demeanor toward his family. And it prompted him to call his dad, thinking, *I've never in my whole life told him the things I want to say now, but I'm going to call and tell him I love him, and all is well with me toward him.* Just think how much courage that call would require! But Earl was learning how to forgive his dad and wanted to get the relationship on a new footing.

Earl's father, who lived across the country, wasn't a real talker, but Earl placed the call. They made small talk for a while, and then Earl said, "Dad, incidentally, I've been thinking a lot about us lately, and even though I've never said this before, I wanted to tell you that I love you."

Click. His dad had hung up on him!

Earl couldn't believe it. So he called him right back and said, "Dad, I was trying to tell you that I love you."

Click.

Earl turned to his wife and said, "I don't understand this! My dad is hanging up on me."

"You just have to keep trying," she encouraged.

So he waited a few days, called his dad again, made small talk for a couple of minutes, and then said, "Dad, don't hang up on me. I want to tell you something. I really love you."

Click. He hung up on Earl again. He just couldn't handle Earl's words, maybe because he had never heard them from his own father. And who knows how many generations of that family had gone without hearing the words "I love you"?

A few weeks went by. Then one day Earl's mom called. "Son, I don't know how to tell you this, but your dad's disappeared. He's gone. No note. He's run away. We've looked everywhere and tried everything. I hate to tell you this, because I know you wanted to do something with him." Earl was crushed.

Everyone in the family was thinking the worst, but a month later, his dad came home. Where had he been? He had checked himself into an alcoholic rehab center. His explanation? "I want to love my son, and I want to be able to talk to my son about loving him and him loving me, and I couldn't do it with what alcohol was doing to me. I've been so messed up all my life, and this is the first time I've really wanted to get help."

Once home, he called Earl, who flew across the country; the father and son determined to learn how to love each other with the help of a counselor. Then they drove to see the other brothers and sisters. They didn't call ahead to say they were coming, and when they arrived at the first brother's house he screamed at the father, "Never come in my home again! I never want to see you as long as I live!" He then ran out of the house, got in his BMW, and left.

Though tragic, I'm not surprised by the second son's reaction. There was a deep, deep anger inside that son toward his dad. His father was trying to clear things up with him, but he wasn't interested. The story is still unfolding; I haven't heard the final chapter, but I know the dad is continuing to try to get through to all his kids and heal their family. Already, he and Earl have a better relationship than they ever had before. And Earl and his wife have drawn closer, their relationship reaping the benefits of Earl's courageous move to try to reach out to his offender.

To return to Linda's story, in time she was able to ask her dad what he was doing to overcome the grandfather's abuse toward him. For both the father and the daughter, their continued conversations went a long way toward healing the intergenerational wounds.

When you're ready to reach out to someone who has hurt you, perhaps a good starting place is to pray for the offender to be released from the anger in his or her own life. As we've seen, any healing actions we take can, in time, drain away some of our own personal anger.

Using These Seven Steps to Drain Your Own Guilt

If you are the offender—if you've "provoked" someone to choose anger because of your hurtful, frustrating actions or words—or if the pain of your own guilt has turned into anger toward yourself, consider this statement as a step that reaches out to heal both the offended one and you, the offender: Each of the seven steps to get rid of your own anger can also be used in reverse to release anger in someone you have offended (as well as anger-produced guilt in you, the offender).

You remember the story of my friend Larry, who was angry with me for nine years? Let's just imagine a different scenario from what actually happened. Suppose right from the beginning I had been aware I had wounded him. Suppose I had called him that very week, met him for coffee, and analyzed or named my offense, apologized and made some explanation for my actions, then sought his forgiveness. I could have helped loosen the lid on his anger—and the guilt that would have been eating at me.

Let's review: Analyzing the offense that gave rise to your anger. Grieving your loss. Understanding your offender. Releasing the offender and turning away from bitterness. Looking for pearls in the offense. Writing a letter. Reaching out to heal. These are all steps that add up to forgiveness and will release you from the anger that can otherwise eat away at your insides.

A Story of Release

Let me close with a story that illustrates many of these elements. I have a friend who once played professional baseball. At one point in his life, he came to a startling realization: *I really didn't enjoy playing baseball as much as my father did. He forced me to play from the time I was a little guy. He was my coach and inspiration. In fact, I didn't even see him a lot except for baseball. And the bottom line is that I'm very angry at him for the way he raised me.*

He came to that understanding in a movie theater. He was in his late forties by that time (his father was in his early eighties), and he and his wife were watching the film *Field of Dreams*. As he sat there watching the movie, he started crying, then sobbing. *What in the world is going on?* he wondered. And his wife was giving him a *What's wrong with you?* look. But he just sat there crying, even after the credits had run.

"Honey, the movie is over," his wife said as the lights came up.

"I don't know what's going on with me," he said, "but this movie brought out all kinds of feelings about my dad. Honey, I don't know if you'll understand this, but I'd like to go see him right away. I really feel I need to. What do you think?"

"That's fine," she said.

My friend called his mother that night and said, "Mom, I'm going to fly up and see Dad. Make sure he's home tomorrow night, because I'm coming up to do something with him."

So he got up there and told his dad what he wanted to do, and the father replied, "What! You flew all the way up here for us to go to a movie?"

"That's right, Dad, I want to watch this movie with you." That's all he told him.

They went to the theater together, and this time they both sobbed all the way through. At the end of the movie, they drove to an all-night restaurant, where they talked over what had happened and how they felt. By early morning, this son had forgiven his father, and they were reconciled in a way that neither had ever before experienced.

I understand *Field of Dreams* has had a similar healing effect for many fathers and sons. In this case, although the whole process took place rather quickly, my friend used many of the steps described in this chapter. He clarified and grieved his loss—as a young man he hadn't realized his own goals and dreams. Then he forgave his father and reached out to heal both him and their relationship.

I trust that these steps of forgiveness can help you or someone you love to drain away all kinds of anger. To the extent that you can experience inner healing, you'll be better equipped to love the people around you. For the sake of our society as well, we need to see families healed and brought back into harmony. We need to say "Enough is enough!" and start learning how to forgive each other. When that spreads, just watch what happens in our world! I pray that you'll be right at the heart of that movement.

The next chapter gives much more insight to help you forgive or reduce your anger level. Just imagine: Whether you've been hurt by life in the past or you're being hurt now or you get hurt in the future, you can use the concept in the next chapter to turn it all into something good for you.

Forever-Love Principles

Our list of forever-love principles continues from the previous chapter:

13. Forever-love listens to the heart's warnings—fear, frustration, and hurt—and makes the choice to get better, not bitter.

14. Forever-love seeks to identify an offense. Name a fear or a loss, and anger begins to lose its debilitating power.

15. Forever-love does not deny a grievance but grieves the harm's loss.

16. Forever-love tries to understand any "why" behind another's hurtful actions.

17. Forever-love chooses to forgive—to untie the knot of anger and release the bitter blame.

4

You Can Turn Your "Sand Storms" into Pearls

Precious memories may remain even of a bad home, if only the heart knows how to find what is precious.

—Fyodor Dostoyevsky

I could be happy; I could be in love with life, if only . . . Most not-yet-happy people have one or more "great" ways to finish that sentence. *If only my spouse would drop dead. If only I had a spouse. If only I lived in a better neighborhood. If only I were to win the lottery.* These people believe they could love life if only they could somehow reduce the number of their troubles, leave behind the frustrating, anger-producing negatives—as a snake slithers out of its skin and leaves it behind.

But just the opposite is true! Without some painful encounters, our quality of life is diminished. Scott Peck begins his classic book *The Road Less Traveled* with a now-famous line: "Life is difficult." He continues: "This is a great truth, one of the greatest truths."[1]

On these two counts I agree, and I also say that contained in every difficulty are good and great things that we can learn to appreciate—that we can use for our benefit and enrichment.

All our trials, great and small, can bring more of the two best things in life: love for life and love for others. But only those who take full responsibility for their responses to trials find these loves in their lasting form.

No one can escape his or her share of life's problems. One might try to, like old Charlie, who thought he could find true happiness by escaping the pressures of life. With this hope, he entered a monastery where silence was the rule—the only exception being chapel prayers. Every five years, however, you could speak two words to the abbot. At the end of his first five years there, Charlie chose his words carefully: "Bad food," he said. After five more years Charlie said, "Hard bed." Finally, after fifteen years, Charlie declared, "I quit!"

Disappointed, the abbot responded, "I'm not surprised. Ever since you came, all you've done is complain."

Trials, hardships, hurts, and all the other painful experiences we encounter are like personal "sand storms." They might blind us, sting us, irritate us, anger us. But as we respond to them, we have a choice I introduced in the previous chapter: *After a trial we can get better or bitter.*

We can find the road to a love that lasts forever as we get to the place where we regularly use our "sand storms" to our advantage. I call the process of transforming hurts into benefits *pearl-counting.* I use that word picture—that image—because the pearl found within an oyster started with an irritating piece of sand.

Those precious jewels are there for us—ours for the taking. In fact, every trial contains several pearls. Once I caught on to this principle, I got excited about seeing how many I could find in each crisis. Some provide a whole "necklace" suitable for prominent display. The more pearls, the greater your riches.

But you might ask, "What good comes out of my business going under . . . or having been abused as a child . . . or my mate's serious illness . . . or . . . ?" Although those situations are initially devastating, they each eventually can produce a set of beautiful, valuable pearls. Usually this process doesn't happen too quickly. It usually takes several months for an oyster to add layer after layer of secretions to make the larger, valuable pearls.

As you dig into your tribulations and discover the gems buried within them, your self-worth will soar, and so will your ability to give and receive love. One of the greatest life-giving principles I've found is that all trials, big or small, can add to our "love chest" if we search for it.

How One Couple Turned Their Trauma into a Pearl

At age thirty-eight Terry Brown had finally found his dream bride, Janna. But one week before their wedding, Terry received a midnight call from his brother: Their mother had been diagnosed with acute cancer; doctors gave her only twenty-four hours to live. Terry flew to Florida the next day to be by her side, where he and his brothers stayed until she slipped into a coma. Meanwhile, Janna came to me in tears, wondering what she could do to support Terry and asking if they should postpone their ceremony.

As Terry's mother lingered on life support, other family members urged Terry to go forward with his wedding plans; no one knew for sure how long she would last.

As it turned out, the mother lived until her son's wedding, which took place as originally planned. That evening, following the ceremony, Terry heard that his mother, without regaining consciousness, had slipped away earlier in the day.

At this point, Terry and Janna's plans did change. The next morning, when they were supposed to be starting their honeymoon, they flew to Florida for what would be the first of three memorial services. Then, still on their "honeymoon," they flew to Chicago for the funeral.

We can all sympathize with Terry's loss and the unfortunate timing. But follow with me and see what they did in response to their tragedy.

Several months after the wedding, I listened as they explained their response to the terrible events. Terry confessed that even though he was losing the mother he had loved for thirty-eight years—and though he knew his mother wanted more than anything to be with him for his long-awaited wedding—he was gaining the closest friend he had ever known. He said it was a strange, conflicting set of emotions: On the one hand, he was losing a most important loved one. On the other hand, he was feeling so encouraged by and such a tender tug toward Janna, who was demonstrating such unconditional love for him. She was far more concerned for him and his feelings than she was for her own honeymoon. Through this terrible situation, he could see her friendship in action—unbelievably supportive, caring, and relaxed.

This traumatic beginning of their life together convinced them that they would be able to go through almost anything. The crisis was so bonding for them Terry later admitted that the whole week was the most encouraging time of his life. His bride's love for him far exceeded anything he had imagined possible.

Because Terry had previously learned the secrets of pearl-counting, he was somewhat aware of these positive possibilities while still in the midst of the funeral (honeymoon) week. He just started looking for—expecting—

something good to come out of that mess. And it did! Terry found pearls: a deeper bond with Janna, the assurance that he has a friend committed to him even in hard times.

Before we get into the specific steps of pearl-counting, let's look at what enables someone to find treasure within pain. Several key foundational issues have been covered in the previous chapter. As you work through the steps to releasing unresolved anger—as you quit blaming others and yourself for your troubles—you're better able to find pearls. Here's another key foundational mind-set: Don't overreact to problems.

Avoid Extreme Thoughts

When we hit hard times, we often overreact and panic, thinking, "This is the absolute worst thing that could happen!" "Nobody has ever gone through anything as devastating as this circumstance!" But the truth is that neither of those statements is true.

Try to refocus some of your energy away from all that's bad and instead search for anything that could possibly be good in the trial you're facing. Try to think of what new opportunities this situation may bring. *What can I learn? What future happiness lies in store as a direct result of this incident?*

As hard as it seems, relax. Again, most trials are not as bad as they seem at the time. As Mark Twain once said, "I am an old man and have known a great many troubles, but most of them never happened."

One extreme but subtle thought we can try to avoid might be boiled down to this: *I am the center of the universe.* A recent *Newsweek* cover featured a big, bold word: "Exhausted." The inside story, titled "Breaking Point," paints a picture of a frazzled America—stressed as never before. Why? Because "we have cell phones in the car and beepers in our pockets, and we carry them to Disneyland, to the beach, to the bathroom."[2] We think the world will fall apart if we don't respond *right now.* When everything becomes an emergency that only we can fix, life quickly lurches out of control.

Facing an emergency, the human body revs up, ready for the challenge: increased heart rate, constricted muscles and arteries, pumped adrenaline. That ready-to-fight stance may serve us well to ward off physical attack, but "it's horribly suited to the unremitting pressures of modern life."[3] Extreme thoughts hurt us physically and psychologically; we too often turn daily challenges into "dog attacks."

Even the threat of a real dog attack can prompt unnecessarily wild thoughts, such as *This is it. I'm dead.* I know. I've been there. Years ago I was at a speaking engagement in Florida and scheduled to stay in a private home. On my very first evening there, well after dark, I was dropped off at my host's home, and my ride drove away. Then I discovered I was locked out of the house. No key. No one at home. I knew I was at the right house. I knew I was expected. What to do?

I walked over to the front window to see if it would open. No. It was locked. I thought I'd try a back door. As I fumbled my way to the back, I saw that the yard was surrounded by a substantial iron fence. I tried to open the gate. Yes. Success.

I entered, closed the gate, made my way up the back walk, and met my worst nightmare—a *huge* dog. Our eyes met, and he immediately saw the fear in mine. Sensing his victory, he bolted toward me with what seemed to be incredible speed. I knew I was a dead man. The adrenaline kicked in. I was ready to fight him off with nothing but my bare hands and maybe my teeth—though I knew his would win.

He sped over to me, put on his brakes, and slid down the walk until he was right on top of my shoes. Then he instinctively did what he was trained to do: He started licking my feet!

I leaned over, petted him, and said, "Nice doggy . . . that's a good doggy!" Meanwhile, my heart was beating so hard, it felt as if my whole body were that one pumping organ!

Anyone would have extreme thoughts with a huge dog racing toward him. I tell the story to illustrate a larger point: that in real life, most of our trials are something like that "dog attack"; the perceived threat or even the perceived damage doesn't match the reality of the actual damage.

Even when the damage is real (even if I had been mauled by the dog), that trial still leads to the creation of one or more pearls—there for the finding.

Several years ago, a guy named Tom went through the most agonizing trial of his lifetime. With no recognized warning, one day his wife left him. She meant business; the separation quickly led to a divorce.

In Tom's own words, it wasn't like a "sand storm," it was more like a "sand *hurricane*." He had always wanted a happy marriage, and he had no clue as to why his wife had aborted their relationship. The accompanying tailspin is not uncommon in such situations. Tom was hopelessly depressed. He questioned why he should even go on living.

But Tom gradually regained a proper focus on life; his extreme thinking at the time his wife left him proved faulty. He realized that his life was not utterly destroyed, and he felt a growing desire to help others facing a trauma similar to his.

So Tom went back to school, eventually completing his Ph.D. He gained extensive counseling experience. In time he started a national organization, Fresh Start, which specializes in helping people through the trauma of an unwanted marital breakup.[4] He told me, "As I look back, my divorce has turned out to be the greatest and most rewarding experience of my life."

During his crisis Tom thought nothing could ever match the pain he felt. But that pain was redeemed. Tom's life-career opened up as a result of his own pain. Tom has remarried, and the relationship he has with his new wife and children is better than he had imagined possible.

As I've grown older I've conditioned myself to avoid extreme "panic" thinking. If we can slowly reverse our thinking from "all that we're losing" in any trial to "all that we will eventually gain," we'll become much more positive and not so easily shaken by negative circumstances. Just think how much easier you'll be to live with once you grasp this principle. Your mate or friends might throw a party in celebration! You might throw your own love-for-life party.

Reminder: Allow Yourself to Grieve the Pain

Even though I urge people to keep an optimistic outlook when confronted by a negative experience, it's still important to allow yourself to figure out what took place, analyze how it makes you feel, and feel the pain associated with the event. If you don't use this last key, you can stuff the feelings so deep within yourself that you think you've solved the problem—when actually you're simply denying the problem.

Remember that "counting pearls" is the fifth step in releasing unresolved anger, one step in a larger process that involves working through grief and accepting the reality of one's trial and one's loss. There are exceptions, but generally we are able to find pearls not before but during and especially following our grief.

How to Find Priceless Pearls in Every Trial

Now we get to the specifics of how to find those pearls in the "sand storms" of our lives. Remember, these steps are not something we use just for a short time after a trial; we continue doing them until our thinking actually changes and we realize the positive results—until we find the pearls that exist in every trial. You will have victory over your pain only when you feel and see the benefits to you. What do I mean by benefits? More connection with others, yourself, your God, and an underlying heart-happiness. New opportunities. Keep reading to identify more pearly gems.

Counting pearls is transforming bitter into better. When you're bitter, you're angry and feel low self-worth. When you're better, you feel grateful and enjoy an elevated sense of self-value and happiness.

Five Practical Steps in Pearl-Counting

To get a handle on the basics of the pearl-counting process, take out a sheet of paper and pencil and get ready to draw yourself a "pearl chart." This entire chart is positive. It may not seem like it at first because the chart will include a list of trials, or crises. But when you've finished filling out the chart, you'll see how your crises have brought you numerous benefits. The benefits aren't simply vague character traits; you'll find specific pearls that fit into every area of life.

With the long edges of the paper as the top and bottom, divide the page into five columns from top to bottom. Each step in pearl-counting will have its own column. Or you might use five separate sheets of paper, one sheet for each column described below. Give a title to each of the five columns:

Column 1: My Lifelong Strengths

Column 2: My Most Painful Trials

Column 3: My Support People

Column 4: My Pearls from Each Trial

Column 5: My Loving Action Because of Each Trial

Now let's discuss what each column is about.

1. My Lifelong Strengths

In the first column, list your strengths—what you're grateful for in yourself and in life in general. To think of things to include in this column, it might help if you finish this sentence: I'm glad I'm alive because . . .

Naming your strengths might be an easy assignment for you, but it's a hard challenge for some people. Self-appreciation is not an unhealthy, narcissistic indulgence but a healthy exercise in personal value. It's a realistic look at yourself.

What do you like about yourself? This is not the time to be overly humble. What we're looking for is an accurate view of the positive things about you and what you truly appreciate about who you are. What types of activities do you do well? How are your people skills? Hobbies? What do you bring to relationships that others appreciate? If you can't think of several strengths about yourself, ask your mate or friends—and read on. It gets better!

2. My Most Painful Trials

Write down the most painful trials you've been through. Think back over your whole life history, and list your personal "sand storms." Include ones that have lowered your sense of self-value or caused you shame or guilt.

It may be too hurtful to list some, but I encourage you to list any—and all—in the future as you're able. If the listing process does become unbearable, focus in on two or three trials and deal with the others at another time.

I have searched for every pearl in each major "storm" of my entire life. Because of that, I can honestly say there is nothing that remains negative about me in my mind. Don't misunderstand me; I don't see myself as even close to perfect, and others may still see negative things about me, but I've done my best to turn everything around to a positive inside my own heart. I get to spend every day bathing in a pool of value about what has happened to me. It's like soaking in "pearl water."

The negatives in my life started early. Let me name one particular negative I've come to see as a positive—a poor academic record and a resulting poor self-image. My parents didn't place a high premium on academics. Neither one of them had gone far in school. And their lack of interest had a discouraging effect on my life. Besides that, we moved often. I'd change schools every year, sometimes twice a year. In first and second grade I was in California, where they were experimenting with some new educational philosophy that didn't last long. It was one of those "the-child-will-learn-when-he's-ready" approaches that didn't suit me well. Apparently I wasn't ready to learn, because by third grade I was far behind my peers.

Further complicating the issue was a move to Washington State. By the time I got to the end of third grade, my parents were told things like, "We'd really like to see Gary be a leader in school," and, "We want to see Gary mature around the others." The translation was clear: *I had flunked third grade.*

To this day, my kids tease me mercilessly over this issue. "Dad, how could you flunk third grade?" they'll ask. Then we all laugh together.

Truthfully, I was deeply embarrassed for many years about having failed a grade. It was a secret I tried to keep as private as possible. Once I completed this pearl-counting exercise, however, I was able to turn it all around. You'll see how this occurs as you read on.

Before you leave this category, you may want to number your trials in the order of their severity. Give the worst pain you endured a number one, the next-worst a number two, and so on.

3. My Support People

In this column, list the people you can turn to for support in helping you pearl-hunt, people who have helped you through some of your more serious trials. I would imagine your spouse would be on top of the list if it's a recent trial. Others would be folks like your parents, a professional counselor, a minister, a friend, or your extended family. In the midst of a trial, it's also possible to pray for God's wisdom and understanding. Maybe God is on your list.

Tremendous support may be nearby, and that support can help you as you move to column 4.

4. My Pearls from Each Trial

Next list all the benefits you can identify from each trial. Here is the very heart and life of finding your own pearls. These pearls are more valuable than the earthly pearls one strings for a necklace; they are so treasured you can encase them on your heart's trophy shelf.

In column 4, start listing the positive aspects of each painful encounter in your life. Besides your own answers, it would be valuable to ask for the input of those who know you and love you—the support team you identified in column 3. They can often add a perspective to your suffering that you may have overlooked.

Also refer back to column 1 and the personal strengths you identified. Have any of those strengths come as a result of particular trials? That column identifies strengths you've gathered—from where? Often from what you've learned by trial and error—in every sense of the phrase.

The next few true stories will give you more specific examples of how a trial can be turned into precious pearls.

Pearls from Flunking. For years I saw nothing positive about my poor academic record. Flunking third grade and being a poor reader and speller were completely negative for me. But I now see positives in my entire educational development. One such benefit is this very book you're reading. Can you imagine how amazed all my elementary-school teachers would be if they knew I've written twelve books? And for reasons beyond my understanding, some of the books have actually won awards! How can this be?

Most of the reason goes back to my being a poor reader. In those years learning disability tests weren't given. But if they had been, I wouldn't be surprised if I had been placed in that category. Since I know the struggle of a poor reader, I realize a book must possess a certain excitement about it that will keep the reader's attention, and I strive to add enthusiasm and excitement to everything I do. My goal is also to make a book as understandable as possible. And I appreciate the concept of "salt," that special "thirst creator" in a book that makes me want to keep on reading.

I work hard at achieving these things in my books. It's not uncommon for me to go through twenty or more rewrites of each chapter to reach that ideal blend of content, excitement, and salt. I'm still not the greatest reader. So if a chapter doesn't interest me or force me on, I redo it until it does. I'm very grateful today that I had that weak childhood training—not that this is license for anyone to do poorly in school, but if life deals you a painful "piece of sand," turn it into a pearl and use it in a way that can benefit you and others.

Throughout this whole chapter I've talked about turning sand into pearls. Consider this equally interesting fact: "The silicon in a computer chip comes from ordinary sand. Yes, sand. What makes the chip so fantastically complex is the amount of human engineering and design that goes into it."[5] When your life is a desert, think again! Consider the possibilities!

Pearls from a Heart Attack. Remember it is always possible to find treasure in physical trauma. One person who learned that lesson was George, a typical hard-driving executive. He looked ten years younger than his age, forty-five. Great job, great family life. It was a classic case of "George is the last guy I thought would have a heart attack!"

But that's exactly what happened.

On a Tuesday afternoon, in the middle of an upper-management strategy session, George complained of chest pains and then collapsed onto the boardroom table. As he was rushed to the hospital by the paramedics, George just kept repeating his wife's name: "Barb, Barb, Barb." And Barb was at the hospital waiting when George arrived.

He was wheeled directly into the operating room from the emergency vehicle. After hours that seemed like days, the surgeon appeared at the waiting-room door to assure Barb that George was going to be all right. "But he must take it slow," the doctor warned.

Barb took it upon herself to ensure that George experienced a full recovery. She helped him with his slow and steady climb back to a normal life. George can barely get through recounting this time in his life without choking up. "Barb was the most amazing helper I had ever seen," he says. "For all the years we were married, I had prided myself on a healthy physique—so much so that I secretly doubted if Barb would even be interested in me if I let myself go—or worse yet, got sick."

George continues, "But it was through this horrible trial that I saw a side of Barb that had been hidden in the twenty-one years we had been married. I was treated to a glimpse of a woman who loved me unconditionally. Her love wasn't dependent on my good looks, firm physique, or good health. She just loves me . . . no matter what. I wouldn't wish a heart attack on anybody, but I do have to say it has been the greatest aid in strengthening our marriage. I now see life so differently. I've slowed down; I smell the roses. I can honestly say I'm glad it happened to me." That's a glimpse of finding very precious pearls as a result of a life-threatening sickness.

Pearls from Depression. Fran is another good example of searching for her own treasures to turn bitter into better. Here is her story in her own words:

"After being married for a while, my husband and I experienced three years of marital upheaval. During this time I stuffed issues down inside, becoming rageful. I cried often. I was sick for a solid ten months, until I 'crashed' emotionally and physically. My word for it was I 'died.' I remember how my body parts felt disconnected from me, and I felt like I was removed from my body. My voice didn't even sound like it was coming from me. I felt like I had been stripped down to the core of me—like a straw house falling down to its tiny foundation."

When Fran was struggling in the depths of this "disconnected" misery, she attended one of my seminars and became acquainted with pearl-counting. As she thought about her bouts with deep depression, she began to see things in a different light.

"Depression is a gift," Fran concluded. "I didn't see it at the time, but depression is your body's way of saying, 'Slow down—no more stuffing anger. Be reflective; take a look at how you take care of yourself.'"

Fran excitedly searched for her pearls. Through this process, she started to see for the first time that every area of her life could bring her something good.

In her family, Fran's depression became like smelling salts, waking her husband to her needs. He hadn't noticed that his busy schedule didn't allow any time for her and the kids. Now Fran can't believe how good their relationship is: a pearl from a problem.

Counting *Your* Pearls. If any of these stories inspires you, take your time listing the benefits that have come as a result of your trials. We usually don't see them all at once; you may have a trainload of pearls waiting to be discovered one carful at a time. The following is a partial list of great qualities of love or benefits to you in general that have been created, enriched, or increased as a result of your painful trials.

You are:

- Patient
- Kind
- Tender
- Forgiving
- Appreciative; praising others more
- Empathetic—feeling the pain of others and caring about them more
- Enjoying the simpler things in life
- Persevering
- Hopeful
- Calm about life in general; relaxed
- Aware that you can live through most trials
- Interested in enriching the lives of others before yourself
- Thoughtful
- Serious about life
- Developing a deeper spiritual life
- In touch with your feelings and the feelings of others
- Careful about what you say because it might hurt another
- Responsible at work

You are much less:

- Fearful
- Jealous or envious
- Arrogant
- Humorous at the expense of others

Let me recommend another resource—a wealth of immediate encouragement whenever you go through "valleys." A hilarious comedian, Andy Andrews, has put together two volumes of letters from famous people telling how trials have bolstered them toward success and happiness.[6] Check it out.

5. My Loving Action Because of Each Trial

In the last column, list ways you can turn pearls into loving action. When major disasters strike, priorities have a way of realigning; in the midst of crises, most people first search for their family members, not their belongings. Suffering has a way of bringing people together; the most important things on earth come into sharper focus. This increased interest in being with and helping others during a crisis is a demonstration of love.

The key to this final column in your chart is understanding how love works. It's as simple as this: We use love or we lose it. We take hold of a new appreciation for "connections," reorganized priorities, and new sensitivities we've gained in hard times, and we share with others the new joy that results from that connectedness—or we lose the joy.

One couple, David and Linda, were attending one of my seminars and realized how they needed to find any value they could in a devastating loss. Five years earlier, their precious daughter, Sara, had died just two hours after birth. David and Linda both lived the following years carrying anger, resentment, and frustration.

After allowing themselves time to feel the pain of their grief—their loss—they gained enough strength to start their own hunt for any good that could come from this tragedy. And what did they discover? David and Linda now realize how they appreciate the little things in life that they once had taken for granted. But Linda found a more specific way to use her search for pearls to help someone else.

She writes, "A friend of mine lost her brother and sister-in-law in a tragic auto accident. As a result, three young girls were left as orphans. But over the last three and a half months, I've been able to talk to this friend. When she expresses hurt, frustration, and agony, I can say, 'I know what you're feeling,' and really mean it!"

Linda goes on to say, "I actually thank God that I had Sara for the short time I did, because I learned so much from her death. I'm so much more alert to the suffering of others. I can be an understanding companion to my friend and her family, and I look forward to helping more because of my experience. When I'm with those three girls, they know that I not only love them but also that I deeply understand their loss as well. I can tell they know I understand and care. Through searching for treasure, I feel my daughter's death has finally given me a purpose. I still miss her a great deal, but I can now help others like I never dreamed I would. And helping them has been so rewarding."

In the previous chapter I told the story of another Linda, a young woman whose father had abused her. Linda's journey was long, but eventually she was able to identify and claim several pearls as a result of her childhood trauma. Again, what the father did was reprehensible, massively unloving. And what happened was beyond Linda's control; it was not her fault. But now, years later, Linda has chosen to walk toward forgiveness and to search for some good that might have been given her by her father.

And she has succeeded. She has seen how extremely sensitive she has become to the hurts and pain of others. She is a very caring, kind person. I helped her see that the greatest gift in life is genuine love. At twenty years of age, she could see that she had been given several key ingredients to genuine love: sensitivity, compassion, empathy, a deep desire to care for others who suffer, and a keen ability to pick up on signs of abuse in other young women. These are all characteristics that make for an effective counselor—and they are priceless pearls gathered from a situation that could have ruined her life had she chosen to let it. Instead she chose to respond by finding pearls and then turning them into loving action and reaching out to others, including her own husband and young child. Her faith in God has greatly increased, and she sees finding the very special man she married as a precious pearl.

Perhaps you are one who has endured the most horrible trial imaginable. You've been put through so much, you feel there can't possibly be any kind of treasure in your circumstances. Pain has been a way of life for you.

But pearl-counting can help! I urge you to give it a try. Imagine yourself as a caterpillar. Your cocoon of pain totally envelops you. You want to be free, but you're afraid. Do you know the secret of a butterfly's breaking free of its cocoon? The very struggle of working to get free from the cocoon is what strengthens the wings to allow it to fly. Imagine the beautiful butterfly that emerges as a butterfly of love. You can emerge as a new person—and the process starts as you take one knock at the enclosing wall, as you take one step toward working through your anger and searching for the positive.[7]

I know of nothing more helpful to those who suffer than to at least begin the slow process of breaking through the cocoon of anger and the feeling of being cheated in life. The crisis of breaking out is the opportunity of a lifetime!

Now Return to Column 1

After you've filled out all five columns of your pearl chart, go back and look again at column 1. Can you now identify new "personal strengths" that you see as a result of your tragedies-turned-to-triumphs? Yes? Then go back and add another pearl to your list: *Increased sense of my own capabilities.*

Actually, with every trial, you can walk up one full flight of a staircase that has five clearly marked "landings," as shown in the illustration below.

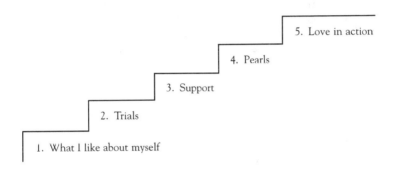

5. Love in action

4. Pearls

3. Support

2. Trials

1. What I like about myself

At each landing, you've increased your capacity for loving life and others.

I've never found an exception to this principle for myself or for anyone I've tried to help. There are pearls in every trial. The bigger the trial, the greater the potential for making your love last forever! And for anyone who truly desires to keep his or her love alive, the next chapter exposes another "iceberg" that can sink your love if you're not careful.

Forever-Love Principles

Our list of forever-love principles continues from the previous chapter:

18.   Every painful trial is like an oyster, and there is a precious pearl—a personal benefit—in every one. Every single one.

19.   Forever-love digs up the pearl buried within every trial.

20. Forever-love avoids extreme thoughts.

21. Forever-love assumes that things will get better, not worse.

22. Forever-love gives a wound time to heal.

23. Forever-love reaches out to share the joy of life.

24. Forever-love: Use it or lose it.

5

How to Balance
Expectations and Reality

If we could first know where we were and whither we were tending, we could better judge what to do and how to do it.

—Abraham Lincoln

Taking responsibility for how you respond to circumstances and keeping your anger levels low—these are major leaps toward a life of love. And choosing to find pearls in all your past failures and difficulties helps you keep your head above water. Now I want to show you how you can prevent the loss of valuable, vital strength you'll need for loving life and for loving your spouse.

The insights in this chapter are based on this foundational insight: *The wider the gap between what we expect and the reality of what we experience, the greater the potential for discouragement and fatigue.* The gap between expectations and reality is like a drain through which we lose the *joie de vivre*—the joy or love of life.[1]

When you hit a crisis situation—when reality opens a trapdoor—don't let your energy drain away. Here's how you can minimize the trauma of any future crisis you face—and crises are inevitable. Some are predictable; they're called life-cycle crises. Some are beneficial. All can be redeemable. But . . . there are specific ways you can protect yourself. As you run with me through the next story, you'll see a truth about life in general, and you may begin to see there is something you can do to prevent energy loss. (Special thanks to Dr. Dan Trathen for his insights and help in this chapter.)

Creeping Sun and Slithering Snakes

When I was about twelve years old, I got the scare of my life. It was the worst thing that ever happened to me. In fact, I'm amazed that I'm alive today to tell this story.

My family was living in the state of Washington, out in the country. One fall day I was outside playing with my best friend. Having great fun, we weren't paying much attention to the clock. As the sun crept toward the horizon, we suddenly realized it was time to be heading home. So, like the two adventurous boys we were, we decided to take a shortcut through a wooded area.

We had no path to follow, but that didn't bother us. We were just running along, the wind whistling past our ears. And then, all of a sudden, we heard this deafening and horrifying rattling sound very close by. We stopped, froze, and listened. The sound was all around us, and it seemed to be coming from everywhere at once.

We looked at the ground. It was moving. We were in the middle of a field of rattlesnakes! Hundreds of them, in all sizes. And they were striking out blindly in all directions.

My friend and I knew we didn't have long to live.

Fortunately, we had the presence of mind to jump up on a snake-free log that was well above the ground. We yelled for help at the top of our lungs, but we were too deep into the woods for anyone to hear.

"What are we going to do?" my friend shouted.

"I don't know," I answered, "but we've got to do something soon because it's getting dark!" *Will the snakes crawl up onto our log?* I wondered.

Then one of us got the idea of breaking long branches off the log and using them as extended arms or "swords" to flip the writhing, rattling creatures out of our way as we cleared a path to make our escape. And that's what we did. One snake at a time—what seemed like one inch at a time— crying all the way, we made a path to the edge of that sea of snakes. The slightest slip or fall would have landed us on top of a half-dozen of them, but we kept moving.

We only had about thirty feet to cover to get into the clear, but it seemed to take forever. When we finally left the last snake behind, we were trembling and exhausted. But we gathered our remaining strength and ran home as fast as we could to report our own near-death experience.

I'd like to use this childhood crisis to symbolize all of life's crises and how we can reduce the energy loss and shorten the duration of the trauma they cause.

Disaster Protection

Whenever a crisis strikes, we can be just like two boys running along near the safety of home and suddenly finding themselves in the middle of a field of deadly snakes—smack in the midst of a seriously unpleasant, potentially disastrous, situation.

As you can imagine, my friend and I weren't prepared to deal with rattlesnakes that day so many years ago. We were just wearing sneakers, jeans, and T-shirts—easy for a snake to bite through—and we had no weapons except our sticks. But suppose things had been a little different. Suppose that instead of wearing low-cut sneakers, we had been prepared for the reality we faced; suppose we had been wearing hip-high boots made of multiple layers of strong, thick leather—so strong that a snake's fangs would break off before they could penetrate to the skin underneath.

If I had been wearing such a pair of boots and knew they would protect me, my whole attitude toward the scene would have been different. Instead of being terrified, thinking I would die at any moment, I would have walked right into that mass of snakes with confidence! I would have simply kicked them out of my path as I made my way to the other side of the field. "Go ahead, take your best bite, make my day!" I would have challenged them boldly. And the protective boots would have kept me safe.

What kind of "hip boots" can we wear to protect us in all of life's crises? What can shield us from the harmful effects of such situations? We *"put on a thick pair of hip boots" by maintaining balance in our life*. To switch metaphors and use a common cliché: If we've put all our eggs in one basket and that basket falls to the ground, our life expectations are dashed. But if we carry several baskets, each holding a different life interest, and then drop one, causing disappointment in one area of life, we are able to maintain strength, hope, and joy because we're still holding several baskets. Let me explain.

When the "Big One" Hits You

Here's an illustration of what can happen when the "hip boots of balance" aren't worn: Two years ago Gene's life fell apart. His small business went bankrupt. The business was most of his identity. He'd given it so much time and attention that his wife and children were "distant" housemates, providing little support in his despair. Gene's friends—business-related contacts—also scattered like frightened birds when he filed his court papers. Nonwork friends? He had none. And where was God? It had been a long time since Gene had paid any attention to faith.

With no intimate friends, distance at home, no spiritual center, and then the loss of his career, Gene felt overwhelmed. Nowhere. Hopeless. At age forty-two, Gene took his own life. A two-word note was found by his body. His message to the world: I failed. Maybe Gene's basic failure was that he had neglected to develop any "life support" outside his business.

Let me contrast that with another story. Granted, this is not as drastic as a foreclosure and a suicide; nevertheless it was a severe career crisis for a young man—my son Greg.

As each of our children formed a career path, we began to share a dream that someday we could all work together, maybe speaking on the same platform.

Not long ago Greg felt he was finally ready to make part of our dream come true. He was prepared to stand in front of a large audience and teach some of the principles I regularly present in seminars. As you can imagine, I was thrilled.

I invited Greg to join me and speak at an upcoming seminar. As I said, Greg was ready—but nervous and apprehensive. He spent hours getting ready for his talk. As the day approached he was losing sleep and feeling nauseous because of performance anxiety.

The big moment soon came for Greg to get up and address the audience. For me—proud papa—it was a magical experience, one I'll never forget. My years of fatherly dreaming were about to be rewarded. As I introduced him to the group, I had to stop for just a second to wipe my misty eyes.

Greg stood, approached the podium to warm applause, and turned to address the audience. He started off very relaxed, saying what a delight it was to share the platform with his dad. Then he added, "It's always good to be with him at times like these when he's sober." After the laughter died down, he added quickly, "Just kidding. He's a teetotaler." Now the crowd was with him. Sitting down in the front row, I thought, *With a start like this, it's going to be awesome!*

Then, halfway through his presentation, Greg experienced a major crisis. He went blank. Right there, standing all alone in front of two thousand people, with every eye in the room on him, he forgot what he was supposed to say next. His dilemma was instantly and painfully obvious to everyone. Greg did the only thing he could, referring back to his podium notes. But since he had memorized his talk and hadn't been following along in the printed outline, he couldn't find his place. His notes were useless.

To make matters worse, I could see he was starting to lose his saliva as he tried to stumble ahead—an understandable case of extreme nervousness. But a dry mouth is death to a speaker. I saw him deflate and lose steam as all the energy seemed to drain from his body and spirit. I'm sure he was thinking, *I'm bombing! I'm going down in flames!*

Watching any speaker struggle that way is hard. As a speaker myself, I would naturally empathize. But this was my son. I was rooting for him, praying for him, and a part of me wished I could run up and rescue him somehow. I knew I couldn't, though. He had to learn to get through the crisis on his own.

Mercifully, Greg's memory finally kicked in, and he resumed his talk. All seemed well . . .

Until he went blank again . . .

And again a third time just a few minutes later.

Fortunately, the audience was behind him 100 percent. The people stayed with him, listened attentively, and pulled for him every time he went blank. He managed to finish his talk, and everyone was happy and relieved—except Greg, of course.

He came up to me afterward as I was chatting with some friends and apologized profusely. Then he pulled me aside and whispered, "Dad, can you give me any helpful advice?"

I looked into his eyes and told him soberly, "Son, remember this: It's always the darkest . . . just before it goes totally black!"

As we laughed together, Greg shot back, "Thanks a lot for your encouragement, Dad!"

I tell that story because it illustrates so well the core message I want to get across in this chapter. For just as Greg found himself in a crisis that drained away much of his energy, so any of us can experience a crisis at any time. If the crisis occurs in one of the most important areas of our life, such as our job, marriage, children, friends, or our spiritual side, we can suffer massive loss of emotional and mental energy. But Greg was already doing something that allowed him to recover quickly from his crisis and regain his strength and the ability to move forward.

Fortunately, there's a way to overcome a crisis and regain equilibrium quickly. It worked for Greg, and it can work for you. Let me explain. Greg experienced a crisis in the career area of his life. For the moment, the failure drained him, frustrated him, caused him pain, and dragged him down. But in four other major areas of his life, he was doing well. As a husband, his marriage was solid and fulfilling. As a father, he had a great relationship with his child. Spiritually, he felt he was on good terms with God. As a friend, he had several buddies who would stand by him no matter what.

Because these other important areas of his life were doing well, they balanced out this crisis in his career. In other words, in the other four "baskets" of life, reality was relatively close to expectations. Remember, the narrower the gap between what we expect and what is actually happening, the more strength we maintain. For Greg, four life areas buoyed his spirits and provided an added reserve of energy that helped him get through his crisis. Not long after suffering probably the greatest embarrassment of his life, he was optimistic again and looking forward to his next chance to speak in public.

How can you protect yourself from a massive loss of energy? The rest of this chapter offers protection and more—tips on how you can replenish your energy.

Three Ways to Balance Your Life

Middle-aged men especially need to understand the importance of balance in life. Imbalance is a major cause of midlife crisis; when career expectations aren't realized, too many people lose vision and hope for the future.

1. Identify Life Priorities

Imagine your life as a large, lush vegetable garden. (I know this may sound strange at first, but trust me—the word picture will help you better understand these concepts that have been of tremendous benefit to me and thousands of others.) Each type of vegetable represents one part of your life. For instance, the carrots are your relationship with your mate. The cucumbers are your role as a parent to your children. The lettuce is your career, whatever that may be. The green beans are the members of your extended family. The tomatoes are your friendships. Then add on your hobbies, your volunteer work, your homeowner responsibilities . . . and your spiritual life seems like sunlight and water.

Now, what I'm about to say may seem so obvious that you're tempted to skip to the next subhead, but stay with me. Far too many of us understand this intellectually but act oblivious to the obvious: *You won't have a very satisfying garden unless you plant several different vegetables.* And once you plant them, you need to nurture them carefully if you're eventually going to enjoy their taste. If you overwater or overfertilize some parts and neglect others altogether, the result can be one sick garden.

I've discovered that we usually need at least five healthy "vegetables" to keep up our vigor and love for life, even in the face of crises.

To help you find the five most important parts of your own garden, take a few minutes right now to think about the main parts of your life. How would you complete this sentence? I am a _____ . Come up with your five top responses. As I ask people to do this all over the country, the most common answers include:

I am a spouse.

I am a parent.

I am a friend.

I am a spiritual person.

I am a son or daughter.

I am a [name of vocation.]

I am a [name of avocation.]

I am a man or woman [a physical being.]

Some of those are my own answers, and they may be yours as well. Whatever your five "I ams" are, write them down:

I am a:

1. _____

2. _____

3. _____

4. _____

5. _____

Now look over your list and prioritize your five key areas. Which is most important, second in importance, and so on?

Why have I asked you to identify five top areas, not just one or two? It's a principle called *diversification*. A wise investor spreads his or her money—diversifies—over a number of different investments. That way, if any one or two of them is in the pits, the overall results can be helped by those that are doing better. If the investor held only one investment, on the other hand, and it took a nosedive, he could be wiped out.

You may have heard or read about the great famine in Ireland in the 1800s. More than one million people starved to death. Why? It had to do with the lack of diversification. Because of the climate and the soil conditions, potato farming flourished, and the peasant population thrived on a diet of potatoes—and not much else. When a fungus wiped out year after year of the sustaining crop, a small country starved.

Similarly (and unfortunately), some of us leave ourselves vulnerable in our personal lives by failing to diversify our interests. When one part of our lives is "hit by a fungus," we are susceptible to emotional starvation.

If we focus most of our energy and effort on just one or two areas of life—our careers and a hobby, for example—and something goes wrong there, we can be dumped emotionally, spiritually, and physically. But if we have five priority areas and a problem develops in one or two of them—like giving a speech that goes poorly and wondering if we'll ever be invited to do it again—our health in the other areas can lift our spirits and restore our energy.

If you're completely wrapped up in one aspect of your life and that area crumbles, you can feel as low as Gene, the small-business owner who committed suicide. How sad to think of all the men and women who can identify with his depression brought on by a career crisis! If you relate to his dilemma at all, it's time to diversify, to give some attention to the other key areas of your life.

Why do I suggest you list *only* five key areas? While life offers many good things, I've discovered there are only a few best, most important things. Those are the vegetables that both deserve and require my most careful attention.

The necessity of focusing on our top priorities can be illustrated visually. (I've actually done this demonstration before seminar audiences.) Take two large jars of the same size. One is filled almost to the top with uncooked rice. Each grain of rice represents one of the many good things we could make a part of our lives. The other jar is filled almost to the top with whole walnuts still in the shell. There are a lot fewer of them, and they represent the top-priority areas of our lives.

If you try to pour the walnuts into the jar that's already nearly full of rice, you'll manage to get in only a few nuts. However—and this looks almost like a magic trick—if you pour the rice into the jar that's virtually full of walnuts, all the rice will fit! Before your very eyes, the rice will fill in the many spaces under, around, and on top of the walnuts.

Here's the point: If we fill our lives and give the majority of our time and energy to *countless* good and worthy things (the rice), we won't have much room left for what is truly important. But if we devote ourselves first to those things that deserve top priority (the walnuts), we'll find we're able to enjoy the many other good things as well. They come as bonus energy-boosters.

2. Compare Expectations against Reality

For example, if the "cucumbers" that represent your relationships with your children could speak, what would they say? Would they tell you, "Hey, you're doing a great job here! We really appreciate all the careful attention"? Or would they say, "Hey, we're dying over here! You haven't watered us in days"?

You've named five key areas of your life—ways you identify yourself. By virtue of identifying these "I ams" as your top priorities, you've admitted that these parts of your garden are important to you. And if they're important to you, they are areas in which you want to do well. They encompass your high hopes. Those great expectations of life provide the happiest moments of our lives. But they also lead to our greatest disappointments— when expectations don't jibe with reality. And that gulf between expectations and reality means crisis.

Think about my son Greg's disastrous first speech. Why was it a crisis? Because his career goals—counseling and public speaking—are very important to him. He wants to do well long-term, and he expected to do well the first time out. After all, he had trained hard to be a good speaker, he had worked hard to develop a good talk, and then he had worked even harder to memorize what he was going to say. Everything was looking positive for an incredible first speaking engagement.

Then he ran into a brick wall called reality.

What Greg actually experienced was far different from—far worse than—what he had expected. As we already mentioned: The wider the gap between what we expect and the reality of what we experience in any important area of our lives, the greater the potential for discouragement and fatigue.

What is the second step in keeping your emotional and mental energy high, in surviving life's crises? Slow down and give your life a reality check. How do your expectations compare to your life's realities? What is the condition of your garden? How is each part doing? The effective gardener has to inspect all areas of his or her garden almost daily.

Another helpful way to picture this is to imagine that each of those top five areas of your life has its own thermostat. You might set the temperature at a comfortable seventy-two degrees in, say, the area of your marriage. In other words, you develop a set of nice, comfortable, satisfying expectations. Everything seems to go fine for a while. Before long, however, you start to notice that your home isn't as warm as you had expected. In fact, it's downright cold, and you reach for a sweater.

What's the problem? You're racing through each busy day without taking time to check the thermometer on the wall. And the fact is that the reality of your marriage isn't meeting your present expectations. Remembering where you set the thermostat isn't enough. You also need to look at the thermometer to see the actual temperature, which may be down around sixty degrees. The gap between the temperature you expect and the real temperature is a crisis that will drain energy from you every day. And that loss of strength will go on day after day as long as you're unaware of the problem.

There's a theory that helps explain this predicament and our need to check the temperature. It says that the human brain is always trying—always working—to close the gap between expectation and reality.[2] To match up the two, the brain labors feverishly to somehow reconcile them. If this theory is true, then it's obvious that the further our reality is from our expectations, the harder the brain has to work to try to bring them together, and the greater the energy drain. And in a crisis, when expectations and reality are very different, you can actually watch the strength drain out of a person.

Part of the process of checking reality against expectations may send you back to look at the way you've prioritized the parts of your life. Is your home life causing you stress—because you're spending too much time at the office and therefore distancing yourself from your spouse or children? If so, look at your priorities. When it comes down to the wire, is your job more important than your family?

Years ago I was forced to check my priorities—comparing expectations with reality. Like a lot of other people, I had gotten caught up in my career. Through church-related service work, I was "doing good"—helping others. I could point with pride to how well I was providing for my family. Fine. Great. Just one problem: In the process I was neglecting the emotional and relational needs of my wife and children, who should have held a much higher priority than my job. (If you'd asked me, I would have said they were my first priority. I would have said I wanted to be a good husband and father. But in reality? Well . . .)

I was finally forced to deal with the situation when our son Michael was born. Besides the extra work that's inevitable when another child comes along, Michael provided added stress because he was born with severe, even life-threatening medical problems.

Now, who do you suppose was suffering the greatest loss of energy during this period? That's right, my wife, Norma. She reasonably expected her husband to be at her side, offering emotional support and also extra help with the older kids while she cared for Michael. But I was still back at the office, absorbed in my job, imposing a reality far different from what she expected and needed.

This problem went on for some time, but gradually I became aware of what was happening and how my focus was almost exclusively on my work. Then I determined that I had to back off from my work somewhat and give more time and energy to my family. I had to find a better balance in the top areas of my life. And, with some effort, that's what I did.

Mind you, it's not that I started to improve my balance because I was some maturing husband or father who wisely assessed the situation and automatically made the necessary changes. Instead, Norma quietly confronted me one day and stated that either I helped her or she would have a complete nervous breakdown. In my line of work, that wouldn't have been good for business!

To this day, I'll say to Michael—who is now a healthy adult—"You brought me back to our family." Much to my surprise, I also found that I could still be effective in my work even while I made my loved ones a higher priority. In some ways, rearranging my priorities made me even more effective on the job.

I could give you example after example from my own experience of the need to check your expectations against reality. Another that stands out in my mind is the physical area of my life. My expectations are that I'm a trim, healthy fifty-something man with a long life ahead of me. Now for a little reality: As I said in a previous chapter, the men in the Smalley family have a tendency to develop heart trouble. A little more reality: A few years back a donut would have been the best symbol to represent my body.

You get the picture. So did I. At a periodic checkup I noticed that picture of the *Titanic* I mentioned at the beginning of the book. And that's when the doctor graphically warned me about the dangers of ignoring warning signals.

He had me right where he wanted me. I had been warned before to change my diet and exercise more, to get my cholesterol under control. I had been taking some pills and exercising almost every day, but considering the results of the tests and the shape of my body, that obviously wasn't working. How many warnings would I need before I made lasting, healthy changes? I wanted to be as strong as possible physically and to live a long life. Fortunately, this time he got my attention and made me slow down and look carefully at this part of my life. I doubled the medication and became more faithful in my exercise and eating habits. I've been doing this with the support of some close friends; I need the support and accountability of a "team" working with me.

When I compared my thermostat to the thermometer in my physical life, I saw they were far apart. And that, in turn, led me to the third step we all need to take to get and keep our gardens healthy, our lives in balance, and our energy high.

3. Align Your Expectations with Reality

There's a saying that if you keep doing the things you've been doing, you can expect to keep getting the same results you've been getting. I needed to relearn that lesson in my physical life. I couldn't go on enjoying the habits of Donut Man and expect my cholesterol level and other health indicators to move in the right direction. I needed to change both my expectations and my reality, gradually but steadily.

Change my expectations? Yes. A fifty-year-old body is not a twenty-year-old body, no matter what the family history is.

Change my reality? Yes. Even at fifty, I can change habits that are proven to affect my heart health. This idea applies in any area of potential stress. And there are many practical, workable ways to change habits.

One of the biggest energy-draining experiences most adults stumble through is a strained marriage. I think back over the number of times

Norma and I have been bent out of shape due to some disagreement. It's amazing how the tone of our relationship could get so dark so fast. One hour things would be great, and then instantly we'd be locked in an angry argument over some earthshaking situations like, "Oh, no, you didn't say that! You said you wanted to stop and eat there, so my mouth has been watering to taste their specialty. How dare you change your mind!"

One morning we were in our camper driving out of Prescott, Arizona. I wanted breakfast at this certain restaurant where Norma had agreed to stop, but as we got close, she remembered this other place and asked if we could eat there instead. We quickly found ourselves locked in a three-hour battle, and all kinds of things came out that had nothing to do with eating breakfast. The "discussion" created a gap between our marital expectations and reality, to say the least! After we ate at a completely different restaurant neither of us liked, we got back in the camper and decided to reexamine the marriage area of our respective "gardens."

I was wiped out, feeling like a failure and as if all our progress in being a loving couple had been washed away in one three-hour torrential downpour. We were never going to make it. In the middle of this type of crisis, my personality tends to see only the negatives. But Norma tends to put things in a more realistic perspective. I remember her saying, "Just look at all the things that go great between us, and this is only a small speck in the scope of all the years we've been married." That knack of pulling our expectations and reality closer together gives me more energy to continue the discussion.

We took a closer look at expectations and reality. Were our expectations unrealistic? Was our reality as bad as it seemed? As for reality, Norma had helped clarify that our whole relationship had not flooded away. She helped me take some of my own advice: Avoid extreme thoughts. No, Chicken Little, the sky is not falling.

As for expectations, we decided that some of my expectations about our marriage—that we would always be at peace—were just not practical or realistic. No couple can live each day without some disagreements or even major conflicts. Conflicts are inevitable and can even be healthy, as you'll see in chapter 13. Even if a couple can't work things out for a few days, that's okay. In our case, we had to develop new expectations, ones that were more pragmatic. And we had to remember:

**Forever-love does not see doom in every gap
between expectations and reality.**

Driving down the highway, we both evaluated our marriage and began making a list of things we expected to receive and what we believed would be acceptable for a mutually satisfying relationship. And it's amazing how just talking and agreeing on those marital basics has increased our levels of energy and love for life and each other.

Remember, it's the gap between what we expect and what we get that drains our energy. When our experience is close to what we anticipated, we're stronger and more content. That bolsters our ability to keep on loving. But unless we talk about those things and bring our expectations to the surface, our mate may not know our wishes, and we may find ourselves facing an energy-sapping gap between our desires and our reality.

If you discover on inspection that your expectations and experience don't match up well in a particular area of your life, you need to determine whether you should try to change the expectations or the reality (or both). In my own life, I've often found that when I took the time to look at them, my expectations were unrealistic and had to be adjusted. What I wanted just wasn't entirely reasonable. But other times, I've seen that there were things I could do to improve my reality and raise it closer to my desires.

When your expectations in a certain area involve other people, a good way to make sure those expectations align with reality is to talk them over with all those concerned. This can be difficult and even a little scary if you're not in the habit of speaking with people candidly. It also seems to be human nature to simply expect that somehow our loved ones can read our minds and know what we want.

Many wives, for example, long to hear their husbands say "I love you" more often. Yet many of those same wives will go for years without telling their husbands that's what they would like. Rather than get upset with their husbands, those women can either lower their expectations or—much better—talk over their need to hear those three magic words with their men. The result can be a richer reality, a stronger marriage, better ability to weather life's crises, and more joy and energy for the whole family.

In my own family, we decided a number of years ago to write a family constitution that would spell out what was reasonably expected of everyone. (You can read more details about this idea in chapter 9.) In the process of writing our constitution, we had to talk through all the expectations each of us had that we each thought made up a mutually satisfying family. By the time we were done and started putting it into practice, we were all happier, because we all knew what was expected of us and that we were generally doing a good job of meeting those expectations. It wasn't perfect, but talking things through and getting our expectations out in the open was a big step in the right direction.

The Best Ways to Change

Before we leave this chapter, I'd like to draw your attention to four simple effective ways I've found to help me "stay the course" of lasting change.

First, I like to read several of the best recommended books on the subject at hand. Second, I find an expert or two in town and discuss the issue with him or her. I simply explain my goals and ask the expert to assist me in changing. Next, I gather three of four others who have the same goal, and we meet weekly for a number of months to give each other mutual support and, most important, accountability. For instance, I'm just finishing up a few months with Weight Watchers. It's the weekly weigh-in that keeps me losing weight. The others in the session are all supportive, which makes it easier to experience lasting change. Finally, but certainly not least, I always seek the strength I receive as I look to God in faith. Each of these four resources has given me the ability to keep going and growing. They help me close the gap between expectations and reality.

It's Always Your Choice

If you choose to take the three steps described in this chapter—identify your life priorities, compare your expectations against reality, and align your expectations with reality—you'll do two things: You'll maintain more of your inner strength in the midst of potential and actual crises. And when the inevitable crises do hit—expectations and reality will never totally align in this world—your balanced life will protect you from utter devastation. When a crisis strikes in one area, the health in the other key parts of your identity will provide balance that can soon restore your energy and *joie de vivre*.

In chapter 4 I suggested you list your personal strengths. Identifying five "I ams" has been the key to chapter 5. In the next chapter we'll look at one more aspect of the "Who am I?" question, this time asked in terms of "Who am I as separate from you?" It's a critical question—one that can stop others from robbing you of satisfaction in life and one that can help you enrich the lives of others.

Forever-Love Principles

Our list of forever-love principles continues from the previous chapter:

25. Forever-love is protected when it grows in a diversified garden.

26. Forever-love identifies and nurtures five priority concerns.

27. Forever-love inspects life—to compare expectations against reality.

28. Forever-love reduces life-strain by closing the gap between expectations and reality.

6

Avoiding Hurt Is My Responsibility

That long [Canadian] frontier from the Atlantic to the Pacific Ocean, guarded only by neighborly respect and honorable obligations, is an example to every country and a pattern for the future of the world.
                                                                    —Winston Churchill[1]

If I could get you to read just one chapter in this book, it might well be this one. I feel so strongly about it because the concept at the core of this chapter has done more to change my life—my positive attitude, my wife's attitude, and the health of our life together—than anything else in the last ten years. Let me relate a disastrous scenario that awakened us to this powerful relational truth: When we are causing each other hurt and frustration, we both are at fault. And we both have a responsibility for maintaining and respecting "neighborly" boundaries.

How to Ruin a Great Day

A couple of years ago, Norma and I were in Hawaii with a lot of our staff members to do a live seminar. Norma was excited about being there—the beach, the sun, the rest, and the relaxation. I always enjoy going there, too, whether to speak or just to have fun, so we both started off in a good frame of mind. Then I did it again—something I had done all too often in our married life.

We had arrived on a Saturday, and now it was Monday morning. We woke up early, around six, and as I started to get going, I was thinking, *Hey, we're all alone, and we haven't had a good discussion for a long time. We've both been so busy. Now would be a great time!*

So I looked at Norma and said, "What do you say we work for an hour or so on our marriage goals for the coming year?" I assumed she would love the idea. We have periodic discussions about our future—a version of the "checkups" I mentioned in the previous chapter. Discussing goals helps us keep expectations and reality in line.

Instead, however, she answered, "No, I don't feel like doing that today."

Well, the word *no* is not one of my favorite expressions, so I persisted. "Look," I said, "we haven't had this kind of meeting for a while. We've always got people around, but here we are all alone for a while. What do you say? Let's do it."

Again she replied, "No, I really don't want to do that this morning."

Now her refusal started to get to me. I thought, *Wait a minute! I'm in the business of working on marriages, and we ought to be making sure our own is tuned up just the way it should be.* So I tried again. "Let's just get started on our goals," I said. "We can talk about them at length later, when we get home."

Norma still wasn't interested, and at that point I got a little upset. So what did I, the marriage counselor and seminar speaker, do? To my embarrassment now, I pushed right ahead against her will and said a few choice words under my breath that she didn't appreciate but that got her to give in. We had our talk, all right, but it was obvious the whole time that we weren't really working on our relationship goals.

Why didn't I recognize that I was doing a wrong thing? Frankly, I'm not sure. I know I was convinced that the subject was important and we needed to talk about it. At the time, I also thought it was getting urgent, because it had been way too long since we had last had a time like that to review our goals. Maybe I was even thinking, *This is hard today, but sometimes good things in life are hard, and you have to push your mate to do them.* That sounds good at one level, doesn't it?

Well, whatever I was thinking, after a couple of strained hours of that discussion, Norma's displeasure was unmistakable. She's really open and honest with me about everything, which I love, though this time it hurt.

"This is just great!" she said. "This is the day that Terry [one of our staff members] is going to ask Janna to marry him. It's supposed to be a happy, festive day."

That remark made me realize that I had wiped her out emotionally with our forced conversation. *Gary Smalley*, I thought, *why did you have to push it this far?* I knew she would walk out of that room, and the staff and our kids would take one look at her and then ask me, "*Now* what did you do to her?" Sure enough, shortly after she left for breakfast without me, the story was out, and my son Greg came to me first and said, "Dad, I can't believe you did this! We're both counselors, right? . . ." and so on. One of the other wives also came and said, "Way to wreck our whole day!"

You can imagine how the rest of my day went! Norma and I weren't really speaking. I tried to be nice to her, to joke and warm things up a little, but nothing worked. She just wasn't ready to respond.

That night, Terry, our staff member, put up a big banner on his outside balcony asking Janna to marry him. It could be seen a long way off, from outside the hotel, and Janna saw it and said yes. So we were all excited and in a good mood, including Norma. I thought, *All right. She's getting warmer. There's hope for me yet. I only have four more days until my marriage seminar.*

A little later the whole staff spontaneously went out for ice cream. We were in high spirits, and I announced to everyone in the ice-cream parlor, "Hey, this couple just got engaged!"

All the people cheered, and the manager said, "All right! Free ice cream for you folks!"

After the ice cream was served and our group had finished eating, I was up at the cash register trying to pay, not sure the manager had meant to give us *all* free food. But she ignored me for the moment and looked instead at Terry and Janna. "Listen," she told them, "I don't really know you, but I'd like to give you some marriage advice. There's this television infomercial running right now by a guy named Gary Smalley. He's selling this video series on marriage, and I got it, and it's really been helpful. I think it would help you guys too. You ought to get it before you get married."

At that point, Janna looked at me, I looked at her, and I knew she was thinking, *Gary set this up.* So before she could say a word, I shook my head and told her, "No, I swear I didn't do a thing."

Janna turned to the manager and said, "Do you know who that is— trying to pay you?"

"No," the woman answered. "Should I?"

"It's Gary Smalley," Janna said.

The woman looked at me closely for a few seconds, and then her face broke into a giant smile. She ran around the counter and gave me a big hug.

It was a nice scene. But the clincher came as we were leaving, when Norma leaned in close with her arm around me and said, "You ought to order those tapes."

That day was a turning point in my life. The disaster helped Norma and me see an unhealthy pattern in our lives and our relationship: We didn't clearly understand the importance of personal boundaries. Today, I can see clearly that I was wrong to force Norma to discuss something she wasn't prepared to talk about that morning. I made a big mistake. But so did she. And the pattern we lived out that morning is repeated in home after home across the country.

My mistake was to barge into Norma's life without her permission. If you're a "Gary," in this chapter I'll give you a method that can help keep you from doing the same thing to your spouse or others.

Norma's mistake was that she *let* me barge in. For the "Normas" out there, I'll give practical advice for keeping others from storming into your life.

What's This Talk about Boundaries?

Let me answer that question by asking another: Do you know where you end and 'others' begin? The question doesn't have to do with physical bodies or skin. It has to do with your emotional being. Think of yourself as having an invisible property line around yourself. Imagine that a land surveyor marked off where you start and end with stakes. Inside the property line is everything that makes up who you are—your personality, your likes and dislikes, your goals and dreams, the various parts that make up your life—like the garden I talked about in the last chapter. That garden has a property line around it, but because it's invisible, others may not know where it is—they may not know if they're about to cross it, or if they have crossed it—unless you tell them where the line is.

Most of us want others to respect our property lines and not enter our gardens without our okay. I call this concept "No visitors without my permission." In short, we want people to respect who we are and see us as separate from them—but also as a loving part of them. We want them to respect the thoughts and values we have chosen that reflect our most personal selves, the part of us that is unique and special, like a fingerprint.

To reduce misunderstanding here, know that I'm not suggesting that a husband and wife should fence out each other or their children. I'm not talking about erecting a barrier so that others can't get close. I certainly support the enriching idea that a man and a woman can become "one flesh" after marriage. But oneness does not mean that one mate dominates the other or that the stronger controls the weaker. I'm also not suggesting that a shy person should use this concept to keep others at arm's length.

What I am suggesting is that each one of us, married or single, is a separate and unique person—worthy of two kinds of respect. (1) Respect from others. Others should treat us as separate people with our own likes and dislikes, feelings, hopes, and tastes. Other people should not cross our property lines unless they're invited to do so. (2) Respect from ourselves. We need to feel strong and whole enough to tell others when they are trespassing—trampling on our gardens.

When people insensitively force their way across our personal boundaries, we get very uncomfortable, frustrated, hurt, and, as a result, angry. If you've realized you've carried around deep-seated, unresolved anger, it may well be that someone in your past bulldozed his or her way into your garden. If you were young, you were particularly vulnerable and defenseless. Someone may be trespassing even now. You may think the border violations are out of your control, but there's hope.

Let's look more closely at how the dynamics work—first at my tendency to bulldoze and then at Norma's tendency not to stand her ground.

Confessions of a Bulldozer

Have you ever wished for something all your life, but you figured it would never happen, and then suddenly your dream came true? That's what took place for me, and it was great . . . for a while.

My dream was to drive a big, yellow, powerful bulldozer and build my own road. I don't remember if I played with toy bulldozers as a kid or what, but that driver dream was old and deep.

My opportunity came when my wife and I bought a small farm. Lo and behold, I needed to build a road about a block long down through some trees. So I got in touch with a bulldozer owner and arranged the date and time for him to come and clear the way for my road.

On the appointed day, I started salivating when I saw that gigantic machine on my own property driven by a burly, weathered guy. I thought, *Ohhh, I'd love to drive that bulldozer! But there's no way he'd let me do it. How many hundreds of thousands of dollars did he spend for it?*

The guy got the bulldozer off the flatbed trailer and fired up that huge engine. The ground shook, smoke filled the air, and I was a kid again!

I figured it was now or never. If I was ever going to have a chance of fulfilling my dream, I just had to ask. Besides, what did I have to lose?

"Excuse me," I said, "but I'd like to ask you a question before you start. Is there any way . . . I mean, I was just wondering . . . would you let me use your bulldozer and make the road myself? I'll pay the same amount. I'd really like to do it. What do you think?"

The guy scratched his head and thought about it. I held my breath, amazed that he was even considering the request. Then he said, "Sure, why not?"

Unbelievable! I thought. *Who would have thought?* I said, "Great! Show me what to do."

We climbed up on the bulldozer together, and he gave me about a two-minute lesson in how to operate the machine. "Here's your transmission," he said. "This lever raises and lowers the shovel, and so on. Then he climbed down, and I was on my own."

Was I excited! This was the thrill of a lifetime! You can keep your yacht; I'll take a bulldozer any day. I actually kept it for an entire week and smoothed down everything that needed smoothing all over my property.

A few days later on the following Sunday, I was sitting in my home with a friend when I heard a knock at the front door. I opened it, and there stood one of my neighbors with his wife and teenage son. "Hi, neighbor," I said with a smile.

Without any greeting or the usual pleasantries, he said, "We've got a problem."

"We do?" I asked.

"Yeah. One of your workmen bulldozed my fence and got into my rocks."

"Ohhh," I managed to say as the full force of his words hit me. As my face turned red and my legs went weak, I was tempted to say, "Yeah, those workmen! It's so hard to find good help today, isn't it?" That was my first instinct. But I forced myself to tell the truth. "You know, I need to apologize," I told him. "I'm the one who did that with the bulldozer. I thought I was smoothing my own land. I pushed down those trees and that fence, and I took those rocks. I really did think I was on my own property, and I'm really sorry. I'll be glad to bring the bulldozer back up there and try to fix things."

"No, no, don't bother with that," he said. "Just fix the fence so my horses don't get out."

We wrapped up the conversation, and he was very nice about it all. But as you can imagine, I was extremely embarrassed.

Here I thought I had done a good job of clearing a part of my land, when I had actually been rather careless, torn down a neighbor's fence, and taken something that belonged to him. That's how bulldozer-type personalities can think when it comes to another person's personal boundaries.

Bulldozer Reform

As I said earlier, the way I treated Norma that day in Hawaii illustrates a tendency I've had throughout my life. With my wife, my children, and my friends, I've often rammed my way into their lives, many times without regard for their feelings, and usually without even realizing what I was doing. I now see that my behavior was a classic example of a major way in which people are robbed of their contentment. True love never demands its own way but searches for ways of enriching the other.

My efforts at reform have not only made life easier for Norma; they have opened up my own "lighter heart." I carry less guilt for having "ruined a day." I see that we're both responsible for our own love and satisfaction. I see a way to reduce the frequency of our conflicts.

Though I use the word *bulldozer* to describe my own mode of operation, don't think that all boundary violators are as easy to recognize as a bright yellow earthmover. Some people are masters at "moving in" with subtle guilt trips: maybe a spouses's, "If you loved me you would . . ." or a child's, "All the other parents are . . ."

Soon after I gained new understanding about boundaries, I sent a letter to all three of our children trying to explain the dramatic changes that were occurring in me. Here's what they read:

> Dear Kari, Greg, and Michael,
>
> I woke up this morning thinking of you and thought I would send you a quick note about a very important lesson I've been learning as I prepare for my new video series.
>
> You came to mind for two reasons. One is that without any choice of yours, you were born into our family. As I see more clearly the way I was raised, I can understand why I treated you and the other family members the way I did some of the time. There were many, many times that I was

like a tank smashing down the important and sometimes fragile property line around you without asking if I could visit inside your life.

When you were younger, there were times I would "bulldoze" into your life even if for some reason you had asked me not to come in. In one sense, I could make you feel like, "Well, I'm coming in because I'm your father." I did the same thing with your mom and your siblings. But something happened yesterday to allow me to see these things I've done more clearly than I ever have. I now know that the way I was raised and my personality contribute to a lot of what I did.

If I could live my life over again, I would change a lot of things, but the one thing I would work on most is controlling what I say to others. I have crashed over people's property lines on so many occasions that I couldn't count them. When I think of the little and major things I have said to you over the years and the things I have uttered to so many people, it's scary.

The second reason I wanted to write you is that even though you will probably never do these things to people because of your maturity and loving nature, I just wanted to warn you that some of the things you may say to your classmates or others may come back to haunt you later in life. People are too precious to jump their property lines without permission. It may really hurt them, and many times we never know until years later.

Positive Role Model

In contrast to my aggressive ways, let me give you an example of someone who knew how to respect the property rights of others—my late mother. Without knowing any formal psychology, she greatly respected my property lines as I was growing up. I remember, for instance, that she did a lot of her family shopping in thrift stores because we didn't have much money. But I, as a typical high-school kid, was greatly embarrassed by this. Under the powerful influence of peer pressure, I had to have clothes with the right labels that came from the right stores. And I worked all the way through high school so I could do just that.

Mom didn't care about any of those status issues. But she did care about me, and she was sensitive to my embarrassment over her shopping habits. One morning she said to me, "I need to buy some shoes. Would you give me a ride down to the thrift store?"

"Mom, I really don't want to do that,"I answered.

"That's okay, I understand," she said. "Just drop me off a block away, and I'll walk the rest of the way. You can wait for me in the car and then take me home when I'm done."

"Nah . . . ohh . . . all right," I finally agreed.

Notice that she wasn't violating my individual feelings and needs; she wasn't walking in my "garden area" by making me do something that wasn't me. She got my cooperation, but she did it in a way that allowed me to maintain my sense of dignity. My feelings were valued and treated with respect.

How can we develop an attitude like my mom's with regard to others? As I already mentioned, the first mistake we can make is to invade another's territory without permission. That's what I had done to Norma in Hawaii and to my neighbor's property at home. But I've learned an effective way to slow down and respect the special "property rights" of others.

Respecting the Rights of Another to Pursue Happiness

This whole idea sounds a little like our country's Declaration of Independence, doesn't it? Our Founding Fathers laid down the truth there that "all men are created equal, that they are endowed by their Creator with certain unalienable rights," among which is "the pursuit of happiness."

With that God-given right of everyone to pursue happiness in mind, how should a person—especially a rather aggressive personality like me—approach others when there's something he or she wants? *It's basically a matter of asking for permission before entering someone else's "space" and then being willing to accept the answer you're given, even if it's not the one you wanted.* (This principle may seem obvious, but for many it's not practiced.) This is the thing I'm learning to do—the one thing that has most changed how I deal with people and has most improved my relationships.

Asking permission is critical, but so is the ability to hear a *no* or *not now* with grace. When Norma says "Not now," I need to respect myself enough to feel that she is not rejecting *me*. What does this mean? It means anger levels need to be low; we need to be constantly working through the principles presented in earlier chapters. If anger levels are low, we're best able to see a particular conversation as an incident unto itself; we're not dragging in excessive baggage from previous encounters.

Here's the approach I've now learned to use when I want to talk about something or do anything with Norma. I'll walk up to her and "knock" at her imaginary gate. I'll say something like, "Could we talk about next week's schedule tonight?" or "I want to go out tonight. What about you?" It can be any subject, feeling, or need I wish to address.

She's free to respond, "No, I don't want to talk about it right now. Maybe later."

Then I'll say, "Okay, when?"

She might answer, "I would love to talk about it later this evening. Or how about tomorrow?"

And I'll conclude, "Good. That's great. Then we go on to something else."

Believe me, my ability to operate that way and respect Norma's wishes—her uniqueness—is a big difference in my life. (And I don't want to misrepresent Norma: If it truly is an urgent matter that must be discussed now, she'll respect the issue and talk immediately.)

My gentler approach has also helped us deal with three or four particular subject areas we don't talk about often because it's so difficult. You and your spouse probably have similar subjects, the kind that get you heated up every time they're broached. It used to be that way when I wanted to discuss something explosive. We would just launch into the subject and hope for the best, and many times we ended up in a hurtful argument. Now we both ask for permission to bring up those topics, and we feel much more comfortable, safe, and loved.

Here's one final and very down-to-earth illustration of how to use this approach in a healthy way: Jim and Suzette, a couple from our support group and close friends of ours, were having lunch with us and practicing this concept one day. Suzette said to Jim, "Can I talk to you about something?" (Notice she's asking for his permission respectfully.)

Jim immediately responded, "Well, I've got a video camera security system on my property today." But he continued, "What do you want to talk about?" (He wanted to know more before he granted permission.)

"Just one thing," she answered.

"What is it? I want to know what you want to talk about before I decide to let you inside my gate."

"All right," she said, "I want to talk about what you're eating for lunch today."

"Okay, come on in and we'll discuss it," he told her, inviting her to come through his elaborate security system. (Remember, Norma and I are good friends with them, and they felt safe enough with us to have a discussion like this in front of us. I recognize that some couples can't imagine discussing a sensitive marital problem in front of others. But we've been doing it for so long it's now second nature, and it has been extremely helpful in both marriages.)

Suzette went on, "I know we've talked about this before, but when you order your favorite kind of spaghetti at this restaurant, by six o'clock at night you really have an unusual odor."

"What do you mean?" he said, surprised.

"Well, this garlic gets in your system, and you really . . . uh . . . smell. It's embarrassing to me when we go to basketball games or other public events. I'm very aware of it, so I find myself trying to keep you away from other people so they don't notice it."

Jim accepted that graciously, if reluctantly, and said, "All right, I won't order that today. If it really bothers you, I'll have something else." (Notice his sensitivity to her feelings and her uniqueness.)

Then Suzette decided to push her luck. "While I'm inside your garden," she continued, "may I talk about just one other thing?"

Now, realize he could have said no to that request. He could have said, "I really don't feel like two in one hour. Maybe later." But he answered, "All right, go ahead."

"Okay, one other thing," she said. "When we go to that high-school basketball game tonight, would you not yell at the officials and the fans from the other school? It really embarrasses me when you pick out a fan and start haggling with him."

"But I'm a coach," he protested. "I know how to work referees, so I do that. It's part of the game."

"Well, it really embarrasses me," she repeated, standing her ground. "You're a community leader, so other people are watching you. And it makes me feel like I want to wilt."

"All right," he said, choosing to be gracious again. "I'll try to be more aware of yelling tonight."

Here again, Jim had the freedom to decide. He could have said, "When I go to a game, I love to yell. That's just me. I can't help it, though I'll try not to be rude." But he had invited her comments, he was in a generous mood, and he gave her what she wanted. For her part, Suzette had respected his property line, asked for permission to speak, and then stated her case clearly. That's a healthy personal property line at work.

This first part of the chapter has covered the kind of mistake made by the Garys of this world, where the strong personalities tend to bulldoze the weaker. Now let's turn to the mistake Norma made.

Claiming One's Own Ground

Early that morning in Hawaii—the disastrous day that woke Norma and me to the reality of our border disputes—I was not the only person who made a mistake. Norma had a choice in how she responded to me. She and many people like her tend to blame their circumstances or others for their discontent with life. Each of us can and should take responsibility for how we allow others to "visit" us inside our "gardens" without permission. The Normas of the world need to understand that love does not always give in to every request, especially to intimidation.

Gaining Strength

As a human being in relationship to another human being, you are not a genie with this life motto: *Your wish is my command.* You have the ability to say no; you have a responsibility to say no if someone bulldozes over you. Allowing that bulldozer to tear down your fence and trees can cause resentment. You'll feel trampled and squeezed. (Think back to the "can of anger," where a dangerous substance was compressed, pressurized.) That unhappiness and unresolved anger you'll blame on the bulldozer. But wait. Have you let the bulldozer onto your property without as much as a warning sign? You are responsible for warning others and then lovingly standing your ground.

But, you say, saying no will cause an unhappiness of its own. "Making waves" is so uncomfortable.

Yes, bulldozers have a way of making it difficult to hold your ground. But let me give some advice:

Work through old unresolved anger. I repeat, if anger levels are low, we're able to see—and deal with—one incident at a time. You don't need to escalate a minor boundary infraction into World War III proportions. But that's what can happen when you've let someone squeeze you in for so long that one day you finally blow—pointing a weapon at someone and screaming "Get off my land!" That's what happens when you let a bulldozer's "few choice words" set off a minefield of emotion.

Remember, at the beginning of the chapter, we said that respect for others was half the boundary issue; respect for self was the other critical ingredient. As you claim your ground, speak in love. Speak with respect for yourself and the other person. Be reasonable but firm. And watch as a new self-respect counters your dis-ease.

A Revised Scenario

That morning in Hawaii, Norma could have claimed her ground and said, "Not now." She didn't have to give in to my intimidation.

Let's go back to that morning and ask what Norma could have done to defend herself from unwanted intrusion. Could she have done something practical to postpone our conversation until she was ready for it?

For one thing, after stating her objection, she could have tried to change the subject. She could have said, "Let's go to breakfast, and let's just have fun while we're here in Hawaii. This is Terry's engagement day, after all. What are you going to wear down to breakfast?"

But suppose I continued to push ahead with something like, "Breakfast can wait," or "Fine, we'll talk about it at breakfast." What then?

In that case, Norma could have emphasized her willingness to discuss the subject later. "Sure I'd like to talk about our marriage goals," she might have said, "but not now and not here. Let's just relax while we're here. This is supposed to be a fun vacation, and having a big, serious discussion now is not my idea of fun."

By that time I should have been getting the message, don't you think? But let's say I was still determined to talk about goals that morning. Then she would have needed to really dig in her heels and take the blunt approach: "What's that saying?" she could have recalled: "What part of no don't you understand? I really don't want to talk about marriage goals today."

At that point, even I would have understood. I probably would have been frustrated for a while, but that would have faded quickly as we got into the fun of the day and the joy of Terry's engagement. (For specific ideas on how to resolve conflict so that frustration doesn't turn to anger, see chapter 13.)

I'm happy to say that since the Hawaii incident, Norma has learned to defend herself much better. Awhile later, we went to Florida together for a conference and writing session. We were on the beach, close to the water where the waves could lap at our feet, and I was rehearsing what I would say in the part of my presentation covered in this chapter. I would ask her opinion of something I planned to say, and she would respond, "Try saying this and maybe this." She gave me a number of great ideas.

We went back and forth like that for about two hours, and I was really enjoying it. In fact, I wanted to keep going for another hour or so. But Norma had reached her limit, so she said something like, "I'm tired of talking about this stuff. I came down to relax by the water."

Well, I was on a roll and I pleaded, "Just a little more?"

"My gate's closed," she said lovingly, looking me in the eyes. "I'd like to read for a while. I'm putting a 'Do not disturb' sign on my gate."

Fortunately, I had learned my lesson by that time, and I got the message. I was frustrated because we were right in the middle of the discussion as far as I was concerned, but I honored her as a special person with her own feelings and needs. I let go of my frustration and moved my chair down the beach a little way. Because I needed an audience and there was no one else around, I started speaking to the sea gulls! But even they didn't seem that interested.

Border Watch

How can you tell if the imaginary line around your life isn't being respected as it needs to be?[2] This is one area where your emotions may be a pretty good guide. For instance, have you been really angry in the last month, an anger that lasted more than a couple of days? Have you been frustrated over a period of time? Have you felt used or abused? Have you felt suffocated in a relationship?

If you're living with any of these negative emotions, your boundary may need to be better marked. Remember, your present quality of life depends upon the choices you make. Claim your ground. Except in cases of extreme abuse, I recommend that you choose to tell others when they're trespassing. (See "Tough Situations" below.)

One caution, again having to do with unresolved anger: If you find that everybody's always frustrating you, your old anger may be making your boundary unnecessarily broad. Remember, anger keeps you distant from others. Love builds bridges to others.

Tough Situations

What do you do if you're in a relationship with someone who constantly bulldozes into your life without permission and just won't take any form of no for an answer? Obviously, that's a tough situation, and there are no easy answers. I recommend that every couple be part of a couples support group. This might give you a safe place to discuss touchy things if your mate is willing. Professional counseling is another tool you might use for yourself or—even better—for both of you together. There are many helpful resources (agencies and counselors) available today in most cities.[3]

In extreme cases, especially where there is any threat of physical harm, you may have to physically separate yourself from the boundary violator. This might involve calling 911 and contacting legal authorities. No one should suffer physical abuse.

Perhaps you're thinking, *I want this person's love, so I had better just leave matters alone or he or she might leave me or harm me further.* Believe me, you're not the first person to think that way. But if you choose to ignore your circumstances, I've found the problem usually gets worse, not better. It's much better to alert an offender to your property line and insist that you will no longer allow trespassing. Take a stand, and defend yourself. In the short term, the other person will probably resist and may give you a hard time. But in the long run, he or she will respect you much more. It's your only real hope for a satisfying relationship.

Final Thoughts

As we've seen, clearly defining who we are is essential. It can make or break our love for life and the satisfaction we receive from relationships built on respect and honor. Learning this concept and beginning to respect the boundaries of my wife, children, and friends has literally changed my life, and I'm glad to say I'll never be the same as before.

But realize that keeping a "garden area" in good repair and defending it is hard work. For people with either tendency—to be too aggressive or too passive—the final word is *moderation.* An age-old rule of life and love is this: "Love your neighbor as yourself."[4] The two loves are intertwined in a tight strand of respect that can temper the aggressive, strengthen the passive, and make for long-lasting peace—with one's neighbor (spouse) and with oneself.

In chapter 7, I give one more warning—how you can avoid the biggest "iceberg" that threatens forever-love. When we quit pretending that our spiritual journey doesn't matter, we're on our way to availing ourselves of the power we need to love life and others.

Forever-Love Principles

Our list of forever-love principles continues from the previous chapter:

29. Forever-love respects another person's personal boundaries.

30. Forever-love never demands its own way but searches for ways of enriching the other person.

31. Forever-love asks permission before entering someone's garden.

32. Forever-love hears "no" or "not now" with grace—not with paranoia.

33. Forever-love is not a genie. "Your wish" is not "my command."

34. Forever-love can hold its ground against intimidation.

35. Forever-love knows the quiet, confident strength that comes with self-respect.

36. Forever-love equally respects self and others.

37. Forever-love tempers the aggressive and strengthens the passive.

7

Finding the Power
to Keep Loving

*To make [things] your masters, to look to them to justify your life and save your
soul is sheerest folly. They just aren't up to it. . . . Having ushered God out
. . . through the front door, the unbeliever is under constant temptation to
replace him with something spirited in through the service entrance.*
—Frederick Buechner[1]

Where do we find added strength to keep loving and enjoying life when difficulties hit or when we just get tired of trying or when life turns into a boring
routine? I've found that one of the key truths lies in "sighting" and avoiding
a deadly cluster of "icebergs" that would block our spiritual journey.

Why is the spiritual journey so important? Marriage researchers are
finding a correlation between one's spiritual journey and one's satisfaction
in marriage. Howard Markman, Scott Stanley, and Susan Blumberg report
that religion has a favorable impact on marriage. They write that religious
couples "are less likely to divorce . . . show somewhat higher levels of satisfaction . . . lower levels of conflict about common issues . . . and
higher levels of commitment."[2] And in worldwide research Dr. Nick
Stinnett found six characteristics common to most happy marriages and
families—one being an active, shared faith in God.[3]

Though a recent Gallup poll revealed that over 90 percent of Americans
believe in God, many struggle to find a personal living faith. Most of us

realize that we don't have it all together and that we do need some outside strength to help us keep our love from fading or to endure the pain caused by others. But often, as I did for so long, we choose some course that drives us in a different direction from developing our spiritual dimension.

Out of my depression twenty years ago, I started learning about the obstacles that kept me disconnected from a personal God. As I've gradually seen how to connect, I've become keenly aware of how vital this spiritual area of life is for anyone wanting to experience greater satisfaction in life and lasting love.

In this final chapter of part 1, I will discuss four main factors that hindered my spiritual journey. I kept hearing that God was a God of love who could somehow give a person the ability to love others and himself or herself. But I couldn't find how this truth could be real *for me*. I seemed to need more than education and support from family and friends to keep my love for life and others alive and growing. I wanted supernatural help, but it wasn't there for me until I turned thirty-five and became very tired of hitting "icebergs."

In my thirties, feeling hopeless and isolated, my anger grew like mold in a damp basement. I distanced myself from my wife and kids, I didn't want to go to my job, and I was ready to quit the profession for which I had been preparing for years.

I felt as if I were floating in a sea of anger, and I kept allowing Norma and my kids to poke more and more holes in my leaky life vest. I realized I was sinking fast. I had to take some steps in a hurry and cry out for help.

It was like the time our family visited a wave-pool water park in Las Vegas; I went out in the deep end without a raft. Wave after wave came, and I finally tired. I was all by myself—the kids were already out of the water—and I decided to swim to the ladder at the side of the pool and climb out. But I couldn't make it! Every time I got close to the edge, another wave would push me away again, and I was too tired to fight it. I swallowed water, began to panic, and realized I was helpless. At that point my only thought was, *I'm going to drown here in Las Vegas in front of my family!* I was sure I was going down for good.

Fortunately, my family had seen what was happening. The next thing I knew, my son Greg was stretching way out, grabbing me by the arm, and pulling me toward that ladder. When I got to it, I wrapped my arms around it and hung on for dear life.

That's kind of what happened to me with God. I kept trying to reach out for some kind of satisfaction in life, but each time a wave of reality would push me back out, and I was sinking. I've heard alcoholics, the addicted, and many other hurting people who were just as miserable as I was, say this same thing. Each of us finally reached out and grabbed God's hand, which had always been there, outstretched and waiting for us.

It's been rewarding because I actually did find what I'd heard so many people say was possible, but had eluded me for so long. I found a way to tap into the spiritual realm and receive the ability to love God, others, life, and myself more. In other words, for the past twenty years my ability to keep loving has not been dependent upon the actions of others or my circumstances, but rather on my choice to stay connected to a personal God. This chapter is about how I was able to tap this supernatural force.

My own outstretched hand came in the midst of my depression and disillusionment. I recalled a verse from the Bible, Psalm 50:15: "Call upon me [God] in the day of trouble; I will deliver you, and you will honor me." I realized that was all I could do then, and it was what I needed to do. Sinking like the *Titanic*, I cried out to God for help, asking him to somehow rescue me from the mess I was in and show me he was real. And deep in my spirit, I kept hoping he heard me. Eventually I did find a personal connection to God, and it's been so rewarding I've never looked back.

Before I get to the four icebergs that kept blocking my ability to find a personal God, let me share what this chapter will *not* do. I obviously won't be addressing all the subtle meanings that you, my readers, bring to this spiritual area of life. I want to present my ideas so you see how wonderful it has been for me, yet I don't want to come across as preachy or saccharin and possibly cause some to further avoid its tremendous benefits. Also, I'm not trying to address all the various doctrines or great concepts about faith in God. I simply want to share the hindrances I encountered in my spiritual journey and why the lack of connection with a personal God affected my ability to love my wife, my family, and others—even myself.

You may have little interest in spiritual things because you've been wounded by someone who claimed to be a "religious person." Perhaps you've been hurt in a past church experience. Or maybe you've had close friends who claimed to be spiritual but lived out hypocritical lives. Well, I've been jerked around and hurt by a lot of "religious" people myself.

But I finally saw that denying the spiritual side of life because we've known some phonies is like refusing to go to a bank where they're waiting to give us one hundred thousand dollars because we know that some of the people who work there or deposit money there are two-faced.

In the spiritual arena, I've found truths that have meant the world to me. This area has been the most enriching part of my entire life's journey. I just couldn't write a book about making love last forever without talking about my faith. It would be like talking about sailing without mentioning the wind.

My faith has become like a powerful turbocharged engine in an old '57 Chevy. God has become like the warmth of a fireplace after being out too long in the cold. Before I found him to be real, I allowed myself to be spiritually hindered, even battered, by four icebergs that blocked my path.

1. My Doubts Kept Me from God

When I was seriously questioning the existence of God back in my college days, someone challenged me to open my mind to the possibility of a personal God by asking me three humbling questions. Those questions were healthy for me, because they caused me to develop my own personalized belief system. Here are those questions:

1. How much knowledge do you think we now have in the world out of all the knowledge that can be known (0 percent to 100 percent)?

   _____

2. How much of this knowledge do you think you know personally (0 percent to 100 percent)? _____

3. Do you think it's possible that a personal God could someday reveal himself to you through the remaining knowledge that you could gain (yes or no)? _____

When I ask these questions of others, the average person admits to having only a small percentage of the available knowledge. And most people then take the position that it may be possible to someday see and experience a personal God.

Again, for me, I was full of doubts about a personal God, and with my level of anger and guilt, even during my college years, there was no way I was going to "see" God. My anger kept him far from me.

I could fill an entire book with my elaborate doubts, many of which left as my anger and guilt subsided. You may not have a lot of doubts about

God's existence, and you may well be on your way with your own spiritual journey, but possibly telling my version of this vital area of life may further enhance yours. From my personal experience as well as that of thousands of others, I'm convinced that you can obtain the single, most important key to lasting love, one that nothing or nobody can ever take away.

2. Hypocrites Kept Me from God

I didn't start attending church regularly until I was a teenager. My older brother and sister got me involved.

At the very first church I attended, the minister was asked to leave because of some moral problem. That was a harsh reminder of the truth that no one is perfect. Nonetheless, I was fairly active in this first church—until I had a fistfight with one of the staff members! Shortly after that scuffle, my father passed away, leaving me in need of someone older to look up to. A new staff member with a sincere, loving nature kept me coming to church, and he proved to be genuine. I still deeply admire this man even though he, too, eventually left the church because of personal struggles. I used to wonder how this vital area of life, our faith in God, could survive with such inconsistencies among its believers.

In spite of the leaders I encountered, my faith remained alive during my college years, and then, as a graduate student, I was hired by a church to work with its youth. I was excited at the opportunity and looked forward to a satisfying, fulfilling ministry. To my dismay, however, the senior pastor never bothered to learn my name. In staff meetings he would call me "Hey, you." I thought, *That's incredible! People who say they serve a God of love are supposed to be more loving.* And I was scratching my head in wonderment a lot of the time.

My first meeting with the youth of this church knotted my stomach. The teenage leader was asked to pray before a noon meal. He rose respectfully to utter these words: "Rub-a-dub-dub, thanks for the grub. Yea, God." Then he sat down amid giggles from the other kids. One evening awhile later, that same teen admitted in a formal youth business meeting that he couldn't find God as a meaningful experience. Several others in the meeting expressed their disbelief as well, along with the adult sponsors. Everyone else seemed to get into the confessional mood, so I joined them. That night after the meeting, I told my wife that I would probably be asked to leave the church because I had just admitted that God was not real to me. I believed God existed; I just couldn't find him to be personal. Nothing ever came of my confession, but the experience certainly motivated me to find out what kept blocking my ability to know God.

My wife's childhood church experience also fed my growing disappointment with "religious people." In her first church, the pastor ran away with Norma's best girlfriend's mother. The church-family members were devastated, and so was the child who would become my wife.

Following graduate school, I worked for a religious organization with which I grew disenchanted, and I finally left that place as a discouraged man. Then, despite my spiritual condition and disillusionment, I went to work—briefly—in another church. I was hired to guide the congregation in setting up a counseling center. But within months that pastor was asked to leave because of marital infidelity.

I stayed there to help out for a while, and when I left there I started my own work teaching a marriage seminar, along with writing books about how to stay happily married. I've since had many wonderful experiences being a member of various churches—but for more than fifteen years I've not had the opportunity again of being a staff member.

You may be wondering how I stayed on a spiritual journey with all I had experienced. I had plenty of reason for skepticism, and you may as well.

I came to realize that I wasn't responsible for the wrongs of those other people. Then also, I wasn't going to let their irresponsibility rob me of my future love for life. I held on to a baseline faith in the "God of hope."[4] I chose to heed the advice of an old friend who reminded me, "If you draw close to God and continue to seek after him, you will find him."[5] And I listened when someone said, "God is still enriching the lives of those who find him." I always wanted to know if it was possible to experience God. I got to the place where I no longer cared how hypocritical the "bank tellers" or the others who "deposited" at church were; I was going to keep up my own search for his treasures and his power.

Powerful Lessons

I finally saw the major hindrances for me in knowing a personal God. I can best explain it by asking you to imagine a life-size baby doll in a store and picture this doll moving and even speaking a limited vocabulary. In her back a battery pack opens up; it holds three D batteries to supply the power so she can function as she was designed to—so she can be all she was meant to be.

We're all somewhat like that doll. God made us capable of doing many good and wonderful things, but we need power to operate. He intends for us to get the main power for living—and the primary things we need in life—from him. If we let him, God can empower our love; it's like having all three D batteries in place. He fits. I find that many people, like me, have had this vague emptiness in their lives; they don't know what will fill it. We can feel a need to be connected to a personal God, a longing for wholeness, or a desire to gain control over our emotions and struggles.

Our spiritual problems only increase when we try to stuff things other than God into our battery packs, hoping these things will fit and empower us. I've found that if we try to gain completeness, strength, love, and joy from any substitutes for God, they don't bring a lasting fulfillment. In fact, when you look closely at negative emotions of hurt, frustration, and fear, they often come as we expect God's creation—rather than God—to "charge" our life.

We can simplify this idea by seeing that these substitutes generally fall into one of two categories: what we expect to get from other people (like AA batteries) and what we expect to get from our jobs (like C batteries). I tried to stuff people and my job into my battery pack for years, and all I kept getting was the very emotions I didn't want—hurt and emptiness.

I'll never forget the day I realized that my lack of connection with God was primarily the result of my own decision to remain angry. My main anger source was my expectations that people and my job would fit nicely into my battery pack, that they would provide me with energy, love, and satisfaction. Unfortunately expectations bring the hurt and frustration leading to anger. People and the things our jobs can bring are great batteries, but just the wrong size for us.

On this particular day, I was casually reading a section of Scripture and my eyes stopped at a verse that seemed to scream this message at me: "If you remain angry with anyone, you'll lose your ability to walk in the light of God and thus the ability to know the love of God."[6] Very angry people seem to be spiritually blind and unable to draw near to God.

3. Expecting Too Much from People Kept Me from God

We try to fit friends and loved ones into our battery packs. We think, *If only I had the right mate. If only I had some good friends who would stand by me and support me, no matter what. If only I had parents who believed in me. If only I had kids who made me proud instead of embarrassing me every time I turn around . . . then I could set the world on fire. I'd have it made.*

We rely on one person or a group of folks to meet our needs for love, purpose, excitement, fulfillment, ego gratification . . . And you know what happens? They eventually let us down because they are human. Their love often proves to be conditional rather than without reservation. Life with even the best mate is boring at times. And no one lives forever—what then? Our kids have a will of their own and may choose words and actions that hurt us rather than fulfill us. A best friend might betray us or just move away to another part of the country in our time of deepest need.

Remember, our supply of energy for dealing with life's daily demands depends on how closely our expectations match the reality we experience. Well, when friends and family let us down, when we've been counting on them, we can suffer a huge energy loss.

This is what happened to me in my period of great discouragement after graduate school, when I went to work in the field of counseling with a reputable religious organization. I thought I had it made. Not long after I joined the staff, however, I grew uncomfortable with what I saw. I felt that top administrators were involved in highly questionable activities. And I developed a special animosity—a hatred, really—toward one individual in particular.

Eventually I had so much anger toward some of my coworkers that there were days I couldn't make myself go to work. I would call in sick. And I distanced myself from my family too. For instance, I couldn't bring myself to sit and eat with them. I hid myself away in a bedroom for days on end. Our kids were only three, seven, and nine at the time, and they needed their daddy, but emotionally I couldn't be there for them.

Norma grew concerned, not only for my health and the family's, but also for our finances when I started talking about resigning.

"But you can't do anything else," she said pragmatically. "You've been trained only in this kind of work."

Her words were like a bucket of ice water thrown into my face. It was painful to acknowledge. I had a graduate seminary degree. What good would it do me if I left the religious milieu? I had no skills I knew of that would get me a job outside the fold. "You're right," I had to admit.

In that moment of realization, I went deeper into discouragement and depression. As Norma walked away, her hand slipped out of mine, and in a sarcastic tone I said, "Thanks for your encouragement."

It was so debilitating, that sense of anger mixed with hopelessness. In every area of my life at the time, including my marriage, my expectations were far from my reality.

Coworkers I had greatly admired eventually disappointed me—a huge difference from what I had expected. So without even realizing it, I leaned more heavily than ever on Norma to meet my needs. But she didn't understand all I was feeling; she was busy being a mom to three young children, and she had only so much left to give me at that time.

That's my point exactly: Some friends and coworkers simply weren't interested in meeting my needs. And even my closest family member, who has a heart of gold and wanted to help me, couldn't supply my need. As someone has rightly observed, spouses make lousy gods. They don't fit our "battery packs," and they simply can't meet our deepest needs or keep us happy all the time.

So I was losing massive amounts of energy, and that was contributing to my depression. Years later I came to realize that going through that trial opened me to a new, deeper compassion for people who are hurting and discouraged (one of my pearls from that sand storm).

As a result of this crisis, I also made massive strides in my own spiritual journey. We've said that anger distances us from God. In time, through forgiveness and pearl-counting, I was able to take inventory of my relationship with God—a God who dwells in a sphere beyond human hypocrisy. And, again, I've found God more than adequate; he supplied far above what I expected from others. Today I'm actually grateful I walked through all that hurt and depression, because it was the main motivation leading me to discover a personal God.

There are many good reasons to forgive the wrongs of others, but the most rewarding is to use it in our spiritual journeys. Consider the words of what came to be known as the Lord's Prayer: "Forgive us our trespasses as we forgive those who trespass against us." This indicates his forgiveness of us is connected to our forgiveness of others. It's because our unforgiveness blocks our ability to receive his strength and love.

Unforgiveness is a sign that we're expecting power from a "false battery." If we're trying to stuff other people into our battery packs, the result is usually anger when they disappoint us. (People are good at not allowing us to use them.) But if we're not trying to use them to somehow energize us—if we know the true source of power, if we know that only God gives the best things in life—we can forgive them and consequently relax our expectations of them. As we understand the limitations of people fulfilling us—they can't compare to what God can do when it comes to energizing us—we can sincerely desire the best for others. That's genuine love.

So if people offend us or let us down, we can release our anger to God and allow the hurtful experience to remind us of our dependency on him.

As we do this, we find freedom—and power—to help others on their own spiritual journeys. Again, that's genuine love.

To summarize this idea, one of the main blockages to our spiritual journey is expecting others to meet our deepest needs, and this sets us up for being hurt and getting angry. But we tend to relax when we realize that God can meet our deepest needs. Then as we actually experience God meeting our needs and doing things that could only be described as miraculous, we gain a peace and happiness that's beyond what we had imagined gaining from other people.

I believe the key to maintaining love and satisfaction in life is not expecting lasting satisfaction and love to come from God's creation. Keep those expectations for God alone. Allow him to be the main-battery power source and expect everything else to be "overflow."

That's not to say I never experience down times anymore. Like you and most others, I still have anger and other defeating feelings at times. But the difference for me is that when I experience those normal negative emotions, I find myself "rejoicing," which means returning to the source of my joy. I'm willing to admit that my anger is a result of expecting to use others for my satisfaction instead of enriching them.

4. Expecting Too Much from My Job Kept Me from God

The other "false battery" I used to squeeze God out was looking for fulfillment and energy in a job.

Think of all the places we can go and the things we can have because of our "positions." The money we earn makes all those things possible. We may think, *If only I had a bigger house or a more modern house . . . If only I lived in the right part of town . . . If only I could vacation in Cancun instead of Cleveland . . . If only I could live in Florida, where I'd never have to shovel snow anymore.*

But once again, this type of expectation is bound to disappoint. In reality, a bigger house means higher costs, more work, and more worry. And when you get right down to it, all homes are just wood, bricks, and mortar. Vacations, as great as they are, are only temporary breaks from the demands of daily living. And Florida, as warm and beautiful as it is, also gets hurricanes and is the land of large roaches.

No matter where we are, we face the challenges and difficulties that are universal to humankind. No matter how big our house, the folks inside have all the failings of the human race. When you stop to think about it, can any home or other location take the place of God in filling our battery packs and meeting our deepest needs? I haven't found any place that rejuvenates as he does.

We may also think, *If only I had a lot of money in the bank* . . . *If only I could drive the right car or wear the latest designer clothes* . . . *If only I had a higher-paying, more prestigious job, one where I was considered invaluable by all my superiors* . . .

Perhaps you've seen the bumper sticker that says "He who dies with the most toys wins." Well, I've been able to enjoy a few nice things in recent years, and while they provide pleasure for a while, they also rust, break, get stolen, or just wear out. And, according to the hundreds of people I've spoken with, when you have a sick child or a troubled marriage, the size of one's bank account doesn't bring the satisfaction one once expected. The more accurate bumper sticker is the one that says, "He who thinks that having a lot of toys brings fulfillment is already dead."

I know rich and poor people alike who are at both ends of a scale of contentment; some are very happy, and some are miserable. Money doesn't seem to be the gauge for happiness. I can honestly say that no amount of money has ever kept me satisfied or in love. Only if I'm allowing God to meet my needs and empower me with his love, joy, peace, and contentment every day am I truly happy regardless of my circumstances.

Nonetheless, our natural human tendency is to expect fulfillment (a personal battery-charge) from friends and loved ones or from what our jobs can buy—where we live or visit and the things we own. And they inevitably disappoint us, leaving us frustrated and angry.

Practical Ways by Which I've Drawn Closer to God

I have talked at length about my crisis twenty years ago and what precipitated my feeling distant from God—how anger had blocked my relationship with God.

To cover the next twenty years of my life in detail, especially how God made himself real to me, would require another book, a book I wrote several years ago titled *Joy That Lasts.*[7] But I can briefly summarize the two main lessons I have learned that have made my journey more than worthwhile. These two truths were first planted in my heart during my college years. But in my midlife-crisis years they really took root, and they form the essence of my faith in God. Actually, these two truths have become the centerpiece in every area of my life. They are the soil that nurtures my marriage, my relationships with family and friends, and my work. But they didn't become personalized until after my discouragement.

These truths are captured in this quick summary of all the biblical laws: "Love God with your whole heart, and love others as you love yourself."[8]

Can We Really Love God?

When I read that commandment as a college kid, I wondered, *What in the world does that mean? Love God?* It was embarrassing even to say it out loud. You can love your wife, your girlfriend, fishing, or golf, but how do you love God? It seemed too ethereal, too strange. But it was a lifesaving truth I recalled in my depression, and then it began to make sense. I certainly don't know how God does it, but he somehow makes himself real to those who wholeheartedly seek after him. I'll try to explain this as I've come to understand it.

I came to realize that the word *love* is an action verb that indicates you're doing something for someone because that someone is very valuable to you. It is closely connected to a word I've used extensively in my seminars and writing and counseling, the word *honor*.

To honor someone means you choose to see a person as being very valuable. In your eyes, he or she is the heavyweight champion of the world, the best, of the highest value possible. *Dishonor*, on the other hand, is when you consider somebody as nothing more than mist from a teakettle; it disappears and is gone and has little value. (I'll share more about this concept in chapter 8).

This word *honor* has helped me draw close to God. As I have established God as my highest value in life, God has miraculously reached out and made himself real to me in many ways. I don't understand how he does this anymore than I understand how my computer works, yet I go on typing . . . And in my spiritual life I still go on honoring and believing, and God continues to make his presence known to me.

Let me illustrate what I mean by "making God my highest value." Imagine that you and your mate are at a concert with thousands of fans, waiting to hear one of your favorite female singers, Crystal Gayle. As you sit and wait for the concert to begin, you think about how all your life you've wanted to meet Crystal and get her autograph.

Your seat is in about the fiftieth row, and once the show starts, you and the thousands of other people listen for hours, just spellbound. Several times you mentally thank the friend who gave you the ticket, and you feel especially valued because this friend gave up his own seat—for you.

And Crystal—you've got all her music, and you're yelling and clapping and treasuring this time with her. She is of great value to you, and you're honoring her with your presence and enthusiasm. That's what the word means.

Now let's go further. Let's say that just before the concert is over, an usher in a tuxedo comes down and points at your seat number, M-52. An announcer calls out, "Would the person in seat M-52 step out and follow the usher at the end of the show? The friend who gave you the ticket wrote Crystal and told how much you like her music. She would like to meet you personally in the green room after the concert."

Well, your heart practically explodes. You just go nuts. For the rest of the show, you're thinking, *This can't be happening. This is too good to be true.* You don't really hear the final songs because of your excitement.

The concert ends, and you ask the usher, "Is this for real?"

And he knows your name! "Crystal got the letter that talked about you," the usher says, repeating the announcer.

So you go backstage and meet her. She asks about you and thanks you for being such a big fan, and the two of you hit it off. You even go out with her whole entourage for something to eat afterward. Then, to your amazement, she says she'd like to see you and your spouse again the next day, so you spend the afternoon together. At the end of the day, to top everything off, she says she'll pay for you and your spouse to take a two-week vacation with her because she really enjoys being with you. So over a period of months, you get to know her; she becomes one of your close family friends, and you just shake your head in wonder at your good fortune.

That's kind of what happened to me in my experience with God. I was like a groupie with God as my idol. I had valued him ever since I was in college. Nothing meant more to me than him and my relationship with him. But I certainly wasn't able to do what I thought he expected of me—love him and others as I did myself. I fell way short of his standard. I needed not only his forgiveness, but also his strength. But having such high honor of him, I was drawing close to him and loving him even when I wasn't aware of it.

I've learned that as I honor God, I learn to love God. As I've sought after God, I've found him. As I set aside the anger that keeps me distant from him, I am ushered into his presence; I am able to experience him in my spirit.

I have hundreds of examples of how he has made himself known to me. Many involve inner assurance—peace and comfort and wisdom—in the midst of crisis, a rejuvenating joy, and an increased desire to love others. I didn't have to work at these things; they seemed to be given to me without effort on my part. All I did was draw closer to him by honoring him. As I honored him, I got to know him and trust him.

This contentment came as I, in faith, experienced the fulfillment of biblical promises such as "My God will meet all your needs according to his glorious riches in Christ Jesus."[9] All the things I will ever need, God can supply! That's quite a promise, especially since a lot of my emotional needs had been going unmet for years, my work had been disappointing rather than fulfilling, and I was wondering how I would provide for my family in the months ahead. But as I got to know God better, I came to trust him more, and I found that he's as good as his Word. Time and again, he has miraculously met my deepest needs in very practical ways.

Can We Love Others?

As I recovered from my crisis, this new awareness that God was taking care of me allowed me to spend more time and energy thinking about the needs of others. It was like, "Well, I'm taken care of, so now I can do more to take care of the needs of those around me." This attitude allowed me to concentrate more openly on the second truth. Remember, the summary commandment was, "Love God with your whole heart, and love others as you love yourself."

When I no longer felt distanced from God, I could better love others (and myself). When I started increasing the value of others—honoring them—my desire to help them increased. It's been said, "Where your treasure is, there your heart will be also."[10] As I treasured people, I loved them. I didn't have to work up a love for people; it just grew as I honored them more.

Practical, Specific Steps

I'd like to present some steps that I take each day to maintain my relationship with God. It's not a rigid set of procedures but just some ideas that help me in a practical way.

I recognize that God's creation can't ultimately give me the kind of contentment that only God can give. So I use my natural negative emotions to remind myself to let him be that source of power for me. Whenever I'm fearful, worried, or angry because someone or something has failed to meet my expectations, I admit it to God. (That's another way of saying I confess my error of seeking contentment from people or the things money can buy.) For example, if I'm angry, I say, "Lord, I'm thankful that I'm angry right now. It shows me how easy it is to expect your creation to charge my battery pack. It also shows me that I've been looking in the wrong place for my fulfillment, because I haven't been looking to you. I haven't been honoring you as the source of my power and life."

Then I tell God, "I'm going to take the time right now to pull that non-God thing out of my battery pack." In other words, I make a conscious decision that I'm going to stop relying on people or my job for fulfillment. I'm not going to keep expecting them to provide my happiness, contentment, and love.

Next, I say to God, "I now invite you to take full possession of my battery pack." I realign myself with God, acknowledging that only he will never disappoint me. I start looking to him, and him alone, as my source of energy and joy. And when I'm aware of how I've "missed his mark" by acting in an unloving way, I seek his forgiveness. That keeps our relationship open.

Finally, and this is the hardest part, I tell God, "I honor you and your ways that are beyond my knowledge. Lord, I'm willing to wait until you 'charge my battery.' I know it may take awhile before I'm content with what you provide rather than secretly expecting my spouse or my house or my job to meet my needs. But I want you to be the source of my life, the source of my strength, my power to love others as I should."[11]

I've found that in praying this way consistently and sincerely, God has been faithful in revealing himself to me. If we're putting anyone or anything other than God into our battery packs, expecting people or jobs or things to energize us and make us happy, we're going to be disappointed—and often. Those people and things simply can't take his place. *The reality is always going to be less than our expectations.*

Can you imagine what it would be like to have two people in a marriage who are both relying mainly on God to fill their "happiness packs"? Then they would both try to outdo the other in meeting one another's needs. They would be following what Jesus called the greatest commandments: Love God with all your heart, and secondly, love others as you value yourself. I don't know of anything better.

Heeding the Warnings to Steer Clear of Disaster

Our spiritual journey concludes the first part of this book. We've seen how our choices in five major areas can make the difference between hitting an iceberg or taking a route that can lead to a deeply satisfying love for life that undergirds a love for our mate. It's our choice:

- To move beyond unresolved anger and learn to forgive,

- To seek the highest value in all of our trials,

- To gain strength from more than one or two life areas,

- To lovingly claim and respect personal property lines, and

- To allow a loving God to meet our deepest needs to empower us to love for a lifetime.

Next, in part II, we'll focus on eight of my favorite ways to enrich relationships, especially with your spouse. I'll show you how you can make a few adjustments in your own life that can transform your marriage. Even if your mate is unwilling to travel this route with you, you can still greatly influence your marriage for good. And the basis for part II is that second truth that has transformed my life: Love others as you love yourself.

Forever-Love Principles

Our list of forever-love principles continues from the previous chapter:

38. Forever-love relies on God as its enduring source of power.

39. Forever-love doesn't ask the impossible of a truelove: "Be my power-pack."

40. Forever-love knows that power isn't in positions and titles.

41. Forever-love gives God the highest value in life.

42. Forever-love admits its failures and asks for grace.

Part II

Forever-Love Principles:
How to Stay in Love
with Your Spouse

Looking for the secret of growing old alongside your spouse? After fifty years of marriage you hope you'll still be smiling when he walks in the door? Still reaching for her hand in the movies? Still eager to snuggle up on the couch or between the bedsheets?

Stay tuned. Part 2 focuses in on the intricacies of personal relationships, especially marriage. How do you learn to balance what you know makes you happy with the things that satisfy your spouse's needs? How do two people maintain their energy for life and their excitement for each other? From the ABCs of effective communication to the XYZs of good sex, the following chapters present principles for making a solid marriage that is defined by the vows made on one's wedding day: to love and to cherish till death do you part. Together forever as partners in love.

Keep in mind that these forever-love principles work to the extent that both parties are trying to live out the love-for-life principles presented in part 1. Two people at peace with themselves have more energy to be at peace with each other. Think about the possibilities: living with a mate who has so much fun in his or her own life garden—and you in yours—that, when you're together, it's overflow. I personally can appreciate the scenario, because it is the kind of relationship my wife and I have cultivated and grown in our garden of love.

I see a different scenario altogether if one spouse has shut the door on the love-for-life factor. For example, a spouse who is spraying unresolved anger at anyone and everyone may not be able to receive a mate's loving words or actions. Why? Because anger can repel love and keep others at a distance.

Having said that, I assure you that there is hope for virtually any relationship if even one party is taking responsibility for his or her own contentment, quitting the blame game, and choosing to go for love in the relationship. Ultimately love-for-life and lasting love for each other are based on the choices we make—choosing our responses to circumstances and to people. *The buck stops with each one of us.*

I urge couples to read part 2 together, if possible aloud to each other, pausing here and there to discuss an idea or its application. If your mate resists the thought of improving the relationship, remember that even small changes by you can make a huge difference in your marriage.

Part 2 presents the tools that have worked best to renew my own marriage and the thousands I've been able to help. Here's how these "tools" are shared in this second half of the book:

- Chapter 8 gives five signs that indicate a healthy relationship and symptoms of relationships that are not healthy.

- Chapter 9 discusses seven ways to enrich your communication, making it possible for you and your spouse to understand each other's meaning and feel each other's emotions. Here you'll see how you can move beyond the superficial levels of communication and get to the deeper levels of intimacy. This is the key to staying lovingly married—meaningful communication.

- Chapter 10 shows how anyone can make himself or herself more lovable—by understanding and working to bring out the best in your own natural personality tendencies.

- Chapter 11 sheds some additional light on five ways you and your mate are different from each other. One of these areas is the fascinating topic of gender differences. How can you bring out the best in your maddening mate?

- Chapter 12 is a high tribute to women in general. Here's how to read a woman's built-in marriage manual. A woman intuitively knows what small steps could be taken to make for a better marriage. To me this is a spectacular insight.

- Chapter 13 describes how normal, everyday conflicts can be used to strengthen your relationship. Instead of tearing you down, they can actually prove to be benefits. You'll see how to reduce the frequency of conflicts and use them to enrich your intimacy.

- Chapter 14 reveals that good sex has four equally important elements—and only one of them is physical.

- Chapter 15 discusses the most powerful way I know to divorce-proof your marriage. You might call the concept "no deposit, no return."

- Finally, chapter 16 describes the best kind of love, the kind that may give you more satisfaction than receiving love from another.

I challenge you to read part 2, "Forever-Love Principles," carefully and discuss which tools would be most useful to you at this time. Then review the book later, as new challenges arise.

And as you read, know that many of these principles will enrich all your relationships at work or at home, especially the potentially explosive relationships with children and teens.

At this midpoint in the book here's the challenge I place before you: Make forever-love your aim, have patience, and watch the fruit of your marriage grow.

8

Five Vital Signs of a Healthy Marriage

Love is an active power in man[kind]; a power which breaks through the walls which separate man from his fellow men, which unites him with others; love makes him overcome the sense of isolation and separateness, yet it permits him to be himself, to retain his integrity. Envy, jealousy, ambition, any kind of greed are passions; love is an action, the practice of a human power, which can be practised only in freedom and never as the result of a compulsion.
—Erich Fromm[1]

Are my relationships healthy? Maybe you can hear someone asking the question of a counselor. Maybe you've asked the question yourself. What does the question mean? What does *health* mean in terms of a relationship?

Here's what I'm learning about what's healthy. It's a relationship where each person feels valued, cared for, safe, and loved. Each person is relatively content with life and is growing toward maturity.

In every relationship, especially in marriage, there are at least five generally accepted indicators, or vital signs, of the health of that relationship.[2] In this chapter we'll take a close look at those signs. To make love last forever, marriage partners must learn how to read their relationship's vital signs.

Symptoms of Ill Health

If we can identify signs of health, we can also see symptoms that indicate "something's not right here." Let's look at some of those symptoms in the story of Jack and Sherry. At one point, all their vital signs were negative. Their marriage seemed to be a terminal case.

About ten years ago, after several years of marriage, Sherry got so fed up with the shape of things that she decided the marriage was over. "This is it!" she said. "I'm not going to put myself through this emotional roller coaster anymore!" Packing a few things, she fled the house.

"I didn't have any mama to run home to," she explains, "so I went to our houseboat and locked myself in."

In a way that boat symbolized the root of the couple's problem. Jack's father, an alcoholic, had never hung on to a job for very long. "I was hell-bent to be the antithesis of that," says Jack, who became a classic workaholic, toiling long hours to build a successful business and provide financial security and comfort for his own family. One of those comforts was the houseboat. He enjoyed this luxurious "toy" and others, paid for by his long days and professional preoccupation. And he assumed Sherry appreciated the boat as much as he did.

She may have enjoyed the boat and what it represented, but it did not satisfy any inner restlessness. What did Sherry want? In her mind she pictured and longed for a loving marriage. Central to that image was a husband who made time for her, talked with her, and cared for her. No comfortable home or big boat could take the place of a loving husband's presence and attention.

Sherry's frustration increased when she knew that Jack was at least somewhat aware of her dissatisfaction. Wanting to be a better husband, he agreed to go to marriage conferences and counselors. They even joined a small group devoted to building up the members' marriages. He would hear some piece of advice—such as a reminder that they needed to spend more time together—vow to Sherry that things would improve, do better for a while . . . and then revert to his old workaholic ways. Sherry, who'd never had a great relationship with or trust in her dad, grew more resentful.

When it came to affection, Sherry felt as if she were living in a perpetual drought. She'd get no rain for months. Then a few sprinkles would drop, and she would think, *Oh, this is so refreshing!* She wanted the sprinkles to turn into a shower, but she was never too hopeful. *No, no, something is going to happen, and he'll stop again.* Those negative thoughts made it impossible to enjoy even the sprinkles. Then sure enough, she soon found herself back in an emotional drought.

Jack's tennis-playing became a particular sore point. He used the game to relax, something he really needed after working such long hours. But to

Sherry, tennis was an intruder competing for her husband's attention. And when he would make space in his schedule for a match and not for her, she grew increasingly jealous.

Sherry's resentment built up over the years. It was hard for her to express her thoughts and feelings to Jack. When she did try, he shamed her into silence. "Why, you have everything wonderful!" he'd insist. "What are you complaining about? We've never had it so good!" And her emotional needs remained unmet, her feelings unacknowledged.

The tension and pressure built until Sherry decided she couldn't take it anymore and ran to the docked houseboat.

Their son Jim came after her as soon as he found out about her disappearance. Knocking on the door, he said, "Mom, I only want to pray with you."

She refused to open the door and let him in. "I knew that if Jim prayed for me, I would start crying and give in," she says, "just like I'd always done with Jack." So she told Jim, "No, I don't want to do that right now. I don't want you out here. I really need some time alone."

Jim respected her wishes and went home. But then Bob, a member of their small group, showed up. He was almost like a son to Sherry, and she had always been able to be open with him in the group setting. When he knocked on the door and identified himself, she still held her ground. "Go away! This is it. I don't want to talk."

"Sherry, I'm not going to try to change your mind," he said. "I just want to be here and make sure you're okay."

"No, I can't see you!" she maintained. "Just go away!" And that, she thought, was the end of it. Nothing more was said, and she assumed Bob had left.

Half an hour later Sherry needed to use the rest room, which meant leaving the houseboat. It was February and bitterly cold—only seven degrees above zero that day—so the water on the boat was turned off. Sherry opened the door to go out, and there sat Bob—no coat, shivering, starting to turn blue! He had never left.

Sherry couldn't believe it. And in her concern for Bob, she immediately forgot her need for a bathroom, dragged him inside, and gave him a blanket. They started to talk, and before long she was pouring out all her frustrations and resentments. She told him every lousy thing Jack had ever done. Bob just listened—no criticism, no defensiveness, no denial of her feelings. He simply gave her the gift of an attentive ear.

As Sherry talked, an amazing thing happened. Having someone listen and understand her frustration "uncorked" her hurtful feelings, and
they seemed to drain away as she spoke. Finally, she couldn't think of any
other negative things to say about Jack. She sat there for a while in
silence. *What's this?* she thought as she sensed a subtle shift in her spirit.
By emptying herself of the clutter of negative emotions, she had discovered a residue of positive feelings. She remembered a few of the good
things Jack had been doing and the small but hopeful changes he had
made. She saw ways he had been trying, in his own way, to reverse the
habits of a lifetime to be more of the kind of mate she needed. He was far
from perfect, but he was making an effort to improve. She felt a new
appreciation for him and, without fully understanding it, a fresh hope for
their marriage.

Within about an hour her feelings toward Jack and the potential for
their marriage had turned around. After talking to Bob a little longer,
Sherry said, "I think maybe there's hope for us after all. I'm going home to
work things out."

Since then Jack and Sherry have experienced the normal relational
bumps that any couple can expect. But her retreat to the houseboat was a
real turning point, and I've watched their marriage continue to grow and
flourish right up to the present. They're such an inspiration to me and so
many others.

Before this momentous day their marriage exhibited the two most
common characteristics—symptoms—of unhealthy relationships: (1) Too
much distance between the partners, and (2) Too much control being
exerted by one person. When both are present in the same relationship, as
they were in Jack and Sherry's case, disaster is almost inevitable.

Too much distance can occur when the husband and wife are not talking enough for both to feel "connected." One person is too often silent,
unable to share deep feelings or simply closing the other person out of his
or her private life. Often a couple gets too busy to stay in touch emotionally; one's job may require too much time away from home. If even one
person feels this "distance," resentment can spread like a cancer.

In a situation of overcontrol, one spouse is dominating the other—
choosing where the couple will live, go to church, and take vacations,
making everyday decisions, and so on. The one being controlled can lose
a sense of personal identity and eventually not know clearly what he or she
wants or who he or she really is. This person's personal boundaries can be

violated until he or she feels squeezed into a little box. And in that box anger is quickly compressed.

Unless they're recognized and understood, these problems—of distance and control—can become deeply ingrained in a marriage. That's exactly what happened with Jack and Sherry. Jack failed to understand that his controlling nature created distance between him and Sherry, who learned not to discuss her negative feelings; rather, she buried them. Until the crisis at the houseboat, neither of them recognized the warning signs of a problem potentially deadly to their marriage.

Now let's turn from ill health to the vital signs of health in a relationship. We'll continue to refer to Jack and Sherry and their "new" relationship to see how several of these signs function. (I thank my friend and psychology professor Dr. Rod Cooper for his insights in this discussion.)

Vital Sign 1: All Feel Safe to Think for Themselves

In any healthy relationship, people have the freedom to think for themselves. Think of a converse situation. If a spouse says things like "That's a stupid idea!" or "Just do what I say and don't ask questions!" the mate soon learns that it's not safe to think for himself or herself. It's not long before that berated person learns to belittle his or her own thinking or grow resentful (or both).

In the case of Jack and Sherry, he routinely made it clear that if she didn't see things his way, there must be something wrong with her. If she said he was working too many hours, he told her she was failing to appreciate the sacrifice he was making for the financial good of the family. If she claimed he was giving tennis a higher priority than time with her, he insisted she was refusing to recognize his need for recreation to relieve the pressures of his job. In short, he communicated that her thinking must be flawed.

In healthy relationships, on the other hand, we encourage others to think. We want our kids to verbalize their plans, ask questions, and then learn to make their own decisions. We want our spouses to use their creativity and intelligence to complement our own. As someone has said of marriage, if both of us think exactly alike, one of us is unnecessary.

I have to admit, with embarrassment, that I was somewhat insensitive to my wife's thinking process in the early years of our marriage. I believed many stereotypes about the female "emotional" way of thinking; at times I would discount her ideas because of my desire to have everything be "perfectly logical." I foolishly assumed my way of thinking was superior.

Now, having been married for more than thirty years, I've learned, not only to listen to Norma's ideas about everything, but also to draw out her thinking as much as I can. That's because I've so often seen her intuitive and logical thinking processes work wonders and keep me out of messes.

Vital Sign 2: All Are Encouraged to Talk and Know Their Words Will Be Valued

In a good relationship, you have not only the freedom to think, but you also are encouraged to talk, to express yourself. When you talk, the other— your spouse, parent, friend, boss, or whomever—listens with the attitude that what you are trying to express is greatly valued, even if the two of you disagree.

(Please understand that I'm not saying it's okay to speak disrespectfully. With freedom comes responsibility, and everything we say should be honoring to those we're addressing. Even strong opinions can be stated in a way that's clear and yet respectful.)

In a lot of homes, unfortunately, spouses and children are literally to be seen and not heard. Or perhaps when they do speak, they're constantly interrupted. Or they know certain subjects are taboo and are raised only at their peril. Getting shut down like that can produce a lot of buried, destructive anger.

Whatever type of communication was used in your childhood home, that's the pattern of communication you'll tend to use as an adult. If you weren't allowed to talk as a child, you'll tend not to give your spouse or children that freedom, either. If you were encouraged to speak, you'll probably give others the same right.

Did you have a distant or controlling parent? Were you never allowed to speak candidly? Were the words "I love you" seldom heard? If you now find yourself repeating such an unhealthy pattern, I have a recommendation that has worked for many of my clients. Go to your husband or wife (or your kids or close friends) and say, "I wish I were talking to you more and listening to what you have to say, but I wasn't raised like that so it doesn't come naturally to me. It's hard for me. But I want to break that habit, that generational pull. Will you help me?" When the people we love begin helping us love them more, they are usually much more tolerant of our ways and forgiving of us.

I've asked for help a lot as a husband and dad. I've had to, because just as soon as I would tell myself I would never jump on Norma or the kids and shut them down again, I would turn around and do it once more. It helped them to understand why I sometimes reacted the way I did, and it helped me to know they were holding me accountable. It also gave us a basis for asking for and extending forgiveness when I "slipped."

In Jack and Sherry's case, he had learned a very unhealthy pattern from his alcoholic father; in turn, Jack was an expert at shutting down Sherry's attempts to express herself. You'll recall that his weapon of choice was shame: "How can you complain? Look at how good you've got it!" So Sherry kept silent and grew more angry and more frustrated until she had finally had enough and ran away.

Anytime I see parents controlling their children in unhealthy ways, I don't think, What rotten people! Instead I usually think, I wonder what kind of parents they had. Almost always, their negative parenting habits can be traced back to the way they were reared.[3] Based on research presented in their book Family Therapy, Irene and Herbert Goldenberg have concluded that the communication skills we learned as children tend to be the ones we use as adults. Again, it's the generational effect: What we got as kids, we tend to give to our mates and kids.

The encouraging evidence for us today is that the pull of our pasts can be broken. And as I suggested above, one of the best ways to accomplish the break is by making ourselves accountable to our loved ones.

To convey acceptance of others' words, I recommend a gentle touch. Whenever you're listening to your spouse or your children, remember to put an arm around them or a hand on their shoulders. That tender touch communicates that you love them, that they're important to you, and that what they're saying is valuable.

Eye contact is also vital, especially with children. When we make the effort to set aside whatever else we may be doing and look them in the eyes, they know they have our full, undivided attention. But if we're trying to talk at the same time we're doing something else, they know we're not really listening.

A friend tells of the time he was looking at the newspaper and his little girl wanted to talk. "Daddy, are you listening to me?" she asked.

"Uh-huh," he said, continuing to read.

Whereupon his daughter reached over, took his face in both her hands, and turned his head so he had no choice but to look her directly in the eyes. "Look at me when I'm talking to you, Daddy," she pleaded.

She knew how to be sure she had his attention. But why wait until someone makes such a desperate plea? Why not make eye contact on your own and show someone—young or old—respect?

Body language can also convey interest and acceptance. Leaning toward the person who's speaking, occasional nods of the head—these are some of the subtle signs of active listening that encourage people to talk.

Vital Sign 3: All Enjoy a Sense of Safety and Value in Sharing Their Feelings

In a healthy relationship, you not only know your thinking and words will be valued, but you also have the freedom to share your feelings, knowing they will be respected. In an unhealthy situation, on the other hand, any attempt to share feelings may be met with a denigrating statement: "Oh, grow up!" "Lighten up!" "You're making a mountain out of a molehill." "Give me a break!"

Recently I was with a husband and wife as they packed the car for a trip during which they were leaving their high-school-aged son with some friends. They hadn't spent a lot of time away from their boy in the past, and the wife expressed some feelings of regret about leaving him behind. "Who's going to make his lunch in the morning?" she said. "Who's going to fix him a snack when he gets home from football practice?"

The husband responded, "Come on, lighten up! We're only going to be gone a few days. I can't believe you're making such a big deal out of this!"

Being a friend of the couple, I put my arm around the wife's shoulder. As I looked at the man to make sure I had his attention, I asked her, "How do you feel about what he just said?"

"It makes me feel silly and like my feelings aren't valid," she said, staring at the ground.

"Would you rather not go on the trip?" he asked, embarrassed.

"No, I want to go," she replied. "But I would love it if you would just let me say what I'm feeling without criticizing."

Then I put my other arm around his shoulder and asked, "Do you hear what she's saying?"

"Yeah, I hear it," he said with a sheepish look.

Do you think he realized what he was doing when he made that harsh comment to his wife? No! He had no idea he was controlling her by belittling her feelings. He was like so many of us who can fail to realize what we're doing unless it's pointed out to us.

I've been in that man's place more times than I care to remember. Norma would express her feelings, and I would reply sarcastically, "I can't believe this! Here we go being sensitive again." If she would cry, I would roll my eyes in frustration and do all I could to win the argument quickly so we could get on to "more important things." For much of our married life, I didn't realize how unhealthy that kind of response was. But as I've learned, I've given her more freedom to share her feelings, and she has grown safer in doing so.

Because the tendency to belittle her feelings has been so ingrained by my background and personality, however, this will probably always be an area of struggle for me. Several years ago, when our kids were pretty much on their own and we had a little extra money for the first time, I said to Norma, "We have the rest of our life together. What do you want from me more than anything else, so that if I gave it to you, you would say, 'This is the best gift you could have given me; I need this most of all'?"

Without hesitation she answered, "I want you to be soft and gentle with me, to understand my feelings and listen to me, not to lecture and be so hard on me."

You see, I was still doing a lot of the controlling things I had learned from my own father, things that were natural for me, considering my personality style. But I told her, "If that's what you want, that's what I want to learn to give." And since that time, I've made it my goal to be the person with whom she feels the safest sharing her feelings. I'm still learning and I still goof up, but I know I've made a lot of progress, too.

I tell the story in another of my books about the time Norma sheared off part of the roof of our mini motor home as she pulled away from our garage after a shopping trip. If I had still been reacting like my father at that point, I would have gone ballistic the way he did one time when I had an accident with his car. In the early years of our marriage, I was capable of saying something like, "That was stupid! Weren't you looking where you were going?"

But because I had been learning and growing a little in this area, I knew Norma felt bad enough already and didn't need a lecture from me. (I also knew that she had already told the neighbors across the street, and they were looking to see how I was going to respond!) She needed me to understand her heart and reassure her I didn't think it was the end of the world. So I put my arms around her and told her I loved her more than campers. We even managed to get the roof fixed within a couple of hours.

How safe do you feel sharing your feelings with your spouse? How safe does he or she feel with you? How safe do you and your kids, your neighbors, your fellow church members, and your coworkers feel with one another? This freedom to share feelings and know they'll be heard and respected is one of the clearest indicators of the health of a relationship.

Vital Sign 4: All Feel Meaningfully Connected

What are the best ways of knowing if you're "connected" to the ones you love? You're connected when you regularly share your deepest feelings with one another, when you're enthusiastic about seeing one another at the end of a long day, when you enjoy being together and doing things with one another. The opposite of this is a situation where a partner is either neglectful—perhaps a workaholic—or controlling. Neglect or control creates distance rather than connection.

The desire for connection is a basic human need. It's so powerful that when people don't feel connected, they're far more likely to develop addictions. The pain of empty relationships is so great that they go looking for some way to medicate the hollow feeling, to cover it over with some numbing pleasure. They get their sense of connection, not from healthy relationships, but from some unhealthy addictive substance. Or even food. Pam Smith, a nationally recognized nutritionist, notes that some compulsive overeaters "eat to 'fill the gaps' in their lives. Food becomes a friend and companion who is always there no matter what. When we're lonely, eating seems to fill the emptiness. It can substitute for love, attention, and pampering."[4]

Think again of Jack and Sherry. Because his alcoholic father had been unable to connect with his children, Jack didn't know how to connect either. (From my experience, it appears that alcoholism disconnects people.) And because Sherry had had a poor relationship with her dad, Jack says, "Some of the suspicions and lack of trust of me didn't come from what I was doing but from her memories of her father." So neither Sherry nor Jack knew how to connect. It's no wonder they had an unhealthy relationship for so long!

Remember, too, that unresolved anger disconnects people. It makes a person want to withdraw, not draw close. If your spouse hates his parents, he's going to have a harder time connecting with you. Hidden anger sabotages a lot of relationships, and that's one of the reasons it's so important that we deal with our anger the right way, through forgiveness and pearl-counting, as we've discussed previously.

How do we build better connections with others? Through shared experiences, intimate conversations, meaningful touch, and—one of the best ways I've discovered—shared crises. As Norma and I look back over our years of marriage, we both realize that one particular type of shared experience was the key to our family being so "connected." Namely, we took time for a lot of outdoor family activities. We did everything from skiing to scuba diving. But of all the things we did, the best one for emotional connecting was our camping trips.

Camping has a way of creating a crisis—hopefully minor—in every outing. And we discovered, by trial and error, that any time a family experiences a common crisis, if the people can overcome the inevitable accompanying anger, they're drawn closer together after the dust settles. At the end of two weeks of mosquitoes, rain, and cold sleeping bags, folks are either more closely connected or very angry at each other! But as soon as the anger subsides and forgiveness is experienced, the shared crisis has driven everyone into close bonding.

Let's take another look at Jack and Sherry: As part of their eventual effort to develop a more healthy sense of connection, they scheduled more activities together. Recently they went boating on a lake and stopped for a romantic picnic on a remote part of the shoreline. By the time they started back to the dock where their car and trailer were waiting, night had fallen. Suddenly, as they were driving through the water, they collided head-on with an unlighted boat. Their boat was thrown about ten feet into the air! Miraculously, no one was hurt. But the whole day, from the romantic meal to the near tragedy in the boat, became an experience that drew them closer as they remembered and retold the story in the weeks that followed.

Just a few months later, Jack and Sherry took a caving trip in Arkansas. As they were climbing out of the deep and long cave, Sherry slipped and fell headlong about twelve feet. She was rather seriously injured and needed two months to recover. But this experience, too, as Jack rescued her and then cared for her as she healed, multiplied their feelings of loving closeness.

I'm not suggesting you have to go on dangerous outings to stay connected, but I do encourage you to plan regular activities that have the potential for minor things to go wrong. Then watch how any shared crises bring you and your mate into a deeper sense of closeness. You don't even have to go on an outing; crises and bonding can occur in your apartment or backyard. The key is to go through the crises together however and whenever they happen.

Connection is healthy. Lack of connection, or distance, is unhealthy. How connected do you feel to your spouse, your children, and other members of your family? Or better yet, how much distance are you putting between yourself and those you love? Just like Jack and Sherry, you can plan activities that you have discovered bring you and your loved ones into closer connection.

Vital Sign 5: The Personal "Property Lines" of All Are Respected

The fifth vital sign of a good relationship is respect for each other's personal "property line." We discussed this in detail in an earlier chapter, so I won't say a lot more here. But honoring and protecting others' boundaries is crucial to the health of both the individual and the relationship.

Let me give you a couple of new word pictures to illustrate the importance of this. One of the primary functions of physical skin is to protect a person's internal organs. If you cut it, disease and infection can get in and threaten the whole body. Now think of your mate's property line as a sort of skin around his or her personality and feelings. Violating it can cause a crack that lets in emotional infection, especially anger, that threatens every area of the person's life.

Or think of your loved one's property line as a fragile robin's egg. If you care for it and nurture it, you'll see a beautiful, healthy bird. But if you're careless and crack it, the growing bird inside may die.

All five of these vital signs are important if you want your relationships to remain healthy. But one of the most important threads running through each of these five signs is a concept that is hidden throughout this entire book, and I believe it is the most important concept of all healthy relationships. When it comes to life itself, think of this concept as the very air you breathe. It's that vital.

Honor: The Weighty Foundation of Good Health

Honor is to any growing and loving relationship as diamonds are to jewelry. For the ancient Greeks, something of "honor" called to mind something "heavy or weighty." Gold for example, was something of honor because it was heavy and valuable. And the word dishonor actually meant lightweight "mist" . . . unimportant things.[5]

If we honor someone, that person carries weight with us, like the "Heavyweight champion of the world." That person is valuable to us. Honor is so weighty and significant in relationships that I've dealt with it at least briefly in every book I've written. It's the theme in all eighteen marriage videos we offer through our national television show.

When we honor someone we give that person a highly respected position in our lives. Honor goes hand in glove with love, a verb whose very definition is doing worthwhile things for someone who is valuable to us.

What's the relationship between honor and love? We first honor— increase the value of—someone, and then we feel the desire to love—do worthwhile things for—the person. Love is honor put into action regardless of the cost. Honor provides us with the energy to stay in love.

Consider the ancient truth: Whatever you treasure, that's where your heart is.[6] When we highly value something, such as a job, car, friend, toy, rifle, or a coat, we enjoy taking care so as not to lose it or harm it. We enjoy "being with it." I've found that as I increase the value of my mate and family, it's easier to love them. I want to be with them, and I feel as though I'm "in love." The feeling of love is simply a reflection of my level of honor for them. So how do you retrieve lost feelings of love? By choosing to increase the value that person has in your mind.

There's a little trick to honoring someone. You can feel as if you're showing honor or doing someone a favor, but your intentions can go awry if you're not listening and communicating well. (Hold on. Communication is the topic of the next chapter.)

Just recently, though I had the best honoring intentions, I actually managed to communicate dishonor to my mate. Here's how it happened: Besides being the keeper of our home, Norma runs the day-to-day affairs of our business. She gets up at five each morning to accomplish everything, and I thought I saw energy draining from her because of overwork. In addition, since she was doing our financial reports manually and not using a computer, I wasn't getting some information I thought I needed.

So I figured I would kill two birds with one stone by suggesting she get some accounting help. That would lighten her workload and get me the financial data I wanted. A good idea, right? I thought so when I proposed it to her.

There was just one problem with my plan to help Norma: It wasn't what she wanted or needed. "Gary," she said, "if you think that's what would make me happy, you haven't been listening to me. I enjoy what I'm doing. I like getting involved in financial details, even if it makes for a long day. In fact, a total high for me would be if all three of our kids [who are all married now] would call a family conference and ask me to sort out their finances and set up budgets for them."

She was right. I don't ever remember hearing just how much she enjoys working with numbers. She really didn't want anyone else taking her jobs away. Then she gave me a word picture that made her feelings crystal clear. "What you're trying to do for me," she said, "is like my suggesting that you have someone else write all your books—the content, stories, word choices, and everything else—because you're working too hard." Since I love communicating the insights I've gained to as many people as possible and books are a great way to do that, I understood immediately what she was talking about. Even if it might lighten my load, I wouldn't want someone else doing my work.

As I said, I started that whole affair with the best intentions. But because I didn't ask Norma what she wanted and what was best for her—I just assumed I knew—I ultimately failed to honor her. Instead of giving her more energy and fulfillment, my idea would have been draining energy away from her.

In one sense, however, I was honoring Norma. I'd made the suggestion to get help because I consider her valuable. But if I value and respect her, I need to ask what she wants and then listen carefully. I can't make decisions that affect her without first getting her input and approval. She's a unique and special person, and I prove she's these things when I listen to her and understand her.

If you consider the principles presented in part 1, you can see that honor and forever-love for your mate grow best out of a healthy respect for yourself. When you have high regard for yourself, you can more easily and energetically—with greater focus, clarity, and insight—do the things that help your mate feel valued.

Many of the things we've already discussed in this book will help you value yourself in a healthier way. For example, draining anger out of your life will increase your sense of self-worth. Pearl-counting can always raise your awareness of personal benefits. As you work to align your expectations with reality in your life garden, you will be renewed—better able to love your mate and your children. This, in turn, honors them and makes you feel more worthwhile as a person. And as you'll see in a later chapter, accepting and appreciating your own unique personality, as well as your mate's, is still another way of valuing and honoring both of you.

Time for a Checkup

Like you—and like Jack and Sherry—I want my marriage to be healthy. I want my family to be healthy. I want my friendships and working relationships to be healthy. And healthy means giving others the freedom to think, to talk, to feel, and to connect with us. Healthy means showing honor by respecting each person's uniqueness.

But let me remind you that we all make mistakes. No one is perfect as a spouse or parent, so don't kick yourself mentally or dismiss yourself as a failure every time you blow it. I hate it when I hear some presentation about relationships and the speaker makes me feel ashamed and guilty. We all struggle in one area or another, and we all need to help each other develop healthy habits. But even if we fail a thousand times along the way, with the help of others new habits can be formed. We can choose to pick ourselves up when we fall. We can choose to check our marital vital signs regularly and make adjustments to move from ill health toward health.

I suggest you use the "Parental Effectiveness Scale" rating system shown on page 138 to take inventory of your life in light of the five vital signs of healthy relationships discussed in this chapter. Where are you? What's healthy about the way you do things, and what's unhealthy? When you've done that, join me in deciding to break those habits from our pasts and to start a new way of life for ourselves, our mates, and our children. Let's launch a wave of healthy relating that will carry generations to come into a positive future.

A big part of launching this relational revolution is learning how to be a better communicator. The next chapter deals with the part of marriage where couples say they need the most help. If we don't know how to communicate effectively, any relationship is jeopardized. According to Drs. Howard Markman, Scott Stanley, and Susan Blumberg, one communication method you'll read about in the following chapter has the potential for erasing the four main causes of divorce.[7] I call it "drivethrough talking."

Parental Effectiveness Scale:
Rating the Way You Were Raised

As we've discussed, unhealthy relational patterns tend to be passed down from generation to generation—unless one makes a conscious effort to change course.

Consider again the line of Abraham Lincoln: "If we could first know where we were and whither we were tending, we could better judge what to do and how to do it."

The ten questions in this inventory will help you judge where you've been so you can better judge where you are and where you should be in terms of relational health.

On a scale of 0–10, use the following statements to rate the way you were reared by your parents (0 = not at all; 10 = all the time).

My parents were:

_____ 1. Like dictators, wanted obedience.

_____ 2. Rigid, forceful with strict rules, values, beliefs, and expectations (shamed us if we differed).

_____ 3. Critical, judgmental with harsh punishment. ("I felt abused emotionally, sexually, physically, mentally, or spiritually.")

_____ 4. Closed to talking about certain subjects: sex, religion, politics, feelings.

_____ 5. Poor listeners about my thinking and feelings.

_____ 6. Like a machine with many demands ("you should" and "you should not").

_____ 7. Degrading with names such as "stupid," "lazy," "no good."

_____ 8. Cold and indifferent toward me.

_____ 9. Resistant to changes and learning new things. (It was not easy to disagree with them and stay "safe.")

_____ 10. Distant (not close friends, and I was not invited to do things with them regularly).

_____ Total score. Add up the numbers of your ten responses.

The higher your score (the closer it is to the max of 100), the higher the potential for your having been raised in an emotionally unhealthy home.

Questions for further thought: How much "old baggage" do you still carry? Do the statements reflect your current relationship to your spouse or children?

Forever-Love Principles

Our list of forever-love principles continues from the previous chapter:

43. Forever-love is handicapped by too much distance between partners and/or too much control by one over the other.

44. Forever-love allows others to think for themselves.

45. Forever-love encourages conversation, listens well, and values the words of others.

46. Forever-love is not afraid to ask for help to break bad habits learned in childhood.

47. Forever-love does not belittle the feelings of others.

48. Forever-love makes a truelove feel safe.

49. Forever-love looks for ways to connect with a truelove.

50. Forever-love thrives on shared, minor crises that, when remembered, prompt laughter.

51. Forever-love highly values a truelove. "With me, you carry weight!"

52. Forever-love is honor put into action regardless of the cost.

9

The Number One Request: Better Communication

The small-talk of everyday life can be a genuine road towards contact, a way of getting to know somebody, a prelude to more profound exchanges, a simple and natural approach. But, let us admit it, it is also often used as a means of avoiding personal contact. It is like a prologue that goes on so long that the play never begins. It allows us to be friendly and interesting with people without touching on subjects that would compel us to enter into real dialogue.

—Paul Tournier[1]

At most of my live marriage seminars, I ask several hundred couples to name one thing they believe could improve their marriage above everything else. Without exception, in more than twenty years and from more than three hundred thousand people, the answer has come through loud and clear: "We need better communication!"

The quality of our communication affects every area of every relationship we have. Review the vital signs of a healthy relationship, and you'll find effective communication at the heart of all five of them. It even influences our physical health. Effective communication reduces occasions for anger to be buried inside. And, as we saw in chapter 2, unresolved anger can disastrously affect one's health. Learn how to be a better communicator, and everyone wins.

Why such a high priority on communication? Because good communication is the key to what all of us who marry basically want . . . to love

141

and be loved. We want to share our lives with someone who loves us unconditionally. We want to grow old with a mate who has valued us, understood us, and helped us feel safe in sharing our deepest feelings and needs. We want to make love last forever. And this type of loving relationship is most often attained by couples who have learned how to reach the deepest levels of verbal intimacy.

Communicating—at What Level?

Marriage researchers have helped us understand that there are five levels of intimacy in communication, moving from the superficial to the most meaningful.[2] The more often a husband and wife reach and remain on the fourth and fifth levels, the more satisfying their marriage.

When we communicate on the first level, we speak in clichés: "How did your day go?" "Fine." "Give me five!" "What's happening?" Think about it. Does conversation at this level mean much? A question like "How are you?" may be more than a cliché, especially in marriage, but it's often asked just as superficially in a domestic setting as it is by a store clerk you've never met before. Some couples who are afraid of conflict spend a lot of time at this "safe" level.

At the second level of communication, we share facts—just information. "Hey, it looks pretty wet today, doesn't it?" "Watch out for that new road construction." "Did you hear the latest about the president?" Like level one, this is pretty shallow communication, and it's still relatively safe. Not many major marital wars start this way.

At the third level, we state our opinions. Here is where communication feels a bit more unsafe and conflict may arise. "How can anyone vote for that person? He has no experience." If we feel insecure in our marriage, we tend to steer clear of this level. Though most couples do get to this level, most of our conversation, even with family, rarely goes beyond it to the deeper levels.

The fourth level is when we say what we're feeling. "I was really hurt by what my father said on the phone last night." Opening up this way can be scary, but we can reach the deeper levels of loving and being loved only when we put ourselves at risk of having our feelings misunderstood or ridiculed. In fact, one of the healthiest questions we can ask is "What are you feeling right now?"

The fifth level is where we reveal our needs. "I just need for you to hold me for a few minutes," you might say after hearing about the serious illness of a good friend. To risk at this level of verbal intimacy, we have to feel secure in the relationship. Let's see how a couple with a strong marriage and good communication skills might work their way quickly to this level.

Suppose, for instance, that a conversation starts at the third level with the husband saying to his wife, "Hey, you're drenched! Why don't you ever remember to put your umbrella in the car?" That's an opinion that his wife should keep an umbrella handy.

She responds at the fourth level by saying, "Do you know how I feel today? I feel like somebody ran over my foot at work. It's been a tough day! And with that cute comment, you're now standing on my foot!"

Instantly he knows how his spouse feels. He can now encourage her to move to the fifth level by asking, "What do you need tonight? What would it take to make you feel as if your foot is being massaged and soothed? What can I do?"

She might respond by saying, "You know that movie we were planning to go see? I don't really feel like going tonight. I'm beat! I would love a hug, and I just want to talk and be with you. But first, I would like to be alone for a while, to relax and kind of cool down."

Those are needs, and expressing them is the deepest level of verbal intimacy.

If the environment is really safe and healthy, the husband might say, "Okay, let's do that. I wanted to go to that movie, but we don't have to go tonight. We can go tomorrow. What do you think?" That's a mutually satisfying relationship, where both people's needs are expressed and they have the flexibility of give and take.

Our goal as a married couple should be to go into those fourth and fifth more satisfying levels of communication more easily and frequently. But again, the key to deep verbal intimacy is feeling safe to share our feelings and needs and sensing that our feelings and needs are valued by our mate. Having the self-control to listen lovingly without overreacting or misunderstanding keeps the lines open. The caution I would interject here is that we need to speak in love, measure our words carefully, and only make requests that we can reasonably expect our mate to respond to favorably.

About ten years ago, a good friend of mine brought up the subject of weight with his wife. He said he really needed her to lose a few pounds. It made perfect sense to him and seemed reasonable because they had both been talking about ways to improve their marriage. But his wife wasn't able to respond positively to this fifth-level request. She was hurt and frustrated, because all her previous attempts to lose weight had ended in failure. She felt trapped. She wanted to please her husband in this way, but she couldn't.

What she wanted from her husband was comfort—not the sense of rejection she felt now. She had been trying for some time to find the underlying reasons for her overweight condition. Some were probably inherited, she concluded, while others were learned. But she couldn't overcome all the various "pulls" she felt to control her eating habits, and his request only seemed to increase her problem. So again, my caution is that you allow honor to regulate when and how your communication goes to the fifth level of verbal intimacy. Sharing needs that require your mate to make too great of a change can be hurtful and actually weaken the relationship.

Now let's take a look at five effective communication methods that can enrich a marriage and help you move into those deeper levels of intimacy more often and with greater ease. Over the years Norma and I—and our children—have tried many communication methods, and I consider these five my favorites. To help give you the flavor of them, I've given them names that relate to eating in a restaurant.

Practice Drive-through Talking

Drs. Howard Markman, Scott Stanley, and Susan Blumberg report that this first type of communication I'm going to describe is the key to overcoming the four main reasons couples divorce.[3] For me, it's the absolute best method I've ever learned. My wife and I use it as a couple and with our family, and our company profits by it as an organization. Communications expert Dr. Dallas Demitt, of Phoenix, taught me this approach several years ago.

I call this first method of communication drive-through talking. Let me explain. I've just driven to one of the fast-food restaurants and pulled up at the speaker. I'm ready to place an order for my whole family. The clerk comes on the intercom and says, "Welcome to the Good Life Cafe. May I take your order, please?"

"Yeah," I say, "I would like three hamburgers, a cheeseburger, three Diet Cokes, one Pepsi, three fries, and one order of onion rings." Then I ask my family, "Is that it, guys?"

They say, "Yeah."

The clerk comes back on the intercom and says, "We have three cheeseburgers, one hamburger, three Cokes, one Pepsi, three fries, and one onion rings."

"No," I say. "That was three hamburgers, one cheeseburger, three Diet Cokes, one Pepsi, three fries, and one onion rings."

The clerk says, "Okay, I think I've got it. Three hamburgers, one cheeseburger, three Diet Cokes, one Pepsi, three orders of fries, and one onion ring."

"You've got it!" I answer. "Thank you."

"Drive through, please," he says.

Then I drive up to the window, get our order, check the bag, and say, "This isn't even close to what I ordered!" And I start all over again.

Have you ever had that frustrating experience at a fast-food place? We all have, I imagine. And it illustrates the best way to communicate what's on your mind. Drive-through talking is when you say something to someone and you wait to hear it repeated back exactly the way you said it. If the other person gets it right—if he or she can tell you accurately what you just said without somehow missing your meaning—you respond, "Yes, you understand me." If it isn't right, you say, "No, that's not what I said," and you repeat your message until the individual gets it right. Once the other person reflects an understanding of what you meant to convey, you know you've communicated.

This method can be especially effective when you're communicating feelings or needs. An incident that took place during the early years of our marriage shows how drive-through talking could have helped Norma and me avoid a misunderstanding. I was jogging early one day, and during the run my mind wandered in a number of areas. Then I thought, *Why don't I do something loving for Norma today?* You know, it was one of those thoughts that can come to a man's mind on rare occasions. Anyway, I started wondering what I could do for her. Then it occurred to me, *We're going camping later today. And she loves to go to breakfast with Helen. I could volunteer to pack the camper while she goes out for breakfast with her. Then, when Norma gets home, we can jump in the camper and be off.*

Now, I want to ask the guys reading this: Don't you think that sounds like a loving, sensitive thing to offer? Yeah? It did to me too. I didn't see anything wrong with it. So when I got home, I told Norma, "Hey, I've got a surprise for you."

"What's that?" she said.

"How would you like to go to breakfast with Helen while I pack the camper? And then, when you get back from breakfast, the camper will be ready and we can go." I added excitedly, "What do you think?"

To my surprise, Norma wasn't very enthusiastic about the idea. And I thought, *Wait a minute! What's wrong here?*

But do you know what she was thinking? Because her personality makes her want to be sure things are done "correctly," she figured I had planned a creative way to get her out of the house so I could finally pack the camper "my way." But that's not what I was thinking. I didn't care one way or the other about how the camper was packed. Her response irritated me. I felt like saying sarcastically, "Okay, you pack the camper, and I'll go to breakfast with Helen." Have you ever had such feelings after you do something that you think is loving and the person nails you for it?

Well, those negative feelings would never have happened if Norma had used drive-through talking. Instead of assuming I had an ulterior motive, she could have repeated my message like this: "Now, let me understand. You're saying you want to pack the camper. And you want me to go to breakfast with Helen. Then when I get back, it's all done?"

I would have said, "Yeah, that's exactly it," because that's what I said and that's what I meant.

Next she might have asked me to confirm the feelings or needs behind the words. "But are you really saying that you want to get me out of here so you can pack the camper the way you like it?"

Then I would have said, "No. That wasn't what I meant. [That's not the order I placed.] I'm really just trying to make your life easier and give you a good time with Helen." In such a scenario we would have been moving back and forth between the fourth and fifth levels of communication. At this level of intimacy, I valued her feelings while she valued my need to be helpful.

This method of communicating—taking the time to repeat back what we think we've heard (or what we think the real meaning was behind the words)—eliminates so many unnecessary hostile episodes. You can practice it with your mate, your kids, your coworkers, and I promise you'll be amazed by the results. You'll understand each other more clearly and feel so much better about the relationship.

Recently I was with a couple who in more than twenty years of marriage had never once tried drive-through talking. When I had them sit together and start practicing it, they were instantly pleased with the results. At first this confirming feedback might seem awkward. But try it. It's the best method I know to enrich communication—with anyone.

Write a Marriage or Family Menu

My second favorite and effective communication technique involves listing the most important "foods" on your marriage menu. It can be like a marriage or family constitution. Sounds like a chore? Keep reading to see the rewards.

What is a marriage or family constitution? It's a written listing of the most important things you and your loved ones want out of your relationship every day. It objectifies your feelings and needs, and it sets guidelines for your family the way a federal constitution sets guidelines for a nation. When you read a restaurant menu, you know what the establishment is all about. You can say the same for a marriage constitution.

My wife and I wrote our own constitution for our relationship, and we order our life according to it. We feel great about it because we each know that our crucial feelings and needs—critical to intimate communication—are understood and in writing. It has evolved over the years and today lists eight items, but yours could have three, five, ten . . . whatever fits your situation.

To give you an idea of what might be in such a constitution, let me summarize ours.[4] We listed eight items significant to our lives together:

- **Honor.** The greatest thing in our relationship and in our parenting is that we honor each other. Honor is woven through all our constitution. It's the foundation, the basis of everything we do, including our communication. Remember, I have defined honor as "choosing to attach high value, significance, and worth to someone or something." When we highly treasure someone, we are honoring that person. We've continued to discover that our lasting feelings for each other follow our honoring of each other.

- **Personality traits.** We want to understand each other's personality traits and value them, especially when they're very different from our own.

- **Resolving anger.** We want to keep unresolved anger out of our house. So we wrote a short paragraph that describes how we will deal with anger. It fits us and our personalities. Briefly, we simply try to resolve any hurt feelings, frustration, or fear before the next day, if possible. We listen carefully to each other, and when necessary, we seek or offer forgiveness. (Chapters 2 and 3 show how to reduce levels of anger; you can write your own paragraph based on what you learned there. See also chapter 13, on conflict resolution.)

- **Touch.** We want a lot of tender, meaningful touch. How many times does your mate, particularly a wife, need to be touched each day? Just recently we were updating our constitution, and I asked Norma, "How often?" A written answer to that question is only a guideline, however; touch shouldn't become a mechanical action. Remember that each person is different. You may need twenty affirming touches a day. Another person may need only five. And each day the need may vary.

- **Communication.** We also want regular and healthy communication. Just how much and what kind do we need? That's spelled out in our constitution.

- **Bonding experiences.** We also place a high priority on bonding experiences—doing fun things together.

- **Finances.** What about our spending, giving, saving, and other financial issues? We have an agreement on those in our constitution as well.

- **Spiritual issues.** Our spiritual life is a vital part of our marriage. So our constitution also states what we agree on here.

A family constitution forces couples to the fourth and fifth levels of intimacy. But it's also the best method I know of in training and disciplining kids. As I go into more detail about how a constitution helps make for a mutually satisfying marriage, let me show you how it works with kids as well.

A Constitution Brings Unity

First, a constitution brings a couple—or a family—into unity. There's terrific strength and consistency when you're united on a course of action that you all believe in and are committed to. When a young couple writes a constitution, it's theirs, both the husband's and the wife's. When a family writes one, the kids have ownership too. Let me illustrate this from my own family's experience.

Our kids helped to write our constitution. That meant the rules it contained were truly family rules and not just a code imposed by Mom and Dad. This caused the kids to become very committed to the whole approach. And then, for more than three years, we had a meeting at our dinner table every night where we reviewed our constitution, which was printed and hanging on the wall. We would just read through it and see how we all did that day.

At that time our constitution included about a half-dozen requirements for the kids, such as, "How well do you obey Mom and Dad in things, like when they tell you not to go up the street?" We had some things about cleaning your room, chores, manners, and honor. (If I had it to do over again, I would put honor at the top, and all the others would be subpoints to honor.)

Finally, our children agreed on three character qualities they had to have to some degree before they dated. (Because a lot of people have asked about the three qualities, I've listed them in the appendix at the end of this book.) Then, when they got to the age where they were about ready to date, they would say, "Can I date? Can I date?"

Norma and I would answer, "Well, remember you agreed that these three qualities need to be present."

And they would have to say, "Oh, yeah." Our constitution saved us a lot of arguments that way.

Likewise, a constitution helps keep everyone together on what the consequences will be when family rules are broken. Just as a restaurant menu lists rules such as "No shirt, no shoes, no service," so a family has rules to meet its needs.

Let's say one of your marriage constitution items is "We'll spend at least twenty minutes a day in meaningful conversation with each other." And it's your turn this week to be the initiator. But by the time you get ready for bed, you haven't fulfilled your commitment. That's when your spouse says, "You were supposed to do this before 10:00 P.M., but you forgot."

Once you're caught, the agreed-upon consequence kicks in. You can choose various penalties for violations of your constitution. Pick things that are realistic but still mildly painful if they're to be effective. For example, you might agree not to watch a favorite TV show or to do extra chores or do something with your spouse that he or she enjoys but you could live without, and so on.

In writing this part of our constitution when our kids were younger, we had them list about fifty things they would be willing to lose for twenty-four hours if they violated one of the rules. Then I said, "Okay, do you guys agree with this?"

"Yeah," they said, and they signed their little names.

I remember when Greg said, as we were working on the consequences, "If we violate the first rule, no dinner for a month." You know how some kids can be harder on themselves than their parents would be.

"No dinner for a month, huh?" I said. "That sounds pretty severe. I don't think I could do that to any of you. Maybe we could make it no dinner for one night."

"Okay," he said. "That's pretty weak, but I suppose it will be all right."

Guess who was the first one to violate that particular rule: Greg, of course! So he was in the next room salivating while we ate dinner that night. Norma was fidgeting the whole time, and finally she said, "You know, this is more punishment for me than it is for him. I'm the one who's hurting. I don't think this is a good consequence."

"I don't like it either," I told her. "It makes me real uncomfortable." We had agreed that if we didn't like the way one of the consequences was working out, we could have a meeting immediately and revise it. So I said to the kids at the table, "Hey, do you like this consequence?"

"No, we don't like it at all," they answered.

Then I called out to Greg in the other room, "Greg, do you like this consequence?"

"No, I hate it!" he yelled back.

"Come on into the kitchen then," I said, and during the meal we picked a different consequence for him to have that night. He didn't get out of being disciplined, but we revised the constitution right on the spot. That's being flexible, which is healthy. Too much control, or rigidity, on the other hand, is unhealthy.

A Constitution Reminds You What's Important

A relationship constitution also helps you concentrate on and stay committed to your most important values. We hung our constitution right on the kitchen wall so we could see it every day. It reminded us of the values we had all agreed were crucial to us.

As I said earlier, our highest value was honor. When our kids were little, we would be driving through town with them, and I would say right out of the blue, "What's the greatest thing in life?" And they would say, "We know it's honor, Dad. Don't keep asking us. It's honor." But today my children— all in their middle and late twenties—agree that honor is their highest value.

A Constitution Acts As Police Officer

A written constitution is vital for a third reason: It becomes the police officer in your home. When you have it in writing, there's no dispute over what the rules are or who agreed to what, because you don't have to rely on anyone's memory. In marriage, for example, it's not uncommon for a couple to be a little angry and distant for a while, but you don't want it to continue for long, and breaking the ice after a conflict is never easy. A marital constitution can help return warmth to the relationship if it contains an article something like this: "We, the Smith family, do hereby swear that we will open up and discuss any hurts within twenty-four hours after the hurt occurs." You may want two or three subpoints to help clarify how things will be resolved, but make sure they're easy to remember or they become useless.

With our kids, I remember a night when Michael was about four years old. We were going down the list in our constitution, and we got to the rule about the kids keeping their rooms clean. "Mike," we said, "how is your room today?"

"Great!" he said. (Everything was always great with Mike.) "My room is spotless."

But Norma said, "Mike, just before dinner, I looked, and it wasn't done."

"I know I cleaned it up, Mom," he said with conviction.

"Well, why don't we just go look?" she suggested.

So we all got up and walked into his room. It was a mess! "I thought I cleaned this up," he said.

We went back to the table and checked the constitution, and his consequence for failing to clean his room was no TV for twenty-four hours. When she saw that, Kari said, "Mike, do you know what night this is? This is *Little House on the Prairie* night!"

"Oh, no!" he said. "Of all the days not to do my room!" He paused for a moment, and then he said, "Oh, I don't care. There's too much sex on that program anyway."

We hoped he didn't know what he was talking about, but you can see how the constitution served as the policeman enforcing the rule in that case. Norma and I were free to hug him and say, "Bless your heart. We love you, but no TV tonight."

That constitution saved us over and over. It cut down on the need to even think about spanking because it became the policeman, and it was in writing, right in front of all of us.

For the constitution to do this part of its job effectively, the key once again is flexibility. Couples in a healthy relationship feel safe to introduce any revisions. And parents especially need to be flexible. When Greg was ten or twelve, he would come and say, "You know, I don't like this constitution idea. I was a little kid when you started this. I think you're taking advantage of us kids, and I think we ought to change it."

"You want to change some part of this?" I'd say.

"Yeah, I'd like to change part of it."

"Which item?"

"Well, I don't know, but I'll give it some thought."

And you know what? He never came up with anything. Just knowing we were flexible was enough to convince him the rules were fair.

Go for an All-You-Can-Eat Buffet

A third effective communication method is what I call an all-you-can-eat buffet. You can use this in a marriage, certainly, but you can also use it in parenting, in a friendship, or in any other relationship. It is like giving someone a huge injection of energy—feeding someone a gigantic meal. Here's how this worked with the Smalleys: We would pick out one member of the family, and then for sixty seconds all of us would barrage him or her with praise. We would say anything positive we could think of and as much as we could think of. After sixty seconds, the person was "stuffed."

To the individual being praised, it was just overwhelming. You would sit there and say, "Oh, oh, okay. Thank you a lot. Okay. I believe that one. Oh, that's a good one." It's fun and very enriching.

I remember interviewing dozens of women years ago and asking, "How often do you need to be praised by your husband?" And I was amazed to hear repeatedly, "As often as he wants to praise me." Almost all women say, "I have a bottomless capacity to be praised."

From those interviews and other evidence, I've concluded that we don't need to worry about praising people too much. Some people say, "If we praise them too much, they'll get a big head; they'll get conceited." But just the opposite is true. If people aren't praised and don't feel valuable, that's when they appear to be conceited. You really can't overdo genuine, meaningful praise, because most of us can't remember to give it as much as we should.

Make Your Spouse Thirsty

What I call the salt principle is a communication method by which you can be sure you have the full attention of the person you want to talk with. This fourth method is great when you're wanting to say, "Hello in there. Is anyone listening? Is anyone home?" I especially recommend this method to wives because I've repeatedly heard wives complain that their husbands don't listen to them. (I've found that it's just naturally harder for many men to connect verbally than it is for women.)

Using the salt principle, you don't try to make your point to someone unless you have that person's full, undivided attention. To get that attention, you pique that person's interest until he or she is "thirsty."

You know the old saying that you can lead a horse to water but you can't make it drink? Well, that's not true. If you dump a lot of salt into its oats before you take it to the water, it will probably be very thirsty. That horse will suck it up as fast as it can. And a wife or husband can do the same sort of thing with a mate. I'm not talking about manipulation here. I see manipulation as a selfish tool, something done to get one's own way. The salt principle could be used to manipulate, but it won't be if honor is the guide and you're trying to com unicate for the benefit of the relationship.

Consider how my wife got my attention and motivated me to listen to her one time: She had a desire—or need—she wanted to communicate to me. She wanted me to spend more time with our children. So she came up to me and said, "I talked to Greg's teacher today. I found out that he's not doing well in reading and spelling. The teacher said part of his problem is that he hasn't developed his hand-eye coordination well enough. That's a real serious thing." Immediately she had salted my interest with the word *serious*. And then she said, "It could cost us a lot of money in the future."

"A lot of money in the future," I repeated, engrossed now.

"Yeah," she said, "because we would possibly have to get some tutors. So the best thing to do is to nip it now." (That's a whole can of salt.)

"What do we have to do?" I asked as I "thirsted."

"I've been thinking about it," she continued, "and I think it would be good, if you're interested, to start playing catch with Greg regularly so he can develop that hand-eye coordination."

"Football, you mean?"

"Yeah."

I thought, *Hey, hey! Saving money in the future and helping my son. Where's the football?* And I started playing catch with him right away. In high school, Greg was a receiver on the football team (not just because I played catch with him, of course), and he's also a great reader, a good writer, and a good speller today. But notice that before Norma made her request that I play catch with Greg, she first got my interest.

This salt principle can be effective in almost any relationship, even when the person knows it's being used. See if the following story doesn't create some "thirst" within you.

Peter Cartwright was a circuit-riding preacher back in the 1800s. When he arrived in a town, news would spread: "The preacher's here; there'll be a meeting tonight." One day he and his horse were both exhausted. Though this wasn't a scheduled stop where he had a loyal congregation, he "parked" his horse and went to an inn—actually a saloon—to get something to eat. A band was playing. The clientele was dancing and boozing it up. As he watched this, Cartwright thought, *I wonder if there's some way I could give my message to these people? But how do you get people in a bar to listen to you, especially if you're a preacher?*

He was sitting there thinking about what to do, his head down, when he felt this warm hand on his. He looked up, and there was a pretty young woman. "Would you be my partner for the next dance?" she asked.

"I'd be honored," he said, and the two of them went out on the dance floor.

Just before the music started, Cartwright said something to the woman. In an instant she dropped to her knees, confessing a newfound belief in God. His words were also heard by others in the room, and several of them—even in the band—walked up to Cartwright thanking him, and God, for changing their lives.

Now, if you're like most people, you probably want to hear the end of this story; you're thirsty for more. What could Cartwright have said that would make such an impact on the patrons of a bar? It amazes me how even simple stories like this one can create a thirst to hear more. But unfortunately I'm in the same boat as you. Because the person who told me the story wouldn't give me the whole ending. If he knew it, he wasn't telling! Like me, you'll have to guess what Cartwright did. You might mull over the story to remind yourself of the power of the salt principle.

Have you ever found yourself telling your spouse, "I've said this to you fifty times! You never seem to remember"? Maybe his or her interest level hasn't been high enough. That's the key. Try dumping some salt in the "oats." Your partner is more likely to say, "Yes! Give me this information. Tell me what you feel. Tell me what you need." You might think that would never happen with your husband or wife, but I've seen it work time and again.

Creatively Title the Recipes

A fifth and powerful method of communication calls for the use of emotional word pictures. Most of us use these already. The poets among us might call them metaphors or similes.

Ever been to a restaurant where a hamburger wasn't just a hamburger but a steamroller? Or read a magazine where a recipe for tuna-noodle casserole was called "Fish 'n' Worms"? (Maybe not.) A cook is giving you a word picture.

In a relationship, word pictures might work like this: When you meet somebody who seems a little off, you might say, "That person seems one taco short of a combination platter." If you've had a really tough day at work, you might come home and tell your spouse, "I feel as if I've been run over by a truck." A little earlier in this chapter, we had the example of one spouse telling the other, "I feel as if you're standing on my foot."

Those are simple word pictures that help one person quickly understand what another is thinking and feeling. Why is this method is so powerful? It helps us "step into the other person's shoes" and experience something emotionally close to what he or she feels. It can move us into and keep us in the fourth and fifth levels of intimacy.

Let me give you another example of how a word picture can help a couple move into the intimate levels of communication. Friends of mine— a husband and wife—have a pretty good relationship. But the husband had a habit that really annoyed the wife. When they had a disagreement, he wouldn't lose his temper and yell at her; he would switch into a lecturing tone of voice that made her feel he thought she was stupid. He wasn't even aware he did it, but it bothered her to no end every time it happened.

Finally, she decided to use a word picture to make him aware of his habit and how it made her feel. The next time he spoke to her that way, she stopped the conversation and said, "Do you realize what I see when this happens? I see you gritting your teeth and speaking deliberately, as if I'm stupid and can't understand you otherwise. I feel like a little girl being lectured by her daddy."

"Really?" he said. "I had no idea I was doing that or that it made you feel that way. But now that you mention it, I can see how you could take it that way. I'm sorry."

And ever since, though the wife says he occasionally needs a "you're doing it again" reminder, he has tried to be much more careful about how he speaks to her in times of conflict. Her word picture helped him see and feel clearly, in just a few words, how dishonoring his way of speaking had been.

Word pictures are powerful. I actually call word pictures the male language system. As a woman, why use more words when one "picture" can open up a man's heart? More times than I can count, I've seen one word picture stop and change people like that husband. If you'd like even more examples, Dr. John Trent and I have created more than three hundred that anyone can use in any relationship; we share them in our book *The Language of Love*.[5]

My son Greg uses a word picture on me that works every time. In an earlier chapter, I described the big moment when he got up to address a large audience for the first time and forgot his speech about halfway through. He was mortified. Neither of us will ever forget it. But now he can simply say to me, "Dad, when you say or do this or that, I feel like I've just forgotten my speech." I instantly feel with him and apologize if I need to.

An effective variation on emotional word pictures relies on a scale from zero (very low) to ten (very high) to rate how you feel or what you need in a particular area. Men especially appreciate how this approach clarifies many relationship situations. And like other kinds of word pictures, it immediately lets your partner know how you're feeling. For example, you can say, "On a scale from zero to ten, this need is an eight." Obviously, that's a strong need. "I only need this at a three level" would indicate a need that's not so urgent.

This rating tool really helps when a couple desires a marital growth spurt or when the relationship is in decay. In either case, husband and wife can ask each other, "Zero to ten, where are we today in our communication . . . touching . . . anger level?" Then they can follow up with the golden question: "What would it take today (or over the next few weeks or however long) to move each area of our marriage closer to ten?" Even in the middle of a conflict with Norma, I've stopped and asked where that dispute had moved us, zero to ten, and what it would take to resolve it.

Go for the Best

There are many other effective communication methods, but the five I've presented in this chapter are my favorites. My family and I have used them all, as have many people I've counseled and addressed in my seminars. I know these methods work.

Try them out, practice them, and improve your communication skills. Remember that your goal is to move through the first three somewhat superficial levels of verbal communication and get down to the more intimate fourth level, where you find out what your mate feels, and finally to the fifth level, where you discover what he or she needs. The more you do this, the healthier your marriage and all your relationships will be. In fact, they'll come alive! Don't settle for anything less. Go for a love that will last forever.

Communication can be a particular challenge if you and your spouse have differing basic personality types, which is usually the case. But an understanding of temperament types leads to more effective communication. The next chapter—about temperament types— can help you understand why your mate behaves in a particular way. It gives insight into why you both get under each other's skin from time to time. You'll also see how making small adjustments to temper the extremes in your personality styles can quickly improve your relationship.

Forever-Love Principles

Our list of forever-love principles continues from the previous chapter:

53. Forever-love is built on communication that gets to the heart of what both people feel and need.

54. Forever-love takes the risk to ask, "What are you feeling right now?"

55. Forever-love thrives on flexibility.

56. Forever-love measures words carefully and only makes requests that are within the realm of reason.

57. Forever-love communication repeats back what has been heard and then asks, "Have I understood your message and motive?"

58. Forever-love clarifies priorities and sets guidelines for the relationship to eliminate unnecessary guesswork and help align expectations and reality. This might be called a family constitution.

59. Forever-love looks for things to agree on.

60. Forever-love communication creates a thirst—piques an interest—for "tell me more."

61. Forever-love communication uses vivid word pictures to make it easy for a truelove to understand feelings and needs.

10

Understanding Personality Types: A Key to Lovability

Almost without exception, our weaknesses are simply a reflection of our personality strengths being pushed to an extreme.

—John Trent, Ph.D.

We're all a blend of four basic personality types, but most of us have one or two dominant styles. Our individual blends make us unique, like fingerprints. And one of the best ways to improve our relationships is to bring balance to any of our traits that we've neglectfully or subconsciously pushed to an extreme. If you're already familiar with one or more categorizations of personality types, stay with me. In this chapter I present a short course in how we can "take the edge off" the extremes that make us less lovable than we could be.

Many unhappy spouses are just like Sam, whom you're about to meet. They create problems for themselves simply because they don't see that their greatest personality strengths pushed just a bit too far out of balance can become their biggest problems when it comes to relationships.

A person's basic blend of personality tendencies seems to be natural or innate. But as we grow older, we can get into the habit of pushing one or more of our natural traits to an extreme that can strain our marriage and hurt others. It's just harder to love some people who push their natural strengths to the limit.

Understanding why people behave a certain way is a great help in working through anger or conflict. And in the same manner, better understanding of the motivations and actions that grow out of our basic personalities can help us achieve personal and marital satisfaction. Sam didn't have that basic self-understanding and self-control, and it was about to cost him his marriage.

The Lion King

One day several years ago, when I was still counseling regularly, Sam called my office. When my secretary buzzed me and said there was a man on the phone who insisted on talking to me directly, I immediately had a clue as to what kind of personality we were dealing with. And when the secretary put the call through, Sam's voice came booming—even barking—over the line.

"My name is Sam, and my wife is getting ready to leave me," he said, getting right to the point. "I'm miserable and depressed. So I need to see you, and I'd like to see you today, if possible."

"I'm sorry," I answered, "my schedule is full for the next two weeks. But I could see you after that."

"You don't seem to understand," he said in a commanding tone. "I have to see you. I'll come over after hours, I'll come to your home, or I'll meet you early, but I won't take no for an answer."

Faced with his aggressive personality and the fact that I really did have a full schedule, I decided to try an approach I had never used before. "Sam," I said, pausing and getting aggressive myself, "I have to tell you that you're one of the pushiest people I have ever talked to! I don't know why your wife is leaving you, and I certainly don't condone it, but I have a strong suspicion I know her motive!"

The phone line was silent for what seemed like a long minute as my words sank in. Finally Sam replied, "I'll call you back later," and he hung up.

A few days went by, and after he had had a chance to cool down, Sam called again, saying, "No one has ever spoken to me the way you did—but it was exactly what I needed to hear. I'm too pushy with my wife and others. I'm too controlling. Would you help me overcome that tendency?"

Sam did become one of my counseling clients, and as I got to know him and his background and present circumstances, we established that his domineering behavior was just an outgrowth of his basic personality. He wasn't carrying deep-seated anger; no one had seriously violated his "property line." But he had a type of personality that I call the lion style (more about that shortly). With no understanding or even awareness of his natural temperament, he had allowed it to get out of hand, and his wife was suffering the bad, sad results.

You Know the Type?

All of us have distinct personalities—not just the aggressive lions—and all of us can, without knowing it, push some of our inborn characteristics to an unhealthy extreme that can wreak havoc in a marriage.

In the late 1970s, Tim LaHaye and Florence Littauer helped me understand, through their books and lectures, that there are four basic personality types.[1] And while all of us reflect a combination of styles, one or two styles usually dominate a personality. LaHaye feels that wives tend to understand their husbands' personality styles better than husbands understand their wives'. But in the many years since I first started talking about personality differences, I've seen too many husbands and wives misunderstand their mates, causing a lot of relational damage.

Then in the mid-1980s, I gained further insight from a personality inventory—a tool for learning what your personality type is—given to me by my dear friend Dr. John Trent. It's called Performax. Thanks to Dr. Trent's personal touch and advanced understanding of personality styles, we were able to write our own inventory and test it on thousands of people. And in 1990, we did an entire book on the subject titled *The Two Sides of Love*. Dr. Trent is still teaching an excellent seminar on understanding how personality affects one's marriage and especially parenting skills.[2]

More than thirty different personality inventories are available today, and you may have already taken one. But because self-knowledge in this area is vital, if you haven't taken a personality inventory in the last six months, I invite you to turn to the end of this chapter and take the inventory. People usually stay pretty much the same for most of their lives, but retaking an inventory can show if you're more balanced than you were the last time. You'll find that taking the evaluation is quick. You can see the results easily and clearly.

You might also encourage your spouse to take the inventory. One word of caution: Use the inventory to strengthen your relationship, not as a tool for criticism or as something to throw in your spouse's face.

Dr. Trent and I came up with a way of describing the four personality types using four animals that capture the common traits of each style. First come those people we call lions. Our friend Sam, whose story began this chapter, is a classic lion. These folks are like the king of the jungle. They're usually the leaders at work, in the civic group, or at church. They're decisive, bottom-line-oriented, and problem solvers. They build big buildings and organizations, and they command armies— but they're normally not intimate conversationalists.

Next come the otters. If you've ever seen an otter frolicking in the water, you'll know why we chose this animal to describe those people who are basically fun-loving and playful. Human otters are essentially parties waiting to happen. They tend to be the entertainers and networkers (they love to talk!), and they're highly creative. They're also good at motivating others.

Then we have those people who are the most sensitive and tender in the world; we call them golden retrievers. Just like that special breed of dog, these folks are unbelievably loving, nurturing, and loyal. They'll stick with something or someone forever. These are the people who buy all the greeting cards. I like to call them the nerve endings of our society. They're great listeners and real encouragers.

Finally we have the beavers—those people who like to do things right and by the book. These folks tend to be hard working, and they actually read instruction manuals! (Those manuals were probably written by beavers to begin with.) They're excellent at providing quality control in an office or factory, and they shine in situations that demand accuracy. They're also the bankers and accountants of this world. They like quality things, too—no junk for a beaver.

Perhaps you've already got a good idea of your basic personality type and that of your mate from your own previous study or from these brief descriptions. The four animals capture the four styles in a way that's easy to understand.

But remember, the same traits that make each type of person unique and valuable often get taken to an extreme, and that's the source of a lot of unhappiness for everyone involved. We may be born with one or more characteristics; even so, the characteristics can be controlled. Want a happily-ever-after marriage? Consciously work to become more aware of your natural tendencies. Go for a healthy balance, tempering any extreme problem area. Focus on the strengths of your dominant characteristics and learn to cultivate the strengths of your less-dominant areas. Let's look at how you can tame the extremes of your dominant personality trait.

Taming the Lion

Lions who push their strong, decisive leadership qualities too far can become overbearing, hyperaggressive, domineering people who trample anyone who gets in their way. They're used to getting what they want, and sometimes they're none too diplomatic in how they go about it.

These traits can start at a very early age. Three-year-old Steve was a lion; his father was not. One day, Dad ducked into the bathroom for a quick shower. As soon as he finished, while he was still toweling off, Steve demanded, "I want my bike out of the garage."

"In a minute," Dad said. "I just got out of the shower."

That wasn't good enough for Steve. "I want my bike now," he insisted.

"You'll have to wait a few minutes," his dad said. "I have to finish drying and get dressed."

But Steve kept pushing and just wouldn't take no for an answer. Finally, Dad decided it was easier to give in than to keep arguing. He threw on the all-purpose terrycloth robe that hung on a peg inside the bathroom door, and without even taking the time to tie it, ran out to open the garage door.

Unfortunately, as Dad began to pull up on the door, the bottom of the robe caught on the lock. As he continued to slide it open all the way to the top, his robe was pulled up and over his head! There he stood, facing the street, arms in the air, fully exposed! Both dad and son learned an important lesson that day about what can happen when lions demand and always get their way.

Bobby was a six-year-old with a lion for a father. One morning as his mom was driving him to school, he blurted out, "Mommy, where are all the idiots?"

His mother was shocked. "Where did you learn to talk like that?" she asked.

"Yesterday Daddy drove me to school," he said innocently, "and we saw six idiot drivers on the way."

Sam, the lionlike husband whose wife had left him, had a lot of what Bobby's dad and Steve had. He had gotten in the habit of demanding what he wanted from everyone in his life. To say he was overly controlling toward his wife is a major understatement.

As I worked with Sam, however, he became more aware of his tendencies and learned to control that natural bent of his. He actually learned all over again how to date his wife, and little by little, she warmed to his efforts at being softer and less demanding. His desire to honor his wife led to a change of actions. It didn't happen overnight, but after watching him for several months, she did decide to come back. I saw that it wasn't easy for him, because natural tendencies are so ingrained, but she eventually did start trusting him again. Yes, she was concerned that he would revert to his old ways, but she responded as he reined in his tendency to control and push and balanced it with some tender golden retriever qualities.

Many lions need to make a conscious decision to relax their control over others. Again, this won't be easy, and it will take some time, but as Sam's case shows, it can and must be done. And one of the best ways of relaxing your grip on others is to look at the best traits of the golden retriever and practice using those same strengths.

Lions also may need to learn that meaningful communication takes time. They need to slow down and discuss decisions with others, not simply charge ahead on their own. For a lion, that's a secret of getting along with people and being enjoyable to live with.

Slowing Down the Otter

Let's-have-fun otters can push their natural tendencies too far as well. As a card-carrying otter myself, I'm a master at getting into trouble. It was a big moment for me when I realized I was 100 percent responsible for my choices and needed to get a handle on some of those traits that created problems for me and others.

We otters are always ready to take chances. Our attitude is *Hey, this will be fun! Let's go for it!* We don't always carefully think through the entire situation. I could give you all kinds of illustrations of this from my own life, but there's a particular incident that stands out in my memory.

Not long ago Norma and I were in Scotland, celebrating our thirtieth wedding anniversary and having a good time. While we were there, Norma decided to tint her hair using a dark brown/reddish dye. The next day some friends were flying in from the States to be with us, and Norma, who also has some otter in her, suggested to me, "Why don't you color your hair too? Then when we go meet our friends at the airport tomorrow, we'll see if they recognize you without your gray head!"

"That's a great idea!" I said without a second thought. So Norma dyed my hair, and everyone enjoyed the gag the next day. It was otter heaven.

The fun didn't last, however. Just a short time after we got home, I was scheduled to speak at a big university in front of several thousand students. Posters had been put up all over campus advertising the event, and they featured a picture of me with my naturally gray locks. You can understand, then, why I didn't want to show up with—and have to explain—my reddish-brown hair.

When I tried to get the color out of my hair, however, I discovered I was in trouble. The box said it would come out in twenty washes at most, but after twenty shampoos, my hair looked the same as before. So I tried Tide, Amway cleanser, and anything else anyone recommended. Nothing worked.

Finally, I ended up going to Norma's stylist to see if he could get the dye out. The process took several hours, during which my scalp was burned and my hair changed colors several times. At one point it was orange, but I didn't know that, and I asked the guy if he was done yet because Norma wanted to go out to dinner.

"Sure, you can go out—to McDonald's," he said. "You look just like Ronald McDonald!"

Well, I decided not to go out right then, and I didn't leave when it was yellow, either. At last he got my hair pretty much back to normal—normal, that is, for a woman in her eighties with that bluish-gray tint. I was able to speak at that university without being embarrassed. At the time I write this, though, you can still see about four different colors in my hair if you look closely. Only an otter would get himself into such a mess!

Otters also love to challenge authority. As far as we're concerned, rules were made for other people. A restaurant menu, for example, is just a group of suggestions to us. Norma will dutifully order number 5 off the menu, but I'll ask the waiter if I can get this part of number 5, half of number 3, and another item out of number 8. "Why can't you just order by the number?" Norma will ask in frustration.

"Because it's no fun that way!" is my standard answer.

As an outgoing, outspoken otter, I love to bargain too. That can be irritating to an accompanying spouse, or it can get someone like me in trouble all by myself. A few years ago, I was speaking in Wichita, Kansas, during a bitter winter storm. When I arrived from warm, sunny Phoenix, I realized I had forgotten to pack my overcoat.

"Well, let's get you a new one," one of my staff members suggested. Our host told us about a factory-outlet store with a large selection of coats, so off we went.

A factory outlet is made to order for a bargainer like me. And as soon as we entered the store, I saw a beautiful navy blue topcoat that I wanted. The tag on the sleeve said the original price—$450—had been cut to $129. That was a great deal, but the otter in me decided to see if I could push it. "Watch me get this coat for $99," I bragged to my friends.

I walked over to a salesman and said, "Excuse me, I'd like to speak to the manager."

A couple of minutes later, an older man came up to me and identified himself as the store manager.

We had exchanged pleasantries, and then I got down to business. "I'd like to buy this overcoat. But look at the condition of it. There's a button missing [it was in one of the pockets], and it looks as if someone has already worn it. It doesn't look quite new anymore."

The manager sighed. Obviously, he wasn't enjoying this game as much as I was.

But since I was far away from home and not worried about seeing anyone I knew, I kept pushing for a special deal. "What do you think, how about this coat for ninety-nine dollars—considering its condition?"

"Normally we wouldn't do that," the manager replied politely. "But I'll let you have it for ninety-nine dollars, Mr. Smalley. My family is watching your videos."

He had recognized me! I was so embarrassed! I assure you I have not tried to work a price down like that since.

As I said earlier, some of my biggest marriage problems and greatest dissatisfactions in life have come from my mouth—talking too much or too quickly without first thinking through what I was going to say. The otter in me saying things spontaneously, attacking verbally when under stress, or talking about people's problems without their permission has sometimes deeply hurt others and me.

To deal with such tendencies, my fellow otters and I need to develop some golden retriever and beaver traits, such as sensitivity to the feelings of others and weighing the consequences of our words or actions before we jump into something. My vow never to embarrass anyone in my seminars is a sign of my growth in this area.

If you have a lot of natural otter tendencies, what do you do that gets you into trouble or irritates those closest to you? To become more balanced, you might consider taking on some of the traits in one of the next two personality types.

Building Backbone in the Golden Retriever

Thank God for golden retrievers! Their love and loyalty are a blessing to us all. But they, too, can push their good inborn traits to an unhealthy extreme.

Norma is primarily a golden retriever, and our family is much the richer for it. But there are times when she needs better balance. For example, she loves and feels so deeply—her empathy for her family is that great—that when I or one of our kids is disappointed or discouraged, she can get very disappointed or discouraged herself. That means her emotions are being too controlled by others, and she is learning to take more responsibility for herself and not just reflect what her loved ones are feeling. Her retriever's concern is wonderful, but she needs to remember that she's not responsible for my happiness or that of her children. She's responsible only for her own. This is a truth all retrievers need to learn.

Sometimes Norma's sensitivity toward others frustrates the otter in me. I remember the time recently when we attended a concert near our home. Norma, a real fan, was especially excited to see this particular popular singer. We were able to get good seats close to the stage for the big event.

I enjoyed myself immensely that evening, and I could see that Norma was having a great time. But then, as the concert neared its end, my otter nature asserted itself. I leaned over close to her and said, "Let's sneak out during the last number and beat all the traffic." Fun-loving otters don't like being stuck in the parking lot!

Norma, however, wasn't on the same wavelength. "No!" she said emphatically.

"Why not?" I asked, genuinely puzzled.

Her answer was pure golden retriever. She didn't want to offend the performer. "She's looked at me several times this evening and smiled, so she'll notice, and it could hurt her feelings to see us walking out on her before she's done."

I just rolled my eyes.

From her many years of experience with me, Norma knows how much of an otter I am, and usually she'll go along with my impulsiveness. But if she thinks someone's feelings will be hurt by my suggestion—well, that's a different story, and she can dig in her heels with the best of them. I've never seen anyone so stubborn as a golden retriever who is protecting someone else's feelings. In this situation, since I know her as well and didn't want to make us both unhappy, I didn't push to leave early but dutifully stayed until the concert was over.

Golden retrievers are often indecisive too. That's why it's rare to find two golden retrievers married to each other—neither of them could have made the decision to get married. A golden retriever will often marry a lion. The retriever likes the lion's willingness to lead, and the lion likes the retriever's willingness to listen and follow. It can be a good match as long as both of them keep their natural tendencies under control. But this combination is the one I've seen most often in my office for counseling. They can have a great marriage, as they grow to be tolerant and forgiving and self-controlled—and these qualities generally come as a result of understanding themselves and each other.

Golden retrievers also can be so eager to please others that they have a hard time saying no. The result can be overcommitment, fatigue, and putting too much time and effort into things that aren't really their highest priorities.

If you're a golden retriever and this is a problem for you, you may need to balance your personality with more lion and otter tendencies. I suggest, for example, that you actually practice saying no. It may be hard at first, but the more you do it, the better you'll get at it and the more you'll enjoy the feeling of freedom and control over your own life. So stand in front of a mirror and say it out loud with several different inflections: "No. No. No." You'll probably never feel comfortable doing that, but keep practicing it with your spouse or another friend. It's one of the simplest yet most helpful skills you can develop.

That skill—the ability to say no—can help you set the boundaries essential for your own well-being, as we saw in chapter 6. And it can balance some of the extreme lion or otter behavior that wounds or pains others, especially the sensitive golden retriever. Sometimes people say or do things that unintentionally offend others; they don't know the effect of their words. But a golden retriever's willingness to articulate feelings and then say no can make others—lions or otters—aware of the pain they may have caused.

Yet another characteristic of golden retrievers is that when they get under pressure, they do the most amazing thing—they slow the pace of whatever they're doing and may even deny that things are as bad as they are. Just becoming aware of this tendency will help a golden retriever overcome it, as will a conscious decision to develop some lionlike determination to push ahead and some beaverlike commitment to getting the job done.

Easing Up on the Beaver

Beavers are the best at getting the details done or even seeing what needs to be done. They seem to be able to spot the smallest piece of dirt in the corner of the room. The room may look okay to everyone else, but not to some beavers if it's not just right.

Overly rigid and organized beavers can make life uncomfortable for others. Take Bonnie, for example. She was single, but if your husband or wife is a strong beaver, you'll identify with Bonnie's friend:

Bonnie had a lot going for her when she came to me for help. An attractive woman in her late twenties, she had a fulfilling career in banking. Yet she was very unhappy and looking for answers.

"I continually have a problem in my friendships," she told me.

"Describe it for me," I said.

"It seems to me that my friendships only go so far, and then my friends pull back," she explained.

"What do you mean, pull back?" I asked.

"Well, we appear to get along fine until I start making suggestions . . ."

"What kinds of suggestions?"

Bonnie looked embarrassed, but she took a deep breath and went on. "My friend Arlene is a good example. I really care about her as a friend, so it bothers me when I'm over at her apartment and I see dirty dishes in the sink and laundry left unfolded. Rather than attacking her, I offer to help her straighten things up, but she always seems offended by that."

"Can't you just enjoy yourself at Arlene's without making an issue of the unfinished chores?" I asked. But I already knew the answer.

"To be honest," she said, looking me in the eyes with a mixture of resolve and resignation, "no, I can't."

"Do you know why you can't?" I asked.

"Why?"

"Because that's an important part of your personality. You thrive on finishing jobs and doing them right. On the other hand, you're frustrated when things go unfinished."

"You're right," she said.

Bonnie is a typical beaver, but her natural desire for neatness and seeing work completed was pushed to such an extreme that she was alienating all her friends. As a result, she was feeling rejected and lonely. The same traits that helped in her career were ruining her social life. And this same trait can put unnecessary strain on a marriage.

I explained the four personality types to her, and she immediately recognized herself. Then I asked, "And what personality type is Arlene?"

She thought for a second and then replied, "Based on what I know of her, I think Arlene is an otter."

"I would agree," I said, "and that's why it would be good for both of you to continue pursuing your friendship. You can really help each other grow."

"How?" she said with a puzzled look.

"Arlene may need someone like you to help her learn the importance of finishing things. Just remember not to be pushy and to offer your help only if she wants it or, better yet, asks for it."

She smiled and nodded her understanding.

"And Arlene can help you," I pointed out. "As an otter, she knows how to relax and have fun. You need someone like her to keep reminding you to lighten up and not take yourself so seriously."

"That's a good idea," she agreed.

Shortly after that, Bonnie and Arlene gave each other the personality-evaluation inventory, which confirmed what Bonnie and I had already determined. They had a good talk about it and a lot of laughs, and their new understanding allowed them to be more honest with one another as well. They really were able to help each other grow and develop better balance.

If you're a beaver like Bonnie, you may have trouble deciding just how much of each personality style you have. After all, you must be accurate. But your focus on doing things right, if carried too far, can hurt you. For example, I've found that beavers have more stomach problems than any other personality type because of the pressure they put on themselves.

Like Bonnie, then, beavers need to develop some otter and golden retriever characteristics. If you're a beaver, relax and have fun with your spouse! It's okay for your closet to be a little messy now and then too. And it's okay if your family and other loved ones don't do things exactly the same as you. Save your stomach, your marriage, and ultimately, your smile.

Tempering Your Natural Tendencies

Let me close this chapter with a couple of final suggestions for each personality type. If you take no other advice away from this discussion, applying these tips can still make your life more pleasant and your marriage more enduring (and endearing) as you take responsibility for tempering your natural tendencies. And if you want more of an in-depth study on personality development, please read my book with John Trent, *The Two Sides of Love*.

Lions: Be softer and more gentle, and include others when making decisions.

Otters: Think before you speak, and consider the consequences before you act.

Golden retrievers: Practice saying no and making firm decisions.

Beavers: Learn to relax, and don't expect others to do things just like you.

Understand that I am not suggesting that you deny your dominant temperament. I've found that if you try to become too different from your natural tendency—from the personality with which you were born—you ineffectively use or drain off an excessive amount of energy. But if you accept yourself as you are and work to accentuate the positive aspects of that temperament while tempering its extreme manifestation (and if those closest to you praise you for that—we'll get to this point in the next chapter), you'll find that you're constantly being energized.

In this chapter we've focused on ways you can improve your marriage by making yourself easier to live with. But when it comes to two unique characters sharing a life, "How can I temper my extremes?" is only half the equation. Another question is just as important, and its answers are just as rewarding for a happy marriage. The question? "How can I bring out the best in my maddening mate?" That's what we'll discuss in the next chapter. But first, take the personality inventory to identify your own strongest temperament characteristics.

Personality Inventory

How to Take and Score the Inventory

1. For each temperament type, circle the positive traits (in the left column) that sound the most like you—as you are at home. Do not score yourself as you behave at work. (If you want to evaluate

your "at-work" tendencies, take the test again later, with that environment—or any other—in mind.) *For now, ignore the right-hand column.*

2. For each trait, add up the number of circled traits (in the left column) and then double that number. This is your score.

3. To graph your temperament "mix," mark your score for each temperament type on the graph with a large dot. If you want, draw a line to connect the dots.

I give special thanks to Dr. John Trent and Dr. Rod Cooper for their insights and help in working on this inventory.

Lion Temperament	*Characteristics*
Likes authority.	Too direct or demanding
Takes charge	Pushy; can step in front of others
Determined	Overbearing
Confident	Cocky
Firm	Unyielding
Enterprising	Takes big risks
Competitive	Cold-blooded
Enjoys challenges	Avoids relations
Problem solver.	Too busy
Productive	Overlooks feelings; do it now!
Bold	Insensitive
Purposeful; goal-driven	Imbalanced; workaholic
Decision maker	Unthoughtful of others' wishes
Adventurous.	Impulsive
Strong-willed	Stubborn
Independent; self-reliant	Avoids people; avoids seeking help
Controlling	Bossy; overbearing
Persistent	Inflexible
Action oriented	Unyielding
"Let's do it now!"	

Lion score (double the number circled):_____

Otter Temperament — Characteristics

Otter Temperament	Characteristics
Enthusiastic	Overbearing
Takes risks	Dangerous and foolish
Visionary	Daydreamer
Motivator	Manipulator
Energetic	Impatient
Very verbal	Attacks under pressure
Promoter	Exaggerates
Friendly; mixes easily	Shallow relationships
Enjoys popularity	Too showy
Fun loving	Too flippant; not serious
Likes variety	Too scattered
Spontaneous	Not focused
Enjoys change	Lacks follow-through
Creative; goes for new ideas	Too unrealistic; avoids details
Group oriented	Bored with "process"
Optimistic	Doesn't see details
Initiator	Pushy
Infectious laughter	Obnoxious
Inspirational	Phony

"Trust me! It'll work out!"

Otter score (double the number circled): _____

Golden Retriever Temperament — Characteristics

Golden Retriever Temperament	Characteristics
Sensitive feelings	Easily hurt
Loyal	Misses opportunities
Calm; even keeled	Lacks enthusiasm
Nondemanding	Weakling; pushover
Avoids confrontations	Misses honest intimacy
Enjoys routine	Stays in rut
Dislikes change	Not spontaneous
Warm and relational	Fewer deep friends
Gives in	Codependent

Accommodating . . . . Indecisive
Cautious humor . . . . Overly cautious
Adaptable . . . . Loses identity
Sympathetic . . . . Holds on to others' hurts
Thoughtful . . . . Can be taken advantage of
Nurturing . . . . Ears get smashed
Patient . . . . Crowded out by others
Tolerant . . . . Weaker convictions
Good listener . . . . Attracted to hurting people
Peacemaker . . . . Holds personal hurts inside
"Let's keep things the way they are."
Golden retriever score (double the number circled):_____

Beaver Temperament   ### Characteristics
Reads all instructions . . . . . . Afraid to break rules
Accurate . . . . Too critical
Consistent . . . . Lacks spontaneity
Controlled . . . . Too serious
Reserved . . . . Stuffy
Predictable . . . . Lacks variety
Practical . . . . Not adventurous
Orderly . . . . Rigid
Factual . . . . Picky
Conscientious . . . . Inflexible
Perfectionistic . . . . Controlling
Discerning . . . . Negative on new opportunities
Detailed . . . . Rarely finishes a project
Analytical . . . . Loses overview
Inquisitive . . . . Smothering
Precise . . . . Strict
Persistent . . . . Pushy
Scheduled . . . . Boring
Sensitive . . . . Stubborn
"How was it done in the past?"
Beaver score (double the number circled):_____

	L	O	GR	B	
40					40
35					35
30					30
25					25
20					20
15					15
10					10
5					5
0					0

How did you do? Remember, this isn't a pass-fail test. This evaluation simply shows your tendencies and traits. As you look at your charted score, you may see a blend of all four categories. That's fine. Or you may see two scores significantly higher than the others. Or you may have one category that's head and shoulders above the other three. No one pattern is "correct."

Now note the right-column extreme for each of your circled characteristics. This might be how your positive trait is perceived by your family or friends.

Forever-Love Principles

Our list of forever-love principles continues from the previous chapter:

62. Forever-love understands how personality type influences interpersonal dynamics.

63. Forever-love isn't afraid to look inside and ask, "What characteristics of mine do others find most irritating?

64. Forever-love tempers temperamental extremes and cultivates the strengths of less-dominant characteristics. "For you, my truelove, I'll rein myself in and go for balance."

65. Forever-love knows that meaningful communication takes time.

66. Forever-love does not charge ahead, making unilateral decisions.

67. Forever-love weighs the consequences of words and actions and doesn't lash out when under stress.

68. Forever-love is not so desperate to please that it says yes to every request.

69. Forever-love knows that life will never be perfect.

70. Forever-love doesn't feel the need to "fix" everything about everybody.

71. Forever-love strives for self-control but knows the grace of self-forgiveness.

72. Forever-love knows that natural temperament doesn't need to control life's temperature. "I can temper my control."

11

How to Bring Out the Best in Your Maddening Mate

Many women could learn from men to accept some conflict and difference with-
out seeing it as a threat to intimacy, and many men could learn from women to
accept interdependence without seeing it as a threat to their freedom.

—Deborah Tannen[1]

I trust some of my readers remember that old love song with one unforget-table line: "You say to-may-to, and I say to-mah-to." That simple phrase can describe the wonderful—and yet maddening—differences between you and your mate. When you were courting, those fascinating qualities may have intrigued you, attracted you. But now, after living in the same house for twenty years—even two years—fascination has turned to frustration; intriguing characteristics are now idiosyncrasies. You may appreciate the more drastic word picture that titled a best-selling book: *Men Are from Mars, Women Are from Venus.*

If you and your spouse are so very different from each other, how do you maintain your energy for love? That's what we'll discuss in this chapter. Again, an understanding of the issues is the basis for a breakthrough in the relationship.

To illustrate differences between Norma and me—differences that go beyond our natural, dominant temperaments—let me walk you through a moving experience we had not long ago.

We were out driving together on a Sunday afternoon, and we both started extolling the virtues of another state thousands of miles from our home in Phoenix. After a bit, she said, "Why don't we just move there? I mean, why are we staying here in Arizona when we both love it so much over there?"

"Great idea!" I said.

So far, so good; we were in agreement on the general idea. But then a lot of the basic differences between us started to come into play. The moment we said we would like to move, I was ready to pack my bags, load the pickup, and hit the highway! I get going in a hurry when I decide to do something. In fact, within two months of that day, I was already living in the Midwest.

Norma, on the other hand, moves more slowly and cautiously. Before she does anything, she thinks of all the ramifications and makes a plan to cover every detail. It took her another eight months to close down our business, sell the house, take care of all the changes of address, and complete the move.

Before she moved east, we had bought a small farm and begun remodeling the house to suit our needs and desires. She had flown out three times to check the building plans and make changes, but by the time she arrived to stay, the renovations were only about half-done. I remember an exchange we had right after she'd moved. She walked into the farmhouse, and with great anticipation I asked, "Do you think we captured what you wanted with the kitchen?"

She took one look and said, "I don't like that. I thought I had explained how I wanted it done, and that's not it."

"Yeah," I said, "we tried to get close to what you wanted. Doesn't it look nice?"

Well, it was obvious from the look on her face that she was not pleased at all. "I have to get out of here for a while and think about this," she said.

"But you need to stay," I insisted. "We should figure this out."

"No, I have to go," she insisted. "I have to be alone." As she was getting into her car, I urged her to stay because decisions were needed the next day. I yelled my last words at her car as she was driving away: "Stay! It's safe. I'm a marriage counselor!"

Clearly that was a time of real stress for us. With my extroverted nature, I wanted us to stay together and work out what to do. But Norma, being much more introverted, needed to get by herself to think things through. I'll say more about this extrovert-introvert difference shortly.

The story goes on. One early afternoon as we were walking around our small farm (we'd moved in and the remodeling was almost complete), she said, "Wouldn't it be great someday to have animals out here—chickens and turkeys and maybe a little lamb?"

"That's a terrific idea," I told her. "Why don't we go get them now?"

"Can we?" she asked.

"Sure," I said with confidence. "There are farmers around here that sell animals—I think. Let's go!"

We impulsively hopped in the pickup, making no provision for carrying animals home. I assumed the farmers would have boxes—or something. So we found a place, bought a few turkeys, chickens, guineas, and a cute baby goat, and put them in a makeshift pen in the rear of the pickup. Actually, we had to put the goat in the cab with us; Norma held it all the way home. And, of course, on our way back, Norma named all the animals.

To say the least, we didn't know how to keep or protect our "pets." As soon as we got home, the goat escaped—gone. Norma felt bad about the loss of her newly named friend, but I just shrugged: "Well, he'll come back when he's hungry, won't he?" Too soon every animal we bought had escaped from the barn or the chicken pen. Most we recaptured.

But then we discovered we had neighbors—foxes, coyotes, and wild dogs—who suddenly made their presence known. They quickly started picking off our birds; if the birds didn't get up in a tree for the night, they were gone by morning. Norma was pretty upset by this. But I took it in stride. "Oh, that's too bad for those precious little animals. I guess we'll have to build a pen."

I recall the day we were walking our new dogs in the woods. Unleashed and roaming nearby, they came back to us dragging this turkey carcass. "That's Carl!" Norma exclaimed.

"Oh, that's Carl," I repeated with considerably less grief.

Fortunately, some of our animals have survived up to the present. Norma loves them. I tolerate them. We're different that way and—as the whole story illustrates—in many other ways too.

It shows the uniqueness of our personalities, our extrovert-introvert tendencies, and the major distinctions of being male or female. After we were married, those and other distinctions irritated both of us for several years. But gradually, with new understanding, we learned to appreciate the other's uniqueness.

Changed Perspective

Part of my goal in this chapter is to have you see your mate's maddening differences from a new and positive perspective. Impossible, you say? Consider this lighthearted story of a church secretary and a rich Texan. Watch how quickly her view changes.

The Texan called the church office in the middle of the week and said to the secretary, "Hello. I'd like to talk to the head hog of the trough."

"Excuse me?" the secretary said, annoyed.

"You heard me, ma'am," the Texan said. "I want to talk to the head hog of the trough."

"Are you referring to our senior minister?" the secretary asked.

"That's what you call him," he said. "But I call him the head hog of the trough."

"Well, sir," the secretary said stiffly, "I'm sorry, but he's out of the building right now. May I take a message?"

"Yeah," he said, "I visited your church last Sunday, and I was real impressed. I see that you're having a building fund drive, and I'd like to give a million-dollar gift if I could."

The secretary hesitated and then answered, "Sir, I think I hear that big old pig coming down the hall right now." Her whole perspective on the Texan changed when she suddenly saw some value in him.

You may not see it yet, but there is great value in your mate's uniqueness. That's because natural tendencies that may be fundamentally different from your own can *enrich* you and your marriage.

In this chapter we'll look at five areas that make people different from each other. We'll briefly consider how natural temperament, birth order, and personal history can affect one's relationships, especially marriage. Then we'll look more closely at two additional areas: extrovert-introvert and male-female differences.

The Sixty-Second Boost

As you learn to understand various differences between you and your spouse, you can spark appreciation for qualities he or she has that you lack. Verbalize that appreciation, and you can bring out the best in your spouse. Try praising your spouse and see what happens. Praise is like a shot of adrenaline that energizes a person. It gives a quick, sixty-second boost to

any relationship. Dr. John Gottman says that long-lasting "in-love" marriages enjoy a regular dose of five positive experiences to one negative.[2]
Praise brings a very positive experience to any marriage.

How do you energize, motivate—bring out the best in—your mate?
Give the gift of praise. Think about it. When someone praises you for some
attribute, like being a thoughtful person, doesn't that instantly give you a
lift and make you feel better about yourself? When you're praised for some
action, like cooking a delicious meal, doesn't that make you want to do
more of the same? It takes only a few words to praise your mate, only a few
seconds of time, but the impact can be monumental.

The opposite of praise is criticism. Think about what criticism does to
you. If you're like most people I talk with, criticism drills a hole in your
emotions and through that hole your energy flows out. Along with it goes
most of your motivation to try to do better. Remember the concept covered
in chapter 5: The further we are from what we expect in any area of life, the
more energy we lose. Criticism causes us to feel that we've let someone
down. We haven't met that person's expectations or our own, because we
expected ourselves to be pleasing or acceptable to the other.

Criticism isn't always blatant; it can be subtle, as with the wife who
wakes each morning and right off gives her husband a honey-do list
("honey, do this; honey, do that"), no hugs, no smile, not even a good morning. No thank you in the evening. She's telling him each day: "I'm not
happy unless you're performing. I'm not happy even when you *are* performing." You can imagine how that implied criticism and lack of love and
appreciation makes that guy feel.

But praise, on the other hand, energizes us because it helps to meet
two of our most basic human needs: (1) a deep need to feel significant—
to feel that we matter, that we're important somehow, that we're needed;
and (2) a great need to feel secure in our closest relationships, to feel that
no matter what happens, we belong to each other and will be there for the
other.

We can give that gift of praise at any time. Don't worry that your
spouse will get tired of being praised. When I ask seminar audiences,
"How many of you would like to be praised more often by your spouses?"
everyone in the room raises a hand. It's just something we can never get
enough of.

Let's look now at five things that make each of us unique, areas in
which we can look for natural things to praise and energize one another.

In Praise of Personality Differences

You'll recall that in the previous chapter, we labeled the four basic personality types as lion, otter, golden retriever, and beaver. I trust you took the self-test and identified which one (or maybe two) of the four is your dominant type. Maybe your spouse also took the test.

We all need to be appreciated and affirmed for the strengths inherent in our dominant types: if a lion, for decisiveness; if an otter, for spontaneity; if a golden retriever, for being kind and steady; if a beaver, for being careful and detailed. Pointing out your mate's uniqueness in this area and expressing appreciation will give him or her a real energy boost.

Even if your spouse's dominant type is the same as yours, the degree of dominance and the overall mix of all four types will vary between any two people.

In Praise of Birth-Order Differences

Research shows that your place in the birth order of your family has a great deal to do with how you live with and relate to others. If you were the firstborn of several children, for example, you probably tend to be a leader type, because you learned to take charge of the other kids. Secondborns are usually somewhat competitive and insecure, because they had to prove themselves—measure up to big brother or sister. On the positive side, middleborn children are good negotiators and adaptable; they often feel little need to "control." And third or lastborn children are often very sociable, knowing how to deal with people.

This discussion hardly scratches the surface of this interesting topic. But can you see birth-order influences in your spouse? Are they similar to or different from yours? Consider discussing your varied family experiences in terms of birth order. This topic can get a couple to that intimate "expressing-feelings" layer of communication. As you better understand your spouse, can you look for a characteristic to praise? Try it—discover its effect in energizing your mate. If you'd like to know more about this subject, I recommend *The Birth Order Book* by Dr. Kevin Leman.[3]

While I urge you to understand these categorizations, again I warn against using them as a weapon against your mate. Instead look for the positives.

In Praise of Personal-History Differences

We all have a unique personal history. That means you. It means your spouse. Was your spouse raised by just one parent? Raised with several brothers and sisters, only sisters, or only brothers? Was your spouse abused? Raised in a tough home? Rejected as a child? All these things made a lasting impact and contributed to the person your spouse is.

And his or her history is different from yours. How can these differences draw you together?

Again, honor and communication are key starting points. Talk about your pasts—events, feelings, resulting needs. Look for positives to praise. How does your spouse's past enrich your relationship? Suppose, for example, that your wife was raised with a couple of brothers. As a result, she may have some understanding of how important sports are to most guys. Perhaps she even likes to shoot baskets with you. Put yourself in her shoes for a minute. Wouldn't it make you feel good to hear, "You know, I'm so lucky to have you. You play this game better than I do! I'm glad you understand me and love my world as much as I do." Sweet music! The positive energy pumps through her system! *Yes. Yes!*

You can also take the hardships your mate endured and together "count pearls." As you see more clearly what your mate learned from past hurts and how those hurts matured him or her, you can reinforce the resulting good through praise.

In Praise of Extrovert-Introvert Differences

As you may have noticed in the opening story of this chapter, Norma has a lot of introvert in her, though she's fairly balanced, while I'm an off-the-chart extrovert. Whichever you are, you need for your spouse to know that part of you, appreciate it, and praise you for it (and vice versa).

Extroverts like to be with people. Even if I've been with others all day, I still like to be with people at night because I get energy from interacting with them. But if introverts have been with others all day, they'll often need some time alone at night. They've had enough of people for one day. A lot of times Norma will come home at the end of a workday (I work out of our house now while she runs the business office), and I'll want to spend time with her right away. "No, just give me a little time by myself first," she'll say.

I used to be bothered by that until I understood this basic difference between us. She's much more steady than I, and part of that trait comes from her desire to be alone and process things by herself. She doesn't have to run from thing to thing or person to person. I'm much more spontaneous, and I like to tell her, "Honey, I love it that you naturally calm me down."

As an extrovert, I'm also happy to tell almost anything to almost anyone. I've been known to reveal our bank balance to perfect strangers! (That really bothers Norma, so I've learned to restrain myself a little.) But introverts like Norma don't like to divulge personal things to people they don't know well. They're just not very open except with trusted friends. Even today, there are some great stories from our marriage that I would like to tell in my books and seminars, but Norma isn't ready to let the world hear about them, so . . . you'll have to wait.

Furthermore, as an extrovert, I love to think and plan out loud. I like to have others around so I can bounce an idea off them and ask, "What do you think of that?" I actually need to think through something by talking to someone. For a long time, however, Norma thought that I fully intended to do whatever I said out loud. Then if she didn't like my ideas, she would react strongly. So we were getting into conflict just because she didn't understand the way I process ideas.

She, on the other hand, likes to think things through on her own for hours or even days. I'll want to talk an issue out with her, but she'll say, "I can't do that." When we were first married, I used to think it would take her a week of "consideration" before she'd do anything "spontaneous," and that really irritated me. But it doesn't anymore, because her more careful, introverted approach has saved me from trouble many times over the years.

I used to feel like one of those clay pigeons they use in skeet-shooting. I'd come flying out with a new and exciting idea, and *boom!*—Norma would blast it out of the sky with her shotgun. "Why do you always do that to me?" I'd ask in frustration. But now I recognize that it's only because of the way she thinks. Can you imagine the trouble I'd be in if I had followed through on all the ideas I've come up with off the top of my head? So now I praise her for her caution.

For her part, Norma praises me for my spontaneity and very visible creativity. Over the last couple of years, we've concluded that she's a dream-maker, meaning she loves to get with me and ask, "What are you dreaming this year? How would you like to be able to help singles or couples or families?"

I'll respond, "Well, I've always wanted to do this or that." So I get to be the idea person.

Then she'll say, "Great, give that to me. Let me go figure out how we can make that happen."

What a match we've turned out to be! And this difference that used to divide us is now one of the things in our relationship for which I'm most grateful and most eager to praise her. Our strengths complement each other and make for a great team.

In Praise of Gender Differences

The first four areas of difference we've considered in this chapter aren't gender specific. But now I want to look at some of the things that research indicates do tend to distinguish men from women. I'm aware of the dangers in stereotyping people, but my hesitation to speak in generalizations is offset by the new understanding that can come as we identify behavior patterns of men and women that do follow certain norms. Not every man and every woman will fall neatly into the categories I'll cover in this section, but from both the present research and my own observations, the majority certainly do. In fact, I find the generalizations to be true 70 or 80 percent of the time, so if you're a skeptic, I ask that you humor my generalized statements that "men do this . . . women do that." It's amazing how our nation is enjoying all the new information about gender differences, and that's because it rings true.

For more than twenty years, I've been speaking and writing about gender-based differences. Some of my most hilarious anecdotes come from those differences. I've actually made my living off the way men and women tend to view life and operate day in and day out. But as I look back over those years, I can see now that I've only been scratching the surface of the vast differences. Research coming out today from specialists like Dr. Deborah Tannen[4] and Dr. Bernie Zilbergeld,[5] along with popular books such as Dr. John Gray's *Men Are from Mars, Women Are from Venus*,[6] are helping us discover that most men and women are in different worlds, and we tend to be confused and sometimes irritated by those differences.

There are thousands of differences between men and women. Here's just one scientific-medical example: In a recent study, brain monitors revealed strong gender differences in brain activity when the subjects were told to "think of nothing."[7]

I could mention many gender-based distinctions that do not need brain monitors for detection. But I'd like to summarize five of my favorites from my own study and observations, hoping that, as you increase your understanding of your complementary strengths you'll have more ammunition with which to praise your mate. Look for the positive; discover the value of variety! After a general look at these differences, I'll give you several specific suggestions in praising your mate.

Difference 1:
Men Love to Share Facts—Women Love to Express Feelings

Men, even in close friendships, tend to be into gathering and expressing facts. Women in the same sort of relationship tend to be better at and more interested in sharing their feelings. This is no rigid rule, remember. Both genders can and do share feelings and facts, but the scale seems to be tipped in favor of facts for men and emotions for women.

A wife might say, "Honey, we need to talk tonight." She is expressing a need, no doubt based on a feeling of "disconnection" from him.

He may answer, "About what?" He wants the facts.

"How are you feeling about your job?"

He scratches his head, wonders where that question came from, and responds, "I feel fine." He isn't as in touch with his feelings or as interested in them as she is. And he thinks his answer finished their talk.

Then she might change the topic and express her need to discuss their older daughter's twelfth birthday party four months away.

It's obvious to him that she's continuing the conversation—but on a new subject—and he wants to know where their conversation is headed. So he asks her, somewhat annoyed, "How long is this conversation going to last?"

She may be offended and suggest he doesn't love her anymore.

Now he's really confused. How did this conversation take this turn? How did his question—asking for facts—turn into "I feel as if you don't love me"?

This differing fact-feeling orientation does not have to tear down a relationship. But it's important that both men and women understand the other's propensity. Your mate is not necessarily irritating you on purpose. Usually the behavior that bugs or frustrates us is just a reflection of the way our spouse is. He or she is not trying to strain the marriage but is just being natural and normal.

Remember, men, we are healthier when we become better communicators. Thank God for your wife. When's the last time you paused and thanked her for wanting to talk about emotions?

Difference 2:
Men Tend to Be Independent—Women Tend to Be Interdependent

A second big gender difference is that men tend to be independent while women are more *inter*dependent. This shows up clearly in the way young boys and girls play and disagree.

Have you ever wondered why it takes millions of sperm and only one egg to make a baby? Maybe it's because not one of those little surfers will stop and ask for directions!

In contrast, girls tend to form small groups or pair off to play games where they share things face to face. In other words, the girls go for community. Female interdependency is evident in the common situation where several women in a group get up together to go to the rest room, something men rarely do.[8]

I realize some men will be more community minded than others, and some women will be more independent than the norm. The key is for you and your spouse to figure out where the two of you are in this area and work together in an understanding way, praising each other rather than ragging on one another for the things that make you unique.

Difference 3:
Men Connect by Doing Things—Women Connect by Talking

This third difference—men connect by doing things together while women connect by talking together—is closely related to the first two: facts/feelings and independence/interdependence. A fascinating aspect of this difference is the way the two sexes define the word *intimacy*. Over the last few decades, women have played the major role in defining intimacy for our culture, with the result that many men have concluded it's just not for them. That definition always includes "talking and touching"—that's what women want when they say they want more intimacy.

What's the male definition of intimacy, according to the latest research? Doing something with another person.[9] There doesn't have to be any talking at all. A couple may just be watching TV together, but the man will think that's getting close or being intimate while the wife is sitting there thinking, *When are we going to say something?*

A woman at one of my recent seminars told me how she used this insight to get her own needs met. "I found that when I wanted my husband to open up verbally," she said, "I could suggest that we do something together, like take a drive or a walk. As soon as we started doing it, he would start talking." Another woman for whom this worked too well told her husband with tongue in cheek, "I roast at baseball games; I freeze at football games; I get bitten by mosquitoes when we're fishing. Why do you always have to do everything with me?"

Most men like just being with someone else. But they tend to avoid togetherness if the woman is critical or insists on communicating the entire time, because that's not their idea of intimacy.

Let's look at how this difference—women connecting through words, men through actions—can affect a typical conversation. Over dinner, after a rough day at work, the wife says, "I hate my job!"

How might a man respond? "Why don't you quit then?"

"No," she says, "it's just that there's so much work to do and not enough people."

"Well, then, tell your boss to hire some help for you."

"Oh, why can't you ever just listen to me?" she asks, getting frustrated.

And he, genuinely confused, says, "I *am* listening to you. If you didn't want my advice, why did you bring up the subject?"

What's going on there that neither of them may understand? By expressing her feelings about her job, the wife is really saying, "I want to *connect with you.* I want to get into community with you. And I do that through conversation. I'm not trying to get anything solved." When the husband fails to respond in keeping with her need to connect, she concludes he isn't really listening to her.

From the man's perspective, however, his response is consistent with his view of intimacy. He wants to *do something* with her. He wants to fix things with her. In this case, that means offering a logical solution to her problem. His comments are factual and aimed at helping with her dilemma.

His comments may also be a reaction to the male fear of being controlled and losing his independence. A conversation focusing on emotions can make him feel inadequate, less in control. So he may try to assert control with a verbal attack and not even realize what he's doing to her.

How can we get past this misunderstanding of one another to develop the connection both partners need? What I'm about to suggest may sound unrealistic at first, but Norma and I have learned to handle such a situation in a way that seems to work. If she complained about her job and I suggested she just quit, she might come back with something like, "I see what you're trying to do. You're doing something with me—helping me, right? You think quitting my job would help, don't you? That's an interesting idea. I appreciate the fact that that's part of who you are. But I'm not really looking for a solution tonight. I just want to talk and connect with you. Is that okay?"

And then I might think, *Oh, I see what's happening. I was trying to help you and at the same time feel significant myself.* But I can respond by saying that I appreciate the way she wants to connect with me; I know that's good for both of us. I might even ask straight out, "Do you feel disconnected from me right now?" If she says yes, I could then ask, "What could we do—or talk about—tonight to get more connected?"

For her part, she might ask me, "What would it take for you to feel significant and helpful to me? How can I best respond when you offer your well-intended fix-it suggestions?" If a wife praises her husband's attempt at trying to be "helpful" when he's giving unsolicited advice, it can push the relationship forward a long way.

In this way, we respect one another's different needs and understanding of intimacy.

Difference 4:
Men Tend to Compete—Women Tend to Cooperate

This difference is very important to understand, because it can help explain why a male may all of a sudden start an argument over something the wife had no idea would lead to a fight.

Why do males tend to be competitive while females tend to be more cooperative? You can see this in the kind of pets the two sexes like. Most men prefer dogs to cats. Think about it; dogs don't engage us in a contest of wills; most dogs are loyal, obedient, and easy to train. They come when you call them. We men want to win and feel we're in charge.

Women, on the other hand, tend to prefer cats. When you call cats, they give you a look that says "bug off" or "I'll come if and when I feel like it, which will be when I want something from you." Women by and large are more willing to tolerate a pet that has to have its own way. Why? They like to stay in harmony whenever possible. It goes back to their concern for community.

Male competitiveness extends to just about every area of life. It certainly applies on the job, where it's vital that a man feel as though he's doing well. If he doesn't, he can be discouraged and experience a massive loss of energy. Wives, one reason we're so sensitive about your jokes concerning our jobs is that much of our identity is wrapped up in what we do. (This may be a reason why many men become ill after retiring.)

My male competitive nature hurt my family from time to time in the early years. When our kids were little and I would play games with them, Norma would get upset with me because I "couldn't" let them win. It was hard for me to bring myself to lose on purpose. "It's terrible that you have to win against your own children," she would say accusingly, sometimes with tears.

I'd try to defend myself with, "Well, they've got to learn that this is a tough world, you know."

But she would insist, "I just can't believe you could treat the kids like that." She was seeing the whole thing from the "community" viewpoint, and I was seeing it from the "status and winner's" perspective.[10]

Male competitiveness also extends to our support of our favorite sports teams. We're tremendously loyal, and we enjoy watching "our team" win. "My team is playing tonight on TV. I can't let my team down"—that's the way a man can reason.

This can lead to a situation where a wife says something like, "Honey, could you pick up Sandy at school after her practice tonight?"

"No," the husband answers, "my game is coming on early, and I want to watch it with the guys."

"She really needs to spend time with you," the wife says. "You've been so busy lately." (She senses he needs to be in "community" with his daughter, and she's probably right.)

"Honey," he says, "I want to watch the game. Let her walk. She needs the exercise anyway. If she gets healthier, it will reduce our medical bills." (That's logical, isn't it?)

"You're impossible!" she says.

"I'm not impossible," he insists. "You're manipulative! I can see what you're doing!"

What's going on here? Two things for the man: (1) Loyalty to his team is important to him; and (2) He wants to win the argument with his wife. He's in competition even during the discussion. If he thinks it's necessary to win, he might even start getting harsh, knowing his wife will probably give in. He realizes intuitively that she's cooperative and helpful and more concerned about the state of their connection than she is about winning an argument. But while he wins the battle, he's not really winning anything, because he's not paying attention to what's going on in the overall relationship. When most men take the time to really think about it, they know the relationship is far more important than the football game or even "winning" the discussion. But in the heat of the argument, the desire to win may dominate.

A wife can be confused when her husband reacts negatively to her attempts at helping him care for their children. Subconsciously, we men think we can do as good a job of rearing them as you women, even though common observation shows that you generally have an edge in knowing how to nurture kids. Your natural advantage can actually annoy us because we reason, *Who does she think she is, anyway?* The fact is, men can learn to be great parents. But we can also get our competitive fires turned up by a mother trying to help us become "a better parent."

Here's a perfect opportunity to offer praise to the mother of our children. Why not just say to her, "Thank God for moms! You sure do a great job with the kids, and thanks for helping me to remember more of what our children need." That will raise her energy level by several notches.

Driving is still another area we men see as a contest. This is also an area where women like to "connect" with us by being verbal. "Aren't you following the car ahead a little too closely?" a wife might say. But we men know that if we back off a bit, some other driver will cut in on us, and then we would be "losing" to that driver!

I remember a winter day recently when, for some reason, Norma and I had switched cars with our good friends Jim and Suzette. Norma and I were driving their van, and they were just ahead of us in our car. There was a bit of ice on the road, and I can enjoy a little ice, though nothing dangerous. But Norma hates any amount of ice.

As we made a left turn, I was thinking about how, if you punch the gas just a hair, you can skid a little and have some fun! I wasn't going to do it much because I know Norma gets nervous (and I made sure there were no cars coming the other way). So I stepped on the gas just a bit, and guess what: We ended up spinning a whole 360 degrees into the other lane!

Norma closed her eyes and screamed, "I can't believe this!"

In the car ahead, Jim and Suzette saw what has happening, and Suzette said, "I can't watch!"

But Jim, getting more into the spirit of the thing, said, "Way to go, Gary! I give you an 8.5 for that spin!"

Likewise, my reaction was "Yes! That was a good one! If you're going to spin, you've got to make it a winner!"

My point is simply that we men are in competition all the time. The encouraging thing about this is that more and more, all over the country, I see men taking up the challenge to be better lovers of their wives and children. It's like being in competition: Who can be the most supportive husband and father? (And wives can jump into this by praising our efforts to "win" at being a better mate and parent.) But it's a friendly competition as I've seen a nation-wide movement of men coming together by the hundreds of thousands in major events to say, "Let's help one another learn how to love our families better. We're going to do whatever it takes." This kind of competition is excit-ing to me and extremely beneficial to our country's welfare and stability. Wives, this is something that's worth supporting. You can say to your hus-band, "I really appreciate your competitive spirit. I love that, because I see everything you're willing to do to make our family better."

And husbands, we can praise our wives and give them that energy lift by saying, "Honey, I'm so glad I married you, because I see your interest in the whole area of staying lovingly connected, and I know I need that con-stantly with you and the kids."

Difference 5:
Men Tend to Be Controlling—Women Tend to Remain Agreeable

This gender difference is closely connected to difference 4—competi-tion/cooperation. You see, most men think that a "boss" of anything is a winner; a wife challenging a husband can be a threat to a man's need to feel like a winner. But I refer separately to this controlling/agreeable difference, as it hits right at the heart of a man's deepest need—feeling significant.

Men usually like to be in control. Research has shown, for example, that when men and women talk, the conversation "follows *the style of the men alone.* . . . When women and men talk to each other, both make adjustments, but the women make more."[11] As we've seen, women desire verbal communication—to create intimacy—and many will let the man lead—to preserve the connection and keep conversation going.

Why do men value being in control? The whys of these differences are impossible to ferret out. We generally equate having control with being highly esteemed. But think about it: When a controlling person—male or female—lightens up his or her attempts to control someone else, isn't that "controller" then perceived to be more "loving"?

When testosterone is flowing, there's one particular thing we men wish we could control about our wives—sex whenever we want it! But as we'll see in chapter 14, that's not how good sex works. Sex is a reflection of the overall state of the relationship. A lot of wives just aren't as interested in this area as their men are. According to my good friend Dr. Kevin Leman, a nationwide Gallup poll discovered that the average woman says sex is only number 14 on her list of favorite things to do with her husband. Number 13 is gardening.[12]

In some circles the word *submission* in the context of marriage is a real hot button. But I've found that it's only an issue when one partner—usually the husband—wants to control and even dominate the relationship, which is not a lasting, giving type of love. When both people love each other in a genuine, honoring way, however, that word *submission* doesn't seem to be a problem. (The word basically means "agreeable.") In my own informal research, I've asked many women, some of them avowed feminists, "How would you respond to the word *submission* if your husband were really loving and sensitive and caring and treated you like a very valuable person?"

Most women say, "I wouldn't have any problem with it at all. I could respond to a man like that." (Some also ask, "Do such men exist?") In fact, I haven't had one woman get after me yet for asking that question. So submission isn't really an issue when our focus is on trying to outlove each other.

One of the best solutions to a "battle of the sexes" is to just understand that it exists. It's a maturing man and woman who can comprehend our basic natures and look seriously at why the male wants to run things and why the female wants to not make waves. As we both see these tendencies and accept them as natural, we can then start to adjust our relationship to what works best for us. This calls for temperance, tolerance, and conflict resolution along the lines discussed in chapter 13.

Drawing Closer, Not Apart

Clearly, there are a lot of potential differences between a husband and wife, and we tend to be attracted to our counterpart. Some of those differences are general in nature; others are male-female distinctions that usually hold true (though "any randomly chosen woman might do better at a 'male' skill than a man, and vice versa"[13]). Men and women can be critical of one another because of these differences, or we can learn to praise the other for his or her unique and complementary characteristics. In doing so, we can energize the other and strengthen our marriage.

Men, when is the last time you looked your wife in the eyes and said, "I appreciate so much your emphasis on relationships and all you do to build ours up. The things you do to make our house into a home and the time you give to the kids—you're terrific"?

Women, when is the last time you looked your husband in the eyes and said, "I really appreciate the way you're always doing your best for our family. Your dedication and hard work mean a lot to me"?

I suggest this exercise. Sit down and ask yourself this question: *How can my mate's differences help me in every area of my life, and especially in our marriage?* Just stop and think about some of the areas that your mate has helped to enrich. If mostly negative things come to mind at first, keep trying this exercise, or refer back to chapter 4 and try counting the pearls your mate has given you. Here are just a few of the advantages my wife has brought to me:

Help with my job. Norma has kept me out of more conflicts with coworkers than I care to think about. She has also helped me restore relationships that were broken. When we were first married, she "tutored" me when I was trying to learn how to talk with and relate to other adults in my first job. With her woman's intuition, she has also helped me understand coworkers and evaluate potential employees for our business, and I'm constantly amazed at how accurate her perceptions are. So I praise her for all these things.

Help with self-confidence. Norma has continually told me, "Yes, you can do it!" When I was stuck in an unfulfilling job, she encouraged me, "You're not using your talents. Just look what you could do!" She has also used her personality, her introvert tendencies, and her energy to help make my dreams come true and boost my confidence that I can reach my goals. Over and over I've tried to get her to pursue dreams of her own, and her reply is "Helping you and the others in our company to be successful is my dream!" For these things I praise her as well.

Help with personal finances. I have a friend who is president of a large chain of banks. He told me that he sees men as being primarily responsible for couples falling into deep financial trouble. Men tend to buy the big things, he says, and women tend to buy the things that keep the families running smoothly. NBC's *Today Show* recently ran a series on marriage. In a segment about the first year of marriage, two young lawyers explained their expectations and adjustments. A key tussle had concerned the husband's wanting to buy a new sports car while the wife wanted a house. (The wife had prevailed and the husband acknowledged they'd done the right thing.) Many women won't buy personal items if their husbands and children are in need. My wife has always been the one to keep us "down to earth" with money. She questions everything I do if it has any potential for weakening the family or threatening our security. Before we met with a financial adviser, she told me, "I'll go, but I'm going to 'sniff him out' and hear what he has to say before I'll go along with his idea." Again, that's one of her strengths, and I also praise her for that.

You can do the same type of thing with your spouse. Think of the many ways your mate enriches various areas of your life. Then praise him or her for each one.

As you get ready to pass into dreamland each night, ask yourself, *How many times have I praised my mate today? How many times have I praised my kids?* We don't often think about it, but I guarantee that every person in your life would love to be praised more and criticized less.

Praise is such a great gift, and it's so easy to give! So look at the things that make your spouse and others unique, and develop the habit of praising them for those very things. It will bring out the best in them. It will energize them instantly—and you too! And that's what makes love last.

Though the next chapter seems to be addressed to "us men," "you women" might want to peruse the pages for some specific positive ways you can "read your own marriage manual" in a way men will enjoy hearing it; it's just one more way to make your love last forever.

Forever-Love Principles

Our list of forever-love principles continues from the previous chapter:

73. Forever-love chooses to appreciate the qualities that make each person different from the other.

74. Forever-love is doubly blessed by the contributions of two unique personalities. It values variety.

75. Forever-love looks for attributes and actions to praise.

76. Forever-love steers clear of manipulative, subtle criticism.

77. Forever-love expresses energizing praise—anytime, anywhere.

78. Forever-love resists the temptation to psychologize or make blanket assumptions about a truelove's motives or reasons for behavior.

79. Forever-love asks, "How can our differences draw us together?"

80. Forever-love thinks in terms of teamwork, accentuating the strengths of both partners that can "cover" the weaknesses of either.

81. Forever-love doesn't jump to the conclusion that a truelove is intentionally trying to exasperate.

82. Forever-love knows the power of the gift of praise.

12

How to Read a Woman's Built-in Marriage Manual

Because of their age-long training in human relations—for that is what feminine intuition really is—women have a special contribution to make to any group enterprise, and I feel it is up to them to contribute the kinds of awareness that relatively few men . . . have incorporated.

—Margaret Mead[1]

We've just spent a chapter seeing how men and women are different from each other. We've discussed how a man's fact-oriented, independent, competitive spirit may serve him well in the work-world, as a provider for his family. On some levels, these characteristics may make the work-world go 'round. But those traditionally masculine qualities may not make for a happy marriage. They may not engender community and cooperation and intimate knowing of another's feelings—all keys to a good marriage. From the beginning of part 2, I've said that control and distance were symptoms of an unhealthy relationship.

What does this mean? It means if we're concerned about nurturing a love that lasts forever, we men may need to take a deep breath and humbly admit how very important our wives' intuitive natures can be to our relationships. C'mon, men, stay with me on this.

I've found that every marriage would be much better off if both partners would learn to read the wife's God-given marriage manual. What do I mean by a woman's natural marriage manual? I mean that every woman has an inborn, intuitive sense of what she needs, what the relationship needs, and what, if anything, is wrong with the marriage. The more in touch with her manual both husband and wife are, the more clearly they can see what they should do to have a satisfying marriage and the sooner they can take appropriate steps.

In this chapter we'll see how both a husband and wife can learn to get in touch with or read that manual. Act on what you read, and you're further on your way to marital delight.

I speak with confidence about this natural phenomenon, because in more than thirty years I've never found a woman who didn't have such a manual. I've had the privilege of interviewing and polling more than fifty thousand women in all sorts of situations and from around the world. And not one has failed to pinpoint what quality of relationship she has with her husband and what two or three things could be done to improve their marriage. This has impressed me as much as anything I've observed as a relationship researcher.

For the average husband, this manual is usually more accessible when the wife's overall anger level is as low as possible. Nothing does more to cloud his ability to read her manual—and block her ability to access the manual within herself—than long-lasting and unresolved anger. On rare occasions when the man does have a better feel for the state of the relationship and how it could be improved, the wife is usually hindered by anger. This is another reason it's so important to drain out as much compressed anger as possible. And remember that anger is a secondary emotion, often caused by fear. So the safer a woman feels in her marriage—safe to think, to feel, to talk, and so on—the more in tune she tends to be with her marriage manual.

How Wives Can Access Their Manuals

Wives might be wondering how to get more in touch with their manuals. Assuming you're in the emotionally and psychologically "normal" range, I'll help you get into it with these few spurring questions:

- What would it take to improve your marriage?

- What's one thing that brings you the most happiness or energy when your husband does it? How could he do it even better?

- If you could wave a wand over your marriage, what would you want your husband to change or improve, knowing it would change (and knowing he would not be upset with you for "waving the wand")?

Now, some husbands reading this section may be feeling very uneasy. I would have, too, in the early years of my marriage. I used to think that Norma had too many ideas about how our marriage should improve. I reasoned that many of her thoughts about us were purely selfish ideas designed to benefit her and certainly not me. But now that I've been married more than thirty years and been in contact with thousand of wives, I'm very relaxed about asking these questions of my wife or any other woman. I can't count the number of times a wife has said to me, "If my husband only knew how much I would do for him if he would just help me to feel secure and valued in our relationship!" When wives feel like queens, they usually relax and overdo themselves in finding ways to make their men feel fulfilled. But, again, they won't do this as well if there's too much anger in their hearts toward their husbands or others.

How Husbands Can Draw Out Their Wives' Manuals

With that background in mind, let's look at eleven possible ways to draw out a wife's built-in marriage manual.

1. Use Three Tried and Tested Questions

For years I've asked the following three questions in my marriage counseling and seminars. They do a good job of drawing out valuable parts of a woman's marriage manual. They bring up and work toward reconciling issues we dealt with in part 1 of this book: expectations versus reality.

A. On a scale from zero (terrible) to ten (perfection), what kind of relationship do we both want?
Maybe the two of you would be satisfied with being at seven or eight most of the time. It's important for both the husband and wife to respond to this first question, which sharpens the print in her manual.

B. On the same scale (0-10), where are we today in our marriage relationship, on the average and with everything thrown in?
This second question opens the cover to her "book." Nearly every

woman has a more accurate answer to this question than her husband, with the man usually rating the marriage a few points higher than does the woman.

C. What would it take to move our relationship from where it is now (question B) closer to where we want it to be (question A)?
This last question is where the words jump out. Almost always, answers involve the kinds of things we're looking at in this book—more security, more affection, less anger, and so on. But one statement from wives surfaces more than any other: "If we could just improve our communication skills!" Many of them say that's all they want for the rest of their marriage; if they got it, they'd be satisfied. The second statement I often hear is, "If my husband could just be more affectionate and tender with me, not lecturing me when I need his emotional support. Gently touching me when I'm down and just listening to me without comment or solutions. And best of all, not getting mad at me when I need him emotionally."

These three questions have continually allowed couples to shorten the time it takes to improve their relationship. As a man and husband, it took me some time to get used to the idea that my wife had a better ability to read our marriage status. Frankly, it used to intimidate me. And at times it irritated me. But today, I've stopped fighting reality. It amazes me how accurate wives are at seeing the condition of their marriages. Instead of resisting this idea, I've found it tremendously helpful to husbands who take the time to listen and understand what women have to say about improving relationships.

I'm not saying that all women are perfect or that any are 100 percent right all the time. I'm saying that they seem to be right *most* of the time. They may appear at times to be selfish, whining, nagging, overbearing, or demanding, but I've discovered that almost always, they're expressing a need within the relationship that's not being adequately met. This need can be with the kids, with themselves, or just in the overall relationship. But, in some ways, wives are like building inspectors; they see things that, if left unnoticed, could damage the building in the future. A husband does himself a real favor in overall health and emotional well-being if he listens to what his wife has to say concerning their marriage. Married men who are satisfied in their spousal relationship tend to take better care of themselves and do better in their jobs.

2. Make Sure She Feels As Safe As Possible
This point was made above, but it needs to be emphasized over and over. If a woman feels safe, secure, loved, and honored in her marriage, she

will find it far easier to get in touch with her needs and her intuitive sense of how things are going.

3. Simply Ask How the Relationship Can Be Improved

Sometimes a straightforward question is the best approach: "What can we do better?" or "What do you think makes for a great marriage?"

Once the question is asked, the husband needs to listen carefully and respectfully. According to Dr. Howard Markman of Denver University, who studied many couples over a long period, the main factor in shutting down a relationship is a husband clamming up—closing himself off and distancing himself emotionally from his wife.[2] But asking, "How can we improve things between us?" goes in the opposite, healthful direction, strengthening the connection and allowing the wife to access her marriage manual.

4. Don't Argue When She Starts to Read Out of Her Manual

And notice that I said the man has to listen *respectfully*. As one woman put it to me, "It's very important, while my husband is listening to me, that he not react or think I'm being critical."

Her comment points to a double "pain" in which many women find themselves. On the one hand, she wants her man to be concerned about the health of the relationship and work with her to make it better. If he's not interested, she feels the hurt. On the other hand, if she says anything about how things can be improved, he may take it as personal criticism and get defensive, and things can easily grow worse rather than advancing. If this happens repeatedly, a woman can close her manual because she no longer feels safe enough to keep it open.

Unfortunately, I sometimes spring this trap on my own wife without even being aware of it. I'll ask, "What would it take to improve our relationship?" When she responds, I'll say, "Wait a minute. That's being too picky."

"Don't ask my opinion if you're going to be critical of my answer," she'll say.

What I can do then is explain that I'm just trying to get a better understanding of what she's saying and ask her not to close her manual. But better still is just to listen and strive to understand her without reacting or arguing.

If you're a husband with an overbearing personality, your aggressiveness or demanding approach can be intimidating, making your wife hesitant to read even a sentence out of her marriage manual. Think of that manual as having a latch with a lock on it. If she doesn't feel safe, she may take only the first step of unlocking it but still may not unlatch it. She may be very sensitive about this, so how much she reveals depends a lot on how safe you make her feel. And most of the time, arguing with her to open it and read it on demand will double-lock it.

If you're a wife, you may be saying, "I could never share my marriage manual with my husband because he would blast me. I could suffer for months, even years, if I suggested anything about wanting our relationship to improve." If you're living with a man who has a strong personality, and especially if he has some perfectionistic tendencies as well, the only way you might be able to get his attention in reading your manual is by hitting him alongside his head with a big stick (figuratively speaking, of course).

I haven't yet had to recommend that a couple divorce, but I do sometimes recommend a brief period of separation in the case of an overly dominant male—to get his attention and force him to deal with the issues. If it's possible for you to do it, taking a few days away from him and telling him the reason, lovingly and firmly, can sometimes be that "stick." Before taking this approach, however, and because this approach can be explosive, it might be well for you to double-check your situation with a trained counselor or possibly with a respected minister who has training in marriage counseling.

Beware, however, of going to the extreme of becoming a nag—of continually reading out of your manual without a request from your husband. I'll say more about this under statement 11.

5. Get the Support of a Loving Team

When you're in a loving, supportive group of three or four other couples, you may feel safer in revealing your marriage manual. It's like going to a counselor, where you feel safe expressing your feelings and opinions. You may even get to see some of the fine print.

A small support group is so important to a marriage that in my video series I have called small-group participation one of four "musts" of a great marriage. (The others? Things we're covering in this book: (1) Honor; (2) Daily resolution of anger; and (3) The monitoring of the wife's marriage manual.) Because of the critical role of support groups to a great marriage, I will return to this subject as I wind up this chapter.

6. Allow Her to Read from Her Manual at the Time When She Feels Most Able to Share

A wife may, for example, feel safer or more in the mood when the two of you are out on a dinner date. Men, ask her when and where is best for her.

I learned the importance of this the hard way. When I discovered that Norma had this built-in marriage manual, I used to demand that she read it to me whenever I wanted so I could grow and we could have an improved marriage. That was not only heavy irony, but it also shut her down from time to time and made her close her book completely.

Just four years into our marriage, Norma and I decided to spend a weekend in a hotel room and concentrate on how we could improve our relationship—my ideas, her ideas, back and forth. We also agreed that over that "retreat" weekend, we would try something new that had been recommended to us by a marriage expert. We would not eat for a day and drink just water so we could spend all our time and energy focusing on our marriage. It sounded like a good idea to both of us at the time. But by Saturday night, a major problem had arisen: Norma was starving! She was desperate to go eat.

I, on the other hand, am so goal oriented that I wanted to stay in the room and stick with our plan. Soon we were in the middle of a serious disagreement and not speaking to each other. So there we were in the coffee shop; she was enjoying scrambled eggs, and I was just staring at her and not speaking. Some love retreat! We had to learn, starting early in the relationship, that because we're both unique individuals, we're going to be different in our approaches to her manual. And we both had to adjust to our differences in order for her to feel safe in reading from it.

7. Discover New Communication Resources

For some couples, having the wife write out some sections of her manual is very helpful; it also serves to give a lasting record of what's going on inside her. Try out the various methods described in the chapter on communication, and then regularly use those that work best for you and your spouse. Learn to use and reuse the method called "drive-through communication." Take extra time to understand it and try it, because the couples I've worked with find that method to be at the top of the list.

Maybe your best method will be using word pictures, such as, "Read me the fine print under the section on improving our sexual relationship." Word pictures are an effective and powerful way to get a point across; you can get your mate to understand you and feel your feelings instantly.[3]

8. Ask Other Women to Share Their Marriage Manuals with You

This might be your mother or grandmother, your sister, your wife's sister, or maybe even a female friend of your family. I've done this myself for years, asking women in groups or individually what they think makes for a great marriage. Some women will feel safer articulating their manuals to someone who is not their spouse. After all, we have few reasons, if any, to criticize what they say, because they're not talking specifically about us. And if one or more of these women knows your wife well, it's amazing what you can learn. When I take the time to explain to a wife that I'm trying to improve my marriage, most have not only tried to help me, but they usually get excited about seeing a man doing something specific to enrich his relationship.

If your wife doesn't feel good about your reading some other woman's manual, her concern is usually filed under the "security" section in her manual. Whenever I find a wife who is somewhat jealous of her husband becoming too friendly with another woman, especially talking about improving their marriage, it usually has something to do with how secure she feels in her husband's love and value for her. If a conflict should come from your friendliness with other women, use the conflict to find out what it would take for her to feel more secure and loved. Listen to her, and look at your own motives. This can be a great opportunity to reestablish your lifelong commitment by assuring her of your love and devotion "till death do us part."

Also, once again, if your wife has too much unresolved anger stored in her heart, then no matter what you say or do, she probably will not become more secure in your love. Her anger needs to drain somewhat before your relationship can improve.

9. Use Reverse Role-Playing

The psychiatrist who wrote the best-selling book *Passive Men, Wild Women* said reverse role-playing is the best method he has ever found to help husbands make lasting changes for the better.[4] This reminds me of the forever-love principle that says:

Forever-love tries to view a situation through the eyes of a truelove.

This is something you can do by yourself in your living room or office. Picture your wife in the room with you, sitting in one of the empty chairs, and ask her what it would take to improve your relationship. Then, if you can, even though you might feel silly, go over and sit in the empty chair where you pictured her, and talk back to yourself as you think she would.

Next, move back to where you started and see yourself listening and responding. If you "get inside her mind" and start saying the things you imagine she would say, you'll be amazed at the insights that come.

10. Ask Her What You Do for Her That Gives Her Energy and What Takes Energy Away
What discourages her, and what gives her hope? This is another way to pull out the fine print in a woman's marriage manual. (We'll discuss this point at greater length in later chapters.)

11. Analyze the Main Points of Criticism You've Heard from Your Wife over the Years
These may have to do with you, the house, the kids, her job or yours, the general state of her life, or whatever. Think of two or three that have persisted for some time, write them down, and look at what they actually reflect.

Norma has criticized some of my manners for most of our married life. What does that tell me about her marriage manual? Well, most women easily and tightly connect to their husbands and become a part of them. The way we look and act can become a reflection on them. So when we bite our nails in public or make loud body noises at home, it can subtly disconnect them from us. It makes them feel, for that moment at least, that they are not a part of us. They can even feel devalued.

Then, too, women are very concerned with their husbands' reputations. They usually want their men to be respected and successful. So when we do something embarrassing in public, they're afraid we're going to be humiliated—and they along with us. This kind of analysis of a wife's criticisms can add a lot to a husband's understanding of her marriage manual.

We've covered eleven ways to draw out a wife's intuitive sense of what's best and enriching for your relationship. Husbands, take what you hear and "go for" a better marriage. Take specific steps to act on your wife's intuitive knowledge of the hairline cracks that could eventually "bring down the house."

A Word of Caution to Wives

Women need to remember that too much of anything can sour the whole process. My grandson Michael, for instance, loves the *Spot* book series, and he's always asking his mother—and me when I go over there—"Read me Spot." That's fine for the first time or two, but after the third or fourth reading of the same book, this grandpa starts to get bored and lose interest in Spot and his adventures.

In the same way, women who read their marriage manuals to their husbands too often—who are constantly reciting them without a request—can become tiresome. They're like a dripping faucet; like a desert sun that beats down on you all day long; or like being trapped in a locked room with someone who just won't quit jabbering. That's the way their husbands can perceive them.

Holding the readings to once a week, once a month, maybe even once a year for some manual chapters is sometimes enough to have a great impact on your marriage. An interesting manual is something your man wants to read. But if he's *forced* to read it (listen to it), then no matter how good it is, he's going to get tired of it, stop listening, and move on to something else.

Wives, how can you tell if you're overdoing it? Well, when you say something that may help improve your relationship but that could be perceived as critical, do your husband's eyes get that "vacant-house" look (you can tell some lights are on but no one's home)? Does he know everything you're going to say as soon as you get the first three words out? While you're talking, does he play raisin and shrivel up before your eyes? In a typical day, how many times are you critical, and how many times do you praise him? Keep track for a few days, and if the ratio isn't seven praises or more for every negative comment, you're being too critical and maybe reading too often. (The same holds true for your husband. If he overdoes it with criticism, you may stop reading your manual to him altogether.)

Wives, appreciate and praise any and all steps he takes in the right direction. In six months or a year, if you get discouraged, think back and consider how far you've come. Occasionally remind yourself that your husband is not your all-sufficient, perfect god (or parent). And remember that your ultimate happiness comes from finding peace based on your internal well-being not on outward circumstances.

A Further Word about Vital Small-Group Support

When we veer off course from time to time, as all couples do, a small group can make the difference between marital life or death. It is critical to making love last forever.

My favorite story is of a couple—Bill and Nancy—whose relationship was in such deep trouble that Bill had decided to walk out and divorce Nancy. But, they didn't divorce; they even turned their crisis into a deeper relationship. Unfortunately, at about the same time, another couple—friends of theirs—headed in the same direction. But this second couple went through with their divorce, it seems because they did not have the advantages Bill and Nancy had; they failed because they tried to fix their marriage on their own. If you're in serious trouble, most often it's just too difficult to make it on your own.

You see, before Bill and Nancy went through their crisis, they had been involved for some time in a weekly meeting with three other couples close to their age. These couples met primarily for friendship and mutual encouragement. Committed to learning what it would take to stay in love, the couples agreed to read various marriage books or watch relationship videos. Then each week, at one of their homes, they would discuss the subject and encourage each other in their separate journeys. They grew to trust each other and eventually felt safe in receiving advice from one another.

They had been meeting for about a year when Bill announced his intention to divorce Nancy. He had been holding his true feelings inside and had been afraid to share his hurt with the group or with Nancy. So when he shocked her with the news, she immediately called those other friends in the group. It was like calling 911. Literally within minutes, one of the other couples was at their house. The wife began to comfort Nancy while the husband took Bill on a jog around the block to talk things over.

As they jogged Bill expressed his frustrations and reasons for wanting to leave. The husband listened attentively, but he also tried to help Bill see things in a fresh light, and he pledged to stand with Bill and Nancy for support as long as it would take to work things out. By the end of their second circuit around the block, Bill was willing and energized to give the relationship another chance. This loving commitment was so overpowering to Bill that he held his face in his hands and cried tears of hope. He wasn't sure things could work out, but he knew others were there for them, no matter what happened.

Bill and Nancy stayed in the group but couldn't make any real promises that things would get better. What Bill discovered, however, was the key to their renewed life together. They received added strength from the other couples to keep working on their marriage. In a sense, the group was like a spare battery. They didn't let them get the divorce. The group members stayed with them, at times into the late evenings, listening and comforting them.

Bill and Nancy worked hard on rebuilding their marriage. And I'm happy to report that today, a number of years later, their marriage is stronger than ever—one of the best I know.

Most of this chapter has dealt with being willing to read a wife's marriage manual. That takes humility. But I propose that joining a small group can be a more humbling challenge for men. Remember, our gender likes the world to think we're in control, on top of it, independent, and self-sufficient. Being part of a support group acknowledges the need for interdependence and calls for a level of vulnerability. It can be scary for some men.

What is so powerful about being in a small, loving support group? I believe there's a dynamic similar to what anyone can find in a healthy family setting, an AA group, a church-family meeting week after week, or the support of a well-trained counselor. I have been amazed at the staying power a small group of friends or couples can give anyone who wants to stay in love in a marriage or build better relationships in a family or friendship.

Let me take a moment to make clear what I'm not saying about small groups. I'm not urging you to pick just any two or three couples to make up your support team. These couples should be friends, people in your local clubs or church, possibly other parents in your children's school. You need to find couples with whom you can feel safe and with whom you would enjoy meeting week after week. On the other hand, after you've been in one or two groups, you may also realize that you can pair up with other couples of different ages and interests. Because our struggles in marriage are relatively common, Norma and I have found it possible to form a group with total strangers. We found common ground and shared a high degree of commitment to seeing our marriages improve. The main problem arises in a group when one or two members are not really interested in growing and maturing or when one person wants too much control.

I witnessed firsthand just how effective support systems can be in strengthening even an entire nation. When I spoke in Ghana, West Africa, I saw thousands of extremely well-behaved young people (elementary and junior-high age) gather at a mass meeting in a field. In fact, they so impressed me that I asked about it. And what I learned is that in Ghana and other parts of Africa, the extended family is very close and is involved daily in raising the children. Grandparents, in-laws, cousins, aunts and uncles, and friends and neighbors, too—all watch over and help emotionally support these children and hold the kids accountable for their actions. If a young child is seen doing something questionable, the entire village gets involved to correct the child. Everyone seems to look out for each other. In other words, families support each other and hold each other accountable.

Here in the United States, where extended family members often live hundreds or thousands of miles away, small support groups fill a real void. One of the best reasons to start or stay in a group is to gain a sense of loving accountability, which we all require if we're to keep growing toward an increasingly mature love. It's amazing how much easier it is to stay on track if you know someone is going to ask, "How has it been going this past week?" Or if, after you report a minor conflict, someone asks, "How would you two do it differently next week?" Because we want to be able to give a good report to the other couples, we're more motivated—energized—during the week to do the things we know we should.

This whole idea of joining a small support group may seem scary, but I've found that the small groups Norma and I have belonged to have all resulted in solid growth for us as a couple, and we've also developed lasting friendships. There's a lot of laughter, too, because we're all so much alike.

Just getting together regularly, encouraging each other and being reminded that you're not alone in your efforts to make a better marriage can be tremendously energizing. In the small groups my wife and I were a part of in one particular city, we didn't lose a single couple to divorce over a three-year period. All together there were more than sixty couples, and many were strained out almost to the point of divorce when we started the groups. Norma and I saw couple after couple getting stronger each week. This was my first exposure to support groups, and it made me a true believer!

Need yet another reason to join a small group? I've discovered that in this context men seem to learn what forever-love means—by watching other men love their wives. Week after week, men get the opportunity to see how it's done. Men are often more receptive to learning what makes a good relationship from other men than from their own wives. The biggest and most lasting changes I've seen in husbands have come through involvement with small support groups.

One of my organizations, a nonprofit corporation called Today's Family, provides a number of helpful materials for couples who want to start or join an existing support group in their area. Write or call for more information.[5]

I've never met a couple doing really well that hasn't had help from others in some way—from extended family, friends, good marriage books, or a qualified marriage counselor. We all need such help to make it through the many barricades that block our attempts to stay together and in love.

There are many other ways of gaining support for your marriage. At least once every few years, it's refreshing to attend a marriage conference. Then, for a good "tune-up" from time to time, I recommend seeing a counselor together. This can give you new insights for improving your relationship, and it can also offer all the same benefits of being in a support group. If couples would spend just a small fraction of their incomes on a counseling session every two or three years, they would be repaid many times over.

If you want to find a marriage counselor, get lots of recommendations from satisfied clients. Don't just pick someone out of the phone book. And look for one who would see you for just a few sessions. What I'm suggesting here is some fine-tuning for a marriage that's not in crisis.

If going to see a counselor makes you too uneasy, you might consider investing in a few additional marriage and family books.[6] One particular book I recommend is *The Good Marriage* by Judith Wallerstein and Sandra Blakeslee.[7]

Summary

In this chapter we've taken a hard look at what can be learned from a woman's intuitive sense. And we've seen that going it alone is not the best route for a couple going for a lifelong love.

The next chapter may well be one you've been waiting for. You may be wishing we'd get down to the brass tacks of how to approach and resolve the inevitable conflicts that can too quickly turn positive emotion—"I love you"—to a negative "I hate you." Dr. Howard Markman says that the divorce rate could be cut in half if couples learned this one set of skills: conflict resolution.[8]

Forever-Love Principles

Our list of forever-love principles continues from the previous chapter:

83. Forever-love stays in touch with a woman's intuitive sense of what the marriage needs.

84. Forever-love is courageous enough to ask, "What would make this relationship better?"

85. Forever-love does not tune out or get defensive in the face of constructive suggestions for improving the relationship.

86. Forever-love is not so goal oriented that it loses sight of relationship and connection.

87. Forever-love analyzes longstanding complaints to find a core of truth.

88. Forever-love steps out and makes adjustments to "go for" a better relationship.

89. Forever-love measures its criticism—giving seven or more praises for every one fault-finding suggestion.

90. Forever-love doesn't make impossible demands, and it accepts the reality that a truelove is not an all-sufficient god or parent.

91. Forever-love stays in tune as it seeks out several other couples for support and encouragement through good days and hard times.

92. Forever-love doesn't go it alone but welcomes the fresh insight of other perspectives.

93. Forever-love maintains energy as it is challenged through loving, supportive accountability.

94. Forever-love welcomes a periodic checkup with a marriage counselor.

13

Conflicts:
The Doorway to Intimacy

The idea that conflict is healthy may sound like a cruel joke if you're feeling over-whelmed by the negativity in your relationship. But in a sense, a marriage lives and dies by what you might loosely call its arguments, by how well disagreements and grievances are aired. They key is how you argue—whether your style esca-lates tension or leads to a feeling of resolution.

—John Gottman[1]

Dr. Howard Markman claims that resolving conflicts is the key area for staying in love and staying married. His twenty years of research indicates that if couples learned to work out their conflicts, the overall divorce rate could be cut by more than 50 percent.[2] Just think of it! For years the divorce rate has been hovering at about one out of two marriages. That sad statistic could be reduced to one out of four—if only couples would learn effective methods of conflict resolution. And one of those saved marriages could be yours![3]

Most of us dislike and try to avoid conflicts, especially with our spouses For peace lovers, this chapter has both bad news and good. The bad news is that we're always going to have conflicts. Our valued individuality—includ-ing our personality and gender differences—make them inevitable. But the good news is that we can not only reduce our conflicts, we can also use them to move into deeper intimacy in any relationship.

To illustrate how conflicts can lead to deeper intimacy, let me relate (with their permission) a story about our daughter, Kari, and her husband, Roger. It was very typical of young married couples. Roger heard that his mom and dad were coming to visit. He was pretty excited about that visit, because he loves to eat. He especially loves a big breakfast, and his mom used to cook him one every day. She's that kind of loving mother, and he was the baby of the family. I know how that goes, since I was the baby of my family. But then I got married and found out that wives don't always wait on you the way your mother did. Well, Roger has learned the same lesson. And also like me, he sometimes says things that have the opposite effect of what he intended.

So, thinking as a male can, when he heard his folks were coming, Roger said, "Finally, I can have one of those big breakfasts again!" He will admit that this comment was in praise of his mother but that it also was meant as an editorial comment about Kari's not cooking him breakfasts. Maybe she'd take the hint. That made sense to him, but it didn't sit well with Kari. Instantly—*wham!*—conflict. Kari went silent.

Fortunately Roger is a sensitive and loving husband. He doesn't want to offend Kari. He wants to make sure everything is going great. This happened before their first child, our grandson Michael Thomas, was born, and already Roger was concerned about providing a healthy family atmosphere. So he opened the door offered by that conflict and asked, "Kari, how did my comment make you feel?" That was level 4 of intimate communication, which we discussed in an earlier chapter.

Now, as I've already mentioned, word pictures are great for expressing feelings. Roger and Kari have developed their own word-picture method that conveys instantly how they're feeling. Their method uses fruit imagery, and it goes like this: If something happens but it's not a big deal, she'll say, "You just hit me with a raisin." If it's a little bigger deal, she'll say he hit her with an orange. If it's bigger still, she'll say it was a cantaloupe. But this time she said, "You just hit me with a twenty-five-pound watermelon—*wham!*—and drove me right into the ground." And he instantly entered into her feelings.

Seeing his desire to work things out, she went on to explain that his comment had made her feel inadequate, not as good as his mom. She thought, *What about all the great dinners I make? How come he isn't saying, "Wow, your dinners are just wonderful! Your dinners blow my mom's dinners away"?*

Roger had a different view. He wasn't saying he had a problem with her dinners. He was saying, "I'm not getting breakfast."

Back to Kari's perspective: It's pretty hard to make a big breakfast when you're a teacher and getting up at six (before he gets up) just to be ready for work on time. And what he said, thinking it was going to motivate her to want to make his breakfast, was not the way to get things done. (I think she had even mentioned to him before they married, "I don't do breakfast," but I guess that's the kind of thing you overlook at the time when you're just starting to grow in love.)

What came out of this conflict? He knew how she felt, he reinforced how much he loved her, and he found out one important way to avoid conflict in the future. I'll add more to their story in a few pages.

That's an example of using conflict as a doorway to intimacy, of getting past opinions to feelings. When conflict is used this way, we don't need to be afraid of it; it actually becomes a good thing that moves the relationship forward.

We actually *need* to have disagreements. That doesn't mean we go looking for fights. Should we keep fighting just so we can enjoy the deeper intimacy of making up? By no means.

But when conflicts do occur, they can bring benefits (produce pearls) if we use them in the right way. With that hope in mind, let's take a closer look at the anatomy of a conflict, beginning with why they happen in the first place.

Why Most Conflicts Occur

Conflicts—disagreements that can escalate into fights—occur for a number of reasons. Part of the following list of primary causes comes from Dr. Carol Rubin, a clinical instructor at Harvard Medical School, and her coauthor, Dr. Jeffrey Rubin, a professor of psychology at Tufts University.[4]

Power and Control

Conflicts happen because there are power and control problems in the home. Who is going to make the decisions? Who's the boss? When there is vying for authority—*boom!* Conflict. It happens when we least expect it.

When one person tries to smother the other with too much control or doesn't let the other think or feel independently, conflict smolders or erupts.

Insecurity

Someone's feeling insecure or unsafe in a relationship causes arguments. If you think your mate is drifting and creating distance, for instance, you're likely to feel insecure, and conflict is a natural result.

Some personalities hold things in for a long time, and then they explode. It might be because they don't feel safe to bring up those things when they first are perceived as a problem. In time the unresolved anger explodes "out of the blue."

Differences in Values

Conflicts arise out of differences in values. He thinks it's okay to drink alcohol at every meal, and she can't stand it. She thinks it's fine to tell people someone's not home when a call comes in, and he thinks that's lying. He wants to attend church every Sunday, and she likes to go only at Christmas and Easter.

It's important to remember here that not all differences can be eliminated. In such cases, it's healthy to say to each other, "We'll never agree on this issue, but I still love you, and I hope we can learn more about each other's feelings and needs through this conflict."

Competition

Conflict can grow out of competition. Some people can't stand to lose at anything, even in a casual game of checkers. Or perhaps the husband is bothered by the fact that his wife earns more than he does, and he's determined to outdo her in that area.

Personal Differences

Couples fight over normal male-female differences and normal personality differences. We can count on those two areas to bring a continual flow of conflicts. That's why I've taken two chapters (10 and 11) to expand on those subjects and show how to understand each other and then use that understanding to make love last rather than to tear the relationship apart.

Misunderstood Feelings and Unmet Needs

I believe this is the major reason for conflict—when one, or more likely both, spouses have unmet needs. Dr. Stephen Covey says this in a different way. He claims that all conflicts are caused by unfulfilled expectations in "roles and goals."[5] One spouse may think, *That's not what you're supposed to do in our relationship. I fix the car, and you fix the meals.* Or one may say to the other, "I've always wanted to go on in my education. You knew that. We'll just have to go without that new couch until I finish." We expect others to know our needs and feelings, in fact, even if we haven't mentioned them.

It's been extremely helpful to me to understand that whenever I'm in conflict with someone, one or two things are occurring: Someone's feelings aren't being valued and understood or someone's needs are not being valued and met.

Knowing and meeting your mate's (and children's) needs is a basic part of intimacy, and it's also important that your needs are understood and that you're reasonably sure they'll be met. (That's why the first part of this book is so vital; it gives us a plan for handling our feelings and needs, including those that cannot possibly be met by a mate.) But needs unnecessarily go unmet when we get too busy—when the spouse and kids aren't getting enough time with us or there's just not enough conversation.

The Circle of Conflict

Growing out of one or more of those causes, conflict tends to go in a circle. Let me show you what I mean with a typical example. A wife with a "perfectionist" personality needs a certain measure of neatness and order in her home, but her "carefree" husband couldn't care less. So the woman might say something like, "I am so frustrated around this house! Look at this mess! Nobody ever picks up anything!"

But the husband, who may be clueless, placing less value in or having less need for neatness, may say, "Yeah, you know what? If you would just get better organized around here, you wouldn't be so frustrated." Or he may ask, "You need more energy? Are you still taking those vitamins we spent all that money for?" "Are you getting your rest?" Or simply, "What's the big deal?" Mr. Fix-it offers solutions and opinions but finds it hard to get down to discussing feelings or needs.

As a pattern, this couple may easily exchange clichés and facts, but when they get to opinions—*wham!*—tension flares, based on disagreement. If they're like a lot of couples (maybe most), they may go silent for a while or escalate to a hotter conflict. They don't enjoy conflict. One spouse may not feel safe enough to get to the deeper levels—expressing feelings or needs. One may have little hope that expressing feelings will make any change. One may express needs inappropriately, in a rage. One, again, may be clueless that feelings and unmet needs have anything to do with the problem.

For any number of reasons, the couple moves back to clichés, because that's real safe. Then they share some facts, followed by opinions again, and *boom!*—back to conflict. They just circle in those three areas and never go to the deep levels of communication where disagreements can lead to a closer, more intimate bond—deeper intimacy.

We're not doomed to an endless cycle of unresolved conflict. But if you're stuck on a merry-go-round, you'll need to take the risk of stepping out of old patterns.

What Doesn't Work in Resolving Conflicts

For a marriage to grow as a result of conflict—for healing to occur after conflict—we need to learn to move toward resolution. But some patterns just don't do the job as well as we'd like.

What doesn't work for healing resolution? For starters, *withdrawing into yourself.* I used to do this because it's what I often saw my father doing. If you withdraw, however, you don't get your needs met, your spouse's needs don't get met, and your relationship suffers. So withdrawing is not the solution. In fact, Dr. Scott Stanley says that the worst thing for a marriage is when the husband clams up and distances himself from the family.[6]

Yielding—giving in—isn't a satisfactory pattern either. While one person wins and therefore peace prevails for a season, the other person loses, and ultimately, the relationship also loses. If both partners don't win, the relationship is weakened.

A third pattern? You could be the winner—the opposite of yielding. But again, one of you ends up a loser, so the relationship loses.

How about *compromise?* Isn't that healthy? Sometimes you just don't have time to resolve the issue right then, so you each settle for half a loaf. But remember that compromise is only a temporary solution because it's still a win-lose situation for both of you and for your relationship. Postponing is okay, but if you don't get back to the dispute, you lose a doorway to a deeper intimacy that we'll discuss in a minute.

Everybody Wins

Let's work through another pattern in which everybody wins—both parties and the relationship. Here you *keep working on the conflict until you both feel good about the solution.* The issue is resolved. You both know your feelings are being understood. And you both feel your needs are being met. It may take some deep conversation over a couple of days or longer, but your attitude and approach are always saying, *Let's work to resolve this issue, where we both feel like winners.*

A few years ago, Norma and I found ourselves embroiled in a dispute. We had taken our youngest son, Michael, to college for his freshman year and had been with him for three or four days. Now we were getting ready to leave, and Norma was sitting on the hotel bed, misty-eyed. We had to get to the airport soon, and I was eager to be on our way. "What's wrong?" I asked.

"I don't know," she said. "It's just real hard for me. This is our baby, and I just hope everything turns out okay here for him."

Oh, brother! I thought. To say I was insensitive to her feelings at that moment would be a major understatement. So I said something like, "We have got to get going. Come on."

But she said, "I'm just sitting here thinking about the empty nest, the trauma a mom goes through in losing all her kids."

I was thinking it might be a fun time for us with the kids all gone, so I wasn't empathizing too well. I replied, "Well, we have to let him go, you know. Let's get moving."

Norma looked across the room into my eyes and said, "You know, what I need right now is what you teach!"

Obviously, we had a conflict of feelings and priorities. Now, at that point I could have become sarcastic or defensive. I could have said, "I can't believe I have to perform all the time! Do I have to go up on the stage now?" Or I could have said, "Which of the twenty areas I teach do you need?" I (or she) could have withdrawn—walked into the bathroom and shut the door to avoid any further tension. One of us could have quickly (or not so quickly) yielded; for me that might have meant saying, "Okay, what do you want?" all the while resenting her condemnation of my behavior. She, on the other hand, could have said, "Okay, let's get going," all the while resenting my unwillingness to listen and understand. As for compromise, if we had been really late for the plane, we could have said, "Let's continue this on the plane or when we get home."

Fortunately, we had a little time to spare, and we had progressed a little beyond the other unhealthy tactics. Swallowing some pride and opening the doorway to intimacy, I walked across the room to Norma, and she scooted over on the bed to make space for me. I sat down next to her, put my arm around her, hugged her, and asked, "If you were the weather right now, what would be happening to you?"

"It's a real drizzle—rainy, cold, and foggy," she said.

"And if you were a flower?" I asked.

"Right now I've lost all my petals," she said, "and they've fallen on the floor. You stepped on them when you walked over here." (*She is so quick!*)

When I asked what she needed, she mentioned some things I might do with Michael that I hadn't even thought of. I listened and made mental notes. She felt better immediately, and we headed home much more at peace with each other and in deeper intimacy.

As I held Norma that day and listened, I felt the tension between us turn to peace. I knew we were working things out. I felt I had won something—new ideas for how I could stay in contact with my son. I'd learned something new about Norma and her fears of the empty nest. I know she felt she was winning, too, because even though I'm still capable of being irritated by the discovery that I'm doing something wrong, she knows she is generally safe in bringing up any issues that are between us. She knew I had heard her out, and she knows I want to resolve any conflicts we have.

It's not always possible to come to a resolution where you both feel good about the outcome. But it is possible to restate your commitment to each other at any point. You can say things like, "I still love you and always will. We can't seem to agree on this issue, but I'm committed to you for life, and I'll never stop loving you over any disagreement." Such commitment and lasting love has a way of softening the dispute.

Reaching Resolution: Developing Personal Keys to Intimacy

If a conflict is ultimately going to draw a couple closer together, they need a set of "fighting rules." That list becomes the key to what I call the doorway to intimacy. If you don't have such boundaries on how you fight, you may say or do any number of things that shut down communication— that slam the door on intimacy.

Even in the best of circumstances, a couple usually walks through the doorway to intimacy after the tension of the conflict is starting to cool down. Most couples I work with can't enter intimacy in the midst of a heated conflict. Nor can Norma and I. It's afterward, when we can think about each other's feelings and needs, that we move closer to each other.

Door Slammers

A few modes of operation predictably shut and lock the doorway to intimacy. One of the most common is the use of accusatory "you statements": "*You* always do this." "*You* never remember that." "As far as I'm concerned, *you'll* never change." These statements immediately put the other person on the defensive. If you want to draw closer, the key is to use "I statements." If the husband is late for dinner, for instance, the wife might say, "*I* feel uneasy, or uncomfortable, when that happens, because *I* don't know where you are. *I'm* concerned about you when you don't call . . . " That's a lot more effective than "*You're* always late. I can't believe it. Why do you do this? *You* never change." Such an approach will only make a person want to run away or fight back.

Sarcasm, disrespect, and screaming are all door slammers too. Denying the conflict isn't the solution, but neither is a temper tantrum. David and Vera Mace report that:

> Studies of the family by Murray Straus have shown that individuals who vent their anger tend, over time, to produce more and more anger and to vent it more and more vigorously until they finally resort to physical violence. . . . Venting anger almost invariably gets the other person angry too, and then you are going to need more and more anger to continue the fight.[7]

Kindness, respect, and calmness, on the other hand, are keys that open the door. Exactly what works best for you and your spouse is something you can work out on your own. Such keys will improve all your conversations, but they'll be especially valuable during times of conflict.

Key Lists

My son Greg and I have developed a set of keys to the doorway of intimacy in connection with his doctoral studies in psychology. I'll show you our list of fourteen suggestions that have worked for us and many others. Then I'll give you a similar list by Dr. Harriet Lerner, who is one of the leaders in the field of conflict resolution. From these two lists, you and your spouse can make your own list of rules in the space provided on page 232. If *rules* seems too harsh a word, think in terms of *keys to intimacy.*

The Smalley *"Fighting Rules"*

1. First clarify what the actual conflict is. Make sure that you understand your partner as clearly as you can before proceeding to a

resolution. Listening is vital here! Endeavor to work for understanding in two key areas: your mate's *feelings*, and then, *needs*.

2. Stick to the issue at hand. Don't dredge up past hurts or problems, whether real or perceived. But if you tend to veer off the issue, you might want to see if there is any other key factor in this conflict, such as fatigue, low estrogen levels, low blood sugar, stress, work problems, or spiritual or emotional issues.

3. Maintain as much tender physical contact as possible. Hold hands.

4. Avoid sarcasm.

5. Avoid "you" statements. Use the words "I feel" or "I think." No past or future predictions ("You always . . ." "You won't ever . . .").

6. Don't use "hysterical" statements or exaggerations. ("This will never work out." "You're just like your father.")

7. Resolve any hurt feelings before continuing the conflict discussion. ("I shouldn't have said that. Will you forgive me?")

8. Don't resort to name-calling. Don't allow the conflict to escalate your tempers. If this happens, agree to continue the discussion later.

9. Avoid power statements and actions. For example: "I quit!" "You sleep on the couch tonight!" "You're killing me!" "I hate you!"

10. Don't use the silent treatment.

11. Keep your arguments as private as possible to avoid embarrassment.

12. Use the "drive-through" method of communication when arguing. (Repeat back what you think the other person is saying.)

13. Resolve your conflicts with win-win solutions; both parties agree with the solution or outcome of the argument. Work on resolution only after both understand feelings and needs.

14. Above all, strive to reflect honor in all your words and actions during the resolution of your conflicts.

Dr. Harriet Lerner's Key Rules

1. Do speak up when an issue is important to you.

2. Don't strike while the iron is hot. (Watch your timing.)

3. Do take time to think about the problem and to clarify your position.

4. Don't use "below-the-belt" tactics.

5. Do speak in "I" language.

6. Don't make vague requests.

7. Do try to appreciate the fact that people are different.

8. Don't participate in intellectual arguments that go nowhere.

9. Do recognize that each person is responsible for his or her own behavior.

10. Don't tell another person what he or she thinks or feels or "should" think or feel.

11. Do try to avoid speaking through a third party (someone speaking for you and you're not there to clarify).

12. Don't expect change to come from hit-and-run confrontations.[8]

The Master Key

When it comes to conflict resolution, everything I say here is based on an underlying rule for a long, happy marriage: Keep anger levels low every day!

Doing that calls for communication—primarily at the deepest level, where one talks about feelings and needs. It calls for openness and for forgiveness—a desire for the relationship to be the best it can be.

The ancient Scriptures are full of amazing insight and wisdom. You may be familiar with the passage about anger: "'In your anger, do not sin': Do not let the sun go down while you are still angry."[9] That is a commentary of sorts on an even older line of poetry:

In your anger do not sin;
    when you are on your beds,
        search your hearts and be silent [be at peace].[10]

If anger and its symptoms of distance and control are an underlying theme of your marriage, I suggest you "search your hearts" and go back and reread the issues I addressed in part 1. If marital conflicts ever resort to violence, see a marriage counselor to work through these issues.

Pearls from Conflict

The disputes—disagreements—in your marriage will never vanish. But there are pearls to be found in those disputes. That's one word picture. Another picture is the one I used above: Conflicts can be doorways to intimacy. Here's how. (I give special thanks to Dr. Gary Oliver for his insights and research in this area.)

Conflicts Reveal Feelings and Needs

Conflict is a doorway into intimacy because it's a way to discover who a person is. As soon as we hit the wall and are in conflict, we have to open a door so we can walk through it to find out what the other person feels and needs. Instead of reverting to silence or clichés, we can adopt an attitude that says, *I'm kind of glad we're having this conflict because it'll result in both of us knowing more about each other and loving each other more.*

Norma and I were recently locked in a prolonged argument about my travel schedule. I still speak a great deal across the country, and we don't live near a major airport. So I wanted to investigate the possibility of leasing a company plane to use on speaking trips. But Norma has been against the idea of small planes for quite some time.

As we went back and forth on this issue, it was increasingly clear that we weren't going to agree. So we stepped back to ask, "What are our deepest feelings about renting a plane?"

I found out that she fears the smaller planes because of all the publicity that comes when one crashes. She feels they're unsafe, so she believes riding in them is taking an unnecessary risk. I also learned that she wants me to value her uneasiness about the plane and to respect her expression of her true feelings.

From me, she found out that flying in a private aircraft would allow me much more time at home and create less stress for me at the airports. I felt the convenience of having our own schedule (as opposed to having to follow the airlines' schedules) would add a lot more pleasure to my job. She listened and did understand, but it didn't resolve the situation.

So we used our "911" group of friends to help us out. A "911" group is two or three very close friends who love us and whom we love in return. On rare occasions we call these friends and ask for their input in some conflicts. We met with our friends, and they helped us sort through the problem. I agreed to drop the discussion for three months while I gathered all the facts about how much a plane rental would cost, how safe it is, and what the actual time savings and convenience would be. Norma agreed that we would bring up the subject again at the end of that time so we could come to a conclusion on the matter.

For me, the meeting provided new insight. I hadn't understood that Norma had been feeling as though I was badgering her over the issue. She felt smothered by my strong interest in renting a plane and also by my lack of awareness of her feelings. She was right—I hadn't seen our talks as smothering to her. But with the help of our loving friends, we were able to be more objective and put the conflict on hold. And we both felt more understood and safer in revealing our feelings because of the dispute.

A few months later, we met again with our support group, and I explained that it's my nature always to be looking for a better way to do things. When I said how tired I was of having to drive an hour just to get to the nearest commercial airport, one member of the group replied that lots of people have to commute an hour each way to their jobs. "You're just a big baby!" she said as we all laughed. But in the end, Norma agreed that if certain safety concerns were met, such as having two pilots in the cockpit, she probably wouldn't be too nervous and could relax with the small-plane idea.

Conflict is one of the best ways to take us beyond our feelings all the way to discussing our needs. In the above scenario, Norma needed assurance that I—her family—was safe, not taking unnecessary, life-threatening risks. I needed to reassure her that I understood her concerns and took them seriously. I needed Norma to understand my desire for greater efficiency and less wasted time spent commuting to and waiting in airports for scheduled airline flights.

Remember the breakfast story from the beginning of this chapter? After Roger asked Kari how she felt and she told him, he then asked what she needed. *What can I do to show you I love you?* She replied, "I need for you to praise me for the things I do and the things I get excited about doing." In other words, she needed him to do more than just avoid insulting her; she needed to hear words of appreciation for the things she does. And since then, he has made an effort to give her that praise. He's become the kind of husband dads hope their daughters will find. (My special thanks to the Gibsons, his parents.)

One of the best ways I know of to meet another person's needs is by developing your own love language. This only works if your relationship is fairly healthy to begin with; if it's not, you might not be willing to give this a try. But if things are going reasonably well, this can be great.

As I've already mentioned, normal conflicts can reveal that my feelings or my needs are not being understood or valued. As we work through a conflict—discovering deep feelings and needs—we can develop a love language based on the alphabet of that new knowledge.

Or think again in terms of pearls: Over years of marriage, this love language becomes like a necklace, made from the pearls hunted and found after conflicts, in answer to the question "What can I do to show you I love you?"

As a result of conflict, over time, you can create a love language. Here's how. You and your spouse should each list five or ten practical and specific things you would like to have the other person do for you—things you believe will really meet your needs. You agree: "This makes me feel as if you love me. I have a need, and when you do this, it meets that need." Your mate's doing one of these for you (or vice versa) expresses love and honor.

Write out this list and post it someplace where it will serve as a daily reminder. It might be in your closet if you don't want everybody in the world to see it. Or you can put it on your refrigerator. But put it in a place where you can be reminded every day.

I've asked seminar participants to write items that would be in their love language. One woman told me she would love to have her husband learn to pick up on her hints better. For instance, if she says "I'm really tired" at the end of the day, she would love for him to pick up on that and respond, "Let's go out to dinner so we don't have to cook tonight." A love-language list is much more effective, however, than hoping your mate will pick up on your hints.

Another woman said she would put this on her love-language list: "On my husband's days off, a lot of times he gets involved with the boys and in doing stuff out in the garage. And when I come home from my really hectic day, I need for him to stop what he's doing for just a few minutes and say, 'I'm so glad to see you. It's great to have you home.'"

A professional woman said, "I need my husband to respect my need to be engaged in activities that he doesn't find fun. For example, I love to just go play in my front- and backyard 'sandbox'—to plant flowers and make our place beautiful. But he has ways of belittling me that are funny to him but hurtful to me. He calls me his little Polish farmer, or he'll tell me I've got a rednecked farmer tan. It would be wonderful if he would praise me for how the yard looks or even join me in the garden."

These comments describe simple yet significant needs. Developing your own love language is a great way to find out what your spouse needs and also to get your own needs met. Conflicts are often an open door to a discussion and an awareness of such needs.

I'll give more specific examples of what might be on your love-language list in chapter 15, where we discuss the energizing concept of "marital banking."

Before I go on, I pause one more time to address any skeptical reader. *Wait*, you say, *you don't know my husband. He knows how I feel, he knows what I need, and he just doesn't give a rip about anything but himself.*

Whoa! If that's your view of life, I make several reminders and suggestions. First, consider this question: Are you sure? Have you really talked about underlying priorities? Have you listened to your mate's feelings and needs? Have you clearly expressed yours? Can you see baby steps of progress you can praise?

On the other hand, start back at the beginning of this book: Your own contentment with life doesn't rely on what your spouse will or won't do. You have the ability to set boundaries and ask that they be maintained. I once more recommend Harriet Lerner's excellent book *The Dance of Anger*, which is subtitled *A Woman's Guide to Changing the Patterns of Intimate Relationships*. If you and your spouse are in an unsatisfying dance, it takes just one of you to change the record. And the new tune could save your marriage. See the endnotes of this book for other helpful resources. At the beginning of this chapter I mentioned a husband and wife who disagreed about how neat the house should be. One recent book even gives principles for living beyond the conflicts presented by those aggravating housekeeping differences.[11]

Conflicts Provide Opportunities to Express Affection

Conflicts can open a doorway to intimacy by surfacing feelings and needs. But conflicts also provide an opportunity to express physical and emotional affection. We all need to be hugged. We all need to be loved on.

To illustrate this point, let me give an example of how *not* to do it. A young husband told me about a conflict he and his wife had before they married. She had invited him to dinner at her place, where she had baked him lasagna. He got to the dinner table, and she served the lasagna—which turned out to be as hard as a brick. So he said, trying to inject a little levity into the situation, "Do you serve chain saws with this?"

As you might imagine, she immediately got up and ran down the hall, crying. He called after her, "And another thing, enough of this sensitivity stuff!"

Believe it or not, he proposed to her later that same night, and she said yes. (Was she blind or what?) But at the moment, this was a big conflict that instantly brought her feelings and needs to the surface.

What could the young man have done at that point to help the situation? He could have put his arm around her, held her, and said, "I can't believe I say things like that. I don't know how I learned to be so sarcastic, but I don't want to hurt you. Will you forgive me?" Now she might need some time to warm up (or cool down). But his contrite spirit and gentle touch would have started the healing and resolving process.

Sorting Out the Big Issues:
A Practical Approach to Reaching Resolution

Norma and I use this practical step-by-step method for conflict resolution every time we get into a big disagreement over some major issue, such as where to live, borrowing for a new car, or changing churches. Our approach involves making two lists. Let me explain.

Suppose our disagreement is about how to parent our children, which was often the case in years gone by. I was a tolerant father in the sense of not having a lot of rules, because that's the way I was raised. Norma, on the other hand, wanted a little more order in the home. As the kids grew older, I would also start pushing them to get out and do various activities. But Norma would say, "I don't think they're old enough. They're not ready yet."

I remember the time she expressed her concern with a great word picture. "You know how this makes me feel?" she said. "I feel like I'm the mother bird in a nest up in the tree. We've got these three little birds in here. And papa bird flies in now and then and says, 'Hey, why don't you guys get out and do some things? It would be boring to me to be in a nest all the time. You've got to jump out and enjoy yourself.' But I know how immature their feathers and bones are. I know where all the cats in the neighborhood are. And if you push our chicks out now, they're going to hit the ground and get hurt or gobbled up in a hurry."

Well, whenever we got into a big conflict like that, we would pull out a blank sheet of paper and draw a line down the middle, dividing it in half. At the top, on one side of the line, we would write, "All the Reasons We

Should Do This." At the top on the other side, we would write, "All the Reasons We Shouldn't Do This."

In listing reasons, we would start by gathering all the facts. Then we would go deeper and find the feelings involved. Each of us would say, "Well, I feel this about that idea." Finally, we'd get to the level of needs: "I have a need, and if we do that, it will mess with my need."

Before long, we would have eighteen to twenty reasons on one side of the paper and maybe fifteen to eighteen on the other. Having it all down on paper—both the pros and the cons—and knowing that we were both heard and valued usually helped us resolve our conflict. We didn't have to win or lose. Maybe it was Norma's idea we went with, or maybe it was mine. But I never felt I was compromising or giving in. I always felt it was the right thing to do. Usually as soon as all the facts were on one piece of paper, it was pretty obvious what ought to happen. The facts won or lost, not us. This method objectified the conflict and took it further out of the emotional range.

Sometimes, however, if we were still deadlocked on an important issue, or if the kids didn't like the outcome, we would need to take this method one step further. We would then rank each statement on both sides of the line. We would ask the question of each statement, "Is that a factor that will have long-lasting effects?" If we believed it would affect us for more than ten years, we'd put an L beside the statement. If we believed there was only a temporary effect, we'd put a T beside the statement. When we were finished marking each item, pro and con, we'd add up the L's and T's and see which side won. This analysis seemed to resolve the issue every time, even with the kids involved.

Sometimes when people come to me for counseling, I'll listen for a while, and then all of a sudden they'll say, "Okay, what shall we do?" If I don't know what to tell them at that point, it's probably because I don't have enough facts yet. The more facts I get, the more pieces of the puzzle I have and the more clearly I can see what the whole picture is and present it to them. And when they see the factual picture, they generally know what to do. I don't have to solve the problem for them. So part of being a counselor is just gathering the facts and laying them out clearly for a person or couple to see. Then I say, "Here it is. What do you think?"

This fact-gathering method has solved so many conflicts through the years for Norma and me. It has a way of calming us down and making us feel safe and highly valued, which is a major factor in resolving conflicts.

Summary

Remember the bad news at the beginning of the chapter? Conflicts are inevitable in any relationship. But the good news overrides the bad: I challenge you to see any disagreements with your spouse as a doorway to intimacy. Let conflicts be that doorway into a better understanding of how you both feel and what you each need.

In the last of his Chronicles of Narnia series (*The Last Battle*), C. S. Lewis describes his characters facing a battle to end all battles. But at a strategic point they walked through a doorway into a stable; some people claimed the stable held a life-threatening creature. But once through that doorway, they discovered "in reality they stood on grass, the deep blue sky was overhead, and the air which blew gently on their faces was that of a day in early summer."[12] Walking through that door had taken them to a heavenly kingdom. And once there, they could continue to go "further up and further in,"[13] making increasingly awesome—wonderful—new discoveries that they couldn't have fathomed before they had walked through that seemingly threatening door.

That's how it can be in a marriage; conflicts have the potential for drawing you and your spouse closer and closer to each other. There's not a monster behind your conflicts. It's a matter of opening the door to intimacy—not closing it, slamming it, or locking it.

Open the door. Walk through—and you learn more about the delights of marriage, including intercourse, than you ever dreamed possible. Intimacy isn't just talking; you know it's much more. When's the last time you both really enjoyed your sexual relationship? Is sex mostly physical? In the next chapter we'll show how good sex is a combination of four important ingredients. Have fun!

But before we move on use the space on page 232 for notes that will begin your own set of "fighting rules." If you are in or starting a small support group with other couples, consider getting input from others as you finalize your rules.

Forever-Love Principles

Our list of forever-love principles continues from the previous chapter:

95. Forever-love knows that marital conflict is inevitable.

96. Forever-love sees conflict as a doorway to greater intimacy and knowledge. "Through this disagreement, what new insights can we gain about us as a couple? How can this eventually draw us closer?"

97. Forever-love doesn't go looking for a fight just to find the joy of making up.

98. Forever-love finds courage to break out of longstanding, circular fight patterns.

99. Forever-love doesn't clam up in the face of verbal conflict.

100. Forever-love doesn't feel compelled to give in and maintain peace at any price.

101. Forever-love doesn't gloat, "I win. You lose."

102. Forever-love approaches conflict saying, "Let's work to resolve this issue so that your needs and mine are met."

103. Forever-love says, "I love you," even when a resolution isn't reached.

104. Forever-love sets down fighting rules—boundaries that aren't to be crossed.

105. Forever-love knows how to say "I'm sorry" and "I forgive you."

106. Forever-love looks beyond disagreement and conflict to identify what needs are begging to be met.

107. Forever-love resolves today's conflicts today—not tomorrow.

108. Forever-love forms a private love language. Both partners develop a list: "These actions make me feel loved and honored." Forever-love reaches out and energizes a truelove by suggesting a love-language activity.

109. Forever-love considers the long-term effects of decisions when conflict is otherwise deadlocked.

Our Fighting Rules

_____

_____

_____

_____

_____

_____

_____

_____

14

Was That As Good for You As It Was for Me?

You must not isolate that [sexual] pleasure and try to get it by itself, any more than you ought to try to get the pleasures of taste without swallowing and digesting, by chewing things and spitting them out again.

—C. S. Lewis[1]

Before Dennis and Lois even sat down in my counseling office, I knew what we were going to be talking about. There's a certain hesitation, a betraying look of sheepishness, that clearly signals when a couple needs to discuss one of the most difficult and embarrassing topics in marriage. Dennis and Lois had problems in their sexual relationship, a situation that isn't uncommon, even in couples that look as if they have it all together. That was Dennis and Lois—one handsome, intense couple. I guessed them to be in their early thirties. Lois was attractive in her jeans and oversized sweater. Dennis was in khakis and a gold shirt from an exclusive country club.

"Where should we begin?" I asked, watching them squirm on the couch as they tried a hundred different ways to get comfortable.

"I'll start," Dennis volunteered. He took a deep breath then said, "I haven't had sex in so long, I forget how it goes!"

Lois burst into tears. After half a minute or so, she regained her composure enough to say, "That's not true. Dennis tends to exaggerate when he's angry."

"Or horny," he muttered.

"Actually, it *is* our sex life that brings us here today," Lois continued. "It has become a real problem in our marriage."

"Tell me about it," I said.

"We've been married for eleven years," she said, "and sex was really good for both of us in the beginning."

"Would you agree, Dennis?" I asked.

"Yeah," he replied, "and that's part of the problem. I know how good it can be, but it's just not that way anymore."

"Go on, Lois," I said.

"Well, I guess our problem is typical stuff. We started having kids, so there were lots of late nights with colicky babies. Then Dennis got promoted, so he started putting in long hours and coming home pretty late. I gained weight while I was pregnant with our second child, too, and I just couldn't lose it after he was born."

"How did all this affect your sexual relationship?" I asked.

"I guess the best way to put it is that we began to feel two very different levels of need for sex," Lois said sadly, looking at the floor. "I was always tired, fighting depression, feeling like a fat, old cow. And Dennis, even with his long hours at the office, still seemed to want sex a lot—or at least a lot more than I did. For a while I tried to keep up with him, but I found I was getting angry at his attitude. I felt he was being demanding and extremely selfish about the whole thing.

"The more we fought about it, the more we distanced ourselves from each other. Even now, when we do have sex, it's not very satisfying for either one of us, but it's particularly unsatisfying for me. I'm just lying there, letting him have his fun."

Silence hung in the air for a few moments before I asked Dennis for his view of their dilemma.

"She's got it pretty straight," Dennis agreed. "I guess I sound like a big heel when I hear how she tells the story. But you know how a man gets . . . We go so long without sex, and I feel like I'm gonna burst!"

He paused, staring blankly at the far wall. "I know Lois has had some hard times, but I think she's overreacting. Take her weight, for instance. I don't think she's overweight, but she's convinced she's fat."

"Do you tell her she looks good to you?" I interrupted.

Lois was shaking her head in the background while Dennis stammered, "Well . . . I guess not as much as I could, but she knows how I feel. What's the big deal?"

"The big deal is that I feel ugly!" Lois snapped. "I don't want to make love to you if I'm feeling all gross-looking!" She was leaning forward on the front edge of the sofa now.

"You just seem to go from one crisis to another," Dennis said unsympathetically. "And it's always our sex life that has to pay the price."

His anger had taken him as far from Lois as he could get. In a matter of moments, this husband and wife who had sat down together were at the opposite ends of my couch.

Dennis and Lois were going through experiences common to a couple married eleven years. Things change. People change. Dennis and Lois had changed. The more they could understand those changes, the better their chances of improving their life together, including their sexual relationship. I used much of the material in this chapter in counseling sessions with Dennis and Lois. We spent several sessions together, and their sexual relationship started to improve before we ever talked directly about that aspect of their marriage.

Nothing in marriage is more misunderstood than the sexual union. It's more than the physical act that sexually unites a couple. And probably the most important thing Dennis and Lois learned is that a sexual relationship is a mirror of an entire marital relationship. They weren't struggling with a sexual problem as much as they were with relational issues that were diminishing their sexual enjoyment. They needed to see sex in the larger context of their whole marriage. There are actually four areas of the sexual relationship that need to be developed in concert with one another if a couple is to achieve maximum satisfaction. As Dennis and Lois concentrated on other areas of their relationship first, their sexual life improved.

Before we look at these four areas, however, a few more words are necessary about differences. Men and women tend to see sex very differently, as they do most other issues.

Male-Female Differences

In an ongoing study I've conducted with hundreds of couples over the years, I ask men and women privately and in groups how they would feel if they knew they would never again have sex with their mates. Almost all the women say, "It's really no big deal if I never have sex again with my husband." But they add quickly that it would be a big deal if they were never touched or kissed or romanced again.

When I ask men the same question, they're almost always incredulous. "Give up sex?" they say. "No way!" To ask a man to give up sex is to ask him to give up eating.

Why this huge difference between the views of men and women? It's not easy for some women to understand what testosterone does to a man. The hormone fires up a man sexually. (I know the image of the male driven by testosterone is a stereotype, but in this case it's an accurate one.) The level of testosterone drops in most men around the age of forty, but many men have been shown to have significant amounts far into their eighties!

To give wives a better idea, imagine you've just been informed by mail that you've won the grand prize in a national contest. You and your husband will be whisked off to a tropical island for ten days of first-class service at a four-star resort. You'll also be given fifteen hundred dollars a day in spending money, unlimited luxury limousine service—in other words, the works! Naturally, you can't wait for your husband to walk in the door so you can tell him the good news.

Now imagine that when he does come home, you greet him by saying you have some wonderful news. But he responds, "Not now, dear. I'm really tired, so I think I'm going to take a nap." As he walks to the bedroom, he adds, "Don't tell anyone else the news. I want to be the first to hear it."

When I ask the women in a seminar audience how they would feel in this situation, most say they would be highly frustrated.

A man's testosterone level makes him feel as if he has won the grand prize . . . almost every day! He can't wait to "tell" you about it. But a disinterested wife responds, "Let's talk about it tomorrow." Imagine the way that makes him feel. Some husbands are so highly testosterone-loaded that they're literally trembling on the other side of the bed while you're drifting off to sleep. Perhaps that will help you understand why he gets frustrated when you put off his physical advances.

Four Areas of Intimacy That Are Vital to Sexual Satisfaction

Sex is more than a physical act. Good sex is the reflection of a good relationship. It's the icing on top of what's right in a marriage. Satisfying sex is admiring a trophy fish after all the skills went into catching it. I've learned that fulfilling sex has at least four separate aspects that work together—they must work together if we are to catch the "biggest ones."

Four aspects of intercourse contribute to good sex. As Denver psychologist Gary Oliver once said to me in terms of marriage, "All of life is foreplay."

Intercourse literally means "to get to know someone intimately." In our culture, we have reduced the word to refer only to the act of sex. Conversely, we've nearly forgotten a traditional meaning of the verb *to know*—which was "to have sexual intercourse." Biblical history starts the whole human lineage with this line: "And Adam knew Eve his wife; and she conceived. . . ."[2] The two words *intercourse* and *knowledge* are closely aligned.

For now, let's return to a simpler day when the word *intercourse* had a broader meaning. A conservative, small town in the middle of Pennsylvania Amish country is named Intercourse—and it's not referring to sex.

Verbal Intercourse

In earlier times, people used the word *intercourse* when speaking of an intimate conversation. Obviously, we have to be sensitive to our current culture, so it's not advisable to have a discussion with your next-door neighbor and then yell over the fence, "It sure was good having intercourse with you earlier today!"

But verbal intercourse is vital to a healthy sex life. It involves getting to know your mate through conversation and spending time together. This is especially significant to most women, who are amazed that men can have sex at almost any time without regard to the quality of the relationship. The women usually want to connect with their partners through verbal intimacy before they can enjoy the physical act. Knowing this, years ago I decided I'd do everything right . . .

The first time Norma and I visited Hawaii, I envisioned a vacation filled with sexual passion. I knew that Norma loved to sightsee, so on one of our first days there, I invited her to drive around the island of Maui. She was thrilled.

We drove from the southern part of Maui, where our hotel was, all the way to the northern beaches. We talked, laughed, saw whales, and discovered roads and little villages that weren't even on the maps! It was a wonderful time of verbal intimacy. And as a male, I knew this might lead to some wonderful sexual intimacy later on.

As we started making our way back to our hotel, however, I discovered that the gas gauge in our rental car was on E. I did my best to keep this information from Norma, not wanting to ruin the moment or jeopardize the rest of the day!

She began to get suspicious, however, when I started coasting down as many hills as I could. "Why are you taking the car out of gear?" she asked. "Oh, no reason," I countered. "Just another way to have some fun!"

But the farther we drove with no gas station in sight, the more nervous I got. Then I suddenly felt as if we were completely out of gas. I went to put the car in neutral again, but thanks to my nervousness, I forgot that this was a rental car, an automatic, not the stick-shift I was used to. Full-force, I hit what I thought was the clutch. Unfortunately it was the brake. The car screeched to a halt in the middle of the road, throwing Norma's head right into the dashboard. (This was before the days of seat-belt laws.)

She wasn't injured, but she screamed, "Gary, what are you doing?"

I didn't have the courage to say what I was thinking, which was, *I'm ruining any chance I had for sex tonight!* Rather, I confessed the gas-tank problem, and we just sat back and laughed together. And I didn't ruin the day or night after all.

What makes a vacation like that so special? For many couples, it's the only time during the year that they carve out interrupted time to talk and listen to each other. Far away from phones, faxes, secretaries, and appointments, it's a rare opportunity for relaxation and getting reacquainted.

What's good for vacations is also good for life. As a couple, work at giving each other the time you need to relax, talk, and listen to each other. Thinking back to the opening story, Dennis and Lois discovered through counseling that they had allowed the busyness of their lives to sabotage their verbal intimacy. As a result, they made talk times a priority, and their relationship showed immediate improvement.

We already discussed communication techniques in chapter 9, but the issue is so important I'd like to summarize here some ways that busy couples can make time for verbal intercourse.

Twelve Ways to Find Time to Talk to Your Spouse

1. You're both home from work at the end of the day? Set aside a fifteen-minute period at some point to discuss—reflect on—your respective day's activities.

2. Make a rule that the TV is off during dinner, encouraging conversation. For that hour, let the answering machine take all phone calls except emergencies.

3. Write a monthly date night into your schedule that *cannot be broken*.

4. If your schedule permits, get together for lunch once a week—even if you're just brown-bagging it in the park.

5. As a couple, attend one of your children's sports games or other performances. It's amazing how conversation can develop while you sit and watch your child or on the way to and from the game.

6. Take a walk together after dinner. It's a good time to talk, and it's also good for you physically.

7. If you are allowed some flexibility in your work schedule, go in late one day—after the kids have all gone off to school. Enjoy the hour with your spouse.

8. Read a magazine article or book together that you both feel will stimulate a discussion.

9. Don't be afraid to use baby-sitters just to give you time alone to talk.

10. Write each other little notes that begin, "I have something really amazing to talk with you about the next time we're together."

11. Once or twice a year, plan a weekend getaway for just the two of you.

12. Ask your best friend to hold you accountable to meet with your mate at least once a week for a meaningful conversation.

(Remember that a certain sex killer is to combine a serious discussion about some conflictive issue while on a fun date, during an intimate talk, or just before or right after the sexual experience. Plan your conflict discussions during the week at a specific time and day and use the ideas presented in Chapter 13 to resolve your arguments.)

For more ideas, ask people whom you respect how they find the time to talk as a couple. You may be surprised at their unique suggestions.

Emotional Intercourse

Sharing deep feelings with each other is emotional intercourse, and it's vital to sexual satisfaction. It's that sense of connectedness that occurs when you're both tracking on the same emotional level. This involves conversations that deal with more than facts alone. Any conversation might start with facts. Then any fact in a relationship can be connected to emotions with the question: "How does that set of facts make you feel?" This is especially significant to women. They are often most responsive to sexual intercourse when the entire relationship is open and loving—when they feel that their husband understands and values their feelings.

Another couple, Dave and Vicki, were struggling with this issue when Dave first came to see me. "I'll shoot straight with you, Gary," he said. "I'm not getting any sex from my wife, and I'm very frustrated."

As I listened to him explain his situation, I suggested he go back to his wife and seek to communicate his feelings through the use of an emotional word picture. "The analogy will get out on the table the deep feelings you have about this issue," I told him.

So that's exactly what he did. And then she responded with a powerful word picture of her own.

"Honey, we have a problem," he told her that night. "I want you to hear how I describe it."

"All right," Vicki agreed.

"When I'm away from you at work, I feel like I'm out in the middle of the desert. It's steaming hot, and I'm slowly baking. But when I get home, I feel like I've entered an oasis."

Vicki smiled and said, "Well, that's good."

"Not really," Dave went on. "You see, when I come home, you look so good to me that I want to enjoy our relationship completely."

"Meaning what?" she asked.

"Sex," Dave answered. "We just don't have sex anymore, so I feel that instead of being in an oasis, part of the oasis is a mirage. The beauty of the oasis doesn't all seem to exist."

He sat there for a moment in silence. As tenderly as he could, he asked her, "How can I make the mirage back into the real oasis we once had?"

Vicki had been listening, and they were connecting on an emotional level. After a minute she responded, "I'll tell you how to return to the oasis. I'll even do for you what you just did for me. I'll paint an emotional word picture to make it clear.

"I feel as if I'm one of your prized rare antique books from the nineteenth century," she began. "Early in our marriage, you would pick me up and admire me, make sure I was free from dust, polish the gold-leaf edges, and just take good care of me overall."

Dave smiled at her knowingly.

"But something has happened to that rare book," she continued. "You don't care for it the way you used to. It has become dusty sitting on the shelf. The gold leaf is covered with a tarnish that could be removed if it just had a little attention. Now I'm just one of many rare books."

She was getting through to him for the first time in a long while, because he responded, "How can I give this book more of the attention it deserves?"

Vicki was able to tell him what was important to her—things like saying "I love you," and even things that Dave considered unrelated, like spending time with the kids. She also remembered fondly the days when Dave used to send her flowers and cards.

The more the two of them talked on a deep emotional level, the more they were able to help each other. This communication at the deep levels of feelings and needs changed Dave and Vicki's sexual relationship into a richer, fuller, and mutually satisfying one. It's still not perfect, but then I've never met a couple for which it was.

Physical Intercourse

Now we get to the real thing, right? Slow down. What we tend to zero in on is actually a small part of the physical relationship. When thinking of physical intercourse, think more in terms of touching, caressing, hugging, kissing, and romancing.

From my interviews and counseling with women, I've concluded that most women need eight to twelve meaningful touches a day to keep their energy level high and experience a sense of connectedness with their mate—a hug, a squeeze of the hand, a pat on the shoulder, a gentle kiss. There are approximately five million touch receptors in the human body—more than two million in the hands alone. The right kind of touch releases a pleasing and healing flow of chemicals in the bodies of both the toucher and the touched. Studies have shown that people get healthier even as a result of tender attention and touch of animals—dogs and cats. Everybody wins when we touch each other in a proper way.[3]

To emphasize just how important good touching is, let me describe some of the research that's been done with people as well as animals. In college, I studied under a professor who was an expert on the sex life of rats. A great specialty, right? But we students learned a lot from him, and in one of our experiments (which would probably not be allowed today), we would take a litter of lab rats and divide the newborns into two groups. Group A was hugged and petted regularly by the students. Group B was never touched. Otherwise, the two groups were fed and watered the same. Then, when they were still small, we put them one at a time on a platform six feet above a cement floor and pushed them off. (The more sensitive students hated this research.)

When the little rats from Group A hit the floor, they were able to get up quickly and scamper away. But Group B's rats all died. The only difference? Loving touch seemed to have made the Group A rats healthier and stronger.

A neurosurgeon friend of mine did his own study on the effects of touch. When he made his daily hospital rounds, he would stand the same distance from all his patients and spend the exact same amount of time with each of them. However, he also touched half his patients on the hand, arm, or face. The other half he didn't touch at all. That touch or lack of touch was the only variable in all the visits.

As the patients were released from the hospital, he had the nurses ask patients how often the doctor had visited them during their stay and how much time he had spent with them. The findings were amazing. Those patients who had been physically touched by the doctor perceived that he had visited them twice as often as those who had not been touched. And the "touched" group perceived the visits to have lasted twice as long as did the other group. Because of studies like this, some medical schools are now teaching the importance of touch.

At Purdue University, a study was conducted with librarians. Half were asked to touch those who came in to check out or return books or ask for information. The other half were to conduct business as usual, with no touching. And the study concluded that those who were touched had higher regard for the librarians and the books in the library, and they followed the rules more willingly.[4]

All of these studies help to make the same point: God has made each of us (even, apparently, lab rats!) to need and appreciate tender touch. And I would add that nowhere is that more important than in the marital relationship.

I know it's difficult for some couples to talk about sexual intimacies. Some marriage experts have reported that the two hardest things for couples to talk about are death and sex. On the lighter side, that explains the shyness of a young minister who always wanted to be invited to speak outside his church. His opportunity came when a women's organization in town asked him to address their luncheon. He was eager to please. "What do you want me to talk on?" he asked.

"We would like to have you talk on sex," they said, and he said okay.

He was home working on his talk when his wife came into his study. "What are you doing?" she asked.

"I've been invited to speak to a women's group," he told her.

"Oh, what are you speaking on?" she wanted to know.

He was too embarrassed to tell the truth, so he said, "Uh . . . I'm speaking on, uh, sailing. I'm going to talk to them about sailing."

She got a puzzled look on her face, but she just said, "Oh, that's good," and walked away.

The next week, after the minister had given his speech, his wife ran into one of the meeting's organizers in the grocery store. The woman came up to the wife and said, "Your husband! Wonderful speaker! He knows so much about that subject!"

"Really?" the wife said. "He's only done it twice. The first time he fell off, and the second time he got sick!"

It's not just difficult for ministers to discuss this topic; it's hard for all of us. But regardless of how tough it is to talk about sex, the whole relationship will be much better if we give each other a lot of tender physical touch throughout the day.

Spiritual Intercourse

Some people sincerely wonder about an old motto: The family that prays together, stays together. But a few years ago as I mentioned earlier, Dr. Nick Stinnett conducted a highly publicized study at the University of Nebraska. After looking carefully at hundreds of families that considered themselves healthy, his research concluded that healthy families possess six common characteristics. And one of those characteristics is "a shared personal faith in God."[5] And surveys taken by sociologist Andrew Greeley indicate that "frequent sex coupled with frequent prayer make for the most satisfying marriages."[6]

Spiritual intercourse may be the highest level of intimacy. A husband and wife can know each other as they both turn to and know God—heart to heart. Scripture writers repeatedly used a marriage metaphor to refer to the relationship God wants to have with those who turn to him. And the Spirit of God has an otherworldly ability to draw two people into harmony, being "one" in spirit.

Consider this saying: "A cord of three strands is not quickly broken."[7] Some writers have seen that truth as a picture of marriage: Man-woman-God bound together in a strong union.

A man and wife can grow spiritually intimate as they pray together, worship God together, attend study groups or retreats together, or simply discuss spiritual lessons and insights. Spiritual intercourse involves knowing one another in the context of a shared faith. And through that faith a couple sees value and meaning to things that would otherwise be meaningless.

Dennis and Lois, our case study at the beginning of this chapter, had always been of the opinion that people—even married couples—shouldn't discuss religion or politics. But after they learned about spiritual intercourse, they had one of their liveliest conversations ever. Then they visited local churches, finally finding one where they felt comfortable. This was a whole new arena for them but a vital link to their marital health and happiness—their union.

In a chapter titled "Praying Together: Guardian of Intimacy," in their book *If Two Shall Agree: Praying Together As a Couple,* Carey and Pam Rosewell Moore quote one couple's strong statement:

> The most important goal of prayer together is that it keeps our relationship as a couple intimate and close, and it keeps our hearts open before the Lord as a couple. There is a lot of unspoken accountability in our walk with the Lord and with each other.[8]

The Moores go on to say,

> Daily prayer can serve as the guardian of the marriage, for the husband and wife who pray together do not pray alone. God Himself is present. . . . He will . . . encourage the formation of an ever-closer bond and He will lend His strength to that bond.[9]

Getting to Know You

Dennis and Lois continued to go through a rigorous examination of their married life to improve each of the four areas of intercourse. As previously mentioned, Dennis had allowed himself to become too busy to talk with and listen to Lois. Purposely cutting back his work schedule was not easy for such a career-minded man, yet he was willing to pay that price, and his decision provided the two of them with some much-needed sharing times.

Through those discussions, they both came to understand the deep hurts they had inflicted on each other unintentionally. Lois was extremely sensitive about her weight, a pain Dennis had virtually ignored. Once he realized the extent of her pain, he was much more supportive. He made a point, for example, of telling her how much he loved her and how very attractive he still found her. Lois, for her part, better understood Dennis's feelings of rejection because of their sporadic sex life, and she made an effort to be more available to him. All these hurts took some time to heal, but it happened.

One problem was Lois felt that Dennis touched her only when he was trying to initiate sex. Dennis admitted that to be true. So I gave them some assignments to touch each other but not allow it to end in consummation. This was particularly helpful to them as they learned to support each other emotionally and express affection.

The blending of these four aspects of intercourse provides the complete context for a healthier sexual relationship. They're like the four sides of a building . . . all are essential for a sound and lasting structure.

Improving Sexual Intimacy

Once you're establishing the verbal, emotional, physical, and spiritual connections, you can follow some additional steps to improve the sexual dimension of your marriage. First I'll give five general suggestions that either a wife or a husband can try to enhance the physical act of sex. Then I'll offer some suggestions that are specific to each of the partners.

Both Partners
Take the initiative sexually. This is generally appreciated by your partner, especially if it's not your usual mode of operation. The change of pace will energize your experience.

Take care with your appearance. Your spouse will value the effort you make to look attractive. I'll say more about this in the specific advice below.

Take more time to enjoy the sexual experience. Routinized sex—relegated to ten minutes after the TV late news on Saturday night—is the kiss of death to a vibrant sex life. Don't be in a hurry. Think in terms of the four areas of intercourse we've discussed, and then take an unhurried walk through all of them. It can make a sexual evening very special.

Pay attention to the atmosphere in which you'll make love. Beyond candlelight, soft music, and a fire's glow (which are all great ideas), don't overlook some basics like a locked door. Visitors aren't welcome, even if they're members of the family. This is a time for husband and wife, and no unpleasant surprises are appreciated.

Express your desire. Many couples feel that the sexual act expresses how much they are attracted to each other, and they use sex in place of verbalizing the desire to be together. But words such as "I love you," "I need you," "I'm crazy about you," "You look great," and "I'd marry you all over again" have an encouraging and stimulating power all their own. So tell your mate often how much you enjoy being with him or her.

For Men

What would your wife say if she were asked how you could improve your sex life? My research shows that women often answer along these lines:

Be romantic. Women love to feel connection with their spouses, and nothing accomplishes this better than romance. By becoming a student of your wife, you can learn the best way to produce romantic feelings within her. For some it is flowers, cards, or a small gift. For others, it's sharing in work around the house and lightening her load. Still others look to a night out on the town, a concert, or dinner in a nice restaurant.

Men can be a little rougher than their spouses in sex. But women love tenderness in a man. They always have, too—this is not just some "sensitive nineties man" fad. Women respond to romance, and most desire more of it.

Take time with foreplay. You cannot lose by spending extra time touching, hugging, and cuddling your wife. These acts are like giving her an injection of pure energy. Ask your wife where and how she likes to be touched, and be responsive to her needs. Conversely, if something you desire makes her uncomfortable, respect her wishes.

Remember also to freely touch your wife with caresses that won't necessarily lead to sex. Praise her, tell her how desirable she is, and give her spontaneous hugs.

Make yourself sexy. Stan is a typical guy. He loves his wife, Andrea, and is always ready to make love at a moment's notice. Andrea is consistently amazed by this attribute. She was recently surprised when he came in the back door after gardening in the muddy dirt for four hours. Sweaty, dirty, smelly, and unkempt as he was, when he saw her bending over in the kitchen, he let out a low wolf whistle and offered her an invitation for some immediate fun.

Andrea, like most women, finds her husband attractive, but that isn't always enough. Did he really expect her to be interested in a sexual encounter after he had just finished four hours in the mud? No way!

At first Stan was hurt by her cool response. He prided himself on keeping in shape and looking good. So Andrea had to explain that she wasn't rejecting him. She just felt more inclined toward making love if there was "a total package," as she put it. That included a clean and scrubbed, freshly shaven ("I hate stubble," she says), cologne-wearing Stan; clean sheets on the bed; soft light; and a classical CD playing softly in the background.

Andrea's reaction had nothing to do with Stan's fear that he was overweight or soft in areas that were once muscular. It was more about *atmosphere*. Stan needed to listen carefully so he could learn how to provide her idea of the perfect evening. It's only fair that he learn from her, because, another time, he'll want her to try his idea of romance (in some room other than the bedroom when the kids are away at their grandparents' house).

For Women

Many wives wish they could find the key to unlock the sexual aspect of their husband's life. So here are some ideas specifically for women.

Understand his tremendous sexual needs. As discussed earlier, the two of you probably view sex from different perspectives. More than likely, he desires sex more often than you.

With that insight, there may be occasions when you're willing to have sex even if all four areas of intimacy are not in place for you. This should only be once in a while, however, not a regular pattern. He needs to be sensitive to your needs just as you're sensitive to his. For example, if your hormones make you wish your husband were in Siberia for several days a month, he needs to understand that and be patient.

If your husband ever struggles with impotence, which is most commonly caused by performance anxiety, refer to the book *Intended for Pleasure* by Ed and Gaye Wheat. It's not uncommon for older men to need stimulation from you to be aroused. Here in the nineties, there are a number of excellent books on the subject of "good sex."[10]

Find out what he really enjoys. A man is thrilled when his wife asks him what he likes in regard to sex and then gives it a try. This does not mean you have to violate your inner convictions or participate in a sexual activity you find offensive. But there may be many things your husband thinks of in his fantasy life that you could fulfill for him and enjoy yourself.

The sexual relationship is a place where creativity should shine. Sex was never meant to be dull, boring, or routine. Take the initiative to instigate some variety in your sex life. Few men will respond, "No, this isn't what I want. Let's go back to doing it exactly the same as we have for the last twenty years."

Make yourself sexy. Having read my account of Stan and Andrea, a woman could conclude that nothing is necessary on her part to keep the sexual fires alive. But the reality is that a balance needs to be achieved. Just as a woman appreciates the "total package" from her husband, so a man is entitled to the same consideration from his wife.

You'll want to have those magical occasions when you take a leisurely bath, slide into something sexy, spray a little perfume around, dim the lights, and turn on the station that plays the late-night love songs. Your husband will enjoy that atmosphere just like you do. It's another way to contribute to the variety that's so helpful to a healthy sexual relationship.

Juicy Fruit

Fortunately, Dennis and Lois were able to bring back some of the passion in their marriage. But it wasn't easy or quick.

Many couples have a hard time discussing sexual matters with each other, so the thought of raising the issues with a third-party counselor is even more stressful. But many qualified counselors can provide confidential assistance in improving this area of your relationship. Add to that the plethora of good books, tapes, and study courses available, and it's exciting to see that so much help is accessible to you and your mate.

"I'll admit," Dennis told me much later in our counseling, "I was angry and embarrassed that our sex life had deteriorated to the point that we had to enlist the help of a counselor. That can be a bitter pill for any person to swallow—especially a man. But it really was one of the smartest moves I ever made. There was so much about Lois that I didn't understand, along with a bunch of stuff I never even knew about her. These discoveries wouldn't have occurred without our reaching out for help."

As Lois summarized in one of our final sessions, "I now see the importance of putting sex in its complete context. Now Dennis and I think, feel, talk, and connect with each other. We're enjoying the fruit of a healthy relationship."

That was a good choice of words on her part, because a couple's sex life can be compared to an apple tree. If we nurture the tree and keep it healthy, we're going to have fruit on it. But if we neglect it and don't nurture it, it's not likely to bear much fruit. If we get impatient for fruit in the springtime, remembering the delicious taste of apples and complaining that we haven't had fruit lately, we might start picking the blossoms off. But they don't taste like fruit, and once you pick them off, you'll never get apples.

A healthy tree needs water, sunlight, air, and fertilized soil—it takes all four ingredients. Likewise, when we nurture a marriage verbally, emotionally, physically, and spiritually, we can watch the love and intimacy and knowledge grow. And as they develop, the marital tree will provide a steady supply of fruit. Then any time we want, basically, we can pick off the fruit and eat it, and it's delicious! Why? Because we've nurtured the sex tree—the relationship. Then we can have cinnamon apple butter from time to time; French apple pie; apple dumplings with caramel sauce; and apple cobbler with ice cream. But we can't have any of those goodies unless we first have the apples.

Don't settle for anything but the best. Don't let your sexual relationship deteriorate into just the physical act. Enrich your life together in all four areas of intimacy and watch your sexual love relationship become forever-alive.

Every engaged couple I've ever talked with has an excited anticipation about married life. They look forward to being together, sharing every aspect of life together—talking, sleeping, hugging, and sexual intimacy. But every married couple knows how reality can change one's hopes and dreams.

The purpose of the next chapter is to help you keep your dreams alive—pulling the threads of the second part of this book into a method that can divorce-proof your marriage.

Forever-Love Principles

Our list of forever-love principles continues from the previous chapter:

110. Forever-love knows that good sex is a reflection of a good relationship.

111. Forever-love makes—even schedules—time for talk. "Tell me about your world. I'll tell you about mine."

112. Forever-love freely expresses feelings in mutual, nonthreatened self-disclosure.

113. Forever-love is renewed and energized by tender touch.

114. Forever-love is bonded by a shared personal faith in God.

115. Forever-love "goes for connection" on four levels: verbal, emotional, physical, and spiritual.

116. Forever-love remembers to romance.

117. Forever-love takes time for play. Foreplay.

118. Forever-love sex thrives on variety within monogamy.

15

Divorce-Proofing Your Marriage

Cast your bread upon the waters,
for after many days you will find it again.
—Ecclesiastes 11:1

I've learned a practical, simple principle that can work wonders in reviving love and keeping a couple together happily. In some ways it underlines most of the principles we've already discussed at length. It's a good method to use—or a mind-set to have—all the time. And it can produce immediate results when a marriage is in crisis.

A story from the early years of my own marriage will introduce the images I use to describe this great tool:

When Norma and I were first married, I was not very responsible financially. Growing up, I had never learned how or even that it mattered. I didn't know anything about keeping a checkbook register or spending wisely. Norma, on the other hand, was a detail-oriented person who worked in a bank. So it was obvious that she should keep the family books and pay the bills, which she was happy to do.

But problems arose right at the start and lasted five years. Each of us had a checkbook and wrote checks on one joint account. (Can you see the conflict brewing?)

I had my own system: I wrote checks as long as I had them in my book—until I ran out of checks; I hoped—or assumed—there was enough in the bank to cover them.

But too often Norma would confront me: "We're overdrawn again."
"We can't be," I'd answer with a grin. "I still have checks in my book.
It's impossible."

Sometimes she would be in tears. "I can't keep track of this. It's driving
me crazy."

We also had a secondary conflict. We disagreed about when to pay bills.
Norma preferred to pay them as soon as they came. But I wanted to hold on
to our money as long as possible, paying our bills at the end of the month,
just before payday. I liked the idea of having money, because you never
know when an emergency might come up. With my check-writing habits,
however, there wasn't always enough left at the end of the month to pay all
the bills, let alone saving for emergencies.

"We have two late notices on this one bill," Norma would say, exas-
perated.

"Don't worry about it," I'd respond, which was not what she wanted to
hear. My philosophy was that you don't have to do anything until you get
the fourth or fifth notice. You just keep shuffling late notices to the bottom
of the pile until they appear at the top again and can't be ignored any longer.

Then the day came when Norma had taken all she could. She tearfully
approached me once more and laid all the bills, her checkbook, and the
budget in my lap. "I've had it!" she declared. "I can't take it anymore. From
now on, this area is all yours. It's up to you whether we sink or swim." Years
later, she admitted her despair that day: She figured she was really giving
away our home, our car, and the rest of our financial life, because there was
no way I would be able to handle it properly.

Fortunately, with the pressure on, I decided to learn how to be
responsible. I got some help, grew to respect a budget, and worked my
way out of the mess I had created. For the next fifteen years, I kept the
books and paid the bills. And as I started to do all this, I learned a crucial but simple principle: You've got to have more money in the bank
than you spend every month. Income has to exceed outgo. That's about
as basic as family finance gets.

Now let me make the application to how you can divorce-proof your
marriage. The principle is simple, yet the impact is powerful. My hope is
that this idea will become a part of your life, just like pearl-counting and the
other principles I've learned to live by and have presented in this book. The
principle is this: To divorce-proof your marriage, make sure you are making
more "deposits" to your spouse than "withdrawals."

Basics of Marital Banking

Before we discuss what I call marital banking, we need to define a few terms.

A *deposit* is anything positive, security-producing—anything that gives your mate energy. It's a gentle touch, a listening ear, a verbalized "I love you," a fun, shared experience; the list could go on and on. Temperament, gender, and birth order influence one's personal definition of a deposit. Going for long walks in the woods with a spouse may energize an introvert in the same way a houseful of holiday company (entertaining) energizes an extrovert.

A withdrawal is anything sad or negative—anything that drains energy from your mate. It's a harsh word, an unkempt promise, being ignored, being hurt, being controlled; the list could be long. Some withdrawals differ from temperament to temperament; something perceived as a withdrawal for one person might be a deposit for another person. But too much control or being absent too much, physically or emotionally, are always major withdrawals, and as I mentioned in chapter 8, these are the two biggest factors in unhealthy relationships.

The more you keep a positive balance in your relationship account, with "giving" deposits exceeding "draining" withdrawals, the more secure that relationship will be. There's something very basic about the saying, "If you're happy, I'm happy." *If you're energized, I'm energized.* Enthusiasm—for life, for romance, for "us"—is contagious.

And if your marriage is in rough shape because you've been making a lot more withdrawals than deposits, beginning now with a concerted effort to make deposits can help you turn things around faster than anything else I've seen. By the way, once again, this will work in any relationship—with your friends, your children, your parents, and your coworkers, as well as with your mate.

I've been promoting this idea of marital "banking" for years, and I'm glad to see other authors offering variations on this same idea.[1]

Now let's look in more detail at how this principle works.

Your Personal Banking History

You and your spouse both have a personal-relationship banking history. As in real banking, your current account balance is the direct influence of past deposits and withdrawals.

The first step in making personal-banking principles work for—not against—your marriage is for you to record and learn to understand your own personal-relationship banking history. Start by thinking through and writing down various withdrawals and deposits you remember from your younger years.

What Are Withdrawals to You?

In one of the TV commercials for my video series, you may have seen a couple, Kevin and Julie. They tell just a little of their story there in the commercial. I'd like to tell you the rest of it here, because Kevin's experience illustrates the impact of childhood events.

Once married, Kevin made all kinds of withdrawals from Julie. For years he was controlling, harsh, critical, arrogant, angry, and abusive. That's when he was home. (He frequently wasn't.) Finally, Julie thought she couldn't take it anymore and got a court order to keep him away. She also had the locks changed on the house. When he arrived home that night and couldn't get in, he was, well, upset.

Kevin went home with a friend who had some of my marriage-help videos. A sobered Kevin watched a few, including the one about marital banking. Acting on the advice to record the withdrawals made in childhood, he started writing phrases—actions, words, and attitudes—that had caused him pain or drained him of energy as a young boy and teen.

When the withdrawals were on paper for him to contemplate, he saw that the withdrawals made from him looked amazingly like the actions, words, and attitudes that Julie complained about. He was passing on to others the abuses that had been done to him,. He determined that he was going to do his best to stop the negative withdrawals and replace them with deposits. (More about that in a minute.)

In my own life, a big withdrawal drained me any time someone—usually my father, later a boss—would exert excess control over me. I mentioned this earlier: I vividly recall my father and I going fishing together. If I started catching fish in one particular place, he would come over, literally shove me out of the way, and say, "Fish somewhere else."

Sadly but not surprisingly, that withdrawal from me became a pattern for how I related to others. In time I became a controlling person with my wife, and I also got in the habit of making the exact same withdrawals from my kids. This was very evident one day when we were fishing in a Colorado stream—and I was reeling them in. When all three of my kids approached with their fishing poles, I said, "No, no!"

Greg knew what I was thinking. Finally he screamed, "Dad, we are not trying to fish here! Kari broke her leg!"

With that news, for a brief second I thought, *Ohhh, I'm going to have to leave this great fishing place!* I handed Greg my pole and said, "You fish here for a while so I don't miss anything." Then I took care of Kari. Even when we're aware of the reality—the record—of our childhood withdrawals, we can still not really understand how influential they are in terms of our current practice.

So jot down some of the withdrawals drained from your emotional-relational account as you were growing up. This exercise can be useful to you in two ways:

1. It can help you, as it did Kevin, identify potential ways you are making withdrawals from your spouse's account. If a parent drained energy from you by doing x, y, and z, are you similarly draining energy from your spouse?

2. It can help you as you think through some of the things that are relational withdrawals from you today. What does your mate do that drains energy from you? Are some of these withdrawals directly connected to—triggered by—things that happened in your childhood?

As opportunities arise, share your childhood and current relational withdrawals with your mate (using "I feel" statements or word pictures, not accusations).

What Are Deposits for You?

What energized you as a child? As a young adult? While withdrawals frequently are caused by elements beyond our control (an emotionally healthy person doesn't seek out draining withdrawals), deposits tend to be things we initiate or search out. And while withdrawals are often seen as being "done to" us, relational deposits are often things "done with" or "done for" us.

As for deposits in my own background, one of the biggest was singing with other people. Starting when I was in third grade, my sister taught me every popular song of the day, and I would harmonize with her. I got so much energy from that! Then I started singing with three or four friends. Rather than dating a lot as teens, we would go for long drives, singing on wheels. I enjoy close harmony so much that sometimes I wonder if I should have been a singer instead of a speaker! (Then I listen to myself sing in the shower, and I know why I'm only *speaking* in public.)

Think through your own childhood and up through the early years of your marriage. Then write down what some of the major relational deposits have been. Again, this exercise can be useful to you as you consider how you tend to make deposits to your spouse's account. Do you "make deposits" that are more suitable to your own needs than to your spouse's? It can also help you as you think through your current-day relational deposits. What does your mate do that energizes you? Are some of these deposits directly connected to things that happened in your childhood?

As opportunity arises, discuss your deposit history and current balance with your mate.

Banking with Your Spouse

The second step in using this principle involves discovering what constitutes a deposit or a withdrawal for your mate.

What Are Withdrawals for Your Mate?

As you might guess from my descriptions of the first years of our marriage . . . when I eventually asked Norma to look back and reflect on those days, she was hard-pressed to think of deposits I had made. Unfortunately she had no problem remembering plenty of withdrawals. She may have been charmed with me in our courting days, but living with me was no energizing venture.

For example, because I was so much into control, her stomach would turn every time I called a family meeting. She would say with her eyes and sometimes with her words, "I hate your meetings." For the longest time, I never understood why. Then I came to learn that too much control or too much distance in relationships drains people of their energy.

Another big withdrawal for her has to do with my driving habits. She's helped me understand the seed of this negative reaction to what I perceive as perfectly passable driving skills. When Norma was in high school, she was in a major car crash with some friends. The car went over a cliff, and two of her friends were killed. Norma suffered a broken neck and was in a cast for a long time. It's perfectly reasonable that she has a healthy fear of a car going out of control. If I'm driving and get distracted and veer a bit too much toward the edge of the road, she'll say, "Oohh, you're over too far." That's a withdrawal. And if I make light of her concern and tension, that's a serious withdrawal. On the other hand, if I make a point of driving carefully, that's a big deposit.

My snoring is another major withdrawal for Norma—keeping her from getting sleep and draining energy from her. This withdrawal doesn't fit the pattern I've previously presented—where something in childhood affects the present. Nor does it involve something I "do to" Norma. But it is something I do—or utter—that affects her negatively. And it is something one can make efforts to stop.

Of course she had to convince me of the reality of this annoying pattern. She once recorded the sounds and played the tape back to me so I couldn't claim my "innocence." Can you imagine sleeping next to a rumbling diesel engine all those years? I've been kicked and told to roll over on my side many times, but nothing has worked so far. I've looked into new approaches to knocking out the noise. And I've just been fitted for a breathing device that completely stops my snoring, and, by the way, I have twice the energy each day.[2]

Think back over your experience with your mate. Write down actions, attitudes, or words (or noises!) you are sure she or he perceives to be withdrawals. But then—to increase the intimacy of your conversation and to confirm your assumptions—ask your spouse whether your memories and perceptions are accurate.

When couples attending my seminars talk to each other about this, common withdrawals for women include "being treated like I don't exist"; "he's never on time," and "he travels too much in his job." Common withdrawals for husbands include "she's always on my case" and "she doesn't initiate sex."

What can you do to reduce the number of withdrawals you make to your spouse's account?

What Makes a Deposit to Your Mate?

Previously I noted that making a deposit in someone's account often involves doing something "with" or "for" someone. I've learned that for Norma, a huge deposit has to do with shopping—especially Christmas shopping. She likes to start shopping for presents in January. Now, I'm not big on shopping in the first place, and I hate to buy a present and then hide it somewhere; I want to give it to the person right away. So for the first several years of our marriage, I frustrated Norma and made big withdrawals by waiting until December 24 to do my shopping.

As we talked and I learned in this area, I came to understand that I could turn things around and make huge deposits just by changing my attitude toward shopping. So now, even though I still don't care to shop by myself, I make an effort to be enthusiastic when I'm doing it with her, whether she's buying presents or looking for a dress for herself. I try not to be like the guy who found out his wife's credit cards had been stolen, yet a year later he still hadn't reported it because the thief spent less than his wife had!

Now, for me, fishing is my shopping. If she suggests taking a picnic on the boat, I know she's saying, "I love you." She doesn't actually go fishing with me. She would rather bring a book along and read. That's okay—I just like to be with her on or near the water.

In chapter 13, on conflicts, I suggested a couple have a love language—actions you both know the secret meaning of: *I love you.* That love language is closely connected with this idea of marital banking. The energizing love language is based on an alphabet of deposits.

Today, Norma and I are best friends. We love finding out new things that make deposits into our accounts with each other. We go out of our way to make sure we're making more deposits than withdrawals.

When I ask seminar attendees for things they consider to be deposits, common responses include "him chatting with me when he gets home from work," "daily verbal expressions of love," "it's a big deposit when she initiates sex," and "I love it when he plays with our kids." That last one is a prime example of something a man might never identify as a deposit unless he asks for feedback. My wife, too, has told me that it's a big deposit for her when I praise and encourage our kids—and especially the grandkids.

Dr. John Gottman has actually figured out through his research the ratio of deposits vs. withdrawals for long-lasting, loving marriages: It's an average of *five positive deposits* for *each negative withdrawal*. In other words, at the end of a week, month, or year, the deposits should outweigh the withdrawals five to one.

Don't Rely on Guess Work

What's the best way to find out what your spouse "receives" as a withdrawal or deposit? Ask! If you're both familiar with this concept, you might say straight out as you do something with honoring intent: "I'm hoping this is a deposit with you. Does it work?" The response you get will tell you if you missed the mark or hit the bullseye.

I've touched on this before, but it bears repeating: In the best of marriages, one spouse may think he or she is making a deposit, but it turns into a big withdrawal. Considering this problem on the lighter side, perhaps you've heard of the couple who decided that a big deposit for them would be learning how to do something together—like duck-hunting. They asked an expert what equipment of "outfit" they needed. He answered, "Well, if you're going to be successful, you've got to have a really good hunting dog."

So they bought a champion dog and then set out on their first hunting expedition. They started before sunrise and stayed with it all day, into the evening, but with no ducks to show for all their time and effort. Finally, exhausted, the man said to his wife, "I don't know. Maybe we're doing it wrong. I think we're not throwing this dog high enough into the air."

Have you tried to make a deposit and it turned out somewhat like the "duck hunt"? You felt as if your "check" bounced?

What really matters to most spouses is that the mate tried to do the right thing. But if you find that your mate is reacting negatively to your well-intentioned deposit attempts, I suggest you allow some time to pass and feelings to cool. Then, by explaining the situation, you can redeposit the "check" in a different way.

Norma has another need that I've had a hard time understanding over the years, and we've been using drive-through talking to help me get it straight. I finally came to realize that she wanted my praise for the great job she does as the manager of our business. But what she had said initially was, "Would you ask me things like, 'Could I do something for you today to help with your job?'"

Now, I wasn't going to ask that kind of question very often, naturally. I've got enough stuff to do of my own. And at first I didn't understand how her question related to her need for praise, either. So I asked, "What exactly are you saying?"

"I don't actually want you to do parts of my job for me," she said. (I wouldn't know how to do them anyway, and I could foul things up in a hurry.) "I want you to notice what I do and praise me for it. And when you ask, 'Is there anything I can do to help?' it gives us an opportunity to talk about what I do." That recognition is a big need to her. But the way she expressed her need needed to be clarified before I could "get it."

When it comes to deposits and withdrawals, *don't guess. Express.* I trust that by talking with your spouse, you'll find out what causes withdrawals and do those things less often. You'll also find out what makes deposits and do those things more often. You'll both be energized in the process.

Thank-You! Thank-You!

Ask your mate to praise you when you intentionally or unintentionally make a deposit into his or her relational account. This will reinforce your positive behavior. Who doesn't thrive on praise? That recognition will energize you, so your energy as a couple spirals upward. A deposit and then a thank-you in return earns a couple *mucho* interest. Let's call it a joint high-interest savings account.

Of course this works two ways. Praise your spouse for deposits—and everybody wins double interest.

Deposits Have the Power to Save a Marriage

Let me give you an update on Kevin and Julie's marriage: Kevin took this marital banking principle very seriously. With his new understanding, he worked hard to reduce his withdrawals from and increase his deposits to Julie's account. Gradually, this tremendous, sustained change in Kevin got through to Julie.

She later told me, "I could tell he wasn't really excited about saying 'I love you,' listening to me, and touching me gently. I could see he was forcing it. As he would listen to something I was saying, he would quickly get preoccupied, but he was trying. When I saw his effort right in front of me, it was a major deposit, and he warmed my heart. That's why it was so easy to say, 'Let's keep going. I think we can make it together.'"

They did keep going, and Kevin did keep trying. If you saw them today, you'd be impressed with how sensitive he is and how responsive she is, and you'd never guess they had been on the brink of divorce just a few years ago.

This simple banking principle can save a marriage—even return that marriage to days of joy.

I once got a call from an irate husband. His wife was divorcing him, and he growled out, "I can't believe it! How can she do this after twenty-five years? I haven't been that bad!"

As I talked further with him and then with his wife, I found that he was a very controlling, belligerent person. Even in talking with me, he exhibited these characteristics. At one point in a phone conversation, as I've done several times now, I interrupted him to say, "I hate to tell you this, but if I were your wife, I don't think I could stay with you either!"

I learned that the wife didn't have any other man in her life, and she actually wanted to get back together with her husband—if only he could understand what he had done to drive her away; if only she could see evidence of change in him. She just couldn't live with him anymore the way he was. Her attitude gave me hope that things could eventually be worked out.

The wife pleaded with me to help them, but she was too fearful to stop the divorce proceedings. I had a gut feeling that there could be a good outcome to this one. Deep down, both wanted reconciliation. This was the best scenario for reuniting a couple. And the husband was motivated. "I don't want a divorce," the husband told me. "Tell me what I need to do."

As I said, there seemed no stopping the divorce, but I could see hope for eventual reconciliation. "There's really nothing you can do to stop the divorce," I told him. "Your wife has a lawyer, and the court date is set. But I'll go with you and support you through the whole process." And I assured him I'd work with him to do what we could to renew the relationship.

We went to the courthouse on the appointed day, and I waited on a bench outside the hearing room. After a while he came flying, furious, out of the settlement room. "That's it!" he shouted. "She wants too much from me, and I won't do it!" He was as angry and controlling as he had ever been.

I admit I got a little upset myself—at him. "What?" I said. "We're talking about trying to get the two of you back together. Give her more than she asked for. Do it! Just remember you're going to get back together, so what difference does it make?"

He thought about that for a minute, and then he went back in and gave her much more than she had requested, which did confuse her. Unfortunately, at that point the divorce went through.

The good news, however, is that his wife agreed to see him—with some small hope that things might still work out. So I started teaching him how to treat her—how to make more deposits than withdrawals. "What does she really like?" I asked.

"She loves for me to be tender and listen to her," he said.

"You can practice doing that," I said. And so we worked on it, and he applied it on their "dates."

This went on for about six months after the divorce. He would do well for a while, making a lot of deposits. Then he would get upset about something and blow his stack, making massive withdrawals. Along the way, he gave me regular reports on how things were going.

At the end of that period, he called one day and said, "Well, I totally blew it last night. I withdrew everything I've deposited since the divorce. It's ridiculous. She'll never want to remarry me now. I'll be surprised if she even wants to talk to me again."

He went on to give me the details of what had happened, and finally I said, "Look, just keep at it. Don't give up. When you see her tomorrow, open up. Admit you were wrong and that you wish you could get all this stuff down quicker. Then you might tell her something like you're sorry she has to go through your stumbling times. Tell her you understand what you did, and explain it to her so she can see you're becoming more sensitive and aware of your behavior."

"All right," he said with resignation. "It's just so humiliating to admit what a jerk I am almost every other day."

"Hey, I have to do it!" I said with a smile in my voice. "If I have to do it, you can. We're in this together. Okay?"

The next day, after meeting with his ex-wife, he called me. "Guess what?" he said. "I went over, admitted I was wrong, and asked if she would forgive me again. I knew she never would, but she did. And then—would you believe it?—she touched me and asked, 'What are you doing this afternoon?'

"'Nothing,' I said.

"And she said, 'How would you like to go back to the same judge who presided over our divorce and ask if he would marry us?'

"'Are you serious?' I asked.

"She said, 'Yes, I think it's time. Don't you?'

"I shouted yes and threw my arms around her."

They did remarry shortly after that, and had twelve more years together—happy years. He had retired and had a lot of time available to make up for the former hurt. In their last two years together, she developed a serious illness. He lovingly cared for her before she passed away. He told me later that she was so tender during their twelve-year "second marriage" that it was worth twice what the first twenty-five years had been. He went on to say, "Those were the greatest years of my life. I can't even imagine being happier. I've lost a great friend, but what treasured memories I'll always have!"

What did he do in those six months of courtship? Deposits, deposits, deposits! And what did he do in those last twelve wonderful years? Deposits and more deposits. Of course he also made some withdrawals, but he would admit them and ask for her forgiveness right away. As a result, they had an incredible marriage, even through days of pain.

What's Your Balance?

What does your marital bank account look like? If you were to ask your spouse today, "What's my balance?" what would the response be?

Whatever the answer, you can start improving your balance instantly by making deposits and by practicing self-restraint—refraining from making costly withdrawals. Do this regularly for a month or two. Then ask the question again. And watch your balance soar.

Another ancient saying summarizes the principle of relational banking: "Cast your bread upon the waters, for after many days you will find it again."[3] Give love and you will receive love back. This concept gives new meaning to the phrase "no deposit, no return." If you make no deposit, you'll get no return. Make deposits and you not only energize your spouse, you energize your marriage and your own life.

Think of this as responsible relationship banking. Practice it and reap the bountiful rewards: the pleasure of seeing your love grow stronger with every passing year—as you and your spouse walk together into the forever.

The type of love that makes the greatest deposits and lasts the longest is featured in the final chapter. We want love to last, but I've found only one kind that can't fail!

Forever-Love Principles

Our list of forever-love principles continues from the previous chapter:

119. Forever-love "deposits" more than it "withdraws."

120. Forever-love seeks to understand its own personal history. "In the past, what actions have consistently drained energy from me?"

121. Forever-love seeks to understand its own personal history and use that insight to energize the marriage.

122. Forever-love asks for feedback. "What energizes or drains energy from you?"

123. Forever-love goes for clarity. Don't guess. Express.

124. Forever-love says, "Thanks. I needed that."

125. Forever-love is energized as one person takes a step to renew the other and the relationship.

16

A Love That Lasts Forever

Greater love has no one than this, that he lay down his life for his friends.
—John 15:13

For years I've been urging the thousands of people who read my books, watch my videos, and attend my seminars to see how much we need to help each other develop the "greatest" love. I call it heroic love—a love that sacrifices itself for the enrichment of the other, that doesn't seek its own good but chooses to satisfy the desires of the beloved.

But don't get the impression that heroic love is all self-sacrifice. From looking at my own marriage and hundreds of others, I've come to understand that enriching the life of another is often more satisfying than doing something for ourselves. As we reach out to another, our own needs for fulfillment and love are met.

I've seen that the most satisfied, joyous couples are those that have learned heroic love and practice it daily. When a husband and wife both want their partner to receive life's best before they do, you have a marriage that's going to exceed every wedding-day dream. Their love not only lasts; it continually grows.

That's the kind of relationship Charlie and Lucy Wedemeyer enjoy. If our world could raise its vision of love to the level of this couple . . . I can hardly imagine what it would be like to live on this planet.

More than fifteen years ago, doctors diagnosed thirty-year-old Charlie Wedemeyer as having progressively debilitating and paralyzing ALS—

commonly called Lou Gehrig's disease. They gave the California high-school football coach one year to live. But Charlie proved them wrong. Despite the relentless, progressive nature of his illness, he continued coaching for seven more years.

When Charlie could no longer walk, Lucy drove him up and down the sidelines in a golf cart. When he could no longer talk, she read his lips and relayed his instructions to the players. And in his dramatic last season as a coach, after he had gone on twenty-four-hour-a-day life support, his team won a state championship!

Lucy Wedemeyer is a heroic lover. She says that from the very beginning of Charlie's illness, they've focused on what they have together rather than on what they're missing. She admits it hasn't been easy, but she says in her book,

> I think we communicate and understand each other better today than we ever did. While I've learned to read Charlie's lips, I find I often don't have to. His eyes almost always tell me exactly how he feels, and his eyebrows punctuate those feelings as they bounce up and down or I watch his forehead furrow into a wrinkle. And if you don't think someone in difficult circumstances can find happiness and contentment, if you doubt the contagious quality of joy, well, you've never seen Charlie smile.[1]

When the ALS struck, the Wedemeyers had two young children and mountains of dreams they would never realize. One week after they were told of his impending death, while watching snow drift by the window of a borrowed mountain cabin, Lucy looked into Charlie's eyes and recognized the same raw emotions she felt churning inside herself. She had never felt more love for Charlie, or more loved by him, than she did that special evening. And yet, she says,

> I'd never in my life felt such pain. Such anguish. Tears filled our eyes. Neither of us dared speak for fear the floodgates would open. So we just sat silently, holding hands across the table, basking in the bittersweet warmth of that moment, wishing the romantic spell could somehow make time stand still. All the while wondering how much time we had left together.[2]

When I first met the Wedemeyers at one of my seminars, I couldn't help but see the radiant joy on Lucy's face and the contentment in Charlie's eyes.

They're the type of heroes I would love to be like someday. No matter what I go through with Norma, we both hope to have people look into our eyes and see a similar enduring fire of love—for life and for each other.

Lucy prays daily for continued strength, because Charlie needs constant care. Some realities of her life are harsh and ever-present, and still she says, "I wouldn't trade my life for anyone else's. It's been so rewarding."[3] How can she mean that? That's the beauty of heroic love. It can move mountains, cross rivers, and overcome any obstacle and for the joy set before it. No one's life is laughing-happy every day, but people like Lucy have such a deep sense of satisfaction and love that, no matter what occurs, they rest on an underlying assurance that everything is still okay.

Every marriage will have its better and worse times, its springs and summers and falls and winters. Forever-love allows that full range of seasons. Enjoy the bright colors and warmth of good days. Accept the dark, rainy days, the cold of winter, and the hot summer winds of disagreement and of waiting for someone to say, "I'm sorry. I was wrong. I love you. Will you forgive me?"

With our society driven more and more by instant everything, many of us are losing the awareness that some of the best things in life take longer and aren't enjoyed until, like ripe fruit, they're ready to be picked. Charlotte, for example, came close to giving up many times with her husband, Mike. But if she had, it would have been too soon.

Mike, like me, didn't know how to love his wife in a way that made her feel loved. He and I struggled through many seasons—many ups and downs—together as we learned the things I teach in this book. And as he grew in his own happiness and in his sensitivity to her needs, she found herself in the kind of relationship she had dreamed about before they married.

Not long ago I got a letter from Charlotte. "I never thought the day would come," she said, "when my life with Mike would be so wonderful. As you know, we've had our 'down times.' But this last year has been worth all we went through. Whatever we didn't have before has long since been forgotten because of what we have today."

Unfortunately, many couples don't wait for that exciting season that wipes out the memory of the difficult times. That good season is like picking delicious fruit after a hard winter, wet spring, and hot summer. The juicy apples need all three seasons to taste delightfully good.

But many other couples have come to realize that it's perfectly normal for a marriage to go through different seasons—of drought, worry, sadness, anger and also times of plenty, happiness, and overwhelming joy and laughter.

I close this book with my personal warranty: No matter what struggle you may have right now that tempts you to leave your marriage, there's a workable solution for you! Start by applying the principles in this book. Get professional counseling if you need it. Through the research and counseling expertise of many people, there's no shortage of excellent help for couples today.

Perhaps this book will give you all the help you need; at the very least, it will give you a big headstart. If you'll work at applying the lessons of this book, and if you'll seek out whatever other assistance you may need, you, too, can one day bask in the delights of forever-love.

Don't give up until you find it.

Appendix

Three Character Qualities:
Prerequisites to Dating for the Smalley Children

Before our children could date, they had to demonstrate that they understood three character qualities: honor, responsibility, and resistance to peer pressure. We watched and constantly assessed them to determine when they understood the concept of honor and when they fully realized *they* were responsible for their actions and the way they handled their emotions. We also wanted to make sure they were able to stand up to peer pressure if they needed to and that they understood the consequences of premarital sex. In this appendix, I'll share with you how we presented those requirements.

1. Honor: The "I'm Third" Perspective

We told our children that honor was to be given in three ways: to God, to others, and to oneself. The "I'm third" perspective involved learning the primary importance of one's spiritual journey. God was to receive the highest honor, a 10 on a scale of 1 (none) to 10 (highest). Other people were to receive high honor, let's say 9.2 to 9.9. Then self should receive a 9.1 rating. You can see we never led our children to think they were unimportant: 9.1 is way up there. It's just that God is worth our worship; the highest commandment in life is to love God with our whole hearts.

We expected our children to respect their church attendance and pay attention to what was taught. They weren't to use degrading names for others, and they were to show regard for people in general as well as the environment/creation. They seemed to have a healthy respect for themselves, which we constantly tried to reinforce.

We tried to watch for growth in this area; as they kept asking if they were ready to date, we would evaluate their progress.

2. Responsibility: For One's Actions and Emotions

We wanted our children to understand that their emotion of anger, springing from fear, hurt, and frustration, was their responsibility. By example, we showed them that it's not what happens to us that determines our emotions; it's how we *respond* to what happens.

We knew they would be hurt and frustrated in the course of the dating process, and learning to take responsibility for their actions and emotions gave them an edge in their teen years.

This is one way I taught them to understand and control their anger: I encouraged them to respectfully ask me a difficult question when I got angry with them (sometimes blaming my frustration or hurt on them). The question? "Dad, are we making you angry, or are we revealing something about you?" This forced me to be honest. Sometimes I had to say, "Yes, you're showing me just how self-centered I am." (And I didn't like seeing this in myself.) Through our example, our children learned little by little how to assume full responsibility for their emotions.

3. Self-Control and Understanding the Consequences of Premarital Sex

We waited to see when our teens would be able to stand up and say no to their peers if they needed to. The stronger their personal convictions, the easier it would be for them to state their beliefs and respectfully stand against peer pressure. Considering the temptations that come with dating, we wanted them not to dishonor someone, especially sexually.

As a family we outlined several consequences of premarital sex. Our kids were very familiar with these, adding to their being ready to date. Here are a few of those consequences:

1. It dulls our soul toward God and God's ways.[1]

2. It reinforces our self-centeredness, our sensual focus, and keeps us away from our loving focus on God and others.[2]

3. It hinders our awareness of the needs of others, especially our future mate or good friends; it tends to make us less sensitive to the needs of others and more concerned about our own sensual needs. When we are preoccupied with our own stimulation, we are more capable

of saying hurtful things and missing opportunities for love. (We have ears and eyes but can't hear or see others.)

4. It makes us susceptible to sexual diseases.

5. It increases our need for greater stimulation in sexual contact, which then can increase the potential for sensual conflict in marriage.

6. It can reduce our satisfaction in the marital sexual relationship, which cannot compete with the backseat of a car. Sexual encounter flashbacks can further hinder our concentration on our mate's needs.

7. Research has found that couples who have had premarital sex have a greater chance of marital dissatisfaction and divorce.

8. It increases one's chances of sexual addiction.

9. It reinforces the notion that sex is an act when sex should be seen as a reflection of a loving relationship. Meaningful sex is a relationship. If this notion is not understood, treating sex as an act can erode a loving marriage.

10. If sex is primarily thought of as a separate physical "act," either the man or the woman can feel like an object instead of the valuable person he or she is in reality and in God's sight.

11. Premarital sex increases the possibility of guilt and resentment building between the two people involved. Either can feel used and after the encounter, discarded.

12. As guilt and resentment build, they can result in a whole host of additional negative consequences. (See chapter 2.)

13. Premarital sex can be a form of medication for lack of love and acceptance from parents. The need for approval or acceptance can be so great that especially a girl can reach out for love as one would for food or vitamins. We must learn how to forgive our parents and past offenders to ensure God's help as we say no to our strong sexual urges.

14. Pregnancy outside of marriage and/or abortion can affect anyone negatively. What's more, it usually hurts parents and friends. Abortion can reduce one's chances of having a normal pregnancy.

The two basic motivations in life are desire for gain and fear of loss. But fear of loss is usually a slightly stronger motivation. Finding more reasons why you should abstain from sex before marriage greatly inhibits becoming sexually active.

Notes

Chapter 1. Love's Best-Kept Secret

1. Clifford Notarius and Howard Markman, *We Can Work It Out* (New York: Putnam, 1993), 29.

2. I credit a number of authors, including M. Scott Peck, Stephen Covey, Michele Weiner-Davis, Howard Markman, and Harriet Lerner, for laying out a "map" that leads to the "buried treasure" of a fulfilling life apart from what others or our circumstances bring us. They've opened our eyes to the truth that we can choose the way we approach life.

3. Stephen R. Covey, *The Seven Habits of Highly Effective People* (New York: Simon & Schuster, 1989), 71.

4. Harriet G. Lerner, *The Dance of Anger* (New York: Harper & Row, 1985), 122–53.

5. Ibid., 64.

6. See Irene Goldenberg and Herbert Goldenberg, *Family Therapy: An Overview* (Pacific Grove, Calif.: Brooks/Cole, 1980, 1985).

7. Howard Markman, Scott Stanley, and Susan Blumberg, *Fighting for Your Marriage* (San Francisco: Jossey-Bass, 1994), 22.

Chapter 2. The Number One Enemy of Love: Unresolved Anger

1. William Stafford, *Disordered Loves* (Boston: Cowley, 1994), 86.

2. Notarius and Markman, *We Can Work It Out*, 237–56.

3. Charles Bass, *Banishing Fear from Your Life* (Garden City, N.Y.: Doubleday, 1986), 18–19.

4. Markman, Stanley, and Blumberg, *Fighting for Your Marriage*, 22.

5. Personal interview with Dr. Scott Stanley.

6. See 1 John 2:9ff.

7. Debbie Barr, *Children of Divorce* (Grand Rapids: Zondervan, 1992), 48.

8. Earl D. Wilson, *Counseling and Guilt* (Dallas: Word, 1987), 42.

9. M. Scott Peck, *Further Along the Road Less Traveled* (New York: Simon & Schuster, 1993), 39.

10. See Richard C. Meyer, "Making Anger Work for Us," *Faith at Work* (Summer 1995), 3.

11. Redford Williams and Virginia Williams, *Anger Kills* (New York: Times Books, 1993).

12. "Anger Can Trigger Heart Attacks, Study Shows," *The American Heart Association Newsletter* 85, no. 23 (11 April 1994): 33.

Chapter 3. Seven Ways to Unload Unresolved Anger

1. John Powell, quoted in Phyllis Hobe, *Coping* (New York: Guideposts, 1983), 127.

2. Peck, *Further Along the Road Less Traveled*, 63.

3. Covey, *The Seven Habits of Highly Effective People*, 29–31.

4. See Proverbs 9:7.

Chapter 4. You Can Turn Your "Sand Storms" into Pearls

1. Scott M. Peck, *The Road Less Traveled* (New York: Simon & Schuster, 1978), 15; *How to Stubbornly Refuse to Make Yourself Miserable about Anything—Yes, Anything!* (Secaucus, N.J.: Lyle Stuart, 1988).

2. LynNell Hancock et al., "Breaking Point," *Newsweek*, 6 March 1995, 59.

3. Geoffrey Cowley, "Dialing the Stress-Meter Down," *Newsweek*, 6 March 1995, 62.

4. For more information about Fresh Start, call 610-644-6464.

5. Charles Colson, "Simple Sand," in *A Dance with Deception* (Dallas: Word, 1993), 123.

6. See Andy Andrews, *Storms of Perfection*, vols. 1 and 2 (Charlotte, N.C.: Internet, 1992, 1994).

7. For more help with pearl-counting, see Gary Smalley, *Joy That Lasts* (Grand Rapids: Zondervan, 1986, 1988).

Chapter 5. How to Balance Expectations and Reality

1. I'm grateful to Dr. Dan Trathen of Denver for helping me work through the lessons in the following preventive plan.

2. Irene Goldenberg and Herbert Goldenberg, *Family Therapy: An Overview*, 152–59.

Chapter 6. Avoiding Hurt Is My Responsibility

1. Winston Churchill, as quoted in John Bartlett, *Familiar Quotations*, 15th ed. (Boston: Little, Brown, 1980), 743.

2. See Henry Cloud and John Townsend, *Boundaries* (Grand Rapids: Zondervan, 1992).

3. See Cloud and Townsend, *Boundaries*. For more direct help, I recommend your nearest Rapha Counseling Center or Minirth Meier New Life Clinic.

4. Matt. 19:19.

Chapter 7. Finding the Power to Keep Loving

1. Frederick Buechner, *Wishful Thinking* (San Francisco: Harper & Row, 1973), 40–41.

2. Howard Markman, Scott Stanley, and Susan Blumberg, *Fighting for Your Marriage*, 285.

3. Nick Stinnett and John DeFrain, *Secrets of Strong Families* (New York: Berkley, 1986).

4. Rom. 15:13.

5. See James 4:8.

6. See 1 John 2:9–10.

7. Smalley, *Joy That Lasts* (Grand Rapids: Zondervan, 1986, 1988).

8. See Deut. 6:5, Lev. 19:18, and Luke 10:27.

9. Phil. 4:19.

10. Matt. 6:21.

11. See Heb. 11:6.

Chapter 8. Five Vital Signs of a Healthy Marriage

1. Erich Fromm, *The Art of Loving*, quoted in *Visions of Faith* (Basingstoke, England: Marshall Pickering, 1986), 315.

2. Irene Goldenberg and Herbert Goldenberg, *Family Therapy: An Overview*, 28–54.

3. Ibid., 55–85.

4. Pam Smith, *The Food Trap* (Altamonte Springs, Fla.: Creation House, 1990), 23.

5. William F. Arndt and R. Wilbur Gingrich, eds., *A Greek-English Lexicon of the New Testament and Other Early Christian Literature* (Chicago: University of Chicago Press, 1957), 119–20.

6. See Matt. 6:21.

7. Markman, Stanley, and Blumberg, *Fighting for Your Marriage*.

Chapter 9. The Number One Request: Better Communication

1. Paul Tournier, The Meaning of Persons (New York: Harper, 1957), 143.

2. Based on a personal interview with Dr. Gary Oliver, Southwest Counseling Associates, Littleton, Colorado. See David Mace, Love and Anger in Marriage (Grand Rapids: Zondervan, 1982).

3. Markman, Stanley, and Blumberg, Fighting for Your Marriage.

4. For additional examples of what a family constitution might look like, see Gary Smalley and John Trent, The Hidden Value of a Man (Colorado Springs: Focus on the Family, 1992, 1994), 182–84.

5. For the three-hundred word pictures, see Gary Smalley and John Trent, The Language of Love (Colorado Springs: Focus on the Family, 1988, 1991).

Chapter 10. Understanding Personality Types: A Key to Lovability

1. See Tim LaHaye, Understanding the Male Temperament (Grand Rapids: Zondervan, 1970), and Florence Littauer, Personality Plus, Updated and Expanded (Grand Rapids: Fleming Revell, 1992).

2. For more information about Dr. Trent's seminar, contact him at Encouraging Words, 12629 N. Tatum Blvd., Suite 208, Phoenix, AZ 85032, 602-953-7610.

Chapter 11. How to Bring Out the Best in Your Maddening Mate

1. Deborah Tannen, You Just Don't Understand (New York: William Morrow, 1990), 294.

2. John Gottman, Why Marriages Succeed or Fail (New York: Simon & Schuster, 1994), 29.

3. Kevin Leman, The Birth Order Book (Grand Rapids: Fleming Revell, 1985).

4. Tannen is the author of You Just Don't Understand (New York: William Morrow, 1990).

5. Bernie Zilbergeld is the author of The New Male Sexuality (New York: Bantam, 1992).

6. John Gray, Men Are from Mars, Women Are from Venus (New York: HarperCollins, 1992).

7. Sharon Begley, "Gray Matters," Newsweek, 27 March 1995, 50.

8. Tannen, You Just Don't Understand, 43.

9. Zilbergeld, The New Male Sexuality.

10. Tannen, You Just Don't Understand, 43–47.

11. Ibid., 236–37.

12. Kevin Leman, *Sex Begins in the Kitchen: The Art of Staying in Love*. Video available from Dr. Kevin Leman, 4585 E. Speedway, Suite 110, Tucson, Arizona 85712.

13. Begley, "Gray Matters," 54.

Chapter 12. How to Read a Woman's Built-in Marriage Manual

1. Margaret Mead, *Blackberry Winter*, as quoted in John Bartlett, *Familiar Quotations*, 15th ed. (Boston: Little, Brown, 1980), 853.

2. Markman, Stanley, and Blumberg, *Fighting for Your Marriage*, 22.

3. For three hundred sample word pictures, see Gary Smalley and John Trent, *The Language of Love* (Colorado Springs: Focus on the Family, 1988, 1991).

4. Pierre Mornell, M.D., *Passive Men, Wild Women* (New York: Simon & Schuster, 1979).

5. Contact Today's Family at 1483 Lakeshore Dr., Branson, Missouri 65616; 800-84-TODAY.

6. See Markman, Stanley, and Blumberg, *Fighting for Your Marriage*; Henry Cloud and John Townsend, *Boundaries*; Gary Smalley and John Trent, *The Language of Love*; Gary Smalley, *If Only He Knew* (Grand Rapids: Zondervan, 1982); and Michele Weiner-Davis, *Fire Your Shrink* (New York: Simon & Schuster, 1995).

7. Judith Wallerstein and Sandra Blakeslee, *The Good Marriage* (Boston: Houghton Mifflin, 1995).

8. Markman, Stanley, and Blumberg, *Fighting for Your Marriage*, 38ff.

Chapter 13. Conflicts: The Doorway to Intimacy

1. John Gottman, *Why Marriages Succeed or Fail*, 173.

2. Markman, Stanley, and Blumberg, *Fighting for Your Marriage*, 38ff.

3. I have long wanted to write a book about the importance of staying together in marriage. I've never written it because other authors have already done it; among them are: Markman, Stanley, and Blumberg, *Fighting for Your Marriage*; Wallerstein and Blakeslee, *The Good Marriage*; Judith Wallerstein and Sandra Blakeslee, *Second Chances* (New York: Ticknor and Fields, 1990); Gottman, *Why Marriages Succeed or Fail*; Michele Weiner-Davis, *Divorce Busting* (New York: Summit, 1992); and Diane Medved, *The Case against Divorce* (New York: Donald Fine, 1989). If you want to be encouraged about your own marriage, let these authors open your eyes wider to the wonderful possibilities (even if you're in a second or third marriage).

4. See Carol Rubin and Jeffrey Rubin, *When Families Fight: How to Handle Conflict with Those You Love* (New York: Ballantine, 1989), 39–60.

5. Stephen R. Covey, *The Seven Habits of Highly Effective People*, audio version (New York: Simon & Schuster Sound Ideas, 1989).

6. Markman, Stanley, and Blumberg, *Fighting for Your Marriage*.

7. David and Vera Mace, *How to Have a Happy Marriage* (Nashville: Abingdon, 1977), 112.

8. Harriet G. Lerner, *The Dance of Anger*, 199–201.

9. Eph. 4:26.

10. Ps. 4:4.

11. Sandra Felton, *When You Live with a Messie* (Grand Rapids: Fleming Revell, 1994).

12. C. S. Lewis, *The Last Battle* (New York: Macmillan, Collier, 1956; 1970), 136.

13. Ibid., 161.

Chapter 14. Was That as Good for You as It Was for Me?

1. C. S. Lewis, *Mere Christianity* (New York: Macmillan Paperbacks, 1952), 96.

2. Gen. 4:1.

3. F. B. Dresslar, "The Psychology of Touch," *American Journal of Psychology* 6 (1984): 316.

4. Helen Colton, *The Gift of Touch* (New York: Seaview/Putnam, 1983), 102.

5. See Stinnett and DeFrain, *Secrets of Strong Families*.

6. "Talking to God," *Newsweek*, 6 January 1992, 42.

7. Eccles. 4:12.

8. Carey Moore and Pamela Rosewell Moore, *If Two Shall Agree: Praying Together As a Couple* (Grand Rapids: Chosen Books, 1992), 200.

9. Ibid., 201.

10. See Ed and Gaye Wheat, *Intended for Pleasure* (New York: Bantam, 1992); Clifford and Joyce Penner, *Restoring the Pleasure* (Dallas: Word, 1993) and *The Gift of Sex* (Dallas: Word, 1981); and Bernie Zilbergeld, *The New Male Sexuality*.

Chapter 15. Divorce-Proofing Your Marriage

1. Some of my favorite writers give a different perspective on this concept, including Willard F. Harley Jr., *His Needs, Her Needs* (Grand Rapids: Fleming Revell, 1986); as well as Covey, *Seven Habits of Highly Effective People; * Weiner-Davis, *Divorce Busting; * Peck, *The Road Less Traveled; * and Henry Cloud and John Townsend, *Boundaries*.

2. I was checked at a sleep-disorder clinic in a hospital. It's been a miracle.

3. Eccles. 11:1.

Chapter 16. A Love That Lasts Forever

1. Charlie and Lucy Wedemeyer, *Charlie's Victory* (Grand Rapids: Zondervan, 1993), 20.
2. Ibid., 60.
3. Personal interview.

Appendix: Three Character Qualities: Prerequisites to Dating for the Smalley Children

1. Eph. 4:17–20.
2. Phil. 2:3ff.

For information on Gary Smalley's speaking schedule,
a catalog of videotapes, books, and cassettes, or a free issue of
Gary's Homes of Honor magazine call **1-800-848-6329** or write:
Today's Family, 1482 Lakeshore Dr., Branson, Missouri 65616.

OTHER RESOURCES INCLUDE:

Books

Love Is a Decision

The Key to Your Child's Heart

The Blessing

Joy That Lasts

The Hidden Value of a Man

The Two Sides of Love

The Language of Love

The Hidden Keys of a Loving and Lasting Relationship

Video Series

Love Is a Decision

Hidden Keys to Loving Relationships

Homes of Honor Small Group Series

About the Author

Gary Smalley is an internationally recognized speaker on family relationships who has sold more than 12 million copies of his books and videos. Best-selling titles include *Love Is a Decision*, *The Blessing* (with John Trent), and *For Better or for Best*. Gary has been featured on hundreds of radio and television shows, including *The Oprah Winfrey Show*. He has presented "Love is a Decision" seminars to hundreds of thousands across the U.S. He is president of Today's Family based in Branson, Missouri, where he and his wife Norma live. Gary and Norma have three children: Kari, Greg, and Michael.

The
Key
To Your
Child's
Heart

Gary Smalley

The Key To Your Child's Heart

THE KEY TO YOUR CHILD'S HEART, REVISED EDITION

Library of Congress Cataloging-in-Publication Data:

Smalley, Gary.
    The key to your child's heart / Gary Smalley. — Rev. ed.
       p.   cm.
    Includes bibliographical references.
    ISBN 0-8499-0947-3
    1. Child rearing—Religious aspects—Christianity. 2. Parenting—
Religious aspects—Christianity. I. Title.
    HQ769.3.S63   1992
    649'.1—dc20   92-12926
                                                      CIP

Printed in the United States of America

In loving memory of our parents,
Uel Jefferson and Eleanor Deck
Frank and Emily Smalley.
And to our children,
Kari, Greg, and Michael,
we present to you our lifetime commitment.

Contents

Acknowledgments

It is with special appreciation that I acknowledge my debt to those without whose help this book could never have been published. To Judy Pitzmier for her dedication, talent, and warm understanding during the many hours of editing. To Al Janssen for his tremendous inspiration, encouragement, and editing skills when I couldn't "see the end." To Bill Yarger and B. John Trent, two of my outstanding and supportive pastors, who carefully evaluated the final draft. Last but certainly not least, to my wife, Norma, who walked with me every step of the way writing this book.

This book represents what Norma and I have learned through God's grace, trial, and error about parenting. It is with grateful appreciation that we express our love and indebtedness to our children—Kari, Greg, and Michael. They have been a tremendous inspiration and blessing to our lives. Each one is a special gift from God. Thank you for helping us to be parents!

Gary Smalley

The Key to Your Child's Heart

We were enduring our twelfth consecutive day of rain while traveling across the country one summer. Everything in our mini-motorhome was damp, and all five of us were tired of each other.

We had taken a drive up into Canada to see the beauty of Banff National Park. I had described the beautiful mountains and rivers we would see, but for three straight days, fog and rain had concealed the scenic beauty. Now, on the fourth morning, we were sitting in a restaurant trying to decide what to do. I urged us to return to our home in Phoenix where it was warm and dry. I'd fly alone from there to my next speaking engagement in Seattle. My wife, Norma, pleaded that we stay a fourth day in Canada and wait for the sun to break through. Kari, our fifteen-year-old daughter, wanted us to continue driving to Seattle. Our two younger boys "demanded" fishing in Washington.

As our volume increased in defense of each plan, Greg, our middle child, shouted, "Stop! I've got the solution!" He was so emphatic that even our neighbors in the next booth stopped to listen. "I think we ought to go out in the camper, get the gun, and shoot each other." All of us burst out laughing and that relaxed us enough to stay put another day during which the sun finally revealed the majesty of the Canadian Rockies.

Why is it that all five of us, and other families similar to ours, can go through very strained times like what we experienced in Canada and still witness a closeness and happiness together? Yet there are many other families that are so divided that even a minor crisis can permanently scatter the members in different directions.

There are many outstanding books on raising children, yet after reading some, I have often wondered "What's the use in trying? It's too difficult!" In my speaking and counseling all across the nation, I have found that many parents experience similar frustration and guilt.

In this book, you'll discover that we're an average family with very typical conflicts. But we have tried to find solutions to those conflicts that can be applied to almost every family. We will recount what has and has not worked in our home and will share with you the main factors that have drawn us into close relationship.

We'll also be summarizing what some of the parenting experts are saying today. For example, there are four basic types of parents. But only one of those four types produces the best results in children. We will examine why the children of these parents have much greater self-worth, are less rebellious, and are generally more successful in life.

You'll read about how we brought order and harmony to our family through the simple method of "contracts."

We will discuss several practical ways to help protect a child from becoming sexually involved before marriage.

If you're wondering how to get your children to clean their rooms, eat healthier foods, and avoid certain harmful activities, we have at least twenty-two ways to motivate your children. We will even share the secret of how you can actually increase your children's desire to listen carefully to you.

This book will give you several basic principles that I believe are *key* to raising children. In particular, the next chapter covers one principle that if diligently applied can virtually guarantee a closer relationship between parent and child. In my opinion, it is *The Key to Your Child's Heart.*

Violation of this principle has undoubtedly destroyed more families than any other single factor. It is the major reason why over one million children have run away from home and why millions more reject their parents' moral values and standards. Fewer teenagers would misuse alcohol and drugs if parents understood and practiced this principle.

Therefore, the concept presented in the next chapter provides the foundation for successful parenting. I suggest that you may want to reread it several times. Master this principle and I can assure that you will make significant progress toward experiencing the joys and rewards of a closer-knit family.

1

How to Overcome the Major Destroyer of Families

- A Closed Spirit
- Manifestations of a Closed Spirit
- Reopening a Child's Spirit
- Five Steps to Reopen a Child's Spirit
- Reasons Why One Might Refuse to Forgive
- Observing Voice Tone and Facial Expressions to Recognize a Closed Spirit
- How Children or Adults Can Reopen Their Own Spirits
- How Open Is Your Child's Spirit?
- Eighty-four Ways We Can Offend Our Children

ONE EVENING, WHILE I WAS in my bedroom on a long-distance phone call, my son Greg, five years old at the time, let out a bloodcurdling scream from the master bathroom. He came running to the door, screaming so loudly that I couldn't hear the other person's voice. I could feel my blood pressure rise as I signaled for him to be quiet. I dramatically patted my bottom to let him know what was coming if he didn't shut up immediately. But Greg continued to scream, so I quickly ended my phone conversation, telling the person I'd get back to him later.

When I hung up the phone, I grabbed Greg by the arm and shook him. "Why are you screaming?" I demanded. "Couldn't you see I was on the phone?"

Without waiting for an answer, I shoved him into the hall and said, "You get into your bedroom right now." He fell when I pushed him, but got back up, still crying, and hurried into his room. I grabbed the paddle we used for spanking—the entire family had helped decorate it—and told him to lie down on his bed. Then I gave him several hard swats. Satisfied with my discipline, I stood back and thought, *That's what you get for violating my rule.* You see, no one was supposed to scream while I was on the phone—I wouldn't want people to think my family was out of control.

It was our custom after a spanking to hold the child and reaffirm our love for him. But this time, something took place that scared me. Greg was still crying. He stood up and the look in his eyes said, "I hate you." He backed away from me to let me know that he didn't want me to touch him. I suddenly realized what I had done, and I knew that if I didn't take immediate action, there might be serious consequences in our relationship. Fortunately, someone had taught me what to do, and within a few moments, we were hugging each other on his bed, back in full fellowship and harmony.

What actually took place has saved our family time and time again from drifting into deep conflict. The principle I am about to share has, without a doubt, been the single most significant factor in establishing and maintaining harmony in our home.

In the United States, we are suffering from an overwhelming epidemic of broken relationships. We don't have to look hard to see the evidence. We see it to some degree in every relationship, both inside and outside of the home. I hope that I can explain in these next few pages what I know can have a very positive effect on all relationships, especially with our children.

I have taken what I've observed during my more than twenty years of counseling, with my own family, and what I've learned from experts in the field of building personal relationships. I've tried to develop a simple system of explaining the major factor that causes disharmony within the home, as well as outside of it. I would urge you again to reread this one chapter many times because I have found it to be *the key* to staying in harmony with *anyone*.

A Closed Spirit

The single most prevalent cause of disharmony within a home is what I have labeled a *closed spirit*.

What do I mean by a closed spirit? What causes it? Let's begin by saying that every person is born with a spirit, soul, and body, and all three are interrelated. I will define spirit as a person's innermost being, similar to one's conscience. It's the area in which people can have fellowship with one another and enjoy each other's presence without a word being spoken. Our deepest relationships are built on the spirit level. The *soul* would include our mind, will, and emotions. The *body* is, of course, our physical makeup. Together, we'll say the three comprise a total person. But the soul and the body are within the spirit.

Very Sensitive Tentacles

To help us understand how the spirit, soul, and body operate together, let's look at an example from nature. When I was a child, I enjoyed observing sea anemones on the California coast. They were often found in tidal pools among the rocks. About four or five inches in diameter, they look like colorful flowers with soft, wavy tentacles. But I noticed an interesting phenomenon. Sometimes I'd take a stick and poke one of them. Immediately the sea anemone would withdraw its sensitive tentacles and close up until it became a shell. It was similar to a beautiful flower closing. Now it was protected from further injury.

What happens with the sea anemone illustrates what happens to a person when he is offended. The tentacles of that sea anemone are similar to the spirit of a person. The sea anemone is completely open and vulnerable. But when the stick pokes him, he closes up. In a similar way, when a person is offended, he closes up. When his spirit closes, it in turn closes his soul and body. If the spirit is open, so are the soul and body. In other words, when the spirits of two people are open, they enjoy talking (soul) and touching (body). If the spirit closes, the soul and body close to the same degree. A person with a closed spirit will usually avoid communication.

Closing Tentacles

This is what I saw happening to Greg. When I pushed him in the hallway and screamed at him in harshness, *I had poked his spirit.* The greater the harshness, the greater the pain a person feels in his spirit. My harshness, pushing, and spanking without finding out the facts were three large poking sticks. Like the sea anemone, Greg closed his spirit to me with each jab. And when he closed his spirit, he closed everything else. He didn't like me. He didn't want to be near me. He didn't want to talk to me. And he resisted my attempts to touch him. These were the keys that told me that his spirit was closing. When a child resists affection—if you touch his hand and it's cold and limp, or if you put your arm around her and she turns her back, shrugs you off, and avoids conversation—that usually means the spirit is closing.

Manifestations of a Closed Spirit

When a child's spirit is closing there are many possible manifestations. He may argue and resist when you ask him to do something. He may be contrary, refusing to like anything you like! He may withdraw, and usually he is not very responsive to affection.

If his spirit is closed further, he may seek friends who are opposite from the kinds of friends you want him to have. He may swear or use disrespectful language. A closed spirit is a major cause for the misuse of drugs and alcohol, and a primary reason why children become sexually permissive.

At the very worst, a child whose spirit has been completely closed may run away from home or commit suicide.

All of these are symptoms of a closed spirit. If we can recognize them, and help to reopen the spirit, we will often take care of the symptoms in the process.

During my years of counseling, I've come to realize that this principle is the key to most relationships. When a man can't stand his boss, it's primarily because his spirit was "stepped on" or "poked." So the employee usually avoids his boss, silently disagreeing and resisting him. I see it all the time with professional athletes. They get offended by management or coaches and suddenly announce they want to be traded. Where once they were thrilled to be on the team, now they want to get away from it.

It happens in dating. When a girl meets a guy, usually her spirit is wide open to him. She likes him. She wants to talk with him. She enjoys doing things with him. When he touches her, she responds positively. Then something happens and suddenly she isn't as open. She guards her emotions more carefully and isn't as free with her affection. Somehow, her boyfriend has been closing her spirit, often without even knowing it.

It happens all the time in marriage. For years I did many little things to close Norma's spirit. I enjoyed telling little jokes about her to my friends or to my audiences when I spoke. I'd say things like "My wife treats me like a God. Every morning she serves me burnt offerings." Or this one: "Being married to Norma is like being married to an angel. Every day she's up in the air, harping about something, and she never has an earthly thing to wear." I'd laugh and others would laugh, but Norma wouldn't laugh. When she tried to express her hurt, I'd answer, "Come on! Can't you take a joke?"

What I didn't realize is that my jokes, kidding, sarcastic comments, and insensitive actions were closing her spirit a little more each time. After several years of marriage, Norma had closed much of her spirit to me. But I didn't know it. I only saw the outward results, like the times when I'd come home from work and she wouldn't greet me. I'd say, "Hi, Hon, I'm home," and there'd be no response. I'd ask, "Is there anything wrong?" and she'd say, "No." Gradually I began to learn that

"No" really meant "Yes." I needed to find out how I had closed her spirit, and take the steps necessary to reopen it.

During my seminars, to demonstrate how sensitive the spirit is, I often ask a man to come forward, close his eyes, and hold out his hand. First I put a large rock in his hand and ask him to identify the object. He usually correctly identifies it as a rock. Then I replace the rock with a pebble. Usually he can't identify it without feeling it for awhile. Most men, when they say something offensive to their wives, think they are only dropping a small pebble on her spirit. But she feels it like a large rock, which can close her spirit.

The same thing can happen in all relationships, especially between parents and their children. This is particularly danger-ous with young children who need a lot of physical affection—touching and hugging. If a parent is harsh with a daughter so that she is offended, she will begin closing her spirit. But she still needs to be touched, and since she won't accept touching from Mom or Dad, she looks elsewhere.

Young men can easily pick up her need for affection and take advantage of her. She may resist at first, not wanting to compromise her standards, but her resistance breaks down with the boy's persistence. Because she has already closed her spirit to her parents and she can't take any more rejection, she has a tendency to give in to the boy. If, on the other hand, her rela-tionship with Mom and Dad is solid, her spirit is open, and there has been a healthy degree of affection and touching be-tween them, she is much more likely to have the energy and desire to maintain her moral standards.

Boys have a similar need for affection. However, some fa-thers won't hug their sons because they think it's not manly. And some have caused their son's spirit to be closed so that their sons reject any affection. It has been determined that this lack of affection may cause boys to find affection in ways that can even lead to a homosexual relationship. Dr. Ross Campbell, a psychiatrist who specializes in working with children, has discovered that in all his reading and experience, he has never known of one sexually disoriented person who had a warm, loving, and *affectionate* father. If, on the other hand, a parent is cold and offensive, a son can close his spirit, and many times adopt rebellious, antisocial behavior.

Fortunately, a child's spirit is somewhat pliable for the first several years. When children are offended, they are willing and ready to get back into harmony. But if we don't recognize when a child's spirit is closing, we can reap disastrous results.

A closed spirit can also occur between children. Once, Michael, our youngest child, exploded in anger at Greg to the point where he was ready to start slugging it out. When I intervened, I learned that Greg had been harsh with Mike, but Mike was responding far more vehemently than was normal. So I knew something else was wrong.

Alone with Michael, I started playing "twenty questions," trying to discover what had caused his spirit to close. I asked, "Did your sister hurt you?" "Was it me?" "Mom?" Finally, when I asked him if anything had happened to him at school, he put his head down and continued crying. Up to this point, Michael refused to tell me anything. Many times children will say they do not want to talk, but they really do. They will often open up when we gently probe to discover their problem.

Michael went on to tell me that his best friend at school had chosen a new friend, and the two of them had turned against him. My heart went out to him as he cried and I wanted to hold him, but he wasn't ready yet. That told me there was still another problem. Then Michael revealed that Greg and his friend across the street wouldn't play with him. The neighbor was taking his brother away from him. It was just like what had happened at school.

I told him that I felt terrible and asked if I could hold him. He scooted across the bed and held me, crying and feeling the full pain of rejection. Later on we got together with Greg, and Michael explained to him how he felt about the neighbor across the street. Together, the three of us were able to resolve the problem by taking the necessary steps to open Mike's spirit.

If I had not learned that Michael's spirit was closing toward Greg and his friend at school, I might have compounded the problem. I could have said, "Michael, shape up. You're getting to be a big boy now. I'm tired of the way you fight with Greg." That would have closed his spirit even more, especially toward me. Being harsh and demanding is like a big stick "poking" a person's spirit and causing it to close.

In the average home, it is impossible to keep from offending each other. Something seems to happen almost every day that will cause someone to be offended. *Yet, it is possible to stay in harmony as long as we resolve each offense.* One offense on top of another, on top of another, can build a wall cementing the spirit shut. It is much easier to reopen a child's spirit when it is closed slightly through one or only a few small offenses. But it is still possible to reopen a child's spirit even in the worst situations.

Reopening a Child's Spirit

There are undoubtedly many ways to help open a person's spirit that has closed toward us. I'll mention five ways that have been the most effective in our family and in my counseling. I'll show them in a particular order because this is how I've observed them to be most helpful. However, you may find it more effective to rearrange them or add other ways to the list.

Each of the five steps was used after I had spanked Greg for screaming while I was on the phone. After applying them, I witnessed his spirit reopen in a matter of minutes. Here is the sequence:

Once I had realized that Greg's spirit was closing toward me, I dropped to my knees and my attitude became *soft and tender*. Gently, I asked him, "Greg, *why* were you screaming in the bathroom?" With his voice trembling as he fought back the tears, he managed to say, "I fell and hit my ear on the bathtub." He showed me his ear which was swollen and bleeding. When I saw what had happened, I felt terrible. I gently said to him, "Greg, *I was so wrong* to have treated you this way. Daddy's the one who deserved the spanking." Greg wiped his tears and added, "Then when you pushed me in the hall, I hit my same ear on the toy box."

By this time, I felt like a child abuser. I was an irresponsible father and I recognized it. "Greg, Daddy was wrong." I handed him the spanking stick. "I'm the one who deserves to be spanked. I'm the one who needs it." He grabbed the stick and dropped it. He backed up again, still not wanting any part of me. I wanted to reach out and touch him, but his spirit was still closed toward me.

Finally, I said, again tenderly, "Greg, I was wrong. I know I don't deserve it, but I wonder if it would be possible for you to find it in your heart to *forgive me*." Immediately he threw his arms around me. We fell back against the bed and he laid on my chest for about a half hour as we held each other tightly. After some time, I looked at his ear again and asked, "Are you sure we're okay now?" "Yes, Daddy, I forgive you," he said, patting me on the back. "We all make mistakes." From the tone of his voice and the way he touched me, I knew his spirit was opening again.

It may take a little more time for some children to reopen their spirits, depending on the circumstances; but a child is certainly worth our time.

Let's go back now and examine more carefully each of the five ways to open a person's closed spirit.

Five Steps to Reopen a Child's Spirit

1. Become Tenderhearted

The first step that I needed to take to open Greg's spirit was *to reflect tenderness and softness*. Gentleness has a way of melting anger.

As we attempt to open one's spirit, our body language, our muscles, our facial expressions, and our tone of voice must become soft, gentle, tender, and caring. By doing this, we are communicating several things to the person whom we have offended:

We're saying:

(a) He is valuable and important. We express this importance in nonverbal ways. We are slow to move toward him. Our heads may be bowed down, and we are obviously grieved that we have hurt him.

(b) We do not want to see his spirit closed; we care about him.

(c) We know there is something wrong. We acknowledge by our softness that an offense has taken place and we are going to *slow down* long enough to correct whatever has happened.

(d) We are open to listen. It is safe for him to share what has happened and we are not going to get angry or hurt him again.

I was counseling a pro football player and his wife, and she was sharing with me how deeply offended she had been by some of the things her husband had said and done. He said he didn't understand why she got so mad and upset about the things he was doing. I could see she was hurting and that her spirit was closing toward him. So I asked him if he wanted to work on opening her spirit. He agreed to try.

"I want you to become really tender right now and put your arm around your wife," I said. "Pretend that your whole body is melting ice cream. Gently tell her that you know you have hurt her and you want to resolve it."

He started to do as I said, putting his arm around her, and she said, "Oh, you don't mean that!" Rather than understanding how hurt she was, he reacted: "I do too mean that. Don't tell me I don't mean this." The athlete was listening to his wife's words, rather than to the tone of her voice which was telling him how closed her spirit was. His anger and harshness were only further closing her spirit.

I suggested he let me demonstrate what I meant. Immediately, my voice softened and I became caring and gentle. I reached across the table and touched her hand and said, "You're really hurting, aren't you? And I know that the things I have done to you have deeply affected you." With my softness her facial muscles began to relax. Her head slightly bowed, her eyes started to fill with tears. Both of us were amazed how quickly her spirit was willing to open.

I find that the same thing happens with our children. Tenderness melts the anger and it begins to open their spirits.

2. Increase Understanding

The second step to open a person's spirit is to *increase our understanding of the pain he feels and how he has interpreted our offensive behavior.* When I asked Greg why he was crying and he said it was because he had fallen against the bathtub, my understanding of his pain immediately increased. I already was soft but my spirit became even softer because I had deeper understanding and could feel his hurt feelings. I probably would have screamed, too, no matter what the rule was, if I had fallen against the bathtub. Many times just these two factors—being *soft* and then *understanding* a person's pain—will open a person's spirit.

Children in various household arrangements often dream

that someday someone will understand what they are feeling and how they are hurting. Where there are single parents or blended families through a second marriage, a child can feel deeply offended by the partner who leaves or by new members of a family he's thrust into. Oftentimes a child will blame himself for a divorce. He may not say anything to either one of the parents, but he begins to express the symptoms of a closed spirit. He is argumentative and avoids his parents, even to the point of not allowing them to touch him. Either parent can begin to solve this problem by softening his or her heart toward that child and gaining more understanding of his pain.

One of the best ways to increase understanding of a child's hurt is through emotional word pictures. They help us feel the child's pain in such a vivid way that some conflicts are resolved in seconds.

One boy, whose father constantly criticized him, told his dad, "I sometimes feel like a bird in a nest. You fly in, and I should feel so encouraged to see you, because you are going to have some food or encouragement for me, but instead you jerk off one of the branches or little fibers that holds the nest together and fly away. I begin to think, 'Wait a minute. He's tearing this nest apart and I'm not ready to fly yet.' I have such an insecure feeling when I see you coming because you're always picking on me, tearing me down, and it's just like pulling those little pieces of string out of that nest." When the boy's father heard this word picture, he felt his son's hurt and insecurity. This one emotional word picture helped this father greatly reduce his criticism of his son.

As parents, we can ask our children to help us understand their feelings by asking them questions like, "If you were a rabbit, what would be happening to you right now because of what I just did?" or, "If you were a piece of cloth what would you look like?" or, "Give me a color to describe how you are feeling." Usually, if we give them time and encouragement, children can tell us exactly how they feel. If my daughter tells me she is feeling really blue, I might ask if it is a dark blue or a light blue, and if there are any cheerful spots in the color. One boy whose father traveled extensively said, "Dad, the way you've been avoiding me lately, I feel like a dishrag under the sink that's had a steady drip on it for the last two months. Nobody has noticed it so now it's rotten and mildewey." Most any parent could feel the pain of mildew.

We can also help our children express their feelings by relating to previous experiences. We can help them by saying, "Remember the time your friend across the street rejected you and wouldn't play with you? Am I sort of making you feel like that?" or, "Remember how you felt in school when you got that F, when you really studied hard for an A? Then your classmates made fun of you, and remember how you were embarrassed? Is that sort of how you felt today when I corrected you in front of your friends?"

Emotional word pictures are such an important tool in communication that we will talk more about using them in another chapter. It is very important that children know we really understand how they feel when they are offended. If a child refuses to talk, it may take a "cooling off" period for both child and parent. After a few minutes, a parent can continue gently probing to discover the level of hurt. Give a child time to understand his own emotional pain.

3. Recognize the Offense

The third step in opening a person's spirit is *admitting that we were wrong*, because what we did was offensive to him. It could even be that what we did was not wrong, but how we did it—our attitude was wrong. For example, I could spank my child for the right reason, but if I spank him in harsh anger, I need to admit my wrong attitude.

Even the world recognizes the importance of confession and admission of guilt. When Soviet fighter planes shot down a Korean 747 killing the more than 250 passengers, the world was shocked. Immediately, a number of the free-world countries demanded that Russia admit it was wrong and apologize. News commentators emphasized a previous example when Israel shot down a Libyan passenger airliner, and how it apologized to the world and paid restitution to all the passengers' families. But when the Soviets failed to admit they were wrong, and failed to make restitution, the free world became even angrier and more hardened toward them.

Children tend to be more aware of their own needs and wants and less concerned about the welfare of others. This self-awareness or self-centeredness increases the possibility of their being offended. As they grow in maturity, they find that people don't offend them as much, because they have become more understanding of people.

As parents, we must be wise enough to know what our child's level of maturity is so that we don't close his spirit unnecessarily. If we offend our child because he is immature, we can say, "I was wrong to treat you this way." We don't add, "You are only hurt because you are so immature." That would only offend him all the more.

One of the hardest things for many parents to do is to admit when they are wrong. It's especially hard for fathers. I do not necessarily like to find out when I am wrong and it's not always easy to admit when I am. But I must remember that a hardened, resistant attitude is extremely detrimental to children.

As a child hears his parents admit it when they are offensive and sees that they understand how he feels, he gains a feeling of importance. He realizes that he is a valuable person. Sometimes this is all it takes to open a child's spirit. But we should be careful because there are two more factors that are important to make sure that the spirit has reopened.

4. Attempt to Touch

The fourth factor is *attempting to touch the offended person.* There are several reasons why we want to touch a child when he has been offended. First of all, he needs to be touched. If he reaches out and responds to our touching, then we know his spirit is opening or has completely reopened. This is an extremely important time to take him tenderly in our arms and hold him for awhile. It lets him know that we care, that we love him, and that he is very important.

Second, touching allows us to find out if the child's spirit is not opening. Perhaps the offense was deeper than we realized. Or he may have been offended by someone outside the family, like Mike with his friend at school, and he has a general resentment toward everyone around him. If I have admitted I am wrong, am soft and understanding, and reach out to touch my child but he pulls back or moves away, it is an indication that he isn't ready to open his spirit. He may need more time or a greater understanding from the one who offended him.

When parents are not accustomed to touching their children, like my own parents who were reluctant to touch each other as well as their six kids, they may want to "warn" or explain to their children why they're starting to touch. A child who hasn't been touched may feel somewhat hesitant to allow touching even if his spirit is open. A gradual adjustment may be necessary.

Obviously, the lack of touching doesn't always mean that we have closed our child's spirit. Children go through stages where they may avoid touching, for example during puberty. However, if a parent is maintaining harmony with his child, he can usually detect if the child is offended or just passing through a stage.

There might be other reasons why our children resist our touch. One summer our family went fishing in the Colorado mountains. I offended Kari by being harsh. She had hurt her knee and I was trying to force her quickly up the bank so I could get back to my fishing. About halfway up the bank, I realized that I had hurt her spirit and that she was far more important than my fishing. So I stopped, took her in my arms, and told her I knew I had offended her and that I was wrong. She wiggled out of my grasp and asked, "Dad, did you use any deodorant today?"

5. Seek Forgiveness

The final step to open someone's spirit is to *seek forgiveness from the one offended.* When we have offended someone, we must give him a chance to respond. For me, the best way is to say something like, "Could you find it in your heart to forgive me?" This is when I knew I had reopened Greg's spirit, for when I asked for his forgiveness, he rushed into my arms. We can say at this point that *true restoration is confession of wrong plus forgiveness granted.*

Reasons Why One Might Refuse to Forgive

If we have followed these five steps and the child refuses to forgive us, there are several possible reasons.

Perhaps the offense was deeper than we realized. Or he may have been offended by someone outside the family and so he has a general resentment toward everyone around him. Maybe we rushed things and the child didn't have time to think through what happened. He may think that a parent can't possibly understand how he has been hurt and that simply asking forgiveness doesn't erase everything. Or perhaps the child might also want to see a real change in the parent's behavior first.

Whatever the reason, I have discovered that the best thing to do is start all over again. Be patient; don't rush. Begin at number one and continue to be soft and tender. Go to number two and increase your understanding. We can even say things like, "You know, I probably don't know how much you are hurting." Repeat that you are wrong. "I don't deserve to be forgiven for the way I have treated you lately, but I pray that you can. I want you to know that I love you and I was wrong. I really mean that." At this point, reach out and touch him on the arm to see if he has softened. If he hasn't, give him some time, but be persistent. And finally, ask for his forgiveness again.

One mistake many parents make is dropping the issue altogether. "Well, if he won't forgive me, that's his problem. I did my part." With that attitude, the problem may never be resolved. It's better to back off for awhile, allow a few minutes or even hours for things to cool down, then come back and repeat these five steps.

As parents, there is one additional effective way we can detect a closed spirit. I've found that if we carefully watch nonverbal expressions, we can add to our understanding of what's going on inside a child.

Observing Voice Tone and Facial Expressions to Recognize a Closed Spirit

One woman said to me after a seminar, "I hate my husband. I hate him so much that I can't even talk about him. I'll never go back to him." Yet four months later, that same woman was back with her husband and they were living together in harmony. I heard one husband say about his wife, "I hate that woman so much I can't even stand to look at her." Within hours that same man was loving his wife and regaining his feelings and desires for her.

Sometimes it takes several months, but I'm finding that regaining harmony is possible. My own hope for families and couples increases almost daily because I'm now aware that surface words like, "I hate you," "I'll never live with you again," "I'll always hate you," are reflections of a closed spirit.

A child may say to his parents, "I hate you. I can't handle any more of this. I'm through with this family. I've had it up to here and I don't want to talk about it. I don't even want to be around here." When people spew forth such words, I find they really are saying that they want to talk about it. They would love to resolve the problem but they want to resolve it in a certain way. We need to listen to how they say it, with what intensity. Learn to watch their facial expressions and listen to their tone of voice instead of limiting your understanding to the words they use.

Imagine for a moment a scale from zero to ten, with zero indicating the spirit is totally open and ten totally closed. If I reach for my daughter's hand after I have offended her and she turns her back to me and says, "Dad, you always do this to me and I just can't handle it anymore," chances are I have closed her spirit to about a three. It is not really major, yet it's still very important to reopen it. If I go to touch her and she jerks away from me and says, "Dad, just leave me alone. You're always doing this to me and I just feel like running away," her spirit is probably closed about halfway. But let's say that I knock on her bedroom door and she asks, "Who is it?" in a very hostile voice. I open the door and she says, "Just get out of here, Dad," and she takes a vase and throws it at me. I duck in time and say, "Hey, I know I was wrong . . ." but she yells, "I'm going to run away from this place. I just hate it around here." Those words and actions tell me that her spirit is closed to probably an eight or nine. Usually, the more violent and hostile the resistance, the tighter the spirit has been closed. Hostility may settle into apathy or indifference indicating "my spirit is cemented closed, don't try to reopen it." But when we realize that one's words don't necessarily reflect how one feels inside, we can continue to gently pry open someone's spirit.

The best way that I know to deal with such surface words is to become soft and understanding and admit we are wrong. Then persevere until we can touch and seek forgiveness. That is what they really want. But it may take time.

I have also found that offenses which happened many years ago can still be resolved in much the same way. A child may remember being hurt by a parent many years before. And if a parent really wants to make sure that a child's spirit is totally open toward him, it is appropriate to go back into the past and bring up these old offenses, *as long as the offenses are resolved once they are brought up.*

How Children or Adults Can
Reopen Their Own Spirits

If parents are not willing to open their child's closed spirit, it would sound as though the child was destined to rebellion. But there are several things that a child or anyone can do to open his own spirit.

This simple but profound truth is taught in a prayer prayed millions of times each year—the Lord's Prayer. I had read this prayer for years, but continued to miss its true meaning. The prayer invites us to forgive those who trespass against us—who offend us—then God will forgive us of our trespasses. But if we refuse to forgive those who trespass against us, then God will not forgive us.

The word forgive comes from a Greek word meaning "to release" or "set free." It means to untie the chains that bind people. Therefore, when we set free those who offend us or trespass against us, God unties us, opening our spirit. He cannot reopen our spirit, however, if we refuse to help those who have hurt us.

Corrie ten Boom, who helped many Jews avoid the German torture camps in World War II, told me a story that illustrated what Jesus meant by His prayer. Sometime after she had been released from a concentration camp, she spoke at a church in Germany. As the crowd filed out after the service, she saw a man working his way forward. With horror, she recognized him. He had been a guard—one of the most cruel—in the concentration camp where she and her sister had been interned. He had actually been instrumental in causing the death of her sister, Betsie. She was almost nauseated by the sight of him. Her spirit had already been closed toward him years before. He reached out his hand and said, "Corrie ten Boom, I have become a Christian and I know God has forgiven me for the cruel things I did. But I've come to ask if you would forgive me." Corrie said her arms were frozen to her side. She couldn't move.

She told me it was the most difficult thing she'd ever done, but she did reach out and accept his hand and tell him that she did forgive him. At that moment, it was like the venom and hatred flowed out of her. "It was God's love flowing through me to him," she told me. "I really did release him from what he had done to me. And as I did, I was set free!"

As parents we can help teach our children that principle. First, a child can begin to recognize *that the person who has offended him has problems of his own.* Everyone who offends us has his own difficulties or unmet needs. He may have low self-worth. He may feel rejected, or guilty, or resentful toward someone. As soon as we start recognizing this, we start being free in our heart and our spirit can begin to open toward that person.

Second, *we can make a commitment to pray for someone who has offended us.* When our children were young, we lived in the Chicago area. When we went through the tollbooths on the expressway, our children would sometimes hand the attendants the money. They would reach over my shoulder to do so, but now and then the coins would drop and I would have to open the door to retrieve them. Some of the attendants became very irritated. As we would pull away, the children often commented about their anger. "You know why that person was mad at us?" I asked. "It's because he has an 'owwie' in his heart. That's his way of saying, 'Would someone please understand me?'" Sometimes we would pray for an attendant, which helped the children realize they shouldn't take someone else's anger personally.

The biggest problem is that people take offenses far too personally. Usually people are offensive because they have their own problems. Maybe they didn't get enough sleep, they've had a bad day, or someone at home or work has rejected them. There are any number of reasons why people can be offensive, and the sooner we recognize this, the less chance we have of being offended and having our spirit closed. However, even if it does close, we can begin to open it by recognizing that the offender has problems. Even if we never get a chance to help the offender with his problems, just wanting and intending to help many times is enough for God to open our spirit and clear our heart of resentment.

How Open Is Your Child's Spirit?

Test yourself with your children to see how open their spirits are. This is a simple, general evaluation that can help a parent detect whether or not a child's spirit is closing. Score each question from one to five. 1 = never; 2 = seldom; 3 = sometimes; 4 = usually; 5 = always.

1. Does my child (age two and above) enjoy touching me? ____

2. Does my child spontaneously touch me when I first see him after school or at home? ____

3. Does my child respect what I respect in life? ____

4. Does my child generally appreciate what I value in life—i.e., the Bible, my vocation, etc.? ____

5. Would my child's friends be my choice for him? ____

6. Does my child wear clothing and hairstyles that I approve of? ____

7. Does my child choose the activities I would choose for him? ____

8. Does my child's music reflect what I approve of? ____

9. Does my child enjoy having conversations with me? ____

10. Does my child agree in general with my opinions? ____

11. Does my child enjoy going places with me? ____

12. Does my child obey me regularly? ____

13. Does my child generally reflect a warm affection for me? ____

14. Does my child naturally enjoy looking into my eyes? ____

Total Score _____

These scores may indicate:

14–20—Danger, resolve immediately.

21–30—Warning, proceed with caution.

31–40—Watch out for falling rocks.

41–50—Things may be bumping along, but okay.

51–70—End of Construction. Drive carefully.

If you believe that one or more of your children are closing or have closed their spirits toward you, one effective way to start reopening their spirits is to take them out to dinner or get away for a weekend. During that time, let the child know you are trying to have the best relationship with him that you can. Then mention a particular incident that you think offended him and ask him if it did. If it didn't, you can ask, "If that wasn't it, what are some things you can think of that I have done in the past that have really hurt you?" Be prepared, however, to hear something that you do not expect. As offenses surface from the past, simply do the same things you would do with an immediate offense. Go through all five steps—being soft, understanding, admitting you were wrong, trying to touch, and seeking forgiveness.

Eighty-four Ways We Can Offend Our Children

As you seek to discover how you might have offended your child, you may need some help coming up with possibilities. In my counseling and work with children around the country, I have asked many of them how their parents have offended them. I took their answers and compiled them. Here are some of their actual responses:

1. Lacking interest in things that are special to me.
2. Breaking promises.
3. Criticizing unjustly.
4. Allowing my brother or sister to put me down.
5. Misunderstanding my motives.
6. Speaking carelessly.
7. Punishing me for something for which I already had been punished.

8. Telling me that my opinions don't really matter.

9. Giving me the feeling that they never make mistakes.

10. Not being gentle when pointing out my weaknesses or blind spots.

11. Lecturing me and not understanding when all I need is some support.

12. Never telling me "I love you." Never showing me physical affection.

13. Not spending time alone with me.

14. Being insensitive, rough, and breaking promises.

15. Being thoughtless.

16. Never telling me "thank you."

17. Not spending time together.

18. Being insensitive to my trials.

19. Speaking harsh words.

20. Being inconsistent.

21. Being taken for granted.

22. Being told how to do something that I was doing on my own.

23. Nagging me.

24. Bossing me.

25. Feeling unnoticed or unappreciated.

26. Being ignored.

27. Not being considered a thinking and feeling person.

28. Being too busy to care for me and listen to me.

29. Dismissing my needs as unimportant, especially when their work or hobby is more important.

30. Bringing up old mistakes from the past to deal with present problems.

31. Teasing excessively.

32. Not noticing my accomplishments.

33. Making tactlesss comments.

34. Liking me only for my physical looks or abilities, instead of what's inside me.

35. Not being praised and appreciated.

36. Being built up and then let down.

37. Getting my hopes up to do something as a family and then not following through.

38. Being corrected without being reminded that they love me.

39. Being disciplined in harshness and anger.

40. Not reasoning with me, and never giving me an explanation of why I'm being disciplined.

41. Misusing brute force.

42. Reacting to me in the opposite way I think a Christian should treat me.

43. Raising their voices to each other.

44. Not being interested in who I am.

45. Cutting down something I am doing or someone I am with as being dumb or stupid.

46. Using foul language when they are upset with me.

47. Being impatient, which often comes across as rudeness.

48. Saying "no" without giving a reason.

49. Not praising me.

50. Sensing a difference between what is said with the mouth and what is said through facial expressions.

51. Making sarcastic remarks about me.

52. Making fun of my hopes, dreams, and accomplishments.

53. Punishing me severely for something that I didn't do.

54. Being distracted when I really have something to say.

55. Insulting me in front of others.

56. Speaking before thinking through how it will affect me.

57. Pressuring me when I already feel low or offended.

58. Comparing me with other kids at school and telling me how wonderful they are and that they wish I could be better.

59. Forcing me to argue with them when I'm really hurt inside.

60. Being treated like a little child.

61. Not approving of what I do or how I do it. I keep trying to get their approval but they just won't give it.

62. Seeing them do the very things they tell me not to do.

63. Ignoring me when I ask for advice because they are too busy.

64. Ignoring me and not introducing me to people who come to the house or we see in public.

65. Showing favoritism toward my brother or sister.

66. Acting as if something I want is of little importance.

67. Not feeling like I am special to them. It's so important to me to have my parents let me know, even in small ways, that I'm special to them.

68. Seeing my father put my mother down, especially in front of company.

69. Seldom touching or holding me.

70. Hearing mom and dad bickering at each other to the point where one of them is really hurt.

71. Not trusting me.

72. Making fun of something physically different about me.

73. Seeing my mom and dad trying to get revenge against each other.

74. Sensing that my dad never approves of what I do or how I do it.

75. Not being able to control their anger.

76. Getting mad at me because I can't keep up with their schedule or abilities.

77. Making me feel like they wish they never had me in the first place.

78. Not having enough time for me.

79. Needing my parents but they are glued to the television.

80. Seeing my parents spend a lot of money on their pleasures, but when I want something, they don't seem to have the money.

81. Making me feel childish.

82. Not spending the time to understand what I am trying to say.

83. Yelling at me when I already know I'm wrong.

84. Making me feel like I hadn't tried to improve at something when I really had.

2

Parenting for Positive Results

- Four Basic Types of Parenting:
    The Dominant Parent
    The Neglectful Parent
    The Permissive Parent
    The Loving and Firm Parent
- The Two Most Important Factors in Raising
  Children

MY HEART SANK WHEN I saw the police car pull into our driveway. I knew why it was there. Too scared to move, I sat still, trying to look innocent while my mother opened the door.

The officer introduced himself, then turned to me. "Have you been with your friend Jimmy today?" he asked.

"Yes," I said, trying my best to hide my nervousness. "I see him all the time."

"Were you down at the river with him?"

"No. I wasn't anywhere near the river."

The officer looked at my mother and then back at me. "Jimmy told me you were down there with him. He also said that the two of you broke into one of the homes there."

I could feel the blood rushing to my face as I shook my head in denial. The officer kept talking: "You're going to have to appear at juvenile court next week. I'll have witnesses there."

I began to cry and then admitted everything. "I was down at the river. We did break into a house. But we only took a couple of small items."

This wasn't my first brush with trouble. A few of the town merchants had accused me of stealing money and items from their stores. I hadn't stolen anything from them, but my reputation was established, so they suspected me anyway. There were rumors going around town that I probably would be sent to reform school. Growing up, I basically did what I wanted to do when I wanted to. I'm sure that I deserved hundreds of spankings for my actions and irresponsible attitude as a child, but my parents never once disciplined me. As a result, there have been many areas where I have had difficulty adjusting as an adult. For one thing, rules never apply to me. If a sign says "no parking," I may park anyway because "I'm an exception." Because there were no rules in my home, I figured rules were for others, not me.

However, the attitude of my parents did have one very positive result in my life; it laid the foundation for a strong sense of self-worth. This fact could sound strange after reading about all of the trouble I was involved in. But as I look back to how I was raised, I can see that my parents were one of four types of parents we'll discuss in this chapter. I now understand how I was able to grow up with a positive self-image in a home void of discipline.

A few years ago, Dr. Dennis Guernsey described four basic categories of parents in an article for *Family Life Today*. His observations were based on a study by three Ph.D.'s at the University of Minnesota. Two types of parents tend to cause their children to resent authority. These children tend to dislike themselves. They may do poorly in school and are often convinced that they never will be successful. These same two types of parents also tend more frequently to close the spirit of their children, resulting in the various problems we mentioned in chapter 1.

The other two categories of parents—one of which characterized my mother and father—tend to produce more positive-acting children. These children are more secure and tend to like themselves. They do better in school and are more responsible as adults.

As we examine each type of parent, it is important not only to examine the kind of parents we would like to be, but also to evaluate our lives in light of how we were parented.

Four Basic Types of Parenting

1. The Dominant Parent. This type of parent tends to produce the most negative qualities in children. Dominant parents usually have very high standards and expectations. But they seldom offer warm, caring support and very few explanations are given for their rigid rules. They tend to be unbending and demand that their children stay away from certain activities because of their strong convictions. But because the children do not know the reasons why these activities are wrong, they may secretly participate in them.

A group of psychologists and psychiatrists studied 875 third graders in rural Columbia County, New York, from 1960 to 1981 and made several conclusions concerning dominant parents. They found that high aggression in younger children is caused by the actions of overly dominant parents. This high aggression usually lasts a lifetime and can lead to major violence. The study also showed that harsh punishment, like washing out children's mouths with soap, coupled with rejection can lead to aggressive behavior.

These are some typical statements and actions by dominant parents:

- "Rules are rules. You're late—to bed with no dinner."
- "I won't stand for your back talk. Apologize." (Or slap the child's face.)
- "You don't need reasons. Just do what I say."
- "I don't care how many of your friends will be there. You're not going and I don't want to hear another word about it, do you hear?"
- "No son of mine is going to goof off. You took the job; you get it done."
- "How many times have I told you to stop that? Get in there—you're going to get it!"

These are some possible reactions by children who have dominant parents:

- They rank lowest in self-respect. They have little ability to conform to rules or authority.

- The rigid harshness of the parent breaks the spirit of the child and results in resistance, "clamming up," or rebellion.

- The child usually does not want anything to do with his parents' rules or values. He tends to reject the ideals of his parents.

- The child may be attracted to other children who rebel against their parents and the general rules of society. They may use drugs and participate in other illegal activities.

- The child may be loud and demanding of his rights.

- In a classroom setting, he may cause disruption in order to gain attention from others.

2. The Neglectful Parent. Neglectful parents tend to lack both loving support and control over their children. They show an uncaring or immature attitude, lashing out at a child when pushed or irritated. These parents tend to isolate themselves from their children by excessive use of babysitters and to indulge in their own selfish activities. Children are viewed as a bother, "to be seen and not heard."

Dr. Armand Nicholi, psychiatric professor at Harvard Medical School, helped me understand that neglectful parents are not only absent when they are away from home. They rob their children of one of the most important factors in their lives—emotional accessibility. When they are home, they usually are not listening or paying attention to their children.

There are four main reasons why our children are being neglected today, according to Dr. Nicholi:

a. *The high divorce rate.* Statistics show that there are more than thirteen million children in single parent homes. The divorce rate has been upwardly spiraling since the early 1960s and has increased 700 percent since the beginning of this century. Most divorces require single parents to work outside the home, allowing less time for the emotional development of their children. It's very difficult for single parents to provide their children with the necessary time each day for listening and emotional accessibility. However, it's not impossible.

b. *The increase of mothers in the work force.* More than 50 percent of all mothers in the United States are working. This also greatly increased in the 1960s, with a strong emphasis being put forth that women were unfulfilled in their homes. The economic pressures of the times also forced many women to seek jobs. By joining the work force, mothers are often less accessible to their children.

The suicide rate among children ages ten to fourteen has tripled in the last ten years. Dr. Nicholi says this can be directly related to changes in the American home. One study he quoted shows that American parents spend less time with their children than parents in any other nation except England. The study quoted one Russian father who said he would not even think of spending less than two hours daily with his children. In contrast, a study at Boston University found that the average father in the United States spends about thirty-seven seconds a day with his children.

c. *Excessive television viewing.* This also increased greatly in the sixties and now more than 90 percent of American homes have at least one television. The problem with television is that even though people are physically together in a room, there is very little meaningful and emotional interaction. As parents neglect their children by watching television or through other activities, the children experience an emotional loss similar to that of losing a parent through death. They often feel guilty when their parents are not with them. Some even believe the reason is because they are bad, and if only they were better, their parents would spend more time with them. Obviously, this awareness lowers a child's sense of worth.

d. *An increasingly mobile society.* More than 50 percent of Americans change addresses every five years. This mobility robs children of their parents' time as well as the emotional strength and accessibility they have from friends and relatives in their former home. Yet even if we have to move our families, we can still provide emotional accessibility to our children. This can be done by setting aside time every day to spend with each of our children or together as a family. Dr. Nicholi stressed that this time should be used to counteract the effects of our mobile society.

To illustrate how prevalent the problem of emotional accessibility is, take a short break and try spending just five minutes concentrating on your family's welfare and how you can help meet each child's emotional needs. You may find it very difficult because we're not used to doing this in our culture.

Listed below are some typical actions and statements made by neglectful parents:

- "Work it out by yourself. Can't you see I'm busy?"
- "No! I'm expected somewhere else tonight. Get your mother to help you."
- "No, you can't stay up. Remember you wanted to stay up late last night. Stay out of my hair!"
- "That's your problem. I've got to get to work."
- "Good grief! Can't you kids be more careful?"
- "Late again, for heaven's sake. Would someone please pass the meat?"
- "So you think I'm stupid, huh? Well, that's your problem, buddy. Just get lost!"

Here are some possible effects on children of neglectful parents:

- The harshness and neglect tend to wound the spirit of a child, resulting in rebellion.
- The neglect teaches the child that he is not worth spending time with.
- The child develops insecurity because his parents are never predictable.
- The child may not develop a healthy self-respect because he is not respected and has not learned to control himself.
- Broken promises break the spirit of the child and lower his self-worth.
- The child tends to do poorly in school because he has little motivation.

3. The Permissive Parent. Permissive parents tend to be warm, supporting people, but weak in establishing and enforcing rules and limits for their children.

This was the type of parents that I had. My mother and father were very warm and loving and accepting of me. But as far as I can remember, there were no rigid rules in our home. They usually gave in to my demands. Even when I was in trouble, they would not spank or discipline me. My mother said she never spanked because her first child died of blood poisoning and she had spanked her two weeks before she died. She made my father promise to never spank any one of their five remaining children.

Although they meant well, that leniency affected me negatively. My parents left all decisions concerning how I would spend my spare time up to me. In fact I didn't start formally dating until . . . the third grade! This caused a number of problems in my life. Once my father caught me in a serious infraction as a young boy. From his firm voice I knew that I was in trouble. But later, he said he would let me off without punishing me if I promised not to do it again. I actually told him that I needed a spanking but he wouldn't do it. There was something in me that wanted to be corrected.

I found the same permissiveness in school. Once a teacher caught me passing notes in the third grade after warning me of the consequences if I didn't stop. She sent me to the principal. He talked to me for awhile, told me I needed to shape up, then said that he was going to spank me. I thought he really meant business, but about fifteen minutes later, he said he was going to give me another chance if I promised not to pass notes again. Of course, I promised the world, but inwardly I can remember being disappointed that he didn't follow through.

One of the major reasons why some parents are too permissive is an inner fear that they may damage their children if they are too strict. That fear of confronting their children may actually produce the very things they fear.

On the positive side, permissive parents are strong in the area of support. I am very grateful that my parents showed me warmth and love. They were very giving, very understanding, very comforting. Effective parents realize that a certain degree of permissiveness is healthy. That means accepting that kids will be kids, that a clean shirt will not stay clean for long, that children will run instead of walk, and that a tree is for climbing and a mirror for making faces. It means accepting that children have the right to childlike feelings and dreams. That kind of permissiveness gives a child confidence and an increasing capacity to express his thoughts and feelings.

Overpermissiveness, on the other hand, allows for undesirable acts such as beating up other children, marking on buildings, and breaking objects.

The following statements and actions are typical of permissive parents:

- "Well, okay. You can stay up late this time. I know how much you like this program."

- "You're tired, aren't you? A paper route is a tough job; sure, I'll take you around."

- "I hate to see you under all this pressure from school. Why not rest tomorrow? I'll say you're sick."

- "You didn't hear me call you for dinner. Well, that's all right. Sit down. I don't want you eating a cold dinner."

- "Please don't get angry with me. You're making a scene."

- "Jimmy, please try to hurry. Mommy will be late again if we don't start soon."

These are possible reactions by children who have permissive parents:

- A child senses that he is in the driver's seat and can play the parent accordingly.

- A child develops a feeling of insecurity, like leaning against a wall that appears to be firm, but falls over.

- A child may have little self-respect because he has not learned to control himself and master certain personal disciplines.

- A child learns that because standards are not firm, he can manipulate around the rules.

4. The Loving and Firm Parent. Loving and firm parents usually have clearly defined rules, limits, and standards for living. They take time to train their children to understand these limits—like why we don't carve love notes on the neighbor's tree—and give clear warnings when a child has transgressed an established limit. But they also give support by expressing

---

55

physical affection and spending personal time listening to each child. They are flexible, willing to listen to all the facts if a limit has been violated.

The loving and firm parent is a healthy and balanced combination of the dominant and permissive parents. There is firmness with clearly defined rules like, "You cannot intentionally harm our furniture or anyone else's," but this firmness is combined with loving attitudes and actions.

Here are some typical statements and actions by loving and firm parents:

- "You're late again for dinner, Tiger. How can we work this out together?" (Parents spend time working out solutions with the child.)
- "Hey, I wish I could let you stay up later, but we agreed on this time. Remember what you're like the next day if you miss your sleep?"
- "When we both cool off, let's talk about what needs to be done."
- "You're really stuck, aren't you? I'll help you this time. Then let's figure out how you can get it done yourself next time."
- "You say all the other girls will be there. I'd like to have more information first."
- "Did you do your piano? I hate to do this, but we agreed—no dinner before it is finished. We'll keep it warm for you."
- "You may answer the phone, but before you answer, you must learn to answer it the right way."

Typical characteristics of children who have loving and firm parents:

- The warm support and clearly defined limits tend to build self-respect within the child.

- A child is more content when he has learned to control himself.

- His world is more secure when he realizes that there are limits which are unbending, and he understands why—the underlying principles.

- Because the spirit of a child is not closed, the lines of communication are open with parents. There is less chance of the "rebellious teen years."

- The children from loving and firm parents ranked highest in: (a) self-respect, (b) capacity to conform to authorities at school, church, etc., (c) greater interest in their parents' faith in God, and (d) greater tendency not to join a rebellious group.

The supportive and firm parent reflects the very specific biblical instruction for parenting. It stresses two important ways that parents must take care of their children. First, they must *discipline* their children, which partly means setting clearly defined limits in the home. Second, they must follow the greatest *instruction* in Scripture—to love one another.

The Two Most Important Factors in Raising Children

I have concluded that the two most important factors in raising children are:

1. Establishing clearly defined and understood rules in the home, limits that the children know they cannot violate without some consequence.

2. A commitment to love each child in a warm, affectionate, and supportive way.

In the chart below, each of these four types of parents is summarized. The dominant parents are lower in their ability to show loving, warm support and higher in the establishment of rigid rules and limitations. Neglectful parents have a tendency to be lacking in warm and loving support and also in establishing rules and limits around the house. Permissive parents have a greater tendency to be loving, warm, supportive, and approving, yet lack the ability to establish clearly defined limits and rules. The fourth type of parent, the loving and firm parent, has established clearly defined limits and is more diligent in communicating warmth and loving support.

Parents	Love and support for their children	Controlling children by limits or rules at home
Dominant	Low	High
Neglectful	Low	Low
Permissive	High	Low
Loving and Firm	High	High

3

Expressing Loving Support— The Most Important Aspect of Raising Children

- Unconditional Commitment
- Scheduled Times
- Availability to Children
- Tender Treatment
- Frequent Eye Contact
- Listening in an Understanding Way
- Meaningful Touching

THE TENSION WAS THICK in the front seat of our car. Greg stared silently out the window. "I know what you've been doing," I said. My thirteen-year-old son was involved in an activity he knew was wrong. But he couldn't admit it.

With tears streaming down his face, he said, "Dad I didn't want to tell you because I knew you'd be so ashamed of me." I held out my arms and he immediately grabbed me and began sobbing. I could feel his body relax as I told him, "No matter what you have done or ever do, remember I will always love you."

With those words, Greg was able to admit what he had been doing. As Greg sensed my love for him, he was able to relax and our communication was open. In this chapter we want to explore several ways of expressing supportive love to our children, the kind of love that builds stronger families and increases a child's sense of personal value.

Unconditional Commitment

One of the most important ways to express warmth and loving support to our children is *to make an unconditional commitment to them for life.* That's the kind of commitment that says, "You're important to me today and tomorrow, no matter what happens."

My family is reminded daily of my commitment to them. At the entryway of our home hangs a wall plaque that I made. It reads: "To Norma, Kari, Gregory and Michael, in assurance of my lifetime commitment to you."

Norma and I frequently tell our children that we love them. In many ways, we let them know that we are committed to them for their entire lives, no matter what they do. We are committed to help them be successful in whatever they want to do. We will be committed to them after they are married. We will be committed to them no matter who they marry. We will be committed no matter what happens during their marriage. We will be committed to their mates and to their children. We tell them we are always available to listen. Should they get into trouble, we will be there to help. That doesn't necessarily mean we will bail them out of a tight situation, for that may not be best for them. But they know how much we love them and that nothing can ever keep us from loving them.

Mark "Golden Boy" Frazie, a professional boxer, told me how his parents demonstrated their commitment to him. When I asked Mark who was the most encouraging person in his life, without hesitation he answered, "My dad." He told me that his father is his very best friend and always will be.

"When I was nineteen years old, I went through a real trial," Mark explained. "Some of my family resisted me and many of my relatives did not understand. But my dad told me that even though he was hurt by what I had done, I was his son. He would always love me and always be there to pick me up."

In contrast, lack of unconditional commitment can result in major conflict. A frightened eighteen-year-old boy standing in front of a stern judge listened as the judge, a close personal friend of the boy's father, told him that he was a disgrace to the community and his family: "You ought to be ashamed of yourself, disgracing your family's name, causing your parents a great deal of anguish and embarrassment. Your father is an upright citizen in this community. I have personally served on numerous committees with him and know of his commitment to this city. I count your father as a close personal friend and it is with deep grief that I have to sentence you this day for your crime."

With his head bowed in obvious embarrassment, the young man listened to the judge. Then, before sentence was passed, he asked if he could speak: "Sir, I do not mean to be disrespectful or to make excuses for my behavior. But I envy you a great deal. You see, there were many days and nights that I wanted to be my father's best friend. There were many times when I needed his help with school work, in some of my dating situations, and in some of the difficult times that I faced as a teenager. But my father was gone a great deal, probably on some of those committees with you, or playing golf. I've always felt like other things were more important to him than I was. I don't mean this disrespectfully, but I truly wish I knew my father like you do."

Stunned by the boy's words, the judge placed him on probation and ordered that the boy and his father were to spend time together every week, getting to know each other. The father obviously was humiliated by the sentence, realizing his lack of commitment to his son, but it caused him to get to know his son better and that was the turning point in his son's life.

Scheduled Times

A second way that we as parents can show our love is to *schedule special times with the family.* Communicating warm, loving approval to our children doesn't just happen naturally. I believe this time should be scheduled on a regular basis—preferably daily—because our children need us.

Schedule times that are meaningful for all persons involved. The activity itself is not so important, but it needs to be something that is enjoyable for both the child and the parent. Often the deepest relationships can be developed during the simplest activities.

As a family, we camp together frequently. It is during those times in the car, or lying in our sleeping bags, or waiting for a fish to bite when things are said that give us a deep understanding about our children. These special times help us understand where they are going in life and what concerns them. Just being with them communicates they are loved. A parent's willingness to wait for conversation to develop further amplifies his or her child's self-worth.

One summer night we were in our motor home driving from Portland, Oregon, to Chicago. It was about 10:00 P.M. and everyone was asleep. I had planned to stop at a campsite around 11:00, but Kari, who was about thirteen years old at the time, was awakened and wandered up front and sat next to me. She brought up the subject of dating and marriage and we got involved in a most meaningful discussion about the consequences of premarital sexual involvement. We had no place to go. There was no telephone to interrupt us. There is no way I could have planned a more meaningful time together. We didn't need to stop for food. And she was, of course, highly interested in the conversation. We stayed up until 2:00 A.M. while everyone else slept. These times seldom occur unless we plan time together. If our children see us neglect other things to spend time with them, they will realize how important they are to us.

I often wonder why we, as parents, are so reluctant to tell our children how valuable they are to us. We need to let them know regularly that they are tremendously important to us. On a scale from zero to ten, where do your children feel they rate in importance to you? My children know that they are about a nine to me. They are the most important things in my life other than my relationship with God and my wife. Sometimes I allow their value to drop to a four or seven, but I keep pushing it back up to nine with a conscious decision to value them. Gloria Gaither and Shirley Dobson have written a book called *Let's Make a Memory*. It is a super resource, filled with ideas for things to do during scheduled times for parents and children.

Availability to Children

Besides unconditional commitment and scheduling meaningful times together we need to *communicate that we are available* to our children both during scheduled and unscheduled times. Sometimes when I'm reading the paper, watching something special on television or heading out the door for a meeting, one of my children will walk up and say, "Dad, you got a minute? I've got this problem in geometry." Or Kari might say to Norma in the kitchen, "Mom, what am I going to do? I can't find anything to wear." We must be careful what we communicate at these times. If we say, "Not now, I'm busy," they'll observe what we are doing and compare their importance to it. Often we can say, "Now isn't a good time to talk, but I can give you my undivided attention in thirty minutes." Sometimes we can drop what we're doing, because our children are simply more important.

Children might go a whole day without asking for our help. But as Dr. Campbell explains in his book, *How to Really Love Your Teen-Ager*, teens have something like a "container" built within them and every once in a while they run out of "emotional gas." This is when they come up and need to be close to us. They need touching, listening, understanding, and our time. After we have filled their "emotional gas tank" they usually say, "Well, see you later." Maybe we haven't finished everything we wanted to say, but they're filled up. And that's okay. I want my children to know they are valuable and that I am available most of the time when they need me.

Being available does not mean that we wait around for our children. It does mean evaluating what is most important to us in life. Is it needlepoint? Golf? Television? Football? Work? How many parents would say that the newspaper is more important than their children? Probably none. Yet many parents appear to be unavailable or even become angry if their children approach them with some special need while they are reading.

It is natural for a father to become engrossed in his work, but a man must evaluate why he is working. Is he primarily working to meet the needs of his family or to meet his own needs? If he is working to meet the needs of his family, he should not rationalize that it is okay to spend many extra hours at work because he is feeding his children or preparing to send them to college. In reality, kids have a much greater need for *time with dad*, than knowing dad is away at work so they can eat or attend college.

Because I can easily get involved with my vocation and rationalize time away from my children, I reevaluate on a regular basis. I often ask my wife if she feels I am spending enough time with our children. I also ask our children the same question, carefully listening to what they say.

Children don't expect that parents give up all of their activities and fun times just so that they are always available for them. But they must see that these other activities are not as valuable as they are to their parents.

Tender Treatment

Another aspect of communicating love to children is how parents act while with them. *Children need to be treated tenderly.* Gentleness and tenderness are of prime importance in dealing with our children. Harshness and angry lecturing communicate to children that they are of little value and in some cases worthless. The phrase "If I meant anything to anyone, they wouldn't be so mean to me" is the frequent subconscious conclusion teens draw.

The calming effect of tenderness in a home has tremendously positive effects. Sometimes, while I'm reading in the evening, one of my kids will climb up on my lap. They may want to talk; other times they're content just to be with me. It's not unusual for Kari to come to me and say something like, "Dad, I'm having a problem with a friend at school. Do you think we could talk about it tonight?" She knows that I am usually open to that situation. And I have learned that when we do get together, she wants me to listen, remain calm, offer some suggestions, and especially try to understand her suggestions. She does not want or need a lecture. Above all, she wants me to be tender while I'm listening.

Recently I violated almost every principle I recommend in this book, but because Kari, now seventeen years old, knows I love her and our relationship is strong, it appeared that she was just barely affected by my insensitivity. Under the stress of finishing this book and several other major responsibilities I launched into a firm and serious lecture with her. "Don't you ever wait until the last day to finish a school report," I ranted. I threatened her social life and anything else that came to mind. I left the house with a close friend and halfway through dinner I excused myself and telephoned Kari. "Kari," I said, tenderly and apologetically, "Dad was wrong, wasn't he?" Often I think children are much more mature than their parents. She answered, "Dad, Mom explained the pressures you are under. The reason I never answered you was because I knew what you're going through. Thanks for calling though. I love you."

In the heat of a family argument I can forget all about being tender. I'm particularly vulnerable when I return home from a trip and am physically and emotionally exhausted. On one such day, Kari said she wanted to participate in some athletic activity but didn't know which one to choose. She had mentioned this on several occasions but never followed through on any of my suggestions. This time, I suggested she go out for track at school. She told me she had no interest in track. That angered me. "I want you to go out for track," I yelled. "If I tell you to go out for track, that means you're going out for track!" She was shocked by my response. Here she was, sixteen years old, a lovely girl with a great attitude, and I was upset because she wasn't going out for track. I knew I was wrong. I could see I was closing her spirit. But I was too upset to deal with it right then.

In situations such as this, it is often best to leave the conflict for awhile. Later that evening, when I'd calmed down, I gently approached Kari. (This was after I had made a deal with my family. Because they are all extremely valuable to me, I had told them I would give ten dollars to anyone if I ever took out my frustrations on him.) I felt so bad about what I'd said to my daughter, I made out a check to her for twenty dollars. I knocked on Kari's door and heard her say very hesitantly, "Who is it?" When I told her it was me, she said, "Oh, Dad, I can't take any more of this right now."

When I told her I needed to talk with her, she unlocked the door. I handed her the check, explaining, "Kari, I know this doesn't buy your love, and it doesn't get me off the hook. But what I did to you was very wrong, and you're too valuable to be treated that way. I want to give you this little gift."

A smile broke across her face and she was a little embarrassed. "Oh, Dad, you don't have to do this." I could tell that her spirit was opening as we spoke. Even if I hadn't given her anything, but had gently apologized, it would have helped begin the process of opening her spirit. When I gave her the money—twice the amount I agreed to give her—I was communicating in a small way how valuable she was to me.

It is easier for me to do this today, because I have been practicing for several years. However it wasn't easy at first. If you are not used to being tender and admitting wrong actions as a parent, it will be difficult for you to humble yourself. But it will pay valuable dividends in the lives of your children.

Frequent Eye Contact

Children need frequent eye contact with us. Frequent eye contact is a very effective way of communicating love to anyone. This can also help a parent evaluate whether or not a child's spirit is closing. A child whose spirit is closing tends to look down or away, or turn his entire body away from the parent. With younger children, it helps to get down on our knees and look them straight in the eye.

I've often heard Norma say, "Now, look me in the eyes," when questioning our children. She says that she can usually sense whether a child is telling the truth. It is difficult for a child to keep his eyes on his parents when he is guilty. He looks down, or away, or his eyes begin to blink. A child may confess something just because of our gentle insistence that we look each other in the eyes.

Listening in an Understanding Way

The sixth aspect of communicating love to our children is *listening in an understanding way.* Listening is one skill that many people take for granted. However, I believe listening is so important that I recommend parents purchase a book or enroll in a course on how to listen. Listening does not come naturally. Most adults are preoccupied with their own needs and problems and therefore have a tendency not to listen carefully to those around them. By not noticing the needs of others, we can communicate that we are not interested in them.

There are several important points to remember about being an effective listener with our children:

A good listener desires *eye contact* with the speaker. That means stopping our activities—putting the newspaper down, turning the television off—and giving our undivided attention.

A good listener *never assumes he knows what the other person is saying.* I have reacted to something one of my children said only to learn later that what I understood wasn't what he really meant. One of the fastest ways to close a person's spirit is to accuse him of something that he doesn't really mean.

I have found it helpful to ask questions to clarify what the other person has said. *I repeat in different words what I think they mean.* Then I ask them, "Is that what you are saying?" If they say, "Well, Dad, that's close, but that's not quite it," I say, "Well, we have plenty of time. Just what do you mean by that?" Then they will repeat what they are trying to tell me.

Greg is our resident comedian. But one time I thought he took it too far when I found Michael, at age three, lying on the bottom of a motel swimming pool. After rescuing Mike, I rushed him to our room so a local doctor could check him. Greg was chasing us when he yelled, "Dad wait, I can't keep up. He's okay, I'm sure!" and he started to laugh. I stopped, snapped my head around, and scolded him, pointing for him to stay with Mom. "What does he know about the seriousness of this situation?" I muttered as I continued running. Later, Greg tried to explain what he meant. Instead of reacting, I asked him to explain himself. He simply was trying to tell me that he wanted to help and in his nervousness he began to laugh without really knowing why.

Another key factor in being a good listener is to *not overreact or take immediate action.* One day I almost ran to Kari's school after hearing what one of her teachers had said about her in class. I was extremely upset that a professional teacher would say what he said to her. Kari immediately started crying and pleaded with me that I not confront the teacher. When I saw her fear I calmed down and reassured her that I would not go to the teacher without her permission. My assurance gave her the added freedom to share the rest of what he had said.

Later, after we'd both had time to think, I asked Kari for permission to see the teacher and she granted it. Norma and I confronted him, repeating what Kari had said he shared in class about her. The teacher confessed it, apologized to us, and asked if he could see Kari immediately. We took him to her and in tears he put his arms around her and sought her forgiveness. It was a special moment for all of us. Because I had not acted impulsively but instead asked for her permission first, Kari has continued to be open in sharing with us what happens in her life at school.

I have found that it is best to go through a whole conversation, then later on, after we have had time to think, take action with the agreement of the child involved. An immediate reaction causes children to fear bringing up things in the future, cutting the lines of communication.

Once I was locked in an argument with Greg concerning one of his grades. In my frustration, I said I was going to ground him from everything, forever. Kari calmly reminded me of my own commitment to wait a few days after a trip before changing or establishing a new rule that affected the kids. She was right. After a few days, I had forgotten all about the situation. Patience is crucial to building trust and openness between the parent and child.

In order to be a good listener, it is also important that we *not ridicule what our children say*. We may not understand what they are saying, but being critical or ridiculing a child lowers his sense of worth and can cut off meaningful communication.

In his book, *The Family That Listens*, Dr. H. Norman Wright outlines some additional ideas about listening:

1. Parents must be careful not to stereotype children. If you feel your child is a complainer, a whiner, a bully, or procrastinator, it may affect what you think he is saying. If we think, "Oh, he's

just a whiner, it's not important what he says," we may miss learning some vital information.

2. People tend to listen five times as fast as another person can speak. If your child talks at one hundred words per minute, and you can listen at five hundred words per minute, what do you do with the remainder of time? Often boredom sets in and we daydream. Or we try to help our children express their thoughts rather than taking the time to listen to what they really mean.

3. We need to listen with our entire body, not just our ears and eyes. We cannot listen effectively as we walk away, fix dinner, or flip through the paper. We listen most effectively with our body turned toward the speaker, leaning slightly forward.

Each of these areas—*unconditional commitment, scheduled time, availability, tender treatment, frequent eye contact,* and *listening in an understanding way*—increases our children's sense of worth and value. As they feel more valued, they feel loved.

Meaningful Touching

The last major way we express love for our children is through *meaningful touching*. There is a great deal of research emerging about the importance of touching and hugging our children.

According to some research, the skin is the largest organ of our body and has a built-in need to be touched. Physiologists contend that the nerve endings of the skin actually are associated with certain vital glands centered in the brain. These glands regulate growth and many other important functions of the body. Research suggests that some children, because of a lack of touching, actually have their growth stunted to some degree. At the University of Minnesota, they have what is called "hugging therapy sessions," where the nurses and attendants spend time hugging and touching neglected children in a meaningful way while telling them they are doing great. Researchers found that these children actually caught up with their peers in physical growth.

In addition to stimulating their growth and aiding their physical health, touching also communicates to children that they are valuable. When I place my hand tenderly on my child's shoulder, I am actually communicating, "You are important to me. I want to spend time with you." On the other hand, pushing our children away or hitting them with our hands communicates rejection. Refusing to touch our children communicates to them that they are "untouchable." Our touching must be meaningful from the child's point of view in order to be effective.

For a wife, a type of meaningful touching from her husband is when he holds her tenderly during a conversation. To find out whether his touch is meaningful to her, a husband can ask his wife. The same is true with children. We can actually ask them, especially as they grow older, if we are too rough, or if we touch too frequently or not enough.

It is important to remember that touching is a two-way street. Not only is it essential for parents to touch their children, but also for children to touch their parents. It is important for children to know that their parents need to be hugged. We don't depend on their hugs and touches like they do ours, but they may not realize that we have the same emotional and physical needs and we appreciate the spontaneity of their affection.

Once we were having our regular family meeting and the discussion turned to touching. During the conversation, we mentioned to Greg, who was fifteen years old, that we needed him to respond when we tried to hug him. He looked embarrassed, so we talked further about it. He said that he didn't realize that by resisting some of our hugs we were feeling that he didn't like us. He changed immediately and became much more receptive to our hugs, even though at times we feel he is trying to rearrange our backbones.

There are several types of touching that are appropriate with children: holding them in our laps while reading to them, hugging them when they arrive home from school, or just holding hands. We have a family hold, where we interlock our little fingers. Every member of our family knows that this is our special, secret, family-tradition hold. Norma and I started holding hands like this when we were first engaged. It is a personal, physical sign of affection in our family. Obviously, as our children have grown older, we seldom hold hands with them. One of the problems in today's culture is that we have associated touching of any kind with sexual connotations. We need to realize that touching does not need to have such overtones.

A real sense of meaningfulness and security comes from touching. At times our children will stay in bed on a Saturday morning. I will go into their rooms and put my arm by their pillow and they will lay their heads on my arm. Other times I will touch them on the shoulder while we talk.

When Greg was about six, we were driving in the Chicago area, and he told me how terrible it would be if we had an accident and I was killed. I obviously agreed with him and told him I would miss him terribly. Greg looked up and melted me when he said, "You know what Dad? If you ever get killed, I want to die right with you. And I want them to put both of us in the same casket and I want to be lying on your arm." As dramatic as that was, it further illustrates how much touching our children means to them.

I haven't always been a touching person. I didn't come from a touching home. I don't recall my parents touching each other and I remember feeling uncomfortable when a relative, who liked to hug a lot, came to visit. Before we were married, I told Norma, "Now, don't expect me to be one of those 'huggy' husbands and fathers, because I'm just not like that." I had to learn over the years how to touch and enjoy it.

But touching has proven to be very meaningful because it builds a sense of value within our children. It helps meet their emotional, mental, and physical needs. To fully benefit from touching, I would say that parents should make a conscious effort to touch their children eight to twelve times a day in a way that is meaningful to them.

Expressing loving support is of paramount importance within the family structure. It is also important to remember that the *attitudes* of a parent in expressing his love are as important as *how* the love is demonstrated. We've discussed ways to express loving support to our children, and in the next chapter we will deal specifically with the second major factor in raising children—developing firm limits and understandable rules. Without the balance of love and limits, children are robbed of the wholeness God intended them to have.

4

Balancing Loving Support through Contracts

- Setting Limits through Contracts
- Enforcing the Contract—Our Experiments
- A Practical Way to Implement Family Contracts
- Don't Expect, Inspect
- Contract for Dating
- Contract for Driving
- Guidelines for Spanking

ONE OF THOSE RARE EVENTS took place when Greg was about seven years old. He awakened me at 6:15 one morning, pushing on me so as not to wake Norma. "Dad, could you get up and read the Bible with me?" he whispered. What could I say? This was a special opportunity few parents could pass up.

We tiptoed downstairs and Greg sat on my lap. We began to read, trying to memorize the short verses as we read. We discussed what it meant to rejoice, give thanks, and pray, and Greg seemed quite responsive. Then we prayed together and thanked God for Greg's messy room that he had to clean up and for all the hard work facing me at the office that day. By then the whole family was up. Amazed by what they saw, they gathered around for a quick time of prayer together. Then everyone scattered and I leaned back in my chair, bathing in the joy of my son's "spiritual maturity."

A sudden racket at the top of the staircase shattered my reverie. While returning to his room, Greg gave Kari a shove against the wall. She shoved back, and the fight was on. After breaking up the combatants I couldn't help but wonder how this could happen so quickly after such a meaningful experience.

Later that week, I related this experience while speaking in another part of the country. A woman in the audience graciously said in front of the group, "Don't worry. Your children are just in one of the stages they all go through. They'll be over it in about thirty to thirty-five years."

We have watched our children go through a number of stages, some of them good, some not so good. Looking back over more than twenty years of being a family, Norma and I have concluded that through all the stages, greatly valuing one another has been the most important ingredient that re-bonds us and "covers all our sins" toward each other. In other words, we have committed to love each other. Part of the meaning of love is "to attach high value or stand in awe of."

In the previous chapter we shared that we want our children to know how valuable they are to us. We try to communicate this value by spending time with them, resolving conflicts, motivating them, and keeping their spirits open. We carefully "listen" to them with our eyes. When they were younger, we got down to their level, on our knees. We take them in our arms, we touch them, we hug them, we talk with them—all to communicate the value we have placed upon them.

Shortly after we married, Norma and I made a very important decision that has affected every aspect of raising our children. We recognized that each of us was an individual, yet an equally important member of a union. Both of us had valuable skills and opinions. But we had also committed in our wedding vows to enter into oneness. Therefore, we determined to always strive to be in agreement.

Our decision to live in agreement does not mean that one of us has to compromise or give in. Rather it means *we will resolve our disagreements so that both of us are satisfied.* This commitment has given us tremendous strength in our marriage and with our children. Sometimes it takes a while to come to a decision, but because we value each other, we are willing to work for a negotiated resolution. We agreed together when we would start having children, the names of our children, and the type of training they would receive.

Before we could resolve how to discipline our children, we needed to do our own "homework." Norma began to read various books on raising children. We interviewed parents who had raised what we believed were successful families. Norma also took a course on raising children. We began to practice what we were learning. We observed which of these ideas seemed to work and which ones the children didn't respond to or caused disharmony in our home. We were constantly adjusting our techniques as we went along.

We studied the ideas of Dr. Robert Coles, one of the nation's most influential psychiatrists. He emphasized that parents seem to have forgotten that children need, perhaps more than anything else, rules of life that clearly establish what is right and what is wrong—practical rules that can govern our daily lives.

We read about a survey conducted several years ago with outstanding linguists, teachers, pastors, evangelists, and medical doctors. They were asked about the influences that led to their vocational choices and why they became so successful in their respective fields. Each said he came from a strict home where there were clearly defined limits. Studies like that encouraged us to establish our own rules and discipline.

We continued to read how children need a sense of discipline and authority in their lives to help them develop emotionally and physically. It gives children a sense of security to know what their boundaries are. Much of our security in life comes from order and regularity. We are relatively confident about entering an intersection when the light is green, knowing that the light for cross traffic is red. Limits are all around us. We know that if we purchase an apple from a grocery store, it has not been injected with a deadly chemical. We can be confident that the chair we sit on will not break, the walls in our home will not collapse, and that the tires on our car, when properly taken care of, will hold air because there are rules and limits regulating their quality. With inconsistency there is insecurity.

We read *Between Parent and Child* by Dr. Haim Ginott, who agrees that children need a definite sense of limits. They need to know what is right and wrong. Dr. Ginott states that one of the greatest philosophies undermining parents has been Freud's psychoanalysis. Freud perpetuated the idea that, "I'm the way I am today because of what my parents did to me." Today's parent is uncertain about how to raise a child. He is fearful that his mistakes will have costly consequences. Therefore a parent may experience paralysis when it comes to setting limits. Dr. Ginott forced us to examine the obvious—there are certain right and wrong limits for children's behavior. These can be as simple as, "You can hit your brother with a pillow, but you cannot hit him with a hammer." This may seem simple, but we read over and over again that *it is possible, right, and essential that parents establish what is clearly defined acceptable and unacceptable behavior for their children.*

Dr. Howard Hendricks, a professor at Dallas Theological Seminary and author of *Heaven Help the Home,* says that parents need to set some clear objectives and priorities for their children. "You can only achieve that for which you aim," Hendricks says. "If you aim at nothing, you will hit it every time." The same goes for setting limits. If we do not have clearly defined limits, and if we change our discipline from week to week, we will not know what we're aiming at or what we want to accomplish in our discipline.

Setting Limits through Contracts

If setting limits is so important, how do parents begin?

For us, it was important to have a *basis* for deciding what is right and wrong. In our family, much of that basis comes from what we believe the Bible says about living our lives. When our children were very young, we realized that it was extremely important that we nail down what we believed to be important family limits. We were even concerned about simple things, like courtesy and table manners.

As we began selecting family limits, we knew it was important not only to set clearly defined limits, but also to have very few limits. From our studies, we came up with two fundamental concepts. They are the same two concepts that Jesus Christ claimed are the greatest commandments in life.

First, we should establish a meaningful relationship with God. This includes an understanding of what He taught about Himself in the Bible as well as how to relate to Him. Norma and I agreed that our relationship with God was the most important element of our lives, and we hoped our children would also have a relationship with Him.

The second concept followed logically from the first. We should love and value people just as we value ourselves. God gave Moses ten very specific and clearly defined commandments, or limits. Each of the Ten Commandments is based upon the two established by Jesus in the New Testament —*valuing God and valuing people.* Jesus said that if a person lived those two commandments, he would naturally obey all the commandments in the Bible. The limits we set were based on these two principles.

When our children were around three years old, our very first and simple limits were:

1. We will obey God as we understand the Bible.
2. We will obey Mommy and Daddy.
3. We will be kind to people and things—God's creation.

With the first rule, we wanted to teach our children that we are not, as parents, the final authority. There is a higher authority. If we were to ask our children to do something that violated the Bible, we wouldn't want them to obey us. We explained to our children that we wanted to have these limits in our home because this would honor God. These were His commandments, not ours. By obeying us, they were obeying God.

The third limit naturally grew out of the first two—being kind to people and things. We didn't want to have the kids calling each other ugly names or doing anything that would make another child feel devalued. We also wanted them to learn that their brothers, sisters, and playmates were valuable because God created them.

As the children grew to six or seven, we began to revise and add to our limits. We included our children in this process and finally, years later, all five of us agree on six limits that are still in force in our home today.

Our entire contract is based on limits we have found in the Bible. We regularly remind our children that these are God's limits for our family. As they operate under the contract, they know that they are obeying God—it is God's learning process, not ours.

1. Learning to obey parents.
2. Learning to put things away after we have used them.
3. Learning to do our chores—responsibility.
4. Learning to have good manners and learning responsibility toward others.
5. Learning to take care of God's creation: people and things.
6. Learning appropriate inner character qualities.

These six limits represented our final draft of an actual written contract that each of us signed and dated. In a very real sense, this was just like any business contract. We discovered that having a written, objective contract greatly contributed to our family's harmony. It made disciplining the children so much easier because we simply pointed to the family contract, and they were much more willing to cooperate and adjust to it.

> Very simply then, discipline in our home consisted of clearly defined limits with our children. These limits became our written family contract.

Most of us live by contracts, but the majority are not written out or signed. Marriage vows and driver's licenses are contracts. Agreeing to do a certain job for an employer is a contract. There are even contracts that no one mentions. For example, you keep your yard in a certain condition or else the neighbors will complain to city officials. Drive your car eighty miles an hour and you will discover that you have a contract with the city or state and it's going to cost you a stiff fine.

The basis of a contract is that all parties participate in the negotiations. All must agree on each point and on the consequences when a point is violated. Then everyone signs the contract, putting himself under its authority.

Our children were very involved in defining the limits. For example, in our first limit, "Learning to obey parents," we asked them what it means to obey. They said it meant two things. First, it meant not complaining. Examples of complaining included, "Why do I have to do it? Why can't Kari do it? I'm always the one chosen. Why is it always me? Why can't you do it?"

The second part of obeying was not nagging. "Please Dad, can I do it? Can I? Please, everybody is doing it. I mean, couldn't I just do it one time?" Constant nagging was interpreted as disobedience and a violation of the command for children to obey their parents. They finally helped us define the word *obey* to mean, "Yes, I will do it and I won't complain."

The second limit that all of us were concerned about was cleaning the house. The house was messy a great deal of the time because the kids would leave their belongings strewn about the floor. At night there was usually a stream of clothing and toys from the bathroom to their bedrooms. Together we agreed it was too much for Dad, and especially Mom, to follow them around and pick up after them. They decided that each person would learn to be responsible for his own property.

The third limitation was responsibility. We talked about the importance of each member in the family and the need to work as a unit. Everyone had responsibilities. There was homework and cleaning the bedroom and feeding the animals. Someone had to take out the trash. Piano practice was part of each child's responsibilities. Once we established all the chores that helped make our home run smoothly we felt it was important for each of us as members of the family to take an active part. This was all part of learning responsibility and sharing our part of the load.

The fourth limit was learning good manners. We defined what that meant. At meals, it meant holding silverware properly, placing a napkin on the lap, and chewing food with the mouth closed, unless of course one had wiry braces or retainers. There were also certain responsibilities for being in public. You didn't run in a grocery store or in church. You didn't crawl under a church pew and bite a sweet old lady on the ankle. *We understood that our behavior in the presence of other people was a reflection of how we valued them.*

The fifth limit dealt with taking care of God's creation—people and things. Part of taking care of God's creation is taking care of our own body. On school nights, for example, that meant the children were in bed between 8:00 and 9:00, depending on their ages. Brushing their teeth after meals was part of taking care of God's creation, as was bathing, washing hair, and wearing clean and neat clothing.

This limit also included taking care of others, such as asking questions instead of arguing. It meant trying to really understand others because what they say is important. It also included playing carefully, not hitting someone with intent to hurt, getting revenge, or calling someone a degrading name.

After writing down these first five limits into a contract (we will discuss the sixth later), we made a place for everyone to sign. If they were not old enough to sign, they scribbled in the appropriate place and I put the date next to it. This showed that we all agreed to the direction we were going to go as a family. Because we involved the children, from the earliest ages, in helping write these limits, they considered them *their* limits, rather than standards their parents were imposing on them.

We never considered any of these limits lightly. We wanted to see these five, simple limits as a part of our children's lives. That meant we had to figure out how to motivate them and what the best means of correction was when they got off course. That's when the fun began. We tried many things that didn't work before choosing a method that accomplished our goal.

Enforcing the Contract—Our Experiments

We tried spanking when one of the limits was violated. But even though spanking is very useful in discipline, it was not effective for us to regulate our family contract daily by spanking.

We tried memory exercises where Norma, the children, and I all memorized the limits. I expected that after they memorized the limits, they would naturally want to follow them. It wasn't that simple.

We tried things like washing their mouths with soap if they called someone a degrading name. We only tried that a couple of times because we found it was actually degrading to the children. It was violating the very thing we were punishing them for.

We tried cutting their allowances and fining them. I had some violation tickets printed, just like a policeman would give. When they violated one of the five rules, I would write out a ticket. Fines ranged from ten to twenty-five cents, depending on the violation. It was cute for a couple of days, but it soon turned into a burden for us as parents.

The list of our punishment experiments is a long one. We tried having them write the limit they violated and how they were going to change fifty times. That was effective to a degree, but again, it only lasted a few weeks. We tried push-ups and running around the block, but both of those only accomplished the loss of weight.

We tried punishing the kids by not giving them dinner. The children thought this would be a good form of punishment because it would make them aware of how important the limits were. The first time we tried it was also the last. Greg sat about fifteen feet away from the dinner table, his tongue hanging out as we ate. Halfway through the meal, Norma said, "This is harder on me than it is on Greg." To Greg's delight, we asked him to join us.

We tried punishing by prohibiting talking, playing with toys, and staying in their bedrooms. We tried turning off the air conditioner in their rooms, no camping trips, no snacks, extra piano practice, and many others. I chuckle now as I write this. But I didn't come from a disciplined home, and there was little written about this area, so we had to experiment.

Unfortunately, nothing seemed to help our children consistently live within these five limits. Plus the methods of correction were difficult on us as parents. Sometimes it seemed like a full-time job trying to keep up with all these little rules and regulations.

In our search to discover how to implement these rules in our home, we met an outstanding pediatrician and his wife, Dr. Charles and Dorothy Shellenberger. They explained how they had implemented their limits in a practical way. It was not only effective, but provided the missing element in training our children.

A Practical Way to Implement
Family Contracts

Using the contract method in a home is a very effective way to balance love and limits. Drs. Charles P. Barnard and Ramon G. Corrales found that a family is forced to clarify limits by writing them out on paper. Before anyone is willing to sign his name, he usually desires to understand what he's putting his name to. The question then, is how to implement the contract on a daily basis.

Here's where Dr. Shellenberger greatly helped us. He taught us that there are three parts to the process:

1. Set clearly defined limits by writing a contract.
2. Supervise the living of these limits regularly.
3. Consistently handle resistance through lost privileges.

Number three was the missing ingredient for us. We had set limits and written the contracts, but we hadn't incorporated the violation consequences in the contract in a practical, workable way. So we gathered again as a family and reworked the contract. Since 1977, though our contract has been amended several times, the format has remained basically the same.

First, we negotiated our family contract into something like Chart #1 on the following page:

Chart #1

Family Limits

1. *Learning to Obey Parents*
Answer by saying "Yes, Dad/Mom" immediately and accomplish the request right away.

- Do not complain: "I don't want to do that." "Do I have to?" "Can't someone else do it?" "This is not fair."
- Do not nag: "Oh, please, please can't we do it?" "Can't I go, Mom? Can't I go, Mom? Can't I go, Mom?"

2. *Learning to Put Our Things Away After Use*
- Toys in our closet or garage
- Clothes in the "dirty" box or hung up in closet
- Towels on the towel rack
- Have a place for everything and everything in its place

3. *Learning to Do Our Chores*
- Clean bedroom before school
- Place used dishes in the sink after meals
- After school: homework and piano before play; take out trash Tuesdays and Fridays; feed cats; bring paper to Mom
- Special chores when Mom or Dad need help

4. *Learning to Have Good Manners*
- Meals: Walk to the table, fold hands in lap, no talking before we pray. Chew food with mouth closed. Say, "Kari, please pass the _____."

- When others are talking, wait for a pause in the conversation and say, "Excuse me Dad, could I _____?"
- When we disagree with someone, do not say so, but rather, be a learner and ask, "What did you say again?" or "I always thought it was _____."

5. *Learning to Take Care of God's Creation: People and Things*

People (Self):

- 8:30 P.M.: Bath, if needed; brush teeth; put school bags by front door; read, listen to record or story

(Others):

- Asking questions—not arguing
- Playing gently—not roughhousing
- Praying for our "enemies"—not hitting
- Being kind and sensitive—not calling names (love and kindness are gifts from God; He changes our heart)

Things:

- Protecting house and furniture: Not jumping and playing on chairs, beds, etc.; not throwing balls in the house or against the house; not climbing the small trees

Second, we decided as a family what lost privileges each member would have when one of the limits was violated. The children had dozens of ideas—no toys, no television, no movies, no eating out, no snacks, no dating, no telephone, no dinners for a month, being grounded. Some of their lost privileges were much harsher than we as parents would have ever put down. After we made a list of thirty or forty possible lost privileges, we went back over the list and agreed on twenty-four hours of lost privileges for each of the five limits. We revised each limit to start with the letter C; the limits came to be known as the "Five C's." See Chart #2.

Chart #2

Our Family Limits

Responsibilities	Lost Privileges for 24 Hours
1. *Conforming:* Obeying Mom and Dad—not complaining, arguing, or nagging	All toys
2. *Cleaning:* Clean room every morning; clean up after using toys or other items	Television
3. *Chores:* Lawn once a week; trash every evening; piano by 5:30 P.M.	After-school snack
4. *Courteous:* At meals; at church and outings	Joining the family the next time they eat out
5. *Caring:* To bed on time; brush teeth; kind to people and things (God's creation); not teasing, hitting, or arguing	Seeing friends

Signed: _____   Date: _____

You can see from Chart #2 that when any of our children violated one or more of the limits they might lose toys or the opportunity to watch television for twenty-four hours.

We met for ten to fifteen minutes each night after dinner to evaluate how everyone was doing in each of the five areas. We kept the chart on the next page by the kitchen table. It was covered in plastic so we could mark on it with a grease pencil and erase it the next evening. We also used this time to correct our children rather than reprimand them throughout the day, unless of course they had committed a serious offense, then we would take care of it immediately.

Chart #3

Responsibilities

	Kari	Greg	Mike	Lost Privilege
1. Conforming	❏	❏	❏	toys
2. Cleaning	❏	❏	❏	television
3. Chores	❏	❏	❏	snack
4. Courteous	❏	❏	❏	eat out
5. Caring	❏	❏	❏	friends

Responsibility is a daily decision.

This chart made keeping up with our contract simple. Each evening as we met after dinner, we would go through this chart with our children. For instance, if Greg had not been responsible with his chores that day, we would place an "X" in that square, and he would not be able to have an after-school snack the next day. He could use that time to catch up on his chores.

Don't Expect, Inspect

For three years, we met every night after dinner, applying the old Henry Brandt proverb, "People do what you inspect not what you expect." We inspected and evaluated their behavior every day. After three years we no longer met daily, because the limits had become a regular part of our children's behavior. However, the contract still serves as our family constitution. It is open for amendments, but we can revise it only if all five of us agree with the recommended change.

As our children entered their teen years we wrote separate contracts to include more specific areas, particularly dating and driving.

This brings us to our sixth and final limit—developing character. We added this as our children became more aware of the opposite sex. We agreed that rather than set a specific age when they could start dating, we wanted instead to see a certain level of maturity in their character. In order to define this, we again looked to the Bible. Our standards of maturity became the nine qualities found in Galatians 5:22–23, the eight beatitudes (Matthew 5:3–10), and the attitude of Christ displayed in Philippians 2:5–8. We'll list a few of the main areas that we discussed with our children.

The first area of importance was that they be able to withstand peer pressure and not compromise the standards they believed were important. Norma punctuated this by relating a story about one of her first dates in high school. She was double-dating with a girlfriend, and they had both agreed not to allow any physical contact on their first date. Norma said that all of a sudden, she looked up and noticed her friend in the arms of this new-found boyfriend. That put pressure on her. Her date began to pursue her, but Norma said "No!" When her date became angry, Norma told him to either take her home or she would walk. It took all the strength Norma could muster.

It takes a great deal of courage for a teenager to be assertive in such situations. But that is the type of character quality we wanted to see in our children before we felt they were mature enough to date.

Another inner quality we felt was important is what the Bible calls being "pure in heart." That means having a single focus on what is most important in life. We wanted our children to understand that having a solid relationship with God is essential to establishing good relationships with people.

The Bible has a certain standard for living that leads to an enjoyable life. Its limits are not designed to restrict us from happiness, but rather to keep us from certain activities that can rob us of joy and peace. For example, the Bible gives us several consequences of premarital sex. We have taught our children that sexual actions from petting on up to intercourse prior to marriage, or after marriage with someone other than our mate, have several negative results. As a family, we discovered in both religious and secular studies at least twenty negative consequences of premarital sex. Here's a sample:

- It immediately reinforces our desires for greater and more frequent sensual fulfillment.

- It reinforces our self-centered nature. As the Scriptures say, it causes us to have a hardened or calloused heart. We become less sensitive to the needs of those around us, because we spend more time looking for ways to have our own sensual needs met. We tend to observe life as a means to stimulate our own senses instead of loving those around us.

- Immorality also reduces our faith in God, because the more we violate God's limits, the more we must rationalize that "God doesn't exist" or His rules are invalid. This can lead to questioning the very creator of those limits. Thus I've observed those who practice an immoral lifestyle have more and greater doubts about the existence of God.

- Sexual "freedom" and promiscuity can actually lead to slavery—slavery to our physical senses and impotency. A certain cigarette company has a slogan that says, "Smoke this cigarette. It *satisfies*." That's a clever twist of the word satisfy. Have you ever known a smoker who could smoke just one cigarette and be satisfied? He has to have another and then another. The same can be true with sexual immorality.

There are so many lies circulating in our world. We're told that we live in a day of sexual "freedom." Implied by the word *freedom* is the opportunity to experience sexual contact before and after marriage with a variety of partners. Just look at the inconsistency of this statement, "We're free to make love." Making love means sexual involvement and the more involved we are the more we lose our freedom to restrain our desires and the more our senses enslave us. It is important for children to understand these consequences of immorality. Even though they have strong and normal sensual drives, they must gain the ability to say "no" for their own long-term benefit and the fulfillment of lasting, loving relationships.

Contract for Dating

The first part of our dating contract deals with a child's character. The second part deals with the actual dating practice. Here are some additional elements in the dating contracts:

With the first few years of dating, we evaluated each dating situation on its own merit, but we especially favored well-organized, school-sponsored activities that were adequately chaperoned. Next, every member of the family must approve of the potential dating partner. This has been a very effective safeguard designed to protect against a potentially harmful relationship. It is a reflection of a close-knit family, each concerned about the well-being of the other.

We also discuss and set a curfew for dates. The greater a child's trustworthiness, self-control, and purity of heart, the greater freedom in dating privileges. Likewise, if any of the character qualities is tarnished or violated, then the dating privilege may be lost for an agreed-upon period of time. For example, if one of the children lies about some activity, even if it has nothing to do with dating, he may lose the privilege of dating for a week or two, depending on the severity of the offense.

We all agreed to this simple dating contract and as the children get older, we will continue to evaluate the contract. We probably will revise it a few times, which is what we encourage families to do. Stay current and up to date with children in the areas of training and correction.

Contract for Driving

Driving a car is another privilege that comes with age and character development. Even before our children were old enough to drive, we agreed as a family on the following contract:

1. Upon receiving my driver's permit, I will be allowed to drive on local errands when accompanied by either parent. I will assist in driving for extended periods of time on long family vacations under all types of driving conditions.

2. Before using the car, I will ask either Mom or Dad if I can use it and explain the purpose.

3. If I want to go somewhere for myself, both my homework and piano practicing or other chores must be completed first.

4. During the first month after receiving my driver's license, the radio will not be used while driving.

5. During the school year, I will be allowed to drive to activities at night but cannot take anyone home without permission.

---

6. I will not allow anyone else to use the car under any circumstances without permission from my parents.

7. I will not carry more than five passengers at a time.

8. I will not give rides to hitchhikers under any circumstances, and I will use extreme caution in accepting assistance if I should have difficulty with the car.

9. I will pay half of the increase of insurance costs whenever my grades fall below a B average. In case of an accident, I will assume half of the deductible costs.

10. If I receive any moving violations, I will lose my license for up to one month. On the second violation, I will lose it for up to three months.

It took us several weeks to negotiate this simple contract and our children signed it only after several revisions. We are certainly open to future revisions, but again any changes must be understood and agreed upon by each of us.

Guidelines for Spanking

Our final contract deals with the important area of spanking. Most violations of our limits are punished by a loss of privileges. But it is part of our written contract that we will use spanking if anyone is obviously resistant or rebellious, especially showing strong defiance against a parent.

Spanking can be very effective to guard against rebellion, but as Dr. Armand Nicholi says, the main problem with spanking is that it can be a release for the parent's frustration, guilt, or anger. It may therefore benefit the parent more than the child. He advises parents to ask themselves who will benefit most from the spanking. Spanking certainly can be used when a limit is violated, but it must be used cautiously.

I have also come to see the effectiveness of spanking on a decreasing scale. It's most effective with preschoolers, but it should rarely be used after age thirteen. If a spanking is necessary, it should be taken very seriously, so as not to close the child's spirit. Usually a loss of privileges is more effective for older children.

Before we developed our contracts, we discovered that the majority of spankings in our home took place before meals. This is often the hardest time because everyone is hungry and tired. Our blood sugar levels are low. The children are restless and impatient, and the aroma of food heightens tension. A number of things can happen at this time to flare up disobedience within children. We found I could reduce some of the tension by simply spending more time with the children when I came home from work.

We also allow our children to call for "court" if they believe that they are being disciplined unjustly by spanking. We started this after I saw Greg push a plate of chips and sandwich across the kitchen table. The plate hit Kari in the chest and the sandwich and chips went all over her and onto the floor. I immediately grabbed Greg's arm and told him, "You're going to be spanked." He was trying to tell me it wasn't his fault and Kari was trying to intervene, but I didn't pay any attention.

Only after I had spanked Greg did I gather the facts—after all, I saw it happen. But I didn't know that Norma had asked Kari to make Greg a sandwich, but Greg said he wasn't hungry. Kari retorted, "Mother told me to make you this sandwich, so you're going to get it whether you like it or not." He shoved it back. The sandwich passed between the two of them at least three more times. I walked into the kitchen just as Greg was shoving it the final time out of complete frustration.

Had I taken the time to get the facts, I would not have spanked him. We initiated the court alternative to avoid similar mistakes. The defendant can call the whole family together, even call in a witness or bring in a friend to act as lawyer if he wants to present his case concerning why he believes he does not deserve this spanking. After all the facts are gathered, we go around the table asking each member of the family for his verdict. If everyone votes "guilty," we ask the person accused what he thinks. Every time we have done that, the guilty party has agreed with the others, admitting his guilt.

Here are ten factors to consider when spanking is used as a method of correction:

1. *Give clear warning before the spanking.* Children need to understand why they are being spanked. We have told our children that they must show obvious signs of rebellion against clearly established rules to get a spanking. Examples might be if they physically harm each other or if a parent tells them not to do something and they say they don't care and do it anyway.

2. *Establish a child's responsibility for his or her disobedience.* When a child disobeys after instructions and warning, the child must assume responsibility for his disobedience. We ask our children *what they have done* so they can see for themselves that they violated our family limits. Sometimes it takes a while for one to admit his wrong. He will want to blame someone else and rationalize his behavior. We must be persistent with our question until he admits what he has done wrong.

3. *Avoid embarrassment and outside interference.* When spanking or correcting a child, make sure you are alone with him, especially when the child's offense occurs in public. If the parent brings up a problem in front of a child's friends and attempts to correct him, the child will be more concerned about his reputation than the offense he has committed. Such a correction demoralizes the child and can produce a closed spirit. It also might motivate a child to figure out ways to justify his action to those who saw him being punished so that they will side with him.

4. *Communicate parental grief over the offense.* This is important because it causes the child and parent to reflect on what has taken place. It also gives them both a chance to calm down. The ultimate goal of this time is to bring the child to a sincere repentance, where he wants to be corrected.

5. *Associate love with spanking. It is important to explain the age-old adage,* "This hurts me more than it does you," to children. My children have questioned that many times, but it is true.

Once when I was going to spank Kari, she tried to talk her way out of it. She promised never to do the offense again. She begged me not to spank her. I decided to take that opportunity to illustrate an example of real love and sacrifice.

I told her how when Christ died on the cross, He paid the penalty for our sin. Then I told her that I wanted to show her a small example of what Jesus did. I was going to let her spank me.

"Someone's going to be spanked today," I told her. "But I'm going to take your punishment for you because I love you and want you to know that I'm not spanking you to hurt you. I'm doing it because I think what you did was wrong and we are correcting it."

Kari stopped crying, her eyes lighted up and she looked at me as if to say, "Are you serious?" I told her I was, gave her the paddle, and lay down on the bed just as I had asked her to do. But when she tried, she couldn't do it. I told her it was okay, but if she didn't want to spank me, I would spank her. She quickly said that she thought she could bring herself to do it. After a long struggle, she gave me a good one. And it stung. I stood up and she gave me a big hug, like we always did with her after a spanking. This only happened once, but it gave Kari some understanding of what her parents go through.

6. *Use a neutral object for spanking.* It is important that a neutral object be used for spanking because a child has a tendency

to associate the pain with the object used to spank him. If a parent uses his hand, the child may feel uncomfortable when that same hand is used to touch, hold and hug, especially if the child is spanked in harsh anger. We have found that it is very effective to use a thin stick that we decorated as a family. We call it the "teacher." Using the "teacher" also helps calm everyone because usually it takes a few minutes to find it.

The first time I used "teacher" was when Kari was about three years old. She jumped on the bed and started screaming. When I reached for her, she jumped behind the bed, then under the bed. I calmly told Kari I was going to follow through with the spanking if it took all day.

Finally, she lay down on the bed and I gave her a swat. As soon as I did, she was jumping on the bed and screaming again. I told her to lie still until I finished. So she lay down again and I gave her another swat. Again, she jumped up and started screaming. I stayed calm, but firm, and the process was repeated three more times. Finally she realized that I was serious and stayed still. Kari never jumped around like that again because she knew I meant business.

From that episode, we both learned that correction can reveal the level of a child's resistance. Persistent correction can break stubbornness, which brings us to the seventh point about spanking.

7. *Discipline or spank until the will is broken.* It is very important that we do not spank our children in harshness or severe anger, even if this means getting away for a few minutes to cool off. We must take the time to communicate love to them, but we must also communicate that we are going to spank them until they understand we mean business. If we spank children in harsh anger, it has a tendency to break their spirit, which can be worse than if we didn't spank them at all.

When Greg was in the seventh grade, he went through a period of blaming a poor grade in school on his teacher, his mother, even the time of day. Everyone and everything was at fault but him. I tried talking to Greg about the importance of assuming responsibility and not blaming those around him. The showdown came when Greg deliberately and willfully told me, "Dad, it's not my fault. It's their fault." He became very disrespectful to me as his father. Then I spanked him. About five minutes later, after I had spanked and hugged him, Greg sat on my lap and said, "Dad, thanks for spanking me. You know, I can see that it really is my fault." Then he sat down, got his books out and started studying. I could see the cleansing in his life because he had been corrected firmly and his stubborn will was broken.

8. *Comfort a child after the spanking.* Kari and Mike almost always crawled into my arms for a hug after a spanking. But with Greg, sometimes it took an hour or two for him to warm up and want to be touched. Once Kari and Greg chose to be spanked in the same room at the same time. They wanted to be together so they could comfort each other. They hugged each other prior to the spanking and asked who wanted to be first. They both took their spanking, they both cried, and we all hugged each other afterward. Hugging reinforces our love for the child.

9. *Discuss any restitution that might be necessary.* If a child is spanked because he hit a neighbor willfully and deliberately, it may be important for you to discuss how he should go and seek forgiveness from that neighbor. Or if he stole money from someone, you may discuss with the child how much and in what manner to repay it.

10. *Evaluate your correction and your child's response to it.* If you have wronged your child in any way, through false accusation, anger, attacking him as a person rather than his wrong behavior, embarrassing him, lacking love, or overpunishing, it is important to go to him and follow the steps of opening his

spirit. This should be done when both parent and child have calmed down emotionally and can evaluate what took place more objectively. A child has a keen sense of fairness and will be highly sensitive to his parents' offenses. One of the most common accusations children have against their parents is that they rarely admit when they are wrong. This pride makes future correction very difficult because it can cause a child to close his spirit.

My worst spanking experience took place when Greg was about two years old and I tried to break what appeared to be his "strong resistant will." I wasn't swatting him hard enough to really harm him physically, but I did persist many times, trying to "break his will." As I continued I could sense his fear, frustration, and inability to explain himself. I finally stopped in grief and held him, seeking his forgiveness because I could see his resentment growing toward me. We waited until he was almost three before he received any more spankings. I felt he wasn't old enough before that to really benefit. It was, and still is, more important for us as parents to have a warm, loving relationship with our children than to have a strict "military" type atmosphere at home. The strictness is important, but I would say in training children, the emphasis should be about 45 percent strictness with limits and 55 percent a loving relationship.

Along with unconditional love and support for our children, successful parents must balance this love by establishing clearly defined rules and limits. This is the area where we had a lot to learn. And we're still learning. What I have shared in this chapter has evolved over years of trial and error.

Parenting is not something we do once and get an "A" and it's over. It would be nice if it were that easy. We must continue to learn and relearn. An NFL quarterback, Jim Zorn, told me that every year for two weeks, the quarterbacks on his team take a class where they review the fundamentals of quarterbacking. Then during preseason training camp, they practice the same techniques over and over again. The same should be true with parents. We need to continually learn, review, practice, and relearn the basics of parenting. Norma and I are still learning. Our children were ten, fifteen, and seventeen years old when this book was first written, and we were committed to continue learning until all of them were raised. Now that they're nineteen, twenty-three, and twenty-five, we look forward to reading, studying, and learning about how grandparents can enrich their grandchildren's lives. We hope we never stop learning.

5

Giving Yourself the Freedom to Fail

- Discipline in the Home
- Communicating Emotionally with Children
- Building Friendships in the Family
- The Value of Being Together without Spending Much Money
- What They Didn't Like
- The Long-Term Effect of Words
- Gaining a New Perspective
- The Principle of Empowerment

YOU REALLY FIND OUT what it means to be vulnerable when you ask your grown children to rate your successes and failures as a parent. That's exactly what Norma and I did last Thanksgiving. We were having a family meeting with just the five of us in the living room, and I said to our children, "I'm thinking about revising our parenting book, *The Key to Your Child's Heart*, and I was wondering if the three of you would like to help?" Kari, Greg, and Michael responded virtually in unison, "Yeah, we'd love to help."

I wasn't sure they would want to help me or have anything to do with the revision, so their sudden, unanimous response surprised me. Getting down to business, I said, "Can I ask each of you a couple of difficult questions? Can you really be honest and share what you appreciated about the way we disciplined you as children and what you appreciated about us as parents? And then can you describe what you wish we had *not* done as parents? What would you have done differently? How would you have done it differently? Tell me what you don't plan to do as parents yourselves because of what your mother and I did when you were growing up. I remember several times when all of you said, 'Boy, I'll never do that with my kids!'"

I said that I thought this was the kind of information a lot of parents would like to know. So in this chapter I would like to share some of the positive and negative aspects of our own parenting.

As parents, Norma and I did what I suspect you are doing as readers. We looked around and saw the large number of families around us who were hurting and falling apart. Like you, we started a search to find reliable training methods for raising our three children. Because our own parents were dead and since every day counted when it came to parenting, we talked to anyone who seemed to know something about parenting or who seemed to be good role models.

One of our best sources turned out to be our own godly pediatrician, Dr. Charles Schellenberger, and his wife, Dorothy. We sought out Charles' advice almost every time we visited his office—which seemed to be practically every week with our kids' runny noses and whatever.

Now that all three of our children are grown and out on their own, our questioning of what they appreciated about our home was a chance to evaluate some of the methods that we had discovered and applied. It was interesting to hear their varied and precise remarks. Before I summarize that, however, it might be helpful to know how the three of them turned out as adults and what they're doing these days. You can see from their "before" and "after" pictures how they changed over the years.

Kari is our oldest. She's twenty-five years old as of this writing and just married to Roger Gibson of Phoenix, Arizona. Basically, she is a practicing missionary school teacher in an inner-city public elementary school in Phoenix. Each year Kari takes a large group of kids from this school to a summer sports program called Kids Across America at Kamp Kanakuk, a Christian camp in Branson, Missouri. During the year she and Roger disciple this group by taking them to church and meeting with them weekly. Norma and I are extremely pleased with the way Kari's life has worked out. Her warm heart, her genuine love for children, and her deep desire to see that they know the Lord and grow up in Him are evidence of the kind of person she is.

Greg, our second oldest, is now twenty-three years old and finishing his first year at Denver Seminary. He's planning to be a clinical psychologist. Greg's gone through some tough times during his university experience. Later in this chapter he'll explain some of the struggles he went through as a young man and how he was able to climb out of a deep hole he had dug for himself. We are very proud of Greg and the commitment he has made to help troubled children and their parents. Greg is also getting married this year, to Erin Murphy.

Mike, our youngest, is nineteen years old now and finishing his first year at Baylor University in Waco, Texas. Michael is our "all-everything" child, and he utilized almost every opportunity to his best advantage during his high school years and especially his summer camp experiences. Mike has often said that he really developed the personal skills and attitudes of confidence, leadership, and dependence upon the Lord that have been his greatest assets when he was at Kamp Kanakuk in Missouri.

Discipline in the Home

Our discussion of discipline focused on the training times and the spanking times. As a parent, it was interesting for me to see that these were what Kari, Greg, and Michael remembered most about discipline in the family. As they looked back, these emotional experiences came to mind immediately; these are the experiences that stick in their minds.

According to our family contract, the only time we ever spanked any of our children was when they deliberately or grossly dishonored something of God's creation. If they used some degrading word against us or against their brother, sister, or even a friend, we said that they were really devaluing God's creation. It was a lack of proper respect, and Norma or I punished them for that.

We never spanked any of our children for something the children didn't know they would be punished for ahead of time. That would have been unfair. If it wasn't in the contract, we stopped and talked about it and pointed out how they were supposed to behave in those situations. The contract was our rule book, and we all had to agree to live by it.

The family contract is a great system. I don't think we can overstress how valuable it was to us in raising our children. If I were raising children again, I would start the contract process when each child reaches five years of age. By then kids are fully capable of understanding how rules work, and they will come to appreciate the fact that there are clear, written guidelines for good behavior in the family.

Our children all agreed that this was an important principle, and when Norma or I talked to them about what they had done, they generally agreed it was wrong, and they understood they would be spanked. It was understood that breaking the contract was grounds for punishment. However, if they didn't think the punishment or the accusation was fair, then we would have a family meeting (a kind of family court) to clarify the situation. Everybody would vote, and if the child was guilty and everybody agreed on that, then the child would usually see it too. If the facts showed that the child was innocent, then we would settle things as quickly and fairly as possible.

There were times when Norma and I *were* wrong, when we made a mistake in assuming what had happened when it wasn't really the case at all. Whenever that happened, we would listen to the child's explanation, hear the other side of the story, and when it was appropriate we would say, "We're wrong. You don't deserve a spanking."

Kari told us that she could not remember any time when we spanked her in anger. "I'm sure there were times when they got angry with us for something we said or did," she said, "but they always took time to cool down before disciplining us. Any time I got a spanking my parents would sit me down and talk to me, remind me of the rules we had agreed to, and also remind me of the consequences. Those certainly weren't happy memories, but I don't remember ever thinking that my parents were bad or unfair. In fact, I felt they were more than fair."

I believe Kari's memory of these occasions is correct. Rarely did we ever spank in anger, as an emotional response, or as a sort of knee-jerk reaction. The children appreciated that. Whenever we had to discipline them, either Norma or I would take them to their room and talk there. We always took the time for them to admit what they had done, and we would always hug them before a spanking and say, "We feel as bad about this as you do," and "I know you agreed with this rule." We'd hug them after the spanking, but we'd never spank any of our children publicly and never in front of the other children.

Physical discipline is a very private, honoring experience, and it was not administered all that often in our house. Over all those years, Greg got the most spankings, and he seems to remember them as daily experiences because it was such an emotional experience for him. Today those spankings are what he remembers most vividly about his growing-up years. On the other hand, Michael got the least. He was our most even-tempered, happy-go-lucky child. Michael always wanted to do what was right.

When we did spank, we were always careful to assure the children that we loved them and that we wanted them to be our friends before, during, and after any disciplining. That was really more important to us than the spanking. Proper training was preeminent in our thinking. We wanted each child to know that honor—which is valuing all of God's creation, people, and things—was the greatest value they could have. And we taught the concept of honor on every occasion.

Now that we look back on those experiences, we realize that honor was truly the most important thing that we taught our children. It was the fifth point in our family contract. If we were just now establishing the contract I think we would make it the first point, because now we see that it covered and over-shadowed everything else we did.

I think it is important to note that we never slapped the children and we never used our hands to spank them. The children's spirit was so important to us, and even when we felt that a spanking was necessary, we were always careful to do it in an honoring way. It's not a very happy time when you have to spank your children, but we spent as much time as we had to with them to ensure that they truly understood the lessons we were trying to teach them. We both felt that it was impor-tant that we discipline them in an honoring way.

Whenever Norma would discipline them, she would take them to their own room and sit down with them. She would look into their eyes and ask, "What did you do?" Their differ-ent reactions were interesting. Kari and Michael would admit immediately what they had done.

It always took longer with Greg. There were times when he was very young that a spanking time might take up to two hours. We knew it was important for him to admit what he had done, but he did not want to do that. After the spank-ing, we wanted to hug him and we wanted him to hug us—this was to affirm him and to assure him that even though he had been given a spanking we still loved him—but he didn't like that at all.

We knew Greg had a strong will, and this was another in-dication of that, but we also knew how important it was to see that he understood and agreed with what we were trying to teach him. On some of those early occasions, Norma would stay in the room as long as it took. It was about a year before Greg was able to bring himself to accept our discipline and to hug us, but that was an important part of the learning experience too.

We did not spank our children after they became teenagers. If parents are consistent in their discipline, by the time the kids are ten or eleven years old they are really obeying you. After that age, as we used our contracts (and when they were allowed to help us set up the rules for the home), the most effective punishment would be the loss of privileges or missing something they would have enjoyed if they hadn't broken the rules. We have counseled with many parents who say they wish they could have used this system with their own teenagers; it is such a fair and logical way of doing things.

Even Greg, our strong-willed child, accepted the rules more easily after he was ten years old. It's sort of like putting a bridle on a young colt: When he knows the restraint and the guidance are going to be there, he actually begins to relax. That's how it worked for us. Greg was constantly probing and testing us when he was small, but he was an easy, fun teenager, and he came to understand the importance of playing by the rules.

After the children became teenagers, our family contract became the family constitution. Decisions of this kind involved the whole family and we had to vote on it. When a serious breach of the rules occurred, it was like having the Supreme Court in session. And since the family constitution provided the guidelines and the law for the family, that meant that spankings, yelling, shouting, and all those kinds of things didn't have to take place.

It was really a wonderful experience then, and I become more and more positive about the idea of a family contract or constitution every year. So I urge every family to write their own constitution. I truly believe that the information on contracts and constitutions in chapter 4 may be some of the most practical and helpful advice we ever received on maintaining discipline in the home.

Most of the time when Greg broke those rules, he would lose certain privileges for twenty-four hours. Spanking was the least-administered punishment, but Greg's spankings are the things that stand out in his mind today because they were the more painful experiences, the physical reminders. With Michael it was different: He received few spankings. Kari received very few because she simply did not like to be out of harmony with the family. If you have read *The Two Sides of Love*, which I wrote with John Trent, you know something about personality types, and you will recall that two of those personalities simply do not like spankings. Children in these categories will go to almost any length not to get themselves in a situation where punishment is necessary. Kari and Michael are like that, and throughout their growing-up years they hated to disappoint their parents.

Now I know that, as a parent, you are praying that if you have any more children they will have personalities like that! These are wonderful children. They are so easy to raise. But in God's providence—or maybe His sense of humor—there often seems to be a mixture of personalities within a family. Kari and Michael were the agreeable ones, and pleasing their parents was very important to them. But we also had Greg. In our house Greg was what John and I called the lion personality. Greg was—and still is in some ways—a strong personality.

To put things in perspective I should add that we didn't have all that many stormy incidents, although it probably seemed like more because of the tensions involved. You know, I wasn't surprised when both Michael and Kari told me that they plan to write a family constitution with their own children. They were both very comfortable with the terms of our agreement. But, believe it or not, Greg also plans to do the same thing. So apparently that was one of the best things we ever did.

As I said earlier, the number one article in your constitution ought to be, "Honor God and His Creation." That was the central principle and central truth we wanted our children to learn. When young people honor God and His creation, they will naturally honor people and things.

Communicating Emotionally with Children

The second outstanding memory our kids had of their childhood was that I told them a lot of stories. I told them all kinds of stories, the typical children's stories, of course, but almost all of them were emotional stories. These were the ones they remembered best. The more drama to a story and the more it involved their own feelings, the stronger their memories are today of that story.

Sometimes I would make up stories, but often I would tell them about my own growing-up adventures. When we discussed these in our family meeting, I found it especially interesting to discover that the stories they remembered most vividly were the stories about my childhood, especially those in which I was in danger. Some of these stories were about my parents, my brothers, my sisters, or just the various dangerous situations that I got myself into while growing up in Washington state. But those stories had a great impact on them.

There were times when I would gather all three kids around and say, "You want to hear a story about what happened to me when I was a little kid?" And to arouse their curiosity, I'd say, "I bet you are going to wonder how I ever got out of that mess!" And I would tell about the time when I stepped into a sawdust pile and discovered it was on fire, or the time when I fell through a bunch of logs. Maybe it was the idea that these were true-life adventures, or that they involved Daddy; whatever it was, my children were fascinated and listened to these stories with real enthusiasm.

Growing up in the Northwest where the lumber industry is so important, there always seemed to be an adventure around every corner. What is really interesting to me today is that my children's memories of these stories are confused and out of sequence! They each remember the facts somewhat differently, and all of them are slightly wrong. What they remember distinctly, however, was that Dad was in danger. They remember the story about the time I ran into a rattlesnake pit during a time when the snakes were all going underground for winter hibernation. They remember the drama, the suspense, and hearing me tell how I narrowly got out of that. Not only do they remember the story, but they still like for me to tell it. And I guess they will probably want me to tell it to our grandkids someday!

I also told a lot of Bible stories during those years, and, again, the ones the kids liked best were the really emotional stories. They liked the one about the time the disciples brought a demon-possessed man to Jesus, and Jesus drove the demon out. You remember, this demon was so powerful it scared the disciples, and they weren't able to cast it out without Jesus' help. So I said to my children, "Do you want to make sure that you never get any demons inside of you?" And, wide-eyed, they said, "No, we don't want any demons in us!" And I said, "Well, make sure that your conscience is clear before God and man." Boy, they confessed every sin they ever had . . . so did I!

In fact, telling the story to the children affected me as much as it affected the children, and I remember that night vividly. I remember lying there in the dark and having a little revival of my own in bed.

Some of the other highlights our children remembered about their growing-up years were the stories I read to them, like C. S. Lewis' Chronicles of Narnia. Whenever the adventure would build up to a peak in those wonderful tales, I'd look at my kids and I could see their little hearts start to pound with anticipation. When something exciting would happen in the story, they would jump under the covers next to Daddy and snuggle up. Isn't it amazing that the casual, comfortable little stories I read or told them during those times have all but faded from their memories, but the stories that gripped their hearts and their emotions remain in vivid detail?

Now as a parent I had a pretty good repertoire of stories. At least I knew some basic endings, and I would just invent the stories to go with them. I'd make them up on the spot, and I would make them as wild and complicated as I could, adding all sorts of crazy things. If I saw that I was losing their attention, I'd say, "Uh, oh. I can't go on. I don't know if I should even tell the rest of this story, it's so scary."

Of course, when I was saying that, I was thinking, *What can I tell them that would be so scary?* I didn't want to scare them into being fearful, but I would say, "Oh, I'm not sure you're old enough for this." And they would always say, "Daddy, we're old enough! Come on, come on. Pleeeeze."

I would always try to give the story a biblical meaning and a good practical point. It might be something about forgiveness, about honoring people, or something about how Jesus loves us, that He'll never forsake us, and that no matter what happens, God always turns the bad things that happen to us into something good if we let Him.

I would use verses like Romans 8:28, 1 Thessalonians 5:16–18, and 1 John 2:9–11. Those verses would give me a certain direction, and I would make up the stories and the plots to try to come to some sort of biblical truth. I think I enjoyed them as much as the kids. Those were wonderful times.

Building Friendships in the Family

Camping was another highlight of our kids' growing-up years. Without a doubt, they said, some of their greatest memories, some of the times they loved best, and some of the times they appreciated most were the family's camping trips. We camped a lot when they were small. As they got older we couldn't go as often because they were all involved in sports—football, basketball, track, everything you can imagine. It was too hard to get away then, but when they were younger, we camped all the time.

In the early years we frequently camped in tents, sometimes in those little pop-up trailers. Later we bought a used motor home, so it was always ready to go. We would just jump in it and take off on a Friday night, drive to a local campground, and camp overnight. We would find a place where we could do a little exploring, tell stories, and have hot dogs around a campfire. They were wonderful, wonderful experiences. Sometimes we would take a week or two, sometimes as much as three weeks, and we would go camping in Canada, Colorado, Texas, or the California mountains.

I remember some disastrous experiences, but those were really the times that bonded us together, as you will see in the last chapter on the secret of a close-knit family. Sometimes the disappointments, the surprises, the battles, even the accidents were the most important parts of the overall experience. But however great or terrible things may have seemed at the time, we all knew that we were in it together. We were a family, and somehow that was enough to hold us together.

In our meeting last Thanksgiving, the kids said that one of the things they appreciated most was the fact that they were all so close in age. There are eighteen months between Kari and Greg and five years between Greg and Mike. That has been a nice age span. Whenever we did do things together, whether it was camping or anything else, they were not just siblings but best friends to boot. That was a big help for Norma and me, and it helped make our outings more fun for everybody.

The real and lasting importance of our camping trips was that it allowed Norma and me to be involved with our children on a personal basis, developing personal friendships with them, and forming memories and bonds with them that would be there the rest of our lives. I cannot overstress how important that has been.

In our family, Kari was usually the one who could come up with the great ideas for fun things to do. Whether it was a family cookout, a talent show, or a night out together, she could always think of fun and original ways to enjoy ourselves. During our family meeting, Norma asked Kari if she would come up with a list of creative ideas for family fun. So, at this point, I would like to give you Kari's list.

Fun Things to Do with Your Family

Home Activities

1. *Lunch Bunch:* Pack a lunch together and "Do Lunch"!

2. *Saturday Blast:* One Saturday a month, do something special, such as visit the zoo or go horseback riding. Whatever you choose, vote on it as a family. If one member votes no, that vote wins the next week.

3. *Lazy Day Saturday:* Before getting up and starting the day, everyone stays in bed and reads a book. (This has been known to be done even when the children are grown and come home to visit!)

---

4. *Let's Cook:* Get matching aprons and once a week (or more) all cook together. You can make dinner, bake cookies, cakes, or even Play-Doh! Get the kids involved.

5. *Sun (Cozy-Bed) Day:* Everyone snuggles up in bed and reads a story, sings a song, or reads Bible verses before getting ready for church.

6. *Kids' Friday Night Bash:* This is an excellent way to start off the weekend. Play a game, cook out, picnic with an early dinner, go hiking (don't forget a snack!), paint rocks that you have collected, watch home movies or a fun video.

7. *Family Talent Show:* (Home or camping) Plan all day what each person will do for a talent. This activity is even better with a whole bunch of "family relations"! That night, "Let the show begin!" Be prepared for lots of laughs.

8. *Dad's (or Mom's) Night:* This night honors Dad or Mom in a very special way. Kids cook their parent's favorite meal! Bring out the candles and set the mood. The honoree even gets to choose the activity for the night.

9. *Dear Dad (Dear Mom):* If one of the parents travels or is out of town, put special notes in his or her luggage, handbag, suit pocket, and other places. Mailing them is even more fun!

10. *Let's Go to the Store:* Give the kids a food list and the fun begins. Remember to get hamburger buns, all the sandwich trimmings, chocolate milk, and dessert. You can even plan ahead to load the food and family in the car and go to a friend's house for "food, fun, and games."

11. *Fancy Sandwiches:* Let your kids cut out their bread, cheese, and meats with different shape cookie cutters. What a fun way to gobble down something healthy!

12. *Warm, Rainy Day Fun:* Load up a few warm blankets and make a tent. Cuddle up and watch it rain. This is especially fun if you have a big porch, but if it's too cold to go outdoors, you can have your tent adventure inside the house. Don't forget a good book.

13. *Time to Wash:* If your little girls love dolls or Barbies, then this activity is for you. Outside, set up a mini laundry line including tiny clothespins. Show them the "old-fashioned" way of washing and drying.

14. *Paper Dolls:* Buy them or make them yourself. I bet you forgot how much fun they are!

15. *Jacks Anyone?:* Another fun game for all ages—all too often neglected these days.

Outings and Outdoors

16. *Let's Go to the Show:* It is so important to give your child a taste of culture: symphonies, museums, science exhibits, community events, the zoo, etc. They may dislike some of these things at first, but they will come to appreciate them if you show your own interest.

17. *Friday Fun:* It's a perfect time to bowl, play miniature golf, or even skate.

18. *A-Z Search:* Hike and look for things that start with each letter. You can write down your list on mini notepads or make it a contest.

19. *Hunting:* Boys love to hunt with their dads, but girls can enjoy it too. Be sure to check local and state regulations; some require certificates of training. As an option, target shooting can be a lot of fun.

20. *Feed the Ducks:* Take leftovers and feed the ducks at the park. A bag of bread crumbs can provide loads of fun.

21. *Fish for It:* On a long drive, make a small fishing pole and tie a clothespin to the end. The children can fish over the car seat and catch all sorts of things, from crayons and coloring books to snacks and treats.

22. *Bait for Bears:* On your next camping trip to a wilderness area, put out some "food bait" for wild animals. National and state parks have regulations about feeding the animals, so be sure to check on the rules, but it can be fun to watch the critters come for the bait.

23. *Backyard Camping:* Can't get away to go camping? Pitch a tent in the backyard and camp for the night. Try having a cookout of hot dogs. Music around the campfire, and s'mores—what could be better?

24. *Fire Tower:* Whenever you go camping or to a wilderness area, visit the local fire tower. Rangers and parks department employees can arrange tours; most are glad to see visitors. The experience is exciting and helps kids realize how important forest rangers and firefighters really are.

I hope these suggestions will help you to think of many other creative ways to have fun with your family. The dividends of this kind of investment in your family relationships are greater than you can ever imagine. Stocks and bonds don't come close.

The Value of Being Together
without Spending Much Money

Recently, Greg told me that knowing that his father and mother considered him to be not just a son but a friend was one of the most important things in his life. He reminded me that way back when, I told him, "You know, Greg, one of the neat things about having kids is that you get a chance to raise your own best friend. And Greg, you *are* one of my very best friends."

Norma and I were very involved with our kids as friends through all the years of their schooling—junior high, high school, and college. We went to all their sporting events, and Norma even went to watch them practice. We planned it into our week. We made it clear that basketball games were more important than board meetings. It was just something that we did automatically. Greg and Michael told me that even though they didn't always acknowledge the fact that we were at those activities, they really appreciated knowing that we were there.

Greg remembers that in high school he didn't want to relate or hug or care, but we kept up a steady pressure on him to do those very things. We never got discouraged. He often resented or resisted the talks we had about the importance of touching and hugging, and the importance of caring between us, to our parents, and to each other as brothers and sisters. But more important than the fact that he resisted it, he would also have *hated* it if we hadn't wanted to talk to him.

He always knew that Mom and Dad wanted to be friends with him and that they accepted him no matter what. Today Greg believes that our desire to be not only parents but friends with our children was a key part of his maturing experience. We always tried our best to treat our children like people, not just kids, but like very valuable people. There had to be a balance. We definitely knew that we were the parents, but we also knew that we were best friends, and our kids later acknowledged that we were able to be not only parents but, at the same time, their best friends.

An important part of our relationship with our children was what we called Family Night. Before they started high school, we would have Family Night every Friday, and these were very important times for us. All our kids agreed. We would play games, have a conversation or a debate, go out for the evening, or maybe we would just have a special dinner.

During most of our kids' growing-up years we didn't have a lot of money, but we still managed to do a lot of things because there was so much we could do that was absolutely free. Camping is about as close as you can get to free entertainment. At one time we could rent a space for about four dollars a weekend. I think campsites run about ten dollars a night these days, but there are still a lot of free campsites around.

Our kids said they never realized we didn't have a lot of money. We could always do the things that mattered. We had food and clothes, and there was plenty of fun. There seems to be a tendency in modern society to believe that money is the only thing that matters. When people don't have very much money they drag around, complaining, feeling underprivileged and depressed because they don't have the things they see on television.

The fact is, we were able to do very simple things that didn't require a lot of money. We might not have money, but we were doing just fine. We made that a point. There were times when we had to buy our kids' clothes at second-hand stores. We would find good quality, name-brand things, and our children didn't know the things we brought home weren't brand new. They were *great* clothes.

It was difficult for Norma and me to go to some of those places at first because we didn't want anyone to see us there. We were struggling with our pride. But after a while we got used to it and it was fine. We felt that it was important not to say that we didn't have a lot of money, or even to make money an issue, because we felt that all of life should be honorable. Money was a convenience: We were glad to have it, but we didn't have to be rich to be happy.

I recently received a testimony from our secretary who was in South America. She said that most of the people she met had no money at all, yet they were happy, loving, hospitable, and gracious. These people know what Norma and I learned many years ago: Money is not the thing that gives honor to a family. Real honor is a decision that we make as parents, and it transfers to our children. It is the attitude that life is worth living, and people have value that doesn't depend on their possessions.

What They Didn't Like

Well, I said I wanted to share some things that our kids didn't like, things they don't plan to do with their own children. I want to preface this, however, by saying that the last item in this discussion concerns what I believe now was about the biggest thing I did wrong as a dad and as a parent. At the time I really didn't realize what was happening under the surface, but I wish I hadn't done it.

This particular problem turned out to be a major obstacle in my relationship with Greg. Even though some great things eventually came about in Greg's life because he responded in the right way, it was nevertheless something I would not do—something I would not say—if I had it to do over again. I would encourage you to consider seriously whether or not you may be saying something like it to your own children.

But the first thing I want to talk about is the matter of discipline: in this case, physical punishment. When it comes to discipline, it is easy for parents to forget what it is like being a child and how fragile children really are. Whenever Greg got into trouble as a child, I would sometimes tell him to go find the spanking stick and bring it to me. The spanking stick was just a little stick that the kids had made and decorated, and we used it to paddle the children, but it stung when they were paddled, and I thought that going to find it would make the kids think about the consequences of what they had done wrong. I thought it would just be beneficial for them to think long and hard about what they had done. I think now that I was wrong, especially in Greg's case.

The problem was that Greg became so fearful inside while he looked for the stick, his little heart would just be pounding. I didn't realize how strongly my plan really affected him. Even though Norma never used this method, I reasoned that he had disobeyed, and if he spent fifteen or twenty minutes looking for the stick then that was fifteen minutes he would have to consider what this was all about. But it was not worth the fear, the hurt, the resentment that this lesson cost. Yes, he was antici-pating the spanking, but in Greg's mind I was a big mean per-son who was about to hurt him. That was a very negative and unproductive message. It did not produce the behavior change I truly hoped for, and I was not even aware of it at the time.

On a couple of occasions Greg has told me that this was the part of his childhood discipline that hurt the most. It was not the physical hurt but the emotional hurt. In fact, in our re-cent conversation about this, Greg said that he remembered a couple of times when he brought the stick to me and I asked, "What's this for?" He'd be standing there, holding the stick, al-ready in tears, and he could tell that I had completely forgotten that I had sent him to get it.

When Greg told me this as a twenty-three-year-old, I just blushed in my heart. I had to ask myself, How could I have been so insensitive? I learned an important lesson. But I think that the point here is that parents need to realize that a child's heart is very fragile. We need to be honoring and careful, especially in the area of discipline and spankings, so that we don't do things in the process of training that are actually dishonoring to them. I know that if I had that to do over again, I surely wouldn't do it the same way.

Another thing that our kids all agreed was a major problem actually developed as a result of our lifestyle and relationships as a family. When the kids were small, we were very active in our church because I was the assistant pastor. We were very involved in the various activities at our church, and Kari, Greg, and Mike were each involved in Sunday school, Bible school, and all the regular church activities. But then I changed jobs.

When I started my full-time ministry in family life, our church in Texas sent me out as a missionary to families, and that meant I was gone a lot of weekends, speaking at conferences, in churches, and at a lot of seminars. Whenever Norma had to stay home with the kids, they were involved in church, but it wasn't the same as before. They went every week, but the sense of family unity had changed. Even when we would take the kids with us when I had to travel on weekends, we ended up visiting a lot of different churches in a lot of different towns. Consequently, we didn't feel that we really had much of a church life.

Sometimes we would wind up traveling on weekends and we couldn't go to church at all. Today the kids feel that, in the long run, this probably hurt them. They weren't involved in our church on a regular weekly basis. They didn't have regular contact with youth groups or youth leaders or church activities, and now they realize they didn't get discipled by our church in the way they wish they could have. That was a serious problem.

In some ways I felt that our family life substituted for church: We had quiet times and devotions and prayer together. But for all the good things that came out of those experiences, I now believe that every family needs a strong local church. Our kids say they really missed the local church experience.

Later the children attended a Christian school and the school became a sort of church for a while, but it wasn't what they really needed. Even very good schools aren't designed for discipleship: That's a job for the local church—the schools will tell you that. So my kids now look back and say they wish they could have had more direct discipleship from older, committed Christian kids. They wish they could have been "plugged-in" to their local youth group.

Looking back now, I totally agree with them, and I wish that we could have done it that way. Even though they are all growing in their relationships with the Lord today, and even though they have strong commitments to God and to other people, I think they missed an important stepping stone in their spiritual walk. In fact, that was probably the area that hurt Greg the most, and that's the area that we will go into with Greg because he was really the one who struggled in this area.

The Long-Term Effect of Words

I made a statement to my kids when they were young. I thought it was a good statement, not really thinking it through carefully, and I thought it was important to say. I said that because of my work and my various responsibilities, we were probably more vulnerable than a lot of families. I said, for example, that if they ever got involved sexually with someone before they were married, then I wasn't sure I would be able to stay in the ministry. In fact, on a couple of occasions I even said that I wasn't sure I would want to.

Now there are a hundred things in life that I could do—and would probably love to try some of them—but they *knew* that I loved what I did. They knew that I was having a definite effect on families all over the world, and they did not want to keep me from doing that. They did not want to be responsible for harming my work in any way. So even though I said that they could always say whatever they wanted to say to their mother and me, the fact that I had said that their behavior could force me to leave the ministry actually became an obstacle to open communication when they were teenagers.

Greg told me, "Dad, you told us we could tell you anything, but we knew that if it was something really bad, it might possibly cause you to leave the ministry. Maybe you would; maybe you wouldn't. We didn't know. But it was an obstacle. When I was in college, I saw a lot of really worldly stuff. There were constant temptations. Sex was all around me: in our dorm, in our room at times. Girls were always talking about it; girls propositioned me; there were magazines. I simply couldn't avoid it."

He went on, "The world is a very different place than when you were a kid, Dad. In our world sex is so prevalent and so talked about that sometimes it is more than a person can ignore. I was away from home, away from my family, and I was struggling with all these problems but I never felt I could talk to you openly about it. I felt that the potential consequences were just too great.

"Sure," Greg told me, "I 'surface' talked to you about it, but not really, not directly. When I went off to the university, I got into serious problems with sex, and before I knew it I was living in two worlds. In one world I was a 'bad person.' In the other world, with my family, everyone viewed me as this 'good kid.' You all loved me and told me how valuable I was, how good I was. But then I would leave your world and go back to my 'bad' world."

When all this first started to come up, I talked to Greg about it to clear the air, to encourage him to just talk things out. This was at Christmas time and we were both relaxing in the Jacuzzi, so it was an honest heart-to-heart talk. Greg said, "You know, Dad, you and Mom saved my life in some ways. I was trapped in sin. I felt guilty and ashamed. There were even times when the thought of taking my own life crossed my mind, but in the end I always knew I had a safe place to come back to. I knew that no matter how bad I felt, I could still get love and support here at home. I suppose I could have gone off the deep end and just gone deeper and deeper, but your support gave me the strength to accept God's love and grace and forgiveness. I am really grateful now that I was able to return to Him and to be able to pull myself out of the ice water I had fallen into."

I could see that Greg had really gotten in over his head. He started to feel like a total "scuzz ball." He said, "I felt like a totally rotten person, and I was so ashamed. But what pulled me out was when I realized that you could screw up and God would still love you and that He could still use you. That didn't mean I didn't feel horrible: I did. But, you know, I made a decision to be better, not bitter. It had to be my own decision. There was nothing my parents could have done."

He continued, telling me, "It always boiled down to my own choice. One reason I decided for a while I wanted to be a lawyer was because I figured that God could never use me in any sort of ministry. But then I remembered the story of Saul of Tarsus. He had killed people, persecuted Christians, and did so many awful things that, by comparison, his sins were so much worse than mine. Yet, God still used him, turned his life around and made him into the Apostle Paul. That seemed to prove that you could never do anything so bad that God couldn't turn you around and use you."

"So, Dad," Greg said, "that's what happened to me. I eventually got my act back together and became best friends with my Savior. I needed to let Him heal me. It was a long process and it has been very painful . . . over two years. But through the pain and the healing I have become what I am today."

I can't tell you how my son's honest confession and his beautiful understanding of what he had been through touched my heart. The shame and the guilt he had felt were so strong that it held him down. He said he felt like he had stepped through the ice into freezing cold water and he couldn't get out. The cold water was immobilizing his muscles, and he was not strong enough to pull himself out of the water.

"The guilt and the shame," he explained, "were the ice, and I couldn't get back through to the good world. I needed some kind of tool to break through it and get out. The Bible became my tool, and I started learning more and more about my personal relationship with Christ and how He could work in my life. I made a deeper commitment to Him at that point, even before I knew all the right things to say. But once I finally made this very real, sincere, personal choice to become a personal friend of Jesus Christ, He gave me the tools to break through the ice."

Our pastor said recently, "When we are in God's will, following His way, then and only then does He empower us." That was the principle Greg discovered. As Greg began to feel the power of God's grace and love, he was able to get his head back above the ice water and start to breath again. He was still freezing and cold and paralyzed, but he was on the way back.

"Months passed," Greg told me, "and I realized that the guilt and the shame were only in my mind. I had to understand that it was okay for me to have done those bad things. I mean, now that they are in the past and I've confessed them, they're not going to hold me down any more. God can truly forgive. He has mercy on us every day, and He can ritualize those old habits and pull us into new patterns. We can actually look back on those old things, and God can turn them into something good."

Greg was so right. Isaiah 61:2–3 says that Christ came to "comfort those who mourn," "to give them beauty for ashes, the oil of joy for mourning, the garment of praise for the spirit of heaviness; that they may be called trees of righteousness, the planting of the Lord, that He may be glorified." God turns ashes to beauty and sorrow to joy if and only if we are dependent on Him. Now Greg was learning all of this on his own.

He said, "I think I have a much greater sensitivity today than I ever did before, a greater love for people. I have a level of understanding that I never had before. I realize now that messing up your life doesn't have to be fatal. I'll soon be married and into my second year of seminary, training for a career in counseling, and I believe that my own past really is a sort of a foundation for my understanding of how to help other people in the future."

Gaining a New Perspective

Now I am not telling these things about our struggles as a family or about Greg's experience to point out how much pain we had to overcome as a family. My purpose is to show how an attitude I had expressed to our children, a verbal caution that they were not allowed to get into any sort of serious trouble, may have been partly responsible for Greg's decision to lead a double life. One of the things we both acknowledged was that my saying that I might have to leave the ministry if he ever told me about those things actually caused him to stay out in the cold.

Greg didn't have access to me and Mom during those lonely nights when he was struggling in the ice water of immorality. That really hurts. But the good news is that because he didn't have me to turn to, he turned to the Lord. It's not exactly the way I would have wanted it to happen, but what a great opportunity my mistake actually became! God turned it into something good: joy for ashes.

Greg and I went to see Dr. Bill Retts, a terrific Christian counselor, and Bill said something wonderful to Greg. He said, "Greg, all of Scripture is the story of how God uses people's lives and their personal stories to tell God's truths. You now have your own story. It's not your dad's story that you are living on, it's your own story. Here's where I was before; here's what happened to me; and here's how God took me out of the ice water. So Greg, I hope you will see this experience as a chance to help other people understand how God changes lives."

Dr. Retts also encouraged me as a parent, just as I now encourage you as parents, to let your kids know that they can tell you the whole truth. You may want to tell your teenagers about your own rocky times, what you were like, and how God pulled you out of the icy waters and put your feet back on the solid rock of Jesus Christ. Tell them the whole story and humble yourself, which I didn't always do. Now I wish I had done more of it. God's walk in our life is a process. It is the story of how God is taking us from victory to victory despite the mistakes and the stumbling we may experience along the way.

Greg's decision to be a youth leader is a real challenge for him. Teaching and leading young people has helped him to grow and it has also helped him to help other kids. It didn't really teach him anything new, but it kept him on that continual upward path. It helped him hold his head above water.

Greg has told me that, looking back, he could say that it was what God did in him through his failure that really turned him around. You can learn those things in many other ways, but he had to go through it because he needed to experience God's grace. Maybe there would have been no other way for him to discover what God wanted to teach him.

Greg knew he was a strong person, very insensitive and very judgmental. I think God knew that and realized that he needed to go through something really humbling in order to soften him up. Now he has a much greater empathy for other people's problems. He can cry with and for people now. Before, he didn't have a clue.

Sometimes when he's talking with kids, either in a counseling situation or just one-on-one, he can feel their pain, their enslavement, their grief. He can see the icy water they've fallen into and know that they are trying to swim out of it. And then, having a new understanding of God's great compassion, he can say, "Here's how I crawled out." He couldn't do that before, and he used to think it was a little wimpy. His reaction would have been to say, "Hey, man, what are you doing? Come on, crawl out! What are you doing in that water anyway!" He had a very hard-hearted attitude toward people he thought were weak. In his own mind he was on a pedestal, and he needed something or someone to take a sledge hammer and bounce him off that block. And that's exactly what happened!

Later I asked Greg, "Did you know that we would accept you even after you told us all this stuff that you'd been going through?" And he said, "Dad, you told me that you'd always accept me no matter what I did, but I never wanted to tell you because I was so proud of what you were doing and who you were. I could see all the people that you were helping, and there was no way on earth that I was going to let my actions make you give up something that I knew was so dear to you. That would have messed me up more than anything else. Home was so good. Whenever I came home I could disassociate myself from what I was doing in my other world. If you hadn't given us that warning about how our mistakes might affect you and your ministry, I would probably have been able to talk to you about it. But despite everything else, I am really thankful now that things worked out the way they did."

Kari's, Greg's, and Michael's comments really confirmed for Norma and me the importance of the concept of honor in the family. We told them that we felt this was the most important concept we had learned as parents.

The truth is, we all go through the experience of parenting as beginners, and we're going to make mistakes. Mistakes are inevitable. God allows us to learn how things are supposed to be done as we go along. As long as we are honest with ourselves and our children, as long as we honor them and are totally honest with them, we have the freedom to make mistakes and still develop character and responsibility in our children.

I sometimes think that the freedom to fail may be the most important lesson we learn as parents, and it is one of the most important things we can teach our kids. We all do it.

The Principle of Empowerment

As I reflect on the lessons my children have taught me and how they have responded to our discipline and our family life, I am truly gratified by the evidence of God's love and protection in our home. I am also humbled to know that the efforts Norma and I made to empower our children with God's love and our own has returned back to us tenfold over the years.

As I spoke with Michael about his thoughts on what we had done positively and negatively as parents, I was struck by his observations.

"Dad, just encourage the parents who read this book to instill godly values in their children *when they are young*. Don't be afraid to take stands on movies or friends, what is right and what is wrong. They need parents *to be parents* while they are in the formative years . . . and then a mom or dad can loosen up and give them the opportunity to adopt these standards as their own as they get older."

There is so much wisdom in what Mike shared. It was King Solomon who wrote the words, "Remember also your Creator *in the days of your youth. . . .*"

When our children are young, we need to be their guides, their encouragers, their teachers and coaches. We need to empower them with the unshakable knowledge of how incredibly valuable they are to us. We need to make stands on right behavior and attitudes and be strong enough to discipline them. But we also have to let them go and grow . . . grounded in our values . . . and secure in our love.

For eighteen years we sought to empower Michael with our efforts and actions. And as Mike talked to me, I realized that he had turned the tables. Now he was empowering *me* to go out and encourage other families by his love and support.

"Dad, I've chosen to follow the guidelines you and Mom set for me. I think you did a great job with us. And I would encourage parents not to spend all their time worrying about what their child 'might' do wrong when they're older, and concentrate on giving them—*when they're young*—the values they'll need to make the right choices on their own."

Norma and I have always taken comfort in the fact that while we haven't done it all right, we've done our best to follow God's will. And you can know that feeling as well. In God's love, you can find the power to be whole and complete yourself and to overflow that love onto your children. This lesson has come back so often and so forcefully in our family, I'm convinced it can be a guiding principle in your home as well.

As we turn now to some practical examples for parents, I would like to offer some useful guidelines and principles for motivating children.

6

Three Powerful Ways to Motivate Children

- Use a Child's Natural Bent
- Use the Salt Principle
- Use Emotional Word Pictures

*I*T WAS 1957, IN SAN FRANCISCO. A tall, skinny ten-year-old boy was waiting to sneak inside Kaiser Stadium. He had waited all year for this game between the San Francisco 49ers and the Cleveland Browns and the chance to see his idol, Jim Brown, the All-Pro running back who held almost every rushing record in the NFL. He knew that at the end of the third quarter the gate guard left and he could slip in. Even that wasn't easy for him because he had trouble walking. Raised in the ghetto, malnutrition had taken its toll and his legs were weak and bowed. He had to walk with the aid of steel splints.

After he made his way into the stadium, he stood right in the middle of the entrance to the players' tunnel, where he patiently waited for the game to end. As the final gun went off, the wiry lad struggled to stand tall so he wouldn't miss this moment. Finally, he saw Jimmy Brown turn the corner and walk toward him. As he passed by, the boy held out a piece of paper, asking politely for an autograph. Brown graciously signed it, then turned for the locker room.

But before he could get away, the boy tugged on Brown's jersey. The great running back turned and was met with this proud confession, "Mr. Brown, I have your picture on my wall. My family can't afford a television set but I watch you on the neighbor's set every chance I get. I know what your records are and I think you're the greatest. You're my idol."

Brown put his hand on the boy's shoulder and thanked him before heading on to the locker room. But the boy reached up and tugged Brown's jersey again. Brown turned and looked into the boy's big brown eyes and asked impatiently, "Yes?"

The boy cleared his throat, held his shoulders back and head high and matter-of-factly said, "Mr. Brown, one day I'm going to break every one of your records."

Brown was so taken aback by the statement that he asked, "What's your name, son?"

The boy answered, "Orenthal James, sir. But my friends just call me O.J."

In 1973, O. J. Simpson broke Brown's long-standing single-season rushing record and became the first player to gain more than two thousand yards rushing in one year. He was second behind Brown in career rushing yardage when injuries forced him to retire. Why was O. J. Simpson so motivated? Why did he have such great success?

There are many, many reasons why people are motivated—it might be the applause, the cheering of a crowd, awards—but as with O. J. Simpson, real and lasting motivation must come from within. If Simpson had viewed Jimmy Brown's records as something he never could achieve, he might have ended up in a wheelchair. But he didn't. He set a goal and believed in himself enough to accomplish that goal.

When a child uses his own energy and drive to achieve a goal he has set, he is truly motivated. That goal may be inspired by parents or friends, but it is important that the child actually set the goal and see that it is attainable and that he will benefit by reaching that goal.

Notice we stress the child setting his own goal. There is a fine line between motivation and manipulation. Dads and moms alike need to be so careful not to use their children as pawns for their own needs. Have you ever witnessed a Dad forcing football on his son because Dad needs it—not his son?

True motivation comes from one or a combination of two factors:

1. Desire for gain.

2. Fear of loss.

Imagine waking a child on Christmas morning. He doesn't need to be motivated to get up. Eagerly he jumps out of bed because he knows there is something waiting for him. That same child will not stick his hand into a fire because he fears pain and loss, and this motivates him to avoid the flames.

Working with young children, teenagers, and college-age young people for more than thirty years has made me aware of over twenty ways to motivate children. At the heart of each of these methods is the desire for gain and the fear of loss. In this chapter, we will focus on motivating through a child's natural personality and the use of two communication tools. In the next chapter we'll cover nineteen other ways to motivate children.

1. Use a child's natural bent.

I could tell that Norma was down in the dumps by her voice on the telephone. It was Mother's Day and I was away from home teaching a seminar. She was lonely and I wished I were home. While we were talking, Greg walked into the house and presented her with a bouquet of flowers. I was pleased with his thoughtfulness, especially since he was only thirteen.

The next day I called Norma again to see how she was doing. "Oh, I'm just sitting here looking at these beautiful flowers Greg gave me," she said. I asked where Greg had gotten the flowers, hoping that he had picked them from our garden and not from the neighbor's.

"Oh, no," Norma said. "He ordered them from a florist."

"He ordered them? Where did he get the money for that?"

"Oh, he just used your charge card."

Greg is very sensitive and helpful whenever his mother is feeling down. He will vacuum the house, wash the dishes, sweep the floor—anything to make his mom happy. But our other children respond differently, and this reflects their different personality types. Kari and Michael tend to empathize with Norma if she's feeling low; they sometimes even get discouraged along with her. But neither one tends to "kick in" like Greg does.

A person's personality type, as I'll be describing, is a result of his total physical make-up, especially his gene structures. I like to call it his "natural bent." Often there is a *combination* of personality types in a child, but usually one is predominant.

Certainly his upbringing and environment affect his "bent," but I have observed that at least five different temperaments can be found in children and it is important to understand each of them. I've arrived at these five through my observation of children through reviewing a number of studies. Each child is motivated differently, according to his or her "natural bent."

Within each of the five personality types, the behavior of children will vary because of birth order. For example, firstborn children tend to be more pushy and prone to give orders. Secondborn children tend to be more sociable. Other factors account for variances within temperaments: being an only child, living with only one parent, being the only boy in a family of girls, and so on. Yet despite these variances, children tend to fall within one of the five general personality types. (For a more complete treatment of a child's and a parent's personality make-up, refer to *The Two Sides of Love*, which I coauthored with John Trent.

The summaries on the following pages illustrate the predominant personality types and general characteristics of each.

Also explained is how to motivate each type of child so that he or she will want to respond in a positive manner.

The Strong-Willed

General Characteristics

- They believe they're usually right
- Often critical, pointing out the mistakes of others
- Perfectionist tendency
- Believe there is a right and wrong way to act
- Prone to "foot-in-mouth" disease
- When doing a task, they want to do it right or not at all
- Negative thinker
- Persistent
- Very loyal
- Good memory of others' actions toward them
- Can be warmly touched by sad stories

Dos and Don'ts in Motivation

- Spend time fully explaining things, because once they see that certain actions are right, they usually comply.
- Be careful not to interpret their ability to be blunt with others as a sign that they can receive blunt, terse words in return. They are much more motivated by sincere grief, even tears, but they are experts in detecting insincere or manipulative motivation.
- They like to know where they are wrong if adequate time is taken, and they know if we are sincere and willing to wait until they really understand.

- Avoid prolonged arguments because the "strong-willed" often feel slightly hypocritical in discussing what they "know" is right—their own opinion.

The Peacemaker

General Characteristics

- Conforms to others
- Pliable
- Dependent
- Supportive
- Tenderhearted
- Agreeable
- Avoids persistent arguments
- Somewhat introverted
- Careful in what they say or do so as not to cause conflict
- Not the flamboyant type

Dos and Don'ts in Motivation

- They need to know that we sincerely like them as a unique individual.
- They react to being stereotyped or placed in a box.
- They respond better to someone they consider a friend.
- Patiently discover their personal goals and motivate them by helping them meet those goals.
- If the peacemaker disagrees, encourage discussion on personal feelings and opinions rather than objective facts.

- Avoid harshness or demanding attitudes because they are very stubborn when offended.
- When disagreement occurs it is better to have a soft, tender conversation as you gently touch them: "You're feeling hurt, aren't you? I sure don't want you to feel badly. Let's resume this later when we can both be calmer."

The Cheerleader

General Characteristics

- Manipulative
- Excitable
- Undisciplined
- Reactive
- Promotional
- Expressive
- Desires to be helpful
- Creative
- Approachable
- Warm
- Communicative
- Competitive
- Impulsive

Dos and Don'ts in Motivation

- Discover their opinions and ideas. Help them figure out how to reach their goals in a realistic way. Many times their goals are not realistic.

- "Cheerleaders" have opinions on almost everything. When motivating them, find out what they are most interested in and develop a friendship on this level of interest.

- They are most responsive to a good friend who likes their ideas.

- When faced with a problem, discuss possible solutions and let them come up with their own solutions, with your help as a parent.

- If you disagree, avoid prolonged arguments because "cheerleaders" have a strong need to win. Look for alternative solutions that you both can live with.

- "Cheerleaders" tend to do what you inspect, not what you expect.

The Pusher

General Characteristics

- Objective
- Uncommunicative
- Cool
- Independent
- Competitive
- Initiates action
- Pushy
- Tough-minded
- Dominating
- Harsh
- Determined
- Decisive

Dos and Don'ts in Motivation

- Help them see the results of their behavior. Be objective.
- They are interested in knowing what will happen, not so much why it will happen.
- When an argument starts, use facts and ideas, not feeling statements. "Pushers" are motivated by cold, objective facts.

The Helper

General Characteristics

- Somewhat like the peacemaker in temperament, but more concerned about assisting people in need rather than empathizing with them
- Tends to be exacting; their way is the only way to do it.
- Undependable
- Impulsive
- Avoids long-range planning
- Conforming because they avoid conflict
- Would rather do a job right than delegate it
- Usually overcommitted

Dos and Don'ts in Motivation

- They run on genuine, sincere praise.
- If you expect them to do a certain job, they'll probably avoid it and do something unexpected for someone else.
- They are stubborn if harsh demands are made.

- They usually try to accomplish more in one day than they can finish so they become frustrated. Help them organize their day, but don't demand that they follow the plan.

- If you want their help with a particular project, it is best to start it in their presence and wait for them to help. They may prefer to finish it by themselves, without your help.

When motivating a child by using his or her "natural bent" it is important to learn the child's basic interests and talents. You can use this knowledge to motivate that child to be a better student, eat healthier foods, read books, and do many other things.

Kari is a lot like the peacemaker and her strong interest is in teaching. We used this goal to motivate her to eat healthier foods, play on the high school basketball team, and study more diligently in school by showing her that she would be better prepared physically and mentally to be a good teacher.

When Michael was ten years old he wanted to be a pro football player. We used this goal to motivate him to eat more nutritional foods and take care of his body. "Have you ever met an unhealthy football player?" I'd ask him. Then he decided that he wanted to be a zookeeper. We visited different zoos and talked about what it takes to be a good zookeeper. Because a zoo must be neat and orderly, we motivated Michael to keep his room more neatly arranged. We gave him books about animals to encourage him to be a better reader which has motivated him to do well in school. And that strong interest in animals helped him to develop his research skills, which helped him throughout his school work and especially now in his college studies.

Our other son, Greg, started taking pilot lessons when he was twelve. He is a good pilot and because of this, his sense of self-worth has increased. Because he wanted to learn more about the history of flying and the various geographical areas over which he flew, his interest in school and reading also increased.

Greg said one of the reasons he wanted to be a pilot was so that we could travel together as a team, speaking together across the country. He took public speaking classes to help him meet this goal. He also became more interested in spiritual matters and living a consistent Christian life, because he realized that if he were going to speak about these matters, he needed to start learning them now.

When parents use their children's interests to motivate them, the resulting progress is often amazing. Motivating a child through his interests is effective because it comes from within him. It reflects his bent.

Parents must be careful, however, not to "force" a child into a particular "bent," especially when considering the child's temperament. People can take on characteristics of other temperaments, so the five general temperaments should only be used as a guide and not as a rigid mold. They can be very useful in communicating with and motivating children, but it can be very harmful to make statements like, "You're the strong-willed type, and this is the way you'll always be." Realize that they can adjust or even change their personality type in time.

2. Use the Salt Principle.

Using a child's interest can motivate very effectively, but what are we as parents to do if we can't even get their attention? What if they avoid our attempts to enter into a serious discussion with them? I have found a simple tool that can grab and keep their attention. It's called the *Salt Principle.*

We were driving back to Phoenix from Los Angeles a few years ago. Norma and the boys were in the back of our motor home, and Kari was sitting up front next to me. "Kari, would you like to date during the upcoming school year?" I asked. Shyly, she answered, "Yes."

"What type of boy would you like to date?"

"Well, he needs to be nice—polite. I want him to be sensitive. He should be interested in a lot of different kinds of things, especially sports."

"Sounds like a hunk," I said. Kari smiled, blushing a little at the name I'd used. "Kari, would you like to be sure that your dream date will come true?"

She looked at me with surprise. "Sure!"

"Well, I've been reading lately about two or three things you can do that will be attractive to a boy like the one you mentioned. Let's talk about them when we get back to Phoenix, okay?"

"Why wait?" Kari asked. "Let's talk about it now."

We spent the rest of our drive talking about several inner attitudes that make a person an outstanding dating partner. We discussed patience in understanding men and how they are different from women. We discussed what it means to have genuine love, and how she will gravitate toward a certain type of boy because of her temperament. It was a very profitable time, and it all happened because I used the Salt Principle.

> Simply stated, the Salt Principle involves using a child's *interests* to teach specific things that a parent believes are important.

We are all familiar with the saying, "You can lead a horse to water but you can't make him drink." But that's not necessarily true. If you dump salt in the horse's oats, he will become thirsty and want to drink. The more salt you dump on his oats, the thirstier he becomes and the more he wants to drink.

When I use the Salt Principle, I'm creating curiosity. That's what I did with Kari. I knew she was highly interested in dating, and I used that interest to share some things that would help her be successful in that area. I was able to hold her interest for hours because she was motivated.

The Salt Principle motivates children to listen carefully and thereby learn some important truths about life. I used it with Kari another time when I said to her: "Do you realize that there is something that could occur in your life this next year that could cause you to doubt God? Just this one thing could cause you to become extremely self-centered and have a difficult time in your relationship with God. You'll have a hard time reading the Bible and praying and you'll find you're less interested in school. You'll also find several other negative things happening to you."

After dumping on all this salt, I asked if she would like to discuss what it is that could cause such a devastation in her life.

"Yes! What's that?" she asked with excitement. "Let's talk about it, because whatever it is, I don't want to do it." At that point, I again shared some of the dangers of premarital sex. It was another very meaningful discussion.

The Salt Principle can be used to teach children many important lessons. Here are some guidelines for using salt effectively:

1. Clearly identify what you wish to communicate.

2. Identify your listener's most important interests.

3. Using their areas of high interest, share just enough of your idea to stimulate curiosity to hear more.

4. Use questions to increase curiosity.

5. Communicate your important information or idea only *after* you see you have your child's full interest and attention.

Not long ago, I wanted to teach Mike an important lesson. If I had said, "Hey, how about a Bible lesson together, just the two of us?" you can imagine the response: "Yeah Dad, maybe later, okay?" or perhaps, "Oh no, not one of those again." We are an ordinary family and I realize that my children often are not interested in what I consider to be important for their lives. But I can salt their interest by relating to things they are interested in. Here's how I used it with Mike:

"Hey, Mike? Want me to tell you a story?" I asked.

"No, Dad. I'm playing right now. Maybe later."

"Well, okay, then I won't tell you about a crazy, wild man who lived in the mountains, and he was so strong he could break chains and no one could hold him down and he made these horrible screams so no one would get near him."

I paused and Mike immediately piped up, "That's in the Bible?"

"Yes. And you won't believe what happened to him. Maybe sometime I'll tell you the story."

"No, tell me now, please!" So I proceeded to tell Mike the story about how Jesus healed the demoniac in Gerasenes.

The Salt Principle is a highly motivating tool when used with a child's natural bent. For example, I could take Greg's interest in being a pilot and use it to motivate him in a number of areas if I combine it with the Salt Principle.

Once I was talking to a commercial pilot, and I learned that you cannot fly commercially if you take certain types of drugs. You must swear to have never taken drugs and pass a lie detector test. I knew this would impress Greg deeply, so I arranged a meeting between the pilot and Greg.

Before the meeting, I salted Greg: "You know, there's one thing you could do which would prevent you from ever being a commercial pilot." Greg naturally was curious about what that could be, but I told him I wanted him to hear it directly from a pilot. When the three of us got together, the pilot asked Greg if he had ever taken drugs.

"Why no, I've never done any of that," Greg replied.

"That's good, Greg, because I want to warn you that if you ever do, you won't become a professional pilot. You can't even experiment with drugs or you can forget about being a pilot."

Talk about motivation. What took place in that discussion was far more effective than anything I could have said. And it was the Salt Principle that motivated Greg to listen to that pilot.

I had a high school English teacher who used salt to motivate us to read books. He would read to the class from a book. Then just when he got to the most exciting part, he'd stop reading and close the book. Naturally, we'd all say, "What happened?"

"It's in the book," would be his reply.

"What page?" we'd beg.

"You'll find it."

And so we'd dash to the library to check out the book, and many times we'd read the entire book to find out what happened. Norma used that same method to motivate our children to read fifty books one summer.

Look around and see how many people use salt. Television shows you twenty- or thirty-second previews of upcoming programs. They show you the most exciting scenes, but don't let you know how they are resolved. They'll show a car flying over a barrier in a chase scene, but in order to find out if it lands or crashes, you have to watch the show.

Gossip is the Salt Principle used in a negative way. You can walk up to someone and say, "You'll never guess what I heard about so and so." The immediate response is "What's that?" If you say, "Well, I promised not to say anything about it to anyone," you have just increased the salt level even more. This negative use of the Salt Principle demonstrates just how effective it really is. It can be used for manipulation, which is very negative, or it can be used in a very positive manner.

It's important to remember that the Salt Principle stems from a desire to serve a child's real or felt needs and interests. It guides that child toward fulfillment of his goals, while helping him gain important information that is vital to becoming a mature adult.

The next area is as equally effective in motivation as using a child's natural bent and using the Salt Principle. However, using it not only motivates a child, but I have never used anything more effective to communicate with children. This is the best method I've found for causing positive adjustments between parents and children.

3. Use emotional word pictures.

During most ordinary days, family members can offend each other and experience hurtful and difficult times. They often wish that another family member could understand how they are feeling. Using emotional word pictures is one of the best ways to have others enter into our feelings and it can motivate them to stop hurting us.

> An emotional word picture is associating our feelings with either a real or imaginary experience.

Using word pictures to motivate others is identifying with them emotionally. It's motivating on an emotional level.

A teenage girl once told me how she motivated her father to listen and understand her. She used an emotional word picture relating to her father's job as an auto mechanic to tell him about something that was troubling her.

"Daddy, you know how sometimes you will tune up a car and it runs okay, but not exactly the way it ought to? Then the owner will bring it back and say it's not running exactly right. Frustrated, you take out all your tools and check everything again and sure enough, you'll make a minor adjustment that makes the engine purr. Well, you're a super dad and our relationship is running along fine, but there's a little part of it that's out of adjustment. I wish we could spend some time so that I could explain from my point of view what we could do together to fine-tune our relationship."

The girl's father understood immediately because he could imagine someone returning a car for an adjustment. Because he understood how his daughter felt, a positive change occurred in their relationship.

I've used word pictures in counseling to help couples open up their lines of communication. Once, the wife of an NFL player used this graphic illustration to describe how she felt about their marriage: "I feel the way you have been treating me lately is like the way a little baby rabbit would feel out in the back yard. It's cold and raining. You've come out of the house and wandered out to the trash can and stepped right on my back and broken both my hind legs. I'm terribly frightened and I'm trying to get away." Tears welled up in her husband's eyes and he said, "I had no idea you were feeling this way. I didn't know I was hurting you like that." Once a person starts to *feel* the pain another is feeling, he increases his understanding and becomes softer in his spirit.

The use of emotional word pictures is useful for children as well as adults. Children can be affected by them at almost any age, as long as they can talk. Here are two steps for successfully using emotional word pictures. First, we need to clearly identify what we are feeling—what's going wrong or how do we *feel* about what's happening around us? Second, once these feelings are identified, we must make up a story that illustrates these feelings. If one is feeling discouraged he can say, "I feel like the color blue," or "I feel like a damp, smelly dishrag," or "I'm in cold water up to my neck in a deep well." Word pictures can be created by using things that are common to our experience: animals, water, mountains, desert, furniture, the seasons.

An example from the Bible demonstrates how powerfully motivating word pictures are. In the story of David and Bathsheba, David became sexually attracted to Bathsheba, lusted after her, and eventually caused her pregnancy. Feeling guilty about his actions, David arranged for her husband, Uriah, to be brought home from the battlefield to be with his wife. David thought this would get him off the hook, but Uriah refused to return home, saying he didn't want to offend his fellow comrades. David was angered, so he arranged for Uriah to be sent to the front lines of the battlefield where he was killed.

David wasn't motivated to repent or change until the Lord sent Nathan, who painted a powerful emotional word picture. Nathan related a story of two men, one very rich with many sheep, the other poor, with nothing but one lamb. The poor man raised the lamb with his children, and the animal became like a member of the family. One day a traveler came to town, but the rich man was unwilling to take one sheep from his flock to prepare for the visitor. So he took the poor man's one lamb and prepared this for his guest.

The story angered David, who said the rich man should make fourfold restitution for the poor man's lamb. David demanded that such a man deserved to die. Boldly Nathan said, "David, you are that man." The emotional word picture was so powerful that David cried out to God in grief and repented of his sin.

Jesus Christ was a master at using emotional word pictures. He used natural things and experiences to teach truth. He said things like, "The kingdom of God is like finding a valuable pearl." Or "Unless we fall to the ground like a seed and die, we will never produce the true fruit of life." "I am the Good Shepherd." "Faith is like a mustard seed." "I am the light of the world." These word pictures illustrate truths that are understandable to man because they are put in the context of human experience and emotions.

I've witnessed the power and effectiveness of emotional word pictures in my own home. It took five minutes to help my son change an irritating habit. I travel frequently throughout the country and am often gone for several days at a time. When I arrive home, the whole family usually greets me. It is an encouragement when they rush out to hug me and yell, "Welcome home, Dad!" When our son Greg was twelve, he would usually join in the welcome, but there was a time when, after the initial greeting, he would avoid me for an hour or two. I would try to touch him or ask him what he'd done while I was gone, but he'd say, "Just leave me alone. I don't want to talk."

That bothered me. He was acting like his spirit was closed toward me, but I hadn't done anything to him. I asked Norma what she thought was wrong and she explained that Greg was probably angry because I had been gone, and this was his way of punishing me.

I wanted Greg to understand how his rejection hurt me, so one evening a couple of days after I'd returned from a trip, I took him out for dinner, just the two of us. After dinner, I made up a story relating to his participation on the school basketball team.

"Greg, suppose you made first string on the basketball team and you were playing well, and suddenly you got an injury. We took you to the doctor and he said you couldn't play for two weeks so the injury would heal. So you don't play, but you show up at practices. Then after two weeks, you're ready to play again, but the rest of the players and the coach just ignore you. They act like you aren't even there. How would that make you feel?"

"Dad, that would really hurt. I wouldn't want to go through that."

"That's somewhat how Dad feels when I come home from a trip and you welcome me home, but then reject me for an hour or two. I want to get back on the family team, but I feel you are ignoring me."

"I didn't know that," he said. "That really makes sense. I won't do it anymore."

About two weeks later, I left for a trip. As I was getting into the car after saying goodbye to my family, Greg yelled, "Have a great trip, Dad. And get ready to be rejected when you get home." We all laughed, but he remembered, and never again did he reject me when I returned home.

Emotional word pictures can be used with anyone. Try using emotional word pictures with your mate or a good friend before trying it on your children. The more you practice, the better you will become, and you will see that this simple motivating force is very powerful.

In the next chapter we'll continue sharing an additional nineteen ways to motivate children.

7

Nineteen Additional Ways to Motivate Children

- Help Children Choose Their Own Goals
- Expect Children to Do Things Right
- Expose Your Children to People You Admire

I REMEMBER LYING DOWN next to our youngest son, Mike, just as he was falling off to sleep. Somehow we began talking about how special he is to me. I asked him the same question I've asked many times, "Why does Dad love you so much?" Unhesitantly he responded, "Because I'm a boy and have blue eyes, right?" "Yes," I answered, "but remember there's one more big reason." He thought and smiled, "I brought you back to the family, huh?" "Yes, but there's an even more important reason" I answered. He had been a major reason I changed vocations in order to spend more time with my family. Mike thought a moment more and said, "Because I'm me." "That's it!" I said. This special time with Mike reminded me of a major problem with motivating children.

Motivating children is a powerful way to change their behavior. However, performance to gain acceptance can cause an emotional drain on children as well as on adults. Parents should be very careful not to withhold acceptance if a child does not perform to their expectations. A healthy parent-child relationship is to accept children for who they are, not what they do. Acceptance adds to their strength and desire to change.

Again, true motivation is from within a child, not from external pressure from parents.

These nineteen remaining ways to motivate are suggested not for manipulation or for performance, but so each child can attain his full potential and experience his own goals.

---

1. Help Children Choose Their Own Goals

The football coach at Texas A&M asked each of his players to write down a number between one and ten, with ten being the best, representing how good he wanted to be. Jeff, a walk-on, wrote down "10" because he wanted to be good enough to play pro football. The coach then asked each player to write down specific goals for the season. Jeff set goals for weight lifting, including a bench press of four hundred pounds, running the one-hundred-yard dash in eleven seconds, and so on. The coach told the players to post their goals in several places, in their lockers and at home so they would be reminded of them at all times. Every week he had them read their goals out loud to each other and evaluate their progress. Jeff said the goal-setting procedure was probably the most motivating force he had ever experienced because the goals he was striving to attain were *his.*

We practice the same type of goal-setting technique with our children, whether it involves sports, school work, or any of their other interests. We say, "From zero to ten, how good do you want to be? We're committed to help you, but we want to understand your goals first."

In the past our children did not set their goals as high as we felt they should, and this led to some conflict. However, once we understood what their goals were, we also understood why they weren't as motivated in some areas. For example, we pushed and shoved Kari for years to be above average in her piano playing. We wanted her to be good enough to play in front of a group. We finally asked her to rate how good she wanted to be from zero to ten. She picked five—average. We had picked eight for her but that was not her goal. Consequently we practically had to sit with her to get her to practice. She finally stopped practicing when she was sixteen years old because she had reached her goal.

Part of loving children is helping them reach *their goals*—not superimposing our goals upon them. If we press our goals, their motivation won't last because it will be from an external pressure rather than true motivation from within themselves.

When helping your children choose their goals, try to expose them to people who have succeeded in areas in which your children are interested. If they're interested in both animals and medicine, set up an appointment for them to spend several hours visiting and watching a veterinarian. Something might be said during the experience to help motivate them. (If they don't faint as the vet patches a broken leg!) The motivational force is often more powerful when it comes from someone outside the family.

2. Help Children Visualize the Positive Results of Achieving Their Own Goals and the Negative Results of Not Reaching Their Goals

It was early in the basketball season and the team was doing quite well. But they were about to face a team which had humiliated them last year by thirty points. The coach knew he had to motivate his players, so he pulled out the film of last year's game. The game looked as bad on film as it had that night. It even captured the fans' shameful expressions, disgusted with their team.

At first that may not sound like the best motivational tool, but then the coach pulled out a film of his team winning a big game. This time the fans were screaming and cheering. "Look how well you played against that other team," the coach said. "This year you can play just as well against the team that embarrassed you last year. What do you say? Let's go get 'em!"

The coach's purpose was to help his players visualize beating the opposing team. He wanted them to see and hear the fans cheering for them, to see themselves out on the court, to recall the joy of beating a tough foe and the pain they would suffer if they failed.

A very popular high school football coach in Southern California motivates his players by finding out what each boy wants out of football. One boy might want to please his father, another wants to impress his girlfriend, while a third hopes to win a football scholarship at a major university. During practice, he might take the boy who wanted to please his father off to one side and say, "You know that play you've been working on? You're not quite getting it right. Now if you use this technique, can you imagine how proud your dad would be when you shoot through the line and make that tackle? Can't you just picture your dad cheering, jumping up and down in the stands?"

To the player who wants a scholarship the coach might say, "College scouts will be impressed if you use this technique. They spend hours trying to teach it to their players. Can you imagine them smiling as they see you make that play? They'll put a special note in their reports about that."

We've watched our son Michael's eyes and facial expressions as he admiringly follows in his older brother's footsteps. We know he wants to be as good as Greg in everything, especially in sports. The main reason we encourage our children in sporting events is because it can help build inner character such as patience, humility, and learning to lose and win graciously.

I witnessed the force of this motivational tool while Mike was telling me how much he wanted to be a tight end on the football team, like Greg. But he was in gymnastics and several years away from being in high school. I said to him, "Mike, can you just imagine how much fun it will be to go out for a long pass in football, catch it, and do a flip completely over the defender because of your gymnastic skills? I can see it now. I'll jab the person in the stands next to me, 'Did you see my son! He jumped completely over that guy—great move!'" Michael was laughing and I could see he was right with me; he was getting motivated.

3. Remember the Power of Praise

If, as a father, you had less than one minute each day to talk to your children, what would you tell them? Studies show that fathers, on the average, spend less than sixty seconds a day talking to their children, and most of that time is spent pointing out negative behavior.

However, the opposite of criticism is one of the most powerful motivating forces available to parents—praise. It can be used in a variety of ways. You might give your children ribbons for good behavior. You could take a picture of your child doing something that you really appreciate and put it in an album or hang it on the wall for everyone to see.

Michael was extremely dejected after his first wrestling match. He had lost and as I walked over to him, I could see tears trickling down his face. "Michael, that was great," I told him, ignoring his tears. "Your opponent has wrestled for two years and just think, the score was only two to one after two rounds. Mike, how did you keep up with such an experienced wrestler?"

Mike looked up and said, "They cheated me. They should let me wrestle someone my own age and with the same experience." He paused and then added, "But I did put him down twice. Did you see that, Dad?" His face began to shine with excitement.

A year later, Mike had decided not to go out for the wrestling team again. But the coach told him, "That's too bad, Mike. You have very good moves and great potential in wrestling." The conversation between Mike and the coach lasted no longer than one minute, but Mike's outlook on wrestling changed completely in those few seconds. That night Mike told me his coach said he was good in wrestling and asked if he could go out for the team.

As parents, we can motivate our children through praise. Instead of mentioning to them the two things they did wrong today, let's talk to them about the ten things they did right. You'll be amazed at the results.

4. Expose Children to a Variety of Activities

Some of the motivational methods that we have discussed so far come from top university students and athletes who serve as staff members at Camp Kanakuk, a nationally renowned sports camp in Branson, Missouri. A top collegiate gymnast at the camp told me that her parents exposed her to a variety of sporting activities when she was young. They introduced her to different people, including a girl who was one of the top baton twirlers in the nation. This personal contact greatly influenced her. Her parents noticed her tremendous interest, paid for her to take lessons, and later she became one of the top twirlers in the nation.

The key is letting the child choose what he wants to do. Expose children to a variety of activities, then carefully watch their response and interest. Wait until they ask to become involved, then support them the best you can.

5. Expect Children to Do Things Right

When I was a youth director for three hundred junior high students in Southern California, I *expected* those kids to show up for activities on time, to leave activities at a certain time, to produce various programs, and to do them well. I demanded the best by my attitude, and I was always fascinated by the outstanding, creative jobs the students did with any assignment I gave them.

I have learned that children can sense whether or not you expect the best from them. If they sense that they can get away with doing less than their best, often they will do just that. If they sense that you expect that they cannot do any better, they may drop to your level of expectation. I also have seen children who were highly motivated when great things were expected of them. I still hear from some of those junior high students I worked with. They tell me that they remember many of the things they were taught because they were *expected* to learn and perform at a high level.

6. Believe Your Children Can Achieve Great Things

Imagine how little you could do if you were only able to use 8 percent of your brain. What things would you have to give up with a 92 percent loss?

Most of us would give up little or nothing at all. Most humans only use about 8 percent of their mental capacity. That helps me realize how much more we are capable of doing. So many of us limit ourselves because we don't believe we can accomplish great things. Doctors say that even if we lose large portions of our brain in an accident, it's amazing what we can relearn through rehabilitation—like learning to walk and talk all over again.

Many of us have watched the television specials where three-year-old children in Japan are trained to be concert violinists. The school attributed the seemingly remarkable feat to the fact that the tots *didn't know* that they weren't supposed to be capable of such a feat.

Our mental capacity is so powerful, but unfortunately we often talk ourselves out of achieving things that are possible. And we can talk our children out of doing what they could accomplish. "Well, I wouldn't try that," we say. "You could never be like that."

Given the right opportunity and encouragement, children can accomplish incredible things. What a miracle when Kari was willing to try basketball in her junior year of high school. She had never played any competitive sports. She didn't even understand the difference between defense and offense. But she tried out for the team and made it. In her first game a teammate threw her the ball and Kari ducked, thinking it was meant for someone else. *Why would anyone want to throw her the ball?* she thought. She was amazed at how much she learned and improved over the year. How thrilled we were when she made her first basket, and when she started for the first time. She was so motivated, she majored in basketball at her summer camp in order to be better prepared for her senior year.

If only we wouldn't limit ourselves. God has created each of us with tremendous potential no matter what level we're starting at. As parents, we must communicate to our children that if they want to give something a try, they should do it. Even strain for it. That is one reason why I ran my first marathon at the age of forty-two. I wanted to show my children that even an "old man" can do things that appear almost impossible.

7. Help Children Develop a More Positive Self-Image

A young boy who looked on the bright side of everything was given a ball and bat by his father. The father told the boy that when he got home from work, he would play a whole inning of baseball with his son. Sure enough, when the father arrived home, he took the son out in the back yard to see what he could do.

The little boy threw the ball up, swung the bat, and missed. "Strike one," the father said. The boy tossed the ball up again, swung, and missed. His father said, "Strike two." With more determination than ever, the boy threw the ball up a third time, swung a mighty swing, missed, and spun around, falling to the grass. His father said, "Strike three. You're out. What do you think?"

To this, the optimistic little boy answered, "Man, am I a good pitcher!"

A little positive thinking can go a long way in motivation. However, the lower a person's sense of self-worth, the less that person tends to accomplish both physically and mentally. A low self-image affects a child in virtually every aspect of life—dress, conversation, facial expression, future employment possibilities, even the future of his or her marriage.

In my counseling of young children, teenagers, and even adults, I have found that certain individuals seem to be programmed to fail. But I also have found there is something we can do to enhance a person's level of self-worth.

It's essential that we get our children involved in at least one activity where they can be successful. The more successful they become in various activities, the more it raises their self-worth. We should literally help them through at least one accomplishment, whether it is playing the trumpet, swimming, painting—anything. A child may say, "I can't do that." But we must find an activity that interests the child and then let the child know that we believe in him and that he is capable of accomplishing the task.

I can still recall when my high school basketball coach yelled at me one day, telling me I was too slow. It took me years to get rid of the memory of those words ringing in my ears, "Smalley, you're too slow." When I went out for track, it was difficult for me to run because I kept reminding myself I was too slow. My low self-image actually inhibited my ability to run.

8. Reward Your Children

Parents who were trying to get their daughter to stop sucking her thumb decided that they would give her a little surprise every time she went seven days without sucking her thumb. When she went thirty days without reverting to the habit, they gave her a bigger surprise. Rewards have a way of motivating and changing behavior and they can be particularly effective with young children.

Of course, we must be careful that children do not learn to expect a reward every time they accomplish something, such as routine chores around the home. Children need to learn that they are part of the family, and that everyone must work together to do things around the home without expecting any reward.

When Greg was fifteen, we discovered a very effective way to motivate him with major chores around the house. We simply placed a list of jobs to be done on the refrigerator with the wage amount written next to each job. These were jobs that were not part of our household chores, such as cleaning the garage, weeding the backyard and garden, and trimming the trees.

These jobs were open to any of our kids, but Greg would rush through as many as he could. It seldom seemed to bother our other two children that Greg earned the most money. But sometimes they would write their name next to a job signifying "Hands off! It's my job."

9. Use the Ol' You-Can't-Do-It-Can-You? Principle

What happens when someone tells you, "You probably don't have time for this," or "You can't do that, so I'll get someone in here who can"? If you're like me, such statements bother you, so you usually jump right in and tackle whatever has to be done. I've seen the same type of motivation work with my children. I'll say, "You probably can't handle this" or "I need someone *strong* to do this. Who can I call?" The result is that the children often get right in there and do the work.

The head of my college math department called me into her office one day and suggested I reconsider my decision to minor in math. "Gary, I know you're having a difficult time in calculus," she said, "I'm not sure you can handle the more advanced courses."

I boiled inside. "Hey, wait a minute," I thought. "Are you telling me that I can't handle math? I'll show you." I politely asked for a chance to prove I could do it. She gave me that chance and, motivated to study harder, I went on to graduate with a minor in math.

While this technique can be very successful, it must be used carefully. If used on a person with a low self-image or someone who has trouble believing in himself, you may only succeed in discouraging him further, or causing him to give up completely.

10. Expose Your Children to People You Admire

My children's inner motivation has greatly increased by exposing them to some very successful people. I've taught at several pro athletes' conferences and my children have come to know Bob Breunig, then an all-pro linebacker for the Dallas Cowboys. Bob and Mary Breunig can talk to our daughter Kari at any time about any subject and she absorbs every word they say. The same thing occurs with Steve Largent, the all-pro receiver for the Seattle Seahawks. Our children already know of his personal faith in Jesus Christ, and when Steve takes time to sit down with our kids and chat, they remember what he says and are motivated by his encouraging words. They never forget these special encounters.

Chuck Snyder, a very successful businessman from Seattle, visits with us a few times each year. When he does, he usually takes Kari out for lunch. Each time he brings her home, it is obvious that Chuck has influenced her life. He carefully listens to her, he praises her, and he really encourages her.

Not long ago, I asked Chuck to help Kari clarify her goals in life. When she came home from their luncheon, she enthusiastically announced that she now knew exactly what her goals were. The impact was tremendous. Not only did she set her own goals, but she began helping us all with our goals. Her motivation level tripled after this one meeting with Chuck. An evening spent dining and conversing with these quality people is such an inspirational experience for my children. I'm not sure I can have the same type of *instant* impact on them. There is no amount of money I could pay Bob Breunig, Steve Largent, and Chuck Snyder or any of the other leaders for what they have taught our kids.

You may be saying, "Well, that's fine for you who know some of these pro athletes and business leaders, but what about me? I don't know people like that."

You might be amazed how easy it is to rub shoulders with some of these outstanding people. Many of them want to share their lives with others, particularly young people. There are many influential people who would love to meet with your children, if only for a few minutes, so that some of the qualities that have made them successful could rub off on your children.

For example, consider inviting your pastor to dinner. Prepare for the time by asking him to share how he started in the ministry and let the discussion after dinner stimulate and inspire your children. Try the same experience with a businessman you admire or an outstanding leader in your community. Let these leaders know what your purpose is. Invite a retired missionary or statesman to your home. Take your children to visit a prison facility. Have them ask some of the administration officials why people generally get into trouble. Try to spend time with someone of influence at least two or three times each year.

11. Be Persistent

As a parent, I never realized how motivational persistence can be. But knowing this, we must be careful to not confuse persistence with nagging. Nagging is basically negative, a criticism of someone who is not acting in the manner in which we would like him to. Nagging usually reflects selfishness: "You haven't started to clean your room yet? You didn't do it yesterday. When are you ever going to get that room cleaned up?" The same topic and the same tone of voice, repeated over and over again, can cause resistance in children and can eventually lower their self-image. They begin to believe what they continually hear—"I can't do anything right."

Persistence, however, is when we creatively and enthusiastically bring up something that we believe to be important. We mention it in different ways and at different times and in different tones of voice.

Many years ago, I came to the conclusion that everyone in our family, myself included, was watching too much television. We were hooked. I was watching too much sports, the kids were watching too many cartoon programs, Norma was hooked on "soaps." I felt uneasy about the control television seemed to be having over our lives. Yet every time I mentioned the subject I was met with a howling reaction. I soon realized it was my fault. I was nagging with statements like, "Let's stop watching television," or, "This television set ought to go." These types of statements did nothing but create negative feelings and reactions to me. No one was motivated to change.

Once I realized what was happening, I decided to become persistent in a calm, loving way. I said things like, "I would really be grateful if we would cut back on the amount of time we spend in front of the television." Then for weeks I would say no more, because I didn't want to pressure anyone. A few weeks later, I made a statement about how much television we were watching, but again, I dropped the matter immediately.

To set an example, I began to spend less time in front of the "tube" myself. Often I'd read in another room. However, I was careful not to appear like I was superior, "Mr. Good Guy." I watched certain programs from time to time, but they were carefully selected. The most powerful statement I made, but didn't realize it until later, was after dinner one evening. I casually mentioned that it would really make me happy if someday we could live in a home where we didn't need a television because we enjoyed life so much without it. But I added, "That's probably not possible."

About a year later, Norma called me at work and mentioned that she and the kids had a surprise for me. When I opened the front door, the kids were all giggling and Norma was smiling. I took a glance around the house, but I couldn't figure out the surprise.

"Don't you see it, Dad?" the kids yelled. "You mean you really can't see it?" I couldn't see "it." Finally, they pointed toward the table where our television used to sit. The table was empty.

"What do you think, Dad?" they asked. I was speechless. They had put the television in the attic. They wanted to go "cold turkey" and forget about television, at least until they had gained control over their habit.

I was overwhelmed and immediately wanted to do something for them since they had changed their life pattern for me. I reached for my wallet and said, "Hey, let's all go out for dinner."

Their reaction astounded me again. They didn't want me to repay them. They didn't put the television away thinking they would get some reward. They told me they did it out of appreciation for my feelings. They did it out of love. I truly felt the love in what they had done. I never sensed that they were pressured into putting the set away. After a year or so we brought the television back, and we watch occasional programs together. But now television doesn't control our lives. We control the television.

12. Be Enthusiastic

Waking up in the morning has never been one of the highlights of my day. I'm one of those people who has to drag himself into the shower to wake up. Norma, on the other hand, is one of those people who wakes up every morning with a smile on her face. She starts singing as soon as her feet hit the floor. She even makes up her own songs. She is excited about seeing the new day, and her enthusiasm fills the whole house. Because of her attitude, everyone feels a lot better about getting up and going to school, to work, or doing whatever has to be done that day.

Being around an enthusiastic person is like being around someone who is laughing. It's contagious. Even when you don't know what someone is laughing about, you start grinning, then chuckling, and before long, you're laughing too.

I have found that, as a parent, if I am really excited about something, my family tends to get excited too.

One year I spent several months trying to convince my family to spend four weeks at an outstanding summer camp. But no one was even interested in hearing about it. Whenever I brought up the camp, I was met with disinterest. Later I met with a musical recording artist who had spent some time at the camp and he gave me all the enthusiasm I needed. That evening, I telephoned home and asked everyone to pick up an extension.

"Are you ready for this?" I asked enthusiastically. "Listen to this great place I just heard about." I went on to describe the camp in full. I told them in detail about all the fantastic activities available, the food, the lakes, slides, and giant water balloons. When I finished, I asked, "Have you ever heard of a place like this?" Their response was "No." They wanted to hear more. Then I told them it was the same place I had been talking about. We all signed up to go that night. Enthusiasm is contagious!

13. Develop Strong Inner Convictions

I believe it is very important that parents periodically evaluate their convictions. What do we believe is right for the family, and what do we believe is wrong? What is right for our children and what is wrong for them? What does the Bible say is proper behavior, and what is behavior that contradicts God's standards?

The average woman probably has no idea how tremendously influential and motivating she can be if she has deep convictions. The Old Testament speaks of a "virtuous" woman. It says that when you find a woman like that, you have found a woman more precious than jewels. In the Hebrew language, a "virtuous" woman was one who had strong convictions and who had influence because of her convictions.

If a woman believes it is very important for children to learn communication skills, for example, she will tend to spend time gathering information on how to teach such skills to her children. She will be *alert* to anything that will help her attain her goal. Her conviction that it's important for her children to know these skills greatly increases the likelihood that they will learn them.

This is a major reason why children learn from their parents nonverbally. When parents approve of what their children are doing, they get excited, and it shows in their eyes, their facial expressions, their nonverbal actions. Our children understand this nonverbal communication, and they tend to get excited, too. When we are displeased, we display negative facial reactions such as frowning and tightening our lip muscles.

Nonverbal communication can be a very motivating factor for children because they are alert to facial expressions and body language. The stronger our convictions, the more our nonverbal language will communicate those convictions.

How many people have had a lasting influence on your life? Think about it. They probably were people with strong convictions. The same is true for us. The stronger our convictions, the greater our influence on the people around us.

When talking with some of the Dallas Cowboys football players, I have learned that former Coach Tom Landry had very strong convictions about how to play football. He had his ideas about how to prepare the offense and defense. The players say they could feel his convictions. Even the television audience could sense his seriousness as the camera scanned the sidelines on Sunday afternoons.

14. Use Contracts

Chapter 4 covered how we involved our children in drawing up our contracts. We have found it very motivating for a child to conform to a contract that he helped prepare. We have watched our children make adjustments in their lives because they have agreed to terms of the contract. For example, Greg decided on his own to change schools, with our blessing, after we had written out a contract that outlined the major reasons children attend school. After he saw the finished contract, he suggested a change. The school he was attending didn't include some of the important areas we had written into the contract. Here's a sample of that contract.

A school should include:

- activities that involve the whole family
- students that I can develop close friendships with because we have many things in common
- an atmosphere where students can pray and interact about their faith in God

There were also several other factors involved. More items were added to this list by our other children. Then together we all chose the school we felt came the closest to our contract on schooling.

15. Encouragement from Peers

When Greg started attending a new high school, he wanted to try out for the basketball team. But he held himself back because he didn't think he was good enough. During the year, he ate lunch with some of the players and shot some baskets with them after school. When the players told Greg he should try out for the team, their encouragement was just the motivation he needed. He did try out the following year and made the team.

Then there was a thirty-second, life-changing experience for Kari. Kari almost dropped out of basketball after practice one evening. I went into the gym to pick her up, and as we walked off the court she announced, "That's it, I've had it. I just can't play basketball!" The front gates were locked so we had to walk around the school and in front of the boys' locker area. When the boys' team saw Kari, they were so excited about her trying basketball that they were patting her on the back and saying things like, "Hey, Kari, go for it!" Thirty seconds later as we were driving home she said, "Dad, I really like basketball. In fact, I can't remember now why I wanted to quit."

16. Create a Positive Successful Experience

Many times we fear that if our children get involved in a certain activity they will fail because they lack some basic skills or knowledge. We have this inner sense that tells us, "I don't think they can handle this," or, "I don't think they're ready for this."

In such cases, I believe it is appropriate for us, as parents, to intervene to help our children gain the *knowledge* or *skills* that they need before attempting an activity that appears to be certain failure.

17. Wait for the Children to Act on Their Own

From time to time, parents must "light a fire" under their children. But there are also times that we need to wait for them to see what we see. We have found, for example, that it occasionally is very motivating to allow our children to let their rooms become extremely messy. Eventually, they get upset with the contrast between their messy rooms and the other orderly rooms in the house. Before long, they become tired of the mess and the room gets cleaned. If a child has never lived with the mess and disorder, it's harder to appreciate order.

It is true, of course, that some children will never clean their rooms without direction from a parent. But the idea is to give a child time to initiate the desired behavior himself.

18. Accountability and Support

When we share our goals with others, whether with family members or friends, we become increasingly motivated to attain these goals because we know we will be held accountable. There is a great deal of discomfort associated with knowing that we have not attained our goals, and that others we care about know this, too. This feeling of accountability, when coupled with support, is a tremendous motivating factor.

When we get discouraged or disappointed that we haven't progressed as far as we would like, the support of our family and friends can generate energy within us. This energy drives us to go forward, even when many times it seems easier to give up. Just having someone say, "How are you doing?" or "You can do it," is tremendously energizing.

19. Tender Touching and Listening

Children can become discouraged for a number of reasons—an injury, lack of progress, knowing there is always someone who is just a little bit better. Any of these reasons can make a child lose his energy. The easiest way for children to regain that energy is for someone who cares to put his arm around them, touch their hand, or pat them on the back. When someone really listens to how they are feeling, it pumps energy into them and motivates them to pick up at the point where they otherwise would have quit in discouragement.

While training for my first marathon, I was running on the shoulder of a major freeway in Portland, Oregon. Lost in my thoughts, I was startled by a motorist shouting at me with his fist clenched in what appeared to be a hostility toward runners. Then I noticed his smile and heard him shout, "Go for it! It's great to see you out here! You can do it!" Tears came to my eyes as he drove off and a burst of energy surged through my body. I literally bounced down the highway. Support like that is highly motivating.

When a child is discouraged, try the touching and listening approach: "Tell me about it," you say as you put your arm around the child. "You're really hurting today, aren't you? Do you want to talk about it?" or "I know it's hard, but you can do it."

As you touch your child, you are not only sharing with him, you are energizing him. You are not pitying him, as that can bring you both down. What you are doing is touching to listen, to understand.

After trying this, let some time go by before you start telling your child how to get back on course. Sometimes we try to get everything corrected too quickly and we drain the child's energy. Give him time. You'll be surprised at just how energizing touching and listening alone can be.

With any motivational tool, we must remember that lasting motivation must come from *within* the child. Motivational techniques such as coercion, threats, and bribing are only temporary. Our job as parents is to help our children set goals and believe in them enough to see them accomplished, and whenever possible, use our resources to help them achieve those goals.

8

The Secret of a
Close-Knit Family

- Six Characteristics of a Close-Knit Family
- Sharing Life Experiences Together
- Dealing with Difficulties in a Positive Manner
- Three Practical Ways to Share Life Together

THE MUSCLES OF MY left thigh were beginning to ache. Pain shot from my knee as I pounded past the fifteen-mile marker. I had been running for two hours, and so far the enthusiasm of this being my first marathon had kept me going. But now, doubts caused by this week-old muscle pull began to creep into my mind as several runners passed me. I started to wonder if I would even make it to the finish line.

The faces of the crowd lining Scottsdale Road were a blur. I was only vaguely aware of encouraging shouts from spectators. Then the words "Way to go, Dad!" broke through the haze. My entire family—Norma, Kari, Greg, and Michael—were screaming and waving at me. As I passed them, they joined in step with me and their enthusiasm filled me with a new surge of energy. Norma and Kari ran a few steps, then said they'd meet me at the finish line, but Michael and Greg wanted to keep me company.

The pain in my leg faded as I enjoyed this special moment with my boys. I was too tired to say anything as we ran, but their company made me feel great. After three more miles, Michael, who was only nine years old, was obviously too tired to continue. I left him at a corner and told him to wait for his mother to pick him up.

Nearly two hours later, I finished the race with Greg not far behind. Exhilarated by my achievement, I claimed my T-shirt and certificate and accepted congratulations and hugs from Norma and Kari. It took me a few moments to notice that their faces were filled with concern. "I'm feeling fine," I told them, but that wasn't the problem.

Norma took me by the arm and pulled me away from our two children. "We've lost Michael," she said. "He's been lost for over two hours."

I started to think back to the thousands of people lining the streets and immediately was concerned about our little blond, blue-eyed boy. I recalled newspaper stories about a child kidnapper and molester in the area and began to wonder if Michael might have become the next victim.

We headed over to the nearest police car and filed a missing person report. As I finished the description, Greg asked if he could talk to me alone. He looked right in my eyes and said very tenderly, "Dad, if we don't find Michael, can I have his bedroom?"

Greg has always had the ability to calm us in the midst of tense situations. However, I was glad Norma didn't hear this comment, for she probably would not have taken it with such amusement. But now I was relaxed. A few minutes later, Michael found us, having walked in with some runners who were late finishing the race.

That evening, we were able to laugh together at the whole incident, and I realized that this was another example of the secret to our close-knit family. This secret is a factor common to every close-knit family that I have observed.

Dr. Nick Stinnett of the University of Nebraska supervised a study of several intimate families nationwide, families that had a great deal of happiness and parent/child satisfaction. For the purpose of the study, he focused only on families with a husband, wife, and at least one child living at home. However, the close-knit secret also applies to single-parent families or any small group for that matter.

Six Characteristics of a
Close-Knit Family

Dr. Stinnett discovered that there were six consistent characteristics among these families. First, family members expressed a high degree of appreciation for each other. Several families even created projects around the house to stimulate praise. For example, one household of five had an event Dr. Stinnett called "bombardment." Every few months, the family members would meet and each would spend one minute praising every other member of the family. Sometimes the sessions were a little embarrassing, but they certainly were stimulating and inspirational.

Second, these families spent a great deal of time together. They genuinely enjoyed being together. They *worked* at doing things that involved every member of the family.

The third characteristic was that these successful families had good communication patterns. They spent time talking to each other. The key to effective communication, according to Dr. Stinnett, was that members listened and worked at understanding each other.

Fourth, the families had a strong sense of commitment. They actively promoted one another's happiness and welfare. An example of this commitment was in how these families handled themselves when things became too hectic, causing them to spend less time together. In one home, each family member made a list of his or her individual activities. The things he or she really didn't want to do or that weren't very important were scratched to provide more time for family involvement.

The fifth common ingredient was a high degree of religious orientation. These families participated in church activities together. They were committed to a spiritual lifestyle.

The final characteristic was that they had an ability to deal with crises in a positive manner. This isn't to say that they enjoyed crises, but even in the worst situations they were able to find some positive element, no matter how tiny, and focus on that.

For the remainder of this book, I want to focus on two of these factors, which I feel are the most important. Together they form the secret to developing intimate families:

1. Spending time together lays the foundation for close-knit families.
2. Close-knit families have the ability to deal with crises in a positive manner.

1. Sharing Life Experiences Together

Several years ago I used to speak to groups of four hundred to two thousand people in fifty cities annually. I began to notice that certain families in the audiences experienced unusually happy interaction among themselves. I was intrigued by this and began to do a study. I would interview the wife, husband, and children separately. Each person was asked the same question: What do you believe is the main reason you are all so close and happy as a family?

What I found amazed me. Each family member gave basically the same answer: "We do a lot of things together."

I found that these families also had one particular activity in common—camping. A minister in South Dakota echoed this idea. He told me that when he has asked each of his children separately what was the best thing they had done as a family, each one answered "camping." I'm not necessarily advocating camping. We've camped as a family for over fifteen years and we've found that *camping* is not the secret! But I believe the secret to being a close-knit family almost always can be found *in* camping.

One reason our family is so close is that we maximize our togetherness and minimize our times apart. That's not to say that we can't be alone as individuals. I work every day. My wife operates our office. Our children pursue their school or career interests. My wife enjoys swimming and going to the gym alone. I enjoy reading a book or watching a television program by myself, and I love running alone. All of us go our separate ways almost every day.

But for the most part, we try to discipline ourselves as a family to organize times when we are all together. For example, every Friday night is family night when the kids are home. We also share our church life together and visit friends' homes together. We share the entire summer together; my family travels with me to various seminars where I speak, and we plan a special vacation. We spend two weeks together at Christmas, another at Easter, and take weekends for various special activities throughout the year. Because of my profession, I am able to take off with the family for extended periods of time, but all-day outings provide the same opportunities for closeness. It just takes a little creativity to find fun things that the whole family will enjoy. But it is very possible!

The principle is also true for husbands and wives without their children. Close-knit marriages result from partners sharing numerous experiences. One summer, Norma asked me if I would take her through a wild animal park. I accepted the suggestion with enthusiasm and borrowed a car at the camp where I was speaking. When we arrived at the park, we were given a brochure that told about the animals and explained that if anything happened to the car, we were to honk the horn and a friendly ranger would come to the rescue.

About halfway through the park, our little convertible overheated. We pulled off the road and I honked the horn. No friendly ranger came to our rescue, but several wild burros wandered over and tried nibbling the convertible top. I honked again and in the rearview mirror I saw a herd of buffalo approach us. Within moments, we were surrounded.

Norma wanted me to honk the horn again, but I was afraid for fear the animals might stampede and crush the car. One of the buffaloes bent down on my side of the car and pushed his head against the window. His nostrils were steaming the window while his big, brown eyes looked to see if we had anything to eat. Norma and I held hands, trying to comfort each other. I couldn't stand to look, but kept asking, "Is he gone yet?" "No," said Norma. "Will you please honk the horn?"

"I can't. Just listen to him breathe."

"That's not him breathing. That's me!"

Gradually, the buffalo lost interest in us and moved on. Forty-five minutes after we had pulled off the road, we were able to start the car and drive through the rest of the park. It is experiences like that which we have shared as a couple or family that provide great memories. Common experiences draw people together.

Professional athletes tell me the hardest part of retirement is that they miss the camaraderie of their team. That unique bond is built through hard training and competition together over months and years. That closeness should be a part of every family.

One summer my sons and I went fishing in Washington. We found an incredible waterfall dropping into a beautiful pool. Having fished since I was in the third grade, I knew exactly how to catch the trout in this water. Michael and Greg weren't experienced, but they insisted on preparing their own lines. Greg did everything wrong. His leader was too long and thick. His hook was too large and his one egg didn't cover it. I had everything just right—a two pound leader, four feet long with a small hook. Although it was difficult, I left the boys and crawled around underneath the waterfall instead of staying at the front part of the pool, where there was no possibility of catching a fish.

I had cast my line and was trying to be perfectly still when I heard Greg scream. He had hooked a twenty-five to thirty inch steelhead. I, the "expert" fisherman in the family, had only caught one steelhead in my entire life. Greg, with his sloppily rigged line, had done the impossible.

I tried to scramble over to Greg to help him reel in his catch. But the rocks were too slippery, so I tried to coach him. He was screaming and reeling in his line too fast. I tried to tell him to slow down, but he was too excited to listen. When the fish reached the bank and Greg was ready to net it, the hook broke away from the line because he hadn't tied the hook properly. The fish flipped back into the water and swam away. Greg threw his pole up the hill, fell on the ground, and began to sob uncontrollably.

My heart sank for him. We both had visions of mounting this catch. In the years since that experience Greg has never hooked another fish like it. We still look back and grieve over it, though now we can also see the humor of it.

Another incident that brought our family closer together occurred in the mountains of California's Sequoia National Park. A small stream running over a large piece of granite about two city blocks long had created a natural, giant water slide. At the end was a dropoff into two pools of water. The boys and I immediately gave the slide a try.

After we'd each taken several turns, Greg asked if I thought he could slide down and make a little turn into a smaller pool. I looked at the slant and the angle and said, "Sure, you can do that." He took off and picked up more speed than we expected. He flew off the edge of a six-foot cliff, but from where Norma was seated, it looked like he had dropped off the mountain. He fell into a ravine, hit the granite abutment, and rolled twenty or thirty feet down into a large pool. When he hit the water, he was motionless.

Michael and I stood frozen in fear. Kari and Norma screamed that I had killed Greg. Finally I rushed down to him and heard him mumble about how his back felt broken. I was amazed he was even alive. After about twenty minutes, Greg was able to get up and walk slowly up the mountain. Within an hour, he was fine.

That experience did something to us as a family. First, *we were together.* Being together provides the basis for shared experiences that become precious memories. Second, facing difficulties draws a family much closer together. This experience particularly made us appreciate being together as we were forced to entertain the thought of life without Greg. The memories of being together on vacation when things went wrong or when we shared adventure is what *knits* the family together. As you read on, you'll see more clearly how a family becomes close-knit when it learns to deal with difficult situations.

2. Dealing with Difficulties in a Positive Manner

When we go camping, we can usually count on something going wrong: rain, mosquitoes, running out of gas, a flat tire, losing the traveler's checks, forgetting the main ingredient to a meal. When families share such conflicts, it can draw them closer together.

We have spent an enormous amount of time together as a family, and not all of our times are difficult. Many times everything runs smoothly. But when something does happen—something caused by an outside force beyond our control—we can recognize and accept it as a major factor that will draw us together.

Confronting such a crisis doesn't usually draw us together immediately. Frequently there is a lot of stress. We can easily become irritable and upset with each other. An important point to remember is that if conflict comes from within the family, if I get harsh and angry and yell at the kids or my wife or they yell at me, that may separate us, because it violates the principles we shared in chapter 1. A certain amount of anger or stress is natural in a conflict or mishap. But family members need to recognize this and not close each other's spirits. If the conflict has come from outside the family and we have not offended each other, we simply realize that in a few days or a few weeks we will look back on the experience and usually, in laughter, see how it has drawn us closer together.

We had an incredibly unifying experience one summer at a camp where I taught in southern Wisconsin. Kari and Greg assisted in the child-care section, teaching the younger kids of the parents who were attending the conference. After the first day, Kari told me, "I can't stand this camp. I want to stay in the cabin with you and Mom." Norma and I gave in and said she could stay with us, not realizing that it was against the rules for the children to stay in our unit.

The director of the camp section in which Kari and Greg were working learned about the problem and talked with Kari for a couple of hours. Finally, she asked Kari if she would be willing to give God a chance to change the circumstances and make the camp meaningful for her. Reluctantly, Kari agreed to do so.

The very next day, the whole experience turned around for her. She met one of the sharpest fellows at camp, and they became good friends during the week. She also developed close friendships with several of the girls, and she had a great experience teaching the younger kids. She learned a valuable lesson: that God can change circumstances, even in the most difficult situations.

We still laugh about that camp experience and are amazed at the complete turnaround in Kari's attitude. She saved her money to fly back to that camp again—the very camp she had wanted to leave.

After understanding the closeness that sharing difficulties can bring, it is almost disappointing when everything goes right. If something does go wrong, we realize it can be exciting, as well as stressful and discouraging. We know the benefit will emerge a few days or weeks later.

This second part of the secret to being close-knit is somewhat like a foxhole experience. Each man together fighting a common enemy will tend to be close the remaining years of their lives. How does this work? Pleasant or unpleasant memories lock us together. They provide common ground for conversation. Imagine being stuck on an elevator with five other people for two days. Each of you will experience common hunger, thirst, cramped conditions, fear, uncertainty, and so on. If reunion occurs several years later, all six of you will share and laugh about your unique experience, "Remember what happened the second day?" "Oh, yeah. That was terrible!" The more challenging, dangerous, and adventurous the experiences, the closer we tend to be with those with whom we share them.

It's very important to be together at various times throughout the year as families, so let's discuss some practical and meaningful ways of actually being together.

Three Practical Ways to Share Life Together

1. Schedule Regular Times Together

Because there is no way that we can effectively develop deep relationships with our children unless we spend meaningful time together, parents need to set aside a few minutes each month to schedule family time.

Spending time together is a decision that must be made and kept. There may be times when we don't want to be with the rest of the family or we feel we don't have time. That is when it is necessary to evaluate how we spend our time and what areas we can eliminate in order to schedule time with the family.

Sometimes we will plan a trip as a family and the day before one of the children will say he or she doesn't want to go. But because we already have agreed together that we will go, we do. As parents we have agreed to avoid saying, "I don't want to go," or "There are too many things to do. Let's plan this another time." Broken promises are a major factor in closing the spirits of our children. We must be careful to follow through when we plan times together.

2. Discover Each Person's Most Meaningful Activity

Once parents have agreed that it is important to spend time together as a family, they should discuss it with their children. If their spirits are closed, they may resist. But most children will say they would like to do things together as a family.

After each family member agrees to the concept of togetherness, the parents should ask each child to list the activities he would enjoy most. You might use the zero to ten scale, with ten being the most fun and fulfilling.

When we tried this in our home, Norma said her "ten" vacation would be at a place where there was shopping, sightseeing, a beach, and cute restaurants. Kari said almost the same thing. Greg wanted a place where he could fish, hike, and scuba dive. Michael's answer was almost the same, except he included playing ball. I said basically the same things as the boys.

We put our lists together and began to discuss places that were financially feasible where we could accommodate all of our "tens." We chose Catalina Island, just off the coast of Long Beach, California. The island has cute shops and places to eat. It has a beach and beautiful water. The boys and I can go hiking, snorkeling, scuba diving, and fishing. We went there for three or four days, two consecutive summers, and had a fantastic time together.

Below is a chart that might help you as a family nail down some specific activities or experiences that you could share together.

What Activities Can We Share
Together in Life?

- Our Church Life
    study classes
    prayer groups
        when?
        where?
        how often?
    witnessing opportunities (mission trips)
        when?
        where?
        how often?
    helping those in our community
        when?
        where?
        how often?
- Trips or Vacations
    What would my dream vacation be?
    What would it include?

What are two of my favorite activities? Write an actual picture in detail of one of these activities.

What is one activity in life that I fear or feel inadequate to face? Ask family members to help me overcome this area of fear.

3. Design Togetherness Times with Each Family Member in Mind

After learning everyone's wishes for family activities and experiences, families can design a trip, vacation, or special outing that meets the needs of all family members.

Some of our family trips were disastrous because I insisted that we travel to the Colorado mountains and camp in the wilderness next to a beautiful stream—miles from any shopping centers or restaurants. It wasn't long before we discovered that to have a meaningful family time, each person must be included—especially Mom. I could find that stream up in the mountains near a cute little village that Norma could walk to in a couple of minutes.

Our family spends one or two months every summer at the sports camp in Branson, Missouri. I'm involved in teaching and counseling while the children participate in the camp activities and are trained to be counselors in the future. There is incredible fishing and shopping nearby. It has everything we could want.

One summer, Michael and I experienced a special time at this sports camp. He had one last event in which to win a letter, archery. He was down to his last arrow and needed seven points, which meant a bull's-eye or the circle next to it. Some of his arrows had missed the entire target and landed in the woods, so he was quite discouraged. I had done well in my college archery class and was trying to encourage him and show him what to do. I felt bad for him, though, because I had this inner feeling that after all his effort, he wouldn't get the letter.

Michael pulled the arrow back, then stopped, relaxing the string. He was very nervous. I patted him on the shoulders, told him to take it easy, and said, "I know you can do it." He drew back the arrow, put it against his cheek, and let go. Bull's-eye! We both jumped up, yelled for joy, and hugged each other.

That kind of experience forms the very fiber that weaves a family into a close-knit unit. But it doesn't happen unless we recognize the value of being together and schedule times with each member's interests in mind.

Resources

Barnard, Charles P., and Ramon G. Corrales. *The Theory and Technique of Family Therapy.* Springfield, Ill.: Charles C. Thomas, 1979.

Brandt, Henry, with Phil Landrum. *I Want to Enjoy My Children.* Grand Rapids, Mich.: Zondervan Publishing House, 1975.

Campbell, D. Ross. *How to Really Love Your Child.* Wheaton, Ill.: Victor Books, 1977.

Coles, Robert. "Our Self-Centered Children I md I Heirs of the `Me' Decade." *U.S. News & World Report.* 25 February 1980. Pp. 80f.

Drescher, John M. *Seven Things Children Need.* Scottdale, Pa.: Herald Press, 1976.

Ginott, Haim. *Between Parent and Child: New Solutions to Old Problems.* New York: MacMillan Company, 1965.

Hendricks, Howard G. *Heaven Help the Home.* Wheaton, Ill.: Victor Books, 1973.

Stinnett, Nick. *In Search of Strong Families.* Lincoln, Neb., Department of Human Development and the Family, University of Nebraska, 1980.

Wright, H. Norman. *The Family That Listens.* Wheaton, Ill.: Victor Books, 1978.

Wright, H. Norman, and Rex Johnson. *Communication: Key to Your Teens.* Irvine, Calif.: Harvest House, 1978.

An interview with R. Armond Nicholi, Psychiatric Professor at Harvard Medical School, February 1982.

GARY SMALLEY
WITH JOHN TRENT

LOVE IS A DECISION

Copyright © 1989 by Gary Smalley and John Trent, Ph.D.

People's names and certain details of case histories related in this book have been changed to protect the privacy of the individuals involved.

Unless otherwise noted, Scripture quotations are from the Holy Bible, New International Version, copyright © 1973, 1978, 1984 by the International Bible Society.

Grateful acknowledgment is expressed to Zondervan Publishing House, Grand Rapids, Michigan, for permission to use selected material from two previous books by Gary Smalley: *The Joy of Committed Love* © 1984 by Gary T. Smalley and *Joy That Lasts* © 1986 by Gary T. Smalley.

Library of Congress Cataloging-in-Publication Data

Smalley, Gary.
    Love is a Decision.

    1. Marriage—United States. 2. Marriage—Religious aspects—Christianity. I. Trent, John T.
II. Title.
HQ734.S686   1989   646.7'8   89-22414
ISBN 0-8499-0721-7
ISBN 0-8499-3362-5
ISBN 0-8499-4268-3 (pbk)
Printed in the United States of America

The material in this book is based largely on the "Love Is a Decision" Seminar, and its success is due largely to the efforts of Terry Brown, our national seminar director.

This book is gratefully dedicated to

Terry

Without knowing it, thousands of couples' lives have been enriched by his years of faithful, loyal service in coordinating the many details for the seminar. We thank God for this special servant and for the unique way he enriches everyone who knows him.

Contents

1

Planning on a Great Marriage?

It was just turning dark when I arrived at the home of a family I was staying with in Tampa, Florida. Exhausted after speaking at a seminar all day, I was looking forward to a restful, uneventful night.

I knew my hosts only slightly, but they lived in a beautiful home in a peaceful neighborhood. But then again, looks can be deceiving. In fact, I would never have expected either event that happened to me over the next few hours.

As I walked up to the front door, I reached into one pocket, then another. That's when I realized I'd left my key inside in my room, and I was locked out of the house. Ringing the doorbell wouldn't have done any good. My hosts had told me they wouldn't be home until late. So I decided to go around to the back yard and see if by chance a window or door had been left open.

As I rounded the back corner, I froze in terror. From out of the dark, a huge black form was racing toward me at breakneck speed. It was the biggest dog I'd ever seen in my life!

Ten feet from where I stood petrified with fear, the dog left the ground with a tremendous leap—and I knew I'd soon be on my way to the hospital. In milli-seconds I'd feel the pain of his teeth tearing into me.

I closed my eyes and braced myself for the collision . . . but nothing happened. At first I thought, *He's toying with me. This dog knows I'm about to die, and he wants to watch me suffer*! But after a moment more, I finally built up enough courage to open my eyes. Unbelievably, he was sitting happily at my feet, his big friendly tongue hanging out and his tail wagging. He was actually whimpering for me to reach down and pet him.

After my heart rate dropped from triple to double digits, I checked the house only to find it securely locked. It was getting late, and I was worn out. I was faced with either camping out on the back porch with my new-found canine friend or thinking of some alternative. That's when an idea hit me.

Another family I'd been introduced to lived in Tampa. Perhaps I could stay with them until my hosts returned. So I jumped into my car and drove across town to John and Kay Hammer's stately home—and into an even more surprising situation.

As I knocked on the door, I was greeted by Kay. "Hi, Gary," she said, flashing her million-dollar smile. She makes anyone she meets feel special and important. I explained my situation to her and John, and they insisted that I stay at their house for the night.

I met their charming children as they piled out of their rooms. Finally, after a little small talk in the living room, we all retired for the night.

My body must have known that my plane didn't leave until the next evening, because it overruled the alarm clock, and I slept late the next morning. By the time I got up, showered, and dressed, the kids and John had already headed off to school and work. Only Kay was left in the kitchen to play short-order cook for her unexpected house guest.

I'd already received one shock when Godzilla the Dog leaped at me, but little did I know I was about to be hit with a second shock that was even more disturbing. As we sat at the kitchen table, the smile quickly fell from her face and down into her teacup. She sat there, her head bowed, staring blankly at the table top. With very little prompting, Kay began pouring out an all-too-familiar story.

For years, this wife had felt neglected. Her husband gave the best of his week to his thriving business, and she and the children were left with emotional left-overs on the weekends. All the family responsibilities for raising four youngsters fell on her shoulders, and she was exhausted from putting out fires between her husband and the children.

At times she would plead with John to work on their disintegrating relationship, but her cries fell on deaf ears. Too consumed with building up his career, he didn't have time to worry about the way his marriage and family were breaking down.

Kay suffered through the "domestic" neglect that many wives do, but with one added heartache. She was a Christian with a genuine faith, but she knew that when her husband went to church it was more for social contacts, not spiritual growth.

Slowly, as the years went by, his insensitivity had eaten its way to the very core of their relationship—and had begun to poison her heart.

The Ruin of a National Treasure

As I sat with Kay that day, I felt like I was watching the wreck of the Exxon tanker, *Valdez.* Here was a beautiful home and a stunning family. Yet with disharmony and heartache steering at the helm, their family relationships had been guided right onto the rocks, just as that ill-fated oil tanker had been.

Day after day, the poison of a ruptured marriage poured onto their lives, covering the natural beauty of a loving family with three inches of sludge. They had tried to clean up some of the disaster (which their relationship had become), but in many ways the damage was already done. The kids were feeling the tensions at home and beginning to reflect it in their lives, and any interest they might have shown in attending church was now falling dormant.

Kay had been listening to her friends—even to Christian friends—who told her, "Quit being a *doormat,* Kay. You've already gone through too much. *God will forgive you.* Get out of this mess of a marriage, and try again with someone else." She'd even gone to her pastor at the time and to a "Christian" psychologist. Both had told her that *with her husband* she could never hope to get the ship off the rocks—their marriage was dead in the water and unsalvageable.

"I'm not rushing you to leave, and I hadn't planned on telling you any of this," she said to me at the breakfast table, embarrassed by the tears that quickly came to her eyes. "But when the children come home from school today, I'm leaving my husband. We're all moving out. . . . "

I'd like to say that John and Kay's story is unusual, but, unfortunately, it isn't. In working with couples and families for almost two decades, I've seen many such disasters. They have ruined our greatest natural treasure—our families.

From every appearance, a few rags or suction hoses wouldn't begin to repair the damage that had taken place in the Hammers' relationship. In fact, the more I listened, the more I could see why certain "advisors" had told her the landscape of their life would never be the same. From a human standpoint, it certainly did look like the better option might be to pack up and move on than try to rebuild the impossible. But God allowed something miraculous to happen over the next few hours with Kay that transformed her relationship with her husband—and my life as well.

It's been almost fourteen years since that fateful morning at John and Kay's home. And today the Hammers are not only some of our closest friends, but members of our National Board! Their relationship has changed from oil-soaked blackness to a crystalclear reflection of Christ's love. Even more, their deep friendship and love for each other is a testimony in itself and has turned back many, many couples from the brink of divorce.

Without a clear action plan that points the way to deep waters of intimacy, and avoids the shallow rocks of marital ruin, we're inviting heartache into our homes.

What brought about the change in their lives? That's what this book is all about. The very verses and concepts I first scratched out on a sheet of notebook paper for Kay that day are the same things I've seen God use in the lives of hundreds over the years. I'll be sharing biblical principles that when applied to a relationship—even one washed up and on the rocks—can turn a mess back into a treasure. Learning specific directions for steering clear of danger can also keep a strong marriage or family from running aground. But change only begins at the place we all must start—at the same point the Hammers had to come to.

Planning to Have a Great Marriage and Family?

Whether it's a family, a school, a company, or a sports team, we cannot possibly guide our relationships safely through the waters of our day without a plan. That's the starting point. Without a clear plan of action that points out the way to the deep waters of intimacy and avoids the shallow rocks of marital ruin we're inviting heartache into our homes. It's critical that we clearly plan our lives and not let chance set their course.

There may have been a time in an earlier day when society itself delineated boundaries clearly enough to substitute for a clear purpose at home. But that's simply not true today. We're asking for a natural disaster of our own if we don't have a specific sense of direction for our families. And that's what this book is all about. It's our best effort to give you a workable, biblically based plan of action for building loving, lasting relationships.[1]

Now we know that asking you to adopt a "plan" of action for your home sounds a great deal like work, but we can assure you that the effort spent on steering your relationship into safe waters is far less work than trying to get it off the rocks would be.

Can having a clear plan of action really bring that much change? In one case, taking the time to learn and practice a plan of action turned a group of defeated individuals into an undefeated team:

The Man Who Made History

When our good friend, Norm Evans, was picked by an expansion National Football League team, they were mired in last place. The owner knew a change was needed, so he hired a new head coach. But that was nothing new. He had already hired several coaches, and hadn't changed their fortunes yet. With the way the team was currently playing, this young "upstart" he'd picked would probably be history himself within a year.

As it turned out, this particular coach *would* go into the NFL history books—but not as a failure. Today, even with ups and downs, he has been in the league longer than any other active coach—and there's a reason. He built his men into a champion team by following a clear plan of action.

The year prior to this coach's arrival, the team had a record of three wins and ten losses. Morale was down, motivation was low, and the players' efforts on the field were lack-luster. Norm remembers standing along the sideline with the other players, wondering how they were going to lose each game they played.

Then the new coach arrived in town, and he wasted no time in getting down to business. His first official act was to call a team meeting—and it was one the players would never forget.

He walked into the room, folded his arms, and stood silently in front of them for several minutes. The moments seemed to stretch into hours. He looked from player to player, and from eye to eye. Finally, he spoke in a clear, convincing voice and said, "Men, you're going to be champions of the NFL."

There was an awkward moment of silence in the room. Several of the veterans had to lower their heads to keep their smiles from breaking into laughter. *Sure, coach . . .* they thought. *Anything you say. . . .* But inside they were thinking, *Who's this guy kidding? We've always been losers in this league. Champions? We're not even challengers!* Then the coach laid out the reason he felt certain the team would be successful—a clear plan of action.

"First," he said, "we're going to give you a great game plan each week that works. I'll guarantee that you'll know more about the person you're playing against than anyone except his wife. *Second,* you're going to *practice* that plan until it becomes a natural part of you. *Third,* you're going to *learn the game plan and practice it—and win."*

Bit by bit, the next season saw the wisdom of his strategy unfold. The players learned a specific plan and then practiced it over and over until they felt a confidence in themselves and between each other that they'd never had before. Now they stood on the sidelines wondering how they were going to *win* games— not lose them. In just one short year, they were a different football team. How different?

It was exactly the reverse of the year before; they came out of the blue to win ten games and lose only three. And the next two seasons, the Miami Dolphins, under head coach Don Shula, won the 1972 and 1973 Super Bowls as the best team in pro football.

"That's a great story if you're a football team," you may say, "but the only similarity our marriage has to an NFL team is that we're always taking cheap shots at each other!" Can having a "plan" really make that much of a difference in a marriage relationship—or even with our children? It did for John and Kay.

Kay Hammer didn't know much about the pro football team in nearby Miami when we sat down that morning, but she still had something in common with them. For years, she and John had let circumstances and the emotions of the moment call all the plays in their relationship—and their lives were on the brink of a last place finish as a result. Yet like this pro team, things started to turn around in their lives once they began to follow a clear plan of action and to practice it consistently.

That morning at the Hammers' breakfast table, I scribbled out for her several biblical principles that I was only then beginning to understand and apply in my own home. The scriptural guidelines that broke through that day and gave Kay hope are the very same ones I'll be sharing with you in this book.

A Marriage Mended . . .

By applying these principles, Kay was able to see her marriage turn around in as dramatic a fashion as I've ever witnessed. Her marriage was doomed for the ashheap of divorce, but because of her willingness to follow a biblically based plan, it's alive, active, and growing today. The man she once couldn't wait to get away from is now her best friend . . . and the one with whom she wants to spend the rest of her life.

The secret doesn't just belong to John and Kay—it's available for everyone who desires to have a strong family and a fulfilling marriage. I look forward to the years ahead and get excited about what can happen in families all over this country. I'd love to see hundreds of thousands of husbands, wives, and children make a commitment to do whatever it takes to honor God by following a clear plan for family intimacy. I believe it can happen; in fact, that's the whole goal of our ministry! One of the places you can start is by putting a biblical plan for relationships into action.

To keep our relationships off the rocks, we need to follow two essential steps: we must gain *knowledge* and then *skills* at applying what we've learned. The more we *learn* and *practice* what we've learned, the more gifted we'll become at developing intimate relationships within our homes. In the chapters that follow, we're going to open God's Word and see what He says about making our relationships strong and fulfilling—beginning with the very foundation of a successful family.

Keys to Building Loving, Lasting Relationships

In the next two chapters, we're going to discover that to have any loving and lasting relationship, we must understand:

- *Honor is at the heart of all healthy relationships—and*
- *Genuine love is a decision . . . not a feeling.*

Are you tired of your feelings of love going up and down like a roller coaster? I'll share with you how you can develop a love that remains consistently strong from season to season, year to year. Contrary to popular belief, love is actually a reflection of how much we "honor" another person—for at its core genuine love is a decision, not a feeling.

Second, you'll see that love can best be put into action by mastering and practicing specific skills like:

- *Recognizing the incredible worth of a woman*

I'll spend an entire chapter helping men in particular see how incredibly valuable women are. In particular, we'll see how God seems to have designed within a woman the very talents that can make her an invaluable resource in the home.

- *Learning how to energize our mates in sixty seconds*

One key to loving relationships is the ability to step in when our loved ones are hurting or discouraged. In this section of the book you'll see a method Christ often used with His disciples and others that can help you reach out to those who are facing discouragement, frustration, or a loss of energy.

- *Keeping a major destroyer of relationships out of our homes*

There is a killer lose in many homes today. It can take the life out of a relationship. One thing that I shared with Kay was how to keep the destructive "tapeworm" of anger out of relationships, and how to re-open the spirit of a loved one who may be closed to you.

- *Understanding the tremendous value of a man*

While many couples don't realize it, a man is not a "second class citizen" when it comes to the ability to have strong, lasting relationships. In this section of the book, you'll discover how to tap into a man's God-given gift for nurturing which can form the basis of genuine love. In fact, you'll see in detail four specific skills with which each man comes "naturally" equipped. These can make a tremendous difference in his relationships. *These same four skills are ones a wife must also master to see her relationships deepen and grow as well,* and they include:

- *Providing security to see a marriage bloom and grow*

If a relationship was like a plant, then security would be the sunlight it needs to grow strong and true. In this section, you'll see not only the results of insecurity, but how to build—or re-build—trust and hope in a home.

- *Uncovering a crucial key to meaningful communication*

For everyone who has ever felt misunderstood, there is a way to communicate with our loved ones that provides the greatest understanding—and the least negative reaction. This communication method is used throughout the Scriptures for praise, correction, deeper understanding, and intimacy—and you'll see it strengthen your relationships as well.

- *Keeping courtship alive in your marriage*

Emotional, romantic times can be a constant part of a courtship—and nonexistent in a marriage. In this important aspect of intimacy, you'll see how to keep or regain the elements of courtship, even years after a wedding.

- *Opening the doorway to physical intimacy*

While many people don't realize it, one book of the Bible focuses specifically on the sexual act of marriage—Song of Solomon. Instead of this important area of marital life being a source of frustration, putting some biblical basics into practice can strengthen a couple's physical intimacy, so that this important aspect of married life is no longer a problem.

• *Discovering how to be best friends with your family*

I've spent years studying and personally interviewing "successful" families, and we've consistently found they share one major characteristic. They've all learned the secret of developing family intimacy in even the most difficult of times. We can use that same secret to draw closer to the Lord personally during difficult times as well.

Kay's life did change the day I spoke with her—or at least she had a dramatic change of heart. But her marriage didn't turn around overnight. It took consistent prayer, time, and energy as she began to learn a specific plan of action and how to put it into practice. Even so, the specific skills I laid out to improve her marriage weren't what ultimately made the lasting difference in her life. Those skills made a major impact on her husband, but in themselves they weren't enough to bring the relationship back from the brink of disaster.

Am I saying that her personal force of will and effort to change weren't enough—even when she learned several specific communication and relationship skills? That's exactly right. You see, if we set out, in our flesh or with our own "will power," to guide our relationship into safe waters, I can guarantee that the day will come when we'll fall asleep at the wheel and run aground.[2] If we want to see lasting change in our lives and the lives of our loved ones, we must learn to rely on the only Source able to guard us "day and night."

Without question, the most important section of this book —and of my life—is found in the final two chapters. It is here that Kay Hammer found the power to put into practice all the relationship skills she learned—even when she didn't feel like doing a single one emotionally. For it is only in learning to depend upon the Lord as the Author and Sustainer of any truly successful relationship, that we'll find the inner strength to make lasting changes. And these changes can come—just as they did for John and Kay—by:

• *Learning the art of tapping into the unfailing power source behind a great marriage*

Most of us expect the "gifts" of life—including our spouse and children—to be the "source" of our life and happiness. In this most important section I'll show that while husbands and wives can make great friends and lovers, they make lousy gods. Learning to plug into the only consistent source of love, peace, and joy is the only way to have the spiritual and emotional stamina to withstand the storms of life. And finally, we need to learn how to . . .

- *Turn trials in our homes into lasting benefits for our lives*

"But what if things don't change around here?" "But you never met my husband!" "But you never tried to live with my wife!" "But *your* kids weren't born with a naturally rebellious spirit!"

In every relationship, there are roadblocks that can seem to stand so high they block out any hope of our ever getting past them to intimacy and oneness. And yet in this last section of the book, *you'll see that even the problems we face can do nothing but benefit our lives.* Even more, they can provide a consistent source of deeper love and sensitivity to pass on to others.

Much of the material in this book comes mainly from the "Love Is a Decision" video and film series which, in turn, is based on much of what John Trent and I do in our conferences. It also includes concepts from other books Dr. John Trent and I have done together as well as books I have written individually. Therefore, if you've had the opportunity to read some of the other books we've written, you may recognize some of it as familiar ground. However, in this book's unique format, I've had the opportunity to rewrite and update almost all the major concepts we share at our marriage and relationships seminar. John and I are only able to do eight to ten "Love Is a Decision" seminars a year, but by providing this information for you in this way, I hope it will give you a comprehensive look at what we teach in a way no single book we've done before could ever do.

It's a scary thought that the twenty-first century is right around the corner. And with a new century breathing down our necks, it's unfortunate that most of us don't have a plan for next week, let alone a plan for the next century.

I hope you're different. I hope you'll work at learning and practicing a plan—any plan—that is based on the Scriptures and grounded in His love. If you do use this book as a guideline, it's my prayer that it will be one of the most sensible, down-to-earth books you've ever read. I also hope that once you've read it, you and those you love will never be the same.

I earnestly pray that spending time in these pages will cause you to fall more deeply in love with God and His Word. As a by-product, I hope that loving God and His Word more deeply will then give you practical tools for constructing a mirror image of God's love to reflect to your family. That building process begins in Chapter 2, where we'll discover that all relationships begin with an essential element to a fulfilling life.

2

The Foundation for All Healthy Relationships

It is winter in Washington state, and a cold, wet wind is blowing. Smoke pours from the chimney of a small, two-story white house that looks warm and cozy in the chill night air. In fact, if you were to come close and peek through the kitchen window, you'd see a scene reminiscent of a Norman Rockwell painting.

Inside are a father, a mother, and five children, seated around the kitchen table having dinner. At first glance, it seems to be a portrait of pure Americana. Like the crackling blaze in the nearby fireplace, the scene gives the illusion of emotional warmth. But if you stayed around for a bit, you'd see that looks can be deceiving. For inside is an emotional chill that can cut to the bone like the northern air whistling through the trees.

The American dream starts to disappear when the father reaches over and pops the nearest teenager on the arm with the back of his hand. The teenager fires back a smart remark, and the two begin their nightly yelling match. The rest of the children all join in with a chorus of jeers—some angry, some laughing.

That is, all except the smallest child . . . the young boy sitting across from his father. He sits wide-eyed, his little heart pounding, watching everything that's happening around the table, wondering why his mother looks so sad, and wishing things would be different tonight.

But at this home, it's always this way—the smart remarks, the challenging looks, the unbridled anger. In most homes, there is a soft side and a hard side to life. But for this little boy, there's just one side of life with his father.[1] The cold, rough side that recalls his Dad decking one of his older brothers in anger . . . but never his giving him or his mother a hug.

Before turning away from the window, we see the father jump up from his chair and slap his napkin down on his plate.

"I never get any respect around here!" he shouts. "I'm leaving!"

"Yea, go ahead! *Get outta here!*" the kids shout back, laughing and taunting their father as he stalks out of the room. But for the little boy, it's been another night of conflict and confrontation at the dinner table, and another layer of painful memories to cover his soul . . . memories that are as vivid today as they were almost forty years ago. . . .

I hope this story doesn't bring back personal memories of a hurtful home for you; but it certainly does for me. For that little boy watching wide-eyed at the dinner table, getting all the wrong messages about family relationships, was me.

Over the years, I've thought quite a bit about what happened in my home growing up. Even as a child, I knew something was very wrong. There always seemed to be something missing from our family that kept us intimate strangers—always together but forever apart. For years, however, I had no idea what it was!

Have you ever wondered at times about the missing ingredient in your own relationships? Have you ever been so hurt that you've felt like throwing up your hands in despair? Have you looked at marital or family unity like candy inside a broken gumball machine—taking nickel after nickel after nickel—but never putting intimacy within your grasp?

Join the club. Most of us—even those from very loving homes and happy marriages—have experienced times when our most important relationships were difficult or unfulfilling. Why is it that the intimacy we want so often seems to be just out of reach?

At times, some of us have felt like John and Kay Hammer in Chapter 1—that the answer to all our family's problems is close at hand. Perhaps she's staring us right in the eye, or he's sitting across the table from us or even sleeping next to us at night. If only "that child or spouse" would change and begin meeting some of our expectations, finally our family life could be all it should be!

The Age-Old Mistake

It's easy for us to get excited about *another* person's need to change. For years, I was like a husband I once heard about. In his personal devotions he was reading Proverbs 31, the section in the

Bible that gives a picture of a practically perfect wife. During the course of an average day, this far-from-average woman buys and sells land, feeds the poor, prepares scrumptious meals for the entire household, hand-sews each child's wardrobe, and basically leaps over tall buildings with a single bound.

The more he read about this godly woman, and the more virtues that piled up about her, the more frustrated this husband became with his own wife. Finally, his emotions reaching the boiling point, he picked up his Bible (making sure he kept his finger on the verse to mark his place), and stomped off to find the "source" of all his problems.

Finding her sitting at the kitchen table, he laid the Bible down in front of her and pointed his finger repeatedly at the verses he'd been reading in Proverbs.

"Honey, do you know about this section in the Bible?" It was less a question than a threat.

She glanced nonchalantly at the open Bible in his hand, recognizing the passage.

"Yes," she said, "I know about that section."

After waiting, unrewarded by any further response, he continued, "Look, I know you want to be a godly person, and if you knew about this section. . . ."

Lifting an eyebrow, she repeated more firmly, "Listen—I *know* about that section."

Then straightening up to his full stature, towering over her as she sat at the table, he said, "If you *know* about this section, how come you don't get up every morning and make me a hot meal?"

"Dear," she said, "if you want a hot meal, *light your corn-flakes on fire!*"

By most people's standards this couple might be classified in the "highly strained" category. The story still points up a key problem in many homes. For years I felt that if only my wife Norma would change, every problem in our relationship would disappear. And during all that time, Norma was feeling exactly the same way I was—with one exception. She wanted *me* to change and then marital intimacy would finally be within reach.

But a funny thing happened on our way to changing each other. As much as I pushed Norma to change, and as much as she pulled me, neither one of us ever budged an inch—and neither did our relationship. For many reasons that we'll look at later, when our best efforts go into trying to change another person, we seem to reap the worst relationship rewards.

15

It's like the wife who noticed the new neighbors who moved in across the street. Every evening, she peeked through the curtains and watched as the husband came home from work.

She couldn't miss the fact that nearly every night, this man would bring home flowers or a little gift for his wife. She'd run to greet him as he got out of the car, and he'd hand her a gift. Then they'd hug and kiss until they had walked inside and closed the door behind them.

> *God's Word contains the only genuine blueprint for successful relationships, both with Him and others.*

One night, after weeks of watching this same gushy scene repeated over and over, the poor neighbor woman finally reached the breaking point. The moment her husband walked in the door, she said, "Have you noticed we have new neighbors across the street?"

As he dropped his briefcase on the floor and fell into the easy chair in front of the television, he replied, "Yeah, I've noticed we have new neighbors."

"But have you noticed what they *do* every night?"

"No, dear," he answered, "I haven't noticed."

She continued, "Every night when he comes home, he gives her a big kiss, he hugs her, and he almost always brings her a special gift." Then she added, "How come *you* don't ever do that?"

Her husband stared at her with a puzzled look on his face and said, "Honey, I can't do that. I hardly know the woman!"

This age-old tactic of trying to get one's mate, friend, child, or boss to change may win a few minor battles, but it never wins the war of unmet expectations. Nonetheless, it was the primary way I tried to improve my marriage for several years.

Looking back now, I deeply regret not having realized how fruitless this approach is. It causes so many more problems than it solves (unhealthy dependency and increased selfishness to name just two). And it forces each marriage partner to be a competitor —not a completer. There have been many times I've wished I could have those years back.

Had I been wiser, Norma and I could have been spared dozens of painful, unnecessary discussions. If only I'd been aware that God had a plan for family relationships—and a personal plan for each one of us—I could have stopped arm-twisting and started arming myself with His wisdom on the family.

The Knowledge and Skills Necessary for a Great Relationship

God's Word contains the only genuine blueprint for successful relationships, both with Him and with others. Yet, for years, I had been looking at the wrong set of plans. As a husband, I based most of my actions on unhealthy family patterns drawn from my past. Instead, I should have been looking to God's unchanging plan for the family where the results would have been far less frustrating and much more fulfilling.

Over the years, in speaking and counseling with thousands of couples, I've discovered I wasn't alone in coming into marriage without the proper knowledge and skills to nurture a growing relationship. In fact, across our country, the average couple spends more than two hundred hours getting ready for the wedding service, and less than three hours in any type of premarital counseling or preparation.[2]

In every state in our country, it is far easier to get a marriage license than it is to get a driver's license! And yet statistics show time and again that even a small dose of training before marriage can positively affect marital satisfaction and outcome.[3]

In talking with hundreds of couples, I've found that my premarital preparation wasn't far from the norm. It consisted of one meeting with a minister who asked me two questions:

"Gary," he asked, "do you love Norma?"

"Well . . . yes," I said. (Norma was sitting right beside me
. . . what else could I say!) But now I realize that I really didn't
understand what it meant to truly love her in the way the Scriptures describe.

Then the pastor asked me a second question, "Gary, would
you lay down your life for her?"

Again I said yes, thinking he was asking if I would throw
myself in front of a truck for her, or step in front of a gunman to
take the bullet meant for her.

The truth of the matter is, when I married Norma I knew the
right words—but not the right answers. I didn't have a plan to go
by, and after marrying a sparky, enthusiastic, godly woman, it
took me about five years of applying the wrong information re-
garding relationships to knock the sparkle right out of her life.

Early in our marriage, I could tell we weren't doing well, so
I decided to try a few quick-fix remedies. As I mentioned, I tried
the "If you'd just change" tactic, and even resorted to the lecture
method of teaching her what the Scriptures say about being a
godly wife. I never used an overhead projector, but I probably
would have if I'd thought about it. Many a night, 99 percent of
my dinner table conversations were actually lectures aimed at
drilling into Norma what the Bible said *she* should do to make
"us" happy.

During all that time, I conveniently ignored the Scriptural
words of wisdom that applied to the husband—probably because
I had never taken the time to truly understand the concepts
behind the words. And to go one step deeper, without realizing it,
I was covering up my own weaknesses and feelings of inadequacy
by pointing out hers.

The Death of a Dream . . .
the Birth of a Genuine Love

Norma kept hoping that I'd "get with it," but I never did. As
she saw her hopes for a warm, fulfilling family life slipping away,
she felt resigned to a marriage that would never match her
dreams.

After nearly five years of watching our relationship grow
more and more strained, I came home one day, walked into the
kitchen, and greeted Norma with the usual, "Hi, I'm home." But
she didn't respond.

"Is anything wrong?" I asked.

I knew from the look on her face and her nonverbal expressions that I didn't need to ask the question. It was obvious that something was drastically "wrong."

Suddenly, I felt tired all over. I had been battling my conscience for years and spent untold energy to keep up a facade of closeness to those at the church. Here I was teaching and counseling each week on relationships, and in my own marriage I felt like a failure. After years of pretending, I knew I didn't need a quick "self-help" gimmick to get through to my wife. I needed the kind of total heart transplant that only God can give. And so I gently put my arm around her and asked, "Norma, what do *you* think is wrong in our relationship?"

"Oh, no, you don't," Norma said, pulling back from me, her eyes filling with tears.

"You're not going to get me to share what I'm feeling and then turn it into another lecture on what I'm doing wrong."

"Honey," I said, trying to stay as soft as I could, "I can see how you'd feel that way, and I'm very, very sorry, but could you *please* just tell me one more time? I promise you, this time you won't hear a lecture."

Reluctantly, Norma did share with me the concerns that had been building up in her heart, and while it may have been her one hundredth time to tell me, I had never heard it the way she explained it that day. Little did I know that this single conversation would become one of the most traumatic—yet one of the most significant—moments in our lives.

Norma said several important things that afternoon, but there was one thing in particular I'll never forget. I now realize that the problem she explained that day is one of the most common reasons many couples and families struggle for years to find a healthy, meaningful relationship, and yet never quite reach it. She told me:

"Gary, I feel like everything on this earth is far more important to you than I am. . . ."

"I feel that all the football games you watch on television are more important than I am, the newspaper, your hobbies, your counseling at the church. Gary, I can spend hours working in the kitchen, and you never say a word. I can even farm out the kids to a baby-sitter and have a candlelight dinner all prepared for you, and the phone will ring and you'll say, 'Oh, I'm not doing anything important. I'm just eating. Sure, I'll be right over.' Then you're gone, telling me to keep something warm for you in the oven.

"I'm not saying that your ccunseling isn't important, but many of those couples you talk to have struggled with their problems for *years!* Taking one night out to spend with your wife isn't going to bother them—but it's killing us!

"It's like I don't matter to you, but other people do. In fact, sometimes I feel that you're more polite to total strangers than you are to me. You'll say the most awful things to me, but never to anyone else, especially not people at the church. . . ."

She went on, but you get the point—and so did I. While it may have been a message that was on continuous play around our house, I was hearing the recording loud and clear for the *first* time.

Before talking with Norma, I would never have stood up in front of a group and said that my counseling or even the nonstop sporting events I watched on television were more important than my wife, but without realizing it, that's exactly what I was communicating to her.

Little did I know that for five years of marriage, I had also been violating a crucial biblical concept which lies at the heart of any strong relationship. Every time I ignored its power to build loving, lasting relationships, I was literally shutting the door to the kind of home and family I'd wanted all my life.

What is this biblical principle that I'd been ignoring for years—and that weakened my marriage as a result? It's a simple, yet incredibly powerful, principle, and it comes wrapped in a single word—"honor."[4]

Honor Is the Foundation for All Healthy Relationships

Without a doubt, the concept of honor is the single most important principle we know of for building healthy relationships. It's important for a husband and wife to begin applying it toward each other. And children to apply it toward their parents, and for parents to apply it toward their children. It even works with friend-to-friend relationships. The results of allowing "honor" to reign can be dramatic and life-changing.

Honor is not only the basis of all our earthly relationships, it's at the heart of our relationship with God (see Matthew 6:19–21,

33). Yet we know so little about it that it's almost as if there's an active cover-up going on to keep it a secret from us.[5] To give you an idea of this crucial concept, let's get a brief thumbnail sketch of what "honor" means in the Scriptures.

During biblical times, the word "honor" carried a literal meaning that has been all but lost by translation and time. For a Greek living in Christ's day, something of "honor" called to mind something "heavy, or weighty."[6] Gold, for example, was the perfect picture of something of "honor," because it was heavy and valuable at the same time.

For this same Greek, the word "dishonor" would also bring to mind a literal picture. The word for "dishonor" actually meant "mist" or "steam."[7] Why? Because the lightest, most insignificant thing the Greeks could think of was the steam rising off a pot of boiling water, or clouding a mirror on a cold winter day.

When we honor particular people we're saying in effect that who they are and what they say carries great weight with us. They're extremely valuable in our eyes. Just the opposite is true when we dishonor them. In effect, by our verbal or nonverbal statements we're saying that their words or actions make them of little value or "light-weights" in our eyes.

When the apostle Paul wanted the Corinthian believers to repent from their immoral life-styles and renew their love for Christ, he told them, "You were bought at a price [literally, with "honor"]. Therefore honor God with your body" (1 Corinthians 6:20).

Every angel in heaven and each of us who make up the heavenly hosts of believers will one day sing, "Worthy is the Lamb, who was slain, to receive power . . . wisdom . . . *honor* . . . glory . . . praise" (Revelation 5:12). In both these verses, honoring God means to recognize that nothing on earth or in heaven is as valuable, as weighty, as significant as He.

But how does the concept of honor specifically apply to a marriage relationship?

How to Bring Honor into Your Home

One of the most powerful statements in all the Bible for husbands is, "You husbands, in the same way be considerate as you live with your wives, and treat them with respect (*honor*) as the weaker partner and as heirs with you of the gracious gift of life, so that nothing will hinder your prayers" (1 Peter 3:7).

In 1 Peter 3:1-2 the apostle states the same idea about a wife's relationship with her husband. Do you want to motivate your husband spiritually? Then the apostle says for a wife to use the powerful shaping tool of "honor" by letting him see your genuine and respectful (or honoring) behavior. Finally, a verse that also communicates the mutual need for honor in a home or in any relationship is Romans 12:10. It clearly states, "Be devoted to one another in brotherly love. *Honor* one another above yourselves."

When I came face to face with the concept of "honor" in a home, I suddenly understood why a major part of my prayer life was being hindered. When it came to Norma, the person who from an earthly perspective should receive the "highest value" I could give, I put a hundred things ahead of her. Work projects were more important to me than my mate, and while it's to my shame to admit it, there were countless times that a mountain trout, a small white golf ball, numerous church meetings, close friends and acquaintances—and almost anything "interesting" on television—took the place of honor which should have been reserved for Norma.

If someone had stopped me on the street or at church and asked me if I loved my wife, I would have answered emphatically "Yes!" The problem was, you could never tell I loved Norma by her place of honor (her priority status) in comparison to a hundred more "important" things in my life.

So right there at our kitchen table, I pledged to change. I didn't realize all the implications of what I was doing, but I had a profound sense that things in the Smalley house would never be the same—and they haven't been.

First, I went alone before my Heavenly Father and asked His forgiveness for my incredible selfishness. I realized that at times many things, even good things like my ministry, had taken on more "weight" to me than my relationship with the Lord. That would have to change. I knew that the first step toward giving my wife honor had to be giving God the place of honor reserved only for Him in my life.

It was hard to admit, but I was coming to realize that the idea of honor was out of balance in my life. At that point, something interesting happened. Almost immediately, I noticed it was easier than ever before to pray and read the Scriptures.

Because I valued too many other things of this world more than my time in God's Word, I didn't naturally dive into the Bible and pray early in our marriage. In addition, I wasn't obeying the command of Scripture to give "honor" to my wife. Today, because of my decision to make God the "weightiest" Person in my life—and my commitment to give Norma the "honor" she deserves—one of the most natural things I do in the course of a day is to pray and spend time in His Word. We'll take time to focus on this important issue in a later chapter.

However, while I had come to grips with the concept of honor in my relationship with my Heavenly Father, like Peter, I couldn't stay on the mountaintop. It was time humbly to go back down in the valley to Norma and ask her to forgive me for the way I'd treated her.

"Honey," I said, "I know that we both want to give God first place in our lives. But from an earthly perspective, I want you to be above everything or everyone else in my life."

When Truth Needs a Track Record

Going to Norma was an extremely traumatic moment for me, and it would prove to be a major turning point in my life and in our marriage. But there was one problem. Norma didn't believe me that day.

I knew I had come face to face with the truth of God's Word, and that my life was going to be different as a result, but she just thought it was more empty words. So she threw out a half-convincing, "Yeah, okay," at my vow to honor her and got up from the table to continue preparing dinner.

It's not that Norma lacked faith in God or His Word. From the first time I met her almost twenty-nine years ago until today, I have always been blessed by her deep faith and commitment to Christ. What she lacked wasn't faith in God, but faith in her husband. She needed a track record of being "honored" from a husband who had never practiced it.

I have to admit that at the time, I didn't know exactly what it meant to put the concept of honor into action in our home, but I knew enough to realize that honor would have to be a daily—sometimes hourly—decision. And I had made that decision. I wasn't going to keep Norma on a starvation diet of praise and three full meals of criticism and unrealistic expectations anymore. I was going to consistently feed her with a nourishing meal of significance and high value in our home.

"Norma," I said, "I know you have every reason to doubt me, but I mean what I'm saying. I never understood this before, and I want to ask you to forgive me for making you think that everything else I'm doing is more important than you. No matter how I've acted in the past, that's not what I really believe."

Our evening discussion was over, and she wasn't dazzled by my promise of change. In fact, because of the five years she had lived with the "old Gary," it took her almost two full years of a consistent track record of honoring acts to finally believe the "new Gary" was for real.

With honor as a permanent resident in a home, there is hope we can restore our relationship with God and with our loved ones.

Norma has never failed to forgive me when I asked her, and she forgave me that day. But she was right to question whether I would actually follow through on my promises. She'd been standing in fifth or sixth place in my life for so long, it was natural for her to be skeptical. It was hard for her to believe she was finally moving to the front of the line.

If you make a decision today to increase the honor in your home, don't be disappointed if your mate doesn't do back-flips until tomorrow or the next month. Remember, he or she has been watching your actions for a long time. They have all your past press clippings cut out and pasted in their memories. And if your previous track record has been less than spectacular—as mine was—emotional scar tissue may cause them to be calloused to your present promises for several months. Hype may sell hamburgers and automobiles, but it doesn't work on your spouse the way time linked with a track record does.

With honor as a permanent resident in a home, there is hope we can restore our relationship with God and with our loved ones. Feelings that have taken years to develop don't change overnight, but persistent honor has the power to win over even the hardest of hearts—particularly as a husband or wife sees affirming actions become a consistent part of a marriage.

Putting Relationships in the Right Order

For me, that fateful conversation with my wife at the kitchen table forced me to get my spiritual and family life in order. In fact, I actually began to prioritize my life from zero to ten, zero being something of little value, ten something of highest value.

I established God and my relationship with Christ as the highest—a ten. On a consistent basis, I began looking at my spiritual life and asking the question, "One to ten, where is my spiritual life with Christ?" "How highly do I value His Word?" "Prayer?" "Sharing my faith?"

Then I placed Norma above everything else on this earth, way up in the nines. With this relationship, too, I often asked myself (and Norma), "How am I doing at making you feel like you're up in the high nines, above every one of my hobbies and friends and favorite sports teams? What can I do to keep you believing you're a high nine?"

How about you? If you were to rate the "honor" quotient of your marriage relationship right now, where would it be? Where do you think your spouse would rate it? Have you asked him or her lately?

You're probably as convinced as I am that we need to give God the honor He deserves first, and then make honor a nonnegotiable item in our home, but you may still have questions about how to honor those you love in a practical way.

Let's bring honor out of the cloudland of theory right down to the cobblestone level where we live. Let me share with you three ways to bring honor off the pages of Scripture and right into your home. Each has been life-tested in my home and in the lives of thousands of people at our seminars. It all begins with practicing the "ah-h-h-h-h-h" principle on a regular basis.

Three Ways to Honor Your Loved Ones

1. The "Ah-h-h-h-h-h" Principle

As I've noted, the most fulfilling relationships in life begin with honor. In fact, the Bible says that the "fear" of the Lord—the honor and respect we give Him—is the beginning of wisdom.

The fear of the Lord is being "awe-inspired." For Moses it happened as he beheld the burning bush (Exodus 3). For Elijah the Prophet it came as he listened for the still, small voice as God's glory paraded by (1 Kings 19). And for Peter the fisherman, it was the result of watching Christ calm a rolling sea with only three words (Mark 4:39). In each case, being in God's presence produced reverence and "awe."

In fact, the fear of the Lord is being so awed that you drop your jaw and inhale a gasp, catching your breath in an audible "ah-h-h-h-h-h." It's a gasp of reverence mixed with a bit of wonder.

In short, honor is a reflex of the heart toward one who is deeply treasured. It's the conviction that you are in the presence of somebody so valuable it's "ah-h-h-h-inspiring." It's important to realize too that this life-changing attitude doesn't start with a feeling—it's a *decision;* and the *feelings* of "awe" eventually follow.

Picture it this way. Let's say you're a homemaker who has taken a well-deserved winter break from housework. It's spring now, and you've decided to pull the house back in order.

You reach into the pantry and take out a can of Johnson's Wax and begin to clean the parquet floor. You've been working an entire twenty minutes when the doorbell rings. Since you were just getting ready to take a break anyway, you cheerfully get up off the floor you've been scrubbing and head to the door.

As it opens and you look up, there stands the President of the United States in the flesh, flanked by two husky Secret Service guards.

"Hi," the president says. "I was just walking in the neighborhood and thought I'd stop in and ask you a few of your thoughts on my foreign policy."

As you stand there with your wet sponge dripping on your

fuzzy slippers, how do you respond? Can you picture the president suddenly showing up at your door to ask a question? No matter what your political viewpoint, having the main occupant of the White House suddenly appear at your doorstep would be cause for a breath-catching gasp of reverence mixed with awe— the "Ah-h-h-h-h-h" response.

Now, I agree that having the president show up at your home for a foreign policy discussion is far fetched, but every day, we see examples of the "Ah-h-h-h-h-h" principle at work. If you've ever been called to jury duty, what does the bailiff say as the judge enters the courtroom?

"Would everyone please rise? The Ah-h-h-h-honorable Judge Wapner is entering the room." It's time to stand up and show ah-h-h-h-honor because someone extremely valuable is about to enter the room.

What do the Orientals do upon meeting someone important or upon signing an important agreement? They bow to each other as a symbol of honor. The gesture means that I have decided you're important and deserve special merit and respect.

Sometimes I walk in the house and see one of my kids sitting in the easy chair watching television. Just for fun, I'll drop to my knees and say, "Unbelieeeevable! I'm actually in the same room with Michael Smalley! I can't believe that I'm living in the same house with somebody as ah-h-h-h-h-mazing as you!"

My kids usually howl, "Da-a-ad." But basically, that is the way you build the "Ah-h-h-h" principle into your relationship. You decide that the people around you—your spouse, your children, your friends, and your parents—are worthy of honor. They are worth an "ah-h-h-h-h-h" on a consistent basis.

Have you ever wondered why the dog is considered man's best friend? As you'll discover in Chapter 5, it's because men, in particular, are extremely motivated by the "Ah-h-h-h-h-h" principle.[8]

Think about the way the average dog greets its owner. Whether you've been gone for two weeks on vacation or ten minutes to the mini-mart, he probably falls all over himself showing his happiness at seeing you. Nonverbally, dogs honor their owners with massive doses of love and enthusiasm. In fact, I'm sure that if the dog could gasp, "ah-h-h-h-h!" when he saw you walk in, he would!

That's probably one reason why men tend to dislike cats. You can call them and they just give you that "Garfield" look of disdain, as if they were saying, "Where do you get off thinking you're valuable enough for me to come running over to you? *I'm the one who gets honored around here!*"

In the book of Proverbs, we're told that even the smallest act of "ah-h-h-h-h" can have a positive effect on a relationship. There we read, "Bright eyes gladden the heart . . ." (Proverbs 15:30, NASB).

Have you ever appeared at a surprise party for a special friend and seen their eyes "light up" when they see you? That same feeling of "I'm really special to them" is at the heart of having "bright eyes." And where do "bright eyes" come from? From a heart that is looking at someone very, very special to us—someone we're delighted to see. Someone we're ah-h-h-h-honoring.

2. Remember That "Ah-h-h-h-h-h" Is in the Eye of the Beholder

When we honor someone, we make a decision that a person is special and important. Biblically (and thankfully), honor was not always something that had to be earned. It was given as an act of grace to someone who didn't deserve it.

An example of this is the verse, "While we were still sinners, Christ died for us" (Romans 5:8). Just like our Lord, we sometimes need to make our decision to honor someone apart from our feelings about that person.

It's amazing how a person's response to something or someone can change dramatically once they've made a decision that the individual is truly valuable. That fact was never more clear to me than after what happened at a special seminar we did that was filmed for a nationwide television audience.

Jim Shaughnessy is a close friend who has been to several of our "Love Is a Decision" Seminars, and he knows that I always teach a section on honoring those we love. Without me knowing it, he planned something for this special seminar that brought about the greatest natural "Ah-h-h-h-h-h" response from a crowd I've ever witnessed.

At most of our seminars, I use a three-inch piece of sparkling crystal cut in the shape of a diamond to give people a word picture of "honor." I usually begin by asking the audience:

"How many of you believe this cut stone is a $100,000 diamond?" A chuckle will ripple through the audience as people look at the crystal. Usually, I have to talk at least one person into raising his hand just so I can continue with the point I'm making. Truthfully, people should chuckle when they hear me put the value of that piece of crystal at $100,000. After all, it's probably not worth more than sixty dollars in any store in the country, but as far as I'm concerned I wouldn't part with it for one penny less than $100,000.

It's kind of like the farmer who crossed fifty pigs with fifty deer—and got a hundred sows and bucks! *It's we who set the value of something.* And that was a fact my friend helped me illustrate better than I could have ever dreamed.

Jim owns a very old Stradivarius violin. Just for the television special, he had it flown in—complete with its own "security guard"! As I began to talk about honor in the seminar, I brought out what looked just like any old, unstrung fiddle or violin.

"This violin is worth over $65,000," I said. I could see by the smiles and nodding of heads that people believed me about as much as they did when I would hold up my "$100,000" diamond. In fact, my holding up the violin didn't produce even one "ah-h-h-h-hdible" gasp in the entire crowd. After all, they could see with their own eyes that it was an old violin. Particularly those sitting close to the speaker's platform could see that it didn't even have any strings.

But as I talked about attaching honor to something, I told them a little bit more about what I actually held in my hand. After all, there are only about 600 violins like it left in the world, and when I angled it so that I could read the inscription inside, and then mentioned the word "Stradivarius," the effect was incredible.

A spontaneous, collective, breath-catching "ah-h-h-h" reflex rifled throughout the crowd. Just a few moments before, it was just an old violin, not worthy of any special honor, but by attaching that one word, "Stradivarius," to it, it suddenly was given a high place of honor by everyone in the room (especially by me as I hoped I wouldn't drop it!).

Remember, people make the decision that something is of high value. Does a Chevy pull up to a Mercedes at a stoplight and gaze at it enviously, wishing it could be a Mercedes? Of course not. Do you think that silver cries itself to sleep each night because it's not as valuable as gold? It doesn't care. *We're* the ones that attach value to a thing—or a person.

Someone came up with a great idea years ago. They decided to take all the old pieces of furniture sitting around in people's attics and garages and call them "antiques." Instantly, people lined up to pay exorbitant prices for all these old pieces of "junk." Then, after spending huge amounts that would make new furniture prices blush, they take home these worn relics and spend countless hours and extra dollars refinishing them!

What happened to all those old sticks of furniture to make them suddenly become antiques? Their value suddenly rose, and that happened for only one reason—we had decided they were more valuable to us. I was aware of this concept everywhere else in life, but I wasn't practicing it in my own home—the most important place for the "Ah-h-h-h-h-h" principle to take root and grow.

Let's say the husband comes home at night and the whole family meets him at the door. Instead of running past him to go out to play or to watch television, he is greeted with a collective chorus of *"Ah-h-h-h-h! Look who's here!!"*

Then, to his amazement, the wife and kids roll out a red carpet runner into the house and as he walks down it, the kids throw rose petals at his feet. Scurrying ahead of him, they usher him into his easy chair, prop up his feet, lovingly hand him his paper, and peel grapes for him, throwing them (at an angle) into his mouth to eat.

What would the average husband think if he was greeted this way when he walked in the door? He'd probably think he was in the wrong house! Honoring actions don't have to be exaggerated the way I've described above. But the attitude of honor does have to be present if our relationships are to grow and develop.

"Hold it," I can hear someone saying, "what if some people don't *deserve* our honor? How can I act in an honoring way toward them when they're not living up to what I want?"

Whether it is a husband or a wife who asks that question about the person they vowed to honor, it takes another question to answer it: Do you want your relationship to blossom instead of wither? If the answer is "blossom," then you can't avoid the issue of honor in a home.

You may be concerned that honoring an undeserving mate will make things worse rather than better. Or you may even be worried your mate will take advantage of you and use you because of your willingness to treat them with respect. However, before you react to what I'm saying and close the book, please try to understand how love and honor intermingle.

I know that God is the only being in life who is always worthy of honor, and yet in His Word we are told to honor others —all others. Children are to give "honor" to their parents. A husband should honor his wife and a wife her husband. We are to prefer "one another" in honor.

Remember, honor is an *attitude* that someone is valuable.

It is not an absolution of all a person's faults, nor a command to be less than honest with who they are. Let me give you an example:

I have a good friend whose father is an alcoholic. I know for a fact that this man "honors" his father by praying for him, encouraging him to accept Christ, and even inviting him to his home consistently.

But "honor" does not mean that he allows his alcoholic father to drive his three-year-old daughter around in his car. Neither does honor dissolve all healthy boundaries in their relationship. There is no swearing allowed, no smoking in the house, and no "teasing" the children. There are times when the father doesn't want to play by the rules—and doesn't come to the house as a result. But he knows and has even admitted—in spite of his complaints—that his son "honors" and even loves him.

"Honor" doesn't cast pearls before swine—but neither does it mean that you treat a person like a swine until he measures up to your standards.

If you're in the situation of having to "honor" a difficult person, you may want to go deeper into several books that John Trent and I have written on this subject and can also recommend.[9] Without exception, be sure to read and absorb everything I cover in Chapters 13 and 14 in this book.

The material in these chapters (on tapping into the very power source of love) will be especially helpful for you. There you will find the secret to really enjoying life in spite of difficult circumstances. The concepts found there are also absolutely crucial for working through the fear of "What if they won't change?"

There have been times when I have been motivated to honor Norma not out of my "feelings," but as an act of my will and in obedience to God's command that I do so. And consistently, once I put honor in its right place, positive, loving feelings will follow.

Is this some type of psychological trick or basis for manipulation? Hardly. It's actually a biblical principle:

In Matthew 6:21 Jesus said, ". . . for where your treasure is, there your heart will be also." In other words, when it comes to our spiritual life, what we treasure—what we place high value upon—is where our feelings reside. The same thing is true in my relationship with my spouse. If I "treasure" or honor a person, my positive, warm feelings about him or her begin to rise correspondingly.

I realize that it isn't always easy to keep one's thoughts and feelings at the "honoring" level. As a wife, you might begin to grumble about the little things your husband does that irritate you. There's the trash can that only gets taken out when you remind him for the tenth time, or the way he remembers to fill up *his* car but always forgets to check out yours. As a husband, you may be frustrated with her weight or her discipline of the children or even with the way she drives at night.

But if an attitude of dishonor is allowed to develop or turn destructive, it's a short step to attaching negative feeling to that *person,* instead of his actions. When men (or women) begin a pattern of consistently dishonoring their spouses—even if it's only in their minds—within a matter of a few weeks they can lose nearly all their loving feelings for them.

That's when you begin to hear the comments, "Why did I pick this guy?" or "Of all the fish in the sea, I got stuck with her!" That's also where small acts of irritation—like squeezing the toothpaste tube from the wrong end—can end up being "grounds" for divorce.

But the opposite is true as well. Time and again, when honor begins to take root in a home, within a matter of a few days or weeks, your feelings will start to change. Your husband may seem like a beat-up old violin, but the moment you begin treating him like a Stradivarius, your world and his can change for the better.

There is a third way to keep honor inside your home. We must concentrate on keeping dishonoring acts—even minor ones —outside of our experience.

3. It's Worth the Hard Work to Keep Dishonoring Actions at Arm's Length

It takes time for honor to take root in our lives, and before it does, all of us are capable of the type of thing I used to do. It violated this crucial principle.

As is typical of all small children, every now and then they need a little "motivation" to behave. Ours were no exception. When the need arose for discipline, I'd often take my thumb and middle finger and "flick" them on the head.

"Greg," I'd say, and flick him on the head, "turn off the television!" or "Michael," flick, "stop bothering the dog."

One night we were in a restaurant, and the kids were acting up. As usual, I reached across the table and flicked my daughter on the head to get her to stop pestering her brother.

"*Gary,*" Norma said, in an icy tone, "we're in a restaurant. Is this any kind of place to flick your daughter?"

Her reaction startled me. After all, flicking my kids had become such a habit, I never stopped to think it was dishonoring, so I turned to my daughter and asked, "Kari, how does it make you feel when I flick you?"

"Daddy, I don't like you flicking me." Without an invitation to comment, my two boys quickly agreed.

"Yeah, Dad. We don't like you flicking us *either.*" Norma didn't say anything at this point because I had never flicked her.

Right there I decided to quit flicking the kids, but I knew that since it was a habit, I'd need some incentive to remind me not to dishonor them. So, after thinking about it for a minute, I said, "I'll tell you what, kids. I don't want to dishonor you any more by flicking you. Will you forgive me?" They nodded their heads.

"To show you how serious I am about wanting to stop, I'll make a deal with you. From now on, anytime I flick you I'll give you a dollar right on the spot."

Their immediate response after looking at each other, was, "Flick on, Dad, flick on!"

Let's start making a mental list of what we do that can dishonor our family or friends. Here's our current list of the top ten dishonoring acts we have reported to us all over the country. They're not in a particular "dishonoring" order, but all of them can be killers of meaningful relationships.

The Top Ten Dishonoring Acts in a Home

- Ignoring or degrading another person's opinions, advice, or beliefs (especially criticizing another person's faith)
- Burying oneself in the television or newspaper when another person is trying to communicate with us
- Creating jokes about another person's weak areas or shortcomings (Sarcasm or cutting jokes act like powerful emotional word pictures and do lasting harm in a relationship.)[10]

- Making regular verbal attacks on loved ones: criticizing harshly, being judgmental, delivering uncaring lectures
- Treating in-laws or other relatives as unimportant in one's planning and communication
- Ignoring or simply not expressing appreciation for kind deeds done for us
- Distasteful habits that are practiced in front of the family —even after we are asked to stop
- Overcommiting ourselves to other projects or people so that everything outside the home seems more important than those inside the home
- Power struggles that leave one person feeling that he or she is a child or is being harshly dominated
- An unwillingness to admit that we are wrong or ask forgiveness

I don't want my wife or children to feel any less loved than God would have them be in my home, and that means that honor must become an everyday activity in my life—like shaving or taking time out for meals. How about you? Are you ready to turn loose the "Ah-h-h-h-h-h" Principle in your home?

In this chapter, we've talked about the decision we all need to make to honor others—that people are worth our time and energy! Now, in the next chapter, let's look at the second greatest aspect of any healthy relationship: love. *You'll discover that love is the action we take to communicate how valuable another is* and, like honor, that love is actually a *decision.*

3

Love Is a Decision

Imagine that you've pulled up a chair next to me as I sit facing Kay Hammer, the woman whose story began this book. Like me, you can sense the tension around the table as it soon becomes obvious that the only thing standing between her and the door are the words that will be shared during the next few hours.

What do you say to a woman who was clinging to the end of her rope when it came to her willingness to hang on to her marriage? As you sit with me, you'd hear me tell her that she should try once more to hold her marriage together, but you'd also hear reason after reason why she should leave John. You would hear me tell her how important it is that God be given every opportunity to keep them together—and sharing the latest research that shows the life-long emotional pain that children and spouses suffer after divorce.[1]

Kay listened and agreed to stay with John after our conversation. But I never realized that things were about to get much worse for her and her husband, not better. In fact, he did something a few weeks later that even caused her Christian friends to say to her, "Kay, *leave* him. You shouldn't take that from anybody. . . ."

At first it took an hourly decision to stay, but with each day, Kay became more committed to do what we share in Chapter 13 and especially Chapter 14. She made a decision to respond to her husband out of the fullness of her love for Christ—not the empty feelings she had about her marriage. And the difference in her attitude instantly began to show. But a severe test was coming of how much Kay was willing to seek God's love first, and then reflect it back to her husband. For a few weeks later, he ripped away the most important thing to her in a moment's notice.

Almost Too Much to Take

John couldn't help but notice the change that had come over his wife. Like many mates who see the first blush of change—he tested her to see how real it was.

For two years, Kay's life-line of support had been her Bible Study Fellowship group. These ladies had prayed for her and encouraged her on those hopeless mornings when she was ready to toss in the towel. As a group leader, the highlight of Kay's year was the annual "leaders' retreat" coming up.

She had already paid her money and arranged for babysitting for the children. Kay was less than twenty-four hours away from heading to the airport and the retreat when John came home from the office.

"Where are *you* going?" he demanded, looking around at the suitcases she'd packed.

"To the Bible study leaders' retreat," Kay said. "You know that I leave tomorrow."

"Well, I've changed my mind," John announced. "I don't want you to go. In fact, I think you're spending way too much time with this group. I want you out of that leadership program right now."

Can you imagine the choice she had to make? To stand against her husband and go to the retreat would be to play the same chorus of "I'll do it *my* way" that she had sung unsuccessfully for years. On the other hand, to follow his leadership—and cut herself off from her primary source of fellowship and spiritual support—seemed equally wrong.

What was she to do? This wasn't a situation where she could change the channel and have her decision go away. She could tell John was waiting for her response. What's more, she knew that this was a major test of her "decision" to show him honor, no matter what the circumstances. Just then the phone rang, and she was saved from having to respond to him on the spot.

It was a friend calling to ask if she and John could come to dinner that night with a noted pastor who was speaking in town—a man named Ray Stedman. John and Kay ended up going to the dinner, and as soon as she could, Kay drew Dr. Stedman aside and explained her situation.

"What should I do?" she asked. "What can I say to my husband that will get him to change his mind about my going to the retreat and being in leadership?"

Kay would never forget what this wise pastor told her:

"Kay," he said, "your first responsibility is to seek the Lord, then your family, and *then* a ministry. I'm not going to talk to you about a way to manipulate John to change his mind. If your husband tells you to get out of Bible Study Fellowship, then when I leave tonight you tell him that you're getting out!"

At the time, she thought someone had tossed four gallons of ice water right in her face. She sat with her mouth open wondering, *How could he say such a thing?* Yet as the evening wore on, she realized that what he said was right. For years, she had tried with varying degrees of success to manipulate her way in and out of things—and now she was being asked to change. It was like hearing an army trumpet sound general quarters. The pastor's words called out that she was in the midst of a spiritual battle— not just a battle with her husband.

When they got home from dinner, Kay's normal response would have been, "There is not enough money in this *world* that could keep me home from this retreat. We already agreed that I could go, and you're breaking that promise!"

But instead, her response was based on a decision that God was in control of her life. "If John doesn't want me to go," she said, "then God must not want me to go this time."

"Father," she prayed, "I don't understand why, but I feel like this is a test. So, Lord, please help me find a reason for my not going."

As she looked at her plane tickets lying on the piano, tears filled her eyes. Yet, in spite of the pain, with all her heart she knew what she was doing was right. It was one of the most difficult things she'd ever done in her life, but she walked up the stairs and told her husband that she would skip the retreat, that she would drop out of her leadership position.

We live in days and times where words like "sacrifice" and "commitment" are four-letter words. I realize that, to many people, Kay's decision to love and honor her husband's wishes might seem unenlightened or even terribly wrong. After all, *she had her rights.* But as Kay was to find out, it was in laying down her rights that she finally broke through to her husband.

In simple terms what Kay literally did was make love a decision. *Genuine love is honor put into action regardless of the cost.* It comes from a heart overflowing with love for God, freeing us to seek another person's best interests. Kay knew that only by loving God first and foremost could she ever hope to pull off loving John

—especially after what he had done. Every "instinct" she had told her to lash out. Yet in spite of her "instincts," her love would be based on a decision to honor her husband—not her emotions. Let me admit that there are situations where either the husband or wife is emotionally unhealthy. In no way am I saying that we are to give a "blanket" yes to a spouse who commands us to do something against the law or in direct violation to God's law. (For a look at the balance between unconditional love and dealing with an emotionally destructive person, we recommend Dr. James Dobson's *Love Must Be Tough*). But Kay believed this was her chance to prove to John what was more important: her husband or her retreat. Perhaps that's why she determined more than ever that her love for Christ would be the basis of her love for her husband. And that's what led to . . . the rest of the story.

The Rest of the Story

Several months passed, and John and Kay were invited to a large Christian conference held in the auditorium at Indiana University. At the conclusion of the seminar, the speaker did something unusual. He opened up several microphones for people in the audience to come up and share what God had been doing in their lives. That's when it happened.

Kay suddenly looked over and noticed that John was getting up from his seat and heading to the front of the auditorium. He waited his turn in line and then stepped up to the microphone.

"Ladies and gentlemen," he said to a group of over a thousand people. *"I just want you to know that I'm here tonight because my wife First Peter three'ed me into coming!"*

The entire place came unglued with laughter as his words sank in. Indeed, as the verse says, Kay's commitment to trust God had won over her husband "without a word" by her godly actions (1 Peter 3:1–6).

"I'm going to tell you all something Kay doesn't know," John continued. "We had this guy named Gary Smalley come to our house and I don't know what he told my wife—but things haven't been the same since. Basically, I'm here tonight because my wife has worn me out with her love.

"I've got to confess that there have been days when I actually sat in my office, thinking up something I was going to tell her to do when I got home *just to see if she would do it*—and she did!

Watching the reality of this woman's love for God is the reason I'm standing up here tonight. . . ." And there was more to come.

John changed so much that soon *he* was in the leadership program of the *Men's* Bible Study Fellowship. And then came the day of *their* men's leadership retreat. Kay drove her husband to where the bus would take him and several others on a weekend retreat. John had never been on a men's retreat, and he was like a schoolboy going to summer camp for the first time.

---

*G*enuine love is honor put into action regardless of the cost.

While she never said anything at the bus station, Kay couldn't help thinking about the retreat she had given up months earlier. And as she drove off, the emotions of the moment finally hit her. She was thankful for the changes in her husband's life, but the hurt of being denied an opportunity to go to her own leaders' retreat brought tears to her eyes—until the phone rang.

Kay had barely gotten back home when John called.

"We're at a truck stop picking up some other people for the retreat," he said, "and I just had to call you."

With his voice choking with emotion, he said, "Kay, I've been thinking back to a time I told you you couldn't go to a retreat. Could you forgive me for asking you to give up something I knew was really important to you? I'm so sorry I asked you to step down from your leadership group. I never should have asked what I did, and I never will again. Can you find it in your heart to forgive me? . . ."

Kay has been to many retreats since the one she missed over thirteen years ago—but none have held as much meaning as the one she never attended. Later, she would say in reflecting on that unforgettable call, "*I gave up a retreat—but I gained back a husband!*"

Over the years, John and Kay have developed a rock-solid love for Christ and each other. This couple whose relationship at one time was dead in the water, held fast by the rocks of insensitivity and bitter arguments, now help countless couples fight back from the brink of divorce. And they do this by sharing the reality of their own story—and by helping others see that genuine love is a decision, not a feeling.

Moving Honor into a Home by Loving Actions

I realize that there are times when love needs to be tough and set firm boundaries with a loved one. But what turned around John and Kay's life was a principle that is true in any home. *The most effective way to open the door to needed changes in a relationship is to honor a loved one. And once we've made that decision to honor, love is the action we take no matter how we feel.*

Genuine love is honor put into action, regardless of the cost. It comes from a heart overflowing with affection for God, freeing us to seek another person's best interest.

In a nutshell, that definition is an outline of this book. We've already seen in Chapter 2 that honor is at the foundation of all healthy relationships. Now we've seen that out of our decision to honor flows loving actions *regardless of our feelings—regardless of the cost.*

Now in the chapters that follow, you'll learn the ten areas that took me all day to teach Kay, and that I've spent fifteen years refining and researching ever since. Each one is a *specific loving action* that expresses the honor and the decision to love that we've made.

The very first loving action that is so essential in any home or relationship is recognizing the incredible worth of a woman. Every woman has two tremendous tendencies that we'll uncover for you. What's more, you'll see that there are three questions any husband can ask his wife that can reveal her built-in marriage manual.

4

The Incredible
Worth of a Woman

One of the greatest joys I have in teaching the "Love Is a Decision" Seminar is sharing with men how incredibly valuable women are. Why? One major reason is that I've spent time learning and asking questions from women. That includes twenty-five years of marriage, and interviewing over 30,000 women at conferences and in counseling sessions across the country. I've seen, first hand, the tremendous relationship skills that God has woven into the fabric of their lives.

But a few years ago, I had an experience that gave me a whole new appreciation for their incredible worth. For on a wind-blown afternoon, one woman's "intuitive" senses quite possibly saved my life, and the lives of several others as well.

A River Gone Wild. . . .

It was mid-May, and time for our annual "staff retreat" where we do more retreating than staffing. We did have one legitimate reason for spending the weekend fishing. We were in the process of interviewing Steve Lyon, now an invaluable associate on our staff, and we decided that spending a weekend quizzing him at our favorite fishing spot was just the place to get to know him—and a few trophy-sized trout at the same time.

We were on our way to Lee's Ferry, located just below Lake Powell on the Colorado River. Lying at the mouth of the Grand Canyon, it offers great fishing and some of the most spectacular scenery in the world.

Early the first morning, we waited at the dock for our two guides. Soon, a truck rumbled up, two figures bouncing in the front seat as it rolled to a stop. The door opened and out stepped a tall, weather-beaten man of about forty. Beside him was his wife, a petite woman only half his size. What I would discover later that day was that anything she lacked in size, she would more than make up for in fishing skill—and her natural female "instincts."

Beautiful canyon walls rose literally two and three hundred feet straight up from the edge of the water as we began a tour of the Grand Canyon at water level. It took our boats nearly an hour traveling upstream to reach the dam which stood as a towering marker to "the end of the line." We shut our engines down and quietly began to drift with the current, letting out line behind us as we trolled for speckled and rainbow trout.

The early morning passed with little success. Then lunch time rolled around and we beached the boats about halfway back to the dock. It had been a fairly calm morning, but by the time we got back to the boats, the wind had changed from a whisper to a stiff breeze. I remember thinking, *We won't catch a thing until these gusts die down.* But they didn't.

With each passing minute, the wind grew stronger and more steady. The once glassy surface of the river was beginning to roll as the water churned with a thousand tiny waves. But we were all seasoned campers and fishermen. *What's a little wind?* I thought.

As we got back in the boats, I noticed our two guides talking. I couldn't hear the words they were saying, but it was obvious they were in the midst of a heated discussion. Finally, the man shrugged his shoulders, nodded his head, and marched over to us with some unwelcome news.

"I'm sorry, guys, but we're going to have to pack it in for right now. I can't explain it, but my wife really feels strongly that this isn't just a minor front coming in—and I've learned to listen to her on these waters. So we're heading back."

It was a good thing we listened to her when we did. Almost instantly the wind began to howl, and the waves were beginning to form whitecaps. Within minutes, we lost the ability to communicate from boat to boat as the fury of a desert windstorm drowned out even the most desperate attempts to shout instructions.

We were all on our own to make it back. By now the wind was blowing with such a galelike force that if we had turned sideways to the current, we would have easily been swamped by the angry swells. The only hope we had of making it back on top of the water was to point the boats directly downstream into the wind, meet the waves head on, and speed full throttle to dock and safety.

For thirty minutes (they seemed like a life-time), our three boats fought a river gone wild. A major storm had turned the narrow Canyon walls into a wind-tunnel. I had no idea at the time what was going on in the other two boats, but I knew that prayer kept ours afloat.

Finally, after stopping to bail out water at one point, all three boats had docked safely with all hands accounted for. I learned later from my two sons, who were in the guide's wife's boat, that she had handled herself beautifully. In fact, she was the first one back to the dock. At one point, a gust of wind caught the front end of the boat and began to flip it over backwards, but her cool-headed reaction, at the very least, saved everyone from an icy swim. At most, she saved my sons' lives.

I walked away from that trip with another reason why women are so incredibly valuable. I know for a fact that if our guide hadn't listened to his wife, we would have been in major trouble.

It's struck me several times since that incident how much I've profited from learning the valuable character traits and natural talents that God has built into my wife. Far from an attempt to erase all differences between the sexes, I feel strongly that God placed the differences there for a purpose.

In this chapter, we'll look at several areas of natural, complementing strengths in men and women. I hope one result for every man will be that he finds new reasons for treasuring and valuing his wife, and I hope that one result for every woman will be to find yet another reason to thank God for the natural gifts she brings to those she loves.

Meeting Our Missing Part

It was a wise and loving God who said, "It is not good for the man to be alone" (Genesis 2:18a). But was a woman designed merely to provide a man with companionship—or does it go deeper than that?

Most people are familiar with the passage that talks about God creating woman and His words, "I will make (him, Adam) a helper suitable for him" (Genesis 2:18b). The Hebrew word for "helper" actually means "completer." The word is used throughout the Old Testament to talk about God being our "helper," the One who "completes what is lacking," or "does for us what we cannot do for ourselves."[1]

One of the things that should increase the "honor" a husband gives to his wife is realizing that God created her to help him in areas he isn't naturally equipped to handle. In other words, a wife is designed to bring strengths to the relationship that the husband does not naturally have himself.

Over the years, I've noted a number of ways in which men and women are different, but there are four areas in particular, I've seen a woman's natural gifts act like missing parts needed to complete a man. That first missing piece comes with a special language that a woman speaks which cannot only strengthen a marriage—it can literally be a life-saving gift to some husbands.

1. Two Languages in the Same Home

One study of little four-year-old boys and girls recorded every noise that came out of their mouths over a period of time.[2] The study concluded that 100 percent of the sounds made by little girls had something to do with literal words. They spent a great deal of time talking to each other, and almost an equal amount of time talking to themselves.

For little boys, however, the figure was only 60 percent words. The remaining 40 percent were simply noises and sound effects (like Bzzzzzzzz!, Zoooooooooom! Baaammmmmm!). In short, the tendency in even little girls is to use more words than little boys, and that early difference in language skills holds up throughout each age level.

Not only are women more verbal, but they often speak a different language than men do. I'm not talking about homes where English and Spanish, or Japanese and English are spoken, but about a much more common family environment where "Womaneise" and "Maneise" are spoken!

In roughly 80 percent of all homes, men primarily relate to their wives using what we call a *language of the head* while women tend to speak a *language of the heart.*

Typically, men tend to be logical, factual, and detail-oriented. In general, when a man runs out of facts to talk about in a conversation, he often stops talking! Usually, men don't have as much of a need to share as deeply or consistently as do their wives. Nor do they have the need to speak the same number of words their wives do. Some studies have shown that the average woman speaks roughly 25,000 words a day, while the average man speaks only 12,500! What this can mean in a marriage is that a woman is often left holding her cup out for meaningful conversation day after day and drawing it back with only a few drops to nourish her.

On the other hand, women often speak a *language of the heart.* In most cases, they love to share thoughts, feelings, goals, and dreams. A woman's natural skills at communicating often will make her wonderfully sensitive to small things others are thinking, saying, or feeling. And her desire for deep relationships usually exceeds what the average man desires.

It's almost as if men are two-humped camels. They can take a little conversation and then go for days across even the most difficult terrain without any need for more "watering" words, but a woman covering the same distances needs a daily allotment of water to survive and flourish—and often double that ration of "watering" words during difficult periods in her life.

Why should a man be interested in having his wife help him learn to speak her "language of the heart"? For one thing, it can actually help him live longer.

In his provocative book, *The Language of the Heart,* Dr. James J. Lynch presents compelling evidence that effective communication skills can do wonders for a person's cardiovascular health.[3] Whether we realize it or not, each time we engage in conversation, whether we are under stress or not, our blood pressure increases. However, when the conversation is stressful—*and especially when we hold our words inside*—our blood pressure can go to extremely high levels. This can be a dangerous situation, especially for people with a history of heart problems such as hypertension.

When a man learns to bridge both worlds—by speaking the language of the head and the language of the heart—it can make tremendously positive changes in his own life and the lives of those with whom he lives and works. Not only that, it can decrease the unnecessary stress that accompanies poor marital or business conversation. In the end, our hearts will thank us for the decreased workloads, and those around us will be thankful for the increased depth and feeling we have added to our communication.

But how does a woman actually help her husband bridge the "language" barrier in a home? If a man opens his eyes to several natural characteristics of his wife, he'll see that her natural strengths can complete him because. . . .

2. Women Tend to Relate on Multiple Levels

When most women are asked to describe the mental capacity of men, their response is, "He has a one-track mind." In a sense, that's pretty close—and not just in the area of sexual relationships. We men usually do concentrate on one thing at a time. It's as if our minds are like the inside of a battleship, with many different decks and compartments. When we leave one deck, we close the water-tight door to the last compartment and busy ourselves with what's close at hand.

Many a wife knows that if she leaves the house for an hour with her husband "in charge" of the kids, she's likely to come back and not see them anywhere in sight.

That's one reason why a wife, when she asks her husband if he thought about her at work that day, is likely to hear:

"Did I think about you today? Well . . . I mean . . . I'm sure I *must* have thought about you sometime!" Take heart, ladies; it's probably not that he doesn't love you, it's just a reflection of his tendency to "compartmentalize" his thinking. A man tends to remain in one world at work that centers around the office or job-site, and when he leaves that one, he enters another that revolves around the family.

A woman's mind, though, is like the war room on that battleship. It's the nerve center, equipped with fancy electronic devices that allow it to monitor all the vital signs on every deck of the house at the same time. Because of the way her mind has been designed, its radar is constantly on and sweeping in all directions.

What this means is that the average woman misses very little about her environment, no matter how crowded it is. That same "radar" system that is so sensitive in Norma is what alerted our fishing guide's wife to the coming windstorm. And it's also the same system that makes it very difficult for the average woman to relax completely if her husband is watching the kids.

Many a wife knows that if she leaves the house for an hour with her husband "in charge" of the kids, she's likely to come back and not see them anywhere in sight. Then when she asks her husband (who's now in front of the television set) where they are, he's liable to say, "Oh, I don't know . . . they're around here somewhere. . . . I think they went down to the pond to play," as he turns back to his game.

She, on the other hand, usually knows exactly what's going on with the kids, no matter what time of day it is, or what part of the house they are in. It doesn't matter if she lives in a three-story Victorian mansion. She can be in the basement when her radar goes off, but she knows the kids are in the attic fighting.

Greg and Mike literally thought that Mom had the house wired when they were out. Invariably, they'd be as quiet as church mice doing something they shouldn't, and still Norma's radar would go off, and she'd catch them.

A woman misses very little about her environment, which is probably the basis for that mysterious gift some have called intuition. We feel strongly that it's more than a natural "hunch." It's just one more way in which a woman can complete her husband—and another reason a man should honor and value his wife.

3. Women Have the Unique Skill of Personalizing Their Environment

Another tremendous strength a woman has is to become personally involved with everything around her. For example, have you ever wondered why the average wife doesn't care that much about watching a football game with you? Most of the time, it's because she doesn't *know* any of the players. There's nothing "personal" going on down on the field. (Now, this may not be true when she is in the stands sitting with you and some friends, but for many women, the battling going on down on the field is not as interesting as who you meet coming and going to the game.)

One way to get a woman to be more interested in a sporting event is to "personalize" it. Take a few moments and share some information with her about one of the players ("Honey, see that guy who just caught the ball? He's the guy I told you about who's been really struggling with his wife and kids . . . "). Then she'll feel more a part of the game and what's going on because she has an emotional tie to it.

How strong is a woman's need for an "emotional" attachment to someone? One indication is the fact that in this country alone, over ten million romance novels will be purchased this year, and 97 percent of them will be bought by women. Why? At least in part because these stories offer a picture of intimacy and deep personal relationships that, unfortunately, many find too infrequently in their own lives.

If a man isn't aware of his wife's tendency to "personalize" almost everything around her, it can lead to friction in a home. That's because for most women, the cat is not just an "animal," but their first baby. The wallpaper isn't just "something to cover the walls," but a reflection of who she is.

As you may have noticed, many men tend to take certain things in their surroundings for granted. For example, the car they drive. Recently, a story appeared in *Reader's Digest* that I really enjoyed.

There was a man with several daughters who owned an old, decapitated convertible. For years, every woman in the house urged him to get rid of the "pile of junk" and even refused to ride in it with him in public. Then one day it happened. He walked out from work, and the car had been stolen.

The man's wife and daughters were celebrating that night that his eyesore of a car had been stolen when the phone rang. The party was over—the police had found the car.

"We found your car only about ten blocks from where they took it," the policeman said. "We don't know who did it, but they left a note saying, '*You can have it back. We'd rather walk!*'"

For a man, a car can often be in the worst of shape because, "It's just transportation" to him, but for a woman, if her car isn't washed it can often leave her feeling incomplete. Why is that? In part, it's because it's usually easier for a man to separate himself from his surroundings than it is for a woman.

This is especially true of the house or apartment you live in. To a man, the home is a place of rest. To a woman, it's an extension of herself.

That's why a woman may feel "trashy" if the trash hasn't been taken out; she may feel dirty if the floors aren't cleaned and the carpet not vacuumed; she may even feel broken down if the fence isn't fixed or the door is falling off the hinges. Each of these things is a part of her; when they aren't right, she feels as if something's not right with her.

Why is this something that can benefit or "complete" a man? In part, it's because a woman's natural sensitivity to her surroundings makes her alert to the things that surround us—and especially the people in her world.

It's like having a quality control expert in the home who can spot lurking problems with her "early warning" system. In addition, her heightened awareness of those around her rarely causes her to make a crucial relationship mistake many men make at the office—and at home.

4. Women Are Generally More Concerned about People Than They Are about Projects.

For the most part, men are conquerors. That means at least some of the time they tend to be less concerned about people and feelings than they are about "getting the job done." This is quite natural for men, because we tend to derive our sense of worth from what we do. The better "job" we do, the better we feel about ourselves.

Women, on the other hand, primarily derive their feelings of worth from those to whom they're related. If a woman is married, she looks to her husband more than any other earthly individual for her personal sense of value and worth.

That natural concern for deep and loving relationships that a woman has can certainly be shared by a man—but it can also be more easily set aside by him as well. Take hunting for example.

The average man can load up his high-powered rifle, go hunting, and blow away one of God's beautiful creatures. Then he can cut off its head, stuff it, hang it on a wall, gather his neighbors around, and triumphantly say, "I did that!" He's conquered something!

But generally women have already made much too deep an emotional attachment to Thumper and Bambi in the movie theater to execute one of their real-life counterparts out in the wild. When those sweet little animals die, a part of the woman is hurt as well.

You can even see this difference between the sexes when men and women go shopping. When the average man hears the average woman say, "Honey, let's go shopping and find a new blouse for me," he hears the word "shopping." But what she usually means is

"Shooooopppppppiiiiinnnng!"

Once a man hears her words, "Let's get a blouse," he is like a bloodhound who has just had an escaped prisoner's scent held in front of his nose. Once he's gotten a "whiff" of what he's going to the mall to hunt for, then it's off to sniff out a new blouse (any blouse), bag it, get back home, and lay on the porch as quickly as possible.

Since men are often more "conquer"-oriented than women, they usually tend to concentrate on the completion of a project—regardless of the personal costs. But because a woman's sense of value is so closely tied to all the relationships around her, she's often gifted in helping a man be more sensitive to what's really important beyond the immediate goal.

Take Brian, for example. For several Saturday mornings, his goal was to get up as early as he could, mow the yard, do his chores, shower, and get in front of the television set just before kickoff of the first football game of the day. As he attacked his objective of getting the yard done and getting in front of the television, he wasn't always concentrating on how to build a strong relationship with his six-year-old son, Mark.

Mark would get up with his father each Saturday and desperately try to help him with the yard. But try as he might, he could never keep up with his father on any of the chores. That was especially true when it came to "helping" his father dump all the grass from the catch bag into the trash can.

"Son, that's enough," Brian would finally say in frustration after having to pick up yet another pile of spilled yard clippings. "I don't need that kind of help right now. Why don't you go inside and see if you can help your mother? *Now.*"

Brian's wife watched each week as little Mark would walk out the door to help his Dad with his chest sticking out—and walk back in a short time later crest-fallen. As a loving wife, she brought what was happening to his attention.

At an appropriate time, she used a word picture[4] to explain to him the way he was killing his son's spirit in his "quest" to quickly mow the yard. He was sacrificing his relationship with his son for a football game that could easily be video-taped and played when his son was in bed. Fortunately, Brian was wise enough to accept her correction. He even expressed appreciation to his wife for what she said:

"Thanks, Honey. Now that you mention it, I've got to admit that I have been pushing Mark aside these past few weeks. I'm not sure why I get so caught up in getting something done my way, but I'm going to learn. My son is a lot more important to me than how quickly I get the chores done—no matter what game is on."

In Brian's home, a sensitive woman received extra honor that night because of her willingness to point out his steamroller tendencies to put projects in front of people. But that's not the only reason he's thankful for the woman God has given him. There's one more reason that outshines them all. Namely, in every marriage, right under a man's roof, is one of the most priceless things God has given him—one that he can tap into almost any time to help him in his responsibility to develop a close-knit family.

The Incredible Worth of a Woman: She Has a Built-In Marriage Manual

Do you know the main reason why men are held back from a promotion at work? Is it a lack of technical skill? Rarely. A lack of education? Occasionally. But the primary reason men fail to be promoted is their lack of relationship skills.[5]

What most men don't realize is that they have the world's greatest instructors in relationships living right under their roofs. A wife is a gold mine of relational skills. If a man wants to take advantage of the "missing part" of the nature that has affected every "Adam" since the beginning, all he has to do is look into the eyes of his wife—and learn to *tap into her built-in marriage manual.*

In talking personally with women in over sixty cities (where we've done our conferences these past five years), I've always asked for—but never found—a woman who was an exception to this rule. Namely, I have never met a woman who by her God-given nature didn't possess a built-in relationship manual.

So here's how a husband can tap into this rich source of relational skills to improve his own marriage—and his skills with his children and others as a result. First, a man needs to realize that his wife comes equipped with two tremendous inner strengths:

1. She has a strong, innate desire for a good and healthy relationship; and

2. She has the natural ability to recognize a great relationship.

These two underlying qualities are the basis for three important questions that a man can use to pull out of a woman her built-in relationship manual.

Three Questions That Can Help a Man Tap into a Woman's Built-In Marriage Manual

Three simple but life-changing questions are all it takes. For the sake of argument, let's say Bob is going to ask Julie these questions:

Julie, I realize that one way God equipped you as a helper was to complete me in the relational side of life. So let's begin with our marriage . . .

Question #1: On a scale from one to ten, with zero being terrible and ten being a great marriage, where would you like our relationship to be?

Naturally, almost every woman (and man, too!) answers that they'd like to consistently be around a nine or a ten. After all, how many of us are into misery? Bob would then go on to question two:

Question #2: On a scale from one to ten, overall, where would you rate our marriage today?

In most cases, a man will rate the marriage two to three points *higher* than his wife will, so don't let the initial difference in perception shock you. Remember, the average woman is much more in tune with the state of the relationship than the average man.

Be sure and give her time to think and share. Use the "quick listen" method described in Chapter 9 to reassure her that you value her opinion and want to understand her as much as possible.

Whether you agree with your wife or not, it's important to honor her by giving her your full attention. The goal is to understand her and to be open to what she may say.

The next question is the crucial one. In fact, in some ways it doesn't matter what she answers to Question Two, for the most important question is this third one—the one that can flip open the pages to her natural marriage and relationship manual.

Question #3: As you look at our relationship, what are some specific things we could do over the next six weeks that would move us closer to a ten?

I have yet to find a woman who cannot paint the answer to that question in brilliant detail. However, I have met numerous men who can't even find the paintbrush!

In some cases, your wife may be reluctant to answer this question, fearing she'll hurt your feelings—or even worse, that you'll hurt *her* feelings by your defensive response. That's why it's important to patiently give her the time to talk and to consistently reassure her about the security of your relationship—no matter what she says or where she rates things. If she feels secure in your love, almost without exception she'll be able to open up with many helpful specifics on how you can more effectively steward the gift of the marriage and family God has given you.

For any of us who are serious about effectively loving those who mean the most to us, honor must characterize our relationships. Nowhere is that more true than for the man who is serious about being a Christlike lover to his wife.

Let me state something clearly. *Valuing his wife's differences, and even tapping into her built-in marriage manual, does not transfer leadership or responsibility away from the husband and place it onto the wife.* Biblically, there is no escape clause from the man being the head of the home—the man is the fact-finder when it comes to building a strong relationship. But to be the type of loving leader God intended, allowing a wife to fulfill her God-given function as a loving "completer," is a must. It can help a man replace insensitivity with sensitivity, and lording it over others with genuine love for them. It can also help men become the observant servant leaders they were always meant to be.

By appreciating the unique and wonderful way God has created a woman, we can add a richness and joy to our marriage that virtually everyone wants, but very few have. The secret is in learning to honor a woman as someone unmatched in God's creation, made especially by Him as a completer, to do things for a man he could never do for himself.

Yet what do you do when your "completer" becomes discouraged or loses energy in your relationship? Or what happens when you do? In the next chapter, we'll see a second loving action that can be a tremendous help to a home. It involves learning a practical method of energizing your mate in as little as sixty seconds.

5

Energizing Your
Mate in Sixty Seconds

My wife Norma has always loved zoos. Regardless of what type of zoo, or how many times she's been through it, she always thrills at the opportunity to go again. On the other hand, having been through dozens of zoos over the years, I rarely get excited about going through another one. But one day on a speaking trip to the Midwest, Norma picked up a brochure advertising a "Wild Animal Park" that actually attracted my attention.

When she saw I wasn't immediately saying "no," her face lit up. Her voice was full of excitement as she read me the brochure and said, "Gary, I know you'll like this one. Will you come with me? *Please.*" Once again, we were off to one of Norma's favorite places in life.

Before we could actually go, there was one minor problem we had to overcome. The brochure described this park as a "drive-through zoo" and we didn't have a car. So with a phone call, I arranged with my close friend and now ministry associate, Terry Brown, to borrow his car for the afternoon. He graciously agreed and delivered to us his tiny Fiat convertible within the hour, and we were on our way to the park.

As we drove up to the main gate, they said convertibles were allowed, but that we would have to keep the top up. The friendly park ranger also gave us some advice on how to feed the animals, when not to feed them, and a strong warning about the one place in the park where we had to keep the windows rolled up. This area was called a "danger zone" because of the very large or very wild animals living there. Emphatically, we were told:

"If anything happens to your car in this section of the park, just pull off the road and honk your horn and a friendly ranger will come and rescue you."

It sounded safe enough to me, so we began our self-guided

tour of the drive-through zoo. Once inside, we quickly discovered that the animals living there were particularly friendly. The giant birds tried to stick their heads inside the car looking for food. One giraffe did manage to stick his twenty-inch gray tongue inside the car and tried to slurp Norma's sandwich out of her lap. At this point I readily agreed with her that this was far better than a "regular" zoo.

Then it happened. Halfway through the park, we finally came to the well-marked "danger zone," and right when we were in the middle of no-man's land, Norma asked, "What's that coming out from under the hood?" Well, it was steam from our overheating radiator, and it was beginning to form an unwelcome white cloud!

"Oh no," I groaned. Glancing at the temperature gauge for the first time, I noticed that it was way beyond the "hot" reading on the gauge and nearing the "melt down" zone.

Great, I thought. *We've only been gone an hour and already I've ruined my friend's car.*

I started to pull over, but Norma cried out,

"You can't pull over here! Didn't you see that sign? *This is a danger zone!"*

"But honey, I can't wreck this man's car. I've *got* to pull over!"

"But not here!" she pleaded. "What if we're both trampled to death or eaten alive? Who'll take care of the children? . . ."

"Now, don't worry," I said as gently as I could. "It says right here in the brochure that if we have any trouble in a danger zone, all we have to do is honk the horn and a friendly ranger will come right over and rescue us!"

Norma frowned, but with the way the car was acting, it was obvious we didn't have any choice. So we pulled over, and I started honking the horn. . . . and honking. . . . and honking. . . .

I honked for forty-five minutes, and no friendly ranger ever came and rescued us. Basically, the guide at the gate had lied to us. We could have been eaten, trampled, or both. But what happened between Norma and me during this time illustrates one of the most important principles I've ever discovered when it comes to developing loving, lasting relationships.

"Don't Look Now, but. . . ."

While all my honking didn't alert a single ranger, it did notify every furry resident of the "danger zone" that we were there—and that we might have (or become) lunch. First, the wild burros ambled up and began nibbling at the top of my friend's convertible. I finally had to get out of the car and yell and chase them away to convince them that hay would be better than our fabric top. I had just gotten back inside the car when I made the mistake of looking into the rear view mirror.

"Norma," I said in my calmest voice, "don't look now, but you're never going to believe what's coming!"

An entire herd of huge, shaggy buffalo were walking out of the woods and soon surrounded our little Fiat. One of them, on my side of the car, wandered over, knelt down, and put his head right up against my window. With those great big brown eyes and a huge head about four inches from my face (the steam coming out of his nose began fogging my window), it was obvious he was saying nonverbally, "Got anything in there for me?"

Then he started pushing on the window, rocking the car as he did. During the whole ordeal, neither of us looked up, hoping our ignoring them would make them go away.

"Listen to that thing breathe!" I said.

"That's not him breathing," Norma said. "*That's me!*"

Finally, our hairy friends wandered off, and our car cooled down enough for us to drive to the main gate for help.

As funny as it seems now, that hour trapped in the car together was actually a very tense situation. In fact, if it had been several years earlier, one or both of us might have responded in a very different way. We could have easily used that tense situation to explode and so weaken our relationship, rather than relying on an important principle that could strengthen it.

Norma could have said to me, "Gary, I can't handle this! I don't care if this thing explodes, get this car moving!" or I could have easily said to her, "Be quiet! You're going to see a wild animal inside this car if you don't hush up!"

Either of us could have done and said things to each other in the "heat of battle" that we would have later regretted; and if we had blown up, it would have drained away the positive feelings and energy we'd stored up in our marriage for weeks as quickly as the water draining from our radiator.

On this trip, however, things were different. They were different because we had finally begun to understand and practice an incredibly important concept in the Scriptures.

We never know when we're going to find ourselves in a frustrating situation with someone we love. During these times, when a high-intensity predicament is threatening to drain the positive energy right out of our relationships, most of us take one of two roads. We either choose to react and blast those near us or we choose to respond in a way that actually helps to strengthen our marriage. It all begins with learning how to energize your mate during a stressful situation in as little as sixty seconds.

Energizing Your Mate in Sixty Seconds

What is the biblical principle that kept our emotions in check during this difficult time? It's really an incredible power that is right at our fingertips—the ability to be gentle and to tenderly touch each other.

What is the biblical principle that kept our emotions in check during this difficult time?—
The ability to be gentle and to tenderly touch each other.

For years I had known intellectually that "a soft answer turns away anger" (Proverbs 15:1), and that a key fruit of the spirit was "gentleness" (Galatians 5:23). But I had never applied either principle in my most important relationships. Now, if softness as a way to energize a person sounds too easy to you, how often do you feel gentle in the middle of catastrophe?

Most people's basic bent during times of stress is to lash out or lecture—or both— especially if the predicament is somebody else's fault. But tenderness, above and beyond the call of our human nature, is a transformer, an energizer of those around us.

Since I wasn't fortunate enough to have a father who knew how to be tender to his wife, I wasn't aware that softness during stressful times was even an option until several years into my marriage. And that's when I learned that one of a person's greatest needs is to be comforted, especially during those moments in life when the roof falls in.

A Creative Way to Add a Skylight to Your Home. . . .

One afternoon I was very late coming home from boating with my son Greg. I had taken the car, which left Norma with only our mini-motor home for transportation. She waited and waited, but when I was several hours later than I had predicted, she decided to take our mini-motor home to the grocery store.

Granted, our motor home is not the easiest thing to handle in the world. I'd already had my share of close calls when it came time to park or back the vehicle out. But Norma re-defined the word "close-call" as she tried to back the camper out of the driveway.

She had almost made it out from under the carport when she turned the wheel the wrong way and sheared off an entire section of the roof. And if that wasn't bad enough, the falling roof bounced off the hood of the camper, scraping away paint and leaving a deep dent in its wake.

When I pulled into the driveway an hour later, I couldn't believe my eyes. Looking at the gaping hole in the roof, my first response was to look at the sky to see if the tornado was still around, but one look at our mobile home told me that it was Mother Norma, not Mother Nature, who had caused this catastrophe.

I instantly felt like ordering her out of the house and asking her questions like, "Where did you get your driver's license? From a gumball machine at Shop-Mart?!"

Instead, I sat in my car, frozen, with my hands on the steering wheel, praying, "Lord, you have to give me strength.

Every fiber in my body wants to lecture my wife now and not be gentle with her. This is one of those pressure situations, and I know I have a choice. Lord, help me figure out what I'm going to do." Turning to my son Greg I asked him, "What do you think I ought to do?"

Greg said, "Dad, why don't you do what you teach?"

"That's a good idea," I said.

But all the while I was praying for the strength to be tender. Being tender at such a moment is definitely not natural. You have to take off the comfortable old nature of lectures and anger, and put on the new nature of tenderness. This can be excruciatingly difficult (Ephesians 4:22–24).

Finally, I got out of the car and walked toward the piece of roof lying in the driveway, but just as I got up to the camper, Norma came flying around the side of the house.

I fought off the voice ringing in my mind, *Lecture her! Lecture her!* and I did what didn't feel "natural" at the time. I simply held her in my arms and gently patted her on the back. I hadn't spoken one word when finally, Norma pulled away and said, "Oh, look what I did! I wrecked the motor home and knocked off the roof," she said. Then she added, "And I told the neighbors across the street what I did, and they're watching to see how you're going to respond."

Thankfully, I hadn't given the neighbors anything to gossip about by exploding at Norma. I just put my arms around her again and gently called her by my favorite affectionate name for her:

"Norm, listen. You know I love you. You're more important to me than campers and roofs. I know you didn't do this on purpose, and you're feeling really bad about it."

At that very moment, I could feel Norma relaxing. What's more, I immediately felt better myself as my own anger drained out of me to be replaced by feelings of tenderness. While it's hard to explain, I could tell that instead of being pulled apart, we were actually growing *stronger* as a result of the trial.

After a few more minutes of talking and holding her, Norma went on with whatever she was doing, and I went out to the garage to lay my hands on the few tools I had. After taking a deep breath, I said to Greg, "Well, I'd better get at it."

Just then, from out of nowhere, a friend from my church pulled up into our driveway. This wasn't just any ordinary friend. He was a local contractor pulling up in his pickup filled with hammers, saws, lumber, nails, paint, and a long ladder. He jumped out and said, "OK, Gary. Let's get at it!"

"Where did you come from?" I asked in disbelief.

Apparently our good neighbors across the street weren't only watching my reactions to Norma. They had also been calling everyone around town to talk about our hole in the roof. Ironically, my friend had been one of the first to hear the news. With his expert help, and without exaggeration, we had our impromptu skylight patched and re-painted within two hours.

As I went to bed that night with Norma snuggled up next to me, I was amazed that I had actually done something right for a change, during a stressful situation. What would I have normally done? I could have zapped the life right out of her emotionally with angry words and lectures, and it would have taken days for us to feel our way back to each other.

If I hadn't known about the power of gentleness, I'm sure I would have acted as I had in the past and blown up. This time I didn't, and amazingly, it made all the difference. The old Gary Smalley might have lost it. The new one followed a biblical blueprint for turning away anger, and it made even a stressful event a time of closeness.

I learned an important lesson that day; it's one I've seen repeated time and time again in my life and in the lives of others. Simply put, that lesson is:

> *Remaining tender during a trial is one of the most powerful ways to build an intimate relationship (James 1:19, 20).*

The power of tenderness is outlined and illustrated from one end of the New Testament to the other. However, from my perspective, Ephesians 4 does the best job of explaining it. In this section of Scripture:

- Verse 15 introduces the concept of gentleness by challenging us to grow up in all aspects "into Jesus Christ." We're to grow up in love and to become mature. That's what each of us wants I'm sure—to be mature, caring people who can encourage those around us.
- Then verses 22 and 23 tell us that to become complete in Christ, we're to take off our "old self," which is the opposite of

godliness, and then put on our "new self." Now the question is, what is it we take off and what do we put on in its place?

• While there are certainly many aspects of our fallen nature that need to be exchanged for godly characteristics, verse 29 gives us one specific we can begin to put into practice today. Without pulling any punches, it says we are not to let "any unwholesome word proceed out of our mouth." Unwholesome words popping out of our mouths are a reflection of our old nature, and they need to be replaced with their opposite—words that are tender, gentle, and nurturing.

The verse continues with the encouragement to speak only words that are "good for edification according to the need of the moment, that it may give grace to those who hear." These are words that build up or strengthen others, words that bring energy and life to people.

Let's look at several practical ways to energize your mate, children, and friends on a daily basis by learning to replace angry, deflating lectures with tender, strengthening words.

Lectures and Tenderness Don't Mix

Let's say a woman is losing emotional energy and reaches the end of her rope. In frustration, she might say to her husband:

"Oooh, I've had it around this house. *Look at this mess.* Nobody ever picks up anything around here. I've got to have some help!"

Now that's a clear sign of a woman who is losing energy. The problem is, her husband may hear only the words, "I need help," and not the feelings or issues behind her frustration. Once a man hears the words, "I need help," his natural desire is to solve the problem at hand. Instantly, he's capable of taking over and saying something like this:

"Honey, I'm really glad you brought this up. You know, if you could just get organized around here, you wouldn't be so frustrated. It's about time you got a system of housework like we have at the office. And by the way, are you still taking those vitamin pills we spent all that money for? Are you getting your rest on a regular basis?"

Or worse yet, we men are capable of hitting below the belt and saying something like, "*Honey, do you think you're being disorganized is an indication that you're not spending enough time in God's Word on a regular basis?"*

Lectures are so natural. Particularly when they make us conquering males feel like we're solving a problem. The real problem, though, is that we've missed the deeper message *behind* her words. In fact, if we do give her a management-effectiveness course on cleaning the house, she tends to resent us, not applaud us. That often leads to a man saying something like:

"Well, what's wrong with you? If you don't want my help, then why did you ask me!"

The problem is, *she never was asking for help in the first place!* At least not the type of help that comes from lectures and object lessons. It only sounded that way because he focused on the words alone. Like many women, this wife was sharing her underlying feelings, her hurt, and her need for support, but what she expressed was her frustration. What a woman needs during times of expressed frustration is not a husband's mouth, but his shoulder. She really needs to be comforted and encouraged. She needs energizing—with a nice dose of meaningful touching tossed in.

We need to understand that when someone is going through a trial, they sometimes express that emotional draining of energy through their anger, discouragement, hurt feelings, or anxiety. The last thing a friend, spouse, or child who's hurting wants from us is a lecture, especially one that's delivered in harshness and anger.

Not only females resist or react to lectures or harsh words. Let's say it's been a very frustrating day at the office and a typical man walks in complaining, "This job doesn't pay enough for what they make me go through." In most cases, he's sharing his frustration—not issuing an invitation to be criticized. Not many men would enjoy hearing their wives say, "Yeah, they *don't* pay you enough, all right. You need to get a real job that pays more so we can make ends meet. In fact, I'll tell you what kind of job you *ought* to get. . . ."

The same thing is true with children. Teenagers rarely appreciate coming home after flunking a test and being met with angry, challenging words. I'm not saying that you can't confront a person in love over areas of error in his or her life, but at the *moment of vulnerability,* and particularly in the midst of the crisis itself, what a person needs first is tenderness.

Tenderness acts as a firebreak to an advancing forest fire. Fire-fighters get ahead of the fire, then clear a wide trail free of all "flammable" material. The fire may roar up to the firebreak, but it can't jump across and keep burning. That's one tremendous benefit of tenderness.

It takes work to "strip" an area clear of emotional kindling —particularly when a fiery trial is closing in on us. But we can head off the negative emotions that are coming and keep from getting "burned" if we do. Or, as we mentioned, we can add more fuel to the already burning fire—in the form of lectures.

Kindness is communicating that someone is valuable through our actions.

To use another word picture, lectures act as an electronic suction device that can suck out all our energy, leaving us emotionally, spiritually, and physically drained. I've sat in numerous counseling sessions where a man was criticizing his wife or vice versa, and you can almost hear the suction machine roaring, pulling the life right out of their relationship.

Lectures may seem right, and occasionally they are an appropriate response to a person, but tender, honoring, "edifying" words can head off an argument before it breaks out in our relationship.

Making Tenderness a Habit in Your Home

Okay, I hear what you're saying: "I'd like to be more tenderhearted. But it's still a little abstract. How about several concrete suggestions on how to practice this new gentle habit?"

Ephesians 4:32 is your instruction booklet for becoming a tenderhearted person. In these verses are two powerful ways to be tenderhearted. The first is, "Be kind . . . to one another," then, "forgiving each other, just as God in Christ forgave you."

In other words, when it comes to being tender, kindness, gentleness, and forgiveness are like battery packs. They are what gives tenderness its punch. Let's look at each of these steps more closely.

Have you ever wondered what being "kind" to someone really means? *Kindness is communicating that someone is valuable through our actions.* There are ways to be kind—like visiting friends at the hospital or going to their home after the loss of a loved one. In these cases, kindness is usually best spoken without a word—by a hug, or a gentle act or touch. Our presence alone says, "I'm so sorry; you're very special to me; I'm praying for you." Combine a "kind" act with a tender touch, and the results can be life-changing.

Recently John Trent and I were on a radio program in California talking about the importance of being "tenderhearted," when a man called in and told us an incredible story about the power of silent tenderness.

A few years back, the caller had had a major heart attack. Though he was only in his early fifties at the time, it was so serious, the doctors at the hospital told his wife to notify the family he probably wouldn't live for more than a few days.

When his seventy-year-old father was called, he flew cross-country to be at what he thought was his son's deathbed. The fact that his father had come at all was a tremendous encouragement to his son. In all his life, he had never once heard the words, "I love you," from his father. Deep down, he always felt he was loved, but for years, he had longed to actually hear the words that would prove he was valuable to his father.

"My father never did come right out and say he loved me," he said. "But after he came out to see me in the hospital, I knew he did—and all because of one thing he did when I was lying in that hospital bed."

"What was it he did?" we asked, glued to our headphones.

"When I was in the hospital," the man continued, "my dad walked in and without saying a word, he took my hand and gently held it for over half an hour. He was tender with me for the first time I can ever remember. He still couldn't bring himself to *say,* 'I love you,' but I know now he really did."

We all teared up just listening to the emotion in his voice as he told us his story. As powerful a story as this was, it was "the rest of the story" that hit us the hardest, for the man went on to tell us that he miraculously recovered from his heart attack. But three days after he had come to visit his son in the hospital, the seventy-year-old *father* passed away!

This man shared with us and the entire listening audience, "If my father had never shown me his love by that one tender act, I don't think I would ever have truly known how much he loved me, but that one act of gentleness spoke more to me than anything he could have said. . . ."

His father's actions communicated kindness in its purest form. Without words—simply by his gentle touch—he shouted out the concept of tenderness in words that will forever ring in his son's heart.

Tenderness and Timing

Often the time to give someone a gentle word of encouragement or a meaningful touch is obvious. Sometimes, though, especially for people like me who do not come from a "high touch" background, it's hard to recognize the not-so-obvious times we need to be tender. What do we do then?

I'll never forget what one woman told me:

"If my husband would only put his arms around me and hold me when I'm feeling blue, and not give me a nonstop lecture or pep-talk about 'counting it all joy,' it would transform our marriage."

"Have you ever *told* him what you need?" I asked.

"Are you kidding? He'd be embarrassed and so would I," she laughed.

"This may come as a surprise to you," I said, "but he probably doesn't know how to be tender with you. He's been trained to lecture. Perhaps he needs some training in what genuine tenderness is."

"That makes sense to me," she said. "Many times when I'm crying and upset, he'll ask, 'What do you want me to *do?*' And I just flare up and say, '*If I have to tell you what to do, then that would ruin it!*'"

A husband should ask his wife, and a wife her husband, to define "tenderness" in their own terms. How he should hold her for her to feel safe and loved—when is the best time for her to be soft and sympathetic with him? A wife or husband shouldn't expect his or her mate to be a mind-reader when it comes to meeting the very important needs in this area.

Most of us aren't good emotional mind-readers anyway, and too few of us come from comforting backgrounds so we don't know the nonverbal signals that say, "Please hold me." While attempting to talk about being tender may seem awkward at first, just being willing to talk about this much needed area tends to bring energy and life to a relationship.

Using Tenderness as an Important Protective Tool for Your Children

We've talked about the need both a woman and man have for tenderness—a willingness to decrease our lectures and increase our tender expressions of love, but if gentleness is a key to marital growth, it is equally powerful when practiced between parent and child.

I know a man who had a very strained relationship with his teenage daughter. Recently, she had been dating a boy he did not care for, and her father had been extremely cutting in expressing his feelings. In fact, every time he brought up the subject (and everything they talked about seemed somehow to lead into it), their exchanges became loud and dishonoring.

At our seminar, he realized for the first time how important tenderness was, and how little of it he was showing to his daughter. He decided that he had to begin putting on the new nature of encouraging words. He still disapproved of the boy his daughter was dating—but he didn't have to blast his daughter at close range every night with angry words just to vent his frustration.

That very night at the seminar, he prayed to be more gentle with his daughter—and the opportunity to put his prayer into practice came to pass. After he got home from the seminar, he walked upstairs to get ready for bed. He passed by his daughter's room and heard her crying as she talked over the phone. It was the boyfriend he disliked so much calling, and it was obvious that they were breaking up over the phone.

Inside, this father felt like jumping for joy. He couldn't think of anything better than what was happening, but something stopped him as he began to enter his daughter's room and pull out the standard "I told you he was a jerk" lecture. As he heard his daughter crying as she hung up the phone, he remembered his vow to God to bring tenderness into his home.

He walked slowly into her room and gently sat down on her bed. She lay with her head buried in her pillow. When she realized he was sitting next to her, she instantly bristled—figuring she knew what was coming, but her father said nothing. Instead, he quietly held her as she cried. When she finally stopped, she looked up at him and said, "Daddy, thank you for just being here with me."

As my friend walked out of his daughter's room, his emotions hit like a sheet of ice water. He realized that he had been so distant from his daughter for so long, it had been years since she had called him "Daddy."

The Master's Use of Tenderness

Our children, our spouse, our close friends, and each of us have a physical and emotional need for tenderness, expressed as words or as meaningful touches. Kindness comes from *honoring* that need in the lives of our loved ones and demonstrating that *love* by doing all we can to fulfill it.

The main reason I've mentioned tenderness and kindness as the second act of love is its great importance in communicating value to others. One of the loudest cries we hear among men, women, and children is the desperate plea for tenderness and gentleness from people who love them.

Jesus was the master at using tenderness to express high value to others. Remember how He greeted the children who came to Him? Mobbed by onlookers and protected by His disciples, Jesus could have easily waved to them from a distance or just ignored them altogether. He did neither. Jesus touched and blessed the children (Matthew 19:13).

His tenderness in dealing with others was graphically displayed when a leper came to Him, described in Luke as a man "with leprosy. . . . Jesus reached out his hand and touched the man" (Matthew 8:3).

To touch a leper in Jesus' day was to flirt with contracting the most terrifying terminal illness known to the biblical world. To have leprosy was to die shunned and untouched, driven away from civilization until finally, mercifully, you died. People in

Jesus' day would literally not get within a stone's throw of a leper—and Jewish law allowed stones to be thrown at a leper if he or she did come any closer.[1]

Yet even before Jesus spoke to the leper, He reached out His hand and touched him. Can't you imagine the people around Jesus recoiling from the sight? *No one* would touch a leper. Yet Jesus, in His wisdom, knew the man's heart, and his need for both spiritual cleansing and physical tenderness (see Matthew 8:1–3 and Luke 5:12).

When Tenderness Is Tied to Forgiveness

I've mentioned several aspects of being "tenderhearted." The first is kindness, and the second is meaningful touch. There is a third element of tenderness, though, that can have incredible power in relationships, namely *forgiving* one another.

It was years before I discovered what "forgiveness" means in the original language, but its meaning has always stayed with me. The literal picture behind the word "forgiveness" is untying a knot.[2] In the confines of everyday life, we can all get tied up in knots because of what others (especially our spouses) have said or done to us.

Part of forgiving someone is actually helping them become untied from their frustrations. No matter if the offense was big or small, forgiveness is saying, "I want this person free! Released! Untied!" For those who want to give encouragement and energy to their spouse or someone else, it can have incredible results.

A doctor friend of mine told me a story about a man who was dying in a nearby hospital. He was very, very ill, and the doctors could give him only hours to live. To all around him he seemed to have given up the fight, but that afternoon, this man's brother appeared in his room. The brother was the same one with whom he had never gotten along and who had always been rough and unkind to him growing up.

"I . . . I just come to ask if you will forgive me for the way I have treated you," the man's brother blurted out. Then he did an extraordinary thing. The rough brother took his dying brother's hand and told him he loved him.

At first when the brother sat and held the sick man's hand, it was rigid and stiff from the years of resentment he'd harbored against his brother. But remarkably, in the moments that followed those extraordinary words, his hand relaxed and the strength of his grip increased.

A moment before, he had felt so weak he did not think he could make it through the night. Yet after that visit, the sick brother steadily recuperated. The doctor couldn't pin-point any single thing that led to his rapid recovery. He told me that there could have been a number of physiological reasons for the man's strange and quick recovery. However, he felt sure that his brother's appearance and this man's recovery were not accidental. Namely, his brother's touch—and especially his words of forgiveness—were an important part in giving this man the energy to have a fighting chance to live.[3]

Are you still hesitating at knocking down old walls of anger and putting in a doorway of tenderness to your home—a door that opens to energizing words, gentle touching, and courageous forgiving? Then start this way.

Begin by spending time listening to your spouse, your child, or your friend—without any lectures. Then, the next time they show signs of losing energy in the midst of a discouraging or pressure-packed time, walk over and, without a word, put your arm around them or gently put your hand on their shoulder.

If you must say something, just say something like, "I can see you're really hurting, and I want you to know that I'm very sorry," or "I'm not sure if I can help you in what you're going through, but I love you, and if you're up to it, you can tell me how you're feeling." Particularly if tenderness hasn't been a hallmark of your relationships, you'll be amazed at how quickly being soft with people in this way can bring positive results.

I often tell people it doesn't take great wisdom to energize a person, but it does take sixty seconds. That's the amount of time it takes to walk over and gently hold someone we love. A few seconds invested in being tender can not only help our relationships —it can become catching in a home as well. But the amazing part of tenderness is that it works wonders even when we're not near our loved ones.

Once, while I was on a speaking trip, my schedule put me out of town on Mother's Day. I called Norma on that special day, telling her how sorry I was not to be there.

"How's your day been?" I asked.

"It's been a horrible day. Mike and Greg have been terrible to me, and everything's gone wrong." Resisting the temptation to tell her "exactly" what to do to make things "right," I simply listened. Soon, she slowed down, and I could tell she felt a bit better.

So I said, "Oh, I wish I was there with you." I said, "I'd just give you a great big hug, ummmmmmmm! In fact," I said, "put your arms around yourself and give yourself a big hug for me. Ummmmmmmmm!"

Now I didn't expect her to say, "Oh, you're such a wonderful husband. Thanks for being so tender." Wives usually don't say that when they're hurting. You've got to do this by faith because there may be times when they say, "Aw, you don't mean that!"

Just as I was getting off the phone, I heard the sound of a door opening, and Norma gasping in delight, "Ohhhh, Greg! They're so beautiful!"

"What's so beautiful?" I asked.

"Greggy brought me flowers for Mother's Day!"

"Hey, that's great," I said. Then it dawned on me. "Say, Norma. Let me talk to Greg a minute."

Once my son was on the phone, I asked him where he got the flowers.

"Oh, I ordered them from a florist."

At that time he was only about thirteen years old, so I said, "But how did you pay for them?"

He said, "Oh, I just used your charge card, Dad."

Let's just say, I tried to remember all about showing tenderness to my son when I got home.

Tenderness is catching when it's communicated in a home —whether it's shared by an encouraging word, a gentle touch, or with an act of forgiveness. And the result between loved ones is energy—and another important way to build a loving, lasting relationship.

It takes practice and relying on God's strength to put on this important aspect of our new nature, but it's worth every ounce of effort we put into harnessing the power of tenderness to energize our loved ones.

As I mentioned earlier, energizing your mate by being gentle and tender is an important act of love, but it doesn't stand alone. It's just one of several ways we can put honor into action and show others how much we love them.

In the next chapter, I'm going to discuss an unbelievably powerful emotion that all of us have, yet few of us master. It's as much a part of our human makeup as our instinct for survival. It shapes the course of human events just as a roaring river carves canyons in sandstone. In addition, it has the potential to make our lives more meaningful and our relationships more fulfilling—or it can literally destroy the very things that are most precious to us.

Understanding it, like understanding the importance of tenderness, is absolutely essential if we want to honor God and others. Let's discover the secrets to mastering what may be the most powerful of all human emotions.

6

A Closed Spirit: Overcoming a Major Destroyer of Relationships

Late one night, while I was sound asleep, the phone rang. It was a man calling long distance who had gotten my number from a close friend. As I was struggling to wake up, he said, "Gary, I'm sorry to call so late, but my wife has left me. Actually, she's thrown me out of the house! She's so hostile toward me, it shocked me. I really didn't see it coming. We've been married almost twenty-five years, and now she's put me out on the street!"

As he continued, he asked, "Could you help me get back together with my wife?"

He sounded so desperate over the phone, I decided to help him if I could. So I asked, "Before I know if I can do anything to help you, I need to talk to your wife."

He immediately shot back, "That's impossible. She's not talking to me. She's not even talking to anyone who knows me. Gary, I don't think you understand. She *hates* me. You have no idea how much she hates me. She has a court order against me right now so that I can't even get into my own home!"

Having talked with many people in similar situations, I replied, "Well, I'll tell you what. I've never been turned down yet by a woman I've called. This could be the first time, but I'm willing to give it a try if you are."

After a brief pause, he said, "Well . . . I have nothing to lose, but please call me back the minute you talk to her and let me know what happens."

The next morning, I did call his wife. When she answered, I said, "Hello, I'm Gary Smalley. Your husband called me last night and really wanted some help, but I told him that in order to do anything for him, I would need to talk to someone who knows him as well as his wife. I was wondering. Could you just spend a couple of minutes with me, helping me understand your husband and why it was so difficult to live with him?"

Instantly she said, "Ohhhhh, I hate that man so much! I don't want to talk about him. In fact, even thinking about him upsets me."

I said, "It must have been horrible living with a man like that."

"You have no *idea* how horrible it was to live with that guy," she steamed. "He was so controlling, it was like I had to get *permission* to go to the bathroom!"

"How did you endure that kind of treatment for so many years?" I asked, trying everything I could just to keep her on the phone!

"I don't know how I managed, and now you're getting me to talk about him—and I don't want to talk about him!"

In the end, she did share several specific things this man had done—beginning with their honeymoon. Many were small, inconsiderate actions that had piled up hurt feelings until molehills became mountains.

After talking with her for only five minutes, I thanked her profusely for sharing her thoughts and time with me and hung up. Immediately I called her husband.

"Did you talk with her?" he asked.

"Yes," I said, "and you're right. *You are in big trouble!*"

Over the years, I could number in the hundreds the husbands who have called or written with a similar story. In each case, the man never "realized" that he was in such bad shape until his marital world came crashing down around him.

While there are unique situations with each person that has called, I can think of one common element in every case. In fact, it's one of the major destroyers of families—*unresolved anger.* Anger, though, is such a "normal" human emotion. How can it be so devastating to a relationship?

Opening the Door to a Major Destroyer of Families

Recently, a close friend told me about a rock star who brought home a cute little lion cub to raise on his ranch in Tennessee. Of course, he had to hire a lawyer to convince the local zoning board to give him a special permit to own a wild animal as a "pet," but with money being no object, he managed to get that detail taken care of quickly enough.

For several years his "tame" lion was quite a hit with his house guests. It never acted like a dangerous predator, only like a big, playful pet. Then one day without warning, a parent's worst nightmare became this man's reality.

His little two-year-old son was playing near the lion cage. The parents heard his screams for help from inside the house, but there was nothing they could do. The lion had broken out of his cage and brutally mauled the little boy before running off into the woods. In a terrible tragedy, the man's son died before they could even get him to the hospital.

I'm sure this man loved his son, and having raised the lion from a cub, he probably never consciously thought that it would one day rob his child of life. But all the reasoning in the world on why it was "safe" to keep a wild animal around the house couldn't erase that animal's nature. For centuries, people have learned the hard way about the dark side of a lion's nature. By allowing a predator into his home, the man was setting the stage for a potential tragedy.

I can't think of a single person I've met who would willingly expose a child or spouse to the fury of a full-grown lion, but I know of many husbands and wives who are letting another deadly killer walk right through their front door without a fight —*unhealthy, unresolved anger.*

Anger can rip the heart right out of a relationship. Without exaggeration, every hour that anger is allowed to stay in a person's life, it acts like an emotional time bomb ticking down to detonation. Like a terrorist bomb placed in an innocent looking shopping bag, it cares nothing for whom it hurts or eventually kills.

"But everyone gets angry. Even Jesus got 'angry' at the people in the temple," some may say. While this is certainly true, there is a major difference between righteous anger (that can have a "corrective" effect on error), and the kind of unhealthy anger that grows wild and, unchallenged, leads to destructive conflicts.

Like that rock star's lion, anger inside a person can never be made a "tame" emotion. Even "righteous anger" can become corrupted if a person is not very, very careful.

The man who called me in the middle of the night learned a crucial skill needed in any healthy relationship. In his case it proved to be a life-saving skill. He realized that by letting anger build up in his wife's life—anger that he was directly responsible for provoking—he had *closed her spirit* toward him.[1]

Like that innocent looking lion cub, he had let his insensitive acts pile up until they finally broke full force on the relationship. What he learned, however, actually helped him begin to repair the damage. He learned how to reopen his wife's closed spirit by getting the anger out of her life—and it made a dramatic change in his situation.

... we'll never be successful in our most important relationships until we learn how to drain the anger out of another person's life.

Unfortunately, my late night friend is not unique. Parents can sometimes leave anger in a child's life when he or she is young, closing the child's spirit to them tightly. These same parents then see that deep-seated anger turns into resistance and rebelliousness in their teenagers. Employers can even close the spirit of their employees and soon meet resistance and a stiffening will in them.

Even though anger is potentially destructive, it can be dealt with, even in cases that may seem humanly impossible. That's what we're going to talk about in this chapter. We don't have to live in continual disharmony with others. We can literally be in harmony with those around us the majority of the time.

But we'll never be successful in our most important relationships until we learn to drain the anger out of another person's life. It's absolutely crucial that we learn how to "open" a person's closed spirit and get back in harmony with them again.

That begins as we learn the skills of putting unresolved anger out of our homes.

Putting Unresolved Anger out of a Home

First, let me define what I mean by unhealthy anger. *Selfish anger is the negative emotion we feel when a person or situation has failed to meet our needs, blocked our goals, or fallen short of our expectations.* It's what we feel when we've placed our needs, wants, and desires ahead of anyone else's. Then we become frustrated if those around us don't react the way we want them to. Let me illustrate more clearly what I mean by "negative" anger by giving a hypothetical example from my own home.

If I walk through the door one night and blast Norma for being five minutes late with dinner, I'd be absolutely wrong. It certainly isn't a sin for her to have dinner ready a few minutes late, and so to "let her have it" only demonstrates I was more interested in my own stomach than her welfare. That's the real problem with anger; it puts "me" ahead of everyone else and shows its displeasure whenever "I" don't get my way.

To clarify even further, there are two things we need to keep in balance. *First,* there is a "righteous" anger that stands up against sin. In Ephesians 4, there is a clear command to be angry over the things that would grieve God's heart (often the kinds of things that fill our newspapers and evening news). "*. . . But in your anger do not sin*" (Ephesians 4:26). Biblically, two wrongs never equal one right. Even if we become righteously angry over some anger-producing situation in our life or the lives of others, we are never justified in reacting in a sinful way.

Second, try as we might by logical reason, we will not always be able to avoid an immediate emotion. If someone accidentally steps on our foot or cuts in front of us on the freeway, our instantaneous reaction may be anger. There's nothing wrong or sinful about anger at this point. But when we let anger remain in our lives, or when we take its energy and direct it toward another person to hurt them, we move from a normal, healthy feeling to a destructive one.

Apply what Martin Luther used to say to negative thoughts: "You can't keep the birds from flying over your head . . . but you can keep them from building a nest in your hair!" We may not be able to keep anger from cropping up as an instantaneous and instinctive reaction to some pain or problem, but we can make a decision to keep it from staying in our lives and poisoning our attitudes or the attitudes of our loved ones.

Putting Healthy Limits on an Unhealthy Emotion

Let's go back to the couple with whom we started this chapter. From the time they were first married, this husband never placed any boundaries around his anger. Whenever his wife blocked any of his goals, or slowed him down in any way, he blasted her without regard to the emotional impact of his words.

One could say that his wife should have been more "spiritually mature" and should not have been hurt by his angry outbursts, but in real life, after a constant stream of angry words and actions over the years, she began to wilt under his treatment. This wife didn't realize that it is possible to be free from anger on our own, as you'll see in Chapters 13 and 14, and her husband didn't realize two things about anger in a home that can cripple a relationship.

1. Anger Eats Away at a Person's Health

Inside the brain, the decision you make to harbor negative feelings toward others can set off a series of physical events you would do well to avoid. When a person becomes angry, his body goes on "full alert." When the inner brain gets the message that there's a stressful situation out there, it doesn't ask questions—it reacts. Your body can easily release as many chemicals and disrupt as many bodily functions when you are angry with your spouse as if you're being attacked by a wild animal.[2]

After several years of living with an angry man, the woman in our story began manifesting several of the symptoms of a person with deep-seated anger locked inside them: early morning awakening, depression, tension, grinding teeth, an unexplainable sense of dread, jumpiness, and increased irritability.[3] None of these negative outworkings of anger is physically helpful. In fact, unresolved anger actually pulls a person's resistance to illness down.

When a person's body is constantly tense and on edge (for unrighteous anger never fully lets a person relax—even in his sleep), this tension will inevitably begin to wear the person down. That's when really undesirable things begin to happen physiologically, such as clinical depression, colitis, bleeding ulcers, anxiety attacks, lowered resistance to colds and flu, and heart and respiratory failure. Several researchers even believe that some types of cancer result from the mega-doses of stress that unhealthy anger carries with it.[4]

Perhaps all these physical manifestations of anger are behind the first commandment with a promise, "Honor your father and mother, so that you may live long . . . "(Exodus 20:12). Anger, however, doesn't just contribute to a poor grade on a health report card. It can also keep us "in the dark" when it comes to loving God and others.

2. The Greatest Problem of All

In 1 John 2:9–11, the apostle says that continual anger toward another results in losing the ability to live in God's light. Being angry with our brother pushes us into darkness—completely isolated from the light of His love. When we live with anger—or provoke it in the hearts of others—we pull a veil of darkness across our eyes that blinds us to the damage we're doing to others.

In part, this is why so many angry men or women don't "wake up" to the damage they've done to a home until the very walls of the family are falling down around them. The anger they have spewed out at members of their family has doubled back and blinded them to God's love and that of others.

Walking consistently in darkness prevents us from being lovingly sensitive toward others. It also kills any interest we have in studying God's Word and puts an icy chill on our desire to pray. Further, it robs us of any desire to please and honor Him or to experience His joy, contentment, and peace.

I've met a number of people who, after years of attending church and seeking God, have still not found peace. And after getting to know them better, the major reason for their failure in many cases is deep-seated anger.[5] They are unwilling to forgive or seek forgiveness, and as a result they hide pockets of darkness inside their lives—black holes in their souls that can expand throughout the years.

Anger does tremendous damage to a person physically and spiritually—and that's not all. It also goes to the emotional heart of a relationship and can bury any feelings of warmth or attachment in its icy darkness as well.

How can we tell that anger has begun to attack our relationship, pushing it into darkness? Our loved ones will begin to withdraw from us on every level—physical, emotional, and spiritual. That withdrawal is something I call a *closed spirit*. Left unchecked, this spirit can drain every bit of sparkle and vitality out of our families and leave them empty, wounded, and alone.

Recognizing a Person's Spirit

Let me get more specific about what I mean about a person's "spirit." It can be explained this way. When you meet someone for the first time, you interact with him on three levels—first with your spirit, then with your soul, and finally with your body.

Imagine with me that I walk up to a person at one of our seminars and meet him for the first time. Before ever we spoke a word, the first thing that would "touch" would be our *spirit*. I'm defining the "spirit" of a person as the innermost, intangible part of our being that tells us if there is any natural connection or friction between us. It's also that part of us that relates to God at times when words aren't enough.

Next, is the *soul* (the Greek word for soul is "psyche"). The soul is made up of three inseparable parts: the intellect, the will, and the emotions. When we communicate with a person, we engage at all three of these levels. For example, with the person I met at the seminar, we would no doubt exchange words when we meet. Later, if we come to know each other better, we would exchange ideas or even dreams. In that way, our "souls" would have touched or interacted.[6]

If our relationship entered the third level, and if it were appropriate, we could physically touch. For example, you and I would probably shake hands if we met for the first time. Now we've had a complete relationship—body, soul, and spirit. Granted, at this point it's a shallow relationship, but at least it has all the elements of a "total" relationship.

In our seminar, I use my hand to illustrate the open and closed spirit concept. To make sure you understand this principle, hold out your own hand right now.

Look at the palm of your hand, with the fingers spread wide apart. Let's say that the fingers wiggling around freely are the spirit of a person. They're the first thing to reach out and touch others. The semicircular ridge where the fingers meet the palm of the hand could represent the soul where people meet intellectually. And the very center of the palm could stand for the body.

When you are happy and all is well in your relationship with your mate, child, or friend, those fingers are wiggling and happy. The palm is open and exposed—ready to reach out and even to lovingly hold someone else's hand. An open hand could have represented the woman whose story we told at the beginning of this chapter. When she first married, she was open and eager for love.

If I offend a person or provoke him to anger, however, that open hand can begin to close. Take time to give yourself a living object lesson. Close your hand slowly and notice what happens. The spirit begins to close over the soul and the body. If it is allowed to tighten up all the way, what do you have? A closed fist —the world-wide symbol of anger and defiance. In short, you have what that man had when he called me in the middle of the night—a wife who was so deeply hurt and so "closed" to him that she lashed back with the force of a rock-hard fist.

As long as everything is healthy in a relationship, the hand is open, the fingers wiggling and happy. The spirit is open and responsive. But hurtful words and actions—allowed to grow into a bitter spirit—can one day lead to our being shut out of someone's life completely.

How Do We Close a Person's Spirit?

While there are probably hundreds of ways to offend someone—and close his or her spirit—we consistently see several that top the list. To repeat just a few, we can close a person's spirit by—

- Speaking harsh words
- Belittling a person's opinions
- Being unwilling to admit that we're wrong
- Taking a person for granted
- Making jokes or sarcastic comments at the other person's expense
- Not trusting a person
- Forcing a person to do something he's uncomfortable with
- Being rude to that person in front of others
- Ignoring a person's genuine needs as unimportant or not nearly as valuable as our own

That's just a sample of the "hit list" of actions that can close a person's spirit.[7] Our loved ones could probably make up their own list. We may not even be aware of what we do to deposit anger into their lives. When it comes to relationships, an important rule of thumb is, *whatever dishonors another person usually closes his spirit.*

While it wasn't my intended goal, I got an early start in closing Norma's spirit. When we were first married, I spoke at a number of youth groups. We were still in college, and we had no children, so Norma always went along with me to these meetings.

I thought I was quite funny at the time, and I would crack jokes at Norma's expense, totally unaware of how it was affecting her spirit. I would say things like, "Oh, it sure is great being married to Norma. She treats me just like a god! Every morning she serves me burnt offerings."

That would get big laughs. So then I'd follow up with something like, "Being married to Norma is just like being married to an angel—she's always up in the air harping about something and she never has an earthly thing to wear!"

And if I was really on a roll, I could always tell the kids about the time I pulled up to the airport with Norma and a sky cap asked, "Can I help you with your bag?" And I said, "No, thanks, she can walk." Later, in the car, you can guess what would happen.

Norma would often say, "I really didn't appreciate your jokes, Gary." To which I'd impatiently wave my hand, and say, "Oh, lighten up. You're *sooooo* sensitive!" I didn't realize it at the time, but each sarcastic comment was beginning to close her spirit to me.

Once again, part of the problem lies with the differences between men and women. Men are usually not aware that God has created most women with a highly sensitive spirit to sarcasm and criticism. I know I wasn't aware of this very important natural difference—particularly during that first important year of marriage.

My Own Valentine's Day Massacre

Six months or so after our wedding, Valentine's Day rolled around. It was our first Valentine's Day as a married couple and Norma had spent hours preparing a fancy meal just for me. In her mind as she was laboring over a hot stove, she was thinking thoughts like . . .

"It's Valentine's Day, and my new husband is going to be coming through the door any minute. He'll have a romantic card for me, and then we'll enjoy a memorable time together!"

What I did was certainly memorable—but it produced the kind of memory I'd like to forget. I called at two o'clock in the afternoon and said "Hon', I forgot to tell you something this morning. I've got a basketball game I'm going to play in tonight."

I could sense the surprise in her voice as she responded, "But this is Valentine's Day!"

"I know, I know, but this game is *really* important."

Then Norma said,

"But I've already made this special dinner, and I've got the new tablecloth on, and candles set out, and . . . and . . ."

"Norma, I have to go to this game. I gave some of the guys my *word* that I'd be there." (Which meant that I wasn't about to embarrass myself by calling up my friends and telling them I had to stay home with my wife instead of playing basketball.)

For a long time, there was only silence on the other end of the phone. Although I'm ashamed of it now, do you know what I thought at the time? *Oh, no. I have a strong-willed woman on my hands!* I mistook a closing spirit for a strong will.

Right then I decided I might as well take advantage of this tailor-made opportunity to straighten her out. So, in a controlled, but firm, voice, I said, "Now, Norma, you know that I'm going into the ministry, *right*? One of the very important things that the Bible says is the wife should submit to her husband . . . ."

I'm sure you know how well my lecture went over. Her spirit began to close on me that very moment because of my total insensitivity—only I didn't realize it at the time. I was so blinded by my own self-interest, I couldn't see the negative writing on the walls of her life, though I would one day be forced to read it.

Bit by bit, month by month, I did more and more of these "little," insensitive things until I knocked the sparkle right out of her precious eyes. It's difficult for me, even after all these years, to think about how unaware I was of her spirit—and how insensitive and wrong I was.

The tragedy is, the more a man steps on the spirit of his wife, the more resistant she becomes toward him. The more resistant she becomes to him, the more he closes his spirit toward her. Soon, you have a vicious circle of two people in the same home who have made a public vow to love each other—now living under a private pledge to have a closed fist, not an open hand. As

I close my spirit to another person, what happens? It closes up my soul and my body as well.

"But how do I know that I'm actually closing someone's spirit?" The state of a child's spirit is the easiest to recognize, because children are not as practiced at hiding their real emotions. When children become closed to us in their souls, they disagree with everything we say, lose their desire to be "with the family," and seem to love to argue. Physically, they stop touching us, or they even resist our touch under any and all circumstances. They may even turn their backs on us when they see us.

To us, our remark may mean nothing. We may not even remember it. To us, our words may seem as light as a pebble. If I dropped a pebble on my spouse's or child's foot, I might think it should bounce right off without their notice. But for our loved ones, what is a "pebble" to us might be a ten-pound weight. And we just dropped it right on their barefoot toes!

Common Marks of a Closed Spirit

Because it's difficult for many of us to recognize when we've closed a family member's spirit, it's worth taking a moment to learn four common warning signs.

Warning sign number one *is a feeling of tension between you that you can't explain away.* That may be the spirit closing.

Warning sign number two *is an argumentative attitude.* They may resist discussing just about anything. They might avoid you, never ask for your advice, or criticize you for little or no reason. Before long, you can say the moon comes up at night and the sun in the day, and they'll find a way to disagree.

Some of us have worked for a boss who has deeply offended us. We know what it's like to disagree with anything he says—even before he says anything! If I have my spirit closed toward someone, I can have negative thoughts whenever I see that person.

The same thing happens when you step on the spirit of your children. Typically, they become resistant. It's the basic attitude of a persistently strong-willed child. Almost all toddlers (and most other kids of various ages) can go through "stages" of being strong-willed. If you win the battle early, then you can avoid facing many battles later in life.[8]

There is a major difference, though, in a child who is going through the normal "stages" of challenging mom and dad, and one who is retaliating out of anger by being stubborn or "resistant." You can tell a closed-fist child to take the trash out, and he won't be "typically" slow about it—he'll be blatantly defiant. "No, I'm *not* going to do it. You do it yourself or make someone else do it."

Warning sign number three *is a loss of physical intimacy.* Hugs and kisses? Forget it; your loved one probably won't want to get within a block of you. Almost all children go through times when "hugging" mom and dad isn't "cool" (or "hot," or "rad"). But even during these times, if parents are persistent and creative, they can fill up their child's "touch" bank with quick hugs and playful wrestling (with the guys). If, on the other hand, his or her spirit is closed to you, it'll be like an armed guard in front of the bank!

Close a spouse's spirit, and watch the romantic feelings all but evaporate. I've had a number of women tell me that emotionally they felt like prostitutes when their spirit was closed to their husbands and they were involved sexually anyway.

I've heard husbands growl, "That woman is totally uninterested or unresponsive!" Yet he may be the primary cause of her low level of sexual response as the one closing her spirit. Physical intimacy for a woman is spirit, soul, and body, not just body alone. All three levels have to be interrelated, otherwise any sexual response, for both men and women, is, at best, mechanical and, at worst, dysfunctional.

Warning sign number four is *negative nonverbal signals.* If a person's spirit is closing toward you, his facial expressions may even be more negative than his words. Physically, he may pull away from you, leave the door to his room shut consistently for "privacy," or even turn his back on you in the middle of a conversation. If your children resent being at home—especially being alone with you—that too may be a sign of a closed spirit.

A Window of Hope

My purpose in writing about a closed spirit is not to heap guilt on spouses or parents who may find themselves battling a fist rather than an opened palm. It is, rather, to give people hope. As I have tried to share in detail, things I've done to both my wife and children have closed their spirits to me for a short time, but the key to maintaining strong relationships over the years is to be able to reopen a loved one's closed spirit. It reminds me of what I had to do with my oldest son, Greg, when he was just a young boy.

Five Attitudes That Can
Help to Open a Loved One's Heart

In my parenting book, *The Key to Your Child's Heart,* I tell about my son Greg when he was about five or six years old. At the time, I worked for a large Christian organization, and I was often on the phone with pastors across the country. This also meant that I would have to take calls at home from a number of Christian leaders at times, so I made a rule in our home that couldn't be violated—nobody screams when I'm on the phone!

One evening I was in my bedroom on a long-distance phone call to a distinguished senior pastor. Suddenly, my son, Greg, let out a blood-curdling scream from the bathroom. He came running into the bedroom, screaming so loudly that I couldn't hear the person on the other end of the line.

"Hush!" I signaled to him emphatically, putting my hand over the mouthpiece of the phone, "Can't you see I'm on the phone?"

But Greg continued screaming, so I quickly ended my phone conversation, telling the person I'd have to call him back later.

When I hung up the phone, I grabbed Greg by the arm. "Why are you screaming and running around the house?" I demanded. "Couldn't you see I was on the phone?"

Without waiting for an answer, I hustled him down the hall and said, "You get into your bedroom right now." Still crying, Greg hurried into his room. Once we were inside, I picked up the little ruler that the kids had all helped to decorate (they affectionately named it the "teacher"). For breaking my inviolate rule, I swatted him on the bottom.

It was our practice after a spanking to hold the child and hug away any resentment, but this time, something took place that startled me.

"Come here so I can hug you," I said.

"No," he said, still crying, and the look in his eyes said, "I hate you." He backed away from me to let me know that he didn't want me to touch me at all.

Then after all that had happened, it hit me.

"Greg, why were you crying?"

With his little voice heaving with his sobs, he said, "I fell in the bathroom and hurt my ear and when you pushed me on the bed, I hurt it again."

He was hurt. That's why he was crying! Why hadn't I asked him earlier? Now I not only felt awful, I also felt like a child abuser. I knew I had closed Greg's spirit tightly at that moment, and if I didn't do something, it could leave an emotional scar on our relationship.

Convicted to my very heart, I got down on my knees.

"Greggy," I said in the softest voice I could. "I'm so sorry that I didn't ask you what was wrong or why you were screaming. You didn't deserve a spanking. I'm the one that deserves to be spanked." I held out the little stick to him, but he dropped it and backed up. It was obvious that he still didn't want any part of me.

So I said, "Greg, I was so wrong. Maybe you can't do it right now, but I wonder if you could forgive me? Would you?" Then it was as if his little heart melted, and he rushed into my arms. I fell back onto the bed with him in my arms and just held him tightly as his sobs slowly turned into regular breathing.

After a long time, I asked him again to be sure, "Greg, are you sure you've forgiven Daddy?"

He just patted me and said, "Oh, Daddy, we all make mistakes."

Do you know what that told me about Greg? It told me that Greg was opening his spirit to me. He was touching me. We were talking. His feelings were coming back. His body, soul, and spirit were reopening.

What was happening between us as we held each other was the result of five attitudes that work together to help open the spirit of a person. Let me state clearly, *these are not steps.* You can't mechanically go down the list and expect to wipe away every hurt or draw out all the anger in a relationship. With Greg, it took only a half-hour to reopen his spirit and put us back into harmony. With Norma, it took almost two years of consistently applying these attitudes to reverse all the closing of her spirit I had done.

The important thing is not the time it takes, but the decision and commitment to do whatever it takes to come back into harmony with a person *to release as much anger as possible.* For years now, I have practiced these same attitudes with my wife and each of my children. They have been a tremendous help in making sure anger is drained out of our home each day. I know they can be an encouragement in your home as well.

Five Attitudes to Reopen a Person's Spirit

1. Become soft and tender with the person

Proverbs says, "A gentle answer turns away wrath" (Proverbs 15:1). My whole problem with Greg started when I became harsh and unreasoning. Things began to turn around when my tone of voice softened along with my spirit. My attitude, nonverbals, and voice said I cared about him. Sometimes softness alone can open a person's spirit. That's the whole message of Chapter 5.

2. Understand, as much as possible, what the other person has gone through (remember, listen to what is said; do not react to the words used)

I would have cried if I had fallen in the bathtub, too. Then to get a spanking on top of that? So I showed Greg by my words, as best I could, that I understood what he felt. I talked with him about how awful it must have been, all the time being careful not to "react" to something he said defensively.

3. Acknowledge that the person is hurting, and be sure to admit any wrong in provoking anger

"Greg," I said, "I was so wrong." As a parent (or a spouse), it can be very hard to say those words at times, but as it did with Greg, it can work wonders. Admitting we are wrong (when we clearly are) is like drilling a hole in our loved one's "anger bucket" and allowing that unhealthy emotion to drain away. Once they hear us admit it, the anger has a way to escape from their lives.

Sometimes we may not think we are wrong, but our attitude might be. Or, it may be the way we've done something that's offensive. If my attitude is harsh and angry when I tell my wife about a legitimate problem, I'm still wrong. ". . . Man's anger (or that of a woman) does not bring about the righteous life that God desires" (James 1:20). Stopping short of admitting we were wrong leaves a dangerous gap between you and your child or mate that may not mend quickly—or at all.

4. Touch the other person gently

If you step on your mate's spirit at ten o'clock at night (or in the morning) and then you get into bed and expect to be amorous, what's likely to happen? Your spouse may move way over to the other side of the bed. That's when you'll hear that she has a headache, it's the wrong year, or she just doesn't want to be touched. The nonverbal message, "No touchie the toes," may mean, "My spirit is closing to you."

If you try to touch someone with a closed spirit, you will find out just how deep the hurt is. If a woman has only been touched in anger or to meet her husband's sexual needs, she may resent *any* touch and pull away, or be stiff and unbending. But persistent softness—expressed in meaningful touches apart from any demands for sex—can go a long way toward draining anger and negative feelings from a relationship.

5. Seek forgiveness—and wait for a response

Say something like, "Could you forgive me? I've disappointed you so many times. I know I don't deserve to be forgiven, but could you try?" or "I don't want you all tied up in knots, not responding to me at all. I know I have a million miles to go before I get everything together in my life, but I love you very much, and I ask you to forgive me. Will you forgive me?"

Try to get a positive response from the person before you quit, but if you need to, start with the first loving attitude of being soft and work your way back down to forgiveness again. Remember, too, *don't just respond to your loved one's words.* In the heat of battle, or if you've deeply hurt someone, that person may say something in retaliation to hurt you: "That's right," they might respond. "You *don't* deserve to be forgiven. I really don't know how I live with you when you mess up so often."

For many people, men in particular, hearing words that may hit below the belt can set off a defensive lecture—or even be an invitation to another round of angry retaliation. But those men and women who are wise enough to reopen a person's spirit have to learn to listen beyond the words to the hurt feelings behind the words.

There have been times when I felt something Norma said to me was unfair, even though I was trying to be soft and ask her to forgive me. Perhaps she misinterpreted my motives or even questioned my character in the process, but when you're asking another person to forgive you, it's not the time to get into a lecture on the precise wording of the problem. Your focus should be on draining away the anger and not on compounding it.

The senior pastor at our home church is an exceptional individual. One of the many things we've learned from Darryl DelHousaye is a biblical admonition on dealing with anger. I've found it to be universally true in relationships. Time and again, Darryl has said from the pulpit, concerning anger and the need for forgiveness, "Biblically, the stronger person always initiates the peace." Are you willing to be the "strong" one who seeks to set things right in a relationship? Sometimes it takes a strong act of the will not to react to someone's words. Remember—in most cases it was hasty reactions that helped to close that person's spirit in the first place.

Biblically, the stronger person always initiates the peace.

Untying Our Own Knots

There is an important reason why forgiveness plays such a pivotal part in opening a person's spirit. It has to do with the very way the Bible defines the word. In the original biblical language, remember, the word for forgiveness means "to release, set free, to untie."

With that picture in mind, when we say or do something offensive to other people, we are actually helping, emotionally and spiritually, to tie them in knots. Perhaps what we've done has come as the result of knots someone else has left in our lives.

Do you know why most "difficult" people are so ill-natured, people who don't like themselves, who are resentful, or who feel rejected? Such people battle forgiving others—or feeling forgiven themselves. The way they tell us that they're tied up is through their negative, obnoxious actions. That's one reason why the

Scriptures say we are to love our enemies. Their negative reactions are warning signals that their lives are tied up in knots. *What about my own knots, though?* someone may be thinking. *How can I get the knots out of another person's life when I'm all tied up myself?* In the Lord's Prayer, Christ answers this important question.

If we could paraphrase a few verses, using the literal definition of forgiveness, it could read like this: "If you are willing to untie the knots of the one who offended you, then God will untie your own knots (forgive you). If you refuse to untie their knotted lives, then God won't untie yours." One major reason why forgiveness is so necessary is that anger blocks the working of God's spirit.

Can you see now that leaving someone angry is allowing them to be in "darkness" and tied up in "knots"? Not only are we damaging a person emotionally when we provoke anger in them, but we are also cutting them off from God's light. There is, however, an antidote to unhealthy anger.

If we are attaching value and honor to the people around us, then we will do our best never to do anything that ties them up in knots. If we do, we will try to untie them. "Do not let the sun go down on your anger" (Ephesians 4:26 RSV).

In Chapters 13 and 15, we'll share specifically about untying the knots that may be in your life. For now, though, keeping harmony in a home comes from understanding the attitudes that can reopen a loved one's life and love to us.

Never . . . Never Give Up

There is one final question we must raise. What if we try our best, and they still don't respond?

Gently persist . . . gently persist . . . gently, lovingly persist.

Near the end of his life, Winston Churchill was asked to give a commencement speech at a noted university in England. His car arrived late, and the jam-packed crowd suddenly hushed as one of the greatest men in British history made his way slowly, painfully to the podium.

Churchill's speech lasted less than two minutes—but it drew a standing ovation. It comprised only twelve words, but it has inspired decades of men and women ever since. What he said is the best advice I can give you when it comes to being persistent in love to open a spouse's or child's spirit. What did he say?

With his deep, gruff, resonating voice, he said, "Never give up. . . Never, never, give up. . . Never, never, never give up."

End of speech, but not the end of the message. If the man who called me at midnight had given up on being persistent in love, he would have sent a wife and family away tied up in knots and still in darkness.

I'm not sure if I have ever heard a more hostile woman than the one I called that morning. Yet a little less than a year later, she called me back and said, "Gary, I just wanted you to know that I'm back together with my husband. . . ."

I'll have to admit I was floored when I received her call. From every human angle, their relationship was dead in the water that fateful evening when she locked her husband out of the house. Obviously she had thought the same thing.

"A year ago," she said, "if you had even *suggested* that there was a possibility we would be back together—that I would even *like* him, much less love him again—I wouldn't have believed you. The amazing thing," she continued, "is that I do love him again. I actually want to be around him. That fascinates me all by itself. . . ."

What happened to bring about such a change? Because this man recognized that he had let anger ruin his home—and learned how to drain it out of his wife's life—he reopened her spirit, and he did one thing more. His commitment to allow God to change him and his attitude toward his family made him never, never give up—even when she said she hated him and never wanted to see him again.

If I had given up any one of a hundred times of working to get the anger out of Norma or one of my children's lives, I probably wouldn't be writing this book now—or enjoying the strong relationships we have at home. What I and my friend learned about opening a person's spirit can work for you too—as it has in my family—to help us all avoid a major destroyer of families.

Now we head into one of my favorite subjects: the tremendous value of a man. For God has given a man exactly what he needs to be a great lover and leader of his home. We men come to the marriage relationship equipped to contribute four essential ingredients that lie at the heart of a rock-solid relationship. Let's discover what those ingredients are.

7

The Tremendous Value of a Man

Just picture the scene. Norma and I are getting ready to begin one of our evening marriage encounter groups—an important part of the early work we did on a church staff. Everyone has been walking around, smiling, drinking coffee, catching up on small talk. Now they're all settling comfortably into the chairs we've arranged around the living room. Then, suddenly, the peaceful atmosphere is shattered.

With a bang, the front screen door swings open. In walks one of the couples from the group. The husband darts ahead of his wife and takes over the couch. Without a word, he crosses his arms and glares at everybody. His wife's eyes are red and puffy, and she walks right past him and sits down across the room, next to one of the other wives.

Only a few seconds had passed, and the evening had gone from easygoing to explosive! Since I was the leader of the group, I decided to get started, thinking that would help.

I opened with a prayer, then looked at the man again. He was still sitting with his arms tightly crossed, looking like Mount St. Helens just before it erupted. Thinking it might relieve some of the tension, I started off with him.

"How's it going this week?" I asked.

"*Terrible!*" he snarled.

"Okay," I said. "What's so terrible?"

"If you really want to know," he replied, leaning forward in his chair and looking me right in the eye, "I've been thinking about getting out of this marriage group.

"No—I'll tell you what," he continued, raising his volume level up a notch, "I've got a better idea. What I'm really thinking about is getting out of my marriage! I *can't stand* that woman over there, and I don't know if I can live with her any longer." His words ripped through the air as he sat back in his chair, a look of defiance on his face.

It was interesting to see what happened the instant he stopped talking. All the women immediately glared at him, and then went over to comfort his wife, and every man in the room instantly did the same thing, only for him. We all looked at each other and thought, *What do we do now?*

As the leader of the group, I knew I had to take charge, so I said, "Why don't we close in prayer?" And that's exactly what I did. It was probably the shortest marriage group meeting on record. As everyone filed into the kitchen, I was able to pull the man aside and asked, "Listen, why don't we get together for lunch tomorrow before you do something drastic?"

Reluctantly, he agreed.

The next day, as we talked at a restaurant downtown, we both discovered something fascinating. In fact, it's something I've used to strengthen my own marriage and have shared with hundreds of men since.

Self-Inflicted Wounds in a Relationship

"Why do you want to leave your wife? What bothers you the most about her?" I asked.

"Gary, there isn't enough time over lunch for me to tell you everything that gripes me. It'd take all afternoon!"

"Just try to hit the high points then," I said. In a few minutes, he had shared five things about her that were particularly irritating.

"She's a sloppy housekeeper . . . she's on the phone all the time . . . she's with her mother constantly . . . she won't take any trips with me . . . she never initiates when it comes to sex."

As the list piled up, his attitude became harder and harder. I threw up a quick prayer for wisdom and then I did something I'd never done before. I began by taking each one of his "gripes" in order and asking him specific questions about them. Questions like: "When it comes to her housekeeping, do you ever encourage her? For instance, do you ever praise her for the good things she does around the house?"

"No," he replied. "She never *does* anything good around the house for me to compliment."

"At least give me an example of what you might say to her when her housekeeping skills don't measure up to where you want them," I went on.

"Well," he said, his tone softening just a little, "the other day I got up and started vacuuming the house at six o'clock in the morning. When I started down the hallway toward our bedroom, she got out of bed and said 'What are you doing?' and I said, 'I'm sick and tired of living in this pig pen! We're cleaning up this place, and we're doing it *now!*'"

"Do you think that motivates her to keep the house clean?" I asked.

"No, I guess it doesn't. But that still doesn't solve the problem of her being a slob," he retorted. Ignoring his barbs, I continued through his list, asking questions.

"After work and on weekends, how much time do you spend actually talking to your wife about something important to her?"

"Well, frankly there's not a lot of time left over in my week. I've got a crushing schedule at the office. I play racquetball three days a week, and then we have to fit in *your* group which takes another night," he said, making sure I knew how much effort he was expending just to be in the group. "And I've got to do something to relax on the weekends, so I usually play golf with some of the guys from work. . . ."

"Do you spend any time talking to her during dinner?" I asked.

Reluctantly he replied, "I usually watch television during dinner. Basically, that's the only time I have to catch the news. But Gary, you've got to understand. In my line of work it's crucial for me to know what's going on, nationally and internationally, to see how it might affect my business."

I said, "Okay, the news may be important, but do you spend *any* time with her during the week, just the two of you, talking together about your lives? About what's important to her, not just your business?"

"No," he said in an emotionless voice, "not really."

I said, "Then it's no wonder she's on the phone day and night and always over at her mother's. A woman comes equipped with a tremendous need for meaningful communication—particularly with her husband. If that need is blocked, she'll find someone else to talk to."

"Oh," he said, a series of tiny lights beginning to switch on inside his mind, "I never thought of it that way."

"You've got your own company now, but in the past have you ever worked for a guy who was very critical?" I asked.

"You bet I have," he said, without pausing even a moment to think about it.

"I had one boss I really hated. He was the kind of guy who couldn't *wait* to come into my office to criticize me. He'd point out anything that was going wrong or even could go wrong in my department. Then he'd yell at me to 'Shape up! Do this! Do that!' After his tirade in front of all the other people I worked with, he'd go back in his office and drink coffee while I worked my head off."

God has built into every man the natural ability to be the very loving leader his family needs.

I said, "How did that make you feel?"

"How did it make me *feel?* I hated working with him," he answered. "I couldn't wait until the end of the day just to get away from him."

"Would you like to go on a vacation with him?" I asked.

"A *vacation?* Are you kidding?" he said incredulously. "That'd be the *last* thing I'd want to do."

I said, "Don, do you realize that you're treating your wife the same way that boss treated you?"

His eyes widened, and he sat straight up in his chair as he took in what I said.

"It's no wonder your wife doesn't want to go on a trip with you, or even to respond to you physically. The way you've been treating her, it's as if she's living night and day with your former boss."

After a long silence, he grudgingly said, "You've got a point there."

We went through all five areas he'd mentioned and made an amazing discovery. With each and every problem he had with his wife, he was at least partially responsible for creating the very attitudes and actions that were so irritating to him.

"What do I do now?" he asked, plaintively.

It's not that this man's negative contributions to his marriage in any way justified his wife's negative behavior, but in many ways, his behavior helped support her actions. Basically, he had no idea he was adding to the very things he didn't want to see in his home. Now that he realized it, he didn't know how to begin to change.

Would you describe this man as a lover? Not really. Would you describe him as a nurturer? Not likely. Could he (and did he) become both? Definitely.

Unlocking a Man's Natural Strength

I am convinced that most men, if they have a plan and know what to do, are willing to take the steps to build a loving, lasting relationship.[1] The problem is that the average man doesn't know intuitively what it takes to do so—nor does he realize the incredible benefits that a strong relationship at home brings to nearly every area of his life.[2]

Remember the women's "built-in marriage manual" we talked about in Chapter 4? In that chapter, we shared how by nature, God seems to equip a woman from birth with important skills a man tends to lack. In part, that is the reason for the special title she bears as a man's "completer" and "helper" (Genesis 2:18).

For some people, a woman's natural edge in relationships can be used as ammunition for blasting men and a man's place in the home. Some people have even read some of my earlier books and felt that I was jumping on the "men-bashing" bandwagon. However, I'd like to set the record straight.

While it is true a man doesn't speak as many words or may not be as naturally sensitive as a woman, that doesn't mean he is incapable of being a great lover in the home. In fact, it seems that *God has built into every man the natural ability to be the very loving leader his family needs.*

Saying that God has designed a man to be the lover in a home may sound a bit strange after all we've said about a man's conquering, logical, fact-driven nature, but that very nature is the foundation for my conviction.

Why? Because the kind of love that lasts, the kind that can grow and thrive apart from feelings, is the kind that comes from a decision. And as I mentioned in Chapter 3, *love*—stripped to its core—is just that, *a factual decision that doesn't have to depend on our feelings.*

There are times in life when we may not feel like doing something that's important, but we still need to do it. We need to give our two-year-old the medicine she needs when she flatly refuses to take it. Or we may have to stay up late to finish the report that has to be done on time—no matter how it bends our schedule or robs us of sleep. Or perhaps it's getting up an hour early each day to exercise and spend time in the Word and in prayer. Whatever the situation, there are times when all our "natural" instincts may say "no," but God's Word or another person's best interest demands we say "yes."

When it comes to family relationships, that same hard-driving, conquering nature that can cause a man to get ahead in his profession, can cause one of two results at home. In many cases, it can create emotional strain and tension if a man tries to blast through his family relationships like so many projects at work. Take that same drive and harness it by giving a man a specific plan of action for the home—and it can be the driving force to bring about the very relationship a woman longs for.

If the truth be known, that man in my marriage group came into his marriage with tremendous *liabilities.* He didn't have a loving father as a child, and the two communication skills his parents modeled for him were anger and silence. Yet, though he didn't know it at the time, in spite of the poor example he'd grown up with, he still possessed a God-given *ability* on which he could draw—anytime—to develop a strong marriage. Namely, once he knew what it took to have a fulfilling relationship, he could tap into his natural drive and desire to "win" and use it to strengthen his marriage.

It's hard for many women to understand how in an intimate relationship, a man is often more motivated to communicate if he puts facts in front of feelings. Normally, a woman will feel something, and then do it. For example, she'll feel an emotional need for communication, and then seek out her husband to meet that need. That's simply not the case with most men.

Usually a man is not driven by an emotional need to relate. Rather, he'll be much more motivated to do something relational (like spending a half-hour in conversation) once he's made a factual decision that it's right. For a man, actions are primarily what dictate feelings, not the reverse.

In large part, I feel that a man's unique ability to blend fact and feeling is a major gift God has given him in order to carry out his responsibility of being the loving leader in a home. When a man is given the right information, told what is right to do and how to do it, he can draw on his natural force of will to make a decision that *stays* while his feelings may come and go.

A Biblical Blueprint for Loving Leadership in a Home

For a man, the first place he should check when it comes to building a strong family is a blueprint found in Ephesians 5. In this important chapter, the man is called to be the "head" of his wife—the primary lover—just as Christ is the head of the church and the lover of the church.

Nowhere does it say that a man is to "lord it over" his wife. In fact, Christ specifically commands that "lording it over" another person has no place in a Christian's relationships. Rather, the Scriptures tell me I am to love my wife as Jesus loves His church.

How did Christ lead in love? By serving, by committing Himself to our best interest, and by doing so regardless of the cost. The greatest among us are simply following a pattern Christ set down—namely serving those He loved and for whom He laid down His life.

Yet let's take the command for a man to be a loving leader in the home, and move it down to the shoe-leather level. What does it mean to be the "leader" in a home?

When it comes to "leadership" and headship in the home, one very specific guideline is found in verses 28–29, ". . . husbands ought to love their wives, as their own bodies . . . . (for) no one ever hated his own body, but he *feeds* and *cares* for it, just as Christ also does the church" (emphasis added).

If we are following the biblical pattern for family leadership, we men are to nurture and cherish our wives (and children). We do so just as we nurture and cherish our own bodies—and as Christ nurtures and cherishes the church.

When a husband makes that first important decision to truly honor those entrusted to him, he takes the first step toward being the loving *nurturer* God meant him to be. As a result he can see his relationship begin to blossom before his eyes and grow.

Growing a Strong Marriage

What does it actually mean to "nurture" one's wife?

The Greek word for "nurturer" means "husbandman."[3] For those of us who haven't grown up on a farm, that's a tiller of the soil, a professional gardener. A nurturer is one who helps things grow, who provides a "greenhouse" atmosphere where the plants are shielded and protected.

In short, that's what I'm called to be as a husband. Like the top gardener at your local nursery, I am responsible for understanding what ingredients cause my marriage to grow and flower —and then for providing them on a consistent basis. The psalmist puts it this way. "Blessed are all who fear the Lord. . . . Your wife shall be like a fruitful vine within your house; your sons like olive shoots around your table . . ." (Psalm 128:3).

Can you imagine what would happen if that gardener at your local nursery went by guesswork when it came to caring for his plants? No wonder in many marriages we see a "Under New Management" or "Gone Out of Business" sign up in the front yard. No less skill is required of the "head" of a marriage. He is called to be a skilled nurseryman, a caretaker of sorts. He is to be the first one to recognize and supply the ingredients needed for growth and well-being in the family and the first to spot and pull any weeds that threaten to do it harm.

In short, *my role as a "nurturer" is to be a fact-finder.* I should interview each member of my family with my fact-finder mind to see what needs should be met that day and then discover how best to meet them. When I do, I nurture, cover and protect them—and get the privilege of watching them grow. In my own life, one word picture has helped to cement this concept of nurturing in my memory.

A Man Has a Natural, Relational "Green Thumb"

After we bought our first little home in Rockford, Illinois, I decided to plant a victory garden. I had heard that the ashes from burned leaves helped the soil, so I gathered a huge pile of leaves from all over the yard. My leaf pile burned all night long, and that's not all. At one point the wind shifted and I nearly burned down my neighbor's garage as well.

Barely escaping disaster, the next day I spread out all the ashes in the back part of the yard where I was planning my garden. I didn't really know what I was doing, but it looked great! The earth was dark and moist, and a few weeks later, the results were even better than I expected. Whatever we planted came up looking like the pictures on the seed packet covers.

Everything grew. In fact, the pumpkins became so enthusiastic about the soil that they grew along the fence and up into a tree and hung down everywhere like Christmas ornaments. After my one experience of gardening in Rockford, I felt that I was gifted with a permanently green thumb. However, one day I discovered that the green on my thumb was disappearing ink.

We had moved a thousand miles away, and I decided to unleash my gardening talents on the Lone Star state. From the first spade of soil I turned, I could tell things were going to be different in Waco, Texas. There the ground was a white, rocky, clayish dirt, not the deep brown I had been used to in Rockford.

Without consulting any of the local nurserymen or gardening books, I simply made the decision that what the soil must need was additional fertilizer. With that in mind, I went out and bought the biggest sack I could find with a label that said "For Gardens" on it. The picture on the sack looked just like the results I'd gotten in Rockford, so I figured this was exactly what I needed in Waco.

Spring came around, we put all the seed into the ground, and sure enough everything came up just like in the pictures. After a short time, the picture began to change radically. The beans started browning around the edge, the tomatoes were rotten in the middle, when we picked them, and our carrots were always spongy and wilted. It was obvious something was very wrong with this garden, but I didn't know exactly what to do.

Take Time to Talk to Your Garden . . .

At the time, I didn't realize that by dumping loads of fertilizer on soil that was already high in nitrogen, I was burning up my plants! Do you know what would have helped immeasurably, were it possible?

If only my garden could talk back to me, it could have let me know exactly what I was doing wrong—and what I could do to correct things. It may seem a little far-fetched, but I could say to my garden for example, "Good morning, down there, how are y'all doing?" And right off, the beans would speak up.

"How are we all doing down here? *We're dying!* That's how we're doing!"

"Come again?" I'd ask.

"We're dying down here! We're choking to death!"

"Hey, what's the problem?"

Then they'd say,

"Mr. Smalley, you know all those white things you poured around our roots? Well, now there are thousands of them, and they're killing us. Didn't you know how much nitrogen is in this soil already, and now you're dumping pounds of it all around us!"

I'd say, "No kidding? I didn't know I was hurting you. I never even thought to check the soil. What can I do to try to solve the problem?"

And they'd say, "Go down to the store and get some chemicals and neutralize this nitrogen. You've got to hurry, Mr. Smalley, we've only got a few days left!"

"Good idea! I'll take care of that." So I start to race off to the nursery when I notice my carrots, and I say to them, "Oh, look at your leaves, they're just wilting all over the place. Bless your pea-pickin' hearts!"

"Mr. Smalley," they cry out, "forget the peas. They're done for, but you can help us if while you're at the nursery, you pick up a nylon mesh to put over us to keep us cooler. Then we could really firm up."

"I never knew that!" I would say. "Listen, you sweet things you, I'll take care of everything, don't you worry."

If only I could have talked to my garden in Waco, I could have solved my green thumb problems in a few hours. Who knows? I could have even landed in a Miracle-Gro commercial. Unfortunately, my garden was for the birds—literally. Because I never took the time or had the wisdom to ask someone what the plants needed in my area, I ruined an entire summer's crop.

I suppose I could have taken a different approach to my "talking" garden. For example, I could have walked down early in the morning, taken one look, and said, "Hey, what's this mess? Look at all your leaves—they're browning out around the edges. Hey, you plants! Any more brown leaves on any of you and I'm going to jerk you up by the roots! Now shape up, all of you, and I mean *now!*"

Would my yelling at the plants have changed things around my garden? In actuality, I had caused much of the damage that my garden now displayed because I relied on wishing, not wisdom.

After almost twenty years of working with couples and families, I can testify that many husbands nurture the priceless relationships in their homes using the same principle that I employed in my gardens—*guesswork*. A husband often enters marriage with a picture of a great home in his mind, but relies on wishing, not hard work and wisdom, to see it come to reality. Unfortunately, when many men wake up to the damage they've done to their families, the summer's crop has almost been wasted and a bitter cold winter is fast setting in.

In short, that's why God calls the husband to be a wise "gardener" of his family. Each season of life, a man needs to prepare the soil of his family's lives, to protect them from the elements, and to mend the damage after any natural crisis. The better a man learns to be the nurturer in his home, the more it will look like the "picture" the Scriptures paint of a successful relationship. Wives and children, like the plants the psalmist talks about, reflect how well they've been gardened.

Going to a Plant for Lessons in Gardening

"Wait a minute," I can hear some men saying. "This nurturing business sounds like it puts all the responsibility on the man. What about the responsibility of a woman, or even the children, to make the home all it can be?"

Whenever I hear this argument, two things come to mind. First, it is true that a man is called to be the nurturer of his family, not a woman. In fact, the Scriptures never tell a woman to "love" her husband, but a man is specifically commanded to "love" his wife.

Throughout the Scriptures, a woman is pictured as the "responder" or reflector of her husband's and God's light. In the Song of Songs in the Old Testament, the bride of Solomon makes this important comment about their relationship, "Draw me after you, and let us run together!" (1:4, NASB).

Can you see the balance in this perspective? The man initiates the loving actions (drawing her after him); the woman responds (let us run together); and then the two of them grow together as a result. As we saw in Chapter 3, a woman's natural calling is to be a completer, a helper, a responder to his love. In addition, she is called to honor her husband (Romans 12:10; 1 Peter 3:1). When it comes to who wears the nurturing shoes in the family, biblically they come in men's sizes.

"But how can I know specifically what my wife needs, so that her life and our marriage blooms and grows?" you may ask. "I barely have time to finish everything I've got going at work. How am I going to learn all it takes to care for her in the way I should? Isn't that asking a lot?"

You're exactly right. It is asking a great deal to see that a marriage becomes successful. Without a doubt, a husband has a high calling in taking on the role of the nurturer in a home, but the task isn't impossible. In fact, it's far from it.

What are those nonnegotiable ingredients to a successful marriage? After years of counseling, researching, and interviewing couples throughout the world, it's apparent a healthy relationship needs at least four things.

As we've mentioned, by nature a woman tends to manifest these actions—and to desire them deeply. But if a husband understands these needs in the home (needs his wife and children have on an everyday basis), then makes the decision to apply them consistently in his marriage, it's almost impossible for healthy growth not to take place. What are these four nonnegotiable ingredients that can form a handbook for a committed nurturer—*man or woman?*

At the heart of "nurturing" our loved ones are providing . . .
1) Deep-seated security
2) Meaningful conversation
3) Emotional/romantic times
4) Positive physical touching

In almost all my books, I've talked about these four factors —and the only consistent power source that underlies each one. But as I speak, study, and talk to people across the country, my understanding of them deepens each year. These four needs are so essential that we'll take several chapters to highlight them all (and then two chapters at the end of the book in particular that talk about where we find the power to grow a love that lasts).

To begin with, let's take a look at the first ingredient in causing a husband, a wife, or child's life to bloom and grow. It's an ingredient that is so essential that with it, a family can experience fulfilling relationships. Without it, they often find nothing but frustration and constant bickering.

8

The First Aspect of Nurturing: Adding the Sunlight of Security to Your Relationships

In some counseling sessions, trying to get a couple to open up about the real issues they're struggling with is like trying to twist the lid off an old honey jar. When all else fails, there's a method that works every time. In fact, it's as effective as holding that honey jar under steaming, hot water.

All you have to do is invite God's little spies—their children —into the counseling session, and it's amazing how they can pop the lid off "hidden" problems in an instant. That's just what happened when Dr. Trent asked the young six-year-old daughter of one couple, "Honey, what makes you feel the worst when Mommy and Daddy argue?"

The little girl frowned and said in a small, hesitant voice, "It's when Daddy takes off his wedding ring and throws it away."

The husband quickly defended himself by saying that he didn't "actually" throw his ring away. Rather, it was only an unusual way of demonstrating his anger during a fight with his wife.

When this couple got into a heated argument, if he wanted to end the discussion he would take his wedding ring off and throw it across the room. As it pinged off the walls and rolled across the floor, the wife and his little girl would watch in silence. Later, someone would pick up the fallen ring and leave it on the counter. Eventually the husband would put it back on.

For this man, "throwing away" his wedding ring provided an immature emotional release from his frustration. For his wife and child, it caused a deep sense of insecurity and fear.

As the people who depended so much on him saw his ring go flying across the room, they saw their security level flying away as well. He didn't actually need to say the words that he was leaving. He let a flying gold band do the talking for him. Each time the ring flew through the air it shouted out, "If things don't go the way I want around here, I'll throw you right out of my life too."

Living Life on an Icy Street . . .

Have you ever endured an ice storm in your home town and then tried to walk down the street? It can be done but there's always the internal tension of knowing a terrible fall is right around the corner.

What many husbands and wives don't realize is that an absence of security in a relationship is like sentencing a person to live on an ice-covered sidewalk.

You're never free to truly relax in a home where insecurity has frozen the relationship in an icy state. It's impossible to enjoy a marriage when you're always fighting to keep your footing.

Unfortunately, in more and more homes across the country, it is always winter and never spring. There are months at a time when the cold January clouds of insecurity are never penetrated by the warm sunlight of security. Yet there is an antidote to living life under a dark cloud cover.

You can warm up your relationship in a dramatic way. In fact, you can actually do something *today* that is like turning the full force of a July sun right on your marriage. What is it? It's providing this first crucial aspect of nurturing our loved ones— unconditional security.

The Warmth to Thaw out a Relationship and Help It Grow

Security is like providing warm, invigorating sunlight to a plant. Leave a plant in the icy darkness of insecurity, and soon its leaves will wilt and turn brown. If a relationship has just been planted, the cold shadows of mistrust can keep any growth from ever sprouting above the surface. A plant must have sunlight if it's to ever be healthy and flourishing. In a marriage, the same thing is true.

Security results when a man and a woman say to each other, "You're so valuable to me that no matter what happens in life, I'm going to commit myself to you. You're so valuable, I'm going to spend the rest of my life proving to you my pledge to love you." In short, it's a reflection of the kind of security we have in our relationship with Christ. Look at Romans 8 for example:

"Who shall separate us from the love of Christ? . . . For I am convinced that neither death nor life, neither angels nor demons, neither the present nor the future . . . nor anything else in all creation will be able to separate us from the love of God that is in Christ Jesus our Lord" (Romans 8:35–39).

Every enduring marriage involves an unconditional commitment to an imperfect person.

God also goes to great lengths to assure us that the plans He has for us are grounded in His security and His protection. "'For I know the plans that I have for you,' declares the Lord, 'plans to prosper you and not to harm you, plans to give you a hope and a future'" (Jeremiah 29:11).

Now, that's security! And the better able we are to reflect the same level of security that we have in Christ to our loved ones, the more we bathe them in much needed sunlight. That goes for mothers who want to see their children feel confident in friendships and later in dating relationships. It's true for fathers who desire these same kids to do well in school and later in their professions. It's especially true for a husband or wife who want to live with the green leaves of a healthy marriage—not the brown leaves of a dying one.

Every enduring marriage involves an unconditional commitment to an imperfect person. This means we can gaze at each other's imperfections and say, "Those brown leaves do irritate me, but I'm going to find out what caused them, and see if I can help. No matter what shape you're in—I'll be around and help you grow." Without this kind of commitment, we're more likely to say, "I can't stand all these brown leaves. They've bothered me for years! That's it! I'm leaving."

If you're in a second marriage, I realize that talking about commitment "no matter what" can be an invitation to guilt feelings. Study after study exposes the long-term negative effects of insecurity that often follow a divorce. However, this still doesn't mean that genuine "security" is somehow out of reach in a remarriage situation.

Men and women who have, biblically and personally, dealt with their divorce and who have remarried have an equal or even greater need to build security in their present marriage. Like love, security is a decision we make on an everyday basis. (For those who may be struggling with guilt or fear from a past relationship, in Chapters 13 and 14 I'll look at ways God can use even something as traumatic as a divorce to make us more loving.)

For all of us, security is an essential prerequisite, not an emotional elective. Let's be even more specific in discussing how we can help our loved ones grow by providing the sunlight of security for their lives. There are at least three things that every man and woman can begin to do to build a secure marriage on an everyday basis.

They can start by 1) building their own "hallway of honor" in their home which in itself can help steer their mate or children away from the doorway of dishonor. Then they can 2) look to the Lord for the strength to make an unconditional commitment and sacrificial choices. Finally, 3) they can become students of their spouses' interests as a tangible way of expressing their commitment.

All are important ways to build security in a home, but the first has a dual benefit. It not only builds positive things into the relationship, it can also help to keep tremendous pain from the people we care about most.

1. A Hallway of Honor . . .

In the hallway of our patio-home, there is a plaque hanging on one wall that proclaims: "In assurance of my lifelong commitment. To Norma, Kari, Greg and Mike. Christmas 1976." Hardly a week goes by that I don't remind those four special people about those words and the commitment behind them.

I realize that words can be cheap. I've spoken with many hurting spouses and children who "believed" the words of commitment of a man or woman whose promises held as much weight as thin air. For them, their spouse walked out on the family leaving a doorway of shame, not a hallway of honor.

I fully realize the only things that will transfer the words of this plaque onto my spouse and children's hearts are my everyday actions and words over the years. Each time I match those words with my demonstrated commitment, I'm adding on to a "hallway of honoring acts" in my home. As a result, I'm leaving a daily legacy of love to my wife and children,[1] not a hurtful inheritance of emotional pain.

A marriage or family can't grow in a healthy way if security is constantly shifting in a home, but loved ones can live without perfection. In fact, the more genuine security a wife or child feels, the more room they allow a person to fail. It's a bit like the farmer who goes to his banker and says, "I've got good news and bad news . . . ."

"Give me the bad news first," the banker says.

"Well, you know all that money I borrowed to buy that farm? I'm not doing well, so I don't have any money to pay you for it."

"Oh?" the banker says.

"Second, you know that money you loaned me for all that equipment, the tractor and everything? I can't pay for that either . . . ."

"No . . ." the banker moans.

"And third, all that money you loaned me for all the seeds? I can't pay that back either. I can't pay you anything."

"Well, what is the good news, for heaven's sake?" the banker wails.

"The good news is, I still want you to be my banker!"

My family knows I'm not perfect; they know I'll lose my temper at times—and they know I'm not always as sensitive as I should be. But one thing that helps them be patient with my imperfections is the knowledge that I'm 100 percent committed to them. I "still want them to be my banker," and I'm trying hard to be the kind of father and husband I should be. With each act of commitment, they see me with hammer and nail, adding on to a hallway of honor in our home.

For your wife or husband, a plaque in your hall may not spell security. But sometimes a loving symbol of our commitment acts like a wedding ring. The ring itself doesn't commit a person to marriage, but it shows to the world that the commitment has been made.

Perhaps for your spouse, security is a special event like a romantic dinner or going to a helpful marriage seminar like Campus Crusade's "Family Life Conference."[2] It may even be something as small as sending a card or calling home from the office each day just to see how your loved one is doing.

Norma has told me often that the way I "date" our kids makes her feel secure. I make it a practice to take my daughter Kari out on a special outing about once a month to show my commitment to Norma. The children are such an extension of her that simply knowing I am spending time with each child individually makes Norma feel secure in the strength and love I hold for our family.

Again, like a wise gardener, ask your spouse, "What is security to you?" Then take careful notes of what he or she says. Security may be spelled, "Let me have a say in the financial decisions," or "Take the time to have family devotions," or "Call me each day when you have to travel."

If you understand what "security" is to them, then you can begin making deposit after deposit into their love bank. This accrues high interest in your relationship. Just begin with a few simple questions like, "On a 1 to 10 scale, one being very '*insecure*' and ten being very '*secure,*' how confident do you feel in my love?" or "What could I specifically do over the next few months that would raise the level of security in our relationship?"

By seeking to build security into your spouse through small, positive acts, you do even more than add positive marks to the marital ledger. You also can help them (and yourself) to guard against the temptation to walk through a doorway named "dishonor."

The more security and honor we build into our homes—the tighter we help to shut the doorway to temptation for our loved ones. Interestingly, it's also the tighter we close the door to temptation for ourselves.[3]

The more "single minded" we are in our commitment to Christ, the less the distractions of the world pull upon us. The more "single minded" we are in building a "hall of honor" for our loved ones through honoring acts, the less room we leave for insecurity to dwell in our homes.[4]

There's a second way to develop security in a marriage that calls for the courage to make and keep an unconditional commitment to one's spouse. That commitment is often best seen in the sacrificial choices we may have to make if necessary.

2. Sacrificial Choices Are Also a Part of Providing Security

Betty waited in a little examination room in the doctor's office, her head lowered. Here it was, only two weeks before their only daughter's wedding, and she'd had another "lock-up" with her arthritis.

Once, Betty had been a cheerleader in the West Texas town in which she grew up. But you could never tell it now. Her heart and bubbly spirit were the same, but today (at fifty-five) they were trapped inside a body that was so crippled, she couldn't walk as well as most ninety-year-olds.

The constant pain from her joints flaring up had been bad, but the "lock-ups" were worst of all. Whenever she had a reaction to one of the "experimental" medicines prescribed for her, it was as if every joint in her body froze in place, and the pain and discomfort were almost unbearable.

Betty was a brave woman, but as she sat in the privacy of the doctor's office, tears rolled down her cheeks. She thought of her marriage to Rusty and all their dreams. She remembered all the plans they'd made for their retirement years . . . that would always remain as dreams. She thought of all the places they wanted to travel . . . but now never could. In her heart she knew that her arms were so battered by arthritis she'd never even be able to hold her first grandchild—the pain would simply be too great.

The door to the room opened, and her husband walked in from talking with the doctor. Looking over at his wife, he could see her chin trembling as she fought to regain her composure.

Try as she might, she couldn't help breaking into sobs.

"Oh, Rusty, please leave me," she begged him. "I'm getting worse, not better. I'm a mess. It hurts too much for you to touch me. I'm spending every cent we've saved toward retirement fighting this thing. I'm a burden to you and the kids and you know it."

Her tall, weather-beaten husband pulled over a chair and sat down beside her. Gently, he took her hand, twisted by arthritis, and said, "Sweetheart, it doesn't hurt to smile, does it? If you'll just smile at me now and then, that's all I need. I really don't even need that. I just need you."

Real love means a sacrificial, courageous commitment—especially when the other person may not be able to give back to you. None of our family members should have to feel what that little girl did when she saw her father's wedding ring bounce off the wall. Security should never be something you take on or off as you see fit. It's an abiding conviction that all is well with our commitment and all will be well—no matter what.

Sometimes sacrificial choices must be made in a marriage —but time and again they can heighten the security level in a home. Take Bill and Brenda for example.

Brenda had always wanted to be a veterinarian. However, she and Bill only had high school educations, and neither could really afford to go back to school. But Bill wouldn't let her dream die. He decided that she would go to school, regardless of the cost.

He knew what it meant to encourage her to get the training she'd need. He was looking at long hours spent on a second job in order for them to have the money for tuition It took seven years of grueling work and sacrifice on both their parts for Brenda to become a vet, but the day finally came when she got her diploma. That meant her diplomas now outnumbered Bill's, three to one, but he couldn't have been happier—and neither could she. Their relationship didn't suffer because he had sacrificed his time and effort for his wife; it flourished.

Why does sacrifice add so much to a growing relationship? It should be obvious to those of us who live on this side of the Cross. That symbol of sacrifice is an unforgettable word picture of God's love for a lost world—and for each one of us who love Him.

Bill was simply following a biblical pattern when he built security into his marriage through sacrifice. After coming through the winter of a tough struggle together getting Brenda's degree, their marriage experienced an Alaskan summer where there's sunlight nearly twenty-four hours a day.

We've looked at building a "hallway of honoring actions" and making sacrificial choices to add sunlight and security to a marriage. There's a third way to raise the security level in a home, and that's to practice the kind of love that gets involved in another person's life in a very special way.

3. Building Security by Going Back to School

Recently, a close friend of ours, Jim Brawner, did a survey of several hundred teenagers at perhaps the top Christian sports camp in this country, Kamp Kanakuk in Branson, Missouri.[5] One of the first questions each boy or girl responded to on the questionnaire was: *"What is one tangible way your mother and/or father demonstrate that you're important to them?"* Can you guess what the number 1 response was, by far?

"I know they think I'm important because . . . they attended my games . . . my practices . . . my concerts . . . my open-houses . . . my band competitions . . . " In other words, with a teenager, security can be spelled with four words, *"Come and watch me!"*

While many men and women may not realize it, we never really outgrow the deep need we have for our loved ones to be excitedly supportive of our interests. What this means in a marriage is that the sunlight of security can shine on a marriage when we show an active interest in our loved one's life.

This was brought home to me in a tangible way when I first met a couple who became special friends. He was a huge offensive lineman for an NFL team when we first met, and his wife was perhaps 5'4" in heels. On the basis of size alone, there probably wasn't a more oddly matched pair. But in terms of their shared interests, this couple was only a heartbeat apart.

I met them at a Pro Athlete's Outreach Conference and was fascinated with a conversation we had at lunch one day. Out of curiosity, I asked this NFL wife how much she knew about the position her husband played on his team. I expected her to say something like, "Oh, he's paid to stand in front of other people." Instead, she gave me a ten-minute presentation on offensive blocking techniques.

Taken aback by her grasp of the sport, I asked how she'd become such an expert on her husband's position on the team. That's when she gave me a real-life lesson on what it does to become one's spouse's biggest fan—by becoming a graduate student of their likes and dislikes.

She explained that when they were first married, she resented the time he spent on the practice field, she resented all the team meetings and the travel. Finally, she grew tired of feeling so negative all the time, and she decided to go on the offensive. She would stop throwing spit-balls from the back row, and get up in the front row and learn about this career that she resented so much.

She began to ask her husband all sorts of questions about playing on the line for a pro team. She even cornered a few of the assistant coaches to learn more intricate details of the game. The more she learned and read, the more of an encourager she became. That's when a funny thing happened.

As her level of encouragement and interest went up, she noticed their marriage improving. While it wasn't her goal to get anything from her husband in return, he began showing more than a passing interest in her likes and dislikes.

What this wise woman had done was to push back the dark clouds of resentment to let the sunlight of security shine on her marriage. She didn't try to "coach" her husband, but her knowledge and interest in his life said clearly, "Because you're so important to me, your interests are important to me, too."

At the end of our conversation, my huge pro-football friend made a comment I've never forgotten: "Sometime I'll have to tell you how much my wife's taught me about refinishing antiques. I wouldn't be surprised if learning about one of her big interests is where I end up after football."

For this couple, being committed to each other meant showing interest in the things they individually valued. The message came over loud and clear that because of that attitude, they felt secure in each other's love and commitment. That security level showed clearly in their lives and the quality of love between them.

Like sunlight to a plant, the warmth of genuine security can be the first element a husband or wife gives to a successful relationship. In the next chapter, we'll look closely at a second crucial ingredient if intimacy is to grow. In fact, we'll introduce you to something we can do in our marriages that can act like life-giving water to our loved ones.

9

Meaningful Conversation: Life-giving Water to a Relationship

Most people take rain for granted—but not farmers. One of the most powerful black-and-white pictures I've ever seen is that of a dust-bowl farmer. He had waited over a year for rain, and now at last he had a chance. His face was turned up to the sky as the desperately needed rain poured down and mingled with his tears.

Every time I see this picture, it calls to mind what happens in many homes. In a marriage, meaningful words are like those raindrops. They can bring life-giving water to the soil of a person's life. In fact, all loving and meaningful relationships need the continual intake of the water of communication, or they simply dry up.

How many couples have I counseled who after fifteen or twenty years of marriage say, "What went wrong? Why is our marriage over?" Time after time, even casual conversation will show that instead of building a spring of consistent, meaningful conversation, they let the well run dry of encouraging words.

If that is the case—if meaningful, intimate conversation is like much needed water to a relationship—why is husband/wife communication often so difficult? Why do couples often learn what *not* to talk about, rather than what *to* talk about?

All too often encouraging words fall as infrequently as a dust bowl storm. Why? There are at least four natural roadblocks to meaningful communication that typically seem to emerge after the wedding day:

Roadblock # 1: Emotional Mind-Reading — or "Please Give Me a Clue!"

Because of a woman's natural sensitivity, nine times out of ten she will be the first one to spot a potential problem in a relationship. However, the problem can be so "obvious" to her that she can legitimately think, *Surely my husband is alert enough to see what the problem is. I'm not going to embarrass him by having to draw him a map.*

Yet, that's the very thing most men need! Give a man a road map of what issues are important to discuss, and often he'll be motivated to talk about them. But expect a husband to "sense" the subtleties (or even bold realities) of a marital or family concern, and often he won't see it as clearly.

Time and time again, I've been thankful for Norma's willingness to point out the "obvious" I've overlooked.

"Did you notice that Greg was acting a little down at the dinner table tonight?" she might ask.

"No, I didn't notice."

"Don't you think you ought to talk with him?" she'd persist.

"About what?" I'd ask. Like most men, I'm motivated to talk about facts. So far, Norma has been cluing me in on "feelings" and nonverbal behavior she's sensed that I've missed. I need "facts" to get really motivated about a conversation.

At this point, Norma could give up, throw up her hands and either go in and talk with Greg herself or chalk up another mark in the insensitivity column for me. But her love—and her knowledge of how to motivate me to communicate—doesn't let her stop here.

"Gary, I'm not sure if it's school, or the girl he's dating, or exactly what it is. But I can tell you that something is bothering Greg. Would you be willing to take your 'fact-finding' nature upstairs and *lovingly* find out how your son is doing?"

Rarely am I able to withstand Norma's call to go on the hunt for a problem to solve, and almost never has she been wrong in her sensitivity about one of the children.

The difference between mis-communication and meaningful communication often comes when a woman is willing to take the extra time to paint the obvious into a picture a man can clearly see or vice-versa. Mind-reading is never encouraged in the Scriptures, and while it may be part of an illusionist's act, it can wreak havoc in the realities of life at home.

Roadblock # 2:
"I No Speaka Your Language . . ."

In Chapter 4, you will recall we discussed the different "languages" that men and women often speak. In short, it seems that there is a "language of the heart" and a "language of the head" often spoken by women and men. Let me paint you a picture. Failing to tap into the unique conversational world of your spouse can cause this kind of frustration. It helps to illustrate a major mistake many women make in dealing with men. Namely, while trying to improve the level of meaningful communication in her home, a woman can inadvertently stifle the very thing she wants so much!

Let's say I walk into an auditorium where in a few short hours, Dr. Trent and I are going to give our "Love Is a Decision" seminar. I'm relaxed and looking forward to a great time with the couples and singles who'll be there, when all of a sudden I get one look at the room and nearly hyper-ventilate.

There's no doubt that this is the room and this is the night of the seminar—but there's also no denying that someone has made a major mistake! The chairs in the room are scattered all over, trash litters the floor, and the stage hasn't been set up. What's worse, with little time left before people begin coming early, I don't see anyone working to get things ready!

Frantically, I begin doing what I can to get the room in shape for the crowd that is bearing down on the auditorium. After ten minutes of going at a whirlwind pace, I notice a petite, bright-eyed woman sitting in a chair near the front row. Elated, I run over to her, and with a smile on my face and excitement in my voice I say, "Pardon me, but in a short time I'm going to be speaking at a conference in here, and I've got a real problem. If you don't have anything to do, could you give me a hand, please? Would you mind setting up some of these chairs while I pick up the trash and get the stage set up? Thank you so much for helping!"

She responds with a warm smile and nods her head, so I bound off like a big puppy, happy to have someone to help. The only problem is—two minutes later she's still sitting there. A little annoyed, I approach her again.

"Pardon me, Ma'am, but setting up chairs must not be your thing, so I'll tell you what. Could you help me with the stage, and I'll worry about the chairs and picking up the trash? Thank you so much for helping!" Once again she smiles and nods her head—but after another few minutes she's still sitting right in the same place.

Now I'm really irritated, and I come storming up to her and say,

"Pardon me, but . . . are you a Christian?"

I could get really angry at this woman and speak unkindly to her. That is until she opens her mouth and the words come out, *"Perdoneme, Senor. Yo no hablo Ingles. Puedo ayudarle a usted?"* If I found out that this woman didn't speak a word of English, it would be pretty insensitive of me to stay angry at her, wouldn't it? But here's the very thing that many women do without even realizing it.

What many women fail to keep in mind is that their husbands genuinely may not see or understand the concerns that they're sharing. In many cases, they simply don't "speak-a" the language!

Getting angry and frustrated with a man to "motivate" him to a deeper level of understanding rarely works. Actually, it can make the surface soil of misunderstanding rock-hard and tougher than ever to penetrate.

Roadblock #3: Test the Soil of a Relationship to Determine Its Needed Moisture Level

As we've said, meaningful communication is like water to a growing relationship, but how do you find out how much "water" is needed in a marriage for maximum growth? Just as we found out that "security" needs are like sunlight to your spouse in the last chapter, in this chapter we'll look at what a nurturing husband or wife can do to encourage his or her partner. We'll find out how much meaningful communication he or she needs to feel fully watered. But let me make an observation.

I've asked hundreds of women in over sixty cities this question, "How much time do you need in meaningful conversation *each day* to feel really good about your relationship with your husband?" And time and again, the average woman answers that she needs at least *one hour a day* in intimate conversation to keep her marriage alive, thirst-free, and growing.

"An hour!" I can hear many men groaning. This can be a mammoth roadblock for many men. "Where am I going to find an hour a day?"

Before you panic, it's important to realize that the hour need not be spent in one block of time. Fifteen minutes in the morning as you trade places in front of the mirror getting ready for work, five minutes on the phone during the day, twenty minutes after work, fifteen minutes after the kids are down, five minutes before bed and then praying together can all be ways to bring needed moisture to your marriage.

We're not suggesting you put a stopwatch on your conversations (as one CPA friend did with the kitchen timer: "OK, Honey. We've got ten more minutes to talk. Now let's talk!") Exact time limits aren't important, but providing sufficient, consistent time to talk about important issues is.

To be accurate, I realize that an hour isn't necessarily the conversational need of every woman. One couple may be content with half an hour of talking, while another may need two hours to work through some difficult issues. Each couple must explore what best meets their needs, and consistently carve out the time from already overcrowded days to make sure their marriage stays a priority. The important thing to realize is that if communication is like life-giving water, a marriage will yellow and brown out if this necessary ingredient for growth is insufficient.

Why Try to Take the Road At All
If There Are So Many Roadblocks?

At this point you may be saying, "What's the use? We're so hopelessly different, we'll never be able to understand each other or be able to reach any kind of intimacy."

That's not true. Time and time again, we've seen the natural "incompatibility" of the two sexes become the very grounds for a great marriage.[1] Rather than retreating into frustration, silence, or verbal explosions, why not take the time to master two specific communication skills that can re-vitalize your communication. These two particular skills help take conversations to a level many never dreamed possible.

The first of these skills is to employ the most powerful communication tool we know of in the Scriptures. We call these emotional word pictures, and without exaggeration, we've seen it turn forty-watt communication into a laser beam of words that hits both head and heart at the same time.

One Emotional Word Picture
Is Worth a Thousand Words

"An emotional word picture is a communication tool that simultaneously activates a person's emotions and intellect. In so doing, it causes another person to not just hear our words, but experience them."[2]

Some of the greatest communicators in history have used word pictures to inspire patriotism, lead nations, and direct the course of history. George Washington and Thomas Jefferson did so in our early history. Abraham Lincoln credited Harriet Beecher Stowe with the North's involvement in the Civil War, claiming that once it got a picture of what slavery was like, there was no turning back. The picture she used? *Uncle Tom's Cabin.*[3] Roosevelt and John F. Kennedy, even Ronald Reagan in more recent times, all salted their political and public speeches with word pictures. For all the good these have done, tragically, many evil leaders like Hitler and Jim Jones have also been masters at using this powerful form of communication.

Without question, the greatest use of word pictures is seen in the Scriptures. Throughout the pages of the Old and New Testament, we are taught the greatest lessons of faith the Bible has to offer through word pictures.

What could be more descriptive of what our attitude should be toward God than King David's picture, "As the deer pants for streams of water, so my soul pants for you, O God" (Psalm 42:1)? Or what could more graphically describe God's love for a stubborn, hard-hearted people than Hosea's relationship with the prostitute Gomer and how it represented God's love for the lost?

What's a clearer picture of the call to a life of faith than of an athlete, training diligently and running hard so as to win the prize (Philippians 3:14)? And, what Christian serious about caring for a lost world has ever casually glanced at the portrait of the Good Samaritan and not been convicted to reach out (Luke 10)?

There's no doubt that word pictures are a powerful way to communicate. They take our words right to another person's heart and also lock them inside their memory. For now, let's look at a few examples of word pictures illustrated in relationships. See if they don't grab your attention more than everyday words.

Let's say a woman usually finds herself saying to her husband: "I'm sick of being ignored around here. You're always watching television." To which he could reply: "Now, honey, am I *always* watching television. Did I watch TV *this morning*? Did I watch it anytime during the day *yesterday*?" (Remember, if you share feelings with a man—the language of the heart)—you're likely to get an answer back in facts—(the language of the head.)

Instead of the same overworked phrases that really don't address the real concern (which is not he is "always" watching television but her feelings of being ignored), you could use a word picture to carry your words.

The wife could ask: "Honey, can we talk sometime soon, right now or tonight if it's better, about something that's been concerning me?" When they do sit down to talk in a quiet setting, the wife could *hand her husband the remote control unit* from the television set. Instead of the standard lecture, she could say:

"Do you know how I'm feeling right now? When you watch TV, you use the remote control device to skip past something you don't like and turn to something really interesting. For the past several weeks, I've been feeling like I'm one of the channels on your set—one of the ones you skip past when you're looking for something really interesting to watch.

"In fact, when my face finally does come up on the screen, you either click the remote to the next channel or put it on 'mute.' On the few times you do leave me on the screen, I feel as if I'm talking and talking to you, but you're just staring at me as if you can't hear a word I'm saying.

"What I want to know is what it would take to have you get your finger off the mute button so I could get some 'air time' to talk about some issues that I feel are very important."

Or instead of a man saying to his wife over and over: "That's it. I've had it with you nagging me. I'll tell you when I'm going to fix the fence. *When I'm good and ready, that's when!* That is unless you keep bugging me—in which case I'll put it off even longer!"

He could use a word picture to communicate his frustration:

"Sweetheart, we've got to talk. Can I ask you a question? How would you feel if you were with the two little ones at the grocery store, and every cash register had a huge line behind it? And not only that, after you finally picked a line, the check-out lady decides to go on a break when you're two people from the front. That means you have to go all the way to the end of another long line and wait all over again, and all the time you're waiting in line, the kids are acting up and arguing with each other and embarrassing you. How would that make you feel?"

Certainly, if she'd experienced such a day at the store she'd be very frustrated, and after hearing her response, he could say:

"Well, you may not realize it, but that's exactly what's going on at work lately. With the move coming up and my having to work with so many different departments and problems, I feel as if I've had to stand in one line to order new equipment, then get in another line to get the space in the new building to put it in. Then I find out that I can't have the space, and I'm back in line, having to start all over again. All the time there are people running around pestering me with little problems and making things really frustrating.

"Finally, after standing in lines all day, I come home from work, and you tell me there's another chore you want me to do. I know that the house and the fence are important to you, but right now, I feel as if I'm standing in so many lines at work, I just can't get in the 'fence' line until we finish our move in three weeks. Can I have a 'time out' from reminders to fix the fence until the move is done at work?"

Do Word Pictures Really Motivate a Person to Change His Behavior?

Word pictures can help make the hard work of a relationship easier by providing the initial motivating factor in getting the process of change started. My own family continually uses word pictures with me because they're so powerful. Recently my daughter Kari shared a word picture with me that motivated me to change an out-of-balance attitude I had with my youngest son, Michael.

We were driving home from a vacation in our rented motor home. We had been gone for about five days, and it was about ten o'clock at night as we finally headed back to Phoenix. Everyone else was asleep when twenty-two-year-old Kari came up to sit by me. It brought back special memories of old times, as it seemed that she was always the one who would "stay up and talk to Daddy to help keep him awake" when she was a little girl. Only this time, instead of talking about her dreams or dating, she said: "Dad, there's something I want to talk to you about. . . . But it can wait until we get back home."

"No, go ahead," I said. "We've got nothing but time."

"But I don't know exactly how to explain this to you," she said.

"Why don't you try to think up a word picture?" I suggested.

"Okay," she said. I jogged her thoughts by saying, "Pick some area that's very familiar to me." We drove on in silence for a few moments as she thought up a word picture.

"Okay, I've got one," she finally announced.

"Pretend that you're giving a seminar somewhere, and it's a really big one. I mean like 2,000 people in the conference. On the first night, you're really funny and warm, and everybody's responded well. They all can't wait for the next day.

"But the next morning when the seminar starts, you're not warm or funny at all. In fact, you spend the whole time criticizing them—even when a lot of them really don't deserve it. You say things like, 'I'm fed up with all of you. You go to church and read the Bible but you don't really love your family like you should!' Or you say, 'I'm so sick of the way some of you wives hound your husbands, it's push, push, push all the time!!! And you men, why don't you grow up and be the lovers you're supposed to be?'

"What would happen to the people in the audience, Dad, if you spent the entire morning criticizing them?"

I said, "Kari, I probably wouldn't have an audience very long. Undoubtedly some of the people would get up and leave as soon as I got started—and many more would begin leaving at the first break. They'd say, 'Why am I sitting here listening to this junk? Who does he think he is? He doesn't even know my situation. . . .'"

I thought for a moment—not realizing that I was digging myself a deeper grave—and said, "You know in Proverbs it says, 'Pleasant words are a honeycomb, sweet to the soul and healing to the bones.' I pray that God will help me speak that way. I don't want to come across harsh."

Kari said, "Dad, I hate to say this to you, but this is probably more true of you than you realize. You see, Michael lives at one of those seminars every day where you are criticizing people —only he's a captive audience. He can't get up and leave like those people when you criticize him."

I couldn't have been stopped any shorter if I had just hit a brick wall with the camper. Perhaps it's because Michael is so much like me, but I have had to battle a tendency to "pick, pick, pick" on little things he does. "Mike, chew with your mouth closed. Mike, don't drink out of that. Mike, don't. . . ." At the time of this writing, it's been a year since Kari hit me with that word picture, and I have yet to forget it.

Kari's word picture literally changed my behavior on the spot, because her words turned into a laser beam and hit me right in the heart. The first thing I did when Michael woke up that morning was to ask his forgiveness. For a year now Kari's word picture has been my constant reminder that I'm to be his greatest encourager—not his strongest critic. Word pictures can be extremely effective, but just as with any skill, we have to learn the basics—and practice them.

Becoming an Expert One Step at a Time

When I first learned to ski, the instructor had to show us how to do it one step at a time. That was frustrating at first, because I saw all these expert skiers gracefully gliding down the slopes, and all the time I was feeling like a pigeon-toed duck with two left feet. He kept drilling us on different skills involved, and after a while I became so dejected that I never thought I'd be able to ski like everyone else, but I was wrong.

Deep-seated problems don't vanish instantly without consistent work by the couple and relying on God's strength for daily endurance.

Bit by bit, as I practiced what he taught, I began to wed one skill to another. Pretty soon, I could get out on the slopes and not have to think, *Plant your pole, pressure on the downhill ski, lean into the turn, turn around the pole, slide the uphill ski alongside.* After practicing time and again, it just came naturally! Now I enjoy skiing more than I ever thought I could.

It's the same way with word pictures. At first, you may feel awkward and discouraged when you try to use them. Each step may seem tedious. But keep at it! You'll get the hang of it quicker than you think. Soon you'll be a master at using them.[4]

Time and again we've seen frustrated, tense relationships transformed as committed couples have used word pictures. This change in their lives doesn't happen by magic. Deep-seated problems don't vanish instantly without consistent work from the couple and a reliance on God's strength for daily endurance. But word pictures can and do bring change—particularly as people discover this powerful pattern of "picture talk" set down in the Scriptures.

If word pictures are the most powerful method of communicating we know, there is a second aspect to communicating that any healthy home shouldn't be without. This method has saved many a conversation from deteriorating into a distasteful argument. It works by slowing down what we say—in order to quick listen!

The Effectiveness of Slowing Down to Quick Listen!

During my morning run one day, I thought of something I could do as a loving act for Norma. I decided that since we were going camping that afternoon, I'd volunteer to pack the camper. She could go to breakfast with her good friend Helen and have a great time while I got our things stowed away.

I increased my pace, and when I got home, I said, "Hey, do I have a surprise for you!"

"What's that?" Norma asked.

"What do you think about calling Helen and the two of you going out to breakfast this morning? I'll do all the packing for the trip."

"Hmmmph," she said as she turned and walked away. It was not exactly the reaction I was anticipating.

"What's wrong?" I said, following her. That's when she said something that I couldn't believe I was hearing:

"You've been thinking for a long time how you could take over the packing, haven't you?"

I was stunned. "No!" I answered emphatically.

She responded by saying, "Then why do I get the feeling you think you can pack the camper better than I'm doing it?"

"WHAT?" At that moment, I wanted to tell her *she* could go ahead and pack the camper and *I'd* go to breakfast with Helen.

When the initial anger subsided, I realized she thought I was coming from a totally different direction, but before we got into a major blowout, I decided we needed to do a little *quick listening* to straighten things out.

"Why are you reacting to me like this?" I asked.

"Because I know that secretly you don't like the way I pack the camper."

"You mean you think I made up the thing about you going to breakfast with Helen so I could get you out of the way and pack the camper. Is that right?"

"Yes, exactly."

"Norma! That wasn't it at all. I was trying to think of something loving I could do for you today."

She paused, "You're saying that you were trying to do something *nice* for me?"

"As strange as it may seem, *Yes!*"

By doing some quick listening, I was able to clarify exactly what she thought the issue was, allow her the opportunity to see that I truly understood her, and then correct the misperception in our communication. By listening rather than reacting, I was able to avoid a major confrontation.

Quick listening is simply one technique you can use to help you understand what the other person is really saying. It slows conversation to a pace that both of you can manage. Surprisingly, in our high-speed world, putting thoughts in low gear can move understanding ahead more quickly.

It's a helpful tool to use when an argument is about to erupt, and it is also very useful in everyday conversation to clarify meaning and enhance understanding. It helps you talk through problems succinctly and more clearly, and forces you to make your statements fairly. There are just three simple steps in mastering the art of quick listening.

Three Steps to "Quick" Listening

1. Try to Recognize the Issue behind the Issue

Let's say you and I are having a discussion and are having difficulty understanding one another. Using quick listening, I can honor you by giving you the opportunity to clarify what you're saying first. It lets you know that I'm genuinely concerned and interested in what you're saying—and that I'm making an effort to understand you. It relaxes you because you realize I'm more interested in comprehending what you say than conquering the discussion. It also allows me another opportunity to hear what you're trying to say.

With Norma, the issue wasn't breakfast with Helen. The issue that was at the heart of her hurt feelings was her sensitivity in thinking I was really criticizing the way she packed the camper. We could have talked all day about my words, but when we slowed the conversation down to talk about the issue *behind* the words and her reaction, we quickly came to an understanding of the real problem.

2. Restate What the Other Person Has Said in Your Own Words

After the other person has had the opportunity to summarize what they've said, I can respond, "Now let me repeat what you've said to make sure I understand." I can then verbalize what they've said to see if I've actually received the message *they* meant to communicate.

If I have it right, they'll say, "Yes, that's it." If not, they can say, "No." Then I can restate what they've said. Again, that's what I did with Norma. I had to slow things down and ask her specifically—by repeating her words—if she felt that I was criticizing her instead of helping her. It's my responsibility at that point to keep asking questions and rewording her statement until I get a "yes." When I do, it's my turn to tell her how I feel. That way we're both honored in what is said.

3. Lovingly Confine What You Say

Using too many words during an important discussion can actually break down intimate conversation. When we talk in long, rambling paragraphs instead of short concise statements, we increase the chances the listener has for reacting to what we say, without really understanding it. If we continue to add words without clarifying the issues and feelings we have, the other person can become so frustrated or bored that he'll tune us out altogether.

Learning to be brief isn't always as easy as it sounds. Not too long ago, I took an intensive two-day course in Los Angeles on how to be interviewed on television, radio, and for a newspaper. The first day I felt like a dismal failure. The instructors kept trying to get me to be brief and to the point, and I just couldn't do it.

"Now, Gary," one said, "you have to summarize the most important part of your message in one sentence." After years of being "wordy" by nature, I couldn't do it. She kept stopping the tape and making me try again and again.

"Gary, you said that in five sentences. I said *one!*" my coach would insist. "If you're going to get your message across on television, you've got to be brief. People may like to read about details, but on television or in person they won't stay with you for five sentences."

By the second day, I was doing much better. When I concentrated on what I was saying, I was amazed that I could use half as many words and say twice as much. I love to talk, so, take heart—if *I* can slow down and summarize my conversations, *anyone* can!

Often, couples need to limit their words to increase their understanding of each other. Once, while counseling a couple where the wife rarely stopped talking to listen, I had to break in on her: "I'm sorry, but if you really want your husband to spend time with you, I have to be honest." We were close enough friends for me to say, "You've got to make a decision to confine yourself to saying things with a fewer number of words. I'm getting bored listening to you, and I'm the counselor! Remember that confining your words and listening to what he has to say is one of the most loving acts you can do."

God has endowed some of us with a love for the spoken word. That's tremendous, but sometimes we can get carried away! As did the wife mentioned above, we can lose our audience of one as a result.

Quick listening has stopped numerous arguments from flaring around the Smalley household, and I know it can make a difference in your family as well. We've made a conscious decision not to let our anger stay around longer than the sun going down and to make every effort to honor one another through greater understanding.

Proverbs 14:29 says, "He who is slow to anger has great understanding, but he who is quick tempered exalts folly." One of the keys to any healthy relationship is a willingness to say, "I'm more interested in understanding what you're saying to me than in thinking of what I'm going to say once you're done talking." Quick listening is one of the best ways I know to help others discover what you're thinking—and what they're thinking as well.

In the previous chapter, we looked at how a husband or wife needs to provide security as bright sunlight in which a relationship can grow. Now we've seen that meaningful communication is like a summer rain shower to encourage such growth. These are two of the four essential elements a loving "nurturer" needs to grow a strong marriage or family.

Now let's go on to discover a third important element of a loving home. It is every bit as important as soil is to a healthy root system. At the same time, we'll be uncovering a secret to keep courtship alive in marriage for years on end.

10

Keeping Courtship Alive in Marriage

Without a doubt, this was going to be the most romantic evening of their entire marriage. Of course, they'd only been married a year, but Greg knew his surprise for Sharon would redefine the word "romance."

Unbeknownst to his wife, Greg had taken off work early to get ready for their anniversary. He knew his wife's favorite thing was to enjoy dinner at a place with a beautiful view, so he came up with the ultimate restaurant—*on top of a nearby mountain!*

Greg spent five hours carrying a table, chairs, a Coleman stove, ice, and drinks up to the pinnacle of a small peak near their home. In his mind's eye, he saw the two of them sharing a wonderful dinner together, complete with thousands of city lights sparkling below them like candles. And after a romantic dinner . . . *who knows?*

All that remained for him to do was to drive to his wife's work-place, surprise her, and make the climb to the intimate nest he'd created on top of the world. Greg had thought of everything . . . except his wife's interests and response. For from the moment he "surprised" her at work, his beautiful plan began to unravel.

First, she was so tired from a grueling day of fighting office politics that she wanted to stay home and rest—not go out for a long evening. Then when he pulled out her climbing boots, she said she was too tired to climb anything—and she wasn't really hungry anyway.

Greg didn't want to give away his carefully arranged surprise. (Besides, he knew they had an hour up-hill ahead of them just to reach the summit.) So he demanded that she "quit griping" and start climbing.

Reluctantly, she trudged up the mountain to where the wind

had kicked up and blown over most of his campsite. Then the campstove wouldn't light . . . and the ice had melted . . . and the wind kept blowing dirt all over the table . . . and he'd forgotten the forks.

Finally, dinner was served but Sharon was so tired from climbing and nearly being blown off the mountain-top, she said she'd pass on eating. In total frustration, Greg ripped off the tablecloth, sending dishes flying everywhere. This only caused her to begin to cry and him to begin to fume.

Instead of walking down the mountain arm in arm in the moonlight that night, they stumbled down the now pitch-dark trail in silence (naturally, he'd forgotten a flashlight). The ice for their drinks may have melted up on the mountain-top—but the wall of ice between them was as thick as a brick wall as they drove home!

Greg had the right idea. He was trying to add an important element to their marriage that is missing for many couples. Unfortunately, he missed some important aspects of this third important way to nurture a marriage.

Keeping Courtship Alive in Your Marriage

During courtship, romance is something that seems to overflow naturally. Let the years of marriage pass, however, and often romance slows to a thin trickle. Yet romance is an essential ingredient of a strong relationship. Most women admit it is lacking in their home, and most men confess inability and failure in supplying it.

Actually, romance is not unique to our day. It has filled stories since the beginning of time, but with our Hollywood images of intimacy, for many of us it's difficult ever to experience the real thing. While it may not seem as important as meaningful communication or keeping a person's spirit open, romance is still an essential element to building the kind of loving, lasting relationships we've been discussing.

Romance finds its place in a marriage right between the chapters that illustrate love as a decision of our will, and the sexual relationship which involves our feelings and emotions. In many ways, romance is the bridge between the two. It's an important way we express honor to our spouse, and it provides the basis for a meaningful sex life.

Poetically, we could say that romance is the flame which glows on the candle of unconditional love; it's the act of honor that soothes and refreshes a marriage like a gentle spring rain; it's the fertile soil in which passion grows. But for those of us who didn't major in poetry, what is it in plain English?

Romance is the act of keeping your courtship alive long after the wedding day. Put another way, romance is an intimate friendship, celebrated with expressions of love reserved only for each other.

Romance is the act of keeping your courtship alive long after the wedding day.

Ground Rules for Helping Romance Blossom

In some ways, romance breaks open the deepest feelings of a person. Greg had hoped that all his special efforts would show Sharon how excited he was that she was his wife. He had sought to create a natural setting that would open up her life to a deeper intimacy. Instead, his relationship took a fall from the mountaintop. Why? For the same reason that many couples struggle in keeping courtship alive in their marriage. They need to follow several practical ground-rules to keep romance on the right trail to intimacy.

The most common reason why romance dies in a relationship is that it gets inseparably linked to physical intimacy. Often this happens because that's the way television or movies paint the scene. It's as if any display of tenderness or emotional intimacy is simply a warm-up for the main act of physical intimacy, but while effective romance may *sometimes* lead to sex, our goal in being romantic shouldn't be sex.

God certainly created men to be goal-oriented initiators. He filled their bodies with a wonderful chemical that heightens their sex drive (see Chapter 11). Sometimes, though, we allow our natural enthusiasm to get the best of us and make the fundamental mistake of substituting emotional closeness with a physical experience.

If the only time I take my wife's hand is to say, "Let's go to bed," I'm ignoring her need for romantic times apart from the bedroom. For most women, it's almost as if God has wonderfully crafted them with a built-in "relational safety switch" that won't allow a few moments of pleasure to be a counterfeit for a meaningful relationship.

If romance is more than just making sure the hallway's clear to the bedroom, what is it? First, it's

Friendship, Not Foreplay

In his book, *Romancing Your Marriage,* Norm Wright quotes a couple who define romance this way:

> Romance is not a setting. . . . It's a *relationship* which can be taken into and out of a wide variety of settings.[1]

I like that! Romance is a *relationship,* not an event. It's not something we do occasionally to stoke the fires of passion. Rather, it should be an ongoing, foundational part of our relationship, something that doesn't come and go like the tide, but flows as steadily as a river. An inescapable aspect of romance is being "best friends" with your spouse.

In the Song of Solomon, Solomon praises his bride saying, "This is my lover, this my friend . . ." (5:16). During the ideal courtship, couples should have time to build their friendship to its peak. Why is friendship so closely linked to romance?

Can you think back to "your song" on the radio, your table at a favorite restaurant, your secret way of holding hands? During courtship, an entire nation may be listening to the same love song on the radio—but that same song creates a special bond between the two of you.

A key to blending friendship with romance is to take the

time to explore each other's interests and then share them together. I recently saw a cartoon that captures this idea. The scene shows a couple walking happily hand in hand, looking deeply into each other's eyes, and obviously enjoying a conversation together. The caption reads, "Romance happens when . . . he asks about her potted plants and she asks about the football scores." As unromantic as "sunflowers" and "screen passes" may seem, that cartoon really captures the essence of one important element of romance.

If you're not growing a friendship based on each other's shared interests—I can almost guarantee you that the romantic soil in your relationship is lacking the essential nutrients it needs. I learned this the hard way one summer when a "romantic" getaway did nothing but push Norma away from me.

Missing the Forest for the Trees

For years one of the things that I thought would be a "10" romantically would be to take a long camping trip to the Colorado mountains with Norma. This would be a special, two-week trip where we took scenic back roads to the most beautiful places in the state, visited historic spots, and stayed in campgrounds or even out in the wild. After years of prodding, I finally convinced my wife it would be a great experience, so we loaded up and headed for the hills.

Less than half-way through the trip, Norma was beside herself. She finally broke down and said, "I don't know how much longer I can take this. There are no malls around, no cute shops, and no restaurants. I can't handle another day of this, much less another week. Can't we camp in the mountains close to a town so we could walk to it and see some other people or shop for the kids?"

At first I was angry that she was trying to ruin my "romantic" dream vacation. I even drove nonstop from Colorado to Flagstaff, Arizona, without saying one word to her on the way home. Later, I apologized for my actions, and I realized I had never thought of asking what would be a romantic trip for *her.* I wasn't interested in what she was interested in; I had my own romantic adventure in mind, even though it was hopelessly boring for her.

Fortunately, even if we feel helpless in picking a romantic

experience, there's something a man or a woman can specifically do to help turn one's spouse into the hopeless romantic we'd like him or her to be.

What's Your Ten?

Contrary to popular opinion, close romantic times don't just happen. With our over-committed lifestyles, if we don't set our schedules, someone or something else will set them for us. Since the chances to make great memories together come and go so quickly, it's important to take advantage of opportunities for romance that come our way.

Planning is the key. I know, some of you are thinking, *But Gary! . . . Planning takes all the thrill out of it. Romance is supposed to be spontaneous!* No doubt spontaneity has its place; we'll look at that in a moment. For now, though, it's crucial we rid ourselves of the false notion that the secret to building a romantic relationship is the five o'clock phone call for a candle-light dinner at six.

By planning, what I mean is using the "twenty questions" method with your spouse. This is something we've done at seminars across the country, and it's amazing the amount of "romantic" information you can get in a short time. If you remember, Chapter 4 listed questions a husband can ask a wife that can revolutionize their relationship. Each question uses the "one to ten" scale to gauge the other's response.

The same is true here. Husbands and wives should begin blending their recipe for romance together with:

"Honey, on a scale of one to ten, what's a romantic ten to you?"

It's a good idea to have paper and pen ready, to jot down each idea that is suggested. Next, "milk" these answers for added information. By "milking" I mean try to find out as much information as possible about what your spouse has told you by asking more questions about the idea.

For instance, if your spouse says, "I think it would be a ten to go on a skiing vacation," then you could ask, "Where would you want to go? What time of the year? What kind of snow would you like best? Would you need new ski clothes? What colors and styles? Where would we eat? Where would you like to stay?

Would we meet friends there or go by ourselves? Would we do anything else besides ski?" The list could go on and on.

Each question you ask makes you a more insightful romantic. The more you know about what would be a "ten" for your spouse, the more you'll be able to understand his or her interests, and become more fully involved in them.

Not too many of us are able to schedule a week's skiing as a vacation, which leads to a very important principle we need to keep in mind. *The success of romantic times together has very little to do with how much money we spend.* If successful, romantic relationships depended on the size of our bank account, most of us wouldn't even have a nodding acquaintance! Focusing on money as the secret to sharing one another's interests will rob us of some of the most romantic times we'll ever spend.

Steve Lyon, one of our invaluable staff members, recently had no money in his pocket and an open Sunday afternoon. Sensing his wife's, Brenda's, need to get out of the house, he loaded her and their baby girl into the car and drove to a downtown civic and arts center.

Sidewalk vendors were selling trendy T-shirts, jewelry, and ice cream; couples and families sat on a plush carpet of green grass listening to a brass quartet. Fountains flowed with the gentle sounds of bubbling water, and the art museum was open free of charge. They didn't buy *anything*—not even an ice cream bar or a glass of lemonade.

Two hours later, they were relationally richer and not a penny poorer. Brenda would later say, "That was one of the most romantic times we've had in months." Surprising, isn't it? Not to a man who knew his wife's love and interest in art and who took time that could have gone into a Sunday nap to create a romantic memory in her life.

So who cares if you can't jet to the Rockies and schoosh down a mountain? Spend a Saturday morning hunting down garage sales or going for a frozen yogurt. Your romance will never be better, even if your wallet isn't bulging with money! (Later, we'll share twenty-five low-cost ideas on keeping courtship alive.)

Why not sit down with your spouse and look at the year ahead? Find out each other's romantic tens, and schedule what you can into the calendar. It's amazing what anticipation does to heighten romance! Be sure to commit to making these dates a priority. If you don't, other things or other people will crowd them out of your schedule.

At our house, we sometimes know what we'll be doing a year in advance. Most families don't plan that far ahead, but my work requires me to plan so that other things don't choke the romance out of our relationship. Norma and I talk about special times we'll have together as a family (something I discuss more fully in Chapter 12), but we make sure we reserve some special time just for the two of us.

Developing a deep level of friendship through shared interests is the first essential ingredient in a romantic relationship. Discovering each other's relational "tens" and making plans to make them happen can also make a huge difference in the quality of our romantic times together. There's a third way of keeping the courtship alive with our spouse. It's found in learning to . . .

Celebrate the Moments of Your Life

Those who are wise romantics will realize that some special date or event every year can be used to fan the romantic flame. I recall one man who did put together a very special celebration for his wife to honor her for a sacrifice she had made for him.

It was the eve of his graduation from a long, grueling master's degree program. Four years of intensive, full-time study had finally found him about to receive his diploma.

His wife planned a special party where many of their friends were to come and help him celebrate the long awaited "day of deliverance." There would be cake, refreshments, banners, streamers, a pool nearby, croquet, and other yard games. Many people had already accepted her invitation to come, and it looked like it would be a full house. Her husband, though, had other ideas. He secretly contacted each person who had received an invitation and told them he wanted to make the party a surprise in honor of *her*. Yes, there would be banners, streamers, and all the rest, but they would bear her name, not his.

He wanted to do something special to let her know how much he appreciated the years of sacrifice she'd devoted to his graduation. Working full time to put him through, and putting off her dreams of a house and family, had, in many ways, been harder on her than the long hours of study had been on him.

When the day arrived, she was busy with preparations and last minute details, still convinced that all was going according to plan. He arranged to get her away from the party site, and while she was gone, he put up a huge banner with her name on it. During that time all the guests arrived as well.

She returned to be greeted with a huge "SURPRISE!!!" and when she realized what was going on, she could barely fight back the tears. Her husband asked a few people to share what they most appreciated about her. Then he stood before them and, with tender words of love and appreciation, expressed his gratitude for all she'd done for him. When he was through, they saluted her with an iced-tea toast.

The rest of the evening was a fun-filled fiesta of laughing, catching up with one another, water volleyball, yard games, and more food than anyone could eat. It was a celebration of an experience they both shared, and by commemorating it in a special way, this husband created a lifelong, romantic memorial to his wife's love and dedication.

Birthdays, anniversaries, or holidays can become more than simply a traditional observance. They can be a personal opportunity to let your loved one know they are very special to you—in ways they'll never forget.

Creative Romance:
Surprise, Surprise, Surprise!

We've seen that building a friendship around shared interests and tapping into times of special celebration, can strengthen the romantic bonds in a relationship. There's another aspect of romance that, if not overused, can also be a real help in a home, for if it's true that the element of surprise has won countless battles, it's equally true that it has won the hearts of untold lovers.

A young man in our home church recently pulled off a romantic surprise that's one of the best I've ever heard. It's something his wife-to-be will never forget, and it will make a great story for his grandchildren one day.

It was a beautiful, clear desert morning. The sun was still minutes away from its grand entrance, but it teased the Eastern sky with a hundred shades of gold. The mountains kept their silent sentinel in the cold, crisp dawn, the brilliant stars shining behind them like silver sequins on black velvet.

"WHHHOOOOOOOSSSHH," the sound of the hot-air balloon's burner broke the desert's quiet with resounding force. In a few heartbeats, its brilliant blue and red canopy sprang to life and lifted off the ground. It floated upward, carrying a basket with Steve, Jan, and the pilot cradled inside.

Going up in a hot-air balloon was something they'd both wanted to do for a long time, and now they were in the air! In just a few moments, they were several hundred feet up, gliding along with the wind's gentle currents.

The scene was spectacular, and while Steve and Jan were busy enjoying the moment, the pilot was making sure the flight continued to go smoothly.

All at once, the incredible quiet was broken by the distinct drone of an engine. At first, Jan thought it must be the sound of a truck on the road below them, but then she realized it was getting louder. Startled, Jan looked up to see an airplane headed right for them! She was paralyzed with fear—but if she had looked at Steve or the pilot, she'd have seen them both smiling.

The plane Steve had hired to "buzz" the hot air balloon was right on time. When it turned close to them, a long tail appeared behind it revealing a message that read, in larger-than-life letters, "*I love you, Jan. Will you marry me?*"

When the words on the banner finally hit her, she was beside herself; she jumped up and down in the confines of the balloon basket like a six-year-old on Christmas morning. "Yes, I'll marry you!" she said, laughing and crying at the same time. For this couple, a special surprise was an indication that creative romance would stay a part of their relationship.

Surprising ways to say "I love you" aren't reserved for restricted air-space. They can be a note put in a lunch-box, a cassette tape with a loving greeting put in the car's tape player in secret, a frozen yogurt that arrives with you at your husband's office on a hot, summer's afternoon. Planning can make sure that romance stays a consistent part of your relationship. But surprises can make the moment a cherished one. These actions all say, *I'm thinking about you, my love for you is secure, you're important to me, we're together for life.*

But I'm Just Not Creative. . . .

I once had a friend who worked with high school students in Young Life. He was one of the funniest, most creative people I'd ever met. One day I asked him his "secret" for being creative, and he told me, "My definition of creativity is forgetting who I borrowed the idea from."

Now, that might not work in writing books, but it certainly points out that even if you're unfortunate enough to have come up with a "zero" in the ingenuity department—there's still hope. Just draw together ideas from the hopeless romantics around, forget where you borrowed them, and put them into practice!

It's not so much coming up with good ideas on your own, it's knowing where to find them and then knowing how to make them work. It's important to have a good resource for creative, romantic ideas. Let me suggest two:

Tapping into Creative Ideas for Romantic Times

The first source is your spouse. Sometimes we overlook this tremendous resource because it's so obvious. If you ask your spouse, "Honey, what's a romantic ten to you?" you can potentially receive a wealth of ideas. Most people have a list of things that will strike them as creatively romantic.

One of the cornerstones of creativity is this: *Ideas give birth to more ideas.* Something your spouse says may trigger an idea in your mind for a creative way to pull it off. Be alert to this possibility as you talk together. Whatever you do, be sure to *write down your ideas.* Try to keep your "Recipes for Romance" notebook within reach as much as possible.

The second is collecting lists of romantic ideas. These can be found in a variety of places, but several of them are right in your local Christian bookstore. *Four Hundred Creative Ways to Say I Love You* by Alice Chapin is a great resource.[2] So is a chapter entitled "Keeping Romance Alive," in *Romancing Your Marriage* by Norm Wright.[3] *Men, Do You Know Your Wife?* by Dan Carlinsky[4] is a helpful way to get to know things about your wife that will no doubt spark some creativity.

Let me add a few ideas of my own . . .

Twenty Creative, Romantic Ideas That Cost under $20

1. Dress up for a meal you bring back from your favorite fast food restaurant. Take out a tablecloth, centerpiece, and a tape

recorder of your favorite romantic music and dine to a "Golden Arches" delight.

2. Buy a half gallon of your favorite ice cream, go to the most beautiful park in town, throw a blanket on the ground, and eat the whole thing.

3. Visit a museum or art gallery. Talk with each other about the art you like and dislike. Use the "twenty questions" method to learn all you can about why your spouse likes or dislikes what you see. Concentrate on listening to the other person and learning all you can from what he or she says.

4. Go to a driving range together. Cheer each other's good shots.

5. Go bowling together. Come up with prizes you can give each other for winning games; i.e., a massage, a week's worth of doing dishes, a promise to paint the fence, etc.

6. Go on a hay-ride with four other couples, singing camp songs from a tape recorder or guitar. Plan a cookout under the stars afterward.

7. Write love notes to one another and hide them in unusual places like the freezer, a shoe, in the car's glove box, in the bathtub, in a makeup kit, or under the bed covers.

8. Go snorkeling in a lake.

9. Collect leaves and pine cones together on an autumn day. Take them home and make fall ornaments for the house.

10. Attend a free outdoor concert.

11. Buy a pass from the Forest Service, go to a National Forest, and cut your own Christmas tree.

12. Buy a modern paraphrase of the Song of Solomon and read it to one another.

13. Walk hand in hand along a nature trail.

14. Watch a sunset together.

15. Make "dough" ornaments together, bake them, and then color them with the kids.

16. Rent each other's all-time favorite movies and play a double feature at home.

17. Go to your favorite restaurant for dessert. Bring a child's baby book or your wedding album and relive some memories together.

18. Throw a party commemorating your spouse's graduation date.

19. Get the children together and make a "Why I Love Mom" and "Why I Love Dad" book, complete with text and illustrations.

20. Take your spouse out for an afternoon spent in her favorite store. Note the items under $20.00 she likes best. Return to the store the next day and buy one of those items as a gift.

Friendship, planning, surprises, and tapping into each other's creativity are all-important aspects of romance, but before we close this chapter, we need to sound one caution. Let's take a brief look at something that can kill a romantic experience faster than a duck can jump on a June bug.

Putting Romance in the Deep Freeze

Imagine the following scene. A man and woman are casually strolling arm in arm along a beautiful white sand beach. The waves gently wash ashore, and the sea-gulls dart back and forth overhead. A full moon glimmers in the night sky, and the sand seems like an endless strand of silver dust. It's a romantic ending to a perfect day, until . . .

If you look more closely, you will see the look on her face. It isn't one of peace and love. It's one of frustration and anger. Why? The setting is all right, but something he did is all wrong.

Ten minutes before, she told him she wanted to take a quiet walk on the beach and talk. He agreed to the walk which excited her—but he destroyed the romantic setting when he held her hand with one hand, and his fishing pole in the other.

"Hey, I've been casting for years," he told her. "I can talk and fish at the same time, *no problem!*"

This man broke two cardinal rules of romance. *1. Make sure the romantic activity you're involved in receives your full, undivided attention. 2. Make sure you're doing the activity for her best interests, not yours.*

Any time I send Norma flowers, or give her a card, or do something special, I'm saying, "I love you." At the moment it's spontaneous and unclouded by hidden motives, but I can quickly ruin it for her. All I have to do is ask a favor or tell her about my plans for fishing with the guys that weekend, or intimate that what I've done "deserves" a romantic response, and it's as if I walked into the house saying, "Gee, honey . . . you're sure looking bad today."

We've seen several ways in which the courtship aura can remain in a marriage. First, romance doesn't just happen "naturally" in a marriage; it's not simply an extension of physical intimacy. It takes work! Second, the winning recipe for romance is found in developing a friendship centered on shared interests—and carefully planned. Third, by using surprise, spontaneity, and creativity in romance, we can celebrate those special moments that bond us in a meaningful way. Finally, we need to make sure we give our full, undivided attention to our loved one during a romantic time. Each of these suggestions on keeping the courtship alive in our marriage can help to insure that this important area of our lives blossoms like flowers after a spring rain.

The key to being romantic, then, is to concentrate on being *relational*! When that happens, and your spouse truly senses you desire a deep, intimate friendship, then the stage is set to enjoy the wonderful pleasures of physical intimacy. Let's now examine what makes the sexual union meaningful and fulfilling for both the husband and the wife.

11

Sex Is Much More
Than Physical Intimacy

Without question, one of the most interesting topics to both men and women is sex. But does physical intimacy mean the same to a man as it does to a woman? Hardly.

What is the basic physical need of a man? In most cases, the sexual act, and then, coming in a distant second, nonsexual touching. What is the basic physical need of a woman? Meaningful communication, nonsexual touching, and then sex.

We've looked at three ways in which a man or woman can nurture a marriage and see it bloom and grow. Each one is an important part of establishing a successful relationship—but the three are incomplete without a fourth. Within the confines of marriage, God has provided a way to meet an important need in a man and woman's life—that of physical intimacy.

Meeting Each Other's Needs

Numerous studies have shown that 70 to 80 percent of a woman's physical need is simply to be touched and held.[1] Just the opposite is true for a man, especially during the first several years of marriage. For most men, until they move into their late thirties, you could paint a big "T" on their T-shirt. The "T" could represent the sex hormone "testosterone" which tends to drive a man sexually.

In laboratory studies, if researchers inject a female Rhesus monkey with the hormone testosterone, she will gather other female monkeys around her and try to reproduce. Then, once the hormone has worn off, she'll go back to her more natural behavior.

(Some men have heard about the effects of testosterone and driven straight to their local druggist to see if they can get a prescription for their wives. However, as a dangerous steroid, the physical side-effects would include her shaving and being able to out arm-wrestle her husband.)

Perhaps a word picture might help to explain the common difference between a man and a woman in the sexual area. When it comes to marital intimacy, men tend to be like microwave ovens—instantly ready to be turned on at any time, day or night, and also ready to hurry through the cooking experience. The average woman, however, is more like a crock-pot. She needs to warm up to the sexual experience and savor the process, and the thing that warms her up the most is a quality relationship.

To get an idea of your husband's sexual appetite, think about your own desire to eat. How often do you feel hungry when you're on a diet? If you're like most of us, it's three times a day —morning, afternoon, and night! The hunger drive hits a woman on a diet about as often as a man's sex drive naturally hits him— especially during the first years of marriage. That's why a man can slip into bed at 10 o'clock at night after not seeing his wife all day, reach over and touch her on the shoulder, and say, "What do you *think?*"

After a hard day at work, with the kids or both—and little or no meaningful relational time spent to prepare her—her response may well be:

"*What do I think!* You *animal.* Don't even *think* about what you're thinking!"

To most women, sex is much more than just an independent physical act. It's the culmination of a day filled with security, conversation, emotional and romantic experiences, and then, if all is right, sex. For the average man, you can reverse the order— or just skip everything that comes before sex!

In many ways, it's just as hard for the average male to initiate intimate conversations and plan romantic activities as it is for his wife to initiate sex. But these two different needs in the physical area can be met—in a fulfilling way—for both a man and a woman. This is true particularly if you're aware of several practical attitudes and actions that can help to fan passion's flame.

Meaningful Touching Outside the Bedroom Can Help the Touching Inside

Recently I read of a survey conducted among several hundred women.[2] In it, nearly 70 percent of the women responding claimed that if they were never again involved in the sexual act with their husbands, they wouldn't complain a great deal. What they would strongly miss was not being touched, held, and caressed. Every area of a woman's life is affected if she's not touched and held by the most important people in her life. As we mentioned earlier, eight to ten meaningful touches a day is really a minimum requirement for a woman to stay emotionally and physically healthy.

One man I know took his wife's need for meaningful touches so seriously that it got him in real trouble. As he was lathering up in the shower, he realized he'd forgotten a towel. Opening the shower door, he made a mad dash for the linen closet in the hallway. As he opened the closet door, he looked and saw his wife standing at the far end of the hall in the kitchen.

An impulsive thought crossed his mind, and he decided he'd give his wife one of those "meaningful hugs" she needed—right in the kitchen—and with soap and water added. So without a stitch of clothing on and dripping wet, he ran down the length of the hallway and burst into the kitchen to give her a great big bear hug—and that's when he saw the neighbor lady sitting at the kitchen table.

Proper timing might need to be taken into account when giving meaningful touches, but they are certainly one important way to grow a strong physical relationship.

Learning to Put Problems at Arm's Length

Do you know what are the two *least* talked-about areas in most marriages? Death and sex. I'm not sure what the relationship is between these two subjects, but I do know many couples don't see anything humorous about either one. Unfortunately, the lack of communication about the physical side of marriage can add to the problems a couple may have—not subtract from them.

To have a healthy sexual relationship, a couple needs to have the freedom to talk about this often "out of bounds" area, the freedom to share their likes, dislikes, expectations, and frustrations. We know of one couple who used the "word picture" method we talked about in Chapter 9 to open up this sensitive area. The method resulted in their becoming closer than ever before.

Darryl was a pro football player on a championship team that wasn't in the habit of losing. Yet when it came to the sexual area of his relationship with his wife, he felt that they were always having a disappointing season. In particular, he was frustrated about how seldom she would respond to his advances—and the negative fallout that would result from his desires being blocked.

Finally, he became so frustrated he decided to come up with a word picture to explain his feelings. So, after being rebuffed again after watching her get ready for bed, and trying to initiate an intimate time, he sat next to her and shared his word picture.

"Honey, we have *got* to talk," he said.

"Do you know how I'm feeling about our sexual life? I feel as if every night we're playing the shell game. Do you know what I mean? It's the game where there are three cups placed in a row upside down on the dresser.

"Under one of those cups is a bean, and if I can just pick the cup that has the bean under it—you'll be in the mood and we'll share some 'you know what!' But the problem is, I *never* pick the right cup. I feel like every day when I'm at practice, you shuffle the cups all around, and no matter which one I pick when I come home, it's always the wrong one. What I want to know is when are you going to quit hiding the bean?"

Darryl sat back, confident that his word picture would run loose through her mind like an all-pro running back. Certainly now that she understood his feelings, his word picture would score a touchdown for his desires. Undoubtedly, it would result in nonstop "availability" on her part. The only problem was that two can play at word pictures, and the one she shared with him in response reversed fields and scored points for her team.

"Darryl, since you asked, let me tell you the reason why we end up playing the shell game most nights. Let's say I'm your favorite fishing reel." Susan instantly had Darryl's interest when she mentioned fishing—one of his favorite activities in life.

"When we were first married, I felt that I was in beautiful shape, having come right from the factory and being wrapped up in a gift box. As soon as we were married, however, you threw me an old rod you had and took me right out and fished me in salt water. Then when you got home, you never washed me off or took care of me.

"When you first got me, you could cast me a mile because my line wasn't all knotted up, and I was oiled and well taken care of. But over the years with the way you've treated me, the reel has gotten salt-corroded and rusted, the line is all frayed, and the eyelets on the fishing rod are all bent and twisted. Now, whenever you have the impulse, you take me out of the corner of the garage where you've thrown me, and without ever taking care of me, expect me to cast as if I'm brand new.

"Can you see now why all you get is knots and backlashes when you try to cast me?"

Her husband answered, "Well, what in the world can I do?"

"You can either leave me in the garage and get the kind of response you're getting now, or you can fix me," she said. "Honey, if you would hold me and listen to me and quit lecturing me when I ask you a question—it would help me respond like a reel with a brand-new line and new eyelets."

That night, Darryl walked into a word picture that hit him harder than an NFL linebacker. For the first time he was able to "see" what the problem was in their sexual relationship in a way that he could understand.

Meaningful touching outside the bedroom can light sparks in a marriage, and meaningful communication can fan the flames.

They ended up on the back porch talking for hours about a "fishing reel." But in actuality, they were talking about the most intimate area of their marriage. Darryl learned what it would take to "maintain" Susan in a way that could actually make her excited about responding to him. On the other hand, she was able to understand how frustrating the "games" they were playing by not talking about this very important area were.

As an unexpected bonus, they both ended up sharing one of the most romantic evenings in months. Why? Because a word picture can help to take even the most difficult subject and put it at arm's length where it can be more easily seen and talked about.

Like many couples, Darryl and Susan were so close to their problems, they couldn't see the forest for the trees. What a word picture did for them was to take them up in a helicopter to where they could get their bearings, see where they first went off the trail, and find the right pathway back to sexual intimacy.

Meaningful touching outside the bedroom can light sparks in a marriage, and meaningful communication can fan the flames. If a couple cares enough to explain their needs, frustrations, and enjoyments to one another, it can help to turn their relationship around. But there's still more that a couple can do.

Purifying Our Character
Increases the Passion Level in a Home

What do you think our "lovesick" society would say is the greatest "love story" ever told? Clark Gable and Vivian Leigh in *Gone with the Wind* during the '30s? Humphrey Bogart and Ingrid Bergman in *Casablanca* during the '40s? Burt Lancaster and Deborah Kerr in *From Here to Eternity* in the '50s? Ali McGraw and Ryan O'Neal in *Love Story* during the '60s? Barbra Streisand and Robert Redford in *The Way We Were* during the '70s? Or Kelly McGillis and Tom Cruise in *Top Gun* in the '80s?

Actually none of these would be right (or even close!). The greatest love story of all times is recorded right in the Scriptures. In fact if junior high kids realized that an entire book in the Bible talks specifically and explicitly about romance, sex, and intimacy, they'd turn to it in droves. (Of course, they would have to understand a little bit about Hebrew poetry.)

How do we know this love story is the greatest? Because we're told so in the title of the book. This book announces itself as "The Song of Songs" in bold letters. For a reader of Hebrew, something significant stands out. When biblical writers wanted to address something as "the very best, the highest, without equal," they repeated it. In other words, that's why we read statements like "the King of kings" and "the Lord of lords!" in reference to Christ. He is the King above all kings and the Lord without equal.

The title's repetition of the words, "The Song of Songs," then, tells us that this is it. It's the greatest love story of all times. It begins with a strong statement of passion.

"Let him kiss me with the kisses of his mouth!" Solomon's bride says to him in the first full verse of the book. For observant readers, that's *her* initiating an intimate response and *her* asking for him to kiss her—repeatedly!

For every man who was ready to inject his wife with testosterone, here is an example of a woman who didn't need any artificial prompting to want to kiss her husband. Interested in what prompted those words of passion from Solomon's bride?

If we look at the very next verse, we're given the reason—and it might surprise us. She tells us that it wasn't his charm or his good looks; it wasn't the expensive cologne or clothes he could afford to wear as the king; it wasn't even his prestige and power. What made his bride responsive to him was his character (Song of Songs 1:3). Her passion came as a direct reflection of the positive qualities in his life.

"May he kiss me with the kisses of his mouth. . . . *For your name is like purified oil,"* she tells him.

Let's not confuse our modern-day techniques for purifying oil with the way it was done in biblical times. The process this woman is picturing involved taking several trays of different size rocks and layering them from large rocks to the smallest pebbles. By the time oil had dripped through all those layers of rocks and pebbles, all the impurities had been filtered out and only "purified" oil remained. To this bride, Solomon's life, his "name," reflected that same process of purification. All the rough edges of indifference and insensitivity had been filtered out, and his wisdom and character reflected purity of "name" and purpose.

What Solomon's wife is telling us is a truth about marital passion. The more purified my character, the more attractive I am to my spouse—and the more responsive she'll be to me as a result. Time and again I've seen this principle working in the relationships of people—for good or for bad.

I remember the case of a man who lost his job with an insurance agency primarily because he wouldn't do something that was clearly illegal. He knew if he refused to comply with the wishes of his superiors, he'd be instantly fired—but he also knew he'd lose far more if he lied.

On the day before he went in to his boss to tell him he couldn't "cooperate," he went home and told his family about what he had to do. Dinner got cold that night as he made it clear to his wife and daughters that losing his job could very well mean they would lose their house as well.

This living object lesson of standing up for the truth distinctly marked his daughters and actually brought the family even closer together in the weeks that followed. But the response from his wife startled him. Even though his dinner got cold that night, her response to him sexually was the warmest, most romantic that he'd ever experienced in fourteen years of marriage. He was totally shocked, but Solomon wouldn't have been. This man's wife had seen her husband's character ring true as a bell, and that promoted far more passion than any flowers or gifts could ever do.

Before we move on, there is another side to this principle to consider. For those who want to see the romantic spark doused with buckets of cold water—all it takes is exposing major impurities in one's character. I remember the case of another person who did this, and it came very close to ruining his marriage.

Bill was a social climber who had to have the best clothes and the best car—but he couldn't afford either. It's not that he didn't make money, it's just that he didn't make nearly as much as he spent. One day, that dishonoring fact came crashing down on his wife.

He and his wife were both working, in large part so that the children could attend an excellent Christian school nearby. With the fall semester beginning, she handed him her endorsed paycheck to cover the beginning cost of their tuition. Without telling her, he cashed the check and spent it on a "need" he had for a new suit.

He fully intended to "rob Peter to pay Paul" and pay the tuition from another account before anyone else was the wiser—but Peter came up broke. That's when the call from the school came to his wife's office. It landed like a bombshell.

It was the school secretary on the phone. Regretfully she informed the wife that her children wouldn't be able to attend class any more until their tuition was paid. The wife confronted her husband when he got home. He lied at first, still trying to cover his tell-tale tracks. Then he made up another lie to cover the first one. Soon his character looked so full of impurities to her that she didn't even want to see him—much less touch him in love. It took months of counseling about his spending problems and re-establishing a track-record of trust before she began to respond to him physically again.

The moral of the story? Our romantic relationship may never be called the "Song of Songs," but we can still sing the chorus with gusto. And a clear stanza from that very helpful song reads, "If you want to raise the passion level in your marriage— increase the purity of your character."

Passion Grows Where a National Average Doesn't

We've all read reports in newspapers or magazines that give an "average number of times" that the "average" couple has sexual relations each day/week/month/year/ or decade. I'm not really sure what the purpose of such averages are, except to increase the counseling rate.

Too many couples who struggle sexually let a phantom national average dictate their loving response. One or both spouses can be so busy chasing after a national average that they forget that the "goal" they're working so hard to achieve is just that— average.

How should couples interpret such figures? Frankly, I recommend that they don't keep track of them at all. In a normal marriage, there will be times of high sexual activity, and periods where it is very low. Trying to keep up with someone else's idea of what "average" is, is an invitation to sexual frustration, not sexual satisfaction.

What's the best marriage guide? The Owner's manual on wise living, namely the Bible. First Corinthians 7:3–5 gives us a healthy "average" to shoot for: "The husband should fulfill his marital duty to his wife, and likewise the wife to her husband. The wife's body does not belong to her alone but also to her husband. In the same way, the husband's body does not belong to him alone but also to his wife."

In other words, a desire to respond to each other in love and a consistent willingness to meet each other's legitimate needs is the best advice on when to be sexually intimate. Don't let anyone set a loving "schedule" for you from a book or newspaper. Look to the Book for the best advice on timing—and on increasing intimacy as well.

Keep "Performance" on the Stage and out of the Bedroom

There are two words that work well on the playing field but are absolute killers in the bedroom. What are they? *Performance anxiety.*

The Diagnostic Statistical Manual, Volume III, is an encyclopedia of psychological dysfunctions. In fact, it lists almost 200 pages of possible sexual problems. Do you know what one of the primary "treatment choices" is for all but a handful of these many disorders? "*Decrease* performance anxiety." In other words, if you can get acting and unrealistic expectations out of the bedroom, you can erase almost every sexual dysfunction that doesn't have a physiological basis, and you decrease performance anxiety by lowering expectations to realistic levels, focusing on genuine love, and seeking to meet the *other person's* needs, comfort, and pleasure instead of your own.

Often a man who has performance anxiety is one who judges the quality of his marriage by his sexual prowess. If, in the normal course of a marriage, he experiences some frustration in his sexual performance, fear can set in, and he can lose all confidence in this area. On the other hand, if a woman "performs" her way through the "act of marriage" by faking her real feelings or responses, genuine intimacy can be a long-forgotten experience. Couples need to stay clear of performance anxiety if they want passion to occur—and not be a memory from the past.

In a way, the sexual side of a relationship can be a barometer to the status of the marriage. In other words, if a wife is not responding to her husband sexually, 99 times out of 100 you can find the reason in their emotional or spiritual relationship. Some men may say, "Forget all these 'relationship' reasons for our sexual problems—I just married a frigid woman."

If you're one of these men, I suggest you honestly check the temperature of your relationship—the security level, the conversation, the sensitivity and romance, and the meaningful touching apart from the sexual act. In reality, *less than three per cent of all women are organically nonorgasmic or truly "frigid."* Of course, I can just hear someone saying, "It figures. I've got one of those wives in the three per cent." If that's your attitude, this is where honor needs to comes in.

Love Does Not Dishonor . . .

Dishonoring words that come up around the sexual area act like red lights to an intimate response. Take the man who would comment on his wife's need to "lose weight" just as she undressed to get into bed. Usually it's the same man who couldn't understand why she was cold and unresponsive. Or what about the woman who "teased" her husband about his sexual endurance until they had a major problem in his responding at all?

Solomon's bride knew she was deeply loved by her husband, but still she says, "Do not stare at me because I am dark . . ." (Song of Songs 1:6). Ever since Adam and Eve hid their nakedness from God and each other, there has been a natural insecurity around the sexual act. That level of insecurity can be multiplied by ten with poorly timed or insensitive words, but it's not only words that can be dishonoring and result in lowered passion. Actions can speak louder and more powerfully in this area.

Not too long ago, a man approached me as I was walking out to my car after a seminar. I could tell he was nervous.

"Gary, could I ask you just one question before you leave?" It was pushing eleven o'clock at night, following the first session of our seminar.

"I didn't want to ask this in front of anyone else," he said. "That's why I didn't come up to you inside. You see, I have a problem in my marriage. For years I've been making my wife do something when we're making love that she has hated doing, and now it's gotten so bad, she doesn't want to have anything to do with me at all. *Gary, isn't my wife supposed to submit to me, or am I reading the Bible wrong?"*

The answers to his questions were yes and yes. Yes, the Bible does say that a woman is to place herself under the loving leadership of her husband, and yes, he was reading the Bible wrong. Nowhere does it say that "submission" gives a man (or woman) the right to make a spouse do something they feel is wrong or terribly "dishonoring"—just to meet a selfish need.

I know that there are books written by Christian leaders who say that basically anything is legal in the bedroom, but I would have to disagree. As we discussed in Chapter 2, at the heart of love is a decision to honor a person—to count him or her as incredibly valuable. Forcing my wife to violate her conscience to please my sexual appetite is absolutely wrong and an invitation to sexual problems.

Regardless of the "no holds barred" pictures of pornography that are painted throughout our culture as being "acceptable," some forms of sexual behavior are dishonoring. To ask a spouse to perform a sexual act that is wrong or repulsive to him or her is to show at least a degree of insensitivity or even a lack of love.

Being "one flesh" in a marriage is a wonderful gift of a happy marriage. But it's only one part of a successful relationship. Security, meaningful communication, emotional and romantic times . . . and physical intimacy go together like pieces of a puzzle to make a nearly complete picture of a fulfilling relationship. As we'll see in the last two chapters of this book, there is still a "missing piece" when it comes to a marriage of true oneness. If a marriage is to really reach its peak, a couple must learn how to tap into the *only consistent power source* for keeping their love alive through each season of life. But before we turn to this most important aspect of intimacy, let's look at one final way to build a close-knit family.

12

Discovering the Secret to a Close-Knit Family

Not long ago, John and I were doing our "Love Is a Decision" seminar right in our hometown of Phoenix, Arizona. Whenever they can, my family makes it a point to attend the seminar, so I wasn't surprised when my oldest son, Greg, told me he was coming. What did surprise me, however, was a special request he made.

"Dad," he asked, "could I take about five minutes and share something I think is really important for the parents to hear?"

Gulp! I was honored that Greg would ask, but I also knew all too well that he is the family clown. With his light-hearted nature, he is basically capable of doing or saying anything once he gets in front of an audience. Now he'd be in front of almost a thousand people, and the possibilities for disaster were endless. Then again, how often does your son ask to join you at a family conference? So I readily agreed.

Just for safe-keeping, I did schedule his five minutes during the afternoon of the second day. That way I figured if he did say something off the wall, it would come after a day and a half of positive input from Dr. Trent and myself.

As the time grew near for him to speak, I'll have to admit I became a little nervous. *They're about to hear some inside stories about the Smalley family,* I remember thinking to myself.

Greg began by saying, "I just want you to know what a privilege it is to be here with my Dad and to share in this seminar. I really enjoy being with him during times like this, *because it's one of the few times he's sober . . . ."*

The audience roared, and of course I thought, *Yep, I shot myself in the foot all right. What's this son of mine going to say next?*

"No, no," Greg laughed, "I'm kidding. My Dad doesn't even drink."

Then he said, "I want to share with you parents for a moment." I had been talking to these people for almost two days, and for the most part they had stayed right with me. When my son began to talk, however, I could see people actually leaning forward to hear what he was going to say.

"I want to encourage you to make every effort to become best friends with your kids—and there's an important reason why. I know firsthand that it can make a big difference in their lives as they get older.

"I'm in college now, and there's temptation everywhere. I've seen many of my friends go to other people they know on campus for advice on sex, drugs, cheating, you name it! And the suggestions they are getting would make your blood turn cold. It's like the blind leading the blind! In many cases, I know why they're going to friends and getting bad advice. It's because very few of them feel that they can go to their parents to ask the hard questions.

"That seems odd to me, because I've always been able to talk to Mom and Dad. Sometimes, I'll call them at two in the morning from school to talk about something I'm struggling with. I'm never afraid to wake them up because I know they really love me, and they want to listen to what's happening in my life.

"If I wasn't confident in their friendship, I would not have been able to call them—and I know I wouldn't be open to their counsel. I can assure you that the advice you give your children will be far wiser than most of what they'll hear from people in their dorms at school. So, please, to make sure they'll listen to you when the time comes . . . do what it takes today to build a strong friendship with your children when they're young, so that they'll *want* to come to you when they're older. . . ."

I've been speaking for years, but I can't think of a time when I've grabbed an audience as Greg did that afternoon. I also don't know when I've ever been more proud of him or more humbled to be his father.

Greg struck a chord on what is one of the most crucial factors in developing and maintaining a loving relationship: *learning to be best friends with your children.* At its heart, a close-knit family is one that respects and honors each member and experiences a deep bond of intimacy.

Almost nothing strengthens a husband and wife's relationship more than when the whole family is united and best friends. The question is, "How does a family take on that kind of personality on a consistent basis?"

What's the Secret to a Close-Knit Family?

Years ago, when our kids were little, I started speaking at family retreats across the country. As I spoke, I'd pick out families who looked happy and seemed to respond well to each other. When I had the opportunity, I'd approach the husband and wife with several questions.

First, I'd ask, "You seem to enjoy each other so much and have a real love for one another! What do you think is the most important thing you do as a family that makes you so close?"

Almost without exception, each family I interviewed said, "We've made a commitment to spend quality *and* quantity time together regularly. We have separate interests, but we make sure we do things together as a family on a regular basis."

Then I'd ask, "What's the one thing you do more than any other that you feel bonds you together?" Time and time again, I'd hear an answer that I simply couldn't believe. What was the common denominator of almost every one of these "successful" families? *Camping!*

At that time, Norma and I had never camped together—by choice. But since learning this secret, we've camped together for over fifteen years. That gives me some authority to speak on the subject, and I can say with absolute conviction—camping is *not* the secret. Before I let our noncamping friends off the hook, though, I do need to say that camping is still the best method I know to *find* the real secret to a close-knit family. You'll see what I mean by looking at our very first camping experience.

Baptism by Lightning

The evidence became overwhelming—we needed to go camping. The kids were small, but old enough to travel, so we decided to give it a try. We bought a tiny, second-hand pop-up tent-trailer, packed our gear, and sped off into the sunset.

We had spent a few nights sleeping in our driveway to "test out" the trailer, but our first night of camping out was in Kentucky. There we discovered a beautiful campground with pine trees everywhere. We set up camp under the shade of the largest pine we could find. That night we built a fire, cooked hot dogs, roasted marshmallows, and had a great time together.

Soon after dark the kids fell asleep in the camper, leaving Norma and me alone to talk the evening away by a nice crackling fire. Finally, we called it a night and crawled inside with the kids. We lay there, peaceful and content. For the life of me, I couldn't think what it was that had kept me from the wonders of camping all these years—but I was soon to find out!

Without any announcement, the wind began to blow steadily. Before long, a row of dark clouds marched overhead, and a gentle rain began to fall softly on the roof. Still, it was only a tranquil "pitter-patter" on the pop-up trailer. I settled back to smell the wonderful fresh scent of rain on a summer's night, and to listen to the soothing lullaby that would send us into dreamland. . . .

Then without warning, Wham! The gentle shower turned into a violent storm. The rain began to come down in sheets, and the wind whipped up to gale force levels. Our little camper, once seemingly anchored on firm ground, began to shake and sway like a break-dancer on television. Within moments, the rain was coming down so hard that it soaked through the seams of the canvas roof and began leaking inside the trailer.

Far worse than the rain was what followed. "Round two" of the storm seemed to throw all its punches at once. Monumental lightning blasts crashed and roared all around us for a solid hour. Each bolt that darted from the sky lit up the night like a Fourth of July fireworks display. The first "near miss" lightning strike instantly blew out all the campground lights, leaving us alternating between blinding flashes of lightning and pitch-black, inky darkness.

About half-way through the thunder storm, Norma and I grabbed each other's hands. Finally, she whispered to me what we both had been fearing, "Do you think we're going to blow over?"

Knowing it was my job to remain calm and relax her, I said, "Naaaa . . . not a chance!" Truthfully, I didn't think we'd blow over. *I thought we were going to blow up!*

It's amazing what kind of thoughts go through your mind at a moment like that. I couldn't help thinking . . . *This is it! We're going home to be with the Lord tonight. When was the last time I told the kids I loved them? Who's going to take care of the dog when we don't get back? I wonder who they'll interview for my position at work?* I just knew that any moment, our shiny metal trailer was going to act like Ben Franklin's key on his kite and draw the next lightning blot right down on top of our heads.

Fortunately, our portable "lightning rod" didn't attract any shocking attention, and we made it through the night with little more than a lack of sleep and rain-soaked sleeping bags. Still the memories of that experience continue as vivid as the night it happened.

The real secret to becoming a close-knit family is shared experiences that turn into shared trials.

Fortunately, not all our camping experiences have been as harrowing as that first one. After we'd gotten a few trips under our belt, a funny thing happened. Just like the couples we'd interviewed, we began to see a deepening bond developing in our home. Why?

Knitting Hearts Together

Going through harrowing experiences as a family draws people together like virtually nothing else. In other words, the real secret to becoming a close-knit family is *shared experiences that turn into shared trials.*

Have you ever noticed the way grown men on a football team will suddenly act like grade school kids, running around screaming and hugging each other, after a close, come-from-behind victory? Or have you ever stood at the Vietnam Memorial in Washington, D.C., and seen the closeness that veterans have there with one another after having gone through the horrors of war? The link people in those situations share is an inseparable relationship, forged from a common experience that stands the test of time.

I can think of one "trying" experience in particular that has marked my life forever—and my family's.

When our third child, Michael, was born, I have to admit I was a little upset. As terrible as it sounds, I wasn't sure I wanted another child. So, initially, I was ambivalent toward him and irritated with Norma for "talking" me into having another child.

I knew my attitude was dead wrong, but honestly, it was the way I felt at the time. During the first three years of his life, I just wasn't as close to Mike as I should have been. I wanted to feel close to him, at times I desperately tried, but nothing I did seemed to spark the emotional fires—that is until the spark of life almost went out of his life.

God's Mercy Creates an Unforgettable Bonding Memory

We were moving to Texas, enroute from Chicago, when Mike was a little over three years old. We had been traveling all day when we decided to spend the night at a motel—with a swimming pool.

It had been a long summer's day with five people stuffed into a tiny car, and the minute the kids spotted the shimmering water, they went crazy. I had to admit the water looked pretty good to me, too. We quickly checked in, dumped our bags in the rooms, and headed for the pool.

Norma took a quick dip and then curled up on a pool-side lounge chair with a *Good Housekeeping* magazine. In no time, the rest of us were in the water, really enjoying ourselves. Kari and Greg were old enough to swim, but Michael needed a small, round inner tube to keep him afloat.

After making sure he was "seaworthy" I turned my attention to the other two, who were screaming for me to play "toss me up," a game where I threw them up in the air and let them land in the water. After a few minutes with them, I looked back over my shoulder to see how our youngest was doing.

I saw the tube floating, but I didn't see Michael. At first, I couldn't believe my eyes. I thought Norma must have gotten him out of the water. Then I saw his tiny little body lying at the bottom of the pool. The only thing moving was his blond hair waving in the water. Instantly I swam underwater, grabbing him in my arms. When we broke the surface, his eyes were dilated, and he was coughing and sputtering.

When I got him on the deck, I began shaking him to get the water out of his lungs. In retrospect, Mike was probably in more danger from me trying to help him than he ever was on the bottom of the pool! After a couple of minutes he was back to normal, with all of us doting over him like a proud mother over a new baby.

When I first looked over and saw my son lying on the bottom of the pool, I was sure we'd lost Michael. During that instantaneous moment of emotion, something took place between us that has never left our relationship. There's something about seeing your three-foot-high son in five feet of water—knowing each second he's down there more life is draining out of him—that melts your hearts together like nothing else. That is, unless it's his first words after nearly drowning.

I'll never forget what Michael said to me when he was finally fully awake and breathing. "Daddy," he said looking at me with tears in his eyes, "I could see your legs, but I couldn't reach you!"

Instantly, my feelings of ambivalence toward my son were gone. I felt closer to him than ever before—and that bond has never been broken.

It was nearly a tragic mistake on my part that I had not kept a closer eye on Michael. As we realize now, it was God's grace that allowed me to go through that traumatic experience with my son. It shook me out of my passive indifference and replaced it with a special love for a very unique and valuable son. Michael has been, is, and always will be a living memorial of God's mercy to me. Each time any of our family brings up that harrowing experience, it unites our hearts in a bond of love and commitment.

Fast-Drying Bonds of Love

None of us would plan disasters just to make our family close knit. If your family is like mine, though, *you don't have to plan them.* They just happen! Because you never know for sure when the next one's coming, you've automatically got the perfect recipe for a "crazy glue" mixture that's perfect for family bonding.

"Crazy glue" experiences are what bonds us to one another in the midst of unexpected crisis. When we're forced by circumstance to go through something trying with another person, the crazy glue gets set in place, and once it hardens the result can be life-changing.

Most of the time, being in the middle of a crisis doesn't find us saying, "Isn't this great! We're all feeling so close right now!" Normally, we're at each other's throats saying things that aren't nearly so positive. The secret is how we'll feel later.

In most cases it takes about three weeks for the "glue" of a shared crisis to set and permanent bonding to take place. Once set, though, it's usually so tight that virtually nothing can tear the memory apart. Let me give you a recent example of a family experience that has "stuck" like glue to our family's emotions.

Famous Last Words: "Trust Me"

We live in a small patio-home in a private subdivision in Phoenix. It's so private, in fact, that the homeowners' association even owns the streets! When Michael was fourteen, he asked if he could drive the car down the street a few houses and pick up some wood we could burn in our fireplace.

Since we lived on a private road, I didn't see any harm in it, so I gave him the go-ahead. But when Norma found out what I'd done, she was beside herself.

"Norma, relax," I said. "This is a private road. It's no problem. *Trust me.*"

A few moments later, we heard a tremendous "BANG!!!" Norma screamed and ran outside, with me just a step behind. When we got there, what we saw looked like something out of the new Disneyland-MGM Studio's theme park.

There was our van, looking as if the garage door had suddenly come to life and attacked it. When Mike started to pull into the driveway, he had accidentally pushed on the accelerator, not the brake. Ramming our van into the garage door made it look like a crumpled soda can. Because of poor judgment on my part, we had a pug-nosed van, one hysterical mother worried if her son was hurt, and one angry father ready to hurt his son's posterior if the accident hadn't hurt him. But there's more.

We'd only recently converted the garage into Greg's bedroom, and "typically," he was asleep inside at the time of the accident. When the van hit the garage door, it knocked a mounted fish off the wall, right onto Greg's head! Scared to death, he thought a massive earthquake had just hit Phoenix, so he jumped up and ran out of the house thinking the apocalypse had come.

At that moment, there was very little bonding going on around the Smalley household. Let's just say that as the neighbors began gathering to view the scene, not one of us felt like laughing. Several weeks later, though, something miraculous happened.

While we never thought it possible during the midst of our "van" crisis, in three weeks time we'd all calmed down, and the garage door was fixed. Today, nearly a year later, it's one of the funniest stories we re-live with each other. Who'd have thought that a smashed garage door could have provided some of the best "crazy glue" for bonding a close-knit family that we've ever experienced? The Smalley family almanac is full of stories that have "crazy glued" us together. It's no wonder we're close.

To make sure the glue sets properly in a home, it's important to remember one thing: *During difficult times, it's vital not to do or say anything that will close the spirit of others.*[1] Harsh words and calloused actions in the heat of battle are the quickest way to dilute the glue.

That afternoon, I realized I had said several things in anger to Michael that I shouldn't have, and I had to apologize to him and ask his forgiveness. It's best when level heads and open hearts work together to cement family "disasters" into positive family memories that can hold you together forever.

Once you know the "stick 'em" power of a well-handled disaster, minor family crises can actually become welcome visitors in your home. While they may knock down the door like an unwelcomed guest at first, once the crisis leaves there is an opportunity for stronger, more intimate relationships.

How do I know this for a fact? Namely, because the same principle that helps draw a family together during times of trial, works in our bonding with our Heavenly Father.

Glued to the Father

One of the most amazing things I've learned is that the same bonding that happens to families in a crisis can happen in our relationship with God when a person of faith goes through trying times.

Have you ever been through a struggle and had to depend totally on the Lord? There's nothing like the helplessness of feeling there's no one on earth to turn to. As Christians, we may often *feel* that way, but the reality is that we can always turn to the most powerful, influential Person in the whole universe and totally depend on Him. Often He allows us to experience that kind of loneliness and desperation so we'll learn lessons about His great love and faithfulness we wouldn't discover otherwise.

Walking through those valleys, you can feel a bonding with God that the "good times" just can't produce. Lessons learned about His loyal love are what inspired David to write: "The Lord is my shepherd, I shall not want. . . . *though I walk through the valley of the shadow of death,* I will fear no evil; for thou art with me . . . " (Psalm 23:1,4 KJV, italics mine). Talk about bonding! David was a man whose heart cleaved to God's because he had faced the fires and yet God saw him through.

In the same way, when disastrous things happen to each of us, we can respond in thankfulness to Him, confident the experience will make us more trusting of Him. (This principle of looking to God to find value in trials is so important, we will take an entire chapter to talk about it.)

Making positive memories out of trying times is probably one of the most powerful ways to develop a friendship I know of today. Remember when Greg stood up in front of several hundred parents and urged them to become "best friends" with their children? Reflecting on past memories is one way to do it. This is especially true if you've suffered through some family crisis that you can look back on and laugh about. This very kind of disaster was one of the worst—but funniest—experiences of my life.

Just Hanging Around

It happened a few months before Christmas. Norma asked me what I wanted her to give me that year. I told her I'd been thinking about a pair of inversion boots, the kind you buckle yourself into and then use to hang upside down to stretch out all your muscles. I told her that before I made the request official, I wanted to try something first.

Norma left for the grocery store, and, thinking this was as good a time as any to try the "invention" out, I went to the garage. I drilled some holes in an old pair of boots, placed a metal hook in each one, and put them on. Then I got out my ladder, climbed up and hung myself upside down from my son's chinning bar. Actually the boots worked fine—my muscles certainly felt as if they were being stretched like never before. But I soon realized I had created a major problem with my new invention.

The problem was, now that I was upside down—hooked to the chin-up bar—I couldn't get down! I was stuck! What's worse, I didn't have enough strength to reach up and loosen the boots to free myself. To top things off, nobody was around. I was left to hang there helplessly like a side of beef in a meat freezer. I had visions of heart failure, and Norma opening the garage door, seeing me, and thinking, *Gary sure chose a weird way to commit suicide!*

The person who finally found me was Greg, the family clown! He had heard my cries for help, opened the door, saw me hanging there, and fell on the ground howling like a hyena.

There I dangled. Dear old Dad. The one who helped to change his diapers, who played ball with him in the park for countless hours, who worked long, hard hours to put food in his mouth and clothes on his back; and all he could do was laugh while I was dying!

Finally, Kari came in and urged Greg up off the floor and tried to help me. Even together, however, they were not strong enough to get me down. By this time, I knew I was going to die. I knew I was about to have a stroke that would finish me. Norma would have to fight the insurance company for years to prove that my death wasn't "suspicious."

At long last, Kari went to get some scissors and cut the shoe strings on my boots. This was certainly helpful in getting me out of the boots, but what they had failed to do was move the ladder I'd used. As a result, I fell onto it and onto the concrete floor and cut and bruised by head and hip.

The moment I hit the floor, the kids scattered—and for good reason. I can assure you, if I had been able to move just then, I would have "laid hands" on them!

It's been several years since my "upside down" adventure, and just like our camping trips, the "crazy glue" of that shared trial has made this story one of our favorite family memories. It was a crisis that everyone in my family enjoyed, even me—after I got over the humiliation.

I have to be honest, though. That's not the end of the story. Two years later Mike and I were visiting some friends in a beautiful home in Seattle. I noticed they had a workout room with a *real* pair of inversion boots.

You know the rest of the story. I got stuck *again*. This time Mike got to do the honors of helping me down. Years after I've gone to be with the Lord, I'm sure my children and *their* children will still get together and talk—and yes, laugh—about "Dad and his boots."

Please Write on Our Walls

To add even more "bonding" glue to your memories, you can actually plan humorous things around your house that will build relationships and create happy times for your whole family as well. We know of a radio talk show host in our city who was a master at creating fun-bonding times when his children were young.

For example, when his son turned ten, he invited all the neighborhood kids over for the party—but not just *any* birthday party. He had saved for months and spent a small fortune in supplying an incredible surprise. Namely, 800 cream pies that he'd ordered for the biggest birthday pie fight that Phoenix has probably ever seen.

His son is grown now, but still recalls that party as one of the greatest highlights of his childhood—and almost every kid who participated does as well. It was terrific fun for everyone, and it created a special bond between father and son that still holds strong today. Still, that's not the extent of this creative man's talents.

As a radio celebrity, he was always being given "promotional" T-shirts when he would do commercials or "live" broadcasts. Even with giving many away to the Salvation Army, his shirt drawer soon began to bulge, and he came up with a creative idea.

When his kids were grade-school age, about once a month he'd pull out an old T-shirt that was ready for the trash (or one he'd been given that he knew he'd never wear). Then when he saw all the kids were home, he'd walk through the house yelling, "*I hope no kids are listening!* I sure hope there aren't any aggressive kids in their rooms that want to be destructive today and tear a T-shirt off of me. Because this T-shirt has a hole in it, and I'm ready to throw it away. . . ."

No sooner had he finished speaking than doors would burst open all over the house and voices screaming with delight would echo down the halls. From everywhere, his four kids would dive all over him and tear this shirt to pieces. He loved it, and they loved him for it.

How about one more example of a creative dad who knows that letting kids occasionally experience something "out of the ordinary" can build lasting, loving memories?

In every home, what is one rule that is always established as soon as a child begins testing his fine-motor skills? That's right. "Don't write on the walls." Just as in everyone else's home, this man's kids also had to obey this rule—until he decided that he'd make one "marked" exception.

One day, he and his wife were struggling over how to redecorate the guest bathroom when he came up with a very creative idea. He called the kids in (after talking to his wife, of course) and told them that whenever they brought home a friend, that child could sign his or her name on one of the bathroom walls. Of course, the wall signing had to begin by having the children put their names in what may have become the largest autograph book in Arizona.

Every other wall in the house was still "off limits" to writing, but soon this guest bath became a focal point of the entire neighborhood. It has stayed that way even now that the kids are all grown and out of the house. Today, when this man's children bring people over to their parents' home, the bathroom is still the first place they visit to have them see or "sign" the wall.

You may not know of many people who spend part of every "family reunion" all jammed into a guest bathroom . . . but now you do. This family loves to gather and look at years' worth of happy memories captured in the names of grade school, high school, and college friends of the kids—and the "grown up kids" who are the parents' friends who also insist on signing the bathroom wall! One creative idea resulted in positive memories shouting from four walls that could have just held wallpaper.

Any kind of fun time you plan, even if it's just wrestling with your kids or playing leapfrog, is something that can bind you in special and significant ways. Don't let "tradition," or fatigue, or a busy schedule, steal all the fun from your family times. It's so important.

John and I have a very close friend named Bill Butterworth who is one of the most outstanding family conference speakers in the country.[2] Often, he asks his audiences this open-ended question: "If you could add anything to your home—what would it be?"

Do you know what answer he has received as the number 1 things many people wish they had more of inside their home? You guessed it—laughter.

Such an answer might surprise you—but then again, after reading this chapter, maybe not. In particular, it shouldn't shock Christians.

A very thought-provoking book came out a few years ago called *Desiring God.*[3] For many Christians, the Christian life can be something so cold and "humorless" it almost begs kids to look for a "cheerful heart" anywhere but in their home or church. Yet that should never be the case. In this author's book, he does a very good job of illustrating that "In the knowledge of God is fullness of joy." In other words, one clear hallmark of a Christian is a joyful life.

I fully realize that joking can sometimes be hurtful. Inappropriate humor can be sarcastic or disrespectful, but let's not leave joy out of a home if we want it to be marked as distinctively Christian. Your kids will always remember you for taking the time and creativity to add a sparkle of fun to the family—even if it costs you a T-shirt or two!

The Family That Decides Together, Bonds Together

Disasters can be great ways for family bonding to take place. For the faint of heart, however, it's also possible to plan times together as a family where neither hardship nor humor are the goals. These are special times for just being together, times that allow the opportunity for relationships to develop simply because you're with someone.

Family outings such as these generally don't happen without effort—particularly in our hectic, fast-paced world. So, the best thing to do is get the family together, talk about what you enjoy doing, and plan an event or activity everyone can enjoy.

But what if you're a group of "individuals" like my family and enjoy different activities? My family solved this situation by deciding to make it a priority to spend time together. That way, when it's time to plan a family activity, we're all open to talk about it.

"Okay, gang," I say, "it's time to plan this year's vacation.

On a scale of one to ten, ten being the best, what would be a ten for you this time?" Each member then has the opportunity to share what would be a "dream activity" for them.

Kari and Norma will usually answer, "A cute beach where I can lay out in the sun, and probably cute little shops nearby." Mike and Greg typically respond, "Water, fishing, snorkeling, rock-climbing—anything adventurous." Then we put our heads together and try to come up with a place or activity that will fit our budget and still accommodate everyone's wishes as much as possible.

Sometimes, we have to make compromises, but that can be a valuable time for our kids to learn the importance of considering each others' needs and wants ahead of their own (Philippians 2:3–8). It may take time to hammer out a solution, but our commitment to doing things together as a family is a great help in urging all of us to bend enough to arrive at a decision everyone is satisfied with.

In the last few years, as our kids have moved through the teenage years, there's been stiff competition between family time and their team sports, clubs, and church trips. Sometimes, we decide *as a family* that we're already busy enough. Still, we try to plan times together as much as our schedules will allow.

It's also important to make a family decision to spend time alone with each of your children. A few years ago Greg and I went to Eastern Europe together on a speaking trip. If you want to bond with someone, just go through a few communist road blocks together as they search and re-search every stitch of you and your luggage! We'll always have the memory of staying in homes where people literally risked their lives to meet and to talk about Christ.

Taking mini-mission trips to your local Salvation Army to serve Thanksgiving dinner or help the poor can be a tremendous bonding time, or plan several years in advance to save up to visit one of your church's missionaries in the field. You can encourage and help them with a specific project or need they may have. Instead of just letting the youth leader get the advantage of all the bonding that goes on during a missions trip, go with the kids as a sponsor yourself. Usually the church is in such need of "sponsors" they may even pick up your expenses to travel with the kids! You'll lose sleep and possibly some hearing (if they're allowed to bring their tape players), but you'll never lose the closeness that can come from trips like these.

We can all waste time on television and movies, but we'll never waste one minute of time giving our children a picture of what God is accomplishing throughout the world.

Let me say clearly that it's not the distance or expense that counts but the personal contact you have with your children during the event. Over the years, Kari and I have made a habit of going out together for yogurt to talk. The warm, intimate father-daughter conversations we've had will always be dear to me.

When Greg got up to share at our conference that day, it made me very aware—and very thankful for—of all the hours we'd spent camping as a family. In many ways, we'd collected a twofold benefit. All the trials and family experiences we had have produced a loving bond with the children stronger and deeper than Norma and I could ever imagine. They've done something else as well. They've also given Norma and me more love for each other—and more positive memories to hold on to now that the kids are grown and moving away.

Whether you do all your "camping" at the nearest Marriott or deep in the heart of the Colorado Rockies, there's no substitute for quality time as a couple—or a family. A close-knit home, like our relationship with our Christ, grows and deepens as we share together moments of trial, tenderness, and laughter.

Now, finally, what I think are the most important chapters await us. I'll never write on more important subjects than the ones you'll find in Chapters 13 and 14, for they provide the insights for us to gain the desire and inner strength to do all the honoring and loving things we've written about in this book. Without these two chapters, this book would be just another "skill-building" book, but in today's world with the pressures we face—skills aren't enough. You need to be able to fully tap into the only power source for a love that lasts—if you want your love to last a lifetime.

13

Finding Fulfillment: More Than Our Cup Can Hold

One morning, a wife was desperately trying to get her husband up for church. She kept pushing and shoving him, trying to get him out of bed. "Get up, George!" she said repeatedly. "We're going to be late for church again!"

Finally, he rolled over in frustration and said, "I told you last night, I am *not* going to church and that's final. Now let me go back to sleep."

"But George," she pleaded, "it's important for you to be there." Finally, she decided to use another approach. "Okay, George. Give me two good reasons why you shouldn't go to church."

"Fine," he said, "I'll give you two reasons. Number one, I don't *like* those people. And number two, they don't like *me* down there either. That's why I'm not going."

There was a long pause as his wife thought over his answer. Finally he spoke up and said, "If you feel it's really so important I go to church, why don't you give me two reasons why I should go?"

"George," she said, "first of all you know that the Bible says it's important for you to go to church, and second, *you're the pastor!*"

Like anyone, pastors can get discouraged. I spent a number of years working at several churches, and I know what it's like to be discouraged. In fact, I know what it's like not to want to get out of bed.

When We Feel Like Never
Coming out from under the Covers

When I was thirty-five years old, there was a time I was so depressed from what I thought life had "dealt" me, that all I wanted was to crawl under the covers and never show my face again.

I blamed all my miseries on this job, and that person, and those circumstances. I can remember being so discouraged over a heart-breaking ministry situation that I lay upstairs in my daughter Kari's room, not eating for almost four days. Each of my children would come up and try to encourage me, but I'd just tell them to go away—I didn't want to face anyone or anything. Norma did her best to break me out of the doldrums as well, but for days I stayed in a darkened room, alone with my misery.

Finally, I remember telling my wife that I had made an important decision. I was getting out of the ministry. I didn't want any part of all the stress and broken promises I'd faced, and I was going to leave and get into some other kind of work.

Norma turned to me and asked, "What would you do?" That's when I realized that I didn't *know* anything else to do. I had been trained for the ministry and nothing else. I really became depressed when I thought about that! In my mind, I was on a dead-end street with no hope of ever finding a pathway that would take me away from my troubles.

During this time, I remember doing something out of desperation that turned out to be the greatest thing that has ever happened to me in my life. This period of personal darkness was the worst experience that had ever happened to me, but it turned into the greatest thing I ever experienced because of what it taught me.

I learned one biblical principle that taught me several important things I may never have learned otherwise. I discovered how to use my emotions—even the negative ones—instead of just being used by them. I learned something that led me to lasting freedom from worry, fear, anxiety, hurt feelings, and depression. I also learned how to take all the negative things that happen to me and actually find positive good and deeper love for others within the trial (I'll focus on this in detail in the next chapter).

Most of all, that terrible experience taught me the secret to experiencing continuing fulfillment in life. This is the very thing any individual or couple must discover if their marriage is to stay strong over each season of life.

Looking for Love, Peace and Joy in All the Wrong Places

What did I learn that had such a dramatic impact on my life? For years before that period of depression, I had spent a lifetime looking to any number of things to give me a sense of significance and security. But I was trying to find the right things in the wrong places.

I learned that we all have similar goals in life. If our lives were like a cup, each one of us would love to have it filled with wisdom, love, joy, and peace. We'd like to have our lives overflow with positive emotions and genuine fulfillment in life. At a very early age, we all begin to look around for what we think can fill up our cup with these positive qualities.

Unfortunately, what most of us do is to look to one of three sources, or all three, to give us the fullness of life we really want. Yet like a mirage, they shimmer with fulfillment, but offer only dust to our souls.

Looking to People to Fill Our Cup

The first place many of us tend to look is toward people. We think to ourselves, *if I'm really going to have my needs met, I've got to have another person in my life.*

Take the average single woman in her early twenties or even thirties. Often, she'll spend hours thinking and dreaming of how that "special" someone will come into her life and fill up her cup. For some women who come from a difficult family background, their personal cup may have so little love, peace, and joy that they long to finally be filled up. So in these cases, there can be a tremendous desire for a "Mr. Wonderful" to come along who can make up for the empty arms and missing love they've experienced.

In her mind's eye, this woman can come home at day's end and find "him" waiting for her. She wants someone who would hold her gently in his arms and spend hours at night in intimate conversation. She is looking for someone who is thoughtful and kind—and can fill up her cup to overflowing.

Many women enter courtship this way, but before a woman has been married a year, panic begins to set in. That's because she begins to discover almost immediately that her husband is not only failing to fill her cup—but often this "special someone" is drilling little holes in her cup by his small, insensitive actions.

Now, in addition to her cup not getting fuller, she's starting to lose whatever positive feelings with which she came into the marriage! Many women have actually told me that they experienced feelings of emotionally "drying up" when they realized that their husband would never fill their cup.

Then something happens. A light can go on in this woman's eyes as she comes to a startling realization. It isn't a husband who fills her cup. *It must be children!* Of course! God's plan. Little children running around the house. So they have little babies running around the house, and soon they discover something that all children have the capacity to do. That is, children can drill *big* holes in the cup!

Now this woman may really face a problem. Neither her husband nor her children are always filling her cup. They can be frustrating and irritating and drain away as much—or more—emotional energy than they give.

For those who look elsewhere, they'll ultimately find the same frustration in any other relationship. Friends can be a tremendous source of help and encouragement at times, but even they can disappoint us over the long haul. We can look to them as the source of positive emotions, but at times they too can punch holes in our emotional lives.

Tragically, some people have even turned to an affair to try to "fill their cup." The sweet taste of stolen waters may seem to fill up one's life, but it's actually like drinking ice-cold salt water. The burning aftertaste of sin can burn huge holes in our cup and leave us emptier and more miserable than we ever imagined.[1]

If people aren't the source that fills up our lives with the positive emotions we want so much, what is?

Looking to Places as the Source of Fulfillment

"We need a home! That's it, we need a place with a beautiful view and trees that are the envy of the neighborhood. If only we had the right place to live, *then* our cup will be full." Then we get that special home and live in it for a short while, and suddenly things begin to go wrong. In part that's true because the bigger our home, the more things there are to fix when they break.

Norma and I live in Arizona where grass front lawns are an exception, but for a period of time we thought, *We need a place that can be an oasis in the desert. We need a house that has a beautiful lawn.* Surely *that* would help our cup be full. Once we got our lawn in, though, we then discovered we were chained to it just to keep it alive.

One year I didn't water it enough, and the grass all died. The next year, I watered it too much and killed the grass again. In fact, there were numerous times when I was tempted to bulldoze the entire yard and pave it over, I was so frustrated with it!

We can put in a swimming pool, a fireplace, or even buy a mountain cabin, and those "places" don't fulfill us. Why? In part because no matter how pretty or fulfilling places look, they don't fit inside our personal cup. Instead they all have sharp edges that cut holes in our lives. What's more, the *people* we share our special places with are the same ones who continue to drain our cup as well!

But if people *and* places don't fill up the deepest part of our lives, where do we turn to finally find love, peace, and joy?

Looking to Things for Fulfillment

How about more money so that we can buy more things? Many of us feel that if we just had more money, we'd be happier in life. But study after study of people who "strike it rich" show this isn't the case.

The more money we make, the more wisdom we must have to handle it. Now I know that many of us wouldn't mind having to come up with that kind of wisdom. But to get money we normally have to pay a personal price. Thomas Carlyle once said, "For every person who can handle prosperity, there are a hundred who can handle adversity." Money alone, and all the things it can bring, can't fill up our lives with the kind of living water we desperately want.

I've met people all over the country who have little money and are miserable. And I've also met those with lots of money who are miserable. I've known people who have mountain cabins and third cars and aren't fulfilled. And some people I know barely have bus fare, but they also feel empty inside.

Most people who depend on "things" to "fill up their cup" end up looking for the one "perfect" job that will be the ticket to all their dreams. All jobs have one thing in common—work! And work doesn't always keep our cup full. It can positively drain us in terms of the people we work with, the place where we do our work, the equipment we must use, and so on.

Some of us try all our lives to get a key to a certain washroom, or a parking space with our name on it. When we get it, however, what do we have? The answer to being filled with wisdom, love, peace, and joy? Hardly. Just the opposite is too often true.

Coming up Empty in Life

At some times in each one of our lives, we run headlong into an inescapable fact. Life is not fulfilling. It's actually often unfair and exhausting. (Try reading the book of Ecclesiastes if you want a picture of someone who had everything, but everything wasn't enough.)

We can never pour enough people, places, or things into our personal cup to keep our lives filled and overflowing with the contentment we want so much. It's no wonder so many people lead lives of emotional desperation, and even consider suicide as a way out.

In fact, by focusing on people, places, and things, we not only miss the positive emotions we want . . . *we end up with the very negative emotions we've been trying all our lives to avoid!* This is true because hurt feelings, worry, anxiety, fear, unrest, uncertainty, and confusion come as a direct result of "expecting" life from a person, place, or thing.

If our ultimate goal in a marriage is saying to our spouse, "I need life from you. Will you cooperate, meet my needs, and fill up my cup?" we're asking for big problems and an empty life.

Many marriages find a husband and wife like two dry sponges, each waiting to soak up life from the other. While we're expecting wisdom, love, peace, and joy from our spouses on a daily basis, they can be sitting across the table expecting us to provide all their needs as well. Then we all come up empty, and major problems can develop.

Why do we get our feelings hurt in the course of an average week? If we're honest and look closely at our circumstances, it's because we've been expecting "life" from someone (or something) who isn't cooperating, and there's one thing more. At the heart of our desperate longing for others to fulfill our deepest needs is a grabbing selfishness that says, "Me first, me first!"

My daughter Kari is a constant source of encouragement to me—and sometimes a loving source of correction as well. I can be frustrated with her over some minor matter and begin to get angry, but she'll always stay incredibly calm. I've often asked her to help me isolate why I'm feeling angry, and she'll say, "Now, Dad, you know that this thing is not really making you angry. It's just revealing your own self-centeredness!"

As much as I hate to admit it, she's generally right! A situation or person doesn't make me angry. I choose to be angry over whatever thing is blocking my goal or frustrating my plan.

We all face the temptation to look to people, places, and things to fill our cup. We're all selfish in wanting others to cooperate in meeting our needs right now. But it's only those who are wise who realize that there is a pathway to freedom from that unfulfilled feeling.

Freedom from Unfulfilled Expectations

Anger, worry, fear, hurt feelings—we wouldn't choose these emotions for anything. Yet we often end up with such feelings starring on our team.

For years, I carried around a great deal of worry and anxiety in my life. At least a part of it came from my background. A few years ago I began to learn what it takes to be completely free from most of the destructive emotions to which I once felt chained. Fear was one of my biggest problems. Here's how it sneaked up on me.

I grew up in a home that was very permissive. Primarily this was because my mother and father lost their first child not long after my mother had given her a spanking. The spanking itself didn't have anything to do with the child's death. A splinter led to an infection and complications that a country doctor and pharmacist in the early forties couldn't heal. Because of the emotional guilt, my mother made my father promise neither one of them would ever discipline us.

This meant that I grew up in a home with no rules. Take dating, for example. Because there were no boundaries in my home, I didn't actually begin my formal dating until the third grade. I did a lot of informal dating before then, but my formal dating started in third grade.

In a climate where "anything goes," my older brothers were left to come up with any "game" they wanted to tease and scare me. One brother loved to wake me up in the middle of the night and stand me up on a chair where he and his friends would laugh at me. He also loved to take his B-B gun and say to me, "I'll give you to *three* to get going." I'd take off as fast as I could because I knew he'd shoot me if I was still in range at the count of three.

He even used to take me out to the middle of a field with his bow and arrow and shoot an arrow up in the air and say, "Scatter!" I never knew where the arrow was coming down, and I was filled with fear and anxiety as I tried to run to safety. Later, every bush became a hiding place to "scare" me. Every time my parents were away was an opportunity to make me jump in some way.

It may seem that all these things were just "childhood games," but they left fearful memories inside my life. While it's hard for me to admit, I was so filled with fear that when I was twenty-four years old I still couldn't take a shower with my eyes closed. I couldn't even stay in a house alone because I'd think I was hearing people breaking in—and I was in graduate school at seminary at the time!

Today, though, it's been almost ten years since I had a fearful thought. Why? Because I've been learning something very specific from God's Word that has taken the fear right out of my life.

Envy, jealousy, comparison. I used to struggle with these emotions constantly, but rarely any more. Why? Because I'm learning how to take these very negative emotions and turn them into a flashing light that illuminates lasting fulfillment. Let me give you an illustration of what I mean.

Using Negative Emotions as Positive Warning Lights in Life

Let's say Dr. Trent and I have just finished our seminar and we've asked Bob, the local chairman, if he'd take us to the airport. As always, we're cutting it close, but if he hurries we'll make the plane just in time.

As we drive to the airport, Bob is having a great time, asking us questions and commenting on how the conference went. He's moving down the highway at a steady clip when suddenly the red light on the dashboard comes on and starts blinking, indicating there's an oil problem with the engine.

I see the light and point it out to Bob right away. After all, this is the last flight out for the day, and we're really anxious to get home to our families.

"Don't worry," Bob assures me. "That thing comes on and off all the time."

Now, though, the light is shining even brighter and is staying on, not flashing. "Bob, are you sure there isn't a problem with your car?" I ask, beginning to wonder if something is actually wrong.

"Naw, nothing to worry about," he says. Just then his engine freezes up, stranding us in the middle of the freeway and causing us to miss our plane.

Actually, Bob had several options when that warning light came on. He could have pulled over and checked the oil, or flagged someone down who could help him fix the problem, or get us to the airport. He could even have done something like this:

When I asked him the second time about the red light on his dash, he could have said, "Gary, do me a favor. Reach into the glove box and hand me that little hammer that's inside there." When I handed him the hammer, he could have taken it and Wham! Wham! Wham!, smashed out the light. "There, now do you feel better? That light won't bother you any more!"

No intelligent person ignores a warning light. It's installed for a purpose. Rather than smash it, you should learn from it. It will alert you to a potential problem. Unfortunately, when it comes to experiencing negative emotions, many people try and "smash them" out of their lives instead of using them as positive warning lights.

Many people feel tremendously guilty when they experience anger, fear, worry, or hurt feelings. I've learned to use them in a positive way. These emotions are actually red lights flashing telling us our focus is in the wrong spot. We're expecting life from the wrong source!

You see, there's a fundamental problem with expecting fulfillment from people, places, and things. These are the *gifts* of life, not the *source* of life. Any time we expect the gifts of life to give us what only God can, we're asking for our cups to be drained of energy and life itself.

Now, when fearful thoughts come into my life, I don't degrade myself for feeling them. I simply say, "Thank You, Lord, for reminding me that you're the only One who can give life." Instead of resenting negative emotions, I can be thankful for their warning-light reminder that I'm looking for something other than the Lord to fill my cup. They can also be the prod that God uses to get us moving in the direction He has chosen for us. How can we learn to harness negative emotions to point us in the right direction?

People, places and things are the gifts of life, not the Source of life. . . .

Seeking First the Source of Life

When the red lights of negative emotions fill my life, they are all ultimately tied into the same sensor. It's a spiritual sensor that is saying, "Smalley, you're expecting fulfillment from people, places, and things—not from the Lord." I'm focusing on the gifts of life and expecting them to be the Source of life.

Matthew 6:33 gives us a clear direction on what our Source of life should be. "But seek first his kingdom and his righteousness, and all these things will be given you as well." When I give God first place in my life, He promises to meet all my needs.

I try to love God with all my heart. In other words, He's the highest priority in my life. When I focus on Jesus Christ alone as the Source of my life, an amazing thing happens. Because He loves me and actually possesses the wisdom, love, peace, and joy I've always wanted—He alone can fill my cup to overflowing! That's exactly what He promises to do for His children. Ephesians

3:19–20 tells us that " . . . this love . . . surpasses knowledge—that you may be filled to the measure of all the fullness of God." Can you get any more filled than full? Absolutely not.

Do you understand now why very few people can hurt my feelings? Because I'm no longer expecting people to fill my cup, I'm not hurt when they don't respond in a particular way. Even if my wife or a close friend says something to hurt me, it is still a reflection that my focus was on what they could give or take away—not on what God gives.

Whenever those warning lights go off, I thank God for them. Then I pray and ask forgiveness for focusing on something that is less than Himself. Finally, I ask Him alone to fill my life. Psalm 62 says that we are to wait and hope in God alone. He's our rock, our salvation, our rear guard, our hiding place. He's everything we'll ever need!

Think of how many wives are manipulated by husbands from whom they "expect" life and vice-versa. The more we place our expectations on another person, the more control we give them over our emotional and spiritual state. The freer we are of expectations from others—and the more we depend upon God alone—the more pure and honest our love for others will become.

Tapping into a Limitless Source of Power

For twelve chapters we've looked at the various "skills" that can move a marriage from rock bottom right up at the top. We've also been careful to say that communication and intimacy skills alone aren't enough to build the kind of lasting love we all want. Why? Because if we really want a relationship "made in heaven," we must learn to appropriate the power of Heaven—and that power is available through prayer.

The key to powerful prayer is found in Luke 18. When I pray, I become a great deal like the little widow woman pictured in this parable of Jesus. He used her as an example to teach the disciples how to pray. Let me tell her story:

There was once a little old widow lady who went before a wicked judge seeking protection from people who were bothering her. The problem was, this judge had no respect for either God or man, and he repeatedly turned her away. Even with that kind of treatment, she never gave up.

Every day she got in line in front of that wicked judge. Finally, through sheer persistence day after day, she got the protection she was looking for. What was the point of this story? Jesus went on to tell His disciples that we have a God who loves us. "How much more will He hear and answer our prayers" when we line up every day with our requests.

That's how I pray. I line up every day before God and wait expectantly for His answer to my prayers. Of course, even before I pray, I make sure that I'm praying as I should. I always pray keeping 1 Timothy 6:3 in mind, checking to see that my petition is consistent with God's will and that it leads to godliness. If I'm careful that my request meets these standards, then I never get out of line—just like that widow woman. How does this apply to a marriage or having a strong family?

Remember John and Kay Hammer, the couple back in Chapters 1 and 3 who went through such terrible struggles? Kay learned all the "skills" I could teach her about how to have a strong marriage, but that wasn't all. She also learned how to tap into the one power source that could fill her cup to overflowing. That source was separate from anything John could ever do. Once her expectations for wisdom, love, peace, and joy were placed on her God and not her husband, she was finally free to love John. She also had the strength to keep persistently, expectantly praying for positive changes to happen in their relationship.

As she practiced the skills of growing a great relationship, she also prayed continually for a positive result in her home, in her own and her husband's lives. It was her attitude of prayer that gave her the power to keep going when all her feelings said, "Give up!"

Standing in line every day before God reminds me of the story of a man who died and went to heaven. The first place St. Peter took him was to a huge warehouse. It stretched for miles, and it was filled with millions and millions of presents.

"What in the world is this room?" the startled newcomer asked.

"This room is full of presents that were for God's children," Peter answered. "But they got out of line too soon."

I know many, many couples who began the work of forging a loving relationship—but they got out of line too soon. They weren't persistent enough. They ran out of strength to keep their relationship together, forgetting that "those who hope in the Lord will renew their strength" (Isaiah 40:31).

Whenever I wake up in the middle of the night and find my stomach knotted over some problem I'm facing, I've learned to do something that puts me right back to sleep. I've learned to thank God for my knotted stomach, because it's telling me that I'm focusing on one of the gifts of life for love, peace, and joy, rather than the Source of life. The level of my cup doesn't vary now from day to day, phone call to phone call, circumstance to circumstance, because His mercies are new every morning—a fresh full cup of life every day.

It's not Norma who fills my cup. It's not Kari, or Greg, or Michael. It's not my good friends or family members. They're "overflow," not my basic needs. John 17:3 says that to know God is life. Just knowing Christ is life. It's not knowing about Him, it's knowing Him. In 1 John 5:12 the apostle says, "He who has the Son has life; he who does not have the Son of God does not have life." It's as simple as that.

Is your life filled with negative emotions? Or all the fullness of Christ? As we close this chapter, let me share with you one example. I hope it will bring this concept closer to your heart. It did for me the first time I heard Linda's story.

A Single Place to Plug in our Lives

Linda was a young woman who had suffered terribly as a child. Her father adored her, but with his untimely death when she was only five, it seemed she was left without anyone to love her. Her mother resented her, and her brothers and sisters rejected her. All through her childhood, Linda could remember crying herself to sleep at night, wanting so much for things to be different, but they never were.

Linda's desires in life were the same as ours. She longed for others to highly value her. She wanted inner happiness, calm, and contentment. Yet growing up in a negative, non-Christian environment, she experienced only anger, bitterness, and defeat.

Up to this point, I've talked about the Lord filling our cup. Let me change the imagery to give us a different perspective. It was as if Linda's life were a lamp with a single cord.

She wanted desperately to see her life lit up with positive

feelings and a warm, inner calm. She wanted the joy of knowing she was accepted unconditionally by her mother and loved by her brothers and sisters. Yet every time she tried plugging into her family, she received a terrible shock.

Over the years, Linda had been shocked so many times by her family, she sometimes felt like giving up. The very people who should have given her love and acceptance had given her only pain and hurt. Thus she often considered taking her own life.

Linda was so tired of darkness and being shocked, so desirous of light in her life, that she went to another extreme. She spent years plugging into anything and anyone she thought might bring her power and warmth.

She tried lighting her life by plugging into friends, dating, school, jobs, houses, even "recreational" drugs and alcohol. Every time she plugged into one of these things, they, too, left her trapped in darkness and afraid she would never see the light she longed for.

Do you know someone like Linda? Has a difficult background or even some present relationship left you searching for the light of love and peace, and full of darkness and fear? Like Linda, there is only one place where any of us can plug in our lives and find the satisfaction we so desperately need.

Plugging into the Source of Life

When Linda finally discovered that she needed to plug into the Source of Life, Jesus Christ, she saw her life light up for the first time. In His love she found unconditional acceptance (Romans 8:38–39; John 10:1ff; Hebrews 13:5). In His power she found the strength to be joyful in spite of her circumstances (Philippians 4:11–14; 1 Peter 1:6–9). Guided by His hand, she found a spiritual family at a nearby church. They loved her unconditionally. Through His Word and Spirit she received the inner peace that had always eluded her (John 14:6, 1 John 5:1ff).

Perhaps you need to ask yourself what your life is plugged into. Many people try to carry around dozens of "extension" cords and plug them in to the Lord as well as many other people and things, but God has designed us with a single cord and only one place where we can plug it in to find lasting life and power—Himself.

One afternoon after a long conversation with a close friend, Linda made the most significant decision anyone can make. For the first time, she plugged her life into the Source of Life. For the next year and a half, she made a daily decision to look only to the Lord to light up her life.

Whenever she found herself angry with her husband or impatient with her children, she took time to realize that she was really plugging in to them, trying to use them for fulfillment or to meet an unmet need in her own life. Most importantly, whenever she thought about her terrible past and her light began to dim, she would immediately unplug from the hurtful memories and plug back into the positive words of Scripture to discover a special future her Heavenly Father had for her.

What happened when Linda found a single, unbroken source of life to plug into? Her life was never again the same.

Her marriage began to blossom as she finally stopped expecting her husband to make up for years of neglect she had experienced with her family. In her early fifties, she even called her estranged mother and began working to restore that relationship. Her mother was in her eighties!

Linda still met with the same painful, discouraging words, but somehow the shock had been turned off. She was finally free to love her mother because she wasn't expecting anything from her—and it made a major difference in their relationship. She never knew the joy of leading her mother to Christ, but at least Linda was free from the choking feelings of hatred and anger she had carried for years.

Are you expecting life from another person? Someone in the past, like your parents? Someone in the present, like your spouse? Are you struggling with forgiving them because they've "taken" something from you? Something only God could ever have given you in the first place?

For some of us, this single concept of plugging into Christ alone for wisdom, love, peace, and joy can be the most freeing experience in our lives. It certainly was for me.

For me, learning that the ministry, other people, and even my spouse would never fill my cup was the very thing that got me up out of bed when I was so depressed. Believing and practicing the fact that Jesus alone is the Source of life, wisdom, fulfillment, and purpose is what has kept me active and excited about life ever since. I've already accomplished more from a human perspective than I've ever dreamed possible—and in large part it's because I no longer look at life from a human perspective. I'm free to succeed or fail because Jesus Christ is the Source of my life, the fullness of my cup that can never be drained away.

There remains only one final area to discuss before we close this book. In many ways, it could be the most important. In addition to learning that Christ alone could free me from unrealistic expectations, I discovered something else during that difficult time. Even the very trials that led me to depression actually contained valuable gold for developing strong, lasting relationships.

14

The Source of
Lasting Love

Some readers may be thinking, *All this talk about having strong relationships and even "plugging" into Christ as my only Source of life is great, it's inspiring. I can even believe it works for other people—but not for me. There's no hope for me.*

I can hear you saying, "You've never met my husband! You've never met my wife! She's been unfaithful! He's left me before! My kids have turned against me! She's turned away from God! I'm a pastor's wife, and I can't tell anyone our problems! I've already been divorced twice! I've had five jobs in the last year and none of them have worked out! . . . ."

In almost twenty years of working with individuals, couples, and families, I've heard terrible stories of heartache and tragedy. Many of these certainly sound like "exception" clauses to God's power to turn a terrible situation into something positive. Let me tell you Diane's story:

Diane came to one of our seminars. In her early sixties today, as a young girl she had lived in a very beautiful home in the Northwest. Her father was a well respected attorney in the community, but he was a terror to live with at home. Verbally and sometimes physically abusive, he was always critical and unreachable.

When she was nine years old, her mother caught her father in the midst of an affair. In a fit of anger, she threatened to expose her husband and ruin his reputation in their small town, but like a wounded lion, he turned on her and successfully sued *her* for divorce first—thoroughly slandering her name in the process. Their "soap opera" courtroom theatrics became so bad, other parents forbade their children to play or even talk with Diane or her older brother at school. Then, one day, circumstances turned from bad to far worse than Diane could ever have imagined.

When Diane and her brother came home from school, the movers were in the house packing all their things and getting ready to cart them away. Their father had won the divorce decree and had even gotten a court order evicting his former wife from the house.

As the mother wept, Diane's older brother became furious. He stormed into the house and up to his father's room, grabbing up a gun he knew his father always hid in his bedside drawer.

When he came out of the house, his grandmother was walking up the porch and saw him with the gun. In a burst of anger, he told her he was on his way to kill his father. She grabbed at him, trying to wrestle the gun away. But in the struggle the gun went off. In a terrible accident Diane's brother had killed his own grandmother.

Tragedy would follow tragedy that day. When the police came to the house, they tracked down the boy who was hiding in a neighbor's garage. A gun battle broke out, and an officer was critically wounded. Diane's brother was killed.

Can you imagine her feelings? Only nine years old, she had lived through the trauma of her parents' hostile divorce. She had lost her grandmother and brother in a single day. The community was blaming her because her brother had nearly killed a police officer. And now she was literally put out on the street after having lived in the lap of luxury.

There was nothing good about what happened to this woman or her family. The pain her father and brother caused will always be with her. And yet she told us, "It's taken many years, but I can actually say that God has used my terrible childhood to make me a much better person, especially with my own family. I've had to work through a lot, but I know God has made me a more loving wife and mother because of what I've been through."

Certainly, you say, her story is an exception. Exceptional perhaps, but an exception? Hardly. Here is another story that may be even worse. We share it to underline that whatever we're personally struggling with, if God can turn a situation like this into something worthwhile, He can bring about a similar result in our trials.

Two Roads to the Same Destination

During the Vietnam War, two very different men were part of a Navy SEAL Team, an ultra-elite group sent on dangerous search-and-destroy missions. One was Dave Roever.

Dave would sit on his bunk and strum his guitar, singing religious folk songs and telling his buddies how much God loved them. The other man occupied the bunk above him. His name was Mickey Block, and along with another soldier, he gave Dave a hard time, constantly telling him to shut up and to knock off his preaching. In fact, as in many combat units, they gave Dave a nickname. During his tour in Vietnam, his handle would be the "Preacher Man." Dave came up with his own nickname for them, calling them Pervert Number One and Pervert Number Two!

One night, while on an ambush raid in their heavily armed patrol boat, another American vessel mistook them for the enemy and started firing. Mickey was hit over a dozen times by shrapnel and large caliber machine-gun bullets. His right leg was shot to pieces, and the top of his left hand was torn to the bone by a grenade blast.

The next year and a half, Mickey spent in and out of the hospital in tremendous pain. The doctors tried valiantly to save his leg, but they couldn't. The rest of his body was held together with pins and tubes for months. He found his only relief in getting high, and he stayed that way until he had become addicted to painkillers.

Life moved on at the front, and Mickey heard little about those he had fought with in his SEAL unit, but he did hear about Dave—and he knew he had to be dead.

Not long after Mickey was wounded, Dave was out on a combat mission with a squad of men when they were pinned down by enemy machine-gun fire. Dave pulled a phosphorus grenade from his belt to light up the enemy's position and stood up to throw it, but as he pulled back his arm, a bullet hit the grenade, and it exploded next to his ear.

Lying on his side on the bank of a muddy river in Vietnam, he watched part of his face float by. The rest of his face and his shoulder alternately smoldered and caught fire as the embedded phosphorus came into contact with the night air.

Dave Roever knew that he was going to die, yet miraculously he didn't. He was pulled from the water by his fellow soldiers, flown directly to Saigon, and then taken to a waiting plane bound for Hawaii. But his problems were just beginning.

In the months that followed, he would have dozens of operations—but he almost didn't make it through the first one. The Navy surgical team had a major problem during that operation. As they cut away tissue that had been burned or torn by the grenade, the phosphorus embedded in his body would hit the oxygen in the operating room and begin to ignite again! Several times the doctors and nurses ran out of the room, leaving him alone because they were afraid the flammable oxygen used in surgery would explode! Roever survived that first operation and was taken to a ward that held the most severe burn and injury cases from the war.

The real struggle for both men came after the war. Roever would start each day putting his wig on his bald head, adjusting his false ear, un-taping his eye which has to be taped closed at night since he has no eyelid, and staring at a face that shows the horror of burned flesh. Mickey, at the same time, was surviving skin grafts, amputation, traction, and plastic surgery only to acquire a bone disease and recurring abscesses and infection.

The two had pain and trauma in common after they came home, but beyond that their lives were very different. Mickey would sit in his house at night with a loaded gun in his lap, hoping someone would try to break in so he could shoot the intruder down. His marriage was ruined, and his addictions were getting worse.

Dave, on the other hand, had fallen back on his faith. Soon he was speaking across the country about his experiences. One special night, I heard him speak on national television, and he said: "I am twice the person I was before I went to Vietnam. . . . I wouldn't trade anything I've gone through for the benefits my trials have brought to my life. . . ."

I know what some of you are thinking now. *These people are crazy! How can a trial like this benefit us?* But before you put down the book, read what happened next.

About the same time that Dave Roever was telling how his trials had given him a better spiritual and family life, Mickey Block decided to kill himself. He sat in a chair in his bedroom and stuck his gun in his mouth. Even though he was not a "religious" person to say the least, he recounted that he suddenly felt as if he had seen a vision.

In his mind's eye, he saw the scene a moment after he'd pull the trigger, his brains and blood splattered over the wall behind him. He saw his children come running into his room after school. He tried to get up out of the chair and tell them not to look, but he couldn't! He saw the horror and fear in their eyes as they found his lifeless body slumped in the chair. . . .

As he sat there, a second away from death, he blinked away

the terrible picture of what he had almost done and began crying for the first time since Vietnam. Then, also for the first time, he prayed. He thought back to all the "preaching" he'd heard from Dave Roever and other Christians he had known and finally surrendered what was left of his broken life to Jesus Christ.

What happened next, he would only explain as a peace settling over him. Nothing drastic changed that day. His marriage was still shattered, his leg was still gone. He still battled his addictions, but now there was hope in his life—and a deep inner knowledge that he was forgiven for a life turned against God. He was no longer alone with his problems. His wife viewed his conversion with skepticism but as the months passed, she knew he was a changed man.

Then the day came when a friend called who happened to be listening to a local radio program. "Hey, Mickey," he said. "There's a guy talking about God on the radio who was a member of the SEALs in Vietnam like you were. Do you think you know him?"

The Preacher Man? Mickey thought. It couldn't be. From the account he had heard from the men who put Dave's body on the helicopter in 'Nam, he knew he was dead.

He called the radio station, his hands trembling as he asked to speak to the Vietnam veteran who had just been on the show. After a few moments, a familiar voice came on the line and said, "This is Dave Roever. Can I help you?"

In a few moments of animated conversation, Mickey found out that the "Preacher Man" was in town to speak at a church that night. Dave warmly invited him to attend the meeting, and he agreed. Mickey hadn't been inside a church in years, but that night he went with his wife. By way of introduction he put a .308 caliber machine-gun bullet in the offering plate—the type of bullet they used on their patrol boats and that had torn off his leg.

When the bullet was given to Dave at the front, he stopped speaking and called for his combat buddy to come up with him. Mickey limped the length of the church to Dave's waiting arms, amidst the tears and cheers of the people in the church.

That night, two men stood at the front of that church. They had both lived through the same excruciating, horrible experience. Each had taken a different road to the same destination. One found a deeper faith through having his face nearly blown away. The other lost his leg and nearly his wife and family—but finally he gained everything worth living for. He had new life in Christ and new hope for his family.

Turning Wrong Around

Not one of us would want to experience the kinds of tragedies that Diane, Mickey, and Dave experienced. Yet in each case, these people became stronger in their personal and family lives as a direct result of their trials.

One of the greatest truths I know is that life is difficult and often unfair. What makes the difference between those people who experience difficulties and grow bitter—and those who find a better life produced by a similar or even more difficult trial?

I experience the joy of sharing all across the country that everyone who knows Jesus Christ as Lord and Savior can have the assurance that their trials will produce good in their lives. In fact, for the believer, I often say, every trial comes gift-wrapped with a treasure ready to be found inside.

When Trials Fall from the Sky

I once heard of a man who was walking along the sidewalk outside his high-rise apartment in New York City. It was very early on a bitterly cold winter morning, and he was hurrying to get out of the wind. Suddenly, from out of nowhere, he was hit on the shoulder by a heavy object and knocked to the ground.

For several moments he lay on the sidewalk, dazed, feeling to see if his shoulder was broken. Finally, he sat up and looked around. The street was deserted, so he ruled out a mugging. He looked up at the apartments above him, but he could see no lights on and no open windows. He glanced around the ground where he was lying and saw a shoe box next to him. It was heavily taped from end to end. He reached over to pick it up, but it was so heavy he had to use both hands.

He took the shoe box back to his apartment, got some scissors out, and cut through the tape. Inside were three fairly large cloth sacks. As he lifted out one of the sacks and opened it in the light he gasped. There were several small gold bars and dozens of gold coins! After a few more moments of gasping, he decided he'd better take this shoe box to the police station.

The police told him that more than likely the gold was stolen jewelry that had been melted down. Whether it had fallen from an apartment or from a plane overhead, they couldn't say. If he'd leave it with them for six months, they told him, it could be his if no one lawfully claimed it during that time.

The six months took forever to pass, but finally the day came. He hurried to the police station and there was the shoe box that had given him the sore shoulder. His shoulder didn't hurt anymore, and soon because of this treasure that fell from nowhere, his pocketbook didn't either.

. . . though apparent trouble may look as if it's destroying our home, it can actually turn into a benefit for us through God's power!

Most of us would gladly suffer through a sore shoulder to end up with a box filled with gold. Yet we may not realize that we have the same chance of benefiting every time we are hit by problems. For every trial is like a box containing valuable treasures. It may knock us to the ground and bruise us, but once we learn how to open the box, we can find a golden opportunity inside.

"Gary, you're either crazy or oversimplifying the problem of pain," some may say. "It's hard to believe that every problem can have a silver lining." After all, what good can come from some serious trial? A trial like having your face nearly blown away? Or from losing your leg and being on drugs? Or from being put out on the street at age nine?

As Diane, Dave, Mickey, Joni Eareckson Tada, Corrie Ten Boom, and many others can testify, trials are often devastating at the time. Yet in spite of the pain, they can produce a gold of sorts in our lives. Like a refining fire, each trial can work to make us more pure and sound. The Bible says God will " . . . bestow . . . a crown of beauty instead of ashes . . ." (Isaiah 61:3).

Don't misunderstand me. I'm not implying that God causes all trials (James 1:13). Neither am I saying that we ought to cause trials for others so that they'll gain from the experience (Romans 6:1–2). But I certainly do believe that in His sovereignty and love, God *can and does* take anything that happens to us and use it for good (Romans 8:28; Isaiah 61:7).

It isn't wrong to avoid painful situations when possible, but it is wrong to deny problems, ignore them, or try to explain them away. As Christians, we are left with a much more positive option than denial or trying to delude ourselves into thinking tragedies didn't happen. Of all people we have a promise that whether we get blasted in the jungles of Vietnam, or in the front yard of our father's home, trials can produce the very things that can make us the most like Christ—His love, peace, and joy.

It's never easy to "welcome" trials as friends, but trials can train us to become more Christlike, if they're experienced in the right light. I've learned to "treasure-hunt" with every difficulty I face. This attitude has been one of the most important tools we can give our children to help prepare them for the large and small trials of life they'll inevitably face.

How God Turns Trials into Triumph

I'm writing this chapter because I know that trials can not only defeat individuals, they can ruin entire families—especially if that family doesn't know how to handle the trials effectively. So here's a summary of this entire book in three sentences.

In Chapters 1 through 12, there's a practical plan we can follow to strengthen our relationships and develop the specific skills necessary to practice that plan. In Chapter 13, we looked at the only consistent power source—the Lord Jesus Himself. Only He can give me the strength to love my spouse as I should over a lifetime. *Now in this final chapter, we have the assurance that although apparent trouble may look as if it's destroying our home, it can actually turn into a benefit for us through God's power!*

That means all trials, over all seasons of the life-cycle. Let me give you a personal example. I'll take you on a treasure-hunting journey through three of my own personal trials and show you the benefits that God ultimately gave me through each one. We'll begin with a trial I faced early in life. It has left a lasting mark upon me.

Being Held Back Moved Me Forward

Until I was in high school, I had moved at least once every year of my life. I'm not proud to admit it, but between bouncing in and out of so many different schools, I flunked the third grade. A number of children are held back before or after kindergarten at an age when it's socially acceptable, but how do you explain to your friends that you're being held back in the third grade because you can't read well enough?

While it may not make anyone's list of all-time trials, I can assure you that at the time, it was one of the greatest traumas I had ever faced. Now, as I look back years later, what did I get from the experience? Humility, to begin with.

Not being promoted with my friends kept me humble for many years. To this day I am self-conscious about my spelling. That's especially true if I have to write a note to one of my children's teachers, because my atrocious spelling was one of the reasons I was held back. Humility may not sound like such a great benefit, but a valuable gift of gold can be added to our character as a result of being humbled. It's found in a verse that says, "God opposes the proud but gives grace to the humble" (James 4:6). While I didn't realize it at the time, God was actually giving megadoses of His grace to me during the third grade!

Flunking third grade also made it difficult for me to read aloud in front of people. One of my most embarrassing moments was the time I was not able to finish reading a section of Scripture at my church. As president of a large college group, I was humbled even more by that experience. It gave me a deep concern for those struggling with dyslexia and other spelling and reading disorders such as mine.

Also, because I was so embarrassed, to this day I am extremely careful to try not to embarrass people who attend my seminars. My experience of embarrassment increased my sensitivity. This is also a fundamental requirement for being a loving person.

At the time I didn't feel there was anything good about flunking a grade, but there was. I received more of God's grace and added sensitivity to hurting people. Two major benefits from one trial, and that's just one trial.

When Our Ship Came In . . . and Ran Aground

During our first few years together, Norma and I lived on the edge of poverty most of the time. My poor accounting skills didn't help.

One year, we had absolutely no money—but we could see our ship coming in any day! Especially since we knew that a tax refund of $2,000 was on its way to us in the mail. When the letter came from the IRS, I hurriedly ripped it open, certain that I'd find a check inside that would be a tremendous help to us financially. Instead, I learned that I had made a major error on our tax form and that we actually *owed* the government $1,700—and they wanted it *now!*

At the time, I couldn't think of a single treasure I was getting out of this particular trial. In fact, I was dying trying to come up with every cent of earthly treasure we had, just to keep the Federal agents away from our door. As Norma and I look back on that experience, however, the real treasure didn't go to the government to play catch-up with the deficit. We learned several lessons more important than money, and they have stayed with us until this day.

The first benefit was the reminder that money is not the source of life. We had focused on our tax refund so much, it had shifted our focus away from Christ. That experience took away everything we had monetarily in life, but God showed us that neither money nor anything money could buy could take away what was more important—our relationship with Him. Because we had to struggle so much to pay the tax bill, the whole family learned the value of trusting God to meet our needs. (Including things like saying "thank you" for care-packages of food that were delivered mysteriously by some close friends.)

Finally, the trial forced me to get professional help with my taxes so that I wouldn't get any "surprises" in the mail again. It also forced me to take a more serious look at the management of our finances. Trial number two, and this time three major positive benefits by nearly going broke! Actually, I could count even more benefits, especially the love we gained through the experience

—remembering that we gain more of God's love in every trial (Hebrews 12:9ff).

A Matter of Life and Death

When it comes to my third example of treasure-hunting trials, to tell you the truth, I'm glad I'm still around to explain it. While it's not easy for me to talk about, for the last two years, my health has not been the best. Basically, at times I've felt I had one foot in heaven and the other on a banana peel here on earth.

You see, my brother died of a heart attack two years ago at the age of 51. My sister had a heart attack last year as well, and another brother had to have triple bypass surgery at age 51. For those who are believers in genetics, it seems that my father's background may have something to do with the hearts in our family giving out when they do. My father died of a heart attack at age 58.

With my family's health history in mind, something happened two years ago—when I was 46—that started me counting my days.

For years, I've jogged a short distance every day and carefully watched my diet, hoping that alone would keep me healthy and fit. Then one morning in Vail, Colorado, during a speaking visit, I walked out of my hotel for a morning jog. Before me were 50 to 60 people, all in running clothes, stretching out and pinning race numbers on their T-shirts.

Recognizing them as people from the convention I was addressing, I said, "Hey, what are you guys doing?"

"This is the annual three-mile race," several people said. "Why don't you come and join us? Everyone at the convention is invited to run."

"You're only going *three miles?*" I asked.

At the time I could do three miles without breaking a sweat in the near sea-level altitude of Phoenix. So I walked over to the sign-up table, got myself a number and joined in. However, I soon discovered that there was a slight problem. This wasn't the friendly three-mile jog I had envisioned. It was a flat-out sprint through two-mile-high Vail. I was a short-distance jogger, not a long-distance sprinter, but the male conqueror mentality inside me kicked in, and I decided I was not going to finish in last place if it killed me.

It almost did.

Before I reached the half-way point, there were small children and senior citizens passing me. It was as if all the breathable air had suddenly been sucked out of Colorado. As I struggled to reach the finish line, I could see that last place was either going to be me or to a woman wheezing alongside me who looked like she'd flunked out of Weight Watchers. So I gave it all I had at the end—and she beat me.

The moment the race was over, I knew something was terribly wrong. I was sick. I spoke that day, then got on the plane with chills and fever. Before I knew it, I was vomiting and bleeding internally. I spent two weeks in bed and even then my blood pressure and cholesterol levels didn't recover. My kidneys were secreting blood, and I was having massive headaches. They were so bad that one doctor wanted to do surgery on my sinuses to drill holes in them so they could drain. Something about the altitude, my health, and my sprint had turned my body inside out.

What good could come out of almost dying? Particularly when John and I had conferences to conduct and books lined up to write? All this required nonstop work.

In the last two years, I have been forced to learn how to balance my life—how to level out the "high-highs" and "low-lows." I have learned even more about healthy food, healthy eating habits, and healthy work habits. I learned what burn-out and stress can do to a body and how damaging out-of-control emotions can be on my system. I also learned how to seek the Lord in a way I'd never done before.

As I learned the concept I described in Chapter 13 (gaining my fulfillment from Christ). I also re-learned the "little widow lady" attitude of prayer. For months, I had to wait daily in that line for my own physical health and strength and to accept that I may not be able to walk through every door of "ministry" that's open to me. The treasure I've gained from that experience is a clearer understanding of how God does give His strength to the weak and of His faithfulness to those who seek Him alone.

These were three trials at different times in my life, some small and some large. Each resulted in similar gains in my store of God's love, peace, and joy. Herein lies the secret to successful treasure-hunting. We can gain a great deal through our trials or nothing at all—depending on our faith. It's not how *much* faith we have, but whether the faith we have takes God at His Word.

Great Faith or "Dinky" Faith

The secret to successful treasure-hunting is understanding two life-changing words: faith and love. The greater our faith in God's Word, the easier it is for us to treasure-hunt trials. The more we treasure-hunt, the more we'll be able to see the ways we're becoming more loving as a result of our circumstances. It all begins with faith, however. We have to take God at His Word. It's not more faith we need, but great faith. Here's what I mean.

Do you remember the story of the centurion who came to Jesus for the sake of his servant? It's one of the clearest descriptions in the Scriptures of exactly what "faith" entails. Read Luke 7 to see if I'm telling the story correctly.

The centurion was a powerful man who commanded an entire garrison of men. Yet one day he faced a problem he couldn't defeat on his own, and he pushed his way through a crowd until he stood in front of Jesus. Coming quickly to the point, he said, "Sir, my servant is lying paralyzed at home, suffering great pain." Even though the man made only a statement, not a request, Jesus answered, "I will come and heal him."

But do you remember the centurion's response?

"Lord," he said, "I am not worthy for You to come under my roof. I am a man used to giving and taking commands. Just say the word, and my servant will be healed." Amazed by the centurion's faith, Christ said to the people around him, "I have not found such *great faith* with anyone in all of Israel!"

Anyone? He was talking about a very religious country. This Roman soldier had greater faith than anyone Jesus knew? Even greater faith than the disciples who would one day die for Him?

"Have you ever wondered what the disciples must have thought about such a statement? Peter was probably saying under his breath, *Sure, Lord, embarrass us in front of our Jewish brethren!* There was no love lost between the Jews and Roman soldiers.

What had impressed Jesus so much about what the soldier had said?

The answer is like a picture-frame around the concept of faith. This soldier believed that Jesus had only to command it and his servant would be healed. "For I, too, am a man under authority," he said to Jesus, "with soldiers under me; and I say to this one, 'Go!' and he goes, and to another, 'Come!' and he comes, and to my slave, 'Do this!' and he does it" (Matthew 8:10). The centurion never doubted for a moment Christ's power and authority to heal his servant. Jesus had said it, and that settled it in his mind.

But why *didn't* he doubt? Problems in life are so quick to produce questions in most of our minds. Perhaps the centurion's faith came from facing the trials of spending many days, on many different battlefields. Perhaps it was a reflection of his own father's faith. We're never told how this man came about his great faith. In contrast, Christ's disciples showed theirs to be of "dinky" proportions almost immediately.

It had been a long day of speaking to the crowds and healing the sick, when Jesus told His disciples to "get into their boat and cross to the other side of the lake." Exhausted from the drain of the crowd, He lay down to take a nap.

When the disciples were halfway across the sea, a storm blew in. Waves crashed over the sides of the boat and the disciples panicked. In desperation, they woke Jesus and cried out, "We're perishing!" Jesus just sighed, stood up, and quieted the waves and the wind with a single command. Then, drawing on the living illustration of the centurion's faith, He said to His disciples: "Why are you so timid, you men of little faith?"

How did the disciples' faith differ from that of the centurion? Why did a Roman soldier have "great" faith and Christ's own disciples "dinky" faith? The difference was that in the midst of the storm, *the disciples forgot what Jesus had said to them.* They quit counting on His Word, and as a result they panicked and counted themselves in the "lost at sea" category.

Jesus specifically said to them before He went to sleep, "We're going to the other side," not, "You guys better hug everybody, because we're fish-food halfway across this lake." He had given them His word they would *all* cross to the other side. Yet they forgot His words when the water got choppy.

I'm not blaming the disciples—I'm too much like them. Many of us make the same mistake in our marriages and families, don't we? During difficult times. we forget that God promises we'll make it to the other side—He just never promises a smooth ride on the way there. *But as the waves crash around us, God promises He will produce maturity, righteousness, patience, endurance, and love in our lives.*

In James 1:2, the writer told us to "consider it pure joy . . . whenever you face trials" and in 2 Corinthians 5:7, Paul told us to "live by faith, not by sight." So questioning the waves and their effect on our trip through life is like saying, "God's promises don't apply to me. God doesn't understand my situation, so how can any good come out of all this suffering?" (Isaiah 40:27ff.).

We're Not the First to Be "Treasure-Hunters"

One look in the Bible shows story after story of gaining treasure from trials. How would you feel if you were hated by your brothers, sold for pennies into a foreign slave market, framed for adultery, thrown into jail without a trial, and then forgotten by the one person who could have saved you?

Joseph, in the Old Testament, knew what that felt like. Yet what did he say years later, when he, the Pharaoh's right hand man, brought his brothers to Egypt? Even as he forgave them he said, "You intended to harm me, but God intended it for good" (Genesis 50:20).

Adam, Noah, Abraham, Isaac, Jacob, Joseph, Moses, Elisha, Elijah, Jeremiah, David, Solomon, Esther, Ruth, Isaiah, John the Baptist, Peter, Paul, Mary Magdalene, James. . . . on and on the list goes. All these are people with whom we can identify. They all faced trials like we have. Even in cases of "failure" (remember, Elisha and Jonah ran away, Peter denied Christ, Paul persecuted Christ's followers, James deserted Him, etc.), God took tragedy and even "dinky" faith and turned it into eternal treasure.

Blocking Trials from Producing Love

I'll be the first to admit that there is a problem with experiencing trials. Namely, their worth to us often comes on a delayed basis. As the waves are bouncing us around, we are just like the disciples. All we can picture is surviving the immediate, not thanking God for how He's shaping us for eternity.

Remember how long it took the average family to turn disasters into "family glue" in Chapter 12? It often takes several weeks for the family to see those disasters in their true light and begin bonding as a result. The same is true with trials. It took time for Dave Roever to say he was a better man for having a hand grenade blow up in his face. Diane didn't stop crying herself to sleep for months after the tragedy she faced at nine years of age—but healing did come one fateful morning.

Experts say that it takes at least thirty days of consistent repetition before a habit becomes ingrained. In other words, don't give up on treasure-hunting when you're only a few feet from shore. When someone's experiencing a trial, it's natural to go through a stage in which anger or doubt takes over, but making a decision to remain angry or even to dwell on being a "victim" can block you from any positive effects the trial could have on your character.

If I wanted to, I could still be angry at my third grade teacher or my parents for not getting me the help I needed to pass the third grade the first time, but hanging on to resentment would simply act as a roadblock to any benefits God could bring me. I could blame Norma or the "Infernal" Revenue Service for a complicated tax system that nearly bankrupted our family—or I could admit my own mistake and look in faith to what God could teach me in what happened.

I could even hate my father's memory—and question God's wisdom—in giving me his genes that may put an early time limit on the years I have to serve Him. To do so, however, would be to kick and scream at a loving and sovereign—and—unfathomable God. (Remember from Chapter 5: Anger blocks God's working in our lives, so we're only cheating ourselves to hold on to feelings of being a victim.)

There's no earthly reason why Dave, Mickey, and Diane should be happy and fulfilled after what's happened to them— but there is a heavenly one. Solomon once said if we live long enough, we'll all see enough sorrow to knock the joy out of life if we let it (Ecclesiastes 12:1). Embracing the value of our trials and mining the constructive good God can bring from them is the only way I know to keep rejoicing for a lifetime.

Passing down the Faith to "Treasure-Hunt"

As I mentioned earlier in the chapter, there are important personal reasons for learning to treasure-hunt trials, but it doesn't stop there. For those of us who have children, it's vital that we begin teaching them lessons in centurionlike faith at an early age—especially if they seem destined to increase their sensitivity level by being slightly (or decidedly) accident-prone.

For whatever reason, my son Michael wins the "I've-experienced-the-most-natural-and man-made-accidents" award in our family. When he was two weeks old, he almost died from severe stomach problems that required major surgery. For the next several years, he suffered through a series of childhood illnesses and came close to death again.

Once when he was three, I was digging in the back yard and unearthed a yellow-jacket nest. Where was my "award-winning" son standing? Right where the nest fell. He was stung repeatedly before I could get to him. Then in the same year, Mike nearly drowned in a motel swimming pool.

He's suffered through a retainer to enlarge his mouth and then braces to pull his teeth in tighter. At age thirteen, he was in a major car accident. He broke an arm and was showered with so much broken glass, it took the doctors two hours to take out all the glass slivers from the side of his face and from his eyelid. Soon he'll undergo an operation in which he will have to get his jaw broken and reset.

What do you say to a child who has gone through so many trials? Why not let him do the talking? When the doctor told Michael that there would probably be some pain involved in his upcoming operation, Mike said, "Oh, don't worry about it. I've had so much pain in my life that this isn't going to faze me."

When people go through painful experiences, it often seems to enable them to go through future experiences with less trauma, as if they understand the process and the refining fire. Michael had already been through so many things that the automobile accident wasn't that traumatic for him. Even during the two hours they worked to take all the glass from his face, he was calm and joking. A week after the accident, Mike's attitude was still positive when he learned that he'd have to go through the entire summer in Phoenix with a cast on his arm and unable to swim. The same will be true when he has his jaw operation. At age sixteen, he's already an avid, well-seasoned treasure-hunter—and he's needed to be!

Teaching Them to Look for
Love in an Unusual Place

When you teach your children what God's Word has to say about troubled times, you're providing a true "lamp unto their feet" for the rest of their trial-ridden life. As John and I explain in detail in our book, *The Gift of Honor,* it all begins with your first reaction during a trial. Calmly comforting them at the beginning of a trial lays the foundation for them to find value in their difficult experiences. It teaches them they can be calm, too.

And how do we remain calm at such a chaotic moment? Calmness comes from our own deep inner confidence in God's abiding care. As we discussed in Chapter 13, it's a deep conviction that will work for good in God's time (Romans 8:28).

Watching Mike's positive attitude through his pain gave us an opportunity to praise him for the way he was handling the situation. Yet we made a mental note to keep tabs, as the months went by, on how he was responding (a bit like watching for aftershocks of an earthquake). By doing so, we'd be able to spot early warning signs like depression or anxiety that could grow into major problems later on. That is a good idea for all parents as they smooth the path toward finding the treasure of their children's trials.

Biblical principles are like powerful beacons that can light up even the darkest trial your children may experience. Teaching your children that Romans 8:28 and Philippians 4:1ff speak of spiritual benefits they can claim in faith is a precious legacy you can leave your loved ones. If you take God at His Word yourself, you'll verbally and nonverbally convey this message to your children as they watch your responses to your own troubles.

Great faith is confidently knowing that what God promises will come true. Great faith is the confidence even during a trial that it will one day turn out to our benefit. "Dinky" faith is complaining or "murmuring" during a trial that there is no benefit on the other side, we're doomed. . . . finished . . . beyond help . . . unrepairable. . . .

I firmly believe that the mark of a person who grows through trials is the degree to which he or she is willing to take God at His Word. That is called great faith in the love of God, and only possible for those who . . .

Don't Bail out of the "Love Boat" When Trials Hit

As we've mentioned, the most precious treasure we discover as we unwrap any trial is gaining more of Christ's love. Troubled times have a way of funneling the love and care of God to us, and the love of God *through* us, to others. Only those who desire God's best, His love, truly benefit from trials. Trials are coming to all of us, and it's crucial that we learn to use them for good, rather than let them get us down.

In the weeks after Mike's accident, I sat down with him several times and discussed some of the benefits that were a part of his trial. Because we've done this with so many of his trials, he jumped in quickly, telling me he could see the ways in which he had already become more sensitive. No longer could he pass an accident site and not begin praying for the people instead of just "looking" at what happened.

There's no question in our home about who is the most sensitive family member. No one feels the hurt of people or even animals as deeply as Mike does, and I believe it has everything to do with how much he has suffered.

Recently, on the way to a doctor's appointment, I asked Mike what he wants to do in life. Do you know what he said? "I think I want to try to help protect people somehow. Maybe I'll be a policeman or in some kind of service organization. Maybe I can be a secret service agent or something. I want to do something to help protect people somehow."

How often in our own lives has someone ministered to us during a difficult time with caring eyes and loving ways—and later we learned that person had been through the same kind of problem? One of the clearest treasures a trial offers us is to make us loving and sensitive in its wake. That wonderful sensitivity is, I believe, a major factor in genuinely loving others. We develop more patience, tolerance, sensitivity and over all we become better lovers of people (Romans 5:3–5).

The apostle Paul understood this mystery when he wrote his famous explanation of love: "Love is patient, love is kind. It does not envy, it does not boast, it is not proud. It is not rude, it is not self-seeking, it is not easily angered, it keeps no record of wrongs. Love does not delight in evil but rejoices with the truth. It always protects, always trusts, always hopes, always perseveres" (1 Corinthians 13:4–7).

These qualities of mature love are given to us through trials better and faster than any other way I know. Trials put us in a "love boat" with Jesus. As the disciples we're able to ride out the storm. Just as with them, it's our choice whether we're going to take Jesus at His Word and believe He'll take us to the "other side" of the trial—and gain more love for Him and others in the process. Or whether we'll wake Him up continually with our cries of mistrust and "dinky" faith—and hear His gentle reproof, "Oh, ye of little faith . . . "

I know I can't keep trials from coming. The Bible promises me that trials will show up on my doorstep (James 1:2ff.). Over the years, though, I'm finally coming to the place where I've quit fighting something the Bible says can "Purify you and make you lacking in nothing" (James 1:4).

> *The qualities of mature love are given to us through trials better and faster than any other way I know . . .*

Another way to look at trials is to treat them like long-term "interest-bearing" CDs. It may take time for them to mature and for God to produce a greater capacity to love through our trial, but there's a promise we can count on. We can take Him at His Word that we can cash in on that love one day. As the writer to the Hebrews says, no one enjoys trials, "No discipline seems pleasant at the time, but painful. Later on, however, it produces a harvest of righteousness and peace for those who have been trained by it" (Hebrews 11:11).

A Promise by Day and by Night

Faith is trusting that God's Word is reliable. If He promises, "We are going to the other side," then we are going to the other side. There are a number of promises in the Scripture that can keep us going, keep us searching for that buried treasure of love with a full and open heart. In fact, here's a quick list I offered in the book, *Joy That Lasts*[1] that contains just a few of the promises to remember as trials come to us day by day. I strongly urge you to memorize a list of scriptural promises like these, so that when the next trial hits—you'll stay in His "love boat" and be able to treasure-hunt more quickly when you reach the other side.

1. "And we know that in all things God works for the good of those who love him, who have been called according to his purpose" (Romans 8:28).

2. "Give thanks in all circumstances, for this is God's will for you in Christ Jesus" (1 Thessalonians 5:18).

3. "Consider it pure joy, my brothers, whenever you face trials of many kinds, because you know that the testing of your faith develops perseverance" (James 1:2–3).

4. "Our fathers disciplined us for a little while as they thought best; but God disciplines us for our good, that we may share in his holiness. No discipline seems pleasant at the time, but painful. Later on, however, it produces a harvest of righteousness and peace for those who have been trained by it" (Hebrews 12:10–11).

5. "Jesus replied: 'Love the Lord your God with all your heart and with all your soul and with all your mind.' This is the first and greatest commandment. And the second is like it: 'Love your neighbor as yourself.' All the Law and the Prophets hang on these two commandments" (Matthew 22:37–40).

6. "The goal of this command is love, which comes from a pure heart and a good conscience and a sincere faith" (1 Timothy 1:5).

7. "Dear friends, since God so loved us, we also ought to love one another. No one has ever seen God; but if we love each other, God lives in us and his love is made complete in us" (1 John 4:11–12).

8. Last, but certainly not least, is my favorite chapter in Scripture as I've gone through physical trials this year (Romans 5). To offer a paraphrase of these verses: "Therefore we have been made right with God through faith, peace with God through Christ, and enjoy the power of God in us through Christ. Not only do we have all we need in Him, but we can also be excited about our sufferings. Because trouble brings us endurance—the power to keep going—and endurance produces character (love), character brings hope, and we won't be disappointed (great faith)

because God will pour out His love in our hearts through His Spirit!"

So the truth remains: No one likes trials, yet no one can escape them. We can let them ruin our lives, allowing ourselves to become bitter, angry, resentful. Or we can look for the treasure that will let us love and serve our family and others better. Again, the choice is ours. *For loving God—like loving one's spouse and children—is first, last, and always a decision.*

Notes

Chapter 1

1. In the years ahead, our goal as a ministry is to produce small group follow-up materials that will provide families everywhere with biblically based resources to strengthen their most important relationships.
2. "Even youths grow tired and weary, and young men stumble and fall; but those who hope in the Lord will renew their strength . . ." Isaiah 40:30–31.

Chapter 2

1. Gary Smalley and John Trent, Ph.D., *Hardside/Softside* (Pomona, CA: Focus on the Family Publishers, to be released Spring, 1990).
2. From a training booklet by Jack Hilger, *Training Married Couples to Work with Premarital Couples,* Prepare/Enrich, Inc., 1987.
3. Joan Druckman, David Fournier, Beatrice Robinson, and David H. Olson, "Effectiveness of Five Types of Pre-marital Programs," *Education for Marriage* (Grand Rapids, MI, 1979). Gerald Cossitt, *Effects of Feedback on Idealism in Premarital Couples,* Doctoral dissertation, University of Alberta, Edmonton, Canada.
4. The biblical concept of "honoring" God and others is so important, Dr. John Trent and I wrote an entire book on the subject called *The Gift of Honor* (Nashville, TN: Thomas Nelson Publishers, 1987).
5. Reading books like Frank Peritti's *This Present Darkness* (Westchester, IL: Good News Books/Crossway Publishers, 1988) can help you believe that there may be a satanic cover-up of honor!
6. William F. Arndt and R. Wilbur Gingrich, eds., *A Greek-English Lexicon of the New Testament and Other Early Christian Literature* (Chicago: University of Chicago Press, 1957), 119.
7. Ibid., 120.
8. Men are motivated by the "awe" principle both negatively and positively. One major reason for the creation of affairs is that a woman outside the marriage will show a man "ah-h-h-h-h," and it draws him after her. See Proverbs 5, 6:20–35, and Chapter 7 for a picture of the adulteress who "flatters with her words" in working her destruction.

9. *The Gift of Honor,* Chapter 3.
10. For more on the tremendously damaging effects of negative word pictures, see Gary Smalley and John Trent, Ph.D., *The Language of Love* (Pomona, CA: Focus on the Family Publishing, 1988), Chapter 15, "The Dark Side of Emotional Word Pictures."

Chapter 3

1. For a long overdue look at the long-term negative effects of divorce on children, see the chilling book, Judith Wallenstein, *Second Chances* (New York: Ticknor and Fields Publishers, 1989); Diana Medved, *The Case Against Divorce* (New York: Donald I. Fine, Inc., 1989), and especially, Gary Richmond, *The Divorce Decision* (Waco, TX: Word Books, 1988).

Chapter 4

1. Allen P. Ross, *Creation and Blessing* (Grand Rapids, MI: Baker Book House, 1988), 126.
2. Robert Kohn, "Patterns of Hemispheric Specialization in Pre-Schoolers," *Neuropsychologia,* 12:505–12.
3. James J. Lynch, *The Language of the Heart* (New York: Basic Books, Inc., 1985).
4. For a definition of "word picture," see *The Language of Love,* 17.
5. Arthur Bragg, "What's Holding Them Back?" *Business Insurance* (March 1989).

Chapter 5

1. Leprosy was such a dreaded disease that one rabbi taught it was all right to throw stones at lepers to keep them "a safe distance away," cf. Alfred Edershiem, *The Life and Times of Jesus the Messiah* (Grand Rapids, MI: William B. Eerdmans Publishing, 1971), 1:495.
2. See *aphieimi*, which has the basic meaning of "let go, send away, cancel, remit, pardon, leave, let go, tolerate," Ardnt and Gingrich, *Lexicon,* 125–26.
3. In *The Blessing,* we discuss the physiological benefit of elevated hemoglobin levels in both people involved in the meaningful touch. When elevated, the hemoglobin levels serve to carry more oxygen to our bodies and actually energize us. For more information, see

Gary Smalley and John Trent, *The Blessing*, p. 40, and "Therapeutic Touch: The Imprimatur of Nursing," *American Journal of Nursing* (May 1975): 784.

Chapter 6

1. For a detailed description of the concept of "closing" or "reopening" a person's spirit, see Gary Smalley, *The Key to Your Child's Heart* (Waco, TX: Word Publishing, 1984).
2. For a detailed look at the negative physiology of anger, see Paul Meier and Frank Minirth, *Happiness Is a Choice* (Grand Rapids, MI: Baker Book House, 1978).
3. Ibid., 23–29.
4. Albert A. Kurtland, "Biochemical and Emotional Interaction in the Etiology of Cancer," *Psychiatric Research Review* 35 (1978): 25.
5. "They can sit through sermon after sermon about forgiveness in church, never once misunderstanding what the pastor says, but still refuse to put their son's or daughter's picture back on the mantle." From Gary Smalley and John Trent, Ph.D., *The Blessing* (Nashville, TN: Thomas Nelson Publishers, 1986), 137.
6. We're using "soul" here in a nontheological way and especially not in the way some new-age people would call a "floating soul" touching another.
7. For a more complete list, see Gary Smalley, *If Only He Knew* (Grand Rapids, MI: Zondervan Publishing House, 1979), Chapter 5, "Climbing Out of Marriage's Deepest Pit," 82–86.
8. For an excellent resource on dealing with strong-willed children, see James Dobson, Ph.D., *The Strong-Willed Child* (Wheaton, IL: Tyndale House, 1979).

Chapter 7

1. There are, unfortunately, exceptions. See Gary Smalley and John Trent, Ph.D., *The Language of Love*, "The Dark Side of Emotional Word Pictures" (Pomona, CA: Focus on the Family Publishing, 1988), 150–62; and M. Scott Peck, M.D., *People of the Lie* (New York: Simon and Schuster, 1983).
2. We'll talk about this more later, but physically, emotionally and spiritually a man benefits by developing relationship skills.
3. From the Greek verb, *epitrepho*. Ardnt and Gingrich, *Lexicon*, 343.

Chapter 8

1. For a very helpful resource on leaving your children a legacy of love, see Tim Kimmel, *Legacy of Love: A Plan for Parenting on Purpose* (Portland, OR: Multnomah Press, 1989).
2. For more information on this outstanding conference, contact the Campus Crusade Family Ministry in Little Rock, AR (501) 223-8663.
3. For an insightful, biblically based book dealing with sexual temptation, see Charles Mylander, *Running the Red Lights* (Ventura, CA: Regal Books, 1986).
4. Ibid.
5. For more information about our #1 favorite Christian sports camp for any youngster aged eight to eighteen, please contact Kamp Kanakuk, Route 4, Box 2124, Branson, MO 65616, (417) 334-2432 or 334-6427.

Chapter 9

1. In fact, one of our favorite marriage books is by our good friends, Chuck and Barb Snyder. It's called *Incompatibility: Grounds for a Great Marriage* (Sisters, OR: Questar Publishers, 1988).
2. This is such an important concept, Dr. Trent and I have written an entire book about it called *The Language of Love* (Pomona, CA: Focus on the Family Publishers, 1988).
3. James Ford Rhodes, *History of the United States*. Vol. 1: *Lectures on the American Civil War* (1913). On meeting her, Lincoln reportedly said, "So this is the little lady who wrote the book that made this big war!"
4. Even though you may not realize it, you probably have been using them all your life. Expressions like "I'm toasty warm," "His elevator doesn't go all the way to the top floor!" or "That went over like a lead balloon" are just three of the hundreds of word pictures that are a part of our everyday speech.

Chapter 10

1. H. Norman Wright, *Romancing Your Marriage* (Ventura, CA: Regal Books, 1987), 41.
2. Alice Chapin, *Four Hundred Ways to Say I Love You* (Wheaton, IL: Living Books, Tyndale House Publishers, Inc., 1981).
3. *Romancing Your Marriage.*

4. Dan Carlinsky, *Do You Know Your Wife?* (Los Angeles, CA: Price, Stern, and Sloan, 1984).

Chapter 11

1. Marc H. Hollender, "The Wish to Be Held," *Archives of General Psychiatry* 22 (1970):445.
2. This survey of several thousand women was conducted by Ann Landers and its findings are recorded in "Is Affection More Important Than Sex?" *Reader's Digest* (August 1985).

Chapter 12

1. See chapter 6 for more on "closing" a person's spirit.
2. If you're interested in contacting Bill to do a family enrichment event at your church or business, you can contact him at P.O. Box 2929, Grass Valley, CA 95945, (916) 447-7738.
3. John Piper, *Desiring God* (Portland, OR: Multnomah Press, 1986).

Chapter 13

1. See Proverbs 7:1ff for a chilling description of the high cost of immoral relationships.

Chapter 14

1. Gary Smalley, *Joy That Lasts* (Grand Rapids, MI: Zondervan Publishing House, 1987).